EVIDENCE

EVIDENCE

ANDREW L-T CHOO

OXFORD

UNIVERSITY PRESS

Great Clarendon Street, Oxford OX2 6DP

Oxford University Press is a department of the University of Oxford.
It furthers the University's objective of excellence in research, scholarship,
and education by publishing worldwide in Oxford New York
Auckland Cape Town Dar es Salaam Hong Kong Karachi
Kuala Lumpur Madrid Melbourne Mexico City Nairobi
New Delhi Shanghai Taipei Toronto

With offices in

Argentina Austria Brazil Chile Czech Republic France Greece
Guatemala Hungary Italy Japan Poland Portugal Singapore
South Korea Switzerland Thailand Turkey Ukraine Vietnam

Oxford is a registered trade mark of Oxford University Press
in the UK and in certain other countries

Published in the United States
by Oxford University Press Inc., New York

© Andrew L-T Choo 2006

The moral rights of the author have been asserted
Database right Oxford University Press (maker) Crown

copyright material is reproduced under Class Licence
Number C01P0000148 with the permission of OPSI
and the Queen's Printer for Scotland

First published 2006

British Library Cataloguing in Publication Data

Data available

Library of Congress Cataloging in Publication Data

Applied for

Typeset by Newgen Imaging Systems (P) Ltd., Chennai, India
Printed in Great Britain
on acid-free paper by
CPI Bath

ISBN 978-0-19-876398-7

3 5 7 9 10 8 6 4

For my parents

Outline Contents

Contents

Preface

I hope that this book provides an appropriately contemporary perspective on the law of evidence in England and Wales. Over the past few years the old debates and issues of concern surrounding the law of evidence have been replaced, or supplemented, by new ones. The continuing influence of the Human Rights Act 1998 and the introduction of new legislation like the Criminal Justice Act 2003 provide just two explanations for the current volatile state of the law of evidence. This book attempts to cover the main topics in evidence law, but in doing so to focus on issues of contemporary concern rather than to achieve a comprehensive treatment of all relevant doctrinal principles. When discussing case law, I frequently allow quotations of clear and pithy judicial statements to 'speak for themselves'. Throughout the book I attempt where appropriate to draw on comparative material and a variety of socio-legal, empirical, and non-legal, such as psychological, material. I provide in the footnotes a large number of references which may be used as a guide to further reading and research.

I generally stopped collecting new material after 1 July 2005, but have been able to take account of some material which became available subsequently. In general, any statutory provisions not yet in force are treated as if they are already in force. Website references have been checked on or after 1 July 2005.

I am enormously grateful to the large number of people who have assisted me, directly or indirectly, to bring this book to fruition. At the Oxford University Press, John Whelan first suggested the idea of the project to me before it fell successively on the desks of Michaela Coulthard, Claire Brewer, Kate Whetter, Jasmin Naim, Angela Griffin, and Hussain Hadi. I would like to express my thanks to all of them (some of whom have since moved on from the Press) for their patience and encouragement. Special thanks are due to Kate, with whom I worked during the most crucial stages of the project. I have also benefited from the courteous efficiency of Gabriella La Cava as production editor, Susan Faircloth as copy editor, and David Carles as proofreader.

In the earlier stages of the writing of the book, a number of anonymous referees read a few chapters in draft on behalf of the Press. These referees made, between them, a large number of important comments and suggestions for my consideration. As the book approached completion Roger Leng of the University of Warwick read a substantial number of chapters and provided me with very pertinent comments on them. I very much appreciated the efforts of all these readers and am of course responsible for any errors or omissions that remain.

I am especially pleased to have this opportunity to acknowledge publicly the support of those with whom I have worked in the law subject group of the School of Social Sciences and Law, and when it existed the Department of Law, at Brunel University. I wish also to acknowledge the provision of funding by Brunel University for the appointment of Afolabi Euba as my research assistant for a year in the late 1990s. By the time the book is published I shall have left Brunel for the University of Warwick. Professor Susan

Nash of the University of Westminster has taken a great interest in the project and helped me refine my ideas on a number of issues. I am very grateful to her for allowing me to draw on work that she and I have published jointly. My colleagues at Matrix Chambers have provided me with valuable opportunities to experience the law in action. Outside the worlds of academia and the Bar, a number of other friends have provided support and encouragement, and helped ensure that I did not forget that there was life outside work. I hope I shall not be offending anyone else by singling out Annelies Dogterom, Mark Kirkbride, and Neil Robinson for special mention in this regard.

Finally, none of this would have been possible without the love and support of my family. My parents, in particular, have maintained an unwavering interest in my work, and, from a very considerable distance, offered constant encouragement.

ALTC

London
November 2005

Acknowledgements

Grateful acknowledgement is made to all the authors and publishers of copyright material which appears in this book, and in particular to the following for permission to reprint material from the sources indicated:

Sweet and Maxwell: extract from A L-T Choo and S Nash, 'What's the Matter with Section 78?' *Criminal Law Review* (1999) DEC, 929–940.

Vathek Publishing: extract from A L-T Choo and S Nash, 'Evidence Law in England and Wales: The Impact of the Human Rights Act 1998', *International Journal of Evidence and Proof* 7 (2003) 31–61. © Vathek Publishing, 2003.

Vathek Publishing: extract from A L-T Choo, 'Case Note: Prepared Statements, Legal Advice and the Right to Silence: *R v Knight*', *International Journal of Evidence and Proof* 8 (2004) 62–67. © Vathek Publishing, 2004.

Every effort has been made to clear the necessary permissions. If notified, the publisher will undertake to rectify any errors or omissions at the earliest opportunity.

Table of Cases

Table of Statutes

Table Of Statutory Instruments

European Materials

1
Introduction

Evidence is the information with which the matters requiring proof in a trial are proved. The study of evidence, therefore, is the study of the process by which such matters are proved in court. In very broad terms, the law of evidence may be said to be concerned with the following questions:

• What is the extent to which particular types of evidence may be considered in a case? In a criminal trial, for example, the issue may arise as to whether evidence that the person accused has previously been involved in other misconduct can be introduced. If it can be introduced, precisely what use may the jury make of the evidence? If it cannot be introduced, what is the justification for this restriction on the free admissibility of evidence?

• Are there principles governing the manner in which evidence which has been admitted is to be evaluated?

• By which party in a case must evidence be presented?

• What are the principles governing the course of evidence in a trial?

Questions such as these will form the basis of the discussions later in this chapter and in subsequent chapters. The law of evidence may prove to be of crucial practical importance in a case. It has been argued that:

> the outcome of cases, whether criminal or civil, is in practice more likely to be affected by procedural rules than by any niceties of substantive law such as those that preoccupy textbook writers. Further or alternatively, . . . parties are more likely to regard their treatment at the hands of the law as unjust because of what they perceive to be defects of procedure than because of what they perceive to be defects of substantive law.[1]

It is important in any study of the law of evidence that powers of critical analysis be actively engaged at all times. If the claim that the English law of evidence is part of a rational[2] system of proof can be sustained, then all evidential principles must have clear and coherent rationales that withstand close scrutiny. There must, to put it simply, be a good reason for the existence of every evidential principle. As we shall see, to say that this is not necessarily the case may well be an understatement.

---

[1] J Lever, 'Why Procedure Is More Important Than Substantive Law' (1999) 48 *International and Comparative Law Quarterly* 285, 285.

[2] See generally M Redmayne, 'Rationality, Naturalism, and Evidence Law' [2003] *Michigan State Law Review* 849.

It is necessary now to turn to an examination of a number of basic concepts and distinctions in the law of evidence. This examination will assist in illuminating the discussions in the rest of the book.

1 Facts in Issue and Collateral Facts

All evidence in a case must be relevant to either a fact in issue or a collateral fact. A fact in issue, or *factum probandum*, is a fact that must be proved by a party in a case in order for that party to succeed in the action. It is, to put it another way, an essential fact. What the facts in issue in a particular case are is dependent on the substantive law and not on the law of evidence. In a murder case, for example, the prosecution must, in order to succeed, prove that (1) the defendant caused the victim's death, (2) doing so with the necessary *mens rea* (that is, with the intention of causing death or grievous bodily harm). Thus (1) and (2) constitute the facts in issue in the case. There are three facts in issue in a tort action for negligence: the claimant must, in order to succeed, prove (1) the existence of a duty of care, (2) breach of that duty, and (3) the consequential loss. A fact that is not a fact in issue but is relevant to a fact in issue is known as a relevant fact or *factum probans*.

A collateral fact is a fact of which proof may be permitted but which does not constitute a fact in issue or a fact that is relevant to a fact in issue. The credibility of a witness, or simply 'credit', is a classic collateral fact. The extent to which a witness is worthy of belief may be an important, and indeed crucial, issue in a trial. Whether particular evidence has relevance to credit is therefore a question that may arise for consideration. The Court of Appeal has noted:

> The assessment of credit is not exclusively a logical process. Juries invariably are directed to use their 'knowledge of human nature' when deciding whether a witness is telling the truth, and the law not only permits but requires them to form their subjective though collective view, taking such account of demeanour, motive, consistency and other characteristics of the person they have seen giving evidence as they think fit. In this broad sense, certain matters can be described as 'relevant to credit', but this is something different from relevance meaning logically probative of an issue.[3]

2 Relevance, Admissibility, and Weight

The applicable concepts can be stated simply. Evidence must be *relevant* before it can be used in court. If it is relevant and does not infringe any exclusionary rule, it will be *admissible*.[4] Admissible evidence can, however, be excluded in the exercise of *judicial discretion*. Any admissible evidence that is not excluded in the exercise of discretion will

---

[3] *Thomas v Comr of Police* [1997] 1 All ER 747, 763.
[4] 'Evidence is admissible if it may be lawfully adduced at a trial': *DPP v Kilbourne* [1973] AC 729, 756.

be admitted, and the *weight* to be attached to the evidence is then a matter for the trier of fact.

Relevance[5] is possibly the most basic concept in the law of evidence. 'The question whether evidence is relevant depends not on abstract legal theory but on the individual circumstances of each particular case.'[6] An item of evidence is considered relevant if it renders the fact to be proved *more probable than it would be without that evidence*. Thus, an item of evidence is relevant so long as it has probative value or probative force,[7] however little.[8] As Lord Simon of Glaisdale explained in *DPP v Kilbourne*:

> Evidence is relevant if it is logically probative or disprobative of some matter which requires proof. . . . It is sufficient to say, even at the risk of etymological tautology, that relevant (ie, logically probative or disprobative) evidence is evidence which makes the matter which requires proof more or less probable.[9]

An alternative approach to relevance is that advocated by Wigmore.[10] On this approach, a distinction is made between logical relevance and legal relevance. Evidence is not prima facie admissible unless it is legally relevant. An item of evidence which is relevant in the normal sense of rendering a fact to be proved more probable than it would be without the evidence is logically relevant, but it is not necessarily legally relevant. To be legally relevant, it may be necessary for that item of evidence to possess some 'plus value' in the shape of additional probative value:

Logical relevance + 'Plus value' = Sufficient relevance / Legal relevance

It would seem that this concept of 'plus value' is simply a vehicle for facilitating consideration of any disadvantages of admitting the evidence. Put another way, plus value is the additional probative value required for the total probative value of the evidence to outweigh such possible considerations as prejudice to the defendant, the introduction of collateral issues, delay, confusion of the jury, and so on.[11] On the orthodox approach to relevance, however, such considerations would be taken into account in the exercise

---

[5] For a general discussion of relevance see Law Commission (Consultation Paper No 141), *Criminal Law—Evidence in Criminal Proceedings: Previous Misconduct of a Defendant—A Consultation Paper* (1996) [6.7]–[6.9], available at http://www.lawcom.gov.uk/docs/cp141.pdf.   [6] *R v Guney* [1998] 2 Cr App R 242, 265.

[7] *R v Harz* [1967] AC 760, 785 per Thesiger J: 'the word "relevant" is to all intents and purposes synonymous with the phrase "of probative value" '; *R v Kearley* [1992] 2 AC 228, 263 per Lord Oliver of Aylmerton: '. . . a fact to be relevant must be probative . . .'.

[8] 'It is enough if the item could reasonably show that a fact is slightly more probable than it would appear without that evidence': E W Cleary, *McCormick on Evidence* (3rd ed 1984) 542.   [9] [1973] AC 729, 756.

[10] J H Wigmore, *Evidence in Trials at Common Law (Vol 1A)* (rev by P Tillers, 1983) 969. Such an approach is also taken by L H Hoffmann, 'Similar Facts After *Boardman*' (1975) 91 *Law Quarterly Review* 193, 204–6.

[11] R O Lempert and S A Saltzburg, *A Modern Approach to Evidence: Text, Problems, Transcripts and Cases* (2nd ed 1982) 153: 'Now this concept of plus value is confusing; it is not clear what it would be. In fact it is probably a less precise way of acknowledging, as modern courts do, that even relevant evidence may be excluded if it seems likely to be prejudicial, misleading or unduly time-consuming. . . . The judge's task is to balance the probative value of and need for the evidence against the harm likely to result from admission.' See also H L Trautman, 'Logical or Legal Relevancy—A Conflict in Theory' (1952) 5 *Vanderbilt Law Review* 385; E W Cleary, *McCormick on Evidence* (3rd ed 1984) 548 ('This notion of "plus value" is at best an imprecise way to say that the probative value and the need for the evidence must outweigh the harm likely to result from admission . . .'); W Twining, *Theories of Evidence: Bentham and Wigmore* (1985) 154.

of *discretion*, rather than in determining whether the evidence is 'relevant' in the first place. The Wigmore approach has often been criticized for obscuring the precise basis on which a decision on admissibility has been reached: the mere fact that an item of evidence is legally irrelevant does not tell us whether it is legally irrelevant because it lacks probative value completely, or because of considerations which do not relate to probative value.[12] On the other hand, a court taking the orthodox approach which treats evidence with some probative value, however little, as relevant, but subject to be excluded on a variety of other grounds, would be more likely to articulate the precise basis on which a particular item of evidence is to be excluded.[13]

Whenever a discussion of 'relevance' is encountered in the cases, therefore, the following question should be asked: in precisely what sense is the court using the term 'relevance'? For example, the notion, accepted by some, that there are 'degrees of relevance'[14] is probably premised on the acceptance of a distinction between logical relevance and legal relevance.

' "Weight" of evidence is the degree of probability (both intrinsically and inferentially) which is attached to it by the tribunal of fact once it is established to be relevant and admissible in law...'.[15] Thus where an item of evidence has been admitted in a criminal trial on indictment, it is up to the jury to decide how much *weight* to place on the evidence. That is, the final decision on how compelling the evidence is, and how far it goes in proving the matter requiring proof, is within the province of the jury.

There may be circumstances, however, where relevant evidence ought not to be left to the jury without an accompanying judicial warning. For example, evidence that the defendant was found with a quantity of money in his possession would

---

[12] E W Cleary, *McCormick on Evidence* (3rd ed 1984) 548 n 45: 'The phrase "legal relevance" is misleading inasmuch as it blurs the distinction between evidence that is excluded because it lacks all probative force as to an issue that is of consequence to the outcome of the case and evidence that has probative worth but is excluded on other grounds.' Roberts forcefully states that 'I remain recalcitrant in the view that "legal relevance" and its functional equivalents, such as "direct and immediate" relevance, are dangerous heresy. The principal purpose of the concept, so far as I can see, is to permit judges to base decisions to exclude proffered evidence on value choices concealed behind an opaque and conclusory judgment of "irrelevance," without the need to explain or justify exactly what they are doing. This is not only a question of increasing transparency in legal decision-making, or of forced articulation improving the substantive quality of forensic outcomes, though both these "process values" are certainly significant. Far worse, in some cases judges actually seem to be making relevance work for value preferences which, were they to be explicitly articulated, would fail to derive support from any (other) rule of evidence. This is especially worrying where an expanded concept of relevance is exploited *sub silentio* to exclude defence evidence in criminal proceedings where no (other) exclusionary rule bites; where, in other words, the evidence would have had to be admitted if the traditional relevance standard had been correctly applied': P Roberts, 'Tyres with a "Y": An English Perspective on *Kumho Tire* and Its Implications for the Admissibility of Expert Evidence', accessible via http://www.law.qub.ac.uk/ice. See also M C Slough, 'Relevancy Unraveled' (1956) 5 *Kansas Law Review* 1.
[13] See, however, the defence of the Wigmore approach in J H Wigmore, *Evidence in Trials at Common Law* (Vol 1A) (rev by P Tillers, 1983) 973–4.
[14] See, eg, *R v Edwards* [1991] 1 WLR 207, 219 ('Relevance... is a matter of degree and has to be considered not by rule of thumb but against the background of each individual case'); *R v Randall* [2003] UKHL 69, [2004] 1 WLR 56, [20] ('The question of relevance is typically a matter of degree to be determined, for the most part, by common sense and experience...').   [15] *DPP v Kilbourne* [1973] AC 729, 756.

be relevant to his guilt of the offence of possession of drugs with an intent to supply them. However:

> where such evidence [is] admitted it [is] incumbent upon the judge to give a direction to the jury as to the way in which they should approach the question of whether the finding of the money is probative of the necessary intent. . . . it is necessary . . . for the judge to indicate that any explanation for the money which has been put forward by way of an innocent explanation by the accused would have to be rejected by the jury before they could regard the finding of the money as relevant to the offence. Again the jury should be directed that if there was any possibility of the money being in the accused's possession for reasons other than drug dealing, then the evidence would not be probative. If, on the other hand, the jury were to come to the conclusion that the presence of the money indicated not merely past dealing, but an ongoing dealing in drugs, then finding the money, together with the drugs in question, would be a matter which the jury could take into account in considering whether the necessary intent had been proved.[16]

3 Direct Evidence and Circumstantial Evidence

The testimony of a witness concerning matters personally perceived by that witness, which if believed would be sufficient to prove a fact in issue without further evidence or the need for inference, constitutes *direct* evidence. This is to be distinguished from *circumstantial* evidence, which is evidence from which a fact in issue may be inferred. To put it another way, circumstantial evidence is evidence of a relevant fact as opposed to evidence of a fact in issue. In *R v Exall* Pollock CB stated:

> It has been said that circumstantial evidence is to be considered as a chain, and each piece of evidence as a link in the chain, but that is not so, for then, if any one link broke, the chain would fall. It is more like the case of a rope composed of several cords. One strand of the cord might be insufficient to sustain the weight, but three stranded together may be quite of sufficient strength.
>
> Thus it may be in circumstantial evidence—there may be a combination of circumstances, no one of which would raise a reasonable conviction, or more than a mere suspicion; but the whole, taken together, may create a strong conclusion of guilt, that is, with as much certainty as human affairs can require or admit of.[17]

While, however, 'it is no derogation of evidence to say that it is circumstantial',[18] such evidence must be approached with caution:

> Circumstantial evidence may sometimes be conclusive, but it must always be narrowly examined, if only because evidence of this kind may be fabricated to cast suspicion on another. Joseph commanded the steward of his house, 'put my cup, the silver cup in the sack's mouth of

---

[16] *R v Grant* [1996] 1 Cr App R 73, 78. See also *R v Morris* [1995] 2 Cr App R 69; *R v Lovelock, The Times*, 5 June 1997; *R v Edwards* [1998] Crim LR 207; *R v Guney* [1998] 2 Cr App R 242; *R v Griffiths* [1998] Crim LR 567; *R v Malik* [2000] 2 Cr App R 8; *R v Patel* [2003] EWCA Crim 3782. See generally M Redmayne, 'Drugs, Money and Relevance: *R v Yalman* and *R v Guney*' (1999) 3 *International Journal of Evidence and Proof* 128.

[17] (1866) 4 F & F 922, 929, 176 ER 850, 853. See generally A Samuels, 'Circumstantial Evidence' (2001) 165 *Justice of the Peace* 682. [18] *R v Taylor* (1928) 21 Cr App R 20, 21.

the youngest,' and when the cup was found there Benjamin's brethren too hastily assumed that he must have stolen it. It is also necessary before drawing the inference of the accused's guilt from circumstantial evidence to be sure that there are no other co-existing circumstances which would weaken or destroy the inference.[19]

The following is an eclectic list of some examples of circumstantial evidence:

3.1 Opportunity

Circumstantial evidence of opportunity to commit a crime may be provided, for example, by evidence of the presence of the accused at the time of, and at the scene of, the crime.

3.2 Fingerprints and Bodily Samples

The fact that an object found at the scene of the crime bore the accused's fingerprints constitutes circumstantial evidence of the identity of the perpetrator, as does the fact that samples taken from the accused's body match those taken from the victim. The following guidelines on fingerprint evidence have been provided by the Court of Appeal:

> When the prosecution seek to rely on fingerprint evidence, it will usually be necessary to consider two questions: the first, a question of fact, is whether the control print from the accused has ridge characteristics, and if so how many, similar to those of the print on the item relied on. The second, a question of expert opinion, is whether the print on the item relied on was made by the accused. This opinion will usually be based on the number of similar ridge characteristics in the context of other findings made on comparison of the two prints.
>
> That is as matters presently stand. It may be that in the future, when sufficient new protocols have been established to maintain the integrity of fingerprint evidence, it will be properly receivable as a matter of discretion, without reference to any particular number of similar ridge characteristics. But, in the present state of knowledge of and expertise in relation to finger-prints, we venture to proffer the following guidance, which we hope will be of assistance to Judges and to those involved in criminal prosecutions.
>
> If there are fewer than eight similar ridge characteristics, it is highly unlikely that a Judge will exercise his discretion to admit such evidence and, save in wholly exceptional circumstances, the prosecution should not seek to adduce such evidence. If there are eight or more similar ridge characteristics, a judge may or may not exercise his or her discretion in favour of admitting the evidence. How the discretion is exercised will depend on all the circumstances of the case, including in particular:
>
> (i)   the experience and expertise of the witness;
>
> (ii) the number of similar ridge characteristics;
>
> (iii) whether there are dissimilar characteristics;
>
> (iv) the size of the print relied on, in that the same number of similar ridge characteristics may be more compelling in a fragment of print than in an entire print; and

---

[19] *Teper v R* [1952] AC 480, 489.

(v) the quality and clarity of the print on the item relied on, which may involve, for example, consideration of possible injury to the person who left the print, as well as factors such as smearing or contamination.

In every case where fingerprint evidence is admitted, it will generally be necessary, as in relation to all expert evidence, for the judge to warn the jury that it is evidence [of] opinion only, that the expert's opinion is not conclusive and that it is for the jury to determine whether guilt is proved in the light of all the evidence.[20]

3.3 Continuance

The fact that an event was taking place at a certain point in time may give rise to the inference that it was also taking place at a (sufficiently proximate) prior[21] or subsequent[22] point in time.

3.4 Post-Offence Conduct

The Supreme Court of Canada has succinctly explained:

Under certain circumstances, the conduct of an accused after a crime has been committed may provide circumstantial evidence of the accused's culpability for that crime. For example, an inference of guilt may be drawn from the fact that the accused fled from the scene of the crime or the jurisdiction in which it was committed, attempted to resist arrest, or failed to appear at trial. Such an inference may also arise from acts of concealment, for instance where the accused has lied, assumed a false name, changed his or her appearance, or attempted to hide or dispose of incriminating evidence.[23]

3.5 Reactions of Tracker Dogs

. . . if a dog handler can establish that a dog has been properly trained and that over a period of time the dog's reactions indicate that it is a reliable pointer to the existence of a scent from a particular individual, then that evidence should properly be admitted.

However, it is important to emphasise two safeguards. First, the proper foundation must be laid by detailed evidence establishing the reliability of the dog in question. Secondly, the judge must, in giving his directions to the jury, alert them to the care that they need to take and to look with circumspection at the evidence of tracker dogs, having regard to the fact that the dog may not always be reliable and cannot be cross-examined [or indeed even examined].[24]

---

[20] *R v Buckley* (1999) 163 JP 561, 567–8 (decision of 1999). See also Morgan Harris Burrows, *The Processing of Fingerprint Evidence After the Introduction of the National Automated Fingerprint Identification System (NAFIS)* (Home Office Online Report 23/04), available at http://www.homeoffice.gov.uk/rds/pdfs04/rdsolr2304.pdf.

[21] See *R v Dalloz* (1908) 1 Cr App R 258.   [22] See *Beresford v Justices of St Albans* (1905) 22 TLR 1.

[23] *R v White* [1998] 2 SCR 72, [19].

[24] *R v Pieterson* [1995] 1 WLR 293, 297–8. See also *R v Sykes* [1997] Crim LR 752 (although it would have been better if the trial judge had expressly directed the jury in accordance with the guidance given in *Pieterson*, in the light of the other directions given to the jury and the entirety of the evidence the conviction could not be regarded as unsafe). See generally M Hansen, 'Smells Fishy' [Aug 2000] *ABA Journal* 22.

3.6 Motive

Motive may constitute important circumstantial evidence. Thus:

> Surely in an ordinary prosecution for murder you can prove previous acts or words of the accused to shew he entertained feelings of enmity towards the deceased, and this is evidence not merely of the malicious mind with which he killed the deceased, but of the fact that he killed him. You can give in evidence the enmity of the accused towards the deceased to prove that the accused took the deceased's life. Evidence of motive necessarily goes to prove the fact of the homicide by the accused, as well as his 'malice aforethought,' inasmuch as it is more probable that men are killed by those who have some motive for killing them than by those who have not.[25]

3.7 Adverse Inferences

In civil trials, the failure of one party to give evidence or call witnesses may give rise to the inference that the *other* party's version of the facts withheld by the first party is correct.[26] As the Court of Appeal has explained:

> (1) In certain circumstances a court may be entitled to draw adverse inferences from the absence or silence of a witness who might be expected to have material evidence to give on an issue in an action.
>
> (2) If a court is willing to draw such inferences, they may go to strengthen the evidence adduced on that issue by the other party or to weaken the evidence, if any, adduced by the party who might reasonably have been expected to call the witness.
>
> (3) There must, however, have been some evidence, however weak, adduced by the former on the matter in question before the court is entitled to draw the desired inference: in other words, there must be a case to answer on that issue.
>
> (4) If the reason for the witness's absence or silence satisfies the court, then no such adverse inference may be drawn. If, on the other hand, there is some credible explanation given, even if it is not wholly satisfactory, the potentially detrimental effect of his/her absence or silence may be reduced or nullified.[27]

The failure of the defence in a criminal trial to call a potential witness (other than the accused) may be able to be the subject of a comment to the jury:

> It is permissible for a judge in an appropriate case to tell the jury that they are entitled to take into account the fact that a potential witness who has not been called has not indeed been called. It is of course clear that in making any such comment, the judge must exercise care...But, it would be wrong and inappropriate to seek to tie the hands of the trial judge by laying down or attempting to lay down any particular formulae, because it must depend essentially upon the infinitely varying facts of different cases....

---

[25] *R v Ball* [1911] AC 47, 68. See also R D Friedman and R C Park, 'Sometimes What Everybody Thinks They Know Is True' (2003) 27 *Law and Human Behavior* 629.

[26] *British Railways Board v Herrington* [1972] AC 877, 930 per Lord Diplock.

[27] *Wisniewski v Central Manchester Health Authority* [1998] PIQR P324, P340.

. . . great care must be taken to avoid the possibility that injustice may be done by leaving the jury under the impression that the failure to call a particular witness is something of importance where in fact there may have been some perfectly good and valid reason why a witness should not be called, which would not bear upon the jury's decision.[28]

Furthermore, in determining the guilt of a defendant, 'such inferences from the refusal as appear proper' may be drawn if 'the appropriate consent to the taking of an intimate sample from [him or her] was refused without good cause'.[29] As we shall see later in the book, adverse inferences may also be drawn, in appropriate circumstances, from:

- the accused's failure to mention facts when questioned or charged;[30]
- the accused's failure or refusal to account for objects, substances, or marks;[31]
- the accused's failure or refusal to account for presence at a particular place;[32]
- one of a number of specified failures in relation to disclosure by the accused, or the fact that the accused at trial acts inconsistently in some way with the defence disclosure;[33]
- the accused's silence at trial.[34]

4 Testimonial Evidence and Real Evidence

Testimonial evidence is oral evidence. Thus, the testimony of a witness consists of the oral statements made in court by that witness. Real evidence, on the other hand, is evidence which may be inspected by the trier of fact. Examples of real evidence are diverse and include the demeanour of witnesses, material objects such as the alleged murder weapon, and evidence from out-of-court inspections of, for example, the scene of the crime. Such inspections are known as 'views'.[35] During the well-publicized trial in the late 1990s of Anthony Sawoniuk for war crimes committed in 1942, a view was taken of the scene of the crimes in what is now Belarus.[36]

Experimentation in the jury room is, however, frowned upon:

Equipment which is required or designed to enable a jury to carry out unsupervised scientific experiments in their room . . . are not permissible. On the other hand, . . . a magnifying glass or

---

[28] *R v Gallagher* [1974] 1 WLR 1204, 1211. On the position in Australia see *Dyers v R* [2002] HCA 45.
[29] Police and Criminal Evidence Act 1984, s 62(10).   [30] See Ch 3.   [31] See Ch 3.
[32] See Ch 3.   [33] See Ch 14.   [34] See Ch 11.
[35] See, eg, Evidence Act 1995 (Commonwealth of Australia), s 53; Evidence Act 1995 (New South Wales), s 53; Evidence Act 2001 (Tasmania), s 53.
[36] *R v Sawoniuk* [2000] 2 Cr App R 220, 232: 'The judge was . . . prepared to consider exercise of his judicial powers to give the jury the best possible opportunity of assessing the reliability of the identification evidence. . . . the judge and jury did travel to Domachevo, and members of the jury had the opportunity to stand where Mr Zan said he had stood when observing the scene at the massacre site, and also to observe him from that position when he was standing where he said he had seen the appellant stand.' See also A Buncombe, 'Jury to Visit Site of War Crimes', *The Independent*, 9 Feb 1999, 5; D Ormerod, 'A Prejudicial View?' [2000] *Criminal Law Review* 452.

a ruler, or come to that a tape measure, do not normally raise even the possibility of any such experiments. Indeed they are the sort of objects which any member of the jury might easily have in his pocket when summoned to serve upon the jury, and there could be no possible objection to his using it in the jury room.[37]

Documents constitute a major category of real evidence. The Court of Appeal has doubted the continued existence of any 'best evidence rule' in civil cases under which, for example, secondary evidence of a document is not admissible unless the party seeking to adduce the secondary evidence proves that it is not reasonably possible to produce the document:

> ...the time has now come when it can be said with confidence that the best evidence rule, long on its deathbed, has finally expired. In every case where a party seeks to adduce secondary evidence of the contents of a document, it is a matter for the court to decide, in the light of all the circumstances of the case, what (if any) weight to attach to that evidence. Where the party seeking to adduce the secondary evidence could readily produce the document, it may be expected that (absent some special circumstances) the court will decline to admit the secondary evidence on the ground that it is worthless. At the other extreme, where the party seeking to adduce the secondary evidence genuinely cannot produce the document, it may be expected that (absent some special circumstances) the court will admit the secondary evidence and attach such weight to it as it considers appropriate in all the circumstances. In cases falling between those two extremes, it is for the court to make a judgment as to whether in all the circumstances any weight should be attached to the secondary evidence. Thus, the 'admissibility' of secondary evidence of the contents of documents is...entirely dependent upon whether or not any weight is to be attached to that evidence. And whether or not any weight is to be attached to such secondary evidence is a matter for the court to decide, taking into account all the circumstances of the particular case.[38]

In criminal cases section 133 of the Criminal Justice Act 2003 provides:

> Where a statement in a document is admissible as evidence in criminal proceedings, the statement may be proved by producing either—
>
> (a) the document, or
>
> (b) (whether or not the document exists) a copy of the document or of the material part of it,
>
> authenticated in whatever way the court may approve.[39]

Photographs and photographic images constitute further examples of real evidence. In *A-G's Reference (No 2 of 2002)* the Court of Appeal, after a thorough review of the authorities on photographic images, provided the following helpful summary:

> ...there are...at least four circumstances in which, subject to the judicial discretion to exclude, evidence is admissible to show and, subject to appropriate directions in the summing-up, a jury

---

[37] *R v Maggs* (1990) 91 Cr App R 243, 247 (decision of 1990).

[38] *Springsteen v Masquerade Music Ltd* [2001] EMLR 25 (p 654), [85].

[39] On the issue of authentication see *R v Skinner* [2005] EWCA Crim 1439, a decision on s 27 of the Criminal Justice Act 1988 (the forerunner to s 133 of the 2003 Act).

can be invited to conclude that the defendant committed the offence on the basis of a photographic image from the scene of the crime:

(i) where the photographic image is sufficiently clear, the jury can compare it with the defendant sitting in the dock...;

(ii) where a witness knows the defendant sufficiently well to recognise him as the offender depicted in the photographic image, he can give evidence of this...; and this may be so even if the photographic image is no longer available for the jury...;

(iii) where a witness who does not know the defendant spends substantial time viewing and analysing photographic images from the scene, thereby acquiring special knowledge which the jury does not have, he can give evidence of identification based on a comparison between those images and a reasonably contemporary photograph of the defendant, provided that the images and the photograph are available to the jury...;

(iv) a suitably qualified expert with facial mapping skills can give opinion evidence of identification based on a comparison between images from the scene, (whether expertly enhanced or not) and a reasonably contemporary photograph of the defendant, provided the images and the photograph are available for the jury...[40]

5 The Allocation of Responsibility

Questions arising in a trial may be classified either as questions of law or as questions of fact, and are determined by the trier of law or trier of fact respectively. In jury trials, the trial judge is the trier of law while the jury is the trier of fact.[41] In trials without a jury, the trial judge or magistrate acts as both trier of law and trier of fact. Questions of law include questions relating to the following matters:

- the substantive law;
- the competence of witnesses;
- whether particular evidence should be admitted or excluded;
- whether an issue should be withdrawn from the jury;
- in a criminal case with a jury, whether particular facts constitute an offence under foreign law;[42]
- the directions which should be given by the trial judge in the course of summing up to the jury. A large collection of specimen directions is provided by the Judicial Studies Board, a body providing 'training and instruction for all full-time and part-time judges in the skills necessary to be a judge'.[43] These specimen directions[44] have

---

[40] [2002] EWCA Crim 2373, [2003] 1 Cr App R 21 (p 321), [19]. See also *R v Gardner* [2004] EWCA Crim 1639.
[41] See generally P Otton, 'The Role of the Judge in Criminal Cases' in M McConville and G Wilson (eds), *The Handbook of the Criminal Justice Process* (2002).
[42] Administration of Justice Act 1920, s 15; *R v Okolie, The Times*, 16 June 2000.
[43] http://www.jsboard.co.uk.
[44] Accessible via http://www.jsboard.co.uk/criminal_law/index.htm.

proved influential and a number of them will be referred to at various points in this book.

Questions of fact include questions relating to the following matters:

- the credibility of witnesses;
- the weight to be accorded to evidence;
- whether the facts in issue have been proved.

In criminal trials on indictment, the jury is usually sent out of the courtroom before discussions take place about whether a particular item of evidence should be admitted or excluded. This is because, in the course of such discussions, reference to the evidence in question is often inevitable. A decision on whether to admit or exclude the evidence may be dependent on the existence of particular facts. For example, as we shall see in Chapter 2, a confession by an accused person is not admissible in evidence unless the following facts are established: that the confession was not obtained by oppression, and that the confession was not obtained in consequence of words or conduct conducive to unreliability. A further example may be provided by an issue which will be examined in detail in Chapter 9. Evidence which would otherwise be inadmissible hearsay is admissible in criminal proceedings under an exception to the hearsay rule if the fact that the hearsay statement was made sufficiently soon after the event which precipitated it, so that the mind of the maker of the statement would still have been dominated by the event, can be established. Where the facts on which the trial judge's decision would depend are in dispute, he or she must hear evidence from witnesses to determine the facts. Such evidence is given on a special form of oath known as a voir dire.[45] A hearing on the voir dire is known also as a 'trial within a trial'.

In criminal trials on indictment, the jury is usually sent out of the courtroom before a voir dire hearing takes place. The Privy Council has spoken of the:

> right of a defendant in appropriate circumstances to require a voire dire to be held in the absence of the jury . . . A judge may not override this right by requiring a jury to stay if the defendant wants them to be excused . . . The reason why the voire dire must take place in the absence of the jury is that the jury should not be made aware of evidence which subsequently turns out to be inadmissible.[46]

In criminal cases the traditional procedure involves determinations of whether evidence should be excluded being made at the point of the trial at which it is sought to adduce the evidence; it is only if the evidence is so crucial that the prosecution cannot even open its case without referring to it that a determination of whether it should be excluded may take place immediately after the jury has been sworn. However, this traditional procedure now stands alongside the provision made by the Criminal

---

[45] 'The title of the procedure comes from the French "vrai dire" and the Latin "veritatem dicere" literally to "tell the truth". "Voir" (sometimes spelt "voire") is the Norman-French for "vrai" and reflects the long lineage of this judicial procedure': J H Phillips, 'The Voir Dire' (1989) 63 *Australian Law Journal* 46, 46.

[46] *Mitchell v R* [1998] 2 WLR 839, 845.

Procedure and Investigations Act 1996 for pre-trial hearings.[47] Such hearings, which may be used to make determinations of whether evidence should be excluded, take place before the jury is sworn.[48] The reporting of matters pertaining to a pre-trial hearing before the conclusion of the relevant trial is prohibited.[49]

The obvious advantage of a pre-trial hearing is that it avoids the need for the jury to be excluded from the courtroom for an indefinite period while a trial within a trial takes place. Further, and perhaps more importantly, a pre-trial hearing would obviate the need for full-scale preparations for a trial which could very well be abandoned later if the accused changes his or her plea to guilty after defence attempts to obtain exclusion fail, or if the prosecution decides not to proceed after defence attempts to obtain exclusion succeed. However, 'it is possible that the parties' knowledge that a jury has not been empanelled means that there is less pressure on them to co-operate at the pre-trial stage than during the trial proper', and thus there is a danger that pre-trial hearings may themselves become slow-moving affairs which do little to alleviate the problem of delay in the criminal justice process generally. Problems in relation to pre-trial hearings may also be caused by the possible 'lack of continuity of judge and counsel, and the [lack of] incentives for lawyers to do more work at an early stage'.[50]

In civil cases the position is as follows:

In general, disputes about the admissibility of evidence in civil proceedings are best left to be resolved by the judge at the substantive hearing of the application or at the trial of the action, rather than at a separate preliminary hearing. The judge at a preliminary hearing on admissibility will usually be less well informed about the case. Preliminary hearings can also cause unnecessary costs and delays.[51]

While there is no requirement that this be invariably done, it is obviously helpful for the precise reasons for admitting or excluding a particular item of evidence to be articulated as clearly as possible:

Undoubtedly there will be occasions when good practice requires a reasoned ruling. For example, where the judge decides a question of law sufficient, but no more, must be displayed of his reasoning to enable a review on appeal. Again, on a mixed question of law and fact the judge should state his findings of fact so that the law can be put in context. Similarly, the exercise of a discretion will often call for an account (however brief) of the judge's reasoning, especially where the issue concerns the existence of the discretion as well as the way in which it should be exercised. These are no more than examples. In every case it will depend on the circumstances whether reasons should be given, and if so with what particularity. Frequently, there will be everything to gain and little to lose by the giving of reasons, even if only briefly. But other situations are different...

...

---

[47] See generally A Edwards, 'The Criminal Procedure and Investigations Act 1996: (2) The Procedural Aspects' [1997] *Criminal Law Review* 321.   [48] Ss 39, 40.

[49] S 41. On the position in magistrates' courts see the Magistrates' Courts Act 1980, ss 8A–8D.

[50] M Redmayne, 'Process Gains and Process Values: The Criminal Procedure and Investigations Act 1996' (1997) 60 *Modern Law Review* 79, 88.   [51] *Stroude v Beazer Homes Ltd* [2005] EWCA Civ 265, [10].

. . . In every instance, it is for the judge to decide whether the interests of justice call for the giving of reasons, and if so with what degree of particularity.[52]

The Court of Appeal has emphasized that it would be desirable, in the interests of avoiding difficulties and ensuring that cases are conducted with clarity, if there were discussion at the end of the evidence of the points of evidence arising, and if an attempt were made to reach, if not agreement, then at least an understanding about how they should be handled. This is as important for counsel to know before addressing the jury as it is for the judge to know before summing up.[53] Furthermore, while it is the judge's duty in summing up to refer to the salient items of evidence,[54] there is no obligation to rehearse *all* the evidence in the case: brevity in summing up, as in examination and cross-examination of witnesses and in counsels' speeches, is a virtue and not a vice. In general, the longer a trial, the greater the jury's need for assistance from the judge in relation to the evidence. Many jurors do not have the experience, ability, or opportunity of a judge to note significant evidence and to cross-reference evidence from different sources which relate to the same issue. Accordingly, in a trial lasting several days it would generally be of assistance to the jury for the judge to summarize those factual issues which are not disputed and, where there is significant dispute in relation to material facts, identify succinctly those pieces of evidence which are in conflict. By so doing, the judge can focus the jury's attention on those factual issues which they have to resolve. It would never be appropriate, however, for a summing-up to be a mere rehearsal of evidence. The Court of Appeal would not look favourably on appeals based merely on a judge's failure to refer to particular pieces of evidence.[55]

6 Exclusionary Rules and Exclusionary Discretions

Relevant evidence is liable to exclusion not only pursuant to the application of an exclusionary rule, but also in the exercise of an exclusionary discretion. Relevant evidence which is not subject to an exclusionary rule and which is therefore admissible, but which is excluded in the exercise of discretion, is sometimes erroneously described as 'inadmissible'. The most important exclusionary discretion is the discretion, in criminal cases, to exclude prosecution evidence on the ground that its probative value is outweighed by its prejudicial effect.[56] The principle that it is only *prosecution* evidence which is subject to exclusion pursuant to the probative value versus prejudicial effect discretion has not escaped criticism.[57] Such criticism may be justified. It is arguable that the existence of

---

[52] *Wallace v R* [1997] 1 Cr App R 396, 407–8.   •   [53] *R v N* [1998] Crim LR 886.

[54] *R v Soames-Waring, The Times*, 20 July 1998; [1999] Crim LR 89.

[55] *R v Farr* (1999) 163 JP 193 (decision of 1998).

[56] *R v Randall* [2003] UKHL 69, [2004] 1 WLR 56, [18]: 'the discretionary power to exclude relevant evidence which is tendered by the prosecution, if its prejudicial effect outweighs its probative value, does not apply to the position as between co-accused. In a joint criminal trial a judge has no discretionary power at the request of one accused to exclude relevant evidence tending to support the defence of another accused . . .'.

[57] R Pattenden, *Judicial Discretion and Criminal Litigation* (1990) 259.

a judicial discretion to exclude defence evidence should be explicitly acknowledged, so that such evidence should not automatically be admitted if it is considered 'relevant' and is not subject to an exclusionary rule. The concept of 'relevance' is, as seen above, an imprecise one. This being the case, it may be desirable to acknowledge openly the existence of an exclusionary discretion in the context of defence evidence, so that the precise reasons for excluding such evidence in a particular case are at least more likely to be articulated, rather than cloaked in a finding of 'irrelevance'. Interestingly, the Court of Appeal stated that 'we should not like it to be thought that we have concluded that such a discretion can never exist, although the authorities make it difficult to hold that it does'.[58]

Another important exclusionary discretion is that provided for by section 78(1) of the Police and Criminal Evidence Act 1984. This enables prosecution evidence to be excluded in the interests of ensuring the fairness of a trial.

While it was traditionally doubted whether there was a discretion to exclude admissible evidence in civil cases, it is now accepted that rule 32.1 of the Civil Procedure Rules gives the court such a discretion. Rule 32.1 provides:

(1) The court may control the evidence by giving directions as to—

    (a) the issues on which it requires evidence;

    (b) the nature of the evidence which it requires to decide those issues; and

    (c) the way in which the evidence is to be placed before the court.

(2) The court may use its power under this rule to exclude evidence that would otherwise be admissible.

(3) The court may limit cross-examination.

The Court of Appeal has commented: 'While we do not think that one should simply read across into rule 32 of the Civil Procedure Rules the jurisprudence relating to the powers long exercised by judges in a criminal trial, it can no longer be argued that the civil court has no jurisdiction to exclude relevant and admissible evidence in a civil case.'[59]

The essential difference between exclusionary rules and exclusionary discretions relates to the attitude of appellate courts. An appeal on the basis of an allegedly erroneous exercise of discretion is not treated by an appellate court in the same way as an appeal on the basis of an alleged misapplication of a rule of law. If, on applying an exclusionary rule, a trial judge in a Crown Court concludes that the evidence should not be excluded, the Court of Appeal will not hesitate to substitute its own conclusion if it disagrees with that reached by the trial judge. It is immaterial that the trial judge may have, in reaching his or her conclusion, taken all relevant factors into account and left irrelevant factors out of consideration.[60] However, where a decision is reached pursuant to judicial discretion

---

[58] *R v Thompson* [1995] 2 Cr App R 589, 597.

[59] *Grobbelaar v Sun Newspapers Ltd, The Times*, 12 August 1999 (transcript from Smith Bernal). See also *Jones v University of Warwick* [2003] EWCA Civ 151, [2003] 1 WLR 954 (discussed in Ch 5); *O'Brien v Chief Constable of South Wales Police* [2005] UKHL 26, [2005] 2 WLR 1038 (discussed in Ch 8).

[60] See *R v Viola* (1982) 75 Cr App R 125, 130–1 (decision of 1982).

and this decision is the subject of an appeal, the appellate court will interfere with the decision only in limited circumstances. In considering the issue of the circumstances in which the Court of Appeal should interfere with a decision reached pursuant to judicial discretion, Lord Denning MR said in *Ward v James*:

> This court . . . will interfere if it can see that the judge has given no weight (or no sufficient weight) to those considerations which ought to have weighed with him. . . . Conversely it will interfere if it can see that he has been influenced by other considerations which ought not to have weighed with him, or not weighed so much with him . . .[61]

In a similar vein, Scarman LJ observed in *R v Scarrott* that so long as a trial judge 'does not err in law, takes into account all relevant matters and excludes consideration of irrelevant matters, his discretion will stand'.[62] And in *R v Quinn*, it was said that 'before . . . reach[ing] the conclusion that the judge was wrong . . . [the Court of Appeal] would have to be satisfied that no reasonable judge, having heard the evidence that this learned judge did, could have reached the conclusion that he did'.[63]

As their label suggests, exclusionary discretions are 'discretionary' in nature, in the sense that the tests to be applied by trial judges in deciding whether to exercise such discretions are typically flexible and open-textured. In other words, a degree of latitude is accorded to the trial judge in deciding whether to exclude the evidence. By contrast, exclusionary rules are traditionally more rigid, often prescribing that where certain conditions are satisfied, a particular consequence will automatically follow. A classic example of this, as we shall see in Chapter 9, is the rule against hearsay in criminal proceedings. Where, in a criminal trial, an item of evidence falls within the definition of hearsay, it must automatically be excluded, unless it comes within one of the prescribed exceptions to the rule.

There has been much debate as to the desirability of allowing trial judges more discretion (whether in the context of exclusionary rules or exclusionary discretions) in determining whether evidence should be admitted or excluded. Wigmore once denounced the idea of increased discretion in the law of evidence in colourful terms: 'Is it not

---

[61] [1966] 1 QB 273, 293. See D Herling, 'Weight in Discretionary Decision-Making' (1999) 19 *Oxford Journal of Legal Studies* 583, 593: 'To weigh a factor is to gauge the force with which it advocates a particular solution to the question which the decision-making process is designed to resolve.'

[62] [1978] QB 1016, 1028. 'In my opinion a judge reaches a decision in the exercise of his "discretion" . . . where, on the facts found by or agreed before him and on the law correctly stated by him, he is required in the exercise of his judicial function to decide between two or more courses of action without any further rules governing the decision which he should make, other than that he should act judicially. It is just because this is the nature of such a task facing a judge that this court is restricted by the authorities to the extent to which it can interfere. Unless his decision is perverse in the *Wednesbury* sense (see *Associated Provincial Picture Houses Ltd v Wednesbury Corp* [1947] 2 All ER 680, [1948] 1 KB 223), it must be one to which a judge, acting judicially, could come': *Viscount De L'Isle v Times Newspapers* [1987] 3 All ER 499, 504 per May LJ. See also *Hindes v Edwards*, *The Times*, 9 Oct 1987; *In re W*, *The Times*, 22 and 23 Nov 1990; *DPP v Godwin* [1991] RTR 303, 308; *R v Glennon* (1992) 66 ALJR 344, 348 per Mason CJ and Toohey J (an exercise of discretion should not be overturned unless the trial judge 'took into account some extraneous consideration, failed to take into account a relevant consideration or mistook the facts . . .').

[63] [1995] 1 Cr App R 480, 489. Cited approvingly by the Court of Appeal in *R v Dures* [1997] 2 Cr App R 247, 261–2.

probable that in these proposed large areas of "discretion" the Law of Evidence will suffer ... a relapse into that primal condition of chaos, described in Genesis 1: 2, when the Earth "was without form and void"?'[64] Courts in earlier times, too, viewed the notion of judicial discretion with some suspicion.[65] The issue of the relative merits and demerits of discretionary, as opposed to rule-based, approaches to the law of criminal evidence and procedure continues to be the subject of a good deal of discussion.[66] The main objection voiced to vesting considerable discretion in trial judges is that the resulting uncertainty and unpredictability would make preparation for trial, and planning and decision-making generally, more difficult.[67] This is an argument on which it is easy to place too much weight. It is unlikely that uncertainty and unpredictability would pose a problem after the emergence of a substantial body of case law which lays down clear guidelines in the form of factors to be taken into account by a trial judge in deciding whether to admit or exclude the evidence. An appropriate balance should be able to be struck between maintaining flexibility, and considerations such as the promotion of certainty and predictability.[68] Further, the objection assumes that there is certainty and predictability where the determination of whether to admit or exclude is governed by rigid tests. This is far from being the case:[69] prior to the fundamental reforms to criminal hearsay doctrine effected by the Criminal Justice Act 2003,[70] courts regularly misapplied the hearsay rule, or evaded it altogether, in order to achieve the admissibility of highly cogent evidence.[71] Paradoxically, therefore, the introduction of a more discretionary approach might well increase, rather than decrease, certainty and predictability.

Where exclusionary discretions are encountered in the law of evidence, it is important to determine whether clear guidelines have been laid down by the courts to govern the exercise of the particular discretion, and if so, to assess whether these guidelines clearly reflect the rationale for the existence of the discretion.

---

[64] J H Wigmore, 'The American Law Institute Code of Evidence Rules: A Dissent' (1942) 28 *American Bar Association Journal* 23, 24.   [65] See, eg, *R v Cargill* (1913) 8 Cr App R 224, 229.

[66] See A L-T Choo, *Abuse of Process and Judicial Stays of Criminal Proceedings* (1993) 119–30, and the references cited therein. See also A M Gleeson, 'Individualised Justice—The Holy Grail' (1995) 69 *Australian Law Journal* 421; C E Schneider, 'Discretion and Rules: A Lawyer's View' in K Hawkins (ed), *The Uses of Discretion* (1992); A Stein, 'Evidential Rules for Criminal Trials: Who Should Be in Charge?' in S Doran and J D Jackson (eds), *The Judicial Role in Criminal Proceedings* (2000); C R Sunstein, 'Problems with Rules' (1995) 83 *California Law Review* 953; Law Commission (Consultation Paper No 141), *Criminal Law—Evidence in Criminal Proceedings: Previous Misconduct of a Defendant—A Consultation Paper* (1996) [9.46]–[9.50], available at http://www.lawcom.gov.uk/docs/cp141.pdf; S Walker, *Taming the System: The Control of Discretion in Criminal Justice 1950–1990* (1993).

[67] See generally C E Schneider, 'Discretion and Rules: A Lawyer's View' in K Hawkins (ed), *The Uses of Discretion* (1992) 76–7.

[68] See generally A M Gleeson, 'Individualised Justice—The Holy Grail' (1995) 69 *Australian Law Journal* 421.

[69] See C T McCormick, 'The Borderland of Hearsay' (1930) 39 *Yale Law Journal* 489, 503 ('[It is assumed that a fixed categorical approach to admissibility] enable[s] the lawyer preparing his case to know in advance with fair certainty what he can get in, and what he cannot. If a question as to admissibility does arise, the judge who has no time for subtle discrimination in the heat of trial can make a decision in his stride, as it were. This is splendid, and the only difficulty is that it does not work').   [70] See Ch 9.

[71] See generally D J Birch, 'Hearsay-Logic and Hearsay-Fiddles: *Blastland* Revisited' in P Smith (ed), *Criminal Law: Essays in Honour of J C Smith* (1987); A L-T Choo, *Evidence: Text and Materials* (1998) 304–15.

7 Free(r) Proof

Allied with the growing reliance on 'discretionary' tests to determine whether evidence should be admitted or excluded has been an increasing embracement of the concept of free proof. The term 'free proof' may be taken 'to refer to natural or common sense modes of reasoning about facts at trial, unconstrained by artificial, mandatory precepts, such as strict rules excluding classes of evidence or witnesses'.[72] Jeremy Bentham argued, in effect, that all relevant evidence should be admitted, with exclusion justified only if admission would result in vexation, expense, or delay.[73] Unsurprisingly, 'no common law country has yet implemented Bentham's proposals for total abolition of the technical rules'.[74] As will be seen throughout this book, however, the courts' response to allegedly unreliable evidence is increasingly to decline to exclude it altogether from the jury's consideration, but to allow the jury to evaluate it after being provided with an appropriate warning by the trial judge.[75] It is notable, as Twining has pointed out, 'that it is the proponents of "Law-and-Order", generally regarded as conservatives or reactionaries, who claim to have reason on their side and who attribute the survival of the technical rules to the sinister economic interests of a privileged group, the legal profession'.[76]

Paradoxically, the move away from reliance on the total *exclusion* of evidence has not been accompanied by any real development of rules governing the *evaluation* of admitted evidence. 'Throughout history Anglo-American triers of fact have been almost entirely free from rules of quantum and weight.'[77] Scholars such as Twining[78] have criticized the English law of evidence for remaining too heavily focused on questions of whether particular evidence is to be admitted or excluded, and for its consequent marginalization of questions of how particular evidence which has been admitted is to be evaluated. As will be seen in the course of this book, this criticism is to a large extent justified. Putting aside the law's expectation that those responsible for evaluating evidence are apprised in appropriate circumstances of its possible unreliability, the actual process of evaluating evidence is considered to be a question of fact with which the law of evidence has little concern. Indeed, Wigmore went so far as to describe any discussion of rules of weight or credibility as 'moral treason'.[79]

---

[72] W Twining, 'Freedom of Proof and the Reform of Criminal Evidence' (1997) 31 *Israel Law Review* 439, 439 n 1.

[73] J Bentham, *Rationale of Judicial Evidence, Specially Applied to English Practice (Vol 1)* (1827) (reprinted 1978) 1.   [74] W Twining, *Rethinking Evidence: Exploratory Essays* (1994) 186.

[75] An analogous development is also evident in the law relating to abuse of process. The abuse of process doctrine allows, *inter alia*, criminal proceedings to be stayed as an abuse of the process of the court if their continuation would compromise the accused's right to a fair trial. Although it is well settled that proceedings may be stayed on account of pre-trial delay, a number of recent decisions have suggested that, in some cases, the right to a fair trial would be sufficiently protected by warnings to the jury about the possible implications of the delay; an outright stay of the proceedings would not be required. See generally *R v M* [2005] EWCA Crim 1226.   [76] W Twining, *Rethinking Evidence: Exploratory Essays* (1994) 186.

[77] W Twining, 'Freedom of Proof and the Reform of Criminal Evidence' (1997) 31 *Israel Law Review* 439, 448.

[78] See generally W Twining, *Rethinking Evidence: Exploratory Essays* (1994).

[79] Book review by J H Wigmore, (1909) 3 *Illinois Law Review* 477, 478.

8 Issues in Criminal Evidence

It is important, given the special position of criminal evidence, to identify the considerations upon which the law of criminal evidence is premised. Essentially, it may be said that underlying the principles of criminal evidence are considerations of both intrinsic policy and extrinsic policy. The concern of intrinsic policy is with the promotion of accurate fact-finding or truth[80] discovery, or, in other words, with what Jeremy Bentham called 'rectitude of decision'.[81] The need to ensure that evidence is as reliable as possible is especially important in the case of prosecution evidence, because the admission of unreliable prosecution evidence could lead to the wrongful conviction of an innocent person. 'People have', in the words of Ronald Dworkin, 'a profound right not to be convicted of crimes of which they are innocent.'[82] The crucial question for the evidence lawyer, however, is how far the law of criminal evidence should go in protecting the innocent from wrongful conviction. If the right of the innocent not to be convicted were to be regarded as an absolute right (in other words, if what we are seeking is maximum protection of the innocent), then it is arguable that the prosecution should not be permitted to rely upon any category of evidence which can be seen to be inherently unreliable (a category which might include, for example, confession evidence and visual identification evidence). A blanket ban on such evidence would, however, probably have the effect of leading to the widespread acquittal of the guilty, and would therefore be regarded as unpalatable. It is clearly not required 'that every conceivable step be taken, at whatever cost, to eliminate the possibility of convicting an innocent person'.[83] In examining intrinsic policy considerations, therefore, it is important not to lose sight of the underlying tension between, on the one hand, the pressure to admit all relevant prosecution evidence, and, on the other hand, the need to protect the innocent from conviction.

As we shall see throughout this book, a number of evidential principles are justified in English law on the ground that they ensure the reliability of evidence. A prime example is provided by the limitations placed on the admissibility of hearsay evidence. Concerns about reliability also underlie the principles relating to corroboration and supporting evidence. Certain types of evidence require to be corroborated by other evidence in order to be admissible,[84] and there is a general principle in the law of evidence:

> that a 'special warning' is necessary if experience, research or common sense has indicated that there is a difficulty with a certain type of evidence that requires giving the jury a warning of its dangers and the need for caution, tailored to meet the needs of the case. This will

---

[80] For a critical discussion of the concept of 'truth' see generally K D Kilback and M D Tochor, 'Searching for Truth but Missing the Point' (2002) 40 *Alberta Law Review* 333.

[81] J Bentham, *Rationale of Judicial Evidence, Specially Applied to English Practice (Vol 1)* (1827) (reprinted 1978) 1.   [82] R Dworkin, *A Matter of Principle* (1986) 72.

[83] *Patterson v New York* 432 US 197, 208 (1977).

[84] See Perjury Act 1911, s 13; Road Traffic Regulation Act 1984, s 89.

often be the case where jurors may be unaware of the difficulty, or may insufficiently understand it.[85]

The strength of the warning and its terms will depend on the nature of the evidence, its reliability or lack of it, and the potential problems it poses.[86]

It should be noted that evidence may be excluded in English law not only because of its potential unreliability, but also because of considerations of *extrinsic* policy which do not relate to reliability.[87] Such considerations as the importance of upholding values and protecting the moral integrity of the criminal justice system may dictate that evidence should sometimes be excluded even if reliable. Thus Galligan has written that:

> there are two distinct issues: (i) one concerns rules about the probative value of evidence; (ii) the other concerns rules about the exclusion of evidence for reasons other than reasons of evidentiary value. The question in (i) is how to deal with evidence the probative value of which is in doubt, or which, although of probative value, contains a degree of risk that it will be used improperly ... The guiding objective in these cases is rectitude of outcome; the question is, given some such uncertainty or defect, how best is rectitude achieved; what is the most rational procedure for obtaining an accurate outcome. These are issues *internal* to proof. In (ii) the issue is whether certain kinds of evidence, which are likely to be of probative value and therefore relevant in achieving rectitude, should be excluded, in order to advance other values or policies ... These are issues *external* to proof; they are based on values which compete with rectitude. The exclusion of evidence in order to uphold those values may mean the loss of probative evidence and thus a lower level of accuracy. The distinction between (i) and (ii) is fundamental, since (i) is concerned with the rationality of proof, while (ii) is concerned with the conflict of values.[88]

The issue of extrinsic policy considerations is best illustrated by reference to the problem of improperly obtained evidence, discussed in Chapter 5. Suppose that a piece of prosecution evidence has been obtained illegally by the police, but that there is no suggestion that this evidence may be unreliable. If the sole concern of the courts were with intrinsic policy considerations, it would have to be said that there is no reason to exclude the evidence. This would be the case despite the seriousness of the police illegality. Yet the courts have acknowledged that improperly obtained, yet reliable, evidence is liable to exclusion in certain circumstances. The exact rationale for such exclusion will be explored in Chapter 5, but for present purposes one should note the extension of the courts' exclusionary jurisdiction beyond the confines of considerations of intrinsic policy. When progressing through this book, it is important to assess how well considerations of intrinsic and/or extrinsic policy are accommodated within the individual doctrines of the law of criminal evidence that are encountered.

---

[85] *R v Luttrell* [2004] EWCA Crim 1344, [2004] 2 Cr App R 31 (p 520), [42].

[86] Ibid, [43]. For example, warnings are required in relation to identification evidence (*R v Turnbull* [1977] QB 224) and evidence of a confession made by a mentally handicapped person not in the presence of an independent person (Police and Criminal Evidence Act 1984, s 77(1)).

[87] Such considerations are not necessarily uncontroversial: see, eg, W T Pizzi, *Trials Without Truth: Why Our System of Criminal Trials Has Become an Expensive Failure and What We Need to Do to Rebuild It* (1999).

[88] D J Galligan, 'More Scepticism About Scepticism' (1988) 8 *Oxford Journal of Legal Studies* 249, 255 (italics in original). See also T J Reed, 'Evidentiary Failures: A Structural Theory of Evidence Applied to Hearsay Issues' (1994) 18 *American Journal of Trial Advocacy* 353, 362.

9 Civil Evidence and Criminal Evidence

There are two fundamental differences between civil procedure and criminal procedure. First, while rectitude of decision is obviously important in civil proceedings, it is not allied to the need to protect the innocent from wrongful conviction. Secondly, extrinsic policy considerations do not, again, assume the same dimension in civil proceedings as they do in criminal proceedings. The peculiar nature of due process considerations in criminal proceedings is well captured by Packer:

> The combination of stigma and loss of liberty that is embodied in the end result of the criminal process is viewed as being the heaviest deprivation that government can inflict on the individual. Furthermore, the processes that culminate in these highly afflictive sanctions are seen as in themselves coercive, restricting, and demeaning.[89]

These differences may suggest that there should, in reality, be not one, but two, 'laws' of evidence. Indeed, numerous illustrations of the manner in which the principles of civil and criminal evidence differ will be encountered in the course of this book. For the present, three brief examples will suffice:

• There is a presumption in criminal cases that every issue be proved by the prosecution as the party bringing the action. In civil cases, however, there is no presumption that the claimant prove every issue.

• The rule against hearsay has been effectively abolished in civil cases, but remains applicable (albeit subject to wide-ranging exceptions) in criminal cases.

• Specific rules of a fairly complex nature apply in relation to evidence of a defendant's bad character in criminal proceedings, but there are no analogous rules in civil proceedings.

10 The Implications of Trial by Jury

Writing in 1898, the great American evidence scholar Thayer described the law of evidence as 'the child of the jury system'.[90] It is still true to say today that the existence of some of the major exclusionary rules of criminal evidence is attributable, at least in part, to the phenomenon of trial by jury. This is despite the fact that, statistically, trials on indictment account for only a small percentage of all criminal trials. Thus, the rule against hearsay in criminal trials is often justified on the ground that juries may lack the ability to assess properly the reliability of hearsay evidence on a case-by-case basis, and thus it is preferable that a general ban on such evidence (albeit one that is now subject to wide-ranging exceptions) be maintained. In a similar vein, the existence of a specific

---

[89] H L Packer, *The Limits of the Criminal Sanction* (1969) 165–6.
[90] J B Thayer, *A Preliminary Treatise on Evidence at the Common Law* (1969; first pub 1898) 266.

statutory regime governing evidence of a defendant's bad character in criminal proceedings may be justified on the ground that such evidence is easily misused by juries.

Are such assumptions about the jury really justified? The short answer to this is that we simply have no way of knowing for certain. Certainly, scepticism about the validity of such assumptions is growing. As Weinstein, an eminent American evidence scholar and later a judge, has noted vividly:

> Many rules of evidence can be understood only in terms of the judge's need to rigidly control a group of ignorant illiterates—the jury. But change is . . . apparent here: the present day juror is much more sophisticated and educated than was the juror sitting when the rules of evidence solidified in the last century.[91]

The problem is that to conduct serious empirical research in England and Wales into how juries handle evidence is a difficult enterprise owing to section 8(1) of the Contempt of Court Act 1981, which effectively makes it illegal to ask juries questions about their deliberations in actual trials: 'Subject to subsection (2) below, it is a contempt of court to obtain, disclose or solicit any particulars of statements made, opinions expressed, arguments advanced or votes cast by members of a jury in the course of their deliberations in any legal proceedings.'[92] Any empirical research on juries and the principles of criminal evidence must therefore be based on simulated 'trials' involving mock jurors. The need to rely on simulations means that subjects are not exposed to the atmosphere, drama, and tension of a real trial, and may not therefore (consciously or otherwise) react in the same way as they would in the context of a real trial. The repeal of section 8 of the Contempt of Court Act 1981, as recommended in 1993 by a Royal Commission on Criminal Justice[93] and as advocated by many,[94] would enable 'real' juries to be questioned about how evidence was evaluated in their deliberations. In a consultation exercise being conducted by the Department for Constitutional Affairs in early 2005,[95] one of the options being consulted upon is whether the law should be

---

[91] J B Weinstein, 'Some Difficulties in Devising Rules for Determining Truth in Judicial Trials' (1966) 66 *Columbia Law Review* 223, 225.

[92] See *R v Mirza* [2004] UKHL 2, [2004] 1 AC 1118; G Daly, 'Jury Secrecy: *R v Mirza; R v Connor and Rollock*' (2004) 8 *International Journal of Evidence and Proof* 186; R Fisher, 'Privacy of the Jury' (2004) 148 *Solicitors' Journal* 158; G Langdon-Down, 'Doing Secret Service' (2004) 101(6) *Law Society's Gazette* 18.

[93] Royal Commission on Criminal Justice, *Report* (Cm 2263) (1993) 2.

[94] See, eg, House of Commons Science and Technology Committee, *Forensic Evidence on Trial* (Seventh Report of Session 2004–05) (HC 96-I) (2005) [166] (bold font removed): 'Jury research is vital to understand how juries cope with highly complex forensic evidence. Jury research would also be instructive for understanding differences in the way that jurors respond to oral and written reports by experts, and how easy they find interpretation of these reports. We recommend that section 8 of the Contempt of Court Act be amended to permit research into jurors' deliberations.' Available at http://www.publications.parliament.uk/pa/cm200405/cmselect/cmsctech/96/96i.pdf. Contrast, however, M Zander, 'The Mystery of the Jury Room Is Best Left Intact', *The Times*, 19 Apr 2005, Law, 5; Lord Justice Auld, *Review of the Criminal Courts of England and Wales* (2001) Ch 5, accessible via http://www.criminal-courts-review.org.uk/.

[95] Department for Constitutional Affairs, *Jury Research and Impropriety: A Consultation Paper to Assess Options for Allowing Research into Jury Deliberations and to Consider Investigations into Alleged Juror Impropriety* (DCA CP 04/05) (2005), available at http://www.dca.gov.uk/consult/juryresearch/juryresearch_cp0405.pdf. See generally J Holroyd, 'Judging the Jury' (2005) 155 *New Law Journal* 398.

amended to permit, subject to safeguards, research into a jury's deliberations. For the moment, however, the lack of definitive empirical evidence has not deterred the law from making (often unstated) assumptions about what juries can and cannot cope with. While, for example, it is assumed that juries may be incapable of evaluating hearsay evidence fairly, they are expected to be able to obey instructions from the trial judge to treat certain evidence as relevant only to 'credit' (credibility), rather than as relevant to the facts in issue in the case. The extent to which juries can comprehend and comply with such an instruction is, at best, speculative.

In a quest for greater transparency, Lord Justice Auld, in a review of the operation of the criminal courts, recommended the introduction of a system under which juries are in effect required to justify their verdicts:

> • the judge should devise and put to the jury a series of written factual questions, the answers to which could logically lead only to a verdict of guilty or not guilty; the questions should correspond with those in the up-dated case and issues summary, supplemented as necessary in a separate written list prepared for the purpose; and each question should be tailored to the law as the judge knows it to be and to the issues and evidence in the case; and

> • the judge, where he considers it appropriate, should be permitted to require a jury to answer publicly each of his questions and to declare a verdict in accordance with those answers.[96]

The introduction of such a system does not currently appear to be under serious consideration.

It might be tempting to argue that, given the uncertainty about whether juries are capable of what is expected of them, it would be fairer to move to a system of trial by judge alone. The obvious problem with this suggestion is that—any considerations pertaining to the intrinsic value of jury trial aside—it is premised on a further assumption: that professional judges would necessarily perform better than lay jurors. As Zuckerman has observed:

> Given that common-sense reasoning and moral sentiment influence fact-finding whether by judge or jury it is difficult to see what can be achieved by a change from lay judges to professional ones. Furthermore, if professional judges become triers of fact, the amount of prejudicial evidence will increase due to the assumption in judicial circles that professional judges are immune from prejudice and need not necessarily be kept ignorant of such evidence.[97]

---

[96] Lord Justice Auld, *Review of the Criminal Courts of England and Wales* (2001) Ch 11 para 55, accessible via http://www.criminal-courts-review.org.uk/. See also J R Spencer, 'Inscrutable Verdicts, the Duty to Give Reasons and Article 6 of the European Convention on Human Rights', *Archbold News*, 14 Feb 2001, 5.

[97] A A S Zuckerman, *The Principles of Criminal Evidence* (1989) 262 n 36. Note also the colourful comment, in relation to evidence of an accused's propensity for wrongdoing, by M R Damaška, 'Propensity Evidence in Continental Legal Systems' (1994) 70 *Chicago-Kent Law Review* 55, 65: 'Unfortunately, there is no solid ground in psychology for the belief that only novice factfinders succumb to the temptation of drawing negative conclusions from a person's unsavory life history, while professional adjudicators are immune, even in close cases, to the syren's call of these inferences.'

Surely, if the system of jury trial is regarded as being of intrinsic value and as a fundamental facet of the criminal justice system, it is the principles of criminal evidence which
should be adapted to fit properly into the system. It is not the system that should be
tinkered with to enable the principles of criminal evidence to be accommodated within it.

Debate has continued for several years on the appropriateness of trial by judge and
jury for complex fraud cases, which are notorious for the complex evidence which they
can generate. Provision is now made in section 43 of the Criminal Justice Act 2003 for
the prosecution to apply for certain serious or complex fraud trials to be conducted
without a jury.[98] In deciding whether an order for a trial without a jury should be made,
account must be taken of the question whether 'the complexity of the trial or the length
of the trial (or both) is likely to make the trial so burdensome to the members of a jury
hearing the trial that the interests of justice require that serious consideration should be
given to the question of whether the trial should be conducted without a jury'.[99]
In determining this question regard must be had 'to any steps which might reasonably
be taken to reduce the complexity or length of the trial',[100] although 'a step is not to
be regarded as reasonable if it would significantly disadvantage the prosecution'.[101]
Section 330(5) provides that a statutory instrument containing an order bringing
section 43 into force 'may only be made if a draft of the statutory instrument has been
laid before, and approved by a resolution of, each House of Parliament'.

Reference will be made at appropriate points in this book to the results of some of
the relevant empirical research on jury decision-making undertaken in England and
abroad.[102] One example of such research on juries and the principles of criminal
evidence is the LSE Jury Project in England. This was a study involving groups of jurors
being invited 'to listen to a tape-recording re-enacted from the transcript of a real
trial, and then to reach a verdict upon what they have heard'. The experiments were
'conducted under laboratory conditions so that the jurors could be observed and their
deliberations recorded for later analysis'. Observations were made of 'how different
applications of particular rules of evidence might affect the verdicts given by jurors'.
The limitations of such a study were acknowledged:

> There are drawbacks in using laboratory experimentation as a means of discovering how actual
> juries operate 'on the job.' If the experimental trial consists of a tape recording of spoken voices
> (as was the case in . . . our own experiments), the 'jurors' are deprived of the myriad impressions

---

[98] See generally Leading Article, 'The Manipulation of Our Legal System', *Independent*, 22 June 2005, 30;
A Samuels, 'Trials on Indictment Without a Jury' (2004) 68 *Journal of Criminal Law* 125; R Verkaik, 'Abolition
of Jury Trials "Is Attack on Justice"', *Independent*, 22 June 2005, 6.   [99] S 43(5).
[100] S 43(6).
[101] S 43(7). The House of Commons Science and Technology Committee raises the possibility that similar
arrangements might be made for 'serious cases that rest on highly complex scientific evidence' to be tried
without a jury: House of Commons Science and Technology Committee, *Forensic Evidence on Trial* (Seventh
Report of Session 2004–05) (HC 96-I) (2005) [167] (bold font removed), available at http://www.publications.
parliament.uk/pa/cm200405/cmselect/cmsctech/96/96i.pdf.
[102] See generally P Darbyshire, A Maughan, and A Stewart, 'What Can the English Legal System Learn from
Jury Research Published up to 2001?', accessible via http://www.criminal-courts-review.org.uk/; P Darbyshire,
'What Can We Learn from Published Jury Research? Findings for the Criminal Courts Review 2001' [2001]
Criminal Law Review 970.

made up of things seen in the court room. Even if the experiment is set up on a grand and expensive scale, using a filmed trial, or even a trial performed by actors, the jury will know that they are not deciding the fate of an actual defendant. . . . [However,] [o]ur observation of the course of [the mock jurors'] discussions showed them to be deeply immersed, entirely serious, often vehemently argumentative, to all appearances oblivious that the situation was only an experiment.[103]

Additionally, in 1995, the Home Office commissioned the Centre for Socio-Legal Studies at the University of Oxford to conduct research, again with mock trials, into the effect on mock juries of knowing that the defendant had a previous conviction.[104]

Of some interest also is the *Crown Court Study* undertaken for the Royal Commission on Criminal Justice that reported in 1993. The *Crown Court Study* was based on every case completed in the last two weeks of February 1992 in all Crown Courts in England but three, and involved administering questionnaires to those regarded as the main actors in each case—the judge, the prosecution and defence barristers, the defence solicitor, the CPS, the police, the court clerk, the defendant, and the members of the jury.[105]

11 Summary Trials

In spite of the fact that the law of evidence has evolved around trials on indictment, the same law is applicable generally to summary trials. The absence of a discrete law of evidence applicable to the proceedings where the vast majority of criminal defendants are tried, and where very different considerations prevail from those prevailing in trials on indictment, may be regarded as a major cause for concern, but it remains an issue which is largely ignored or overlooked.[106]

12 Law Reform

English courts were traditionally reluctant to engage in reform of the law of evidence, preferring to leave such matters to the legislature. This is well illustrated by the 1992 decision on hearsay of the House of Lords in *R v Kearley*[107] (discussed in Chapter 9), in which the majority, while deprecating the result they reached, felt nonetheless constrained into reaching it by the law, which in their view could be changed only by Parliament. Parliament acted only in 2003. In contrast, the courts in Canada and Australia

---

[103] LSE Jury Project, 'Juries and the Rules of Evidence' [1973] *Criminal Law Review* 208, 210.

[104] Law Commission (Consultation Paper No 141), *Criminal Law—Evidence in Criminal Proceedings: Previous Misconduct of a Defendant—A Consultation Paper* (1996) App D, available at http://www.lawcom.gov.uk/docs/cp141.pdf.

[105] M Zander and P Henderson, *The Royal Commission on Criminal Justice: Crown Court Study* (1993).

[106] See, however, P Darbyshire, 'An Essay on the Importance and Neglect of the Magistracy' [1997] *Criminal Law Review* 627.   [107] [1992] 2 AC 228.

have been generally far more innovative and reformist in their approach to evidence doctrine. Some references will be made in this book to developments in these countries.

A new trend may, however, be emerging slowly in England and Wales. The Human Rights Act 1998, discussed below, has caused the senior judiciary to take a more principled and comparativist approach to the consideration of evidence doctrine than was the case previously. The Criminal Cases Review Commission is also assuming an increasingly important role in generating interesting case law from the Court of Appeal on a variety of evidential issues. The Commission is an independent public body set up to investigate suspected miscarriages of justice. It assesses whether convictions or sentences should be referred to the Court of Appeal.

In England and Wales, legislation is occasionally passed which makes fundamental changes to the law of evidence. Examples in recent years include the Criminal Justice and Public Order Act 1994 (which changed the law in relation to the right to silence at both the pre-trial and trial stages, and the law relating to corroboration), the Civil Evidence Act 1995 (which effectively abolished the hearsay rule in civil proceedings), the Youth Justice and Criminal Evidence Act 1999,[108] and the Criminal Justice Act 2003.[109] A Royal Commission on Criminal Justice chaired by Lord Runciman recommended in 1993 that the law of criminal evidence be subjected to a review by the Law Commission.[110] The Law Commission issued its reports on criminal hearsay[111] and evidence of bad character[112] in 1997 and 2001 respectively. A review of the operation of the criminal courts by Lord Justice Auld was published in 2001.[113]

Finally, it is noteworthy that the Criminal Procedure Rules 2005, which came into force on 4 April 2005, identify their 'overriding objective'[114] (and associated considerations) as follows:

THE OVERRIDING OBJECTIVE

1.1

(1) The overriding objective of this new code is that criminal cases be dealt with justly.

(2) Dealing with a criminal case justly includes—

    (a) acquitting the innocent and convicting the guilty;

    (b) dealing with the prosecution and the defence fairly;

[108] See generally A Samuels, 'New Law on Criminal Evidence' (2000) 164 *Justice of the Peace* 857.

[109] See generally E Cape, 'Criminal Justice Act 2003—No Debate?' [Jan 2004] *Legal Action* 6; B Gibson, 'The Criminal Justice Act 2003—Part 2' (2004) 168 *Justice of the Peace* 207; G Robson, 'The Criminal Justice Act 2003: A Possible Prognosis' (2004) 168 *Justice of the Peace* 11.

[110] Royal Commission on Criminal Justice, *Report* (Cm 2263) (1993) 125, 126.

[111] Law Commission (Law Com No 245), *Evidence in Criminal Proceedings: Hearsay and Related Topics* (1997), available at http://www.lawcom.gov.uk/docs/lc245.pdf.

[112] Law Commission (Law Com No 273), *Evidence of Bad Character in Criminal Proceedings* (2001), available at http://www.lawcom.gov.uk/docs/lc273.pdf.

[113] Lord Justice Auld, *Review of the Criminal Courts of England and Wales* (2001), accessible via http://www.criminal-courts-review.org.uk/. See generally I Dennis, 'The Auld Review—Part II' [2002] *Criminal Law Review* 1; J McEwan, M Redmayne, and Y Tinsley, 'Evidence, Jury Trials and Witness Protection—The Auld Review of the English Criminal Courts' (2002) 6 *International Journal of Evidence and Proof* 163.

[114] See generally I Dennis, 'Criminal Procedure Rules—An Update' [2005] *Criminal Law Review* 335; P Plowden, 'Make Do and Mend, or a Cultural Evolution?' (2005) 155 *New Law Journal* 328.

(c) recognising the rights of a defendant, particularly those under Article 6 of the European Convention on Human Rights;

(d) respecting the interests of witnesses, victims and jurors and keeping them informed of the progress of the case;

(e) dealing with the case efficiently and expeditiously;

(f) ensuring that appropriate information is available to the court when bail and sentence are considered; and

(g) dealing with the case in ways that take into account—

(i) the gravity of the offence alleged,

(ii) the complexity of what is in issue,

(iii) the severity of the consequences for the defendant and others affected, and

(iv) the needs of other cases.

THE DUTY OF THE PARTICIPANTS IN A CRIMINAL CASE

1.2

(1) Each participant, in the conduct of each case, must—

(a) prepare and conduct the case in accordance with the overriding objective;

(b) comply with these Rules, practice directions and directions made by the court; and

(c) at once inform the court and all parties of any significant failure (whether or not that participant is responsible for that failure) to take any procedural step required by these Rules, any practice direction or any direction of the court. A failure is significant if it might hinder the court in furthering the overriding objective.

(2) Anyone involved in any way with a criminal case is a participant in its conduct for the purposes of this rule.

THE APPLICATION BY THE COURT OF THE OVERRIDING OBJECTIVE

1.3 The court must further the overriding objective in particular when—

(a) exercising any power given to it by legislation (including these Rules);

(b) applying any practice direction; or

(c) interpreting any rule or practice direction.

In contrast with the piecemeal legislative reform being witnessed in England and Wales, there has been legislative activity of a more fundamental nature in Australia.[115] On 18 April 1995, the Evidence Act 1995 (Commonwealth of Australia), covering nearly all aspects of the law of evidence, came into force in the Australian Federal jurisdiction and the Australian Capital Territory. It was expected that the Act would provide a model for similar legislation in other Australian jurisdictions. Indeed, virtually identical statutes have been introduced in New South Wales (Evidence Act 1995 (New South Wales)) and Tasmania (Evidence Act 2001 (Tasmania)). For convenience the three Acts are commonly referred to as the 'Uniform Evidence Acts'.[116]

---

[115] See generally I Dennis, 'Codification and Reform of Evidence Law in Australia' [1996] *Criminal Law Review* 477.

[116] For a discussion of the Acts see J Anderson, J Hunter, and N Williams, *The New Evidence Law: Annotations and Commentary on the Uniform Evidence Acts* (2002).

13 The Implications of the Human Rights Act 1998

The Human Rights Act 1998, which came fully into force on 2 October 2000, has the effect of 'incorporating' the European Convention on Human Rights into domestic law by making certain Convention rights directly enforceable in domestic courts.[117] This constitutes one of the most important developments in the English law of evidence, and indeed English law, in the past few decades. Lord Hope of Craighead stated in *R v DPP, ex p Kebilene*: 'It is now plain that the incorporation of the European Convention on Human Rights into our domestic law will subject the entire legal system to a fundamental process of review and, where necessary, reform by the judiciary.'[118]

In very brief terms, the purport of the Human Rights Act is as follows. Despite preserving the principle of Parliamentary sovereignty as far as primary legislation is concerned,[119] the Act provides that, in so far as it is possible to do so, all legislation must be read and given effect in a way that is compatible with the Convention rights.[120] If, however, primary legislation cannot be read in a way that renders it compatible with the Convention rights, the court must still apply it, but will be able, if it is a superior court, to issue a declaration of incompatibility.[121] Public authorities, including courts and tribunals,[122] are obliged to act in a way which is compatible with the Convention rights[123] unless provisions in primary legislation require them to act differently.[124] 'A court or tribunal determining a question which has arisen in connection with a Convention right must take into account any...judgment [or] decision...of the European Court of Human Rights...whenever made or given, so far as, in the opinion of the court or tribunal, it is relevant to the proceedings in which that question has arisen.'[125] Although such case law is not binding on domestic courts, Lord Woolf CJ observed that 'it would be most unfortunate if the approach identified by the European Court of Human Rights and the approach of [the Court of Appeal] continued to differ unless this is inevitable because of provisions contained in this country's legislation or the state of our case law'.[126]

As we shall see in the course of this book, one of the major current debates concerns the extent to which criminal evidence doctrine has been reshaped by Article 6 of the European Convention on Human Rights, which guarantees[127] the right to a fair trial.

---

[117] See generally A L-T Choo and S Nash, 'Evidence Law in England and Wales: The Impact of the Human Rights Act 1998' (2003) 7 *International Journal of Evidence and Proof* 31 (on which I have drawn heavily in the paragraphs that follow); D Friedman, 'From Due Deference to Due Process: Human Rights Litigation in the Criminal Law' [2002] *European Human Rights Law Review* 216; P Mirfield, 'Silence, Innocence and Human Rights' in P Mirfield and R Smith (eds), *Essays for Colin Tapper* (2003); C Ovey, 'The European Convention on Human Rights and the Criminal Lawyer: An Introduction' [1998] *Criminal Law Review* 4; S Sharpe, 'The European Convention: A Suspects' Charter?' [1997] *Criminal Law Review* 848; B Emmerson and A Ashworth, *Human Rights and Criminal Justice* (2001).   [118] [1999] 3 WLR 972, 988.
[119] S 3(2)(b).   [120] S 3(1).
[121] S 4(2). The superior courts are the House of Lords; the Judicial Committee of the Privy Council; the Courts-Martial Appeal Court; the High Court of Justiciary in Scotland; and the High Court or Court of Appeal in England and Wales or Northern Ireland. See s 4(5).   [122] S 6(3)(a).
[123] S 6(1).   [124] S 6(2).   [125] S 2(1)(a).   [126] *R v Togher* [2001] 3 All ER 463, 472.
[127] In Art 6(1).

While many judges stress that the concept of a fair trial has long been an integral part of the law and practice of the United Kingdom,[128] some have recognized that in giving the Human Rights Act its full effect 'long or well entrenched ideas may have to be put aside, [and] sacred cows culled'.[129] It is noteworthy that, although the Act requires courts to have regard to decisions of the European Court of Human Rights where appropriate, that Court has stressed on several occasions that, in determining whether Article 6 has been breached, it will not concern itself directly with the principle(s) of evidence at issue: 'While Article 6 of the Convention guarantees the right to a fair trial, it does not lay down any rules on the admissibility of evidence as such, which is therefore primarily a matter for regulation under national law.'[130]

Other specific rights guaranteed by Article 6, all of which are closely allied to the right to a fair trial, include the rights of a person charged with a criminal offence:

- to 'be presumed innocent until proved guilty according to law';[131]

- 'to be informed promptly, in a language which he understands and in detail, of the nature and cause of the accusation against him';[132]

- 'to have adequate time and facilities for the preparation of his defence';[133]

- 'to defend himself in person or through legal assistance of his own choosing or, if he has not sufficient means to pay for legal assistance, to be given it free when the interests of justice so require';[134]

- 'to examine or have examined witnesses against him and to obtain the attendance and examination of witnesses on his behalf under the same conditions as witnesses against him';[135] and

- 'to have the free assistance of an interpreter if he cannot understand or speak the language used in court'.[136]

14 Organization of the Book

The order of the rest of the book is as follows. Chapters 2 to 5 are concerned, broadly speaking, with topics that highlight the relationship between the principles of evidence and pre-trial procedures. Chapters 6 and 7 examine two doctrines which allow a party to refrain from disclosing or giving evidence of material, not on the basis of its actual or potential unreliability, but because of considerations of extrinsic policy. These are, respectively, the doctrines of public interest immunity and legal professional privilege. The following two chapters, Chapters 8 and 9, are concerned, respectively, with evidential topics of fundamental importance that have been radically affected in the criminal context by the Criminal Justice Act 2003: character evidence and hearsay evidence.

---

[128] *R v Togher* [2001] 3 All ER 463, 472.   [129] *R v Lambert* [2001] UKHL 37, [2001] 3 WLR 206, [6].

[130] *Schenk v Switzerland* (1991) 13 EHRR 242, [46] (judgment of 1988). The Court has reiterated its position in several subsequent cases.   [131] Art 6(2).

[132] Art 6(3)(a).   [133] Art 6(3)(b).   [134] Art 6(3)(c).   [135] Art 6(3)(d).   [136] Art 6(3)(e).

Chapter 10 deals with expert evidence, a topic that continues to generate considerable controversy. A number of issues pertaining to witnesses are considered in Chapter 11. Chapter 12 examines how it is to be determined which party bears the burden of proving a particular issue in a trial, and to what standard the burden of proving a particular issue requires to be discharged. Chapter 13 considers a number of 'shortcuts' employed by the law of evidence. Chapter 14 looks at the principles governing the course of evidence in a trial, and a number of concluding comments are provided in Chapter 15.

2

Confessions

This chapter explores the extent to which evidence of a confession by an accused person may be utilized by the prosecution at his or her trial.[1] A study published in 2000 found that 55 per cent of suspects made confessions during police interviews.[2] To adduce confession evidence is to adduce hearsay evidence, as the accused's out-of-court statement is being tendered in court as evidence of the matters stated.[3] An important exception to the hearsay rule, however, allows an accused's confession to be adduced in evidence by the prosecution in certain circumstances. An examination of these circumstances will be the focus of this chapter.

1 Confessions and Miscarriages of Justice

The traditional justification for the confession exception to the hearsay rule is that only a guilty person would make a statement against his or her own interest: 'admissions made by [a defendant] are admissible against him for the obvious reason that he would be unlikely to have made them unless they were true'.[4] Thus, a confession may be presumed to be reliable. One need, however, only state this traditional justification for the admissibility of confession evidence to see the flaws inherent in it. Cases such as those of the Guildford Four, Birmingham Six, Judith Ward,[5] and Bridgewater Three have brought dramatically to public attention the sorts of miscarriages of justice which can occur as a result of the admission of confession evidence. In broad terms, three possible problems with confession evidence may be identified. First, the confession may have been totally *fabricated* by the police; it may never have been made at all by the person to whom it is attributed. This practice of, in effect, putting confessions into the mouths of accused persons who never made them is sometimes termed 'verballing'.

---

[1] See generally P Mirfield, *Silence, Confessions and Improperly Obtained Evidence* (1997). Statements against interest made out of court by parties to the proceedings are known in civil cases as 'admissions', and are discussed in Ch 13.

[2] T Bucke, R Street, and D Brown, *The Right of Silence: The Impact of the Criminal Justice and Public Order Act 1994* (Home Office Research Study 199) (2000) 34, available at http://www.homeoffice.gov.uk/rds/pdfs/hors199.pdf.   [3] Hearsay evidence is discussed in detail in Ch 9.

[4] *R v Hayter* [2005] UKHL 6, [2005] 1 WLR 605, [82].

[5] On such cases, see generally I Dennis, 'Miscarriages of Justice and the Law of Confessions: Evidentiary Issues and Solutions' [1993] *Public Law* 291; G H Gudjonsson, 'Unreliable Confessions and Miscarriages of Justice in Britain' (2002) 4 *International Journal of Police Science and Management* 332.

Secondly, while the suspect may indeed have confessed, he or she may have made a *false confession*. There are different ways of categorizing false confessions, but the most common categorization distinguishes between three different types of false confession:[6]

1. *Voluntary False Confessions.* These 'are given without any external pressure from the police'. Such a confession may be made because the confessor (1) has 'a "morbid desire for notoriety", that is, a pathological need to become infamous and to enhance self-esteem, even if it means the prospect of imprisonment'; or (2) has feelings of guilt about a real or imagined previous transgression; or (3) is 'unable to distinguish fact from fantasy'; or (4) wishes to assist or protect the real culprit (a phenomenon that is more common in the case of minor offences than in the case of serious offences); or (5) sees no possible way of disputing guilt, and confesses in order to obtain a reduced punishment; or (6) wishes 'to pre-empt further investigation of a more serious offence'; or (7) wishes 'to hide other, non-criminal facts'.[7]

2. *Coerced-Compliant False Confessions.* Such confessions occur when 'suspects believe that the benefits of confessing outweigh the costs. People confess in order to escape from the police interview, which they consider to be stressful and intolerable (Paddy Armstrong, one of the Guildford Four, said he confessed for this reason); they confess because of police tricks in which they have been promised a reward to confess; or they confess because of a combination of the two.'[8]

3. *Coerced-Internalized False Confessions.* These 'occur when people come to believe, during police interviewing, that they have committed the crime they are accused of even though they have no actual memory of having committed the crime.... Carole Richardson (one of the Guildford Four) reported such an experience.'[9] It has been noted:

> Internalised false confessions do not imply that suspects become convinced that they have committed a crime.... internalised false confessions occur because suspects have formed the opinion that it is *more likely than not* that they are guilty. They typically have no memory of having committed the crime, but the tactics used by the police aiming to diminish suspects' confidence in their memory make them less certain of their innocence and make them wonder whether it might be possible that they did commit the crime.[10]

The third possible problem with confession evidence is that, even if the confession in question was in fact made, and even if it is true, there may be considerations of *extrinsic*

---

[6] See G H Gudjonsson, *The Psychology of Interrogations and Confessions: A Handbook* (2003) Ch 8, G H Gudjonsson, *The Psychology of Interrogations, Confessions and Testimony* (1992) 226–8, and A Memon, A Vrij, and R Bull, *Psychology and Law: Truthfulness, Accuracy and Credibility* (2nd ed 2003) 77–81, on which I have relied in the succeeding paragraphs. See also L F Lowenstein, 'Aspects of Confessions: What the Legal Profession Should Know' (1999) 163 *Justice of the Peace* 586; C Sherrin, 'False Confessions and Admissions in Canadian Law' (2005) 30 *Queen's Law Journal* 601, 622 ff; L J Taylor and S E Henderson, 'Confessions: Consensus In Idem?' [2002] *Scots Law Times* 325; G T Trotter, 'False Confessions and Wrongful Convictions' (2003–4) 35 *Ottawa Law Review* 179, 182–7; J McEwan, *The Verdict of the Court: Passing Judgment in Law and Psychology* (2003) 174–5.

[7] A Memon, A Vrij, and R Bull, *Psychology and Law: Truthfulness, Accuracy and Credibility* (2nd ed 2003) 78.

[8] Ibid, 79.   [9] Ibid.

[10] Ibid, 80–1(italics in original). See also J Pearse and G H Gudjonsson, 'Measuring Influential Police Interviewing Tactics: A Factor Analytic Approach' (1999) 4 *Legal and Criminological Psychology* 221.

policy which dictate that it is still inappropriate to use the confession in evidence, because of the unacceptable methods by which it was extracted.

As we shall see, exclusion remains the primary mechanism utilized by English law to deal with the problem of confession evidence. Despite many exhortations that confession evidence should be inadmissible unless corroborated, or at least supported, by other evidence, a requirement for supporting evidence has not been introduced into English law and it is now extremely unlikely that it will be.

An argument that confession evidence should be excluded totally from the jury's consideration raises a question of law to be decided by the trial judge. An argument that confession evidence was fabricated, however, is a question of fact, and is therefore to be decided, in a trial on indictment, by the jury.[11] Both questions may, of course, arise in the same case. Thus:

> where the prosecution alleges that the defendant made an . . . admission, and the case is raised on behalf of the defendant that he did not make the . . . admission and that he was ill-treated by the police before or at the time of the alleged admission, two issues are raised which are not mutually exclusive. The first issue, which is for the judge to decide, is whether, on the assumption that the alleged admission was made, it is inadmissible . . . The second issue, which is for the jury to decide if the judge rules that the alleged admission is admissible in evidence, is whether the admission was in fact made.[12]

The rationale for the respective roles of judge and jury in this context has been explained in detail by the Court of Appeal:

> The method adopted by domestic law of providing different functions for the judge and the jury in relation to disputed confessions is in our judgment one with significant advantages for ensuring that justice is done. The obvious one is that it removes from the jury what may be a difficult task of disregarding a confession obtained by oppression where it may be patently obvious from its content that it is true and so avoids the risk they might not fully and properly put it out of their minds. The system provides that unless the prosecution can satisfy the judge to the high criminal standard of proof that it was not obtained by oppression, the jury never hear a word of the confession.[13]

> There are other practical advantages to the separate functions. Evidence highly relevant to the issue of voluntariness may be particularly prejudicial to an accused person. Because the jury do not hear the evidence on the voir dire, matters of importance to the issue being examined may the more readily be expressed because there is no fear that the jury will be affected by them. By way of example, the previous experience of an accused in police stations may have a considerable bearing upon how he would react to a given situation in custody since someone with no such experience might react differently. Issues of this kind, potentially of great relevance to the admissibility of the evidence, can be explored before the judge alone.[14]

> The division of functions also, we think, complies with the requirement of the Convention of an adequate safeguard against the prosecution deploying against an accused person evidence which was obtained from him by oppression. A question whether evidence was so obtained is

---

[11] See *Ajodha v The State* [1982] AC 204; *R v Flemming* (1988) 86 Cr App R 32 (decision of 1987).
[12] *Thongjai v R* [1997] 3 WLR 667, 673.   [13] *R v Mushtaq* [2002] EWCA Crim 1943, [31].
[14] Ibid, [32].

to be determined by a judge, without the jury being present. Not only does this, as we have said, allow a defendant to present such objections without being inhibited by the presence of the jury, the tribunal who are to determine the factual questions on the charges that he faces. It also means that the decision as to whether the convention rights have been protected is given in a reasoned judgment, which may therefore be subjected to scrutiny by the appellate court . . .[15]

2 'Confession'

Section 76(1) of the Police and Criminal Evidence Act 1984 provides that 'a confession made by an accused person may be given in evidence against him in so far as it is relevant to any matter in issue in the proceedings and is not excluded by the court in pursuance of this section'. A confession is defined in section 82(1) as *including* 'any statement wholly or partly adverse to the person who made it, whether made to a person in authority or not and whether made in words or otherwise'. It does not, therefore, have to have been made orally or in writing, and may have been made by conduct. Thus a video recording of a re-enactment by the accused of the crime, or a demonstration by the accused of how the crime was committed, clearly constitutes confession evidence. The Privy Council observed in *Li Shu-Ling v R*, however, that, in order that the accused not be prejudiced by 'lack of acting skill':

> the video recording should be shown to the accused as soon as practicable after it has been completed and he should be given the opportunity to make and have recorded any comments he wishes about the film. If the accused says the film does not show what he meant to demonstrate there will then be a contemporary record of his criticism which the judge and jury can take into account when assessing the value of the film as evidence of his confession.[16]

In *R v Hasan*[17] the following question arose for consideration by the House of Lords: 'Whether a "confession" in section 76 of the Police and Criminal Evidence Act 1984 includes a statement intended by the maker to be exculpatory or neutral and which appears to be so on its face, but which becomes damaging to him at the trial because, for example, its contents can then be shown to be evasive or false or inconsistent with the maker's evidence on oath.' The House answered this question in the negative:

> Properly construed section 76(1), read with section 82(1), requires the court to interpret a statement in the light of the circumstances when it was made. A purely exculpatory statement (eg 'I was not there') is not within the scope of section 76(1). It is not a confession within the meaning of section 76. The safeguards of section 76 are not applicable. But the safeguards of section 78 are available.[18]

Such a literal interpretation of the provisions was not considered to violate Article 6 of the European Convention on Human Rights:

> There is . . . nothing in the text of article 6 or in the corpus of European jurisprudence which supports the view that sections 76(1) and 82(1) create any incompatibility with article 6. Given

---

[15] *R v Mushtaq* [2002] EWCA Crim 1943, [33]. The decision of the Court of Appeal was affirmed by the House of Lords: [2005] UKHL 25, [2005] 1 WLR 1513.   [16] [1989] 1 AC 270, 279–80.
[17] [2005] UKHL 22, [2005] 2 WLR 709.   [18] Ibid, [58].

the unrestricted capability of section 78 to avoid injustice by excluding any evidence obtained by unfairness (including wholly exculpatory or neutral statements obtained by oppression), sections 76(1) and 82(1) are ... compatible with article 6.[19]

3 Mandatory Exclusion

Section 76(2) of the Police and Criminal Evidence Act 1984 provides that there are two grounds[20] on which a confession sought to be used at trial by the prosecution must be excluded from evidence:

> If, in any proceedings where the prosecution proposes to give in evidence a confession made by an accused person, it is represented to the court that the confession was or may have been obtained—
>
> (a) by oppression of the person who made it; or
>
> (b) in consequence of anything said or done which was likely, in the circumstances existing at the time, to render unreliable any confession which might be made by him in consequence thereof,
>
> the court shall not allow the confession to be given in evidence against him except in so far as the prosecution proves to the court beyond reasonable doubt that the confession (notwithstanding that it may be true) was not obtained as aforesaid.

If no 'representation' is made by the defence that the confession was obtained in a manner proscribed by subsection (2), the court may of its own motion require the prosecution to prove that it was not obtained in such a manner.[21]

The two grounds for the mandatory exclusion of confession evidence will now be considered in turn.

3.1 Oppression

A confession must be excluded from evidence if it was obtained by *oppression* of the person making it. The word 'oppression' is defined in section 76(8) of the Police and Criminal Evidence Act 1984 as *including* 'torture, inhuman or degrading treatment, and the use or threat of violence (whether or not amounting to torture)'. The decisions of the Court of Appeal in which the meaning of this word has been considered suggest that it connotes fairly harsh treatment of the confessor, and therefore that it is only in rare cases that the prosecution would be unable to prove that a confession was *not* obtained by oppression. In the leading case of *R v Fulling*, the Court of Appeal held that:

> 'oppression' in section 76(2)(a) should be given its ordinary dictionary meaning. The *Oxford English Dictionary* as its third definition of the word runs as follows: 'Exercise of authority or

[19] Ibid, [62].

[20] See generally A V Bicak, 'Police and Criminal Evidence Act 1984, S 76(2): Re-Emergence of the Involuntariness Test' (2001) 65 *Journal of Criminal Law* 85.   [21] Police and Criminal Evidence Act 1984, s 76(3).

power in a burdensome, harsh, or wrongful manner; unjust or cruel treatment of subjects, inferiors, etc; the imposition of unreasonable or unjust burdens.' One of the quotations given under that paragraph runs as follows: 'There is not a word in our language which expresses more detestable wickedness than oppression.'

The Court suggested, in addition, that oppression will almost certainly entail bad faith on the part of the interrogator. Fulling's allegation in this case was that the police had behaved oppressively by informing her that her lover had been having an affair with another woman, and that this woman was in the next cell. Fulling contended that she confessed because these revelations distressed her so much that she could not bear to remain in the cells any longer. The Court of Appeal confirmed that the actions of the police in giving Fulling the information about the woman in the next cell did not constitute oppression.[22]

In a similar vein, the Court of Appeal found no oppression in *R v Emmerson* where one of the interviewing officers, giving the impression of impatience and irritation, 'raised his voice and used some bad language'.[23] By contrast, in *R v Paris*, the case of the 'Cardiff Three', one of the co-accused, Miller, was:

> bullied and hectored. The officers, particularly Detective Constable Greenwood, were not questioning him so much as shouting at him what they wanted him to say. Short of physical violence, it is hard to conceive of a more hostile and intimidating approach by officers to a suspect. It is impossible to convey on the printed page the pace, force and menace of the officer's delivery . . .[24]

The Court of Appeal held that this conduct clearly amounted to oppression.

At issue in *Mohd Ali bin Burut v Public Prosecutor* was the 'special procedure' applicable in cases of suspected firearms offences in Brunei, involving suspects being manacled and hooded during interrogation. The Privy Council considered that 'for the police to interview an arrested person while he is manacled and hooded is plainly oppressive conduct', and that the statements which were made could be said to have been obtained *by* oppression even though they had not actually been obtained *during* the application of the 'special procedure': 'the relatively short gaps between the application of the "special procedure" and the taking of the statements, inferentially suggested that the statements were, or may have been, obtained by oppression'.[25]

Further assistance on the meaning of 'oppression' in section 76(2)(a) may be provided by decisions of the European Court of Human Rights[26] on Article 3 of the European Convention on Human Rights, which prohibits both torture and 'inhuman or degrading

---

[22] [1987] QB 426, 432–3.

[23] (1991) 92 Cr App R 284, 287 (decision of 1990). See also *R v Foster* [2003] EWCA Crim 178.

[24] (1993) 97 Cr App R 99, 103 (decision of 1992).   [25] [1995] 2 AC 579, 593.

[26] See, in addition to the cases referred to below, *Ireland v UK* (1979–80) 2 EHRR 25 (judgment of 1978); *Selmouni v France* (2000) 29 EHRR 403 (judgment of 1999); *Egmez v Cyprus* (2002) 34 EHRR 29 (p 753) (judgment of 2000); *Lorsé v Netherlands* (2003) 37 EHRR 3 (p 105) (judgment of 2003); *Van der Ven v Netherlands* (2004) 38 EHRR 46 (p 967) (judgment of 2003); *Yöyler v Turkey*, Application no 26973/95, 24 July 2003; *Yankov v Bulgaria* (2005) 40 EHRR 36 (p 854) (judgment of 2003); *Kmetty v Hungary* (2005) 40 EHRR 6 (p 134) (judgment of 2003); *Çolak v Turkey*, Application nos 32578/96 and 32579/96, 8 Jan 2004; *Önder v Turkey*, Application no 28520/95, 8 Jan 2004; *Mayzit v Russia*, Application no 63378/00, 20 Jan 2005; *Öcalan v Turkey*, Application no 46221/99, 12 May 2005; *Aydın v Turkey*, Application no 25660/94, 24 May 2005; *Kişmir v Turkey*, Application no 27306/95, 31 May 2005; *Novoselov v Russia*, Application no 66460/01, 2 June 2005.

treatment'.[27] As seen above, section 76(8) makes it clear that either torture or 'inhuman or degrading treatment' will constitute oppression. The Court has held:

> ... Article 3 enshrines one of the most fundamental values of democratic societies. Even in the most difficult circumstances, such as the fight against terrorism and organised crime, the Convention prohibits in absolute terms torture and inhuman or degrading treatment or punishment. Unlike most of the substantive clauses of the Convention and its Protocols, Article 3 makes no provision for exceptions and no derogation from it is permissible under Article 15 § 2 even in the event of a public emergency threatening the life of the nation ...[28]

> However, to fall under Article 3 of the Convention, ill-treatment must attain a minimum level of severity. The assessment of this minimum level of severity is relative; it depends on all the circumstances of the case, such as the duration of the treatment, its physical and mental effects and, in some cases, the sex, age and state of health of the victim ...[29]

More specific guidance on the meaning of the terms 'inhuman' and 'degrading' has been provided by the Court:

> The Court has considered treatment to be 'inhuman' because, *inter alia*, it was premeditated, was applied for hours at a stretch and caused either actual bodily injury or intense physical and mental suffering. It has deemed treatment to be 'degrading' because it was such as to arouse in the victims feelings of fear, anguish and inferiority capable of humiliating and debasing them ... In considering whether a particular form of treatment is 'degrading' within the meaning of Article 3, the Court will have regard to whether its object is to humiliate and debase the person concerned and whether, as far as the consequences are concerned, it adversely affected his or her personality in a manner incompatible with Article 3. However, the absence of any such purpose cannot conclusively rule out a finding of a violation of Article 3 ...[30]

> The suffering and humiliation involved must go beyond that inevitable element of suffering or humiliation connected with a given form of legitimate treatment or punishment. Measures depriving a person of his liberty may often involve such an element. ... the State must ensure that a person is detained in conditions which are compatible with respect for his human dignity, that the manner and method of the execution of the measure do not subject him to distress or hardship of an intensity exceeding the unavoidable level of suffering inherent in detention and that, given the practical demands of imprisonment, his health and well-being are adequately secured. When assessing conditions of detention, account has to be taken of the cumulative effects of those conditions and the duration of the detention ... In particular, the Court must have regard to the state of health of the detained person ...[31]

> An important factor, along with the material conditions, is the detention regime. In assessing whether a restrictive regime may amount to treatment contrary to Article 3 in a given case, regard must be had to the particular conditions, the stringency of the regime, its duration, the objective pursued and its effects on the person concerned ...[32]

[27] See generally J Vorhaus, 'On Degradation. Part One: Article 3 of the European Convention on Human Rights' (2002) 31 *Common Law World Review* 374; J Vorhaus, 'On Degradation. Part Two: Degrading Treatment and Punishment' (2003) 32 *Common Law World Review* 65.

[28] *Khashiyev and Akayeva v Russia*, Application nos 57942/00 and 57945/00, 24 Feb 2005, [170]. See also, eg, *Ayder v Turkey*, Application no 23656/94, 8 Jan 2004, [107]; *Tepe v Turkey*, Application no 31247/96, 21 Dec 2004, [47].   [29] *Labzov v Russia*, Application no 62208/00, 16 June 2005, [41].

[30] *Kehayov v Bulgaria*, Application no 41035/98, 18 Jan 2005, [63].

[31] *II v Bulgaria*, Application no 44082/98, 9 June 2005, [68].   [32] Ibid, [69].

The Court has also noted that 'in respect of persons deprived of their liberty, recourse to physical force which has not been made strictly necessary by their own conduct diminishes human dignity and is in principle an infringement of the right set forth in Article 3 . . . .'[33] Thus 'where an individual is taken into custody in good health but is found to be injured at the time of release, it is incumbent on the State to provide a plausible explanation of how those injuries were caused and to produce evidence casting doubt on the victim's allegations, particularly if those allegations were backed up by medical reports, failing which a clear issue arises under Article 3 of the Convention'.[34]

The word 'torture', unsurprisingly, carries a stronger meaning than the words 'inhuman or degrading treatment':

> In order to determine whether a particular form of ill-treatment should be qualified as torture, the Court must have regard to the distinction, embodied in Article 3, between this notion and that of inhuman or degrading treatment. . . . it appears that it was the intention that the Convention should, by means of this distinction, attach a special stigma to deliberate inhuman treatment causing very serious and cruel suffering . . . However, . . . certain acts which were classified in the past as 'inhuman or degrading treatment' as opposed to 'torture' could be classified differently in the future: the increasingly high standard being required in the area of the protection of human rights and fundamental liberties correspondingly and inevitably requires greater firmness in assessing breaches of the fundamental values of democratic societies . . .[35]

3.2 Potential Unreliability

In essence, section 76(2)(b) is directed at the issue of potentially unreliable confession evidence. It requires the court to determine whether:

- the confession was obtained *in consequence of* something *said or done* which,
- taking into account *all the circumstances* prevailing at the time,
- was *likely* to cause any confession which might be made to be *unreliable*.

Bad faith on the part of the interrogator is not a prerequisite to the successful invocation of section 76(2)(b).[36] However, the condition that the confession be one made in consequence of something 'said or done' has been interpreted narrowly. In *R v Goldenberg*, the defendant, a heroin addict, had *himself* requested the interview with the police during which the relevant confessions were made, apparently because he was suffering from withdrawal symptoms and wished to obtain bail in order to feed his addiction. It was contended that, given these circumstances, the confessions were likely to have been unreliable. The Court of Appeal held, however, that as there was no suggestion that Goldenberg had confessed in consequence of anything said or done *by the*

---

[33] *Elci v Turkey*, Application nos 23145/93 and 25091/94, 13 Nov 2003, [633].
[34] *Karakaş and Yeşilirmak v Turkey*, Application no 43925/98, 28 June 2005, [35].
[35] *Elci v Turkey*, Application nos 23145/93 and 25091/94, 13 Nov 2003, [634].
[36] *R v Fulling* [1987] QB 426, 432.

interviewing officers, section 76(2)(b) could not be invoked. The words 'anything said or done' 'do not extend so as to include anything said or done by the person making the confession', but, rather, are 'limited to something external to the person making the confession'.[37] It would appear that this narrow interpretation[38] continues to be taken in the Court of Appeal; in *R v Wahab* the Court commented: 'In the present case, when the appellant instructed his solicitor to see whether some convenient arrangement could be procured with the police, he was uninfluenced by anything said and done by anyone else. Everything thereafter originated from the appellant himself.'[39]

Breach of a provision of the Police and Criminal Evidence Act 1984, or one of the associated Codes of Practice, may be tantamount to something 'said or done' under section 76(2)(b). Examples include the unlawful denial of access to a solicitor under Code C and breach of the Code provisions governing the recording of interviews.[40]

The confession must have been obtained *in consequence of* whatever is alleged to have been 'said or done'. In *R v Law-Thompson*[41] the Court of Appeal thought that section 76(2)(b) could not have been invoked because there was no suggestion that the confessions had been obtained in consequence of the absence of an appropriate adult during interview.[42] The Court of Appeal was content to assume in *R v Crampton* that 'the mere holding of an interview at a time when the appellant is withdrawing from the symptoms of heroin addiction is something which is done within the meaning of section 76(2)', but doubted the correctness of this: 'The reason why we say it is doubtful is because the words of the subsection seem to postulate some words spoken by the police or acts done by them which were likely to induce unreliable confessions.'[43] It is submitted that the broader approach on which the Court in *Crampton* was prepared to act is preferable: there is no logical reason why the mere holding of an interview should not in appropriate circumstances constitute the words or conduct likely to induce unreliable confessions. Necessarily to have to point to more specific words or conduct would be contrary to a literal interpretation of the provision.[44]

---

[37] (1989) 88 Cr App R 285, 290 (decision of 1988).

[38] It is arguable, however, that the confession evidence should have been excluded under s 78(1) of the Police and Criminal Evidence Act 1984, discussed below. The Court of Appeal remarked in *R v Goldenberg* (1989) 88 Cr App R 285, 289 (decision of 1988): 'It does not appear...that in the present case any submission was made to the judge at the trial to the effect that the evidence should be excluded in accordance with section 78. In these circumstances it does not appear to us that it would be right for this Court to give effect to a submission which depends on the failure of a judge to exclude evidence by a discretion which at the trial he was not asked to exercise.'   [39] [2002] EWCA Crim 1570, [2003] 1 Cr App R 15 (p 232), [41].

[40] *R v McGovern* (1991) 92 Cr App R 228 (decision of 1990).   [41] [1997] Crim LR 674.

[42] See also *R v Samuel* [2005] EWCA Crim 704, [45]: 'In our view there is no doubt that the appellant was doing what he had decided was necessary to secure his release from detention and to remain in Nigeria free from the threat of extradition to the UK. As part of his reasoning he "factored in" information from his fellow inmates and acted in such a way as would best achieve his goals. Thus, whilst he may have amplified his account on the 22nd "in the light of" that information, it cannot be said that it was "in consequence" of it. It remained a voluntary statement by a person who was in control of his own destiny and who did not seek outside help in the form of a solicitor. Accordingly there is no basis for contending that the judge would have concluded other than that the prosecution had satisfied him to the criminal standard that his statement of the 22nd was not made in consequence of anything said which was likely to render any confession contained in it unreliable. On that basis there was no error of law in his ruling.'   [43] (1991) 92 Cr App R 369, 372 (decision of 1990).

[44] See also *R v Walker* [1998] Crim LR 211.

In determining whether what was said or done was likely to render any resulting confession unreliable, the court must consider the circumstances *actually* existing at the time. It is relevant to have regard, for example, to the suspect's physical condition and emotional state at the time;[45] the suspect's mental condition (including his or her mental age,[46] his or her suggestibility and vulnerability,[47] and the presence of any personality disorder[48]); the suspect's fitness to be interviewed (a suspect under the influence of drugs[49] or suffering from withdrawal symptoms may obviously be unfit, although 'the mere fact that someone is withdrawing, and may have a motive for making a confession, does not mean the confession is necessarily unreliable'[50]); and the absence of an appropriate adult.[51]

An unreliable confession is one which 'cannot be relied upon as being the truth'. The concern of section 76(2)(b), therefore, is with 'the nature and quality of the words spoken or the things done by the police which are likely to, in the circumstances existing at the time, render the confession unreliable in the sense that it is not true'.[52] The fact that the *actual* truth or otherwise of the confession is irrelevant is made clear by the phrase 'notwithstanding that it may be true' in section 76(2), and has been affirmed by the Court of Appeal.[53] Clearly, it is considered that for the judge to be required to assess the *actual* reliability of the confession would be to usurp the function of the jury.[54]

3.3 Direction to Jury where Confession Passes Section 76(2) Tests

In *R v Mushtaq*[55] the following question was certified for consideration by the House of Lords:

> Whether, in view of Article 6 of the Convention for the Protection of Human Rights and Fundamental Freedoms, a Judge, who has ruled pursuant to Section 76(2) of the Police and Criminal Evidence Act 1984 that evidence of an alleged confession has not been obtained by oppression, nor has it been obtained in consequence of anything said or done which is likely to render unreliable any confession, is required to direct the jury, if they conclude that the alleged confession may have been so obtained, they must disregard it.

This question was answered in the affirmative. In the words of Lord Rodger of Earlsferry: 'the logic of section 76(2) of PACE really requires that the jury should be directed that, if they consider that the confession was, or may have been, obtained by oppression or in

---

[45] *R v McGovern* (1991) 92 Cr App R 228 (decision of 1990).
[46] Ibid; *R v Sylvester* [2002] EWCA Crim 1327.   [47] *R v Sylvester* [2002] EWCA Crim 1327.
[48] *R v Walker* [1998] Crim LR 211.   [49] Ibid.
[50] *R v Crampton* (1991) 92 Cr App R 369 (decision of 1990).
[51] *R v Sylvester* [2002] EWCA Crim 1327.
[52] *R v Crampton* (1991) 92 Cr App R 369, 372 (decision of 1990).
[53] *R v McGovern* (1991) 92 Cr App R 228 (decision of 1990); *R v Crampton* (1991) 92 Cr App R 369 (decision of 1990). See also *R v J* [2003] EWCA Crim 3309, [44]: 'The words "notwithstanding that it may be true" are important and have been repeatedly said by this court to show that what the court is concerned with on admissibility is the reliability of the confession, given the circumstances in which it was obtained, and not its veracity...'.   [54] See P Mirfield, *Silence, Confessions and Improperly Obtained Evidence* (1997) 99.
[55] [2005] UKHL 25, [2005] 1 WLR 1513.

consequence of anything said or done which was likely to render it unreliable, they should disregard it'.[56]

4 Discretionary Exclusion

Even if a confession cannot be excluded from evidence under section 76, it may still be possible for it to be excluded in the exercise of discretion, on the ground that it was improperly obtained, either under the general common law duty to ensure a fair trial[57] or pursuant to section 78(1) of the Police and Criminal Evidence Act 1984. Indeed, 'it is evident that many cases which could have fallen to be decided under section 76 are instead being considered by the courts under section 78(1)', and it is for this reason 'that the jurisprudence on section 76 remains surprisingly underdeveloped given the difficulties of interpreting it'.[58] Section 78(1), which has been judicially described as a provision which 'is by now known almost by heart by most people who have anything to do with the law',[59] and which is certainly by far the most cited provision of the Act,[60] states:

> In any proceedings the court may refuse to allow evidence on which the prosecution proposes to rely to be given if it appears to the court that, having regard to all the circumstances, *including the circumstances in which the evidence was obtained*, the admission of the evidence would have such an adverse effect on the fairness of the proceedings that the court ought not to admit it.[61]

The common law discretion is a narrow one, and it has been expressly acknowledged by the House of Lords that 'the power conferred by s 78 to exclude evidence in the interests of a fair trial is at least as wide as that conferred by the common law'.[62] To all intents and purposes, therefore, the common law may be regarded as having been rendered otiose in this context by section 78(1): at least the same range of improperly obtained evidence may be excluded under section 78(1) as can be excluded at common law. There is one situation, however, in which it would be necessary, in order to secure the exclusion of confession evidence, to have recourse to the common law discretion. This is where section 76 and section 78(1) are inapplicable because the confession has already been given in evidence.[63] The Court of Appeal suggested in *R v Sat-Bhambra* that the phrases 'proposes to give in evidence' and 'shall not allow the confession to be given' in section 76, and the phrase 'proposes to rely' in

---

[56] Ibid, [47].   [57] *R v Sang* [1980] AC 402.

[58] K Grevling, 'Fairness and the Exclusion of Evidence Under Section 78(1) of the Police and Criminal Evidence Act' (1997) 113 *Law Quarterly Review* 667, 667–8.

[59] *Hudson v DPP* [1992] RTR 27, 34 per Hodgson J.

[60] K Grevling, 'Fairness and the Exclusion of Evidence Under Section 78(1) of the Police and Criminal Evidence Act' (1997) 113 *Law Quarterly Review* 667, 667.   [61] Italics added.

[62] *R v Khan (Sultan)* [1996] 3 All ER 289, 298.

[63] See generally D J Birch, 'The Pace Hots Up: Confessions and Confusions Under the 1984 Act' [1989] *Criminal Law Review* 95, 99.

section 78(1), do not connote evidence which has already been heard by the jury.[64] Thus, where the trial judge decides to exclude from the jury's consideration confession evidence which has already been heard by the jury, the common law discretion would need to be invoked to achieve such exclusion, with the jury being directed to disregard the evidence.

The appellate courts have exhibited a marked reluctance to provide guidelines for the exercise of the section 78(1) discretion. The following comment is typical: 'It is undesirable to attempt any general guidance as to the way in which a judge's discretion under section 78 . . . should be exercised. Circumstances vary infinitely.'[65] Furthermore, 'the Court of Appeal does not set aside the exercise of the trial judge's discretion under section 78 unless it concludes that the decision to admit the confession was unreasonable in the *Wednesbury* sense'.[66] An examination of the cases reveals, however, that a number of general principles have indeed emerged:

• A 'significant and substantial' breach of the rules will weigh heavily in favour of exclusion, but will not lead automatically to exclusion. Exclusion is unlikely to be ordered if the defendant is not considered to have been actually disadvantaged by the breach.[67] The court may consider, for example, that the confession is likely to have been made even if the breach had not occurred.

• A breach may, by its very nature, be significant and substantial; in other words, it will be significant and substantial even if the police acted in good faith. Bad faith can, however, convert a breach which is not otherwise significant and substantial into one which is.[68]

• Section 78(1) is not to be used directly to discipline the police.[69]

A closer look will now be taken at the application of these principles.

4.1 Breaches of the Police and Criminal Evidence Act 1984 and/or the Codes of Practice

Defence attempts to obtain exclusion of confession evidence under section 78(1) are often premised on the argument that the confession was obtained in breach of the Police and Criminal Evidence Act 1984 and/or its associated Codes of Practice.

---

[64] (1989) 88 Cr App R 55, 62 (decision of 1988).

[65] *R v Samuel* [1988] QB 615, 630. See also *R v Jelen* (1990) 90 Cr App R 456, 465 (decision of 1989): 'The circumstances of each case are almost always different, and judges may well take different views in the proper exercise of their discretion even where the circumstances are similar. This is not an apt field for hard case law and well-founded distinctions between cases.'

[66] *Thompson v R* [1998] 2 WLR 927, 949. See also *R v O'Leary* (1988) 87 Cr App R 387, 391 (decision of 1988); *R v Christou* [1992] QB 979, 989.

[67] *R v Samuel* [1988] QB 615; *R v Alladice* (1988) 87 Cr App R 380 (decision of 1988); *R v Parris* (1989) 89 Cr App R 68 (decision of 1988); *R v Keenan* [1990] 2 QB 54; *R v Walsh* (1990) 91 Cr App R 161 (decision of 1989); *R v Canale* [1990] 2 All ER 187; *R v Dunn* (1990) 91 Cr App R 237 (decision of 1990); *R v Dunford* (1990) 91 Cr App R 150 (decision of 1990).   [68] *R v Walsh* (1990) 91 Cr App R 161 (decision of 1989).

[69] *R v Mason* [1988] 1 WLR 139; *R v Delaney* (1989) 88 Cr App R 338 (decision of 1988).

4.1.1 Denial of Access to Legal Advice

The question has arisen whether a breach of section 58, and/or the provisions of Code C which relate to access to legal advice, should lead to the exclusion of confession evidence under section 78(1). Section 58 of the Police and Criminal Evidence Act 1984 makes provision for access to legal advice for persons arrested and held in custody. Subsection (1) provides: 'A person arrested and held in custody in a police station or other premises shall be entitled, if he so requests, to consult a solicitor privately at any time.' Subsection (4) states: 'If a person makes such a request, he must be permitted to consult a solicitor as soon as is practicable except to the extent that delay is permitted by this section.' Section 58 is supported by detailed provisions in Code C of the Codes of Practice issued pursuant to section 66. Significantly, paragraph 6.6 of Code C provides that a detainee who wants legal advice may not be interviewed until he or she has received it, unless (in very general terms)

- delay in providing access to legal advice is permitted in the circumstances; or
- an officer of at least superintendent rank authorizes the interview; or
- a solicitor acceptable to the detainee cannot be found or is unavailable.

The right of access to legal advice has been described by the Court of Appeal as 'one of the most important and fundamental rights of a citizen'.[70] It has also observed that 'the main object of section 58 of the Act and indeed of the Codes of Practice is to achieve fairness—to an accused or suspected person so as, among other things, to preserve and protect his legal rights; but also fairness for the Crown and its officers so that again, among other things, there might be reduced the incidence or effectiveness of unfounded allegations of malpractice'.[71] Given that the law now permits adverse inferences to be drawn, in appropriate circumstances, from silence in the face of police questioning,[72] access to legal advice would seem to assume particular importance in contemporary criminal procedure.

The courts have taken the view that a clear breach of section 58 and/or the associated Code provisions would be likely of itself to be considered significant and substantial, and that, prima facie, the admission of confession evidence obtained as a result of the breach would adversely affect the fairness of the proceedings. What section 78(1) requires, however, is that the trial judge determine whether admission would adversely affect fairness to *such an extent* that the evidence ought not to be admitted.[73] It is here that the precise implications of the particular breach must be considered. Only if the breach could have 'made a difference' in the case would exclusion appear to be justified. In *R v Samuel*[74] the Court of Appeal considered that the refusal of access to a solicitor could have resulted in a confession which would not have been made had the breach not occurred. The appellant's solicitor asserted that, as his client had already strenuously denied his involvement in the crime in four previous interviews, and had already been

---

[70] *R v Samuel* [1988] QB 615, 630.   [71] *R v Walsh* (1990) 91 Cr App R 161, 163 (decision of 1989).
[72] See Ch 3.   [73] *R v Walsh* (1990) 91 Cr App R 161, 163 (decision of 1989).   [74] [1988] QB 615.

charged with two serious offences, he would probably have advised him not to answer any further questions. This led the Court of Appeal to hold that the refusal of access to a solicitor ought to have resulted in the exclusion of the confession evidence under section 78(1). In a similar vein, the Court of Appeal held in *R v Walsh* that the confession evidence in question ought to have been excluded under section 78(1), since, 'having considered the matter, we can see nothing in this case which could properly lead the court to the conclusion that the breach of section 58 made no difference; or in other words that it was likely that the appellant would have made the admissions in any event. The very highest it could be put, to our minds, was that it was perhaps uncertain whether or not the presence of a solicitor would have made any difference.'[75]

By contrast, in *R v Alladice*:

> the appellant himself said in evidence . . . that he was well able to cope with the interviews; that he had been given the appropriate caution before each of them; that he had understood the caution and was aware of his rights. . . . His reason for wanting a solicitor was to have some sort of check on the conduct of the police during the interview. . . . It may seldom happen that a defendant is so forthcoming about his attitude towards the presence of a legal adviser. That candour does however simplify the task of deciding whether the admission of the evidence 'would have such an adverse effect on the fairness of the proceedings' that it should not have been admitted. Had the solicitor been present, his advice would have added nothing to the knowledge of his rights which the appellant already had.[76]

It had not, therefore, been wrong for the confession evidence not to have been excluded under section 78(1).[77]

The notion that a confession will not be excluded from evidence under section 78(1) if it is determined that the presence of a legal adviser would have 'made no difference', since the defendant would have made the confession in any event, is a problematic one. It is clear that such a determination can involve courts in a certain amount of *post hoc* rationalization of events. The desirability of this may be questioned. In any event, as Doherty points out, 'in finding that the defendant was not prejudiced by denial of a legal adviser in *R v Alladice* the court presumed that the adviser's role was simply to tell the suspect of his right to silence. The other roles of the adviser, general support, checking aggressive questioning, being a witness to the defendant's version of events, which may have been both helpful and necessary to an 18-year-old charged with robbery were ignored or dismissed by the court.'[78]

4.1.2 Absence of a Caution

Paragraph 10.1 of Code C provides: 'A person whom there are grounds to suspect of an offence . . . must be cautioned before any questions about an offence, or further

---

[75] (1990) 91 Cr App R 161, 163 (decision of 1989). See also *R v Parris* (1989) 89 Cr App R 68 (decision of 1988).
[76] (1988) 87 Cr App R 380, 386–7 (decision of 1988).
[77] See also *R v Dunford* (1990) 91 Cr App R 150 (decision of 1990).
[78] M Doherty, 'Judicial Discretion: Victimising the Villains?' (1999) 3 *International Journal of Evidence and Proof* 44, 51.

questions if the answers provide the grounds for suspicion, are put to them if either the suspect's answers or silence . . . may be given in evidence to a court in a prosecution.' The Court of Appeal has explained: 'The rationale of paragraph 10.1 of Code C is . . . to ensure that interviewees are informed of their rights, one of which is not to answer questions, and to inform them of the use which might be made of their answers in criminal proceedings. . . . it seems to us that the principal purpose of such a procedure is to ensure, so far as possible, that interviewees do not make admissions unless they wish to do so and are aware of the consequences.'[79]

In *R v Kirk*,[80] the defendant was convicted of robbery and manslaughter. The incident involved an old woman who had her shopping bag snatched, fell, and sustained injuries requiring surgery. Complications arose during the surgery and she later died. Kirk was formally arrested in relation to an offence of assault on the victim, and in relation to the theft of the bag. He was not arrested for either robbery or manslaughter, although by that stage all the material information was in the possession of the police. The Court of Appeal held that the failure to caution Kirk in relation to robbery and manslaughter before questioning him constituted a breach of paragraph 10.1:

> . . . as it seems to us, where the police, having made an arrest, propose to question a suspect . . . in relation to an offence which is more serious than the offence in respect of which the arrest was made, they must, before questioning . . . , either charge the suspect with the more serious offence, . . . or at least ensure that he is aware of the true nature of the investigation. That is the thrust and purport of paragraph 10.1 of Code C . . . They must do that so that he can give proper weight to that factor, namely the nature of the investigation which is being conducted, when deciding whether or not to exercise his right to obtain free legal advice . . . and in deciding how to respond to the questions which the police propose to ask of him.[81]

Furthermore:

> It seems to us that the Act of 1984 and the codes of practice which exist under it proceed upon the assumption that a suspect in custody will know why he is there and, when being interviewed, will know at least in general terms the level of offence in respect of which he is suspected and, if he does not know, and as a result does not seek legal advice and gives critical answers which he might not otherwise have given, the evidence, as it seems to us, in normal circumstances, ought to be excluded pursuant to section 78 . . .
>
> . . .
>
> Because we cannot say that there are relevant admissions which would have come into existence if the proper procedure had been followed, it seems to us that neither the conviction in respect of the offence of manslaughter nor the conviction in respect of the offence of robbery ought to stand . . .[82]

On the other hand, in *R v Gill*, the Court of Appeal did not consider that exclusion would have been justified. The Court remarked: 'There was a breach of Code C which we would characterise as significant but it was certainly not caused by any bad faith and could not fairly be regarded as involving a flagrant disregard of the code's provisions.'[83]

---

[79] *R v Gill* [2003] EWCA Crim 2256, [2003] 4 All ER 681, [46].   [80] [2000] 1 WLR 567.
[81] Ibid, 572.   [82] Ibid, 572–3.   [83] [2003] EWCA Crim 2256, [2003] 4 All ER 681, [44].

More crucially, and in a manner consistent with the approach taken in *Alladice*, the Court also commented: 'We do not think that it is arguable that, if a caution had been administered, the appellants would have done anything different from what they did. They had time to consider their position.'[84]

4.1.3 Absence of an Appropriate Adult

R v Aspinall[85] concerned a breach of what is now paragraph 11.15 of Code C, which provides: 'A juvenile or person who is mentally disordered or otherwise mentally vulnerable must not be interviewed regarding their involvement or suspected involvement in a criminal offence or offences, or asked to provide or sign a written statement under caution or record of interview, in the absence of [an] appropriate adult unless paragraphs 11.1, 11.18 to 11.20 apply.'[86] In his interview, which was conducted in the absence of an appropriate adult, Aspinall told some lies. The Court of Appeal allowed his appeal against conviction, effectively on the basis that the presence of an appropriate adult might have made a difference:

> Not only was this mentally disordered appellant deprived of the assistance, guidance, and protection of an appropriate adult, but was also without any legal advice, apart from the brief conversation with a duty solicitor over the telephone many hours previously. . . . A significant part of the duty of an appropriate adult, is to advise about the presence of a solicitor at interview, and this appellant was deprived of such advice which in all likelihood would have urged him to have legal representation.
>
> . . .
>
> . . . the appropriate adult or legal adviser would have urged him to tell the truth, because patent lies could only harm his defence. The appellant's credibility was undermined by his lies . . .[87]

4.1.4 Breach of Recording Requirements

Breaches of the requirements in Code C for the recording of interviews may also result in the exclusion of confession evidence under section 78(1). An 'interview' is defined as the questioning of a person regarding that person's involvement or suspected involvement in a criminal offence or offences, for the purpose of eliciting evidence (whether of answers or silence) which may be given in evidence in court.[88] In an attempt to protect suspects from the possibility of fabrication, provision is made in the Codes for the recording of interviews. These recording requirements 'provide[ ] safeguards against the police inaccurately recording or inventing the words used in questioning a detained person. . . . Again, equally importantly, the provisions, if complied with, are designed to make it very much more difficult for a defendant to make unfounded allegations that he has been "verballed" which appear credible.'[89]

---

[84] [2003] EWCA Crim 2256, [2003] 4 All ER 681, [48]. See also *R v Doyle* [2002] EWCA Crim 1176; *R v Senior* [2004] EWCA Crim 454, [2004] 3 All ER 9.

[85] [1999] 2 Cr App R 115; see generally K Kerrigan, 'Mentally Disordered Suspects: The Lessons of *R v Aspinall*' (2000) 64 *Journal of Criminal Law* 80.   [86] Italics removed.

[87] [1999] 2 Cr App R 115, 121–2.   [88] See Code C, paras 10.1 and 11.1A.

[89] *R v Keenan* [1990] 2 QB 54, 63.

What is required is that an 'accurate record' be made of each interview with a suspect, whether or not the interview takes place at a police station.[90] Code E provides that tape recording is generally required of any interview conducted at a police station with a person who has been cautioned in respect of an indictable offence.[91] Tape recording is to 'be carried out openly to instil confidence in its reliability as an impartial and accurate record of the interview'.[92] Two tapes are to be produced: a master copy which is to be sealed in the suspect's presence, and a working copy.[93] At the start of the interview 'the interviewer shall put to the suspect any significant statement or silence . . .'.[94] At the conclusion of the interview, the time is to be recorded and the tape recorder switched off. The master tape is to be sealed with a master tape label which is to be signed by all present.[95] The suspect is to be handed a notice explaining the use which will be made of the tape recording and the arrangements for access to it, and explaining that a copy of the tape will be supplied as soon as practicable if the person is charged or informed that there is to be a prosecution.[96] After the interview the interviewer is to make a note in his or her pocketbook of the fact that the interview has taken place and has been tape recorded, as well as its time, duration, and date, and the identification number of the master tape.[97] Tape recording may not be required where it is not reasonably practicable to tape record and it is considered on reasonable grounds that the interview should not be delayed; or where it is clear from the outset that no prosecution will ensue. In such cases the interview is to be recorded in writing in accordance with Code C.[98]

The provisions of Code C relating to written records of interview apply where Code E does not. A written record is to be made on the forms provided for this purpose or in the interviewer's pocketbook.[99] It must be made during the interview unless this would not be practicable or would interfere with the conduct of the interview.[100] If a record is not made during the interview the reason for this must be recorded in the interview record,[101] and it must be made as soon as practicable thereafter.[102] A written interview record must be timed and signed by its maker.[103] Unless it is impracticable the interviewee is to be given the opportunity to read the record and to sign it as correct or to indicate the respects in which it is considered inaccurate.[104]

The importance attached to the recording requirements means that clear breaches of these provisions, like clear breaches of the access to legal advice provisions, will typically be considered significant and substantial and thus a good ground for the exclusion under section 78(1) of confession evidence obtained as a result of the breaches.[105] It seems clear, however, that even serious breaches would not lead invariably to exclusion. As in the case of breaches of section 58 and the provisions of Code C relating to access to legal advice, the courts appear willing to engage in assessments of whether the

---

[90] Code C, para 11.7(a).   [91] Para 3.1.   [92] Para 2.1.   [93] Para 2.2.   [94] Para 4.6.
[95] Para 4.18.   [96] Para 4.19.   [97] Para 5.1.   [98] Para 3.3.   [99] Para 11.7(b).
[100] Para 11.7(c).   [101] Para 11.10.   [102] Para 11.8.   [103] Para 11.9.   [104] Para 11.11.
[105] See generally R v Keenan [1990] 2 QB 54 and R v Canale [1990] 2 All ER 187. See also R v Miller [1998] Crim LR 209.

defendant was likely to have been actually prejudiced by the breaches. In *R v Dunn*, for example, the Court of Appeal acknowledged that:

> there were serious breaches of the code by the police . . . First, there was no contemporaneous note of the disputed conversation. Secondly, the reason for the absence of a contemporaneous record was not recorded in the police officer's notebook. Thirdly, and most important, the appellant was not given the opportunity to read the subsequent record said to have been made within a few minutes of the completion of the interview, so that he could either sign it as correct or indicate the respects in which he considered it inaccurate.[106]

It was held, however, that the *presence of the solicitor's clerk* during the disputed conversation could be taken into account in the exercise of discretion, and that this factor was ultimately of sufficient weight to tip the balance in favour of not excluding the evidence. The clerk was there to protect Dunn's interests; she 'could have intervened during the conversation, before the relevant answers were given. Secondly, her mere presence would inhibit the police from fabricating the conversation which did not in fact take place. Thirdly, if they were to fabricate a conversation despite the inhibition, then it would not simply be a question of their evidence against the evidence of the appellant.' Had she not been present, it would have been appropriate to exclude the evidence.[107]

The notion that the serious breaches could be overlooked simply on account of the presence of the clerk seems somewhat crude and simplistic. Such an approach requires a court to engage in the rather artificial task of determining whether tangible prejudice has been caused to the defendant by the breach or breaches in question. In a similar vein, the breach in *Watson v DPP* was held not to justify exclusion on the basis that the defendant had not been tangibly disadvantaged thereby. *Watson* concerned a prosecution for driving with excess alcohol, and at issue was a breach of what is now paragraph 11.11 of Code C in a context succinctly summarized by the Administrative Court as follows:

> The appeal now effectively raises one issue: were the magistrates right to admit an admission allegedly made by the appellant that he was the driver of the motorcar at the time of the accident? The admission was not recorded in contemporaneous notes made by the officer who spoke to the appellant, and the appellant was not given an opportunity to read the officer's subsequently written up note and either sign it as correct, or indicate any inaccuracies.[108]

The Court held that the justices had been entitled to admit the evidence: Watson had not been deprived of any reasonable opportunity to deny that he was the driver, and indeed had a series of opportunities at the police station to make such a denial.[109] Furthermore, 'the justices are entitled to have regard to the fact that the police officer was, as they found, called away in an emergency'.[110]

Even if it is decided that a breach of the recording requirements does not justify exclusion under section 78(1), it may nevertheless be incumbent upon the trial judge to

---

[106] (1990) 91 Cr App R 237, 241 (decision of 1990).   [107] Ibid, 243.
[108] [2003] EWHC 1466 (Admin), (2004) 168 JP 116, [2].   [109] Ibid, [10], [12].   [110] Ibid, [12].

direct the jury on the significance of the breach. In the context of a dispute between the prosecution and defence over what had been said by the accused in an interview, the Court of Appeal noted in *R v Dures*: 'It was essential that he make clear to the jury, as he did, that the Code was based on an Act of Parliament, that there had been a breach of the Code, that it was for the jury to decide whose evidence they accepted in relation to what had been said, and that only if they were sure that the officers were telling the truth should they rely on the disputed parts of the cell interviews.'[111]

4.2 Other Improprieties

Confession evidence may be excluded under section 78(1) on account of an impropriety which does not constitute a breach of the Police and Criminal Evidence Act 1984 and/or its associated Codes of Practice. In *R v Mason*,[112] the police deliberately lied to Mason and his solicitor that Mason's fingerprint had been found on a fragment of glass at the scene of the crime. The solicitor, influenced by this false information, advised Mason to answer police questions and to give his explanation of any involvement he had had in the incident. The Court of Appeal held that the confession evidence ought to have been excluded under section 78(1): 'It is obvious from the undisputed evidence that the police practised a deceit not only upon the appellant, which is bad enough, but also upon the solicitor whose duty it was to advise him. In effect, they hoodwinked both solicitor and client. That was a most reprehensible thing to do.'[113]

It is interesting to speculate whether the result in *Mason* would have been the same if the police had deceived the accused only, rather than both the accused *and his solicitor*. The tenor of the judgment of the Court of Appeal certainly suggests that the fact that the solicitor was also deceived was considered important. What is unclear is whether it was regarded as crucial, so that in its absence the Court of Appeal would have come to a different conclusion. The seriousness with which the Court of Appeal in *Mason* took the fact that the solicitor had been misled may be viewed in one sense as a logical corollary of the importance which is accorded to the right to legal advice in the decisions examined earlier on the consequences of section 58 and associated Code breaches. The right would certainly ring hollow if solicitors were to provide legal advice on the basis of false or misleading information deliberately provided by the police.

Finally, and in a slightly different context, the decision of the Privy Council in *Mohammed v The State*[114] is noteworthy. In breach of the rights of a suspect under the Constitution of Trinidad and Tobago, the police obtained a confession from the appellant without informing him of his right to communicate with a lawyer. The trial judge exercised his discretion in favour of admitting the confession in evidence.

---

[111] [1997] 2 Cr App R 247, 264.

[112] [1988] 1 WLR 139. See A Ashworth, 'Should the Police Be Allowed to Use Deceptive Practices?' (1998) 114 *Law Quarterly Review* 108, 113–14.   [113] [1988] 1 WLR 139, 144.

[114] [1999] 2 WLR 552. See generally D O'Brien and V Carter, ' "Don't Look Back": The Exclusion of Evidence and the Constitutional Rights of the Accused. A Caribbean Commonwealth Perspective' (2000) 4 *International Journal of Evidence and Proof* 45.

Although the Privy Council upheld the appellant's appeal against conviction on other grounds, a number of observations were made about the confession evidence. It was held that, fundamental as the rights of a suspect to communicate with his or her lawyer are, it does not follow that such rights can be given due recognition only by an absolute exclusionary rule such as that enunciated by the US Supreme Court in *Miranda v Arizona*.[115] Such an absolute rule does not fit easily into a system based on English criminal procedure. The judge's discretion to admit or exclude confession evidence was not entirely abolished by the relevant constitutional provision. But while this discretion is neither prima facie exclusionary nor prima facie inclusionary, it is not a completely open-textured discretion. The judge must perform a balancing exercise in the context of the circumstances of the case: he or she must, on the one hand, weigh the interest of the community in securing relevant evidence bearing on the commission of serious crime so that justice can be done, and, on the other hand, weigh the interest of the individual who has been exposed to an illegal invasion of his or her rights. In the exercise of the discretion, the fact that the right infringed is enshrined in a constitution, and is not simply a common law right, *is* a relevant factor.[116] Indeed, the fact that there has been a breach of a constitutional right is a cogent factor militating in favour of exclusion of confession evidence; it would not generally be proper to admit confession evidence where the police have deliberately frustrated a suspect's constitutional rights. In the present case, however, the judge had been entitled to conclude that the police acted in good faith; the judge had taken into account the competing considerations and the exercise of his discretion had not been shown to be flawed.

It remains to be seen to what extent English courts will be influenced by this 'balancing of competing considerations' approach to the exercise of the judicial discretion to exclude confession evidence which is admissible as a matter of law.

4.3 Analysis

The above review of the mechanisms for excluding confession evidence raises a number of points. Section 76(2) of the Police and Criminal Evidence Act 1984, which requires that certain types of confession evidence *must* be excluded, is interpreted narrowly. 'Oppression' in section 76(2)(a) is given a restricted meaning, as is the concept of something 'said or done' in section 76(2)(b). Section 78(1), in spite of a number of oddities associated with the manner in which it has been approached by the courts in the context of confession evidence, is certainly a great deal more flexible. It is to be noted, however, that trial judges may well not be required to adopt as proactive a stance in relation to section 78(1) as in relation to section 76. It was seen earlier that a trial judge may, even in the absence of a defence submission, require the prosecution to prove that a confession was not obtained in a manner inconsistent with section 76(2); presumably

[115] 384 US 436 (1966).
[116] The previous view of the Privy Council on this issue, articulated in *King v R* [1969] 1 AC 304, 319, was considered no longer to represent good law.

this means that if the prosecution fails to do so, the confession will be excluded from evidence of the trial judge's own accord. Where, however, no submission is made that evidence ought to be excluded under section 78(1), the trial judge would appear to be under no obligation to consider the issue of exclusion of his or her own accord.[117] This would seem to be the case even where there has been flagrant abuse by the police of their powers in breach of the Police and Criminal Evidence Act 1984. Such a principle of non-intervention 'does not mean that if he feels it appropriate the judge should not make a pertinent enquiry of the advocate in the jury's absence in certain circumstances, but beyond that he need not go'.[118]

5 'Tainting' of Subsequent Confessions

It will be clear from the discussion of *Mohd Ali bin Burut* above that a confession may effectively be 'tainted' by earlier oppression. Similar principles would seem to apply in relation to section 76(2)(b) and discretionary exclusion. Thus the fact that something 'said or done' has caused a confession to be inadmissible under section 76(2)(b) may mean that a later but properly obtained confession is similarly tainted and thus also automatically inadmissible under section 76(2)(b).[119] Equally, an earlier impropriety may render a later but properly obtained confession liable to be excluded from evidence under section 78(1).

Whether a later but properly obtained confession will be deemed to be 'tainted' by an earlier impropriety will depend, of course, on the circumstances of the particular case. Some improprieties will obviously be of such a nature that they cannot be 'cured'[120] by a properly conducted later interview, with the result that there 'must inevitably be a continuing blight'[121] on any confessions subsequently made. The question for the court is whether there is any suggestion of oppression, inducement, stress, or pressures in the earlier interview which may have continued to exert a 'malign influence' during the later interview.[122] A relevant consideration is whether the earlier breach was a flagrant or merely technical one.[123] Ultimately, however:

> where an early interviewing is excluded admission of a later interview must be a matter of fact and degree. It is likely to depend on a consideration of whether the objections leading to the exclusion of the first interview were of a fundamental and continuing nature, and, if so, if the arrangements for the subsequent interview gave the accused a sufficient opportunity to exercise an informed and independent choice as to whether he should repeat or retract what he said in the excluded interview or say nothing.[124]

---

[117] *R v Goldenberg* (1989) 88 Cr App R 285, 289 (decision of 1988).
[118] *R v Raphaie* [1996] Crim LR 812; transcript from Smith Bernal.
[119] *R v McGovern* (1991) 92 Cr App R 228 (decision of 1990).   [120] *R v Ismail* [1990] Crim LR 109.
[121] *R v Glaves* [1993] Crim LR 685.
[122] *Y v DPP* [1991] Crim LR 917. See also *R v Canale* [1990] 2 All ER 187; *R v Gillard* (1991) 92 Cr App R 61 (decision of 1990).   [123] *R v Wood* [1994] Crim LR 222.
[124] *R v Singleton* [2002] EWCA Crim 459, [10].

Thus in *R v Neil*[125] the Court of Appeal held that the judge should have exercised his discretion to exclude the evidence, since Neil would have considered himself bound to the admissions in the first statement, and the circumstances of the second interview were insufficient to provide him with a safe and confident opportunity to withdraw the admissions.[126] In *R v Singleton*, on the other hand, 'the objections leading to the exclusion of the earlier interviews were not continuing and the appellant plainly had ample opportunity to decide whether or not to volunteer a repetition of what he had earlier said'.[127]

6 Mentally Handicapped Defendants and Warnings

Section 77(1) of the Police and Criminal Evidence Act 1984[128] provides:

Without prejudice to the general duty of the court at a trial on indictment to direct the jury on any matter on which it appears to the court appropriate to do so, where at such a trial—

(a) the case against the accused depends wholly or substantially on a confession by him; and

(b) the court is satisfied—

(i) that he is mentally handicapped; and

(ii) that the confession was not made in the presence of an independent person,

the court shall warn the jury that there is special need for caution before convicting the accused in reliance on the confession, and shall explain that the need arises because of the circumstances mentioned in paragraphs (a) and (b) above.

Analogous provision is made in section 77(2) for summary trials: if a warning would be required if the trial were on indictment, the court is to treat the case as one in which there is a special need for caution before convicting the accused on the confession. An 'independent person' is one *other than* 'a police officer or a person employed for, or engaged on, police purposes', and a 'mentally handicapped' person is one 'who is in a state of arrested or incomplete development of mind which includes significant impairment of intelligence and social functioning'.[129]

In *R v Campbell*[130] the Court of Appeal noted, somewhat unhelpfully, that a case depends 'substantially on a confession' if it would be substantially less strong without the confession. In determining whether a person is 'mentally handicapped' for the purposes of section 77, a court must not place undue weight on figures produced by intelligence tests. Thus it does not necessarily follow, from the fact that someone who has achieved certain scores has been held to be mentally handicapped in one case, that another person who has achieved similar scores must also be held to be mentally

---

125 [1994] Crim LR 441.

126 See also *R v Nelson* [1998] 2 Cr App R 399, in which *Neil* was distinguished.

127 [2002] EWCA Crim 459, [11]. See also *R v Ahmed* [2003] EWCA Crim 3627.

128 I have drawn in this section on A L-T Choo, *Evidence: Text and Materials* (1998) 405–7.

129 S 77(3).   130 [1995] 1 Cr App R 522, 535.

handicapped. Each case must be decided on its own facts.[131] The 'independent person' must be a person who was independent of the person to whom the confession was made; they cannot have been the same person.[132]

An illustration of the application of section 77 is provided by *R v Lamont*.[133] The defendant was mentally subnormal, with a reading and comprehension ability of a child of eight and an IQ of 73. The trial judge failed to issue a section 77 warning. The defendant's conviction for attempted murder was quashed by the Court of Appeal on the basis that such a warning should have been given. The dearth of reported case law on section 77 is probably attributable to the fact that in many cases where section 77 was potentially applicable, section 76 or section 78(1) might have been utilized instead to exclude the confession evidence altogether. The relationship between the exclusion of confession evidence and section 77 warnings was discussed briefly in *R v Moss*. The trial judge in this case had treated the defendant as mentally handicapped and given the jury a direction in accordance with section 77. The defendant's appeal against conviction was allowed by the Court of Appeal on the basis that the confession evidence should have been excluded altogether:

> Section 77 simply deals with 'a confession,' and in the simplest case a confession may well be obtained from a defendant in one interview during a comparatively short period of custody; that situation is clearly to be distinguished from one such as existed in the present case where there were in all some nine interviews. It was not until the fifth interview that any admission was made and all those interviews where admissions were made, were made in the absence of a solicitor or any other independent person.[134]

It should be noted that, ultimately, section 77 is of only limited value in addressing the problems associated with confession evidence. Most notably, the provision applies only to the mentally *handicapped*, and does not extend to the mentally ill. The reason given for this was that the mentally ill, unlike the mentally handicapped, are not a readily identifiable group. Even if this reasoning were to be accepted, it fails to explain why juveniles, who clearly constitute a readily identifiable group, are also excluded from the operation of section 77. The exclusion of juveniles creates the anomaly that section 77 applies to an adult with a mental age of 10, but not to a 10-year-old.[135]

7 Withdrawal of the Case from the Jury

The Court of Appeal has held that:

> where (1) the prosecution case depends wholly upon confessions; (2) the defendant suffers from a significant degree of mental handicap; and (3) the confessions are unconvincing to a point where a jury properly directed could not properly convict upon them, then the judge,

---

[131] *R v Kenny, The Times*, 27 July 1993.   [132] *R v Bailey* [1995] 2 Cr App R 262.

[133] [1989] Crim LR 813.

[134] (1990) 91 Cr App R 371, 377 (decision of 1990). See also *R v Cox* [1991] Crim LR 276.

[135] See A L-T Choo, 'Confessions and Corroboration: A Comparative Perspective' [1991] *Criminal Law Review* 867, 869; P Mirfield, *Confessions* (1985) 166.

assuming he has not excluded the confessions earlier, should withdraw the case from the jury. The confessions may be unconvincing, for example, because they lack the incriminating details to be expected of a guilty and willing confessor, or because they are inconsistent with other evidence, or because they are otherwise inherently improbable. Cases depending solely or mainly on confessions, like cases depending upon identification evidence, have given rise to miscarriages of justice. We are therefore of opinion that when the three conditions tabulated above apply at any stage of the case, the judge should, in the interests of justice, take the initiative and withdraw the case from the jury.[136]

To confine this judicial power to cases of mental handicap would seem, however, to constitute an unnecessary limitation. It is strongly arguable that the power to withdraw the case from the jury should be exercisable wherever the prosecution case depends wholly on confessions which are so unconvincing that no properly directed jury could properly convict on them. It should be irrelevant whether the unreliability of the confessions is attributable to mental handicap or to some other factor.

8 Partly Adverse Statements

Statements made by accused persons may contain both exculpatory and inculpatory remarks. Such statements are known as partly adverse statements or mixed statements. It has been held that, assuming that the inculpatory part of the statement is admissible in evidence as a confession, the exculpatory part will also be admissible as evidence of the facts contained in it.[137] This principle applies to oral statements as well as to written ones.[138] In *R v Sharp*,[139] the House of Lords approved the following statement of Lord Lane CJ in *R v Duncan*:

> Where a 'mixed' statement is under consideration by the jury in a case where the defendant has not given evidence, it seems to us that the simplest, and, therefore, the method most likely to produce a just result, is for the jury to be told that the whole statement, both the incriminating parts and the excuses or explanations, must be considered by them in deciding where the truth lies. It is, to say the least, not helpful to try to explain to the jury that the exculpatory parts of the statement are something less than evidence of the facts they state. Equally, where appropriate, as it usually will be, the judge may, and should, point out that the incriminating parts are likely to be true (otherwise why say them?), whereas the excuses do not have the same weight.[140]

Not only may the judge point out that the exculpatory parts do not carry the same weight as the inculpatory parts, but the House of Lords has also made it clear that

---

[136] *R v McKenzie* [1993] 1 WLR 453, 455. *R v Galbraith* [1981] 1 WLR 1039, discussed in Ch 14, was applied. See also *R v Wood* [1994] Crim LR 222.

[137] See generally D Birch, 'The Sharp End of the Wedge: Use of Mixed Statements by the Defence' [1997] *Criminal Law Review* 416.　　　　　　　　　　　　　　[138] *R v Polin* [1991] Crim LR 293.

[139] [1988] 1 All ER 65. See also *R v Grayson* [1993] Crim LR 864 and *R v Downes and Rawlinson*, *The Times*, 10 Dec 1993.

[140] (1981) 73 Cr App R 359, 365 (decision of 1981). See also *Von Starck v R* [2000] 1 WLR 1270; *R v Holloran* [2003] EWCA Crim 3282, [28]; *R v Lazarus* [2004] EWCA Crim 1962.

'a judge is entitled to comment adversely on the quality of the exculpatory parts of a mixed statement which has not been tested by cross-examination' because of the accused's failure to testify.[141]

The Court of Appeal in *R v Holloran* expressed the view, without deciding the matter definitively, that, in the interests of ensuring a fair trial, 'once an interview transcript has gone in before the jury and it contains a defence put forward by a defendant, the jury's attention should normally be directed to that defence when the defendant does not give evidence, even if the interview is wholly self-exculpatory'.[142]

9 Use of Confession Contravening Section 76(2)

While a confession obtained in contravention of section 76(2) may not be used by the prosecution to prove the accused's guilt, there are permissible uses to which it may be put.

9.1 Facts Discovered in Consequence of Confession

Suppose that non-confession evidence has been discovered by the police in consequence of a confession that is inadmissible in evidence under section 76(2).[143] Does this derivative evidence or 'fruit of the poisonous tree' constitute admissible evidence? If so, is the prosecution permitted to mention that it was discovered in consequence of a confession?

The effect of section 76(4)(a), read in conjunction with section 76(6), is as follows. The fact that a confession is wholly or party excluded pursuant to section 76(2) 'shall not affect the admissibility in evidence...of any facts discovered' as a result of the wholly excluded confession, or the excluded part of the confession, as the case may be. In other words, derivative evidence is admissible as a matter of law. The prosecution is, however, forbidden by section 76(5) from introducing evidence that the fact which was discovered was discovered as a result of a statement made by the accused; only the defence may introduce such evidence if it so wishes.

This legislative strategy is consistent with a number of judicial decisions at common law. In the old case of *R v Warickshall*,[144] Warickshall confessed to receiving stolen property, and as a result of this confession the stolen property was discovered hidden in her bed in her lodgings. It was held that the confession was inadmissible in evidence, but that this did not affect the admissibility of the evidence of the discovery of the stolen property. No reference could, however, be made to the fact that the stolen property was discovered as a result of the inadmissible confession.

In *R v Berriman*, the accused was charged with concealing the birth of a child. She was asked by a magistrate where she had put the child's body, but her answer was not admitted in evidence. The prosecution then sought to ask a witness whether, in

---

[141] *R v Aziz* [1995] 3 WLR 53, 59.   [142] [2003] EWCA Crim 3282, [30].
[143] I have drawn in this section on A L-T Choo, *Evidence: Text and Materials* (1998) 408–9.
[144] (1783) 1 Leach 263, 168 ER 234.

consequence of the answer improperly elicited by the magistrate from the accused, a search had been made at a particular spot and relevant facts discovered. Erle J said: 'No! *Not in consequence of what she said*. You may ask him what search was made, and what things were found, but under the circumstances, I cannot allow that proceeding to be connected with the prisoner.'[145]

In the Scottish case of *Chalmers v HM Advocate*,[146] the accused, who was suspected of murder, was interrogated at a police station, making a confession that would have been inadmissible in evidence. He was then taken to a cornfield where he pointed out the place where a purse belonging to the deceased was found. The High Court of Justiciary held that evidence adduced by the prosecution of the visit to the cornfield had been incorrectly admitted by the trial judge.

In *Lam v R*,[147] the three defendants were charged with murder. The prosecution case was that they had stabbed the deceased to death with a knife which they had then thrown into the sea. The trial judge held that the defendants' confessions were inadmissible in evidence, but admitted evidence of a video recording which showed the first defendant directing the police to the waterfront, where each of the defendants in turn made gestures indicating the throwing of the knife into the water. The judge also admitted police evidence describing these actions of the defendants which led to the recovery of the knife. On appeal to the Privy Council, it was held that the evidence of the video recording, and the police evidence, had been incorrectly admitted.

The prohibition of the introduction by the prosecution of evidence that the non-confession evidence was discovered as a result of a confession by the accused can have important practical implications, and prove a substantial impediment for the prosecution. In cases where the non-confession evidence was discovered in a 'neutral' place unconnected with the defendant, such evidence will be of little relevance or value in the absence of evidence of what led the police to its discovery. In *Chalmers v HM Advocate* Lord Justice-General Cooper said:

> If the police had simply produced, and proved the finding of, the purse, that evidence would have carried them little or no distance in this case towards implicating the appellant. It was essential that the appellant should be linked up with the purse, either by oral confession or by its equivalent—tacit admission of knowledge of its whereabouts obtained as a sequel to the interrogation.[148]

And the Privy Council noted in *Lam*:

> Of course in the case of Jane Warickshall the fact that the stolen property was found hidden in her bed implicated her as the receiver without introducing any part of her confession in evidence, whereas in the present appeal the mere finding of the knife in the sea in no way

---

[145] (1854) 6 Cox 388, 389 (italics in original).   [146] [1954] SLT 177.

[147] [1991] 2 AC 212. See also *Timothy v The State* [2000] 1 WLR 485, 493: '. . . the prosecution cannot rely on the fact that the guns were found as a result of the police being taken to the site and the guns being pointed out to them any more than the prosecution could rely on the knife having been found as a result of the appellants' directions in *Lam Chi-ming's* case once the finding of the guns is seen to be the result of an involuntary confession whether by writing, orally or by conduct.'   [148] [1954] SLT 177, 183.

implicated the defendants. What implicated them was their admission that they had thrown it into the sea.[149]

9.2 Evidence of Manner of Speech, Writing, or Expression

Section 76(4)(b) of the Police and Criminal Evidence Act 1984 provides that, where a confession 'is relevant as showing that the accused speaks, writes or expresses himself in a particular way', the fact that the confession is wholly or partly excluded pursuant to section 76(2) 'shall not affect the admissibility in evidence ... of so much of the confession as is necessary to show that he does so'. In *R v Voisin*,[150] a body was found together with a piece of paper with the words 'Bladie Belgiam' written on it. In the police station, the defendant, at the request of the police to write the words 'Bloody Belgian', wrote 'Bladie Belgiam'. It was held that the writing was admissible in evidence to show that the defendant spelt the words in that way. Under section 76(4)(b) this evidence would be admissible even if the written words were part of a confession inadmissible in evidence under section 76(2).

9.3 The Role of Section 78(1)

Two points should be made. The first is that, even though admissible as a matter of law, evidence of facts discovered in consequence of an inadmissible confession, and evidence of manner of speech, writing, or expression derived from an inadmissible confession, may still be liable to be excluded in the exercise of discretion under section 78(1) of the Police and Criminal Evidence Act 1984 (or at common law).[151] If, for example, a confession is held to be inadmissible under section 76(2) because it has been obtained in a particularly egregious manner, serious consideration should be given by the trial judge to whether evidence of facts discovered in consequence of the confession should be excluded under section 78(1). It is true that, as discussed above, the derivative evidence will in many cases be of little or no use to the prosecution because of the inadmissibility of evidence of how it was obtained. However, there will always be cases like *Warickshall* where the derivative evidence can, in effect, 'stand alone'. It is in the context of such cases that consideration of whether the derivative evidence should be excluded in the exercise of discretion will be particularly important.

The second issue concerns the prohibition in section 76(5) of the introduction by the prosecution of evidence that the fact which was discovered was discovered as a result of a statement made by the accused. This prohibition relates only to confessions inadmissible in evidence as a matter of law under section 76(2), and does not extend to confessions excluded from evidence in the exercise of discretion under section 78(1).

---

[149] [1991] 2 AC 212, 217. All the preceding cases may be contrasted with *R v Gould* (1840) 9 Car & P 364, 173 ER 870, in which a lantern was found as a result of an inadmissible confession made by a prisoner charged with burglary. A witness was permitted to give evidence that he had made a search for the lantern as a result of something that the prisoner had said.   [150] [1918] 1 KB 531.

[151] See P Mirfield, *Silence, Confessions and Improperly Obtained Evidence* (1997) 225.

The discussions earlier in the chapter have demonstrated, however, that there is a considerable overlap between the operation of section 76(2) and section 78(1): in many instances, the same confession may be legitimately excluded from evidence under either section 76(2) or section 78(1), and it is often a matter of chance whether a particular confession is excluded from evidence under section 76(2) or under section 78(1).[152] Surely consistency requires, therefore, that an analogous principle to that in section 76(5) should apply in relation to confessions excluded from evidence in the exercise of discretion under section 78(1). This result can be achieved by using section 78(1) itself to exclude evidence that the fact which was discovered was discovered as a result of the statement already excluded from evidence under section 78(1).

10 Confession Admissible in Evidence only against Maker

A confession is admissible in evidence only against its maker, and not against anyone else that the statement may inculpate. Thus if the confession of an accused ('A') also inculpates a co-accused ('C'), the prosecution may use the confession only against A. As Lord Steyn explained in *R v Hayter*:

> In a joint trial the prosecution may not rely on what the maker of a confession said against a co-accused. This is a general rule of law. It is buttressed by a rule of practice requiring a trial judge to direct the jury to ignore a confession made by an accused in considering the case against a co-defendant.[153]

Given that a confession (or a mixed statement) made by A is not admissible in evidence against C, the trial judge may permit the statement to be edited so that, for example, C's name is disguised or deleted, or the part of the statement incriminating C is excised altogether. But in deciding whether to permit editing, the trial judge should keep in mind that in certain circumstances editing may result in confusion of the jury. As the Court of Appeal observed in *R v Jefferson*:

> For example, in a case involving many defendants whose names are sought to be excised and substituted by some other designation, such as letters of the alphabet, it could confuse the jury. Equally, the editing of descriptive passages and their substitution by others may leave the jury with a false impression—a bowdlerised version—of the statement credited to the defendant concerned. There can also be problems of selection in which [the non-confessing defendant] seeks to have excised from his co-defendant's statement in interview unfavourable references to himself but to retain favourable ones. There may be other problems for the fair conduct of a trial in a trial judge agreeing too readily to editing ...[154]

---

[152] See also D J Birch, 'The Pace Hots Up: Confessions and Confusions Under the 1984 Act' [1989] *Criminal Law Review* 95; D Feldman, 'Regulating Treatment of Suspects in Police Stations: Judicial Interpretation of Detention Provisions in the Police and Criminal Evidence Act 1984' [1990] *Criminal Law Review* 452; R May, 'Admissibility of Confessions: Recent Developments' (1991) 55 *Journal of Criminal Law* 366.

[153] [2005] UKHL 6, [2005] 1 WLR 605, [7].   [154] [1994] 1 All ER 270, 285.

It would appear, moreover, that C has no *right* to demand that the statement be edited in such a manner. A is entitled to refuse to consent to any proposed editing, and to insist that the statement be heard by the jury as a whole. This principle was affirmed by the Court of Criminal Appeal in *R v Gunewardene*[155] and, more recently, by the Privy Council in *Lobban v R*.[156] In the words of the Court of Criminal Appeal:

> It not infrequently happens that a prisoner, in making a statement, though admitting his or her guilt up to a certain extent, puts greater blame upon the co-prisoner, or is asserting that certain of his or her actions were really innocent and it was the conduct of the co-prisoner that gave them a sinister appearance or led to the belief that the prisoner making the statement was implicated in the crime. In such a case that prisoner would have a right to have the whole statement read and could, with good reason, complain if the prosecution picked out certain passages and left out others.[157]

This is a consequence of the principle, encountered and criticized elsewhere in this book, that there is no discretion to exclude evidence sought to be relied upon by a defendant. The evidence incriminating C, being relevant to A's own defence, cannot be excluded in the exercise of discretion.[158] The Privy Council remarked:

> Inevitably, the legal principles as their Lordships have stated them result in a real risk of prejudice to co-defendants in joint trials where evidence is admitted which is admissible against one defendant but not against the other defendants. One remedy is for a co-defendant to apply for a separate trial. The judge has a discretion to order a separate trial. The practice is generally to order joint trials. But their Lordships observe that ultimately the governing test is always the interests of justice in the particular circumstances of each case. If a separate trial is not ordered, the interests of the implicated co-defendant must be protected by the most explicit directions by the trial judge to the effect that the statement of one co-defendant is not evidence against the other.[159]

It is doubtful, however, that giving a defendant an absolute right to object to his or her confession being edited is likely to serve the interests of justice in the long run. Surely, where reference to the name of a non-confessing defendant is in no way exculpatory of the confessing defendant, the latter ought not to have the right to object to editing. It is the danger of prejudice to the non-confessing defendant which should be the prevailing consideration in such a situation.

A radically different approach is taken by the US Supreme Court to the issue of a confession that implicates a co-defendant. In contrast to the position in England and Wales, much less faith is placed in the ability of the jury to follow an instruction to use

---

[155] [1951] 2 KB 600.   [156] [1995] 1 WLR 877.   [157] [1951] 2 KB 600, 610–11.

[158] See generally *Lobban v R* [1995] 1 WLR 877 and the discussions in Ch 1. The Privy Council in *Lobban* thought that in so far as the decisions in *R v Silcott* [1987] Crim LR 765 and *R v Mathias* [1989] Crim LR 64 'suggest that a judge in a criminal trial has a discretionary power at the request of one defendant to exclude evidence tending to support the defence of another defendant they are contrary to well established principles and do not correctly reflect the law' ([1995] 1 WLR 877, 889). In *Silcott* and *Mathias* the view was taken that to require a jury to follow a direction, even a strong direction, not to use the evidence against a non-confessing defendant is to require mental gymnastics of Olympic standards.

[159] *Lobban v R* [1995] 1 WLR 877, 889.

the confession against the confessor only. The leading case of *Bruton v US*[160] was succinctly described in a more recent decision of the US Supreme Court as follows:

> *Bruton* involved two defendants accused of participating in the same crime and tried jointly before the same jury. One of the defendants had confessed. His confession named and incriminated the other defendant. The trial judge issued a limiting instruction, telling the jury that it should consider the confession as evidence only against the codefendant who had confessed and not against the defendant named in the confession. *Bruton* held that, despite the limiting instruction, the Constitution forbids the use of such a confession in the joint trial.[161]

The Court in *Bruton* thought that 'there are some contexts in which the risk that the jury will not, or cannot, follow instructions is so great, and the consequences of failure so vital to the defendant, that the practical and human limitations of the jury system cannot be ignored.... Such a context is presented here, where the powerfully incriminating extrajudicial statements of a codefendant, who stands accused side-by-side with the defendant, are deliberately spread before the jury in a joint trial.'[162]

It would appear that even editing will not suffice to allow the prosecution to use the confession, if it remains possible for the jury to infer that it is the co-accused whose identity is being concealed. In the words of the Supreme Court in *Gray v Maryland*:

> Consider a simplified but typical example, a confession that reads 'I, Bob Smith, along with Sam Jones, robbed the bank.' To replace the words 'Sam Jones' with an obvious blank will not likely fool anyone. A juror somewhat familiar with criminal law would know immediately that the blank, in the phrase 'I, Bob Smith, along with   , robbed the bank,' refers to defendant Jones.[163]

The reasoning and general approach of the US Supreme Court, being more cognizant of the potential prejudice to the non-confessing defendant, has much to commend it.

The principle that the prosecution cannot use a confession by a defendant against a co-defendant does not, however, affect the following principle. In a situation where a defendant's guilt is relevant to whether a co-defendant is guilty (such as where they 'had been in each other's company at the time of the offence'[164]), it is permissible for the jury to use the defendant's confession as the basis for establishing the defendant's guilt *and then* to use that finding of guilt in determining whether the co-defendant is also guilty.[165]

11 Use of Confession by a Co-Defendant

If the prosecution has succeeded in giving a defendant's confession in evidence against him or her, then any co-defendant of the defendant will be at liberty to rely on the confession for the co-defendant's own purposes. Disputes about the admissibility of

---

[160] 391 US 123 (1968).   [161] *Gray v Maryland* 523 US 185, 188 (1998).

[162] *Bruton v US* 391 US 123, 135–6 (1968).   [163] 523 US 185, 193 (1998).

[164] *R v Hayter* [2005] UKHL 6, [2005] 1 WLR 605, [84] per Lord Brown of Eaton-under-Heywood.

[165] *R v Hayter* [2005] UKHL 6, [2005] 1 WLR 605. See generally A Metzer, 'Life in Crime' (2005) 149 *Solicitors' Journal* 290.

a defendant's confession on behalf of a co-defendant may however arise where the confession has not already been admitted in evidence for the prosecution. Following the common law position as explained in R v Myers,[166] section 76A of the Police and Criminal Evidence Act 1984, inserted by the Criminal Justice Act 2003, now provides that the same two grounds for mandatory exclusion of confession evidence sought to be introduced by the prosecution apply to confession evidence sought to be introduced by a co-defendant against the defendant.[167] The difference is the obvious one that the presumption of inadmissibility, once it is 'represented' that the confession was or may have been obtained by one of the two proscribed methods, is to be rebutted by a co-defendant on the balance of probabilities rather than, as in the case of the prosecution, beyond reasonable doubt. As what is at issue is defence evidence, the court may not exclude in the exercise of discretion (for example, because of breaches of the Codes of Practice) evidence that is admissible under section 76A.[168] The operation of section 76A 'raises the intriguing possibility that, given the difference between the two standards of proof, if both prosecution and co-defendant sought to adduce a confession on the *voire dire*, the Judge might be persuaded to allow its adduction by the latter but not by the Crown. ... Thus, and rather confusingly, a trial Judge would have to direct the jury that it was not evidence for the Crown but only for the co-accused.'[169]

12 The Voir Dire Hearing

The question whether a confession is to be admitted in evidence may be determined at a pre-trial hearing.[170] If such a hearing has not taken place, then the determination will typically be made at a voir dire hearing, in accordance with the following procedure:

> It is primarily the responsibility of defence counsel to inform the prosecution and the judge in advance and in the absence of the jury of an intended objection to the admissibility of statements of a defendant. . . . At the appropriate time counsel must ask the judge to request the jury to withdraw so that a matter can be raised on which the ruling of the judge is required. No discussion of an intended objection must take place in front of the jury. The judge should simply tell the jury that a matter has arisen on which his ruling is required and that they must please retire for the time being.[171]

It was seen earlier that section 76(3) of the Police and Criminal Evidence Act 1984 permits a court of its own motion to require the prosecution to prove that a confession

---

[166] [1997] 3 WLR 552. See generally J Hartshorne and A L-T Choo, ' "Hearsay-Fiddles" in the House of Lords' (1999) 62 *Modern Law Review* 290; M Hirst, 'Confessions as Proof of Innocence' [1998] *Cambridge Law Journal* 146; J D Jackson, 'The Law on Defence Use of Confessions: Some Clarification and Some Confusion', *Archbold News*, 8 May 1998, 5.

[167] See J Hartshorne, 'Defensive Use of a Co-Accused's Confession and the Criminal Justice Act 2003' (2004) 8 *International Journal of Evidence and Proof* 165.   [168] *R v Myers* [1997] 3 WLR 552.

[169] G Durston, 'The Admissibility of Co-Defendants' Confessions Under the Criminal Justice Act 2003' (2004) 168 *Justice of the Peace* 488, 488–9.   [170] See the discussion of pre-trial hearings in Ch 1.

[171] *Mitchell v R* [1998] 2 WLR 839, 846.

was not obtained in a manner proscribed by section 76(2). A trial judge would be unlikely, however, to insist upon the holding of a voir dire hearing against the wishes of defence counsel, who may for tactical reasons prefer the grounds for inadmissibility to be aired before the jury in the trial proper. This course of action would mean, of course, 'that the jury [would] hear the impugned statement whether admissible or not'. It would therefore be necessary for the trial judge, if he or she doubts that the statement is admissible in evidence, to 'direct the jury to disregard it, or, if the statement is essential to sustain the prosecution case, direct an acquittal'.[172]

It would appear that, in a trial on indictment, 'the jury ought not to be informed of a judge's decision on a voire dire held to determine the admissibility of a confession'. This is because:

> the decision on the admissibility of a confession after a voire dire is the sole responsibility of the judge. There is no logical reason why the jury should know about the decision of the judge. It is irrelevant to the consideration by the jury of the issues whether the confession was made and, if so, whether it is true. There is also no practical reason why the jury need to be informed of the judge's decision. ... Moreover, ... the knowledge by the jury that the judge has believed the police and disbelieved the defendant creates the potentiality of prejudice. A jury of laymen, or some of them, might be forgiven for saying: 'Well the judge did not believe the defendant, why should we believe him?'[173]

May the prosecution utilize, in the trial proper, statements made by an accused in a voir dire hearing held to determine whether a confession should be excluded from evidence?[174] This remains unsettled. The position at common law[175] was as follows:

• Irrespective of whether the confession evidence had been admitted or excluded, the prosecution could not adduce, as part of its case in chief, evidence of statements made by the accused in the voir dire hearing.

• If, however, the voir dire hearing had resulted in the *admission* in evidence of the confession, then the prosecution could cross-examine the accused on any inconsistencies between his statements in the voir dire hearing and his testimony in the trial proper, with a view to discrediting that testimony.

The common law position has arguably been reversed by section 76 of the Police and Criminal Evidence Act 1984: it is arguable that any incriminating statements made by the accused in the voir dire hearing would themselves constitute confessions which may be given in evidence by the prosecution so long as they were obtained in a manner consistent with section 76(2) (as would presumably be the case). If this argument is correct, then it is surely in the interests of justice that the trial judge's exclusionary discretion (either at common law or under section 78(1)) should be invoked in appropriate cases to exclude such statements from evidence.

---

[172] *Ajodha v The State* [1982] AC 204, 223.

[173] *Mitchell v R* [1998] 2 WLR 839, 845–6. See also *Thompson v R* [1998] 2 WLR 927, 954; *Constance v The State*, unrep, 16 Dec 1999 (PC).

[174] For a fuller discussion, see P Mirfield, *Silence, Confessions and Improperly Obtained Evidence* (1997) 71–5.

[175] *Wong Kam-Ming v R* [1980] AC 247; *R v Brophy* [1982] AC 476.

13 Reform

In the first few years of the new millennium, the topic of reform of the law of confessions provoked far less debate and discussion than it had done a decade earlier. Hopes that the Runciman Royal Commission on Criminal Justice might make fundamental recommendations for improvement were dashed when its *Report* in 1993 recommended no substantial change at all in the law in the area. Since that time, other topics in the law of criminal evidence and procedure have tended to take centre stage.

It has been seen in this chapter that a number of mechanisms are currently available in English law for dealing with confession evidence. Apart from the obvious devices of mandatory and discretionary exclusion, section 77 warnings and withdrawal of the case from the jury may be relevant in certain situations. A question worth pondering is whether the grounds for mandatory exclusion should be extended. It is questionable, for example, whether an exclusionary discretion is sufficient where fundamental issues like access to legal advice and the tape recording of interviews are concerned. It is certainly arguable that an absolute rule rendering inadmissible in evidence any confession made in the absence of a legal adviser, or any confession that is not tape recorded, should be introduced. Such a rule would go some considerable way further in ensuring that unreliable confessions are not given in evidence. The counterargument, which found favour with the Runciman Royal Commission, is that such a rule would be undesirable as it would lead to the exclusion of reliable evidence: confessions made in the absence of legal advice, or which are not tape recorded, will in some circumstances be perfectly reliable.[176] This seems to miss the point. An inevitable consequence of any rule designed to ensure that unreliable evidence is inadmissible is the exclusion of *some* reliable evidence. And the more rigid and absolute the rule, the more likely this is to happen. The issue, surely, is whether the introduction of an absolute rule is justified in the special context of confession evidence, the admission of which has resulted in so many major miscarriages of justice.

The United States, it is to be noted, continues to adhere strictly to a general rule prohibiting the admission in evidence of a confession obtained without '*Miranda* warnings' having been administered. *Miranda v Arizona*[177] is a landmark decision of the US Supreme Court. 'Prior to *Miranda*', the Court has noted, 'we evaluated the admissibility of a suspect's confession under a voluntariness test.'[178] In *Miranda*, however, the Court held that:

> the admissibility in evidence of any statement given during custodial interrogation of a suspect would depend on whether the police provided the suspect with four warnings. These warnings (which have come to be known colloquially as '*Miranda* rights') are: a suspect 'has the right to remain silent, that anything he says can be used against him in a court of law, that he has the right to the presence of an attorney, and that if he cannot afford an attorney one will be appointed for him prior to any questioning if he so desires'.[179]

---

[176] Royal Commission on Criminal Justice, *Report* (Cm 2263) (1993) 60–2.

[177] 384 US 436 (1966). See generally S O'Doherty, '*Miranda* Rights—A View Across the Pond' (2004) 168 *Justice of the Peace* 647.   [178] *US v Dickerson* 530 US 428, 432–3 (2000).

[179] Ibid, 435, quoting *Miranda v Arizona* 384 US 436, 479 (1966).

The Court confirmed more recently, in *US v Dickerson*,[180] that it was not possible for Congress to overrule *Miranda* and reintroduce a simple voluntariness test by means of a legislative enactment providing that 'a confession … shall be admissible in evidence if it is voluntarily given. Before such confession is received in evidence, the trial judge shall, out of the presence of the jury, determine any issue as to voluntariness. If the trial judge determines that the confession was voluntarily made it shall be admitted in evidence …'.

There were many suggestions in the early 1990s for the introduction of a requirement that confession evidence should be corroborated, or at least supported, by other evidence in order to be admissible. It is certainly arguable that the introduction of such a requirement would, together with the general requirement in Code E that interviews be tape recorded, go some considerable way in reducing the likelihood of confessions being fabricated in the future.[181] Would, however, a corroboration, or supporting evidence, requirement for confessions lead to the widespread acquittal or non-prosecution of the guilty? Studies have shown that the introduction of such a requirement would affect only a tiny percentage of cases. One study, which looked solely at magistrates' court cases, revealed that in less than 1.4 per cent of cases did the prosecution rely on confession evidence alone, or on evidence of admissions falling short of a confession.[182] A more detailed study examined 305 cases in which there was confession evidence. This revealed that:

- in 264 (86.6 per cent), there was actually corroborating evidence in the case;
- in 12 (3.9 per cent), corroborating evidence was certainly available and could therefore have been brought to court to satisfy a corroboration requirement;

---

[180] 530 US 428 (2000). See generally P G Cassell, 'The Paths Not Taken: The Supreme Court's Failures in *Dickerson*' (2001) 99 *Michigan Law Review* 898; Y Kamisar, 'Foreword: From *Miranda* to § 3501 to *Dickerson* to …' (2001) 99 *Michigan Law Review* 879; S R Klein, 'Identifying and (Re)Formulating Prophylactic Rules, Safe Harbors, and Incidental Rights in Constitutional Criminal Procedure' (2001) 99 *Michigan Law Review* 1030; R A Leo, 'Questioning the Relevance of *Miranda* in the Twenty-First Century' (2001) 99 *Michigan Law Review* 1000; L Magid, 'Deceptive Police Interrogation Practices: How Far Is Too Far?' (2001) 99 *Michigan Law Review* 1168; P Mirfield, '*Miranda* Exclusionary Rule Re-Affirmed: *US v Dickerson*' (2001) 5 *International Journal of Evidence and Proof* 61; S J Schulhofer, '*Miranda, Dickerson,* and the Puzzling Persistence of Fifth Amendment Exceptionalism' (2001) 99 *Michigan Law Review* 941; D A Strauss, '*Miranda,* the Constitution, and Congress' (2001) 99 *Michigan Law Review* 958; W J Stuntz, '*Miranda*'s Mistake' (2001) 99 *Michigan Law Review* 975; G C Thomas III, 'Separated at Birth but Siblings Nonetheless: *Miranda* and the Due Process Notice Cases' (2001) 99 *Michigan Law Review* 1081; C D Weisselberg, 'In the Stationhouse After *Dickerson*' (2001) 99 *Michigan Law Review* 1121; W S White, '*Miranda*'s Failure to Restrain Pernicious Interrogation Practices' (2001) 99 *Michigan Law Review* 1211.

[181] It should be noted that even if a corroboration, or supporting evidence, requirement were to be introduced, careful consideration would need to be given to the issue of what exactly should constitute sufficient corroborative or supporting evidence. The experience of some jurisdictions suggests that, if the requirement were too easy to satisfy, its protective value might be illusory. See generally A L-T Choo, 'Confessions and Corroboration: A Comparative Perspective' [1991] *Criminal Law Review* 867; R Pattenden, 'Should Confessions Be Corroborated?' (1991) 107 *Law Quarterly Review* 317; M McConville, *Corroboration and Confessions: The Impact of a Rule Requiring That No Conviction Can Be Sustained on the Basis of Confession Evidence Alone* (Royal Commission on Criminal Justice Research Study No 13) (1993).

[182] Royal Commission on Criminal Justice, *Report* (Cm 2263) (1993) 65.

- in 10 (3.3 per cent), corroborating evidence was probably available;
- in 4 (1.3 per cent), corroborating evidence was possibly available;
- in 15 (4.9 per cent), corroborating evidence was probably unavailable.[183]

The Runciman Royal Commission said of these studies: 'Taken together these studies suggest that a supporting evidence requirement would affect only a very small percentage of cases. But the absolute numbers would nevertheless be quite high, since over 100,000 cases a year are tried in the Crown Court and between 1 million and 1 1/2 million in the magistrates' courts.' On the basis of this the Commission recommended, by a majority, against the introduction of a supporting evidence requirement. With respect, it seems rather flimsy reasoning to recommend against a reform designed to protect the innocent on the basis that it would mean that a *numerically* large number of confession cases would collapse, even though these cases would constitute only a very small *percentage* of all confession cases. A Royal Commission set up in the aftermath of a spectacular miscarriage of justice—the case of the Birmingham Six—might have been expected to have been more sensitive to the dangers of confession evidence, and less influenced by crime control considerations.[184] It must not be forgotten that the cases which would collapse would include precisely those cases which a supporting evidence requirement *should* frustrate.

The majority of the Commission recommended, instead, that:

> the judge should warn the jury that great care is needed before convicting on the basis of the confession alone, and should explicitly refer, giving examples ..., to the possible reasons for persons confessing to crimes which they did not commit. The judge should also draw attention to any such reason advanced by the defence and say where appropriate that cases have been known in which persons have confessed for similar reasons to offences which they did not commit. The judge would then direct the jury as to what evidence, if any, had been given that was capable of supporting the confession. If there were no such supporting evidence, the judge would so direct the jury. Where the confession had not been tape-recorded, the warning would draw attention to this fact and to any possible motive that the person to whom the confession was made might have for fabricating the confession. Finally, since supporting evidence would not be an absolute requirement, the judge would explain that if, after giving full weight to the warning, the jury were nevertheless satisfied that the confession was true, they could convict even in the absence of supporting evidence.[185]

Even this rather modest proposal was not implemented,[186] and little has been heard of it since.

---

[183] M McConville, *Corroboration and Confessions: The Impact of a Rule Requiring That No Conviction Can Be Sustained on the Basis of Confession Evidence Alone* (Royal Commission on Criminal Justice Research Study No 13) (1993) Ch 6.

[184] See generally S Greer, 'The Right to Silence, Defence Disclosure, and Confession Evidence' (1994) 21 *Journal of Law and Society* 102; A Sanders and R Young, *Criminal Justice* (2nd ed 2000) 310–13. Ashworth and Redmayne argue that 'there are simply too many doubts about the processes which lead suspects to confess for a conviction on a confession alone ever to be justified': A Ashworth and M Redmayne, *The Criminal Process* (3rd ed 2005) 104.   [185] Royal Commission on Criminal Justice, *Report* (Cm 2263) (1993) 66–7.

[186] Of course, warnings about confession evidence may be given in the exercise of *discretion*: cf *R v Causley* [1999] Crim LR 572; *Benedetto v R* [2003] UKPC 27, [2003] 1 WLR 1545; *R v Stone* [2005] EWCA Crim 105. See discussion in Ch 11.

3

The Right to Silence and the Privilege against Self-Incrimination

1 The Right to Silence

1.1 The Development of the Law

Prior to the Criminal Justice and Public Order Act 1994, no evidential significance could be attached to an accused's exercise of the right to silence at the stage of police investigation.[1] For over twenty years debate took place about whether the law should be changed. The issue was considered by four bodies:[2] the Criminal Law Revision Committee in 1972,[3] the Royal Commission on Criminal Procedure in 1981,[4] the Home Office Working Group on the Right of Silence in 1989,[5] and the Royal Commission on Criminal Justice in 1993.[6] Their answers to the question of whether a change to the law should be made were respectively yes, no, yes, no. It is ironic that the change of the law by Parliament followed so closely on the heels of the Runciman Commission's recommendation that the existing law be preserved.

In support of a change in the law, it was argued by some that the old common law provided an incentive to suspects to mount ambush defences—that is, to withhold information from the police at the stage of investigation, and then to take the prosecution by surprise at a late stage by springing a defence based on the withheld information. Against this it was argued that to allow an accused's pre-trial silence to be used against him or her at trial would indirectly place undue pressure on suspects, especially vulnerable suspects, to speak. Not only might this be regarded as unjustifiable in principle, but it might also result in the production of unreliable evidence. Those who are innocent might in effect be pressured into incriminating themselves. As has been succinctly explained:

... the common-sense view that confronted with an accusation an individual would normally give an explanation is problematic. Common sense may be unreliable, impressionistic and

---

[1] See generally J D Jackson, 'Silence and Proof: Extending the Boundaries of Criminal Proceedings in the United Kingdom' (2001) 5 *International Journal of Evidence and Proof* 145. The position at common law is discussed briefly in *R v Webber* [2004] UKHL 1, [2004] 1 WLR 404, [16]–[17].

[2] See generally S Easton, *The Case for the Right to Silence* (2nd ed 1998) Ch 2.

[3] Criminal Law Revision Committee, *Eleventh Report: Evidence (General)* (Cmnd 4991) (1972).

[4] Royal Commission on Criminal Procedure, *Report* (Cmnd 8092) (1981).

[5] *Report of the Working Group on the Right of Silence* (1989).

[6] Royal Commission on Criminal Justice, *Report* (Cm 2263) (1993).

unsystematic. . . . Common sense may wrongly equate silence with guilt and fail to take account of other possible factors which underlie the silence, including fear, anxiety, confusion, the desire to protect someone else, embarrassment, outrage and anger. All these emotions may be reflected in silence but juries may not be able reliably to distinguish the 'suspicious' silence from the innocent silence. Silence may be a rational response in certain circumstances but this may not be apparent to the jury or to the trial judge.[7]

Part I of the Criminal Procedure and Investigations Act 1996, which imposes general pre-trial disclosure obligations on the defence in trials on indictment, may be expected to go some considerable way in curbing any problem of ambush defences. In any event, in a research study conducted for the Runciman Commission, Roger Leng found little evidence of an 'ambushing' problem even prior to the 1996 Act:

The right to silence was exercised by 4.5 per cent of suspects who were interviewed. About half of these were convicted. Thus, about 2 per cent of all suspects who were interviewed exercised the right to silence and escaped conviction.

The right to silence was exercised in about 4 per cent of cases which ended with no further action, and in about 10 per cent of cases which ended in acquittal (including cases in which charges were dropped before trial). This indicates that any reform of the law would have a potential impact on 2 per cent of all interviewed suspects, 4 per cent of NFA cases and 10 per cent of acquittals.[8]

The Runciman Commission's *Crown Court Study* revealed that all categories of respondent agreed that just over 10 per cent of defendants had said nothing at all during police questioning.

After a review of the research evidence, the Runciman Commission concluded:

The research evidence may be summarised as follows. The right of silence is exercised only in a minority of cases. It may tend to be exercised more often in the more serious cases and where legal advice is given. There is no evidence which shows conclusively that silence is used disproportionately by professional criminals. Nor is there evidence to support the belief that silence in the police station leads to improved chances of an acquittal. Most of those who are silent in the police station either plead guilty later or are subsequently found guilty.[9]

Thus, to change the law would increase the possibility of convictions of the guilty in only a very small percentage of cases. The Commission accordingly concluded, by a majority, 'that the possibility of an increase in the convictions of the guilty is outweighed by the risk that the extra pressure on suspects to talk in the police station and the adverse inferences invited if they do not may result in more convictions of the innocent'.[10] Parliament, however, effected a fundamental change in the law in

[7] S Easton, 'Legal Advice, Common Sense and the Right to Silence' (1998) 2 *International Journal of Evidence and Proof* 109, 114–15. Cf D J Seidmann and A Stein, 'The Right to Silence Helps the Innocent: A Game-Theoretic Analysis of the Fifth Amendment Privilege' (2000) 114 *Harvard Law Review* 430.

[8] R Leng, *The Right to Silence in Police Interrogation: A Study of Some of the Issues Underlying the Debate* (Royal Commission on Criminal Justice Research Study No 10) (1993) 73–4. The findings of previous studies are also reviewed in this publication. See also S Easton, *The Case for the Right to Silence* (2nd ed 1998) 137–43.

[9] Royal Commission on Criminal Justice, *Report* (Cm 2263) (1993) 53–4.   [10] Ibid, 54.

THE RIGHT TO SILENCE 69

sections 34, 36, and 37 of the Criminal Justice and Public Order Act 1994.[11] These provisions will be considered below. Prior to that, however, a brief account will be given of certain common law principles relating to pre-trial silence which stand alongside the provisions of the 1994 Act.

1.2 Silence in the Face of Accusation

The common law principles on the evidential consequences of an accused's silence 'in the face of anything said in his presence relating to the conduct in respect of which he is charged' are expressly preserved by the Act.[12] These principles[13] may be stated briefly as follows. If the accused:

- remained silent in the face of something said in his or her presence relating to the conduct in respect of which he or she is now charged,

- in a situation where the accused and the speaker were on equal terms, and

- where, in the opinion of the jury, the accused could reasonably have been expected to deny what was said, so that by not doing so he or she accepted its truth,

then the accused's silence is admissible as evidence and it may be inferred from it that the accused accepted the truth of what was said.[14]

---

11 See generally D Wolchover, *Silence and Guilt: An Assessment of Case Law on the Criminal Justice and Public Order Act 1994* (2001), as updated: updates accessible via http://www.davidwolchover.co.uk. For earlier discussions see generally D Birch, 'Suffering in Silence: A Cost-Benefit Analysis of Section 34 of the Criminal Justice and Public Order Act 1994' [1999] *Criminal Law Review* 769; J S W Black, 'Inferences from Silence: Redressing the Balance? (1)' (1997) 141 *Solicitors' Journal* 741; J S W Black, 'Inferences from Silence: Redressing the Balance? (2)' (1997) 141 *Solicitors' Journal* 772; E Cape, 'Sidelining Defence Lawyers: Police Station Advice After *Condron*' (1997) 1 *International Journal of Evidence and Proof* 386; I Dennis, 'Silence in the Police Station: The Marginalisation of Section 34' [2002] *Criminal Law Review* 25; S Easton, 'Legal Advice, Common Sense and the Right to Silence' (1998) 2 *International Journal of Evidence and Proof* 109; A Jennings, 'Adverse Inferences from Silence— An Update', *Archbold News*, 30 Nov 2001, 6; A F Jennings, 'More Resounding Silence—Part 1' (1999) 149 *New Law Journal* 1180; A F Jennings, 'More Resounding Silence—Part 2' (1999) 149 *New Law Journal* 1232; A Jennings, A Ashworth, and B Emmerson, 'Silence and Safety: The Impact of Human Rights Law' [2000] *Criminal Law Review* 879; P Mirfield, 'Two Side-Effects of Sections 34 to 37 of the Criminal Justice and Public Order Act 1994' [1995] *Criminal Law Review* 612; M Nichols, 'Liberal Democracy and the Emergence of Law: The Right to Silence' [1997] *UCL Jurisprudence Review* 239; R Pattenden, 'Inferences from Silence' [1995] *Criminal Law Review* 602; R Pattenden, 'Silence: Lord Taylor's Legacy' (1998) 2 *International Journal of Evidence and Proof* 141; P Plowden, 'Silence at the Police Station' (1998) 148 *New Law Journal* 1598; A Samuels, 'The Right of Silence and Adverse Inferences' (1998) 162 *Justice of the Peace* 201; A J Turner, 'Inferences Under Section 34 of the Criminal Justice and Public Order Act 1994: Part One' (1999) 163 *Justice of the Peace* 243; A J Turner, 'Inferences Under Section 34 of the Criminal Justice and Public Order Act 1994: Part Two' (1999) 163 *Justice of the Peace* 323; A J Turner, 'Inferences Under S 34 of the Criminal Justice and Public Order Act 1994 Revisited' (1999) 163 *Justice of the Peace* 924; D Wolchover and A Heaton-Armstrong, 'Labour's Victory and the Right to Silence—1' (1997) 147 *New Law Journal* 1382; D Wolchover and A Heaton-Armstrong, 'Labour's Victory and the Right to Silence—2' (1997) 147 *New Law Journal* 1434; S Easton, *The Case for the Right to Silence* (2nd ed 1998); P Mirfield, *Silence, Confessions and Improperly Obtained Evidence* (1997).   12 S 34(5).

13 See generally S Easton, *The Case for the Right to Silence* (2nd ed 1998) 29–33.

14 *R v Mitchell* (1892) 17 Cox CC 503; *R v Norton* [1910] 2 KB 496; *R v Christie* [1914] AC 545; *Hall v R* [1971] 1 WLR 298; *Parkes v R* [1976] 1 WLR 1251; *R v Collins* [2004] EWCA Crim 83, [2004] 1 WLR 1705.

In *Parkes v R*,[15] the defendant, who was accused of murder, had been confronted by the deceased's mother, Mrs Graham, who said to him: 'What she do you—why you stab her?' The defendant did not reply and failed to do so again when Mrs Graham repeated the question. She then boxed him twice and seized him, saying that she would keep him there until the police arrived. The defendant thereupon made to strike Mrs Graham with the knife he had in his hand. The Privy Council held:

> Here Mrs Graham and the defendant were speaking on even terms. Furthermore, as the Chief Justice pointed out to the jury, the defendant's reaction to the twice-repeated accusation was not one of mere silence. He drew a knife and attempted to stab Mrs Graham in order to escape when she threatened to detain him while the police were sent for. In their Lordships' view, the Chief Justice was perfectly entitled to instruct the jury that the defendant's reactions to the accusations including his silence were matters which they could take into account along with other evidence in deciding whether the defendant in fact committed the act with which he was charged.[16]

1.3 The Criminal Justice and Public Order Act 1994

The provisions of the Criminal Justice and Public Order Act 1994 that affect the right to silence prior to trial[17] will now be examined. The Court of Appeal has acknowledged that these provisions have 'caused a considerable amount of thought and some trouble'.[18]

1.3.1 Section 34

'Until the enactment of section 34, judges and juries were severely constrained by a common law rule applicable in England and Wales against drawing an adverse inference against a defendant if he failed to mention during police questioning a matter on which he later relied in his defence.'[19] It is accepted that 'the purpose of s 34 is to encourage speedy disclosure of a genuine defence and to permit adverse inferences to be drawn where a defence has been fabricated later'.[20] Acknowledged to be 'a notorious minefield'[21] and 'a very difficult area',[22] section 34 provides in pertinent part:

> (1) Where, in any proceedings against a person for an offence, evidence is given that the accused—
>
> > (a) at any time before he was charged with the offence, on being questioned under caution by a constable trying to discover whether or by whom the offence had been committed, failed to mention any fact relied on in his defence in those proceedings; or
> > (b) on being charged with the offence or officially informed that he might be prosecuted for it, failed to mention any such fact, being a fact which in the circumstances existing at the time the accused could reasonably have been expected to mention when so questioned, charged or informed, as the case may be, subsection (2) below applies.

---

[15] [1976] 1 WLR 1251.   [16] Ibid, 1254–5.

[17] See generally K Grevling, 'Silence, Lies and Vicious Circularity' in P Mirfield and R Smith (eds), *Essays for Colin Tapper* (2003).   [18] *R v Adinga* [2003] EWCA Crim 3201, [27].

[19] *R v Webber* [2004] UKHL 1, [2004] 1 WLR 404, [16].   [20] *R v Lowe* [2003] EWCA Crim 3182, [22].

[21] *R v B* [2003] EWCA Crim 3080, [20].   [22] *R v Bresa* [2005] EWCA Crim 1414, [51].

(2) Where this subsection applies—

. . .

      (d) the court or jury, in determining whether the accused is guilty of the offence charged,

may draw such inferences from the failure as appear proper.

(2A) Where the accused was at an authorised place of detention at the time of the failure, subsections (1) and (2) above do not apply if he had not been allowed an opportunity to consult a solicitor prior to being questioned, charged or informed as mentioned in subsection (1) above.

(3) Subject to any directions by the court, evidence tending to establish the failure may be given before or after evidence tending to establish the fact which the accused is alleged to have failed to mention.

(4) This section applies in relation to questioning by persons (other than constables) charged with the duty of investigating offences or charging offenders as it applies in relation to questioning by constables; and in subsection (1) above 'officially informed' means informed by a constable or any such person.

1.3.1.1 'On Being Questioned under Caution'

There must have been *questioning*[23] under caution. The terms of the caution are prescribed by paragraph 10.5 of Code C of the Codes of Practice issued pursuant to the Police and Criminal Evidence Act 1984:

> You do not have to say anything. But it may harm your defence if you do not mention when questioned something which you later rely on in Court. Anything you do say may be given in evidence.

This is rather more complex than the old caution: 'You do not have to say anything unless you wish to do so, but what you say may be given in evidence.' In the light of evidence that even the old and simpler caution was misunderstood by many suspects,[24] the likelihood of the 'new' one being properly understood may well be questionable. A research study has found: 'Police officers and legal advisers both expressed doubts about the extent to which suspects understand the content and implications of this statement. . . . even if police officers explained the caution in lay terms, they expressed a degree of scepticism about whether suspects fully comprehended it.'[25]

1.3.1.2 'Failed to Mention'

The issue of what constitutes a failure to mention received detailed consideration in the decision of the Court of Appeal in *R v Knight*.[26] When the police sought to interview

---

[23] See *R v Johnson* [2005] EWCA Crim 971, [27]: 'we do not feel able to regard what occurred as coming within the ambit of the phrase "on being questioned". No question was, in fact, put. What occurred was a precursor to that stage of the process.'

[24] M Zander, *Cases and Materials on the English Legal System* (7th ed 1996) 122.

[25] T Bucke, R Street, and D Brown, *The Right of Silence: The Impact of the Criminal Justice and Public Order Act 1994* (Home Office Research Study 199) (2000) 27, available at http://www.homeoffice.gov.uk/rds/pdfs/ hors199.pdf.

[26] [2003] EWCA Crim 1977, [2004] 1 WLR 340. See generally A L-T Choo, 'Prepared Statements, Legal Advice and the Right to Silence: *R v Knight*' (2004) 8 *International Journal of Evidence and Proof* 62; A Keogh, 'The Right to Silence—Revisited Again' (2003) 153 *New Law Journal* 1352.

Knight, a prepared statement was read out to them by his solicitor at the beginning of the interview process. This statement, which was eventually admitted in evidence and read by the judge to the jury as part of the summing-up, provided a narrative account that was wholly in line with Knight's later testimony before the jury. He declined to answer any of the questions that the police asked him. The Court of Appeal asked itself the following question: 'Is the distinct purpose of s 34(1)(a) not only to encourage a suspect to give his full account to the police in response to the accusation made against him, but also (on pain of a distinct inference being later drawn if he does not do so) to have that account subjected to testing questions—in effect cross-examination—by the police in interview?'[27]

The Court held[28] that this question should be answered in the negative: 'the aim of s 34(1)(a) does not distinctly include police cross-examination of a suspect upon his account over and above the disclosure of that account'. The Court pointed out that the relevant failure is described by Parliament as a failure to *mention facts* rather than a failure to *answer questions*. 'A requirement to submit to police cross-examination (so long as the questions are proper), or at any rate an encouragement to do so on pain of later adverse inferences being drawn, is a significantly greater intrusion into a suspect's general right of silence than is a requirement, or encouragement, upon the suspect to disclose his factual defence.' Such an intrusion could, the Court thought, be justified only if it were expressed much more clearly in the legislation.

Furthermore, where a full account of the defence has been provided in a prepared statement, it is not obvious what inference could be drawn from the refusal to respond to police questioning:

> It cannot be recent fabrication of his defence: he has stated his defence in full before or at the beginning of the interview. It could only be that the defence, although thus revealed in full, ought not to be believed, or at least is of doubtful veracity, because it was not tested by police questioning. But it is very difficult to see how such a distinct inference could properly be drawn in the *milieu* of the trial process. If the defendant gives evidence at his trial, plainly the jury will assess the quality of that evidence not least in light of the defendant's answers in cross-examination. If (having given in full his account at the earliest stage by way of a pre-prepared statement) he acquits himself well in the witness box in the eyes of the jury, it would surely be neither realistic nor fair for them then to draw back from that conclusion in light of the fact that he did not subject himself to police cross-examination in interview. If on the other hand the defendant declines to give evidence at his trial, then adverse inferences may be drawn against him where appropriate under s 35. In that situation there can surely be no sensible room for *further* inferences under s 34.[29]

In this case, as Knight had disclosed his full defence to the police by way of his prepared statement, 'there was in our judgment no legitimate room for an adverse inference to be drawn against him under s 34. The learned judge was therefore in error in directing the jury that such an inference was available.'[30] On this basis, Knight's appeal was allowed and his conviction quashed.

---

[27]   [2003] EWCA Crim 1977, [2004] 1 WLR 340, [9].   [28]   Ibid, [11].
[29]   Ibid, [12] (italics in original). S 35 is considered in Ch 11.
[30]   [2003] EWCA Crim 1977, [2004] 1 WLR 340, [15].

The Court of Appeal was careful, however, to issue the following caution:

> The making of a pre-prepared statement is not of itself an inevitable antidote to later adverse inferences. The pre-prepared statement may be incomplete in comparison with the defendant's later account at trial, or it may be, to whatever degree, inconsistent with that account. One may envisage many situations in which a pre-prepared statement in some form has been put forward, but yet there is a proper case for an adverse inference arising out of the suspect's failure 'on being questioned under caution . . . to mention any fact relied on in his defence . . . '. We wish to make it crystal clear that *of itself* the making of a pre-prepared statement gives no automatic immunity against adverse inferences under s 34.[31]

> Nor does it follow that, in a case in which it is not suggested that any adverse inference should be drawn under s 34, the prosecution can be required to adduce as part of their evidence a pre-prepared wholly self-serving statement.[32]

In a subsequent case, *R v Turner*, the Court of Appeal observed:

> This court notes a growing practice, no doubt on advice, to submit a pre-prepared statement and decline to answer any questions. This, in our view, may prove to be a dangerous course for an innocent person who subsequently discovers at the trial that something significant has been omitted. No such problems would arise following an interview where the suspect gives appropriate answers to the questions.[33]

However, even where discrepancies exist between a prepared statement and the defendant's evidence at trial, it may not be appropriate for section 34 to be invoked:

> Where there are differences between what a defendant says in a pre-prepared statement and the evidence he gives at the trial it may be that the jury would be better directed to consider a difference as constituting a previous lie rather than as the foundation for a s 34 inference. It will depend on the precise circumstances.[34]

In sum, any uncertainty surrounding prepared statements that provide a *full*[35] account of the defence later relied on has now been resolved in favour of the defendant. The Court of Appeal has taken a pragmatic approach to the interpretation of section 34 on this point, paying due attention to the rights of the defence and clearly acknowledging that the right to silence is not to be interfered with lightly.

1.3.1.3 What Is a 'Fact'?

What constitutes a 'fact' for the purposes of section 34 has received considerable judicial attention. The House of Lords has stated that the word:

> 'fact' should be given a broad and not a narrow or pedantic meaning. The word covers any alleged fact which is in issue and is put forward as part of the defence case: if the defendant

---

[31] Ibid, [13] (italics in original).   [32] Ibid, [14].

[33] [2003] EWCA Crim 3108, [2004] 1 All ER 1025, [25].

[34] Ibid, [35]. Evidence of a defendant's previous lie is considered in Ch 11.

[35] 'It is of course of paramount importance that the prepared statement covers all of the points to be relied upon in the accused's defence, as he can reasonably at that stage be expected to mention': A Keogh, 'The Right to Silence—Revisited Again' (2003) 153 *New Law Journal* 1352, 1353.

advances at trial any pure fact or exculpatory explanation or account which, if it were true, he could reasonably have been expected to advance earlier, section 34 is potentially applicable.[36]

Consistently with this, the Court of Appeal takes a pragmatic approach on the basis of its perception of the purpose of the provision:

... it seems to us necessary to approach the meaning to be attributed to 'any fact' having regard to the apparent purpose of the statute and, in particular, the context and stage of proceedings with which s 34(1)(a) is concerned, that is to say the questioning of a suspect at a stage when the facts available to the prosecution *without* the benefit of any explanation of the defendant give rise to a suspicion or inference of his involvement in the crime under investigation, and the questioning is being directed to establishing whether such suspicion or inference is well founded in fact. The facts relevant to establishing whether or not the defendant is guilty of the crime in respect of which he is being interrogated go far wider than the simple matter of what might have been observed to happen on a particular occasion and frequently involve what reasons or explanations the defendant gives for his involvement in the particular event observed which, if true, would absolve him from the suspicion of criminal intent or involvement which might otherwise arise.[37]

The word 'fact' is not therefore to be construed as referring solely to specific acts: 'the words "any fact" do not fall to be read only in the narrow sense of an actual deed or thing done...'.[38]

1.3.1.4 Reliance on a Fact

The House of Lords has held authoritatively that:

a defendant relies on a fact or matter in his defence not only when he gives or adduces evidence of it but also when counsel, acting on his instructions, puts a specific and positive case to prosecution witnesses, as opposed to asking questions intended to probe or test the prosecution case. This is so whether or not the prosecution witness accepts the suggestion put. Two considerations in particular lead us to that conclusion.

(1) While it is of course true that questions put by counsel are not evidence and do not become so unless accepted by a witness, the effect of specific, positive suggestions put by counsel on behalf of a defendant is to plant in the jury's mind the defendant's version of events. This may be so even if the witness rejects the suggestion, since the jury may for whatever reason distrust the witness's evidence. ...

(2) Since subsection (2)(c) of section 34 permits the court to draw proper inferences when determining whether there is a case to answer, the section may apply at a stage of the trial when the defendant has had no opportunity to give or adduce evidence, and when it will not be known (perhaps not even decided) whether the defendant will give or call evidence or not. But the court is likely to know, from questions put to prosecution witnesses, what (if any)

---

[36] *R v Webber* [2004] UKHL 1, [2004] 1 WLR 404, [33].

[37] *R v Milford* [2001] Crim LR 330; transcript, [32] (italics in original), cited approvingly in *R v Chenia* [2002] EWCA Crim 2345, [2003] 2 Cr App R 6 (p 83), [26].

[38] *R v Milford* [2001] Crim LR 330; transcript, [32], cited approvingly in *R v Chenia* [2002] EWCA Crim 2345, [2003] 2 Cr App R 6 (p 83), [26].

positive case the defendant advances. It would be surprising if subsection (2)(c) were intended to apply only when, unusually, specific suggestions put to a prosecution witness are accepted by the witness.[39]

Had subsection (1) been intended to apply only where evidence properly so called is given or adduced or elicited by a defendant, we would expect the draftsman to have made that clear by using the language of evidence. As it is, the words 'relied on in his defence' suggest a wider import.[40]

1.3.1.5 Was it 'a fact which in the circumstances existing at the time the accused could reasonably have been expected to mention'?[41]

1.3.1.5.1 *Legal Advice to Remain Silent*

An issue that has proved troubling for the courts is the extent to which adverse inferences may be drawn where the suspect *acted on legal advice* in failing to mention a fact in interview. In *Condron v UK*, discussed below, the European Court of Human Rights remarked that 'the very fact that an accused is advised by his lawyer to maintain his silence must . . . be given *appropriate weight* by the domestic court'.[42] Following *Condron v UK*, the Court of Appeal in *R v Betts and Hall*[43] took the view that to satisfy Article 6, section 34 should be interpreted as permitting adverse inferences only where the jury was satisfied that the suspect had no innocent explanation to offer. The approach advocated in *Betts and Hall* was therefore that adverse inferences could not be drawn from a no-comment interview if the jury accepted the defendant's claim that the 'silence' was attributable to legal advice to give a no-comment interview, rather than to the defendant's having no adequate answer. The issue for the jury was whether the defendant's claim was genuine. While the reasons for the legal advice were not directly relevant, the defence might well have to point to such reasons in attempting to establish the genuineness of the claim that he or she remained silent because of the legal advice. As will be discussed below, *Betts and Hall* has since been referred to in the judgment of the European Court in *Beckles v UK*,[44] where the Court once again found a violation of Article 6 on the basis that the judge had failed to give an appropriate direction to the jury on the drawing of adverse inferences under section 34.

The reasoning in *Betts and Hall* was not, however, adopted in *R v Howell*.[45] The Court of Appeal in *Howell* held, in effect, that genuine reliance on legal advice to remain silent

---

[39] *R v Webber* [2004] UKHL 1, [2004] 1 WLR 404, [34].

[40] Ibid, [35]. See generally S Nash, 'Drawing Inferences from Positive Suggestions Put to Witnesses: *R v Webber*' (2005) 9 *International Journal of Evidence and Proof* 50.

[41] See generally R Leng, 'Silence Pre-Trial, Reasonable Expectations and the Normative Distortion of Fact-Finding' (2001) 5 *International Journal of Evidence and Proof* 240.

[42] (2001) 31 EHRR 1, [60] (judgment of 2000) (italics added).

[43] [2001] EWCA Crim 224, [2001] 2 Cr App R 16 (p 257). See generally D Wolchover, 'An Obituary for Inferences on Police Station Silence', *Archbold News*, 8 July 2002, 3.

[44] (2003) 36 EHRR 13 (p 162) (judgment of 2002).

[45] [2003] EWCA Crim 1, [2005] 1 Cr App R 1 (p 1). For other discussions of this case see R Brown, 'The Benign Continuum?', *Archbold News*, 3 Feb 2003, 7; A L-T Choo and A F Jennings, 'Silence on Legal Advice Revisited: *R v Howell*' (2003) 7 *International Journal of Evidence and Proof* 185; F Fitzgibbon, 'Life in Crime' (2003) 147 *Solicitors' Journal* 287.

was *not* of itself sufficient to prevent the drawing of adverse inferences. The Court considered that the effect of provisions like section 34 is that:

> [the] benign *continuum* from interview to trial, the public interest that inheres in reasonable disclosure by a suspected person of what he has to say when faced with a set of facts which accuse him, is thwarted if currency is given to the belief that if a suspect remains silent on legal advice he may systematically avoid adverse comment at his trial. And it may encourage solicitors to advise silence for other than good objective reasons. We do not consider, *pace* the reasoning in *Betts & Hall*, that once it is shown that the advice (of whatever quality) has genuinely been relied on as the reason for the suspect's remaining silent, adverse comment is thereby disallowed. The premise of such a position is that in such circumstances it is in principle not reasonable to expect the suspect to mention the facts in question. We do not believe that is so. What is reasonable depends on all the circumstances. . . . The kind of circumstance which may most likely justify silence will be such matters as the suspect's condition (ill-health, in particular mental disability; confusion; intoxication; shock, and so forth—of course we are not laying down an authoritative list), or his inability genuinely to recollect events without reference to documents which are not to hand, or communication with other persons who may be able to assist his recollection. There must always be soundly based objective reasons for silence, sufficiently cogent and telling to weigh in the balance against the clear public interest in an account being given by the suspect to the police. Solicitors bearing the important responsibility of giving advice to suspects at police stations must always have that in mind.[46]

The Court in *Howell* considered that its reasoning was not inconsistent with the decision of the European Court of Human Rights in *Beckles v UK*.[47] This, however, overlooks the fact that the European Court in *Beckles v UK* referred expressly to *Betts and Hall* in the following terms:

> In the Court's opinion, the jury should have been . . . directed that if it was satisfied that the applicant's silence at the police interview could not sensibly be attributed to his having no answer or none that would stand up to police questioning it should not draw an adverse inference. It notes in this connection that the case law of the domestic courts in this area has steadily evolved and that the Court of Appeal in *R v Betts and Hall* has recently noted the importance of giving due weight to an accused's reliance on legal advice to explain his failure to respond to police questioning.[48]

This constitutes a clear expression of approval of the post-*Condron v UK* evolution of domestic case law as encapsulated in the decision in *Betts and Hall*. Thus, the attempt in *Howell* to undermine the reasoning in *Betts and Hall* flies in the face of the decision of the European Court in *Beckles v UK*. While it is true that all that is required by *Condron v UK* is that 'appropriate weight' be accorded to the fact that silence was advised, what is significant is the manner in which this requirement of 'appropriate weight' has been subsequently interpreted. The quotation from *Beckles v UK* demonstrates that the European Court effectively endorsed the *Betts and Hall* view that genuine reliance on legal advice to remain silent, regardless of the quality of that advice, must be sufficient

---

[46] [2003] EWCA Crim 1, [2005] 1 Cr App R 1 (p 1), [24] (italics in original).
[47] (2003) 36 EHRR 13 (p 162) (judgment of 2002).   [48] Ibid, [64].

of itself to prevent the drawing of adverse inferences. The merit of consistency aside, such an approach would be clearly justifiable from the viewpoint of principle: it would undermine the fundamental importance accorded by the law to the right to legal advice[49] if a suspect who was advised to remain silent was required in effect to make his or her own assessment of the quality of that advice.

The decision of the Court of Appeal in *R v Knight*,[50] examined above in the context of prepared statements, also addressed the question of silence on legal advice. While emphasizing that any comments on this question would be *obiter*, given that the resolution of the appeal turned on the question of prepared statements, the Court thought that 'in the hope that it may be of some assistance we shall express our view about it'.[51] The Court's view was that, if there was any conflict between *Betts and Hall* and *Howell*, then *Betts and Hall* should be disavowed and *Howell* taken to represent a changed approach: 'A shift of view upon such a matter is not to be ruled out of court on grounds of *stare decisis*. The rules of precedent, not least in the field of our criminal law, by no means require so rigid an approach.'[52] Thus, in the view of the Court in *Knight*, proven reliance on legal advice to remain silent will not, in the absence of a consideration of the quality of that advice, immunize the suspect from adverse inferences under section 34. It follows from this that where the advice is considered to have been of doubtful quality then other factors will need to be relied upon to prevent the drawing of adverse inferences: '. . . we consider that it will perhaps be useful if we make it clear that we do not intend to exclude altogether the possibility of a case arising in which, although the solicitor has given no reasons or bad reasons to stay silent, still it would be wrong to draw a s 34 inference against the defendant: he may in the particular circumstances of the case be distinctly weak or vulnerable, so that it would not be reasonable to expect him to give an account to the police. It would be a matter for the jury.'[53]

It is disappointing that in *Knight* the approach in *Howell* was that which found favour with the Court of Appeal. On the very day that the decision in *Knight* was handed down, however, the Court of Appeal, with a differently constituted membership, handed down its decision in *R v Robinson*.[54] Citing *Betts and Hall*, the Court stated in *Robinson*:

> If it is a plausible explanation that the reason for not mentioning facts is that the particular appellant acted on the advice of his solicitor and not because he had no, or no satisfactory, answer to give, then no inference can be drawn. This does not give a licence to a guilty person to shield behind the advice of his solicitor. The adequacy of the explanation advanced may well be relevant as to whether or not the advice was truly the reason for not mentioning the facts. A person, who is anxious not to answer questions because he has no, or no adequate, explanation to offer, gains no protection from his solicitor's advice because that advice is no more than a convenient way of disguising his true motivation for not mentioning facts.[55]

It would appear, however, that the approach in *Howell* and *Knight* has now prevailed, and that there is no longer any prospect for the time being of the conflict in the case law

[49] In fact, as we have seen, s 34, as amended by s 58 of the Youth Justice and Criminal Evidence Act 1999, prohibits the drawing of inferences unless the accused has been granted access to legal advice.
[50] [2003] EWCA Crim 1977, [2004] 1 WLR 340.   [51] Ibid, [16].   [52] Ibid, [17].
[53] Ibid, [18].   [54] [2003] EWCA Crim 2219.   [55] Ibid, [55].

being resolved in favour of the approach taken in *Betts and Hall*. In 2004 the Court of Appeal confirmed, in *R v Hoare*[56] and *R v Beckles*,[57] that *reasonable* reliance on silence was necessary to prevent adverse inferences from being drawn. The Court stated in *R v Beckles*:

> . . . in a case where a solicitor's advice is relied upon by the defendant, the ultimate question for the jury remains under section 34 whether the facts relied on at the trial were facts which the defendant could reasonably have been expected to mention at interview. If they were not, that is the end of the matter. If the jury consider that the defendant genuinely relied on the advice, that is not necessarily the end of the matter. It may still not have been reasonable for him to rely on the advice, or the advice may not have been the true explanation for his silence. . . . If . . . it is possible to say that the defendant genuinely acted upon the advice, the fact that he did so because it suited his purpose may mean he was not acting reasonably in not mentioning the facts. His reasonableness in not mentioning the facts remains to be determined by the jury. If they conclude he was acting unreasonably they can draw an adverse inference from the failure to mention the facts.[58]

The Judicial Studies Board specimen direction on section 34 has also been amended to take account of the new approach. The direction provides in part:

> The defendant has given evidence that he did not answer questions on the advice of his solicitor/legal representative. If you accept the evidence that he was so advised, this is obviously an important consideration: but it does not automatically prevent you from drawing any conclusion from his silence. Bear in mind that a person given legal advice has the choice whether to accept or reject it . . . If, for example, you considered that he had or may have had an answer to give, but *genuinely and reasonably relied on the legal advice to remain silent*, you should not draw any conclusion against him. But if, for example, you were sure that the defendant remained silent not because of the legal advice but because he had no answer or no satisfactory answer to give, and merely latched onto the legal advice as a convenient shield behind which to hide, you would be entitled to draw a conclusion against him . . .[59]

The existence of good reason for legal advice to remain silent would support a defendant's argument that his or her reliance on the advice was reasonable. In any event, as noted above, even if it were the case that genuine reliance on legal advice would be sufficient to prevent adverse inferences, the existence of good reason for the advice may provide evidence of genuine reliance. By revealing the reason for the advice, however, the accused may well be waiving legal professional privilege.[60] The consequence of this

---

[56] [2004] EWCA Crim 784, [2005] 1 Cr App R 22 (p 355). See generally D Emanuel and A Jennings, 'Legal Advice to Remain Silent', *Archbold News*, 15 June 2004, 6.

[57] [2004] EWCA Crim 2766, [2005] 1 All ER 705. See generally B Malik, 'Silence on Legal Advice: Clarity But Not Justice?: *R v Beckles*' (2005) 9 *International Journal of Evidence and Proof* 211.

[58] [2004] EWCA Crim 2766, [2005] 1 All ER 705, [46].

[59] Available via http://www.jsboard.co.uk (italics added).

[60] 'If a defendant states the basis or reason for the advice to go no comment . . . and if a suspect goes beyond saying that he declines to answer on legal advice and explains the basis on which he has been so advised, or if his solicitor acting as his authorised representative gives such an explanation, a waiver of legal professional privilege is involved . . .': *R v Wishart* [2005] EWCA Crim 1337, [21]. 'It is well-settled that merely by saying he gave a no comment interview on legal advice a defendant does not waive privilege': ibid, [15].

is that 'the defendant or, if his solicitor is also called, the solicitor can be asked whether there were any other reasons for the advice, and the nature of the advice given, so as to explore whether the advice may also have been given for tactical reasons'.[61] This would seem to place the accused in an unenviable 'catch-22' situation. To prevent adverse inferences from being drawn it may be necessary to provide reasons for the advice. Yet this may be interpreted as a waiver of legal professional privilege, so that the accused, or the legal adviser, may be cross-examined on whether there were additional, tactical reasons for the advice.[62] This state of affairs was not regarded as problematic by the European Court in *Condron v UK*:

> . . . the fact that the applicants were subjected to cross-examination on the content of their solicitor's advice cannot be said to raise an issue of fairness under Article 6 of the Convention. They were under no compulsion to disclose the advice given, other than the indirect compulsion to avoid the reason for their silence remaining at the level of a bare explanation. The applicants chose to make the content of their solicitor's advice a live issue as part of their defence. For that reason they cannot complain that the scheme of section 34 of the 1994 Act is such as to override the confidentiality of their discussions with their solicitor.[63]

Such considerations have led the Law Society to recommend that solicitors give any advice to remain silent, and the reasons for it, *during the police interview itself*.[64]

1.3.1.5.2 Other Relevant Factors
Some general observations have been made by the Court of Appeal on the determination of whether the failure to mention a fact was one:

> which in the circumstances existing at the time the accused could reasonably have been expected to mention . . . The time referred to is the time of questioning, and account must be taken of all the relevant circumstances existing at that time. The courts should not construe the expression 'in the circumstances' restrictively: matters such as time of day, the defendant's age, experience, mental capacity, state of health, sobriety, tiredness, knowledge, personality and legal advice are all part of the relevant circumstances; and those are only examples of things which may be relevant. When reference is made to 'the accused' attention is directed not to some hypothetical, reasonable accused of ordinary phlegm and fortitude but to the actual accused with such qualities, apprehensions, knowledge and advice as he is shown to have had at the time. It is for the jury to decide whether the fact (or facts) which the defendant has relied on in his defence in the criminal trial, but which he had not mentioned when questioned under caution before charge by the constable investigating the alleged offence for which the defendant is being tried, is (or are) a fact (or facts) which in the circumstances as they actually existed the actual defendant could reasonably have been expected to mention.

[61] *R v Condron* [1997] 1 WLR 827, 837.

[62] Of course, it is entirely possible that in practice juries will be sympathetic to defendants who remained silent on the advice of their solicitors. As Pattenden has written (R Pattenden, 'Silence: Lord Taylor's Legacy' (1998) 2 *International Journal of Evidence and Proof* 141, 152): 'In practice we may find that jurors are less critical than judges of defendants who remained silent on their solicitor's advice. Jurors may think that if they were arrested they would not try to second-guess their lawyer.'

[63] (2001) 31 EHRR 1, [60] (judgment of 2000).

[64] E Cape, 'Police Station Advice: Defence Strategies After *Condron*' [Oct 1997] *Legal Action* 17, 19.

Like so many other questions in criminal trials this is a question to be resolved by the jury in the exercise of their collective common-sense, experience and understanding of human nature. Sometimes they may conclude that it was reasonable for the defendant to have held his peace for a host of reasons, such as that he was tired, ill, frightened, drunk, drugged, unable to understand what was going on, suspicious of the police, afraid that his answer would not be fairly recorded, worried at committing himself without legal advice, acting on legal advice, or some other reason accepted by the jury.

In other cases the jury may conclude, after hearing all that the defendant and his witnesses may have to say about the reasons for failing to mention the fact or facts in issue, that he could reasonably have been expected to do so. This is an issue on which the judge may, and usually should, give appropriate directions. But he should ordinarily leave the issue to the jury to decide. Only rarely would it be right for the judge to direct the jury that they should, or should not, draw the appropriate inference.[65]

The examples of relevant circumstances given by the Court of Appeal are very important in establishing that the process of drawing an inference from the defendant's silence is a subjective exercise which requires the court to consider closely what meaning can be attributed to the silence of that particular individual in the light of all of his or her relevant characteristics. Empirical research has shown that the following three factors are, by far, the most commonly cited by solicitors as reasons for advising a client to exercise the right to remain silent: insufficient disclosure by the police, insufficient prosecution disclosure, and the physical or mental condition of the client.[66]

1.3.1.6 Directions to the Jury and Inferences which May Be Drawn

The Court of Appeal has emphasized that what inferences it would appear proper to draw from silence is ultimately a question for the jury:

Subsection (2)(d) empowers a jury in prescribed circumstances to draw such inferences as appear proper. That must mean as appear proper to a jury because the jury is the tribunal of fact and the drawing of appropriate inferences from the facts is the task of the tribunal of fact. The trial judge is of course responsible for the overall fairness of the trial and it is open to him to give the jury guidance on the approach to the evidence. There will undoubtedly be circumstances in which a judge should warn a jury against drawing inferences, but the judge must always bear in mind that the jury is the tribunal of fact and that Parliament in its wisdom has seen fit to enact this section.[67]

'Ordinarily, where the Crown is proposing to invite the jury to draw an inference under s 34 the alleged discrepancy [between what was said in interview and the facts relied upon at trial] should be ventilated in cross-examination so that the defendant has an opportunity to deal with it.'[68] In addition, directions to the jury on section 34 are of vital importance:

The guidelines are only guidelines and on any view must be tailored to the particular facts of the case. It cannot therefore be a matter of criticism simply that the judge has not followed slavishly

---

[65] *R v Argent* [1997] 2 Cr App R 27, 33.

[66] J Williams, 'Inferences from Silence' (1997) 141 *Solicitors' Journal* 566, 566.

[67] *R v Argent* [1997] 2 Cr App R 27, 32.

[68] *R v Turner* [2003] EWCA Crim 3108, [2004] 1 All ER 1025, [33].

the guidelines. However the guidelines have been prepared in this notoriously difficult area, giving consideration to the many different points which arise, including striking the fair balance between telling the jury of a defendant's rights and telling the jury of the defendant's choice not to rely on those rights. It is thus critical that the key features of the guidelines appear in any direction, and it must be the safer course to follow them as nearly as the circumstances of the case allow.[69]

The essential ingredients of a direction have been clarified by the Court of Appeal as follows:

(i) The facts which the accused failed to mention but which are relied on in his defence should be identified . . .

(ii) The inferences (or conclusions, as they are called in the [specimen] direction) which it is suggested might be drawn from failure to mention such facts should be identified, to the extent that they may go beyond the standard inference of late fabrication . . .

(iii) The jury should be told that, if an inference is drawn, they should not convict 'wholly or mainly on the strength of it': see para 2 of the model direction . . . The first of those alternatives ('wholly') is a clear way of putting the need for the prosecution to be able to prove a case to answer, otherwise than by means of any inference drawn. The second alternative ('or mainly') buttresses that need.

(iv) The jury should be told that an inference should be drawn 'only if you think it is a fair and proper conclusion': para 3 of the model direction. . . .

(v) An inference should be drawn 'only if . . . the only sensible explanation for his failure' is that he had no answer or none that would stand up to scrutiny: para 3 of the model direction . . . In other words the inference canvassed should only be drawn if there is no other sensible explanation for the failure. That is analogous to the essence of a direction on lies.

(vi) An inference should only be drawn if, apart from the defendant's failure to mention facts later relied on in his defence, the prosecution case is 'so strong that it clearly calls for an answer by him': para 3 of the model direction. This is a striking way to put the need . . . for a case to answer. A note, note 16, to the JSB guideline explains that it reflects 'a cautious approach'.

(vii) The jury should be reminded of the evidence on the basis of which the jury are invited not to draw any conclusion from the defendant's silence . . . This goes with point (iv) above, because it is only after a jury has considered the defendant's explanation for his failure that they can conclude that there is no other sensible explanation for it.

(viii) A special direction should be given where the explanation for silence of which evidence has been given is that the defendant was advised by his solicitor to remain silent . . .[70]

The Court of Appeal has emphasized that 'before drawing an adverse conclusion or inference . . . for . . . failure to mention a matter in interview, the jury must be sure that the prosecution's case was so strong that it clearly called for an answer'.[71]

[69] *R v Bresa* [2005] EWCA Crim 1414, [41]. See also *R v Turner* [2003] EWCA Crim 3108, [2004] 1 All ER 1025, [28]; *R v Salami* [2003] EWCA Crim 3831, [25], [34].
[70] *R v Petkar* [2003] EWCA Crim 2668, [2004] 1 Cr App R 22 (p 270), [51].
[71] *R v Parchment* [2003] EWCA Crim 2428, [12], approving *Condron v UK* (2001) 31 EHRR 1 (judgment of 2000); *R v Gill* [2001] 1 Cr App R 11 (p 160); *R v Francom* [2001] 1 Cr App R 17 (p 237); *R v Bromfield* [2002] EWCA Crim 195; *R v Chenia* [2002] EWCA Crim 2345, [2003] 2 Cr App R 6 (p 83).

'In circumstances where there is no evidence [contradicting the fact not mentioned], or the evidence is weak, it is the more important that the limited function of an omission to state something in interview is spelt out to the jury.'[72] However, 'where it is clear that there is a compelling case for a defendant to answer and so the jury must have been of that view[,] . . . a failure to direct the jury that they should only take an omission to rely on something in interview as support for the prosecution case if they are satisfied that there is a case to answer . . . is unlikely to render a conviction unsafe'.[73]

Conversely, 'where a judge has concluded that the requirements of section 34 of the Criminal Justice and Public Order Act 1994 [are] not satisfied, so that he [cannot] properly leave to the jury the possibility of drawing adverse inferences from the defendant's silence in interview, then he [is] positively obliged to direct the jury that they must not in any way hold the defendant's failure to answer questions against him'.[74] This is known as a 'McGarry[75] direction'.

An interesting question is whether it should be permissible for a court or jury to draw an inference under section 34 where, if that inference were to be drawn, guilt would, without more, be established. Suppose that A and B are found in a small flat containing drugs. The evidence is such that one or the other must have been the possessor of the drugs. A remains silent at interview. B speaks at interview and incriminates A. At trial, A's defence is that B possessed the drugs, and A asserts that the explanation for his silence at interview was an unwillingness to incriminate B. In these circumstances, if the jury were permitted to draw an inference from A's silence in interview that his story in court was not to be believed, the jury would effectively conclude his guilt (that is, if the jury disbelieved his story that B was the drug possessor, this would imply that A himself was the guilty possessor). It is arguable that this reasoning (inferring guilt from silence) is implicitly prohibited by section 38(3) which provides that a person is not to be convicted of an offence solely on the basis of an inference drawn from silence. While this argument was employed successfully to resist the drawing of inferences in some early cases,[76] the current approach of the courts is that inferences may be drawn in these circumstances.[77] This shift in approach has been justified on the basis of 'the clear statutory intention of s 34, manifest from its wording'.[78] It has been vaguely noted that the earlier approach would rarely be appropriate, being likely to be appropriate only 'in the simplest and most straightforward of cases'.[79]

---

[72] R v Parchment [2003] EWCA Crim 2428, [14].   [73] Ibid, [18].

[74] R v Dow [2003] EWCA Crim 3621, [21]. See also R v Rahman [2003] EWCA Crim 3554.

[75] R v McGarry [1999] 1 Cr App R 377.

[76] R v Mountford [1999] Crim LR 575; R v Gill [2001] 1 Cr App R 11 (p 160).

[77] R v Milford [2001] Crim LR 330; R v Gowland-Wynn [2002] 1 Cr App R 41 (p 569); R v Chenia [2002] EWCA Crim 2345, [2003] 2 Cr App R 6 (p 83).

[78] R v Milford [2001] Crim LR 330; transcript, [35], cited approvingly in R v Chenia [2002] EWCA Crim 2345, [2003] 2 Cr App R 6 (p 83), [34].

[79] R v Chenia [2002] EWCA Crim 2345, [2003] 2 Cr App R 6 (p 83), [35].

1.3.1.7 Evidence of No-Comment Interviews

In *R v Griffin*,[80] the Court of Appeal considered the principle that the prosecution should limit evidence about a police interview to the fact that the defendant had remained silent, and that it is inappropriate to spend time going through the questions asked. The Court of Appeal considered that this principle did not, however, constitute a binding rule the non-compliance with which would necessarily be prejudicial to the defendant. It was simply an indication of what would be the appropriate way of dealing with no-comment interviews. In the case at hand, even if prejudice had been suffered initially when the interview summary was given to the jury, the Recorder had later made it clear in his final directions that they should not draw adverse inferences from the failure to answer questions generally, but should limit inferences to failures to mention particular facts later relied upon.

1.3.1.8 The European Human Rights Dimension

In essence, provided that it is interpreted in a manner which ensures that a fair balance is achieved between the exercise of the suspect's right to remain silent and the drawing of adverse inferences by the jury, section 34 will be regarded as Convention-compliant. In *Murray v UK*[81] the European Court of Human Rights addressed the drawing of inferences under the Criminal Evidence (Northern Ireland) Order 1988,[82] which contains provisions similar to section 34 of the Criminal Justice and Public Order Act 1994. The Court was satisfied that, having regard to the weight of the prosecution evidence, and provided appropriate safeguards are in place, pre-trial silence may be taken into account by the tribunal of fact when assessing the persuasiveness of the prosecution case without compromising Convention rights. It was stressed, however, that domestic law and practice must strike a balance between the exercise of the suspect's right to remain silent and the circumstances in which an adverse inference might be drawn from silence.

In *Murray*, the tribunal of fact was an experienced judge who was obliged to give a judgment setting out the reasons for the decision to draw inferences and the weight attached to them. Furthermore, this judgment and thus the exercise of the judge's discretion were subject to review by the appellate courts. In the subsequent case of *Condron v UK*[83] the Court acknowledged that these factors provided important procedural safeguards against unfairness. In this case, which concerned the drawing of inferences under section 34, it was noted that this provision specifically entrusted the task of assessing the evidential value of silence to the jury. The Court considered that in the absence of a mechanism to assess the evidential weight attached to silence, it was of paramount importance that the jury be properly directed. The Court was unanimous in finding fault with the trial judge's summing-up, which had left the jury with the option of drawing adverse inferences. It considered that 'as a matter of fairness, the jury

---

[80] [1998] Crim LR 418.   [81] (1996) 22 EHRR 29 (judgment of 1996).   [82] SI 1988 No 1987.
[83] (2001) 31 EHRR 1 (judgment of 2000). See generally A F Jennings and E Rees, 'Is Silence Still Golden?', *Archbold News*, 14 June 2000, 5; P Stanley, 'European Briefing' (2000) 144 *Solicitors' Journal* 512.

should have been directed that it could only draw an adverse inference if satisfied that the applicants' silence at the police interview could only sensibly be attributed to their having no answer or none that would stand up to cross-examination'.[84] Accordingly, on the basis of the inadequacy of this direction rather than any inherent deficiency in the legislative scheme, the Court concluded that the applicants had been denied the right to a fair trial under Article 6.

Likewise, the European Court later found a violation of Article 6 in *Beckles v UK* on the basis that:

> the trial judge failed to give appropriate weight in his direction to the applicant's explanation for his silence at the police interview and left the jury at liberty to draw an adverse inference from the applicant's silence notwithstanding that it may have been satisfied as to the plausibility of the explanation given by him . . . Quite apart from the fact that the trial judge had undermined the value of the applicant's explanation by referring to the lack of independent evidence as to what was said by the solicitor and by omitting to mention that the applicant was willing to give his version of the incident to the police before he spoke to his solicitor, it is also to be noted that he invited the jury to reflect on whether the applicant's reason for his silence was 'a good one' without also emphasising that it must be consistent only with guilt.[85]

1.3.2 Section 36

In essence, section 36 is concerned with the failure or refusal to account, in the police station, for a particular object, substance, or mark. Section 36(2) provides that 'such inferences from the failure or refusal as appear proper' may be drawn where, in the words of section 36(1),

(a) a person is arrested by a constable, and there is—

    (i)   on his person; or

    (ii) in or on his clothing or footwear; or

    (iii) otherwise in his possession; or

    (iv) in any place in which he is at the time of his arrest, any object, substance or mark, or there is any mark on any such object; and

(b) that or another constable investigating the case reasonably believes that the presence of the object, substance or mark may be attributable to the participation of the person arrested in the commission of an offence specified by the constable; and

(c) the constable informs the person arrested that he so believes, and requests him to account for the presence of the object, substance or mark; and

(d) the person fails or refuses to do so . . .

Subsections (3), (4), (4A), and (5) are also pertinent:

(3) Subsections (1) and (2) above apply to the condition of clothing or footwear as they apply to a substance or mark thereon.

---

[84] (2001) 31 EHRR 1, [61] (judgment of 2000). This quotation is taken from the website of the European Court of Human Rights. The wording of the passage as reported in EHRR is slightly different.

[85] (2003) 36 EHRR 13 (p 162), [64] (judgment of 2002).

(4) Subsections (1) and (2) above do not apply unless the accused was told in ordinary language by the constable when making the request mentioned in subsection (1)(c) above what the effect of this section would be if he failed or refused to comply with the request.

(4A) Where the accused was at an authorised place of detention at the time of the failure or refusal, subsections (1) and (2) above do not apply if he had not been allowed an opportunity to consult a solicitor prior to the request being made.

(5) This section applies in relation to officers of customs and excise as it applies in relation to constables.

1.3.2.1 'Offence Specified' (Section 36(1)(b))

There is no requirement that the precise terms of the offence, let alone the relevant statutory provisions, should be specified. This was made clear by the Court of Appeal in *R v Compton*, where it was held to be immaterial that a defendant who had been told when cautioned that the officer was investigating 'drug trafficking' was later charged with conspiracy to supply cannabis and heroin. The Court stated:

> The purpose of this provision is one of basic fairness, first that the defendant should know the offence-context in which the question is being asked; and second that the reply cannot be used against him in the context of a different prosecution. Both of those objectives were fulfilled by what the officer said in this case. And Robert himself never for a moment said that he did not understand why he was being asked the questions, nor could he have done.[86]

1.3.2.2 'Account for' (Section 36(1)(c))

The meaning of this phrase was also clarified in *Compton*:

> It is . . . important to note that section 36, unlike section 34, invites no comparison between the statement in interview and the evidence at the trial, since section 36 contains no parallel to the question under section 34(1) of whether it was reasonable for the defendant to mention a particular fact: reasonableness usually being judged from the starting point of whether the fact was mentioned at the trial. The sole question under section 36 is whether the defendant did 'account for' the presence of the substance, as put to him by the officer. In the circumstances of Robert's money, stowed away in a safe, the presence of heroin on it is far from accounted for by a bare statement that Robert was a heroin user.[87]

Furthermore:

> It is the defendant who has to account, and account for a specific state of fact. It is not enough for him to refer to other states of fact, from which it can be inferred what his account might be.

Thus:

> *Sean*, when interviewed before the heroin had been detected, said that his wife was a heroin addict, and that the money found at his house came partly from his father, and partly from the sale of a motor vehicle. When re-interviewed after the heroin had been detected he gave a no comment interview. The question is whether Sean failed to account for the presence of the heroin on the money. It was submitted on his behalf that he had done so. The investigating authorities should have been, or were, aware that the heroin could have come from handling by

---

[86] [2002] EWCA Crim 2835, [33].   [87] Ibid, [32].

his father, known by the police to be a dealer in heroin; or from the purchaser of the car, who was similarly known; or from his wife. We do not agree.[88]

A study published in 2000 found that 70 per cent of suspects failed or refused to provide accounts pursuant to section 36. Accounts considered by officers to be satisfactory were given in 19 per cent of cases, while in the remaining 11 per cent of cases accounts considered to be unsatisfactory were given.[89]

1.3.3 Section 37

In essence, section 37 is concerned with a person's failure or refusal to account, in the police station, for his or her having been present at a particular place. Section 37(2) provides that 'such inferences from the failure or refusal as appear proper' may be drawn where, in the words of section 37(1),

(a) a person arrested by a constable was found by him at a place at or about the time the offence for which he was arrested is alleged to have been committed; and

(b) that or another constable investigating the offence reasonably believes that the presence of the person at that place and at that time may be attributable to his participation in the commission of the offence; and

(c) the constable informs the person that he so believes, and requests him to account for that presence; and

(d) the person fails or refuses to do so . . .

Subsections (3), (3A), and (4) are also pertinent:

(3) Subsections (1) and (2) do not apply unless the accused was told in ordinary language by the constable when making the request mentioned in subsection (1)(c) above what the effect of this section would be if he failed or refused to comply with the request.

(3A) Where the accused was at an authorised place of detention at the time of the failure or refusal, subsections (1) and (2) do not apply if he had not been allowed an opportunity to consult a solicitor prior to the request being made.

(4) This section applies in relation to officers of customs and excise as it applies in relation to constables.

A study published in 2000 found that 77 per cent of suspects failed or refused to provide accounts pursuant to section 37. Accounts considered by officers to be satisfactory were given in 13 per cent of cases, while in the remaining 10 per cent of cases accounts considered to be unsatisfactory were given.[90]

1.3.4 Concluding Remarks

While, on one view, the right to remain silent in England remains technically unaffected by sections 34, 36, and 37 of the 1994 Act, it is clear that the right has been substantially

---

[88] [2002] EWCA Crim 2835, [34] (italics in original).

[89] T Bucke, R Street, and D Brown, *The Right of Silence: The Impact of the Criminal Justice and Public Order Act 1994* (Home Office Research Study 199) (2000) 39–40, available at http://www.homeoffice.gov.uk/rds/pdfs/hors199.pdf.   [90] Ibid.

attenuated. Allowing adverse inferences to be drawn is—to quote a comment made in a different context—'tantamount to imposing a penalty for relying upon a procedural right'.[91] Unsurprisingly perhaps, the 'new' provisions may well have had the effect of reducing the extent to which the right to silence is exercised during police interviews. A study conducted just over a year before the introduction of the provisions found that 77 per cent of suspects answered all questions, 13 per cent refused to answer some questions, and 10 per cent refused to answer any questions. A study conducted after the introduction of the provisions revealed figures of 84 per cent, 10 per cent, and 6 per cent respectively.[92] Interestingly, however, the percentage of suspects who had refused to answer some or any questions and who were subsequently charged actually *fell* slightly, the relevant figures being 70 per cent in the earlier study and 64 per cent in the later one.[93] Predictably, empirical research has shown that fear of adverse inferences is the factor most mentioned by solicitors as a reason for advising suspects to speak.[94] The fact that solicitors are now having to spend significantly longer periods in attendance in order to discharge properly their duty of advising clients whether to speak has also led to a substantial increase in the costs of the duty solicitor scheme.[95]

It may be argued that the considerable difficulties involved in administering the provisions that restrict the right to silence are wholly disproportionate to any benefits to the prosecution that the provisions may bring. Such concern has been expressed in relation to section 34 both by commentators[96] and by the Court of Appeal, which remarked that 'it is a matter of some anxiety that, even in the simplest and most straightforward of cases, where a direction is to be given under Section 34 it seems to require a direction of such length and detail that it seems to promote the adverse inference question to a height it does not merit'.[97]

In stark contrast to the contemporary English position, there is a far greater commitment in Australia to the right to silence at the pre-trial stage. For example, section 89(1) of the Uniform Evidence Acts in Australia plainly states:

> In a criminal proceeding, an inference unfavourable to a party must not be drawn from evidence that the party or another person failed or refused:
>
> (a) to answer one or more questions; or
>
> (b) to respond to a representation;
>
> put or made to the party or other person in the course of official questioning.[98]

---

[91] S Nash, 'Silence as Evidence: A Commonsense Development or a Violation of a Basic Right?' (1997) 21 *Criminal Law Journal* 145, 151.

[92] T Bucke, R Street, and D Brown, *The Right of Silence: The Impact of the Criminal Justice and Public Order Act 1994* (Home Office Research Study 199) (2000) 31, available at http://www.homeoffice.gov.uk/rds/pdfs/hors199.pdf.   [93] Ibid, 40–1.

[94] J Williams, 'Inferences from Silence' (1997) 141 *Solicitors' Journal* 566, 567.

[95] D Wolchover and A Heaton-Armstrong, 'Labour's Victory and the Right to Silence—2' (1997) 147 *New Law Journal* 1434, 1435.

[96] See, eg, D Birch, 'Suffering in Silence: A Cost-Benefit Analysis of Section 34 of the Criminal Justice and Public Order Act 1994' [1999] *Criminal Law Review* 769.   [97] *R v Bresa* [2005] EWCA Crim 1414, [4].

[98] See generally M Chaaya, 'The Right to Silence Reignited: Vulnerable Suspects, Police Questioning and Law and Order in New South Wales' (1998) 22 *Criminal Law Journal* 82; E Stone, 'Calling a Spade a Spade: The Embarrassing Truth About the Right to Silence' (1998) 22 *Criminal Law Journal* 17; J White, 'Silence Is Golden?

1.4 Exclusion of Evidence of Silence

It is to be noted that all powers to exclude evidence in the exercise of discretion are preserved by section 38(6) of the Criminal Justice and Public Order Act 1994. Thus it would be open to a trial judge to exclude the evidence of silence altogether pursuant to section 78(1) of the Police and Criminal Evidence Act 1984 or the common law discretion to exclude evidence to ensure a fair trial.[99] From the viewpoint of the defence this would obviously be a preferable outcome to one involving consideration of the evidence by the jury and the possibility of adverse inferences being drawn. Presumably the considerations which would be taken into account in determining whether evidence of silence ought to be excluded in the exercise of discretion would be analogous to those identified in the previous chapter as being of relevance to the discretionary exclusion of confession evidence. 'If the circumstances are such that it would be unfair to permit the prosecution to rely on admissions, it should be equally unfair to allow them to rely on failure to mention relevant facts.'[100] As the Court of Appeal has noted:

> . . . there will be some situations in which a judge should rule against the admissibility of evidence [of silence]. For example (and only by way of example), the judge might so rule in the case of an unlawful arrest where a breach of the Codes had occurred, or if the situation were one in which a jury properly directed could not properly draw an inference adverse to a defendant. Again such a situation might arise if, in application of section 78, the judge concluded that the prejudicial effect of evidence outweighed any probative value it might reasonably have. However, save in a case of such a kind the proper course in our judgment is ordinarily for a trial judge to allow evidence to be given and direct a jury carefully concerning the drawing of inferences.[101]

2 The Privilege against Self-Incrimination

2.1 Civil Proceedings

The position with respect to the privilege against self-incrimination in civil proceedings is discussed briefly in Chapter 7.

The Significance of Selective Answers to Police Questioning in New South Wales' (1998) 72 *Australian Law Journal* 539. Cf G L Davies, 'The Prohibition Against Adverse Inferences from Silence: A Rule Without Reason?—Part I' (2000) 74 *Australian Law Journal* 26; G L Davies, 'The Prohibition Against Adverse Inferences from Silence: A Rule Without Reason?—Part II' (2000) 74 *Australian Law Journal* 99. For a discussion of the position in South Africa see P J Schwikkard, 'Sanctions for Silence—Constitutional Issues in South Africa: *S v Thebus*' (2004) 8 *International Journal of Evidence and Proof* 120.

   [99] Cf *R v Pointer* [1998] Crim LR 676; *R v Odeyemi* [1999] Crim LR 828.

   [100] E Cape, 'Sidelining Defence Lawyers: Police Station Advice After *Condron*' (1997) 1 *International Journal of Evidence and Proof* 386, 388.

   [101] *R v Argent* [1997] 2 Cr App R 27, 31. See also *R v Dervish* [2001] EWCA Crim 2789, [2002] 2 Cr App R 6 (p 105), [50]: 'If allowing an inference would in counsel's words nullify the safeguards contained in the 1984 Act and the Codes, clearly that would be a basis upon which the judge should not permit the jury to consider drawing such an inference. Equally if there was bad faith by the police deliberately breaching the safeguards "in the knowledge that they would still have the benefit of section 34(1)(b) to fall back on", it would be likely that the judge would not invite consideration of any adverse inference.'

2.2 Criminal Proceedings

By permitting adverse inferences to be drawn in certain circumstances, section 34 of the Criminal Justice and Public Order Act 1994 may be regarded as imposing an *indirect* sanction for a defendant's failure to mention a fact in interview. On occasion, however, a statutory provision may prescribe a criminal sanction for refusing to provide information to the authorities. The jurisprudence of the European Court of Human Rights on the privilege against self-incrimination[102] is notable for its uncertainty and inconsistency.[103] Some general principles may, however, have emerged from the relevant decisions. In *Funke v France*,[104] the European Court held that fair trial guarantees derived from Article 6 include the right to remain silent and the privilege against self-incrimination, rights which could not be restricted without significant justification. Attempts by French customs authorities to compel the applicant to produce bank statements were found to contravene Article 6. In *Saunders v UK*,[105] a case involving statements made to DTI inspectors acting under compulsory powers provided by the Companies Act 1985, the Court held that the privilege against self-incrimination:

> presupposes that the prosecution in a criminal case seek to prove their case against the accused without resort to evidence obtained through methods of coercion or oppression in defiance of the will of the accused.[106]

Regardless of whether the transcripts were directly self-incriminating, the fact that the authorities made use of them in subsequent criminal proceedings constituted a violation of Article 6.[107]

---

[102] On the privilege against self-incrimination, see generally S Penney, 'What's Wrong with Self-Incrimination? The Wayward Path of Self-Incrimination Law in the Post-Charter Era—Part I: Justifications for Rules Preventing Self-Incrimination' (2003) 48 *Criminal Law Quarterly* 249; S Sedley, 'Wringing Out the Fault: Self-Incrimination in the 21st Century' (2001) 52 *Northern Ireland Legal Quarterly* 107. For a discussion of the US position see M Berger, 'American Perspectives on Self-Incrimination and the Compelled Production of Evidence' (2002) 6 *International Journal of Evidence and Proof* 218.

[103] See generally A S Butler, '*Funke v France* and the Right Against Self-Incrimination: A Critical Analysis' (2000) 11 *Criminal Law Forum* 461; A L-T Choo and S Nash, 'Evidence Law in England and Wales: The Impact of the Human Rights Act 1998' (2003) 7 *International Journal of Evidence and Proof* 31, 37–43 (on which I have drawn in this section); I Dennis, 'Instrumental Protection, Human Right or Functional Necessity? Reassessing the Privilege Against Self-Incrimination' [1995] *Cambridge Law Journal* 342; S H Naismith, 'Self-Incrimination— Fairness or Freedom?' [1997] *European Human Rights Law Review* 229; B Sudjic, 'Self Incrimination: Has the Fat Lady Sung Yet?' [2002] *Scots Law Times* 328; T Ward and P Gardner, 'The Privilege Against Self Incrimination: In Search of Legal Certainty' [2003] *European Human Rights Law Review* 388; B Emmerson and A Ashworth, *Human Rights and Criminal Justice* (2001) paras 15-63–15-81.

[104] (1993) 16 EHRR 297 (judgment of 1993). See generally A S Butler, '*Funke v France* and the Right Against Self-Incrimination: A Critical Analysis' (2000) 11 *Criminal Law Forum* 461.

[105] (1997) 23 EHRR 313 (judgment of 1996).   [106] Ibid, [68].

[107] See also *Kansal v UK* (2004) 39 EHRR 31 (p 645) (judgment of 2004). As a consequence of the *Saunders* decision, legislation was introduced which restricted the use of compelled statements in criminal proceedings. Thus the Youth Justice and Criminal Evidence Act 1999, through s 59 and Sch 3, made amendments to the following legislation: Insurance Companies Act 1982; Companies Act 1985; Insolvency Act 1986; Company Directors Disqualification Act 1986; Building Societies Act 1986; Financial Services Act 1986; Companies (Northern Ireland) Order 1986; Banking Act 1987; Criminal Justice Act 1987; Companies Act 1989; Companies (Northern Ireland) Order 1989; Insolvency (Northern Ireland) Order 1989; Friendly Societies Act 1992; Criminal Law

Two separate questions arise for consideration. First, would a prosecution, under the statutory provision in question, for the failure to provide information breach Article 6? Secondly, if information is in fact provided, would the use in evidence of the 'compelled information' constitute a violation of Article 6? It is convenient to consider the second question first.

2.2.1 Use of 'Compelled Information'

In *Saunders v UK*, referred to above, the European Court considered that the public interest in the prosecution of complex and serious cases was insufficient to justify the admission of the evidence.[108] In *Brown v Stott*,[109] however, the Privy Council[110] was satisfied that the subsequent use at trial of a statement obtained under section 172(2)(a) of the Road Traffic Act 1988 was not contrary to Article 6. Section 172(2)(a) imposes a duty on the registered keeper of a vehicle to provide the police with information which would lead to the identification of the driver. The penalty for failing to comply is a fine of not more than £1,000. The circumstances of *Brown v Stott* were that, in response to police questioning, Brown admitted driving her car and was subsequently prosecuted for driving with excess alcohol. The Privy Council found that treating the right not to incriminate oneself as absolute did not fit easily into 'the balanced Convention system',[111] which recognizes the need for a fair balance between the interests of the community and the individual. In purporting to distinguish *Saunders*, the Privy Council observed:

> It is true that the defendant's answer, whether given orally or in writing, would create new evidence which did not exist until she spoke or wrote. In contrast, it may be acknowledged, the percentage of alcohol in her breath was a fact, existing before she blew into the breathalyser machine. . . . it is not easy to see why a requirement to answer a question is objectionable and a requirement to undergo a breath test is not. Yet no criticism is made of the requirement that the defendant undergo a breath test.[112]

Applying *Brown*, the Divisional Court held in *DPP v Wilson*[113] that the use in evidence of the defendant's compulsory admission that he was the driver of a vehicle at the time a road traffic offence was committed was not contrary to Article 6. The Court considered that the right against self-incrimination could in appropriate circumstances be effectively qualified or restricted by statutory provisions. *Wilson* was followed in

---

(Consolidation) (Scotland) Act 1995; Proceeds of Crime (Northern Ireland) Order 1996. See generally S Knights, 'Examinations, Investigations and the Right to a Fair Trial Post *Saunders v UK*', *Criminal Bar Association Newsletter*, Jan 2004, 6, accessible via http://www.criminalbar.com.

[108] (1997) 23 EHRR 313, [74] (judgment of 1996).

[109] [2001] 2 WLR 817. See generally A Ashworth, 'Drivers in the Frame?', *Archbold News*, 22 Dec 2000, 3; P Mirfield, 'Silence, Innocence and Human Rights' in P Mirfield and R Smith (eds), *Essays for Colin Tapper* (2003) 135–7; R Pillay, 'Self-Incrimination and Article 6: The Decision of the Privy Council in *Procurator Fiscal v Brown*' [2001] *European Human Rights Law Review* 78.

[110] Although this case originated in Scotland it is relevant for our purposes as it concerns legislation that is also applicable in England and Wales, and the Privy Council is essentially the alter ego of the House of Lords.

[111] [2001] 2 WLR 817, 844 per Lord Steyn.   [112] Ibid, 837 per Lord Bingham of Cornhill.

[113] [2001] EWHC Admin 198, (2001) 165 JP 715.

Charlebois v DPP, where it was held that 'the use of sections 172(2)(a) and (b) for alleged offences of speeding and going through a red light is a proportionate legislative response to the problem of maintaining road safety. Offences of speeding and going through a red light not only lead to the endorsement of a licence and the award of penalty points, but may, in certain circumstances, lead to a driver being disqualified from driving.'[114] The argument that these were not serious offences but merely offences of a regulatory nature was accordingly rejected.[115] Similarly, it was stated in *Mawdesley v Chief Constable of Cheshire*: 'Speeding may present the gravest danger to the public. It cannot sensibly be argued that it is disproportionate to admit an incriminating answer to a section 172 request in a speeding case, but not in a drink/driving case.'[116]

2.2.2 Prosecutions for Failure to Provide Information

It would appear necessary to distinguish between a criminal investigation and a purely administrative investigation or inquiry.[117] The decision in *R v Hertfordshire County Council, ex p Green Industries Ltd*[118] concerned the latter. Taking account of the European Court jurisprudence, the House of Lords held here that the relevant provisions of the Environmental Protection Act 1990, which effectively required local councils to provide regular detailed reports on their waste management activities, and made it an offence to fail to provide information, were not incompatible with the Convention. While noting obscurities in the European Court's reasoning in *Funke*,[119] Lord Hoffmann was satisfied that the *Saunders* judgment was 'perfectly clear' on the issue of the use of compulsory powers in preparatory investigations:

> . . . European jurisprudence under article 6(1) is firmly anchored to the fairness of the trial and is not concerned with extrajudicial inquiries. Such impact as article 6(1) may have is upon the use of such evidence at a criminal trial. Although it is true that the council unlike the

---

114 [2003] EWHC 54 (Admin), [12].   115 Ibid, [13].

116 [2003] EWHC 1586 (Admin), [2004] 1 WLR 1035, [41]. Canadian law similarly does not recognize 'an abstract and absolute rule that would prevent the use of information in all contexts in which it is statutorily compelled . . . A court must begin "on the ground", with a concrete and contextual analysis of all the circumstances, in order to determine whether or not the principle against self-incrimination is actually engaged . . . This analysis necessarily involves a balancing of principles. One must, in assessing the limits on compellability demanded by the principle against self-incrimination, consider the opposing principle of fundamental justice suggesting that relevant evidence should be available to the trier of fact in a search for truth . . .': *R v Jarvis* [2002] 3 SCR 757, [68]. See also *R v White* [1999] 2 SCR 417 and, generally, S Penney, 'The Continuing Evolution of the S 7 Self-Incrimination Principle: *R v White*' (1999) 24 *Criminal Reports (5th)* 247. Cf *R v SAB* [2003] 2 SCR 678 and see generally D Stratas, '*R v B (S A)* and the Right Against Self-Incrimination: A Confusing Change of Direction' (2004) 14 *Criminal Reports (6th)* 227.

117 See generally A Cowell, 'The ECHR and Company Investigations', *Archbold News*, 26 Oct 2000, 5. For a historical perspective see C Sherrin, 'The Privilege Against Self-Incrimination in Regulatory Proceedings: Beginnings (That Never Began)' (2004) 30 *Manitoba Law Journal* 315.

118 [2000] 2 WLR 373. See generally H Davies and B Hopkins, 'Environmental Crime and the Privilege Against Self-Incrimination' (2000) 4 *International Journal of Evidence and Proof* 177; J Fisher and E Schulster, 'Finding the Right Balance' (2000) 150 *New Law Journal* 988; M Scanlan and R Monnick, 'Investigatory Powers and the Right to a Fair Trial' (2000) 144 *Solicitors' Journal* 652; M Stallworthy, 'The Regulation and Investigation of Commercial Activities in the United Kingdom and the Privilege Against Self-Incrimination' [2000] *International Company and Commercial Law Review* 167.   119 [2000] 2 WLR 373, 382.

> DTI inspectors, had power to prosecute in criminal proceedings, I do not think that the request for information under section 71(2) could be described as an adjudication, 'either in form or in substance.' The *Saunders* case is therefore no authority for allowing the appellants to refuse to answer.[120]

Thus, using compulsory powers to take statements in the course of an administrative investigation is not in conflict with Article 6.

In a similar vein, the Court of Appeal in *R v Kearns*[121] expressed its approval of a legislative strategy which obliged individuals to supply information. The Court found 'ample justification' for concluding that the demand for information by the Official Receiver under section 354(3)(a) of the Insolvency Act 1986 was a proportionate legislative response to the problem of administering and investigating bankrupt estates:

> The relevant part of the Insolvency Act 1986 is designed to deal with the social and economic problem of bankrupts. It is in the public interest that the affairs of bankrupts should be invest-igated, that the assets are traced and got in, and that the assets are then distributed to creditors. . . . The bankrupt is frequently the only person who can provide the necessary information about the bankrupt estate. There is, in our view, an obvious need for a statutory regime that imposes a duty on a bankrupt to co-operate in providing full and accurate information . . . Equally clearly that duty should be backed up by appropriate statutory sanc-tions to ensure that the duty is carried out properly.[122]

In both *Ex p Green* and *Kearns*, then, the demand for information was made in the course of an extra-judicial procedure and there was no suggestion that any compelled statements would be used in subsequent criminal proceedings. These decisions would appear to be consistent with the distinction drawn by the European Court of Human Rights in *IJL v UK*[123] between criminal investigations and administrative inquiries. The Court considered that 'a legal requirement for an individual to give information demanded by an *administrative body*' would not, of itself, infringe Article 6. Thus, an examination of 'the nature and purpose of investigations conducted by DTI inspectors' suggested that:

> the functions performed by the inspectors appointed under section 432(2) of the Companies Act 1985 were essentially investigative in nature and that they did not adjudicate either in form or in substance. Their purpose was to ascertain and record facts which might subsequently be used as the basis for action by other competent authorities—prosecuting, regulatory, disciplinary or even legislative. . . . a requirement that such a preparatory investigation should be subject to the guarantees of a judicial procedure as set forth in Article 6(1) would in practice unduly hamper the effective regulation in the public interest of complex financial and commercial activities.[124]

It is clearly important that a careful determination be made in individual cases of the true character of the investigation or inquiry in question. There is at times no sharp

---

[120] [2000] 2 WLR 373, 381–2.
[121] [2002] EWCA Crim 748, [2002] 1 WLR 2815. See generally A Henderson, 'Defining the Limits of Silence (2)' (2002) 146 *Solicitors' Journal* 508.   [122] [2002] EWCA Crim 748, [2002] 1 WLR 2815, [55].
[123] (2001) 33 EHRR 11 (p 225) (judgment of 2000).   [124] Ibid, [100] (italics added).

distinction between criminal and non-criminal inquiries, particularly in the context of financial investigations.

Prosecutions for failure to provide information in *criminal* investigations clearly have the potential to engage Article 6. What is unclear, however, is whether Article 6 will indeed be violated. On this point the domestic courts would appear to resort once again to a rather unsatisfactory and vague approach of 'balancing competing interests' to discover whether Article 6 has been violated. Commenting upon the regulatory scheme imposed by section 172 of the Road Traffic Act 1988, Lord Bingham of Cornhill noted in *Brown v Stott* that the penalty for non-compliance was moderate and required the suspect to answer one simple question.[125] Referring to the high incidence of death and injury on the roads,[126] he considered that when, in assessing the situation,

> one asks whether section 172 represents a disproportionate legislative response to the prob-lem of maintaining road safety, whether the balance between the interests of the community at large and the interests of the individual is struck in a manner unduly prejudicial to the indi-vidual, ... I would feel bound to give negative answers.[127]

This approach may be contrasted[128] with the rather more robust approach taken by the European Court in *Heaney v Ireland*.[129] The applicants were arrested in connection with serious terrorist offences and questioned under legislation which required them to give an account of their movements and made it an offence to fail to do so. They complained, *inter alia*, that their convictions for refusing to answer questions amounted to a violation of Article 6(1). Citing *Saunders* and *Funke* with approval, the Court found that the security and public order concerns of the Irish Government did not justify:

> a provision which extinguishes the very essence of the applicants' rights to silence and against self-incrimination guaranteed by Article 6(1) of the Convention.[130]

While prepared to accept that this right was not absolute and in appropriate circum-stances could be subject to some restriction, the Court considered that the threat of a prison sentence for non-compliance amounted to a degree of compulsion which effectively destroyed rather than restricted the right.

In *Shannon v UK (Admissibility)*[131] the European Court declared admissible the applicant's complaint 'that the requirement to attend an interview with ... Financial Investigators [appointed under the Proceeds of Crime (Northern Ireland) Order 1996] to answer questions, after he had been charged with a criminal offence, and the resulting prosecution and conviction for failing to attend the interview, infringed Article 6 of the Convention, in particular as he was subjected to criminal sanctions aimed at compelling the production of incriminating evidence'.

It would seem, however, that the European Court requires, for a finding that the imposition of a criminal sanction for not providing information violates Article 6, some

---

[125] [2001] 2 WLR 817, 836–7.   [126] Ibid, 836.   [127] Ibid, 837.

[128] See J Seddon, 'Is the Privilege Against Self-Incrimination Protected?' (2002) 146 *Solicitors' Journal* 50, 60.

[129] (2001) 33 EHRR 12 (p 264) (judgment of 2000).   [130] Ibid, [58].

[131] Application no 6563/03, 23 Nov 2004.

degree of possibility that, if the information had been provided, it would have been used in a subsequent criminal prosecution. Thus, to prosecute a person for failing to provide information about the identity of the driver of his car would not violate Article 6 if:

> the link between the . . . obligation under [the relevant legislation] to disclose the driver of his car and possible criminal proceedings for speeding against him remains remote and hypothetical. . . . without a sufficiently concrete link with these criminal proceedings the use of compulsory powers (ie the imposition of a fine) to obtain information does not raise an issue with regard to the applicant's right to remain silent and the privilege against self-incrimination.[132]

It is questionable whether so much should turn on whether any compelled information might be used in a subsequent criminal prosecution:

> . . . might it be objectionable [, for example,] to require that someone give an account of their movements . . . even if the information so revealed is not used against them at trial? It might perhaps be thought enough if the information would help the prosecution, for example by leading to other evidence that could be used at trial. One might also take the view that the requirement is objectionable in itself, even if there was a guarantee that no prosecution would follow.[133]

2.2.3 Production of Documents

Some doubt remains about whether the privilege against self-incrimination applies to documentary evidence. In *Funke* the European Court was satisfied that this right attached to bank documents and chequebooks in the applicant's possession. However, in *Saunders* the Court drew a distinction between compelled statements and real evidence, finding that the right against self-incrimination did not apply to material having:

> an existence independent of the will of the suspect such as, *inter alia*, documents acquired pursuant to a warrant, breath, blood and urine samples and bodily tissue for the purpose of DNA testing.[134]

Evidently adopting *Funke* in preference to *Saunders* on this point, the Court in *JB v Switzerland*[135] found that a prosecution for failing to produce possibly incriminatory documents breached Article 6(1). Where the penalty for failing to provide a statement was 'essentially punitive and deterrent in nature',[136] it was immaterial that the provision was contained within non-criminal legislation. The quality of the Court's reasoning in this case has been subjected to some criticism.[137] Noting the inconsistencies in the European Court jurisprudence, the Court of Appeal in *A-G's Reference (No 7 of 2000)*[138]

---

[132] *Rieg v Austria*, Application no 63207/00, 24 March 2005, [31], quoting from *Weh v Austria* (2005) 40 EHRR 37 (p 890), [56] (judgment of 2004).

[133] A Ashworth and M Redmayne, *The Criminal Process* (3rd ed 2005) 136–7.

[134] (1997) 23 EHRR 313, [69] (judgment of 1996).   [135] Application no 31827/96, 3 May 2001.

[136] Ibid, [48].

[137] A Ashworth, 'The Self-Incrimination Saga', *Archbold News*, 27 June 2001, 5; I H Dennis, *The Law of Evidence* (2nd ed 2002) 141.

[138] [2001] EWCA Crim 888, [2001] 2 Cr App R 19 (p 286). See generally A Henderson, 'Defining the Limits of Silence' (2001) 145 *Solicitors' Journal* 432.

suggested that where no clear answer could be found there, it would be appropriate to follow national authorities.[139] Drawing a distinction between compelled statements on the one hand, and the production of a pre-existing document or real evidence on the other, the Court of Appeal accepted that it would be objectionable to use evidence which the accused was forced to create by the use of compulsory powers. However, using compulsory powers to oblige the defendant to deliver up evidence which was already in existence and had an existence independent of the will of the accused would not be contrary to the fair trial guarantees provided by Article 6.

In *R v Allen*[140] the House of Lords held that a prosecution for submitting a tax return containing false information would not be contrary to Article 6. The House observed that citizens had an obligation to pay taxes and a duty not to cheat the Revenue. In order to ensure the payment of taxes, the State had to have the power to require individuals to provide information about their annual income, and to have sanctions available to enforce the provision of this information.[141]

[139] Those particularly identified were the decisions of the House of Lords in *R v Director of Serious Fraud Office, ex p Smith* [1993] AC 1, *AT & T Istel Ltd v Tully* [1993] AC 45, and *R v Hertfordshire County Council, ex p Green Industries Ltd* [2000] 2 WLR 373.   [140] [2001] UKHL 45, [2002] 1 AC 509.

[141] Ibid, [29]–[30]. An application to the European Court of Human Rights was held to be inadmissible: *Allen v UK (Admissibility)*, Application no 76574/01, 10 Sep 2002. See also *King v UK*, Application no 13881/02, 8 April 2003.

4

Identification Evidence

1 Mistaken Identifications

It is well known that identification evidence, like confession evidence, has contributed to a number of significant miscarriages of justice. The infamous case of Beck at the end of the 19th and beginning of the 20th centuries provides a striking example, but such cases continue to come before the courts.[1] In 1998, the Court of Appeal, on a reference by the Criminal Cases Review Commission, quashed the 46-year-old murder conviction of Mahmoud Hussein Mattan on the basis that the purported identification of Mattan by a key witness was demonstrably flawed.[2] Mattan had been hanged for the murder in 1952.

Essentially, there are three categories of factors which may contribute to the mistaken identification of the defendant as the perpetrator of the offence. These may be termed witness factors, event factors, and post-event factors.[3] Witness factors relate to erroneous perception on the part of the witness at the time of the event. Possible witness factors include the witness's defective eyesight, the witness's expectations, the witness's stress or arousal level at the time of the event, and the activity in which the witness was engaged at the time of the event. The possible contribution of defective eyesight to faulty perception is obvious.[4] Further, a witness may 'perceive' what he or she actually *expects* to perceive; this expectation may be the result either of his or her biases and prejudices,[5] or of his or her past experience.[6] Stress or arousal is relevant, according to the so-called 'Yerkes–Dodson' law, in the following way. Perceptual ability may not be impaired at low levels of arousal, and will be at its optimum at moderate levels of arousal, but will begin to decrease at high levels of arousal.[7] As for perceptual activity, it is clear that the

---

[1] For discussions of the Beck case, see B Cathcart, 'The Strange Case of Adolf Beck', *The Independent on Sunday*, 17 Oct 2004, 19; P Hill, 'A Century of Consistency' (1998) 148 *New Law Journal* 1028; J Hunter and K Cronin, *Evidence, Advocacy and Ethical Practice: A Criminal Trial Commentary* (1995) 394–5.

[2] *R v Mattan, The Times*, 5 March 1998.

[3] See generally B L Cutler and S D Penrod, *Mistaken Identification: The Eyewitness, Psychology, and the Law* (1995) Chs 6 and 7; M R Kebbell and G F Wagstaff, *Face Value? Evaluating the Accuracy of Eyewitness Information* (Police Research Series Paper 102) (1999), available at http://www.homeoffice.gov.uk/rds/prgpdfs/ fprs102.pdf.

[4] See A D Yarmey, *The Psychology of Eyewitness Testimony* (1979) 39.

[5] See, eg, the classic experiments conducted in the 1940s by Allport and Postman: G W Allport and L Postman, *The Psychology of Rumor* (1947) (reprinted 1965) 111. See also E F Loftus, *Eyewitness Testimony* (1979) 40.

[6] See K D Williams, E F Loftus, and K A Deffenbacher, 'Eyewitness Evidence and Testimony' in D K Kagehiro and W S Laufer (eds), *Handbook of Psychology and Law* (1992) 144.

[7] See B L Cutler and S D Penrod, *Mistaken Identification: The Eyewitness, Psychology, and the Law* (1995) 103–4.

ability to perceive accurately may be dependent upon the activity in which the witness is engaged while 'perceiving': 'for example, an eyewitness to a robbery could spend a good deal of time examining the individual features of the face, or he could spend most of his time staring in the direction of the face but might actually be trying to figure out how to escape from an unpleasant situation'.[8]

Event factors relate to the actual event itself, and include *exposure duration* (the longer the perpetrator is seen, the more reliable a subsequent identification is likely to be); the *presence of a weapon* (if the perpetrator is carrying a weapon, the witness's attention is likely to be focused upon the weapon rather than upon the perpetrator's facial and physical characteristics); and the *ethnicity and gender* of the perpetrator (same-race and same-gender identifications are likely to be more reliable than cross-race and cross-gender identifications).[9]

In relation to post-event factors, the following comment is pertinent:

> The widely held belief of the general public is that people store visual and sound memories rather like a video recorder. However, general research on memory, and more specific research on eyewitness identification, have shown that human memory and perception do not work like that.[10]

Pre-eminent amongst post-event factors is the passage of time. The identification of persons may be expected to be more reliable if the event in question is recent rather than one which occurred in the more distant past.[11]

Over the past two decades, two main mechanisms for dealing with the issue of evidence of identification of the defendant have evolved in English law. First, there is a requirement that warnings about identification evidence be given to the jury in certain circumstances. Secondly, Code D of the Codes of Practice issued under the Police and Criminal Evidence Act 1984 makes provision in relation to different methods of generating identification evidence, and breaches of this Code may lead to the discretionary exclusion of identification evidence under section 78(1). Each of these mechanisms will now be considered in turn.

2 *Turnbull* Warnings

In *R v Turnbull*[12] in 1976, the Court of Appeal laid down the famous '*Turnbull* guidelines' on judicial warnings to the jury about identification evidence.[13] Although specifically directed at evidence of visual identification, the Court of Appeal has since

---

[8] E F Loftus, *Eyewitness Testimony* (1979) 48.

[9] See B L Cutler and S D Penrod, *Mistaken Identification: The Eyewitness, Psychology, and the Law* (1995) 101–5.

[10] I McKenzie and P Dunk, 'Identification Parades: Psychological and Practical Realities', 178, in A Heaton-Armstrong, E Shepherd, and D Wolchover (eds), *Analysing Witness Testimony: A Guide for Legal Practitioners and Other Professionals* (1999).

[11] See B L Cutler and S D Penrod, *Mistaken Identification: The Eyewitness, Psychology, and the Law* (1995) 105–6.

[12] [1977] QB 224.

[13] For interesting anecdotal evidence about the influence on juries of strong judicial warnings about identification evidence, see E Crowther, 'Return to *Turnbull*' (1997) 161 *Justice of the Peace* 885.

acknowledged that these guidelines also apply, with any necessary adaptations, to evidence of voice identification.[14] The following are the main considerations pertaining to *Turnbull* warnings.

2.1 When Should a Warning Be Administered?

A warning is required whenever the prosecution case

- depends *wholly or substantially* on the
- correctness of one or more identifications of the accused
- which the defence alleges to be *mistaken*.[15]

It is not necessary that the trial judge recite the actual words used in *Turnbull*; 'it is the substance of the warning which matters'.[16] Thus 'the *Turnbull* principles do not impose a fixed formula for adoption in every case, and it will suffice if the judge's directions comply with the sense and spirit of the guidelines. The provision of a sufficient direction in cases which depend on identification evidence is nevertheless an essential principle....'[17]

2.2 The Content of a Warning

A warning should comprise three elements. The jury should first be warned:

of the special need for caution before convicting the accused in reliance on the correctness of the identification or identifications.... [The judge] should instruct them as to the reason for the need for such a warning and should make some reference to the possibility that a mistaken witness can be a convincing one and that a number of such witnesses can all be mistaken. Provided this is done in clear terms the judge need not use any particular form of words.

Secondly, the judge should direct the jury to examine closely the circumstances in which the identification by each witness came to be made. How long did the witness have the accused under observation? At what distance? In what light? Was the observation impeded in any way, as for example by passing traffic or a press of people? Had the witness ever seen the accused before? How often? If only occasionally, had he any special reason for remembering the accused? How long elapsed between the original observation and the subsequent identification to the police? Was there any material discrepancy between the description of the accused given to the police by the witness when first seen by them and his actual appearance?... [Thirdly and] finally, he should remind the jury of any specific weaknesses which had appeared in the identification evidence.[18]

The requirement that the jury be reminded of specific weaknesses in the evidence is not satisfied simply by inviting the jury to take into account what was said by defence counsel about those weaknesses. What is required is that the judge 'deal with the specific

---

14 *R v Hersey* [1998] Crim LR 281. See 2.7 below.   15 *R v Turnbull* [1977] QB 224, 228.
16 *Ricketts v R* [1998] 1 WLR 1016, 1023. See also *R v Qadir* [1998] Crim LR 828.
17 *Langford v The State* [2005] UKPC 20, [22].   18 *R v Turnbull* [1977] QB 224, 228.

weaknesses in a coherent manner so that the cumulative impact of those specific weaknesses is fairly placed before the jury'.[19] A summary by the judge of the weaknesses is not necessarily required.[20] For example, 'it may well be more convenient, especially in the course of a lengthy summing-up where the evidence is reviewed in some detail ..., to give specific reminders in relation to specific parts of the evidence as they are dealt with in the course of the summing-up, rather than to attempt any form of summary or shorthand which might itself be misleading either at the beginning or the end of that detailed review'.[21]

An important point to be made is that a *Turnbull* warning is required, as seen above, where the defence alleges the identification(s) to be *mistaken*. This is a challenge to the *accuracy* of the identification (that is, an allegation that the identifying witness was mistaken), and is to be distinguished from a defence challenge to the *credibility* of the identifying witness. Thus, 'in cases where the defence challenges the credibility of the identifying witnesses as the principal or sole means of defence, there may be exceptional cases where a *Turnbull* direction is unnecessary or where it is sufficient to give it more briefly than in a case where the accuracy of identification is challenged'.[22] It has been emphasized, however, that it will be very rare to encounter cases in which credibility is genuinely the sole cause for concern. Such an exceptional case may arise where, for example, the only allegation which is made pertains to credibility rather than to accuracy, and 'the witness's identification evidence is that the accused was his workmate whom he has known for 20 years and that he was conversing with him for half an hour face to face in the same room and the witness is sane and sober'.[23] Because of the danger that accuracy may be a cause for concern even though this has not been raised by the defence, 'the cases in which the warning can be entirely dispensed with must be wholly exceptional, even where credibility is the sole line of defence. In the latter type of case the judge should normally, and even in the exceptional case would be wise to, tell the jury in an appropriate form to consider whether they are satisfied that the witness was not mistaken in view of the danger of mistake ...'.[24]

The courts would also appear to take the view that, even where the accuracy of identification is at issue, something less than a full warning may suffice in certain circumstances. A full warning would be of the utmost importance in a case where, for example, the only identification evidence relied upon by the prosecution is contained in the deposition of a deceased person who claimed to have seen the defendants only fleetingly as they ran away.[25] In some circumstances, however, a simpler warning will suffice. Thus the distinction has been drawn between a case where the eyewitness glanced at the subject only fleetingly, and a case where the eyewitness purportedly saw a familiar face over a considerable period of time in perfectly good conditions. In the

---

[19] *R v Fergus* (1994) 98 Cr App R 313, 318 (decision of 1993). See also *R v El-Hannachi* [1998] 2 Cr App R 226, 239.   [20] *R v Pattinson* [1996] 1 Cr App R 51, 56; *R v Qadir* [1998] Crim LR 828.

[21] *R v Mussell*, unrep, 27 Feb 1995, quoted in *R v Pattinson* [1996] 1 Cr App R 51, 56.

[22] *Shand v R* [1996] 1 WLR 67, 72. See also *Daley v R* [1994] 1 AC 117, *R v Cape* [1996] 1 Cr App R 191, and *R v Macmath* [1997] Crim LR 586 on the accuracy/credibility distinction.

[23] *Beckford v R* (1993) 97 Cr App R 409, 415 (decision of 1993).

[24] *Shand v R* [1996] 1 WLR 67, 72.   [25] *Scott v R* [1989] 1 AC 1242, 1260.

former case a full warning would be required, while in the latter case it would be unnecessary.[26] But although the identification evidence in the latter case may be more reliable than in the former, the jury should nevertheless be reminded that even close relatives and friends are sometimes misidentified.[27]

The extent to which a warning is required where the defendant admits his or her presence at or near the scene of the crime would be dependent upon the circumstances of the particular case. If there is a possibility of mistaken identification then a warning is required. This will be the case where, for example, there were two or more people present with similarities in face, build, or clothing, with the consequence that one person could have been mistaken for another.[28] On the other hand:

> purely by way of example, such a direction would not... generally be necessary if the defendant admitted he was the only person present when the complainant received his injuries, or if a woman and a man were present and the complainant said the man caused his injuries, or if a black man and a white man were present and the complainant said the white man caused the injuries, or if four men were present, three dressed in black and one in white, and the complainant said the man in white caused his injuries. Of course, in all but the first of those examples, an appropriate warning would need to be given if in a particular case, for example, the lighting was bad or there were other circumstances giving rise to the possibility of mistake.[29]

2.3 Withdrawal of Case from Jury

A distinction is drawn by the Court of Appeal in *Turnbull* between identification evidence of good quality and of bad quality. An example given of the former is evidence of identification 'made after a long period of observation, or in satisfactory conditions by a relative, a neighbour, a close friend, a workmate and the like'.[30] In *R v El-Hannachi*, the Court of Appeal considered identification evidence resulting from the following circumstances to be of good quality:

> . . . Eve Robertson had watched a group of young men for some time within the public house earlier in the evening. She had been in a good position to see the fight and, since she knew the victims personally, she was likely to pay special attention to the attackers. The evidence indicated that the attackers had walked away along East Acton Lane. This was a long straight road with relatively high railings on each side. The lighting when the fight occurred was good. The identification itself took place under a street light. Eve Robertson looked carefully for quite a

---

[26] *R v Bentley* [1991] Crim LR 620.

[27] *R v Turnbull* [1977] QB 224, 228. The Court of Appeal in *R v Wait* [1998] Crim LR 68 also emphasized the need to give *Turnbull* warnings even in cases where the person identified had been recognized by the witness rather than seen by him or her for the first time. Equally, the Privy Council remarked in *Langford v The State* [2005] UKPC 20, [24]: 'Where... the identification depends upon the recognition by the witness of a person or persons previously known to him, the jury should be reminded that there is room for mistake in such cases as well as in those which turn on the identification of a person thitherto unknown to the identifying witness who is recollected by description.... the need in recognition cases for an appropriate *Turnbull* direction is not diminished.'   [28] *R v Slater* [1995] 1 Cr App R 584, 589. See also *R v Thornton* [1995] 1 Cr App R 578.

[29] *R v Slater* [1995] 1 Cr App R 584, 590.   [30] [1977] QB 224, 229.

long time before she made her identification and when she did she picked out only four of five people.[31]

The jury can safely be left to evaluate good-quality identification evidence even though there is no other evidence to support it, so long as an adequate warning has been given about the special need for caution. An example of poor-quality identification evidence is evidence depending 'solely on a fleeting glance or on a longer observation made in difficult conditions'. Where the identification evidence is of poor quality, the judge should 'withdraw the case from the jury and direct an acquittal unless there is other evidence which goes to support the correctness of the identification'. What is otherwise good-quality identification evidence does not become poor-quality identification evidence on the basis of the lack of credibility of the identifying witness, which is considered a matter for the jury.[32] Evidence will be deemed to be supporting evidence so long 'its effect is to make the jury sure that there has been no mistaken identification'. Thus:

> the trial judge should identify to the jury the evidence which he adjudges is capable of supporting the evidence of identification. If there is any evidence or circumstances which the jury might think was supporting when it did not have this quality, the judge should say so. . . .
>
> Care should be taken by the judge when directing the jury about the support for an identification which may be derived from the fact that they have rejected an alibi. False alibis may be put forward for many reasons: an accused, for example, who has only his own truthful evidence to rely on may stupidly fabricate an alibi and get lying witnesses to support it out of fear that his own evidence will not be enough. Further, alibi witnesses can make genuine mistakes about dates and occasions like any other witnesses can. It is only when the jury is satisfied that the sole reason for the fabrication was to deceive them and there is no other explanation for its being put forward can fabrication provide any support for identification evidence. The jury should be reminded that proving the accused has told lies about where he was at the material time does not by itself prove that he was where the identifying witness says he was.[33]

The precise relationship between *Turnbull* warnings and the complete withdrawal of the case from the jury (or the outright exclusion of the identification evidence) remains unclear. We have seen that the Court of Appeal in *Turnbull* stated that the case should be withdrawn from the jury, and an acquittal directed, if the identification evidence is poor and there is no supporting evidence. The suggestion, therefore, is that 'at some point the adverse conditions for observation cannot be cured by a caution'.[34] Evidence which depends solely on a fleeting glance, or on a longer observation made in difficult conditions, is given by the Court in *Turnbull* as an example of poor identification evidence. As has been noted, however, by Wilson J in the Canadian Supreme Court case of *Mezzo v R*:

> No one would take issue with the 'fleeting glance' test; it represents the extreme of frailty which cannot be cured by a caution. The real difficulty is with 'a longer observation made in difficult conditions'. In this sense *Turnbull* is more significant for what it does not lay down. If it sets out

---

[31] [1998] 2 Cr App R 226, 237.   [32] *R v Macmath* [1997] Crim LR 586.
[33] *R v Turnbull* [1977] QB 224, 230.   [34] *Mezzo v R* (1986) 30 DLR (4th) 161, 194 per Wilson J.

any principle with regard to the test for a directed verdict, it is the principle that the quality of a witness' identification is directly related to the extent of the witness' opportunity for observation. However, *Turnbull* offers no workable criteria for determining when conditions are so difficult that an eyewitness' testimony should not be relied on . . .[35]

2.4 Appeals

What are the consequences on appeal of the failure to administer an adequate *Turnbull* warning? A difference would seem to have emerged between the views of the Privy Council and the High Court of Australia on this matter. The Privy Council has apparently taken the view that a conviction can stand so long as the appeal court considers the quality of the identification evidence in question to be 'exceptionally good'.[36] The Australian High Court, on the other hand, would appear to require that the appeal be allowed unless the appeal court concludes that the jury must inevitably have convicted the defendant on the basis of the *other* prosecution evidence in the case.[37] This view would seem rather more consistent with the protection of the defendant from the consequences of possibly mistaken identifications.

2.5 *Turnbull* Appraised

There is no doubt that *Turnbull* represents a serious attempt by the judiciary to prevent wrongful convictions arising from the admission of identification evidence. It is notable that the approach prescribed in *Turnbull* had been recommended a year earlier in a report on identification evidence in criminal cases.[38] A few of the difficulties and uncertainties associated with the *Turnbull* guidelines have already been referred to above. More generally, it is to be noted that the entire approach is premised on the assumption that juries will actually comprehend and take cognizance of the warnings administered by trial judges. As has been observed: 'It is all very well to tell a jury to be careful, and run through a check list of considerations they should take into account, but a 10-minute lecture on identification evidence does not make a juror an expert in assessing its probative value.'[39]

Research conducted on this question in the United States, where instructions to the jury on identification evidence are also employed, is illuminating. A model instruction is provided in the seminal decision of the US Court of Appeals for the District of Columbia Circuit in *US v Telfaire*.[40] A number of empirical studies examining the effect of *Telfaire* instructions on mock jurors have been conducted. These studies were analysed by Cutler and Penrod and found to show that *Telfaire* instructions may well

---

[35] Ibid.   [36] *Freemantle v R* [1994] 1 WLR 1437; *Shand v R* [1996] 1 WLR 67.

[37] *Domican v R* (1992) 173 CLR 555.

[38] Departmental Committee on Evidence of Identification in Criminal Cases, *Report to the Secretary of State for the Home Department of the Departmental Committee on Evidence of Identification in Criminal Cases* (1976).

[39] Editorial, 'Identifying Problems with Identification' (2004) 28 *Criminal Law Journal* 69, 69.

[40] 469 F 2d 552 (1972).

be of limited efficacy. Cutler and Penrod conclude:

> In summary, the experiments we have reviewed here provide little evidence that judges' instructions concerning the reliability of eyewitness identification enhance juror sensitivity to eyewitness identification evidence. Manipulations of timing and content of the instructions did not improve the impact of the instructions. In a couple of instances there was increased skepticism following instructions . . . , but the effect is not systematic. And, there is no substantial evidence for enhanced sensitivity among jurors who received *Telfaire* instructions in these studies . . . Rather, the evidence indicates that the *Telfaire* instructions—perhaps because they confuse jurors—actually reduced juror sensitivity to witnessing and identification conditions compared to uninstructed jurors. Indeed, . . . careful scrutiny of these results—especially a comparison of conviction rates in good eyewitnessing conditions for uninstructed versus instructed jurors . . . — will suggest that the defense should be especially eager to request *Telfaire* instructions when an identification has been made under good witnessing conditions![41]

In any event, the extent to which the *Turnbull* guidelines are being actually complied with by trial judges is also speculative. The *Crown Court Study* found that there was 'fairly important' or 'very important' identification evidence in close to about 25 per cent of contested cases. Interestingly, *Turnbull* warnings were given in just over 50 per cent of those cases in which there was 'fairly important' or 'very important' identification evidence.[42]

2.6 Evidence of Description

The requirement for a *Turnbull* warning does not apply where the evidence in question is 'evidence of description' rather than identification evidence. The Court of Appeal noted in *R v Gayle* that there is a:

> qualitative difference between identification evidence and what the judge called 'evidence of description'. The special need for caution before conviction on identification evidence is because, as experience has often shown, it is possible for an honest witness to make a mistaken identification. But the danger of an honest witness being mistaken as to distinctive clothing, or the general description of the person he saw (short or tall, black or white, etc., or the direction in which he was going) are minimal. So the jury can concentrate on the honesty of the witness, in the ordinary way.[43]

Thus, the requirement for a *Turnbull* warning applies only where a witness purports to be able to identify the defendant. Where, as in *Gayle*, the witness is able to describe the perpetrator's clothes but expressly states that he would not be able to recognize him, there is clearly no identification and hence no requirement for caution before relying upon an identification. For the same reasons, the police are under no duty to hold a formal identification procedure unless a witness has purported to identify the

---

[41] B L Cutler and S D Penrod, *Mistaken Identification: The Eyewitness, Psychology, and the Law* (1995) 263.

[42] M Zander and P Henderson, *The Royal Commission on Criminal Justice: Crown Court Study* (1993) 92–3.

[43] [1999] 2 Cr App R 130, 135. See also *R v Doldur*, The Times, 7 Dec 1999; *R v Hassan* [2004] EWCA Crim 1478.

suspect or there is an available witness who might reasonably be expected to identify the suspect.[44]

2.7 Voice Identification

There has been increasing recognition of the potential dangers of voice identification.[45] As the Court of Appeal has acknowledged:

... research shows that voice identification is more difficult than visual identification. Voice identification is more likely to be wrong than visual identification. Nevertheless, by the use of mock jurors researchers have shown that ordinary people show themselves to be as willing to rely on identification by ear witnesses as they are on identification by eyewitnesses.[46]

Thus in cases of voice identification a modified *Turnbull* warning would be required:

... a judge should tailor his directions to the jury on the lines indicated by this court and in the specimen directions issued by the Judicial Studies Board in respect of visual recognition or identification, but tailored for the purposes of voice identification or recognition. The judge should follow, suitably adapted, the guidelines laid down in *R v Turnbull* ... and the cases which have followed. Above all, it is vital that a judge should spell out to the jury the risk of a mistaken identification, the reason why a witness may be mistaken, pointing out that a truthful witness may yet be a mistaken witness, and dealing with the particular strengths and weaknesses of the identification in the instant case.[47]

3 Discretionary Exclusion of Identification Evidence

It is considered unjust to ask a witness to identify a defendant for the first time in court because of the inherent likelihood that any witness asked to do this would point to the single person occupying the dock. Accordingly, Code D of the Codes of Practice issued under the Police and Criminal Evidence Act 1984 lays down detailed procedures to be followed for the pre-trial identification of suspects. The evidence of the pre-trial identification would then be admitted at trial to support the in-court identification of the defendant. In trials on indictment a 'dock identification' is strictly admissible in evidence,[48] but any attempt by the prosecution to rely on such a tactic would invite a defence application to exclude the identification evidence on grounds of unfairness under section 78 of the Police and Criminal Evidence Act 1984. The Crown Court is

---

44 Code D, 3.12.

45 See generally R Bull and B Clifford, 'Earwitness Testimony' (1999) 149 *New Law Journal* 216; R Bull and B Clifford, 'Earwitness Testimony' in A Heaton-Armstrong, E Shepherd, and D Wolchover (eds), *Analysing Witness Testimony: A Guide for Legal Practitioners and Other Professionals* (1999).

46 *R v Roberts* [2000] Crim LR 183 (transcript from Smith Bernal).

47 *R v Hersey* [1998] Crim LR 281 (transcript from Smith Bernal). See also *R v Gummerson* [1999] Crim LR 680; *R v Roberts* [2000] Crim LR 183; *R v Chenia* [2002] EWCA Crim 2345, [2003] 2 Cr App R 6 (p 83). See generally D C Ormerod, 'Sounds Familiar? Voice Identification Evidence' [2001] *Criminal Law Review* 595.

48 *R v Reid* [1994] Crim LR 442.

likely to admit evidence of dock identifications only exceptionally, for instance where a defendant has refused to take part in any identification procedure.[49] A more liberal approach would appear to be taken in summary trials. The Divisional Court has said of road traffic cases that:

> every day in a magistrates' court those charged for instance with careless driving, who have made no statement to the police, are entitled to sit back and in the absence of identification to submit that it has not been proven that they were the driver. . . . To deal with that it has been customary . . . for a police officer or other witnesses to be asked, 'Do you see the driver in court,' and for him to identify the defendant. . . . If in every case where the defendant does not distinctly admit driving there has to be an identification parade [or other pre-trial identification procedure], the whole process of justice in a magistrates' court would be severely impaired.[50]

Thus in driving cases:

> it is permissible to permit the prosecution to seek and rely upon a dock identification of the accused . . . where there has been no prior notification that identity is an issue. . . . It is not a breach of the Human Rights Act or Article 6 of the European Convention for the court to expect, and in that sense require, an accused to indicate prior to trial that identification as the driver is in issue. In the absence of such prior indication, it is fair to permit the prosecution to seek and rely on a dock identification of the accused as the driver for the purpose . . . of preventing an unmeritorious, purely formal objection being taken to the prosecution case and an unmeritorious submission of no case to answer being made at the close of the prosecution evidence.[51]

3.1 Formal Identification Procedures and Circumstances in which they Should Be Used

Three categories of cases are distinguished in Code D:

3.1.1 Cases where the Suspect's Identity is not Known

'In cases when the suspect's identity is not known, a witness may be taken to a particular neighbourhood or place to see whether they can identify the person they saw.'[52] The suspect may 'be shown photographs, computerised or artist's composite likenesses or similar likenesses or pictures (including "E-fit" images)', but this must be done in accordance with Annex E.[53]

3.1.2 Cases where the Suspect is Known and Available

A suspect is 'known' if 'there is sufficient information known to the police to justify the arrest of a particular person for suspected involvement in the offence'. The suspect is

---

[49] *R v John* [1973] Crim LR 113. A more permissive approach prevails in Scotland: *Holland v Her Majesty's Advocate* [2005] UKPC D1. See generally P Tain, 'In the Dock' (2005) 149 *Solicitors' Journal* 739.

[50] *Barnes v Chief Constable of Durham* [1997] 2 Cr App R 505, 512.

[51] *Karia v DPP* [2002] EWHC 2175 (Admin), (2002) 166 JP 753, [40].

[52] Para 3.2. See generally D Wolchover, 'Ending the Farce of Staged Street Identifications', *Archbold News*, 3 Apr 2004, 5.   [53] Para 3.3.

'available' if he or she is immediately available to, or will within a reasonably short time be available to, and is willing to, take an effective part in at least one of the following three identification procedures which it is practicable to arrange: video identification; identification parade; group identification.[54]

Where 'the suspect disputes being the person the witness claims to have seen, an identification procedure shall be held unless it is not practicable or it would serve no useful purpose in proving or disproving whether the suspect was involved in committing the offence. For example, when it is not disputed that the suspect is already well known to the witness who claims to have seen them commit the crime.'[55] If an identification procedure is to be held, the suspect is to be initially offered a video identification unless:[56]

- 'a video identification is not practicable' (for example, 'because of factors relating to the witnesses, such as their number, state of health, availability and travelling requirements') or
- 'an identification parade is both practicable and more suitable than a video identification' or
- 'the officer in charge of the investigation considers [a group identification] more suitable than a video identification or an identification parade and the identification officer considers it practicable to arrange'.[57] In this event a group identification may initially be offered.

A video identification involves the witness being 'shown moving images of a known suspect, together with similar images of others who resemble the suspect'.[58] 'Video identifications must be carried out in accordance with *Annex A*.'[59]

An identification parade takes place 'when the witness sees the suspect in a line of others who resemble the suspect'.[60] 'Identification parades must be carried out in accordance with *Annex B*.'[61]

A group identification takes place 'when the witness sees the suspect in an informal group of people'.[62] 'Group identifications must be carried out in accordance with *Annex C*.'[63]

3.1.3 Cases where the Suspect is Known but Not Available

Where a known suspect is not available, 'the identification officer may make arrangements for a video identification . . . If necessary, the identification officer may follow the video identification procedures but using **still** images. Any suitable moving or still images may be used and these may be obtained covertly if necessary. Alternatively, the identification officer may make arrangements for a group identification.'[64] If a video

---

[54] Para 3.4.

[55] Para 3.12. See also P Bogan, '*Forbes* Alive and Well', *Archbold News*, 3 Nov 2003, 5; A Roberts, 'Questions of "Who Was There?" and "Who Did That?": The Application of Code D in Cases of Dispute as to Participation but Not Presence' [2003] *Criminal Law Review* 709; D Wolchover, 'Farewell to *Forbes*', *Archbold News*, 5 Aug 2003, 4. [56] Para 3.14.

[57] Para 3.16. [58] Para 3.5. [59] Para 3.6 (italics in original). [60] Para 3.7.

[61] Para 3.8 (italics in original). [62] Para 3.9. [63] Para 3.10 (italics in original).

[64] Para 3.21 (emphasis in original).

identification, an identification parade, and a group identification are all not practicable, the identification officer may arrange for the suspect to be directly confronted by the witness. 'A confrontation does not require the suspect's consent. Confrontations must be carried out in accordance with Annex D.'[65]

3.2 Exclusion for Breaches of Code D

Code D seeks, then, to provide for the detailed regulation of identification procedures for two main purposes: to optimize the reliability of identification evidence and to enforce procedural rights for the suspect. Reliability is protected by a number of rules preventing contamination—for instance, witnesses should not be shown photographs of the suspect prior to the procedure, investigating officers cannot be present, and witnesses may not view parades or videos in the company of other witnesses. The suspect is granted rights to have his or her legal representative present, to object to other members of a parade or video line-up, and to pick his or her own place in any line-up.

Like breaches of Code C in the context of confession evidence, breaches of Code D may constitute one factor for consideration in determining whether identification evidence should be excluded in the exercise of discretion under section 78(1). As the Court of Appeal has put it:

> At a trial, the trial judge has to consider any question of compliance with the Code in deciding the question of fairness under section 78. But it is not a simple relationship between a question of compliance and the question of fairness. Even where the Code has been complied with, a proper exercise of the discretion under section 78, or the related inherent discretion that the judge has in relation to prejudicial or inherently unreliable evidence, may require the judge to rule that the evidence should not be admitted. Compliance with the Code is a factor but it is not the only factor, nor is it a decisive factor. Similarly non-compliance with the Code is not decisive. It is again only a factor, maybe a cogent factor, in the decision to admit or exclude evidence.[66]

The reliability of the identification evidence in question is obviously an important consideration. 'The overall purpose [of Code D] is one of adopting fair identification practices and adducing reliable identification evidence. Where insufficient regard is had to these purposes the discretion to exclude evidence under section 78 is likely to be exercised . . .'.[67] Thus, in one case, the fact that a street identification was used in preference to the 'much better form of procedure' of an identification parade weighed in favour of exclusion.[68] On the other hand, exclusion was not considered by the Court of Appeal to have been required in a case where 'there were a number of other sources

---

[65] Para 3.23.

[66] *R v Popat* [1998] 2 Cr App R 208, 212–13. See also *R v Kelly* (1998) 162 JP 231 (decision of 1998); *R v El-Hannachi* [1998] 2 Cr App R 226, 232.   [67] *R v Popat* [1998] 2 Cr App R 208, 224.

[68] *R v Nagah* (1991) 92 Cr App R 344 (decision of 1990).

of evidence which went to confirm, in greater or lesser degree, the identification of the appellant as the offender'.[69]

It would appear, however, that bad faith on the part of the police is also a relevant factor to be considered. In *R v Nagah* the police deliberately engineered matters so that the defendant, despite having agreed to appear on an identification parade, was released from the police station in order that the complainant could identify him in the street. The Court of Appeal considered exclusion to be justified in these circumstances. 'It would drive a coach and horses through [the provisions in Code D] if all the police had to do was to say: "Well we are now going to release you and then you can be made the subject of a street identification outside the police station." '[70] On the other hand, a good-faith breach by Trading Standards officers who did not appreciate that the Code applied to their activities was tolerated in *R v Tiplady*.[71]

It would seem that, even if breaches of Code D may not justify the exclusion of identification evidence in the circumstances of a particular case, they may require appropriate warnings to be given to the jury. The House of Lords has authoritatively held:

> In any case where a breach of Code D has been established but the trial judge has rejected an application to exclude evidence to which the defence objected because of that breach, the trial judge should in the course of summing up to the jury (a) explain that there has been a breach of the Code and how it has arisen, and (b) invite the jury to consider the possible effect of that breach. . . . The terms of the appropriate direction will vary from case to case and breach to breach. But if the breach is a failure to hold an identification parade when required . . . , the jury should ordinarily be told that an identification parade enables a suspect to put the reliability of an eye-witness's identification to the test, that the suspect has lost the benefit of that safeguard and that the jury should take account of that fact in its assessment of the whole case, giving it such weight as it thinks fair.[72]

For example, in *R v Quinn*,[73] the Court of Appeal held that, although the trial judge had been entitled to admit the evidence, he ought, in view of the centrality of that evidence and the criticisms which had properly been made about the breaches, to have made a specific reference to the breaches and left it to the jury to consider what their approach should be in the light of the breaches.[74] Conversely, the fact that such a direction was given by the trial judge has been used by the Court of Appeal as a reason for not allowing an appeal against conviction.[75]

---

[69] *R v Tiplady* (1995) 159 JP 548, 554 (decision of 1995). See also *R v McEvoy* [1997] Crim LR 887; *D v DPP*, *The Times*, 7 Aug 1998 (a witness informally identified suspects by reference to clothing and approximate ages; the suspect requested but was not given an opportunity to participate in an identification parade, in breach of the previous version of para 2.3 of Code D; held that exclusion of the evidence of informal identification under s 78 had not been required because the breach was not of such substance, having regard to the nature and quality of the identification evidence, for the court to conclude that by the admission of the evidence any unjust prejudice had been caused to the defendant).   [70] (1991) 92 Cr App R 344, 348 (decision of 1990).

[71] (1995) 159 JP 548 (decision of 1995).   [72] *R v Forbes* [2001] 1 AC 473, [27].

[73] [1995] 1 Cr App R 480.

[74] See also *R v Macmath* [1997] Crim LR 586; *R v Wait* [1998] Crim LR 68; *R v Popat* [1998] 2 Cr App R 208; *R v El-Hannachi* [1998] 2 Cr App R 226; *R v Bell* [1998] Crim LR 879.

[75] Eg, *R v Khan* [1997] Crim LR 584; *R v McEvoy* [1997] Crim LR 887; *R v Kelly* (1998) 162 JP 231 (decision of 1998).

The decision of the House of Lords in *R v Forbes*[76] provides a good illustration of the application of the above principles. At issue was the failure to hold an identification parade, in breach of paragraph 2.3 of the previous version of Code D. The question was whether evidence of the street identification of the defendant could be admitted. The House of Lords confirmed that the breach of Code D did not require the exclusion of the evidence under section 78, agreeing with the conclusion of the Court of Appeal that:

> The evidence was compelling and untainted, and was supported by the evidence (which it was open to the jury to accept) of what the appellant had said at the scene. It did not suffer from such problems or weaknesses as sometimes attend evidence of this kind: as, for example, where the suspect is already visibly in the hands of the police at the moment he is identified to them by the complainant.[77]

The House of Lords accepted that there had been a failure to give an appropriate direction to the jury on the breach and its consequences, but upheld the conviction on the basis that a reasonable jury, properly directed, would have reached the same conclusion.[78]

Clearly, the relationship between exclusion and warnings in the context of Code D violations now requires to be properly clarified. Otherwise, there is a danger that warnings will come to be regarded as an adequate judicial response to such violations even in those cases where nothing less than outright exclusion is warranted. One commentator has succinctly observed that:

> the jury might be considered a less dependable means of safeguarding the fairness of the proceedings, being ill-equipped . . . to take an informed and objective view of the sort of breach which should not be tolerated. Furthermore, their findings on the matter are never explicitly stated, and so provide no guidance for the future either to legal practitioners or to senior police officers who seek to set appropriate standards within the police force.[79]

Perhaps the way forward would be to move away from the present approach of relying solely on discretionary exclusion and discretionary warnings as a response to violations of Code D. In particular, consideration could be given to adoption of an approach analogous to that taken in relation to confession evidence in section 76 of the Police and Criminal Evidence Act 1984. Thus, it may be possible to identify procedures in Code D which are of such fundamental importance that it should be provided in a statute that non-compliance with these procedures *must* lead automatically to the exclusion of any resulting identification evidence. The present approach of relying upon discretionary exclusion and discretionary warnings (with, perhaps, a clearer indication from the courts of the precise relationship between these measures) could continue in relation to other breaches of Code D. Adoption of such an approach would at least ensure that the

---

[76] [2001] 1 AC 473. See generally D O'Brien, 'When is an Identification Parade Mandatory?: *R v Forbes*' (2001) 5 *International Journal of Evidence and Proof* 127.

[77] [2001] 1 AC 473, [26], quoting [1999] 2 Cr App R 501, 517.   [78] [2001] 1 AC 473, [28].

[79] Commentary by D J Birch on *R v Khan* [1997] Crim LR 584, 586.

response to violations of Code D is somewhat less dependent upon the vagaries of judicial discretion than is the case at present.[80]

4 Photographs and Video Recordings

It is accepted practice for incriminating photographs or video recordings of the offender to be shown to the jury, and for the jury effectively to be asked whether it can 'identify' the defendant as the offender from the photograph or recording.[81] But research has shown that identification of persons from video recordings (even good-quality recordings) may be less reliable than it is thought to be.[82] What, then, has been the response of the law of evidence? In the context of a discussion of photographs, the Court of Appeal in *R v Dodson* held that:

it is ... imperative that a jury is warned by a judge in summing up of the perils of deciding whether by this means alone or with some form of supporting evidence a defendant has committed the crime alleged. According to the quality of photographs, change of appearance in a defendant and other considerations which may arise in a trial, the jury's task may be rendered difficult or simple in bringing about a decision either in favour of or against a defendant. So long as the jury having been brought face to face with these perils are firmly directed that to convict they must be sure that the man in the dock is the man in the photograph, we envisage no injustice arising from this manner of evaluating evidence with the aid of what the jurors' eyes tell them is a fact which they are sure exists.

What are the perils which the jury should be told to beware of? ... We do not think the provision by us of a formula or series of guidelines upon which a direction by a judge upon this matter should always be based would be helpful. ... What is of the utmost importance ... , it seems to us, is that the quality of the photographs, the extent of the exposure of the facial features of the person photographed, evidence, or the absence of it, of a change in a defendant's appearance and the opportunity a jury has to look at a defendant in the dock and over what period of time are factors, among other matters of relevance in this context in a particular case, which the jury must receive guidance upon from the judge when he directs them as to how they should approach the task of resolving this crucial issue.[83]

In the subsequent case of *R v Blenkinsop*, however, the Court explained that, while 'there is ... a general and invariable requirement that the jury shall be warned of the risk of mistaken identification, and of the need to exercise particular care in any identification which they make for themselves', what is required is not a full *Turnbull* warning. 'The process of identifying a person from a photographic image is a

---

[80] See also A Roberts, 'The Problem of Mistaken Identification: Some Observations on Process' (2004) 8 *International Journal of Evidence and Proof* 100.

[81] See generally D W Elliott, 'Video Tape Evidence: The Risk of Over-Persuasion' [1998] *Criminal Law Review* 159.

[82] J Laurance, 'Security Cameras "Distorting Justice"', *The Independent*, 27 March 1998, 10; K Worsley, 'Close-Circuit Cameras Short-Circuit Justice', *The Times Higher Education Supplement*, 27 March 1998, 23.

[83] [1984] 1 WLR 971, 979.

commonplace and everyday event—. . . it is done on innumerable social and domestic occasions.'[84] Thus:

> one factor which the jury must take into account is the question whether the appearance of the defendant has changed, or not, since the visual recording was made, and in general terms this is something which should be brought to their attention. In other respects, the *Turnbull* direction is inappropriate or unnecessary; for example, the jury does not need to be told that the photograph is of good quality or poor; nor whether the person alleged to have been the defendant is shown in close-up or was distant from the camera, or was alone or part of a crowd. Some things are obvious from the photograph itself, and *Dodson and Williams* laid down guidelines which do not have to be applied rigidly in every case . . .[85]

The Court of Appeal has held that a non-testifying defendant cannot be required to stand up and turn around so that the jury can have a better view of him or her.[86] It would seem, however, that there is no objection in principle to the admissibility of evidence aimed at interpreting what the jury can see on a film, or purporting to identify actors on the film. Thus it was held in *R v Clare* that evidence of a police constable could be adduced in order to help the jury to pick out significant events from a very chaotic video recording of a large-scale disturbance outside a football ground. The constable in question was an 'expert *ad hoc*' in the sense that he had special knowledge which the court did not possess. This knowledge had been acquired by lengthy and studious examination of the recording, which was itself admissible as evidence. The Court noted that:

> to afford the jury the time and facilities to conduct the same research would be utterly impracticable. Accordingly, it was in our judgment legitimate to allow the officer to assist the jury by pointing to what he asserted was happening in the crowded scenes on the film. He was open to cross-examination, and the jury, after proper direction and warnings, were free either to accept or reject his assertions.
>
> . . .
>
> If admitting evidence of this kind seems unfamiliar and an extension of established evidential practice, the answer must be that as technology develops, evidential practice will need to be evolved to accommodate it. Whilst the Courts must be vigilant to ensure that no unfairness results, they should not block steps which enable the jury to gain full assistance from the technology.[87]

A video recording played in court may be the original or an authentic copy.[88] Where, however, a copy of the recording is no longer available, a person who viewed the recording may give evidence of what he or she saw on the recording. If the identification of the defendant depends wholly on this evidence, then a *Turnbull* warning would be required.[89]

---

[84] [1995] 1 Cr App R 7, 12.   [85] Ibid, 11. See also *R v Downey* [1995] 1 Cr App R 547.

[86] *R v McNamara* [1996] Crim LR 750.   [87] [1995] 2 Cr App R 333, 338–9.

[88] *Kajala v Noble* (1982) 75 Cr App R 149 (decision of 1982).

[89] *Taylor v Chief Constable of Cheshire* [1986] 1 WLR 1479.

Summarizing the legal position on photographic images, the Court of Appeal held in *A-G's Reference (No 2 of 2002)* that:

> there are ... at least four circumstances in which, subject to the judicial discretion to exclude, evidence is admissible to show and, subject to appropriate directions in the summing-up, a jury can be invited to conclude that the defendant committed the offence on the basis of a photographic image from the scene of the crime:
>
> (i) where the photographic image is sufficiently clear, the jury can compare it with the defendant sitting in the dock ... ;
>
> (ii) where a witness knows the defendant sufficiently well to recognise him as the offender depicted in the photographic image, he can give evidence of this ... ; and this may be so even if the photographic image is no longer available for the jury ... ;
>
> (iii) where a witness who does not know the defendant spends substantial time viewing and analysing photographic images from the scene, thereby acquiring special knowledge which the jury does not have, he can give evidence of identification based on a comparison between those images and a reasonably contemporary photograph of the defendant, provided that the images and the photograph are available to the jury ... ;
>
> (iv) a suitably qualified expert with facial mapping skills can give opinion evidence of identification based on a comparison between images from the scene, (whether expertly enhanced or not) and a reasonably contemporary photograph of the defendant, provided the images and the photograph are available for the jury ...[90]

In recent times the use of video surveillance cameras in public places has become commonplace. In *R v Roberts* the Court of Appeal, referring to the increased availability and use in criminal trials of video recordings of the alleged commission of offences, considered whether a video recording which comes to light after an eyewitness to the incident has already given a statement to the police may be shown to that eyewitness. The Court provided the following guidance on the issue:

> Viewing the matter quite generally, it seems to us plain that the duty of any witness when giving a statement is to describe the relevant events to the best of his or her honest recollection and certainly not to invent or fabricate evidence to assist the prosecution or the defence. If, after the giving of such a statement, a relevant video comes to light, it is not in our judgment wrong in principle that the witness should be permitted to see that video. On seeing it the witness may find that in some respects his or her recollection had been at fault, and the witness may wish to correct or modify earlier evidence. It is however, in our view, a matter of the utmost importance that nothing should be done which amounts to rehearsing the evidence of a witness, or coaching the witness so as to encourage the witness to alter the evidence originally given. The acid test is whether the procedure adopted in any particular case is such as to taint the resulting evidence. It is, we would stress, necessary to preserve equality of arms so that facilities are not made available to the prosecution which are not made available to the defence. On the prosecution side we see no

---

[90] [2002] EWCA Crim 2373, [2003] 1 Cr App R 21 (p 321), [19].

reason to distinguish between police and non-police witnesses. They should be treated the same.

The Court was also of the view that 'the growing use of video evidence merits detailed consideration of such evidence by the appropriate authorities with a view, after necessary consultation, to devising a code of good practice'.[91]

[91] (1998) 162 JP 691, 694 (decision of 1998).

5

Investigatory Impropriety: Violations of Article 8 and Undercover Police Operations

This chapter examines two further examples of the interplay between the principles of evidence and pre-trial practices and procedures. The first part of the chapter considers the evidential consequences of pre-trial violations of Article 8 of the European Convention on Human Rights, and the second part the implications of the use of undercover police operations.

1 Violations of Article 8 and the Exclusion of Evidence

One of the most unsettled (perhaps deliberately unsettled) issues in the law of evidence is the extent to which evidence obtained in violation of Article 8 of the European Convention on Human Rights may be used in court. Article 8, which essentially guarantees the right to privacy, provides as follows:

> 1. Everyone has the right to respect for his private and family life, his home and his correspondence.

> 2. There shall be no interference by a public authority with the exercise of this right except such as is in accordance with the law and is necessary in a democratic society in the interests of national security, public safety or the economic well-being of the country, for the prevention of disorder or crime, for the protection of health or morals, or for the protection of the rights and freedoms of others.

Consideration of the evidential consequences of Article 8 violations brings into sharp focus the possible rationales for the exclusion of improperly obtained evidence.[1]

---

[1] For general discussions of improperly obtained evidence see J Allan, 'To Exclude or Not to Exclude Improperly Obtained Evidence: Is a Humean Approach More Helpful?' (1999) 18 *University of Tasmania Law Review* 263; C J W Allen, 'Discretion and Security: Excluding Evidence Under Section 78(1) of the Police and Criminal Evidence Act 1984' [1990] *Cambridge Law Journal* 80; A J Ashworth, 'Excluding Evidence As Protecting Rights' [1977] *Criminal Law Review* 723; T Carmody, 'Recent and Proposed Statutory Reforms to the Common Law Exclusionary Discretions' (1997) 71 *Australian Law Journal* 119; A L-T Choo, 'Halting Criminal Prosecutions: The Abuse of Process Doctrine Revisited' [1995] *Criminal Law Review* 864; A L-T Choo and S Nash, 'What's the Matter with

Academic commentators have identified a number of principles capable of explaining why it may be appropriate for an item of improperly obtained prosecution evidence to be excluded.[2] The more important of these are as follows. First, there is the *reliability principle*: an item of improperly obtained evidence may be excluded because of its questionable reliability. Secondly, there is the *protective principle*: an accused person should be protected from the consequences of the infringement of his or her rights by being put in the position in which he or she would have been had the infringement not occurred; this can be achieved by excluding evidence obtained as a result of the infringement. Thirdly, the *disciplinary principle* sees exclusion as a means of deterring the police from future improprieties by depriving them of the fruits of the transgression in question. Finally, the *integrity principle*[3] sees exclusion as a means of repudiating the impropriety and thus preserving the purity of the court and of the criminal justice process generally. The court, whose duty is to apply and uphold the law, must dissociate itself from the illegality or impropriety rather than effectively to become complicit in the executive's attempts to profit from it. A secondary concern of this principle may well be with the desire to be seen by the public to be upholding values. More will be said about these principles later in the chapter.

Reference has already been made in previous chapters to section 78(1) of the Police and Criminal Evidence Act 1984, a notorious provision which 'is by now known almost by heart by most people who have anything to do with the law'[4] and which is by far the most cited provision of the Act.[5] Section 78(1) states:

> In any proceedings the court may refuse to allow evidence on which the prosecution proposes to rely to be given if it appears to the court that, having regard to all the circumstances, *including the circumstances in which the evidence was obtained*, the admission of the evidence

Section 78?' [1999] *Criminal Law Review* 929; G L Davies, 'Exclusion of Evidence Illegally or Improperly Obtained' (2002) 76 *Australian Law Journal* 170; I H Dennis, 'Reconstructing the Law of Criminal Evidence' (1989) 42 *Current Legal Problems* 21; B Fitzpatrick and N Taylor, 'Human Rights and the Discretionary Exclusion of Evidence' (2001) 65 *Journal of Criminal Law* 349; M A Gelowitz, 'Section 78 of the Police and Criminal Evidence Act 1984: Middle Ground or No Man's Land?' (1990) 106 *Law Quarterly Review* 327; K Grevling, 'Fairness and the Exclusion of Evidence Under Section 78(1) of the Police and Criminal Evidence Act' (1997) 113 *Law Quarterly Review* 667; D Ormerod, 'ECHR and the Exclusion of Evidence: Trial Remedies for Article 8 Breaches' [2003] *Criminal Law Review* 61; D Ormerod and D Birch, 'The Evolution of the Discretionary Exclusion of Evidence' [2004] *Criminal Law Review* 767; D M Paciocco, 'The Judicial Repeal of S 24(2) and the Development of the Canadian Exclusionary Rule' (1990) 32 *Criminal Law Quarterly* 326; A Samuels, 'Illegally Obtained Evidence: In or Out?' (2003) 67 *Journal of Criminal Law* 411; R Stone, 'Exclusion of Evidence Under Section 78 of the Police and Criminal Evidence Act: Practice and Principles' in M J Allen (ed), *Web Journal of Current Legal Issues Yearbook 1995* (1996); A Ashworth and M Redmayne, *The Criminal Process* (3rd ed 2005) 11.3; A L-T Choo, *Abuse of Process and Judicial Stays of Criminal Proceedings* (1993); P Mirfield, *Silence, Confessions and Improperly Obtained Evidence* (1997); P Roberts and A Zuckerman, *Criminal Evidence* (2004) Ch 4; S Sharpe, *Judicial Discretion and Criminal Investigation* (1998); S Sharpe, *Search and Surveillance: The Movement from Evidence to Information* (2000) Ch 6.

[2]   See especially A Ashworth and M Redmayne, *The Criminal Process* (3rd ed 2005) 316 ff; P Mirfield, *Silence, Confessions and Improperly Obtained Evidence* (1997) Ch 2.

[3]   See generally A Ashworth, 'Exploring the Integrity Principle in Evidence and Procedure' in P Mirfield and R Smith (eds), *Essays for Colin Tapper* (2003).   [4]   *Hudson v DPP* [1992] RTR 27, 34 per Hodgson J.

[5]   K Grevling, 'Fairness and the Exclusion of Evidence Under Section 78(1) of the Police and Criminal Evidence Act' (1997) 113 *Law Quarterly Review* 667, 667.

would have such an adverse effect on the fairness of the proceedings that the court ought not to admit it.[6]

Yet the extent to which the senior judiciary in England is willing to sanction the use of section 78(1) to secure the exclusion of improperly obtained *but reliable* evidence remains unclear, even after the introduction of the Human Rights Act 1998.

1.1 The Position prior to the Human Rights Act 1998[7]

Prior to the Police and Criminal Evidence Act 1984, the common law position—at least as it appeared from the decision of the House of Lords in *R v Sang*[8]—was effectively that improperly obtained evidence could be excluded only in the exercise of the court's discretion to ensure a 'fair trial', and in the exercise of this discretion such evidence could be excluded only if the impropriety affected the reliability of the evidence or constituted an infringement of the accused's right against self-incrimination. Evidence could not be regarded as having been obtained in violation of the accused's right against self-incrimination unless it had been obtained *from the accused after the offence*. The extent to which section 78(1) of the 1984 Act would affect the common law was initially a matter of speculation. The ordinary principles of statutory interpretation, requiring as they do a consideration of the plain meaning of the words of the provision, would seem to have permitted courts to develop a fresh approach unencumbered by the common law: the reference to 'the circumstances in which the evidence was obtained' is a general one which does not in any way imply that courts are restricted to a consideration of circumstances which cast doubt on the reliability of the evidence obtained, or circumstances involving the obtaining of evidence from the accused after the offence.

Certainly, as discussed in Chapter 2, a number of landmark cases on confession evidence in the late 1980s saw the Court of Appeal making strong statements about the utility of section 78(1) in addressing the issue of breaches of the rules of police investigation. Although exclusion under section 78(1) must not be used directly to discipline the police,[9] 'significant and substantial' breaches would be taken seriously in the sense that they would weigh heavily in favour of the exclusion of evidence obtained as a result of the breaches.[10] Also evident from the cases is the notion that a breach may, by its very nature, be significant and substantial—in other words, it will be significant and substantial even if the police acted in good faith—but that bad faith can effectively convert a breach which is not otherwise significant and substantial into one which is.[11]

The cases provide instances of strongly worded judicial condemnations of improper police practices. In *R v Mason* the Court of Appeal, in holding that the confession

---

[6] Italics added.

[7] I have drawn heavily in this section on A L-T Choo and S Nash, 'What's the Matter with Section 78?' [1999] *Criminal Law Review* 929.   [8] [1980] AC 402.

[9] *R v Mason* [1988] 1 WLR 139; *R v Delaney* (1989) 88 Cr App R 338 (decision of 1988).

[10] See, eg, *R v Keenan* [1990] 2 QB 54.

[11] See, eg, *R v Walsh* (1990) 91 Cr App R 161 (decision of 1989).

evidence ought to have been excluded under section 78(1), observed: 'It is obvious from the undisputed evidence that the police practised a deceit not only upon the appellant, which is bad enough, but also upon the solicitor whose duty it was to advise him. In effect, they hoodwinked both solicitor and client. That was a most reprehensible thing to do.'[12] In *R v Samuel* the Court stated: 'In this case the appellant was denied improperly one of the most important and fundamental rights of a citizen.'[13] In *R v Dunn* the Court 'stress[ed] yet again the importance of the police complying strictly with the Codes of Practice. There were serious breaches in this case.'[14] Again, the breaches in *R v Canale* were described by the Court as 'flagrant', 'deliberate', and 'cynical';[15] the police conduct 'demonstrate[d] a lamentable attitude towards the 1984 Act and the codes made thereunder. ... If, which we find it hard to believe, police officers still do not appreciate the importance of that Act and the accompanying Codes, then it is time that they did.'[16]

Unsurprisingly, the confessions cases gave rise to the expectation that section 78(1) would also prove a useful vehicle for securing the exclusion of improperly obtained real evidence. Certainly, initial indications were that this might well be the view taken by the courts. In the early 1990s, decisions of the Divisional Court in road traffic prosecutions appeared to advocate an approach in relation to evidence of breath specimens which was analogous to that taken in relation to confession evidence.[17] Thus an impropriety could be considered 'significant and substantial', and hence strong grounds for exclusion under section 78(1), in the absence of bad faith on the part of the police, and simply because it constituted a breach of an important right of the accused. In one case, for example, the Court declined, despite the absence of bad faith, to interfere with the justices' decision to exclude evidence of a positive breath specimen provided after an unlawful arrest:

> The justices were entitled to conclude that the substantial breach by the constable [meant that] the protection afforded to members of the public by section 6 [of the Road Traffic Act 1988] was denied to the defendant, that as a result the prosecutor obtained evidence which he would not otherwise have obtained, and that as a result the defendant was prejudiced in a significant manner in resisting the charge against him.[18]

Finally, the 1990s saw a marked expansion of the doctrine of abuse of process.[19] The House of Lords confirmed in *R v Horseferry Road Magistrates' Court, ex p Bennett*[20] that criminal proceedings could be stayed as an abuse of process on account of improper police or prosecutorial conduct at the pre-trial stage.[21] Thus, a stay would be appropriate if it was shown that a defendant had been forcibly abducted and brought to the

---

[12] [1988] 1 WLR 139, 144.   [13] [1988] QB 615, 630.
[14] (1990) 91 Cr App R 237, 243 (decision of 1990).   [15] [1990] 2 All ER 187, 192.   [16] Ibid, 190.
[17] *DPP v McGladrigan* [1991] RTR 297; *DPP v Godwin* [1991] RTR 303. See also *DPP v Kay* [1999] RTR 109.
[18] *DPP v Godwin* [1991] RTR 303, 308.
[19] See generally A L-T Choo, 'Halting Criminal Prosecutions: The Abuse of Process Doctrine Revisited' [1995] *Criminal Law Review* 864.   [20] [1994] 1 AC 42.
[21] For further discussion see C Gane and S Nash, 'Illegal Extradition: The Irregular Return of Fugitive Offenders' (1996) 1 *Scottish Law and Practice Quarterly* 277.

United Kingdom to face trial in disregard of the extradition laws.[22] The doctrine was refined by the House of Lords in *R v Latif; R v Shahzad*.[23]

The willingness of the House of Lords to breathe life into the abuse of process doctrine may be viewed as an expression of its recognition that it is now completely outdated to regard judicial responsibility as being confined to ensuring the non-conviction of an innocent person. There are, as the House put it simply in *Latif; Shahzad*, 'broader considerations of the integrity of the criminal justice system'.[24] Considerations of extrinsic policy are as much a concern as considerations of intrinsic policy. Even if there is no danger of the conviction of an innocent person, a court has the duty to act if failure to do so would compromise the legitimacy of the adjudicative process and the moral authority of a guilty verdict if such a verdict were to ensue.[25] It would therefore be anomalous if a court were to be permitted to act by staying 'tainted' proceedings (a fairly drastic measure), but were not to be permitted to act by simply excluding an item of 'tainted' evidence (a potentially less drastic measure[26]).

Some decisions of the Court of Appeal on improperly obtained evidence in the mid- and late 1990s appear, however, to have signalled a move away from the approach, taken in the confessions cases referred to above, of focusing on the *nature of the breach*, and towards an approach which takes the *nature of the evidence* as its central consideration. The fact that non-confession evidence is often of undoubted reliability was considered a strong factor in favour of not exercising the exclusionary discretion. At issue in *R v Cooke*,[27] a prosecution for rape and kidnapping, was evidence of a DNA profile obtained from hair roots and sheaths plucked from the accused's head. The Court of Appeal held that this evidence had not been obtained illegally,[28] but even assuming that it had been, the trial judge had not erred in declining to exclude the evidence under section 78(1). The Court noted[29] that 'the vast majority of cases in which the court has ruled such evidence inadmissible have been cases in which what was challenged was an alleged confession obtained from the defendant in breach of one of the Police and Criminal Evidence Act Codes of Practice'. In this case the DNA profile constituted very strong evidence that Cooke had had sexual intercourse with the complainant. Any illegality involved in the way in which the evidence was obtained would not have 'in any

---

[22] See also *R v Mullen* [1999] 2 Cr App R 143, discussed below. Cf *R v Staines Magistrates' Court, ex p Westfallen* [1998] 4 All ER 210; see generally S O'Doherty, 'Home Thoughts from Abroad' (1998) 148 *New Law Journal* 1802. The position in Scotland is discussed in P Arnell, '*Male Captus Bene Detentus* in Scotland' [2004] *Juridical Review* 251.

[23] [1996] 1 WLR 104. See generally A Ashworth, 'Should the Police Be Allowed to Use Deceptive Practices?' (1998) 114 *Law Quarterly Review* 108, 119–20; K Grevling, 'Undercover Operations: Balancing the Public Interest?' (1996) 112 *Law Quarterly Review* 401; S Sharpe, 'Judicial Discretion and Investigative Impropriety' (1997) 1(2) *International Journal of Evidence and Proof* 149.   [24] [1996] 1 WLR 104, 112.

[25] See generally I H Dennis, *The Law of Evidence* (2nd ed 2002) 41–9.

[26] Of course, if the evidence were the only prosecution evidence, or perhaps a crucial part of the prosecution evidence, then its exclusion would be tantamount to a complete stay of the proceedings.

[27] [1995] 1 Cr App R 318.

[28] Hair plucked from the scalp constituted a non-intimate sample under s 65 of the Police and Criminal Evidence Act 1984, and could therefore be taken without consent under s 63(3).

[29] [1995] 1 Cr App R 318, 328.

way cast doubt upon the accuracy or strength of the evidence. In this way evidence of this kind differs from, for example, a disputed confession, where the truth of the confession may well itself be in issue.'

In *R v Chalkley*,[30] Chalkley and Jeffries were charged with conspiracy to commit robbery. The prosecution proposed to adduce evidence of covertly obtained tape recordings of highly incriminating conversations between the defendants. The Regional Crime Squad had obtained the necessary authorization, under the Home Office guidelines, to place a listening device in Chalkley's home.[31] In order to instal the device, they arrested Chalkley in connection with crimes about which no action had previously been taken, seized his house key, and used it to enter the house. They also arranged the cutting of a copy of the key, which was later used on two occasions to enter the house to renew the battery on the device. The Court of Appeal held that the arrest of Chalkley had not been unlawful,[32] but that even if it had been, the trial judge's decision not to exclude the evidence under section 78(1) should stand. The Court suggested, in effect, that the discretion to exclude evidence on the ground that it had been obtained improperly was applicable only in relation to:

- evidence of a confession obtained from the accused; and
- other evidence obtained *from the accused* after the commission of the offence; and
- evidence obtained in an undercover police operation; and
- evidence the quality of which had been, or might have been, affected by the way in which it had been obtained.

As for the evidence in this case:

> there was no dispute as to its authenticity, content or effect; it was relevant, highly probative of the appellants' involvement in the conspiracy and otherwise admissible; it did not result from incitement, entrapment or inducement or any other conduct of that sort; and none of the unlawful conduct of the police or other of their conduct of which complaint is made affects the quality of the evidence.[33]

The Court referred to the decisions of the House of Lords in *Ex p Bennett* and *Latif, Shahzad*, but took the view that section 78(1) could not be used to 'exclude [evidence] as a mark of disapproval of the way in which it had been obtained', since section 78(1) and the abuse of process doctrine did not share the same juridical basis. 'The determination of the fairness or otherwise of admitting evidence under s 78 is distinct from the exercise of discretion in determining whether to stay criminal proceedings as an abuse of process.'[34]

---

[30] [1998] 2 All ER 155.

[31] There were, at the time, no statutory provisions governing the authorization of entry on or interference with property. See now Police Act 1997, Pt III, on which see generally M Colvin, 'Part III Police Act 1997' (1999) 149 *New Law Journal* 311; S Uglow and V Telford, *The Police Act 1997* (1997) Ch 3.

[32] '...a collateral motive for an arrest on otherwise good and stated grounds does not necessarily make it unlawful. It depends on the motive': [1998] 2 All ER 155, 176.   [33] Ibid, 180.

[34] Ibid, 178.

A balancing approach was accordingly not appropriate to a determination of whether improperly obtained evidence should be excluded under section 78(1).

The decision in *Chalkley* was thus potentially far-reaching. It suggested that evidence of the type in *Chalkley*, and real evidence not obtained from the accused, such as evidence obtained as a result of a search, must be admitted if it was reliable; such evidence *could not* be excluded on the ground that it was improperly obtained.[35] Real evidence obtained from the accused, on the other hand, was subject to discretionary exclusion, although *Cooke* suggested that courts generally *would not* exclude such evidence, given its inherent reliability. Such a narrow approach seems contrary to the plain meaning of the words of section 78(1), discussed earlier. That *Chalkley* was not a mere aberration, however, is demonstrated by a subsequent decision where, in approving *Chalkley*, the Court of Appeal held in very clear terms: 'Here the quality of the evidence is simply unaffected by the … illegality and in our judgment the decision under section 78 therefore *had to go in favour of the prosecution*.'[36]

The tendency of the appellate courts immediately prior to the Human Rights Act 1998 was therefore to interpret section 78(1) narrowly, and in effect as being concerned primarily with ensuring accurate fact-finding. The prevailing view appeared to be that improperly obtained evidence should in general be excluded under section 78(1) only if its reliability had been compromised by the manner in which it was obtained.

1.2 Article 6: The Contribution of the European Court of Human Rights[37]

There can be no doubt about the courts' views of the effect of the Human Rights Act 1998 on the law pertaining to the exclusion of improperly obtained evidence. The stance consistently maintained is that compliance with Article 6 of the European Convention will be secured by the appropriate use of section 78(1) of the Police and Criminal Evidence Act 1984. The courts' maintenance of this approach has been assisted in no small measure by the May 2000 decision of the European Court of Human Rights in *Khan v UK*.[38] Having failed in both the Court of Appeal[39] and House of Lords,[40] Khan took his case to Strasbourg. The essential facts were that on being interviewed at a police station after his arrival from Pakistan, Khan denied any offence

---

[35] Cf, however, *R v Stewart* [1995] Crim LR 499 and *R v McCarthy* [1996] Crim LR 818, in which the Court of Appeal appeared to suggest that evidence obtained as a result of an illegal search *was* subject to discretionary exclusion, although the discretion was unlikely to be exercised because of the inherent reliability of such evidence.

[36] *R v Bray*, unrep, CA, 31 July 1998 (italics added).

[37] I have drawn heavily in this section and in the following one on A L-T Choo and S Nash, 'Evidence Law in England and Wales: The Impact of the Human Rights Act 1998' (2003) 7 *International Journal of Evidence and Proof* 31.

[38] (2001) 31 EHRR 45 (p 1016) (judgment of 2000). See generally S Nash, 'Secretly Recorded Conversations and the European Convention on Human Rights: *Khan v UK*' (2000) 4 *International Journal of Evidence and Proof* 268; P Tain, 'Fair Trial and the ECHR' (2000) 144 *Solicitors' Journal* 590.   [39] [1995] QB 27.

[40] [1997] AC 558.

and declined to answer most of the questions put to him. He was released without charge. Some six months later he visited the home of a person whom the police suspected of involvement in the supply of heroin on a large scale. As a result of these suspicions they had installed an aural surveillance device on the exterior of the property, without the knowledge or consent of the owner or occupier of the property. A tape recording was obtained of a conversation which took place between Khan and others in which Khan made statements plainly demonstrating his involvement in the importation of heroin. The European Court of Human Rights found that Article 8 of the Convention had been violated.[41] On the issue of exclusion the Court commented as follows:

> With specific reference to the admission of the contested tape recording, the Court notes that . . . the applicant had ample opportunity to challenge both the authenticity and the use of the recording. He did not challenge its authenticity, but challenged its use at the 'voire dire' and again before the Court of Appeal and the House of Lords. The Court notes that at each level of jurisdiction the domestic courts assessed the effect of admission of the evidence on the fairness of the trial by reference to section 78 of PACE . . .[42]

> The Court would add that it is clear that, had the domestic courts been of the view that the admission of the evidence would have given rise to substantive unfairness, they would have had a discretion to exclude it under section 78 of PACE.[43]

> In these circumstances, the Court finds that the use at the applicant's trial of the secretly taped material did not conflict with the requirements of fairness guaranteed by Article 6(1) of the Convention.[44]

The fact that the evidence 'was in effect the only evidence against the applicant' was considered irrelevant in the circumstances of the case:

> The relevance of the existence of evidence other than the contested matter depends on the circumstances of the case. In the present circumstances, where the tape recording was acknowledged to be very strong evidence, and where there was no risk of it being unreliable, the need for supporting evidence is correspondingly weaker.[45]

In a strong dissent on the Article 6 issue, Judge Loucaides appeared to advocate the mandatory exclusion of any evidence obtained in breach of a Convention right. He was unable to 'accept that a trial can be "fair", as required by Article 6, if a person's guilt for any offence is established through evidence obtained in breach of the human rights guaranteed by the Convention'. He considered that the United Kingdom courts had an obligation 'not to admit or rely on evidence in judicial proceedings which was obtained contrary to the Convention. This applies *a fortiori* in cases where such evidence is the only evidence against an accused person in a criminal case like the present one.'[46]

---

[41] (2001) 31 EHRR 45 (p 1016), [28] (judgment of 2000).   [42] Ibid, [38].   [43] Ibid, [39].
[44] Ibid, [40].
[45] Ibid, [37]. See also *PG v UK*, Application no 44787/98, 25 Sep 2001; see generally S Nash, 'Balancing Convention Rights: *PG and JH v United Kingdom*' (2002) 6 *International Journal of Evidence and Proof* 125.
[46] The view of Judge Loucaides was endorsed by Judge Tulkens in her dissent on the Article 6 issue in *PG v UK*, Application no 44787/98, 25 Sep 2001.

The later decision of the European Court in *Allan v UK*[47] is especially noteworthy. It brings into sharp focus the respective approaches of the Court to different types of evidence obtained in violation of Article 8. When Allan was in custody with one Leroy Grant on suspicion of having committed a robbery, the police received information that Allan had been involved in a murder. Authority was accordingly granted by the Chief Constable for the cell and visiting areas used by Allan and Grant to be fitted with audio and video equipment. When Allan was subsequently arrested for the murder he exercised his right to remain silent. However, recordings were made of Allan's conversations (1) with a friend, JNS, in the prison visiting area, (2) with Grant in the cell in which they were held, and (3) with H, a police informant who was placed in Allan's cell for the purpose of eliciting information from him. He argued, *inter alia*, that the use of the evidence of these recordings (which, together with the testimony of H, constituted the principal evidence against him) violated Article 6(1).

The European Court was 'not persuaded that the use of the taped material concerning Leroy Grant and JNS at the applicant's trial conflicted with the requirements of fairness guaranteed by Art 6(1) of the Convention':

> ... the applicant's counsel challenged the admissibility of the recordings in a *voire dire*, and was able to put forward arguments to exclude the evidence as unreliable, unfair or obtained in an oppressive manner. The judge in a careful ruling however admitted the evidence, finding that it was of probative value and had not been shown to be so unreliable that it could not be left to the jury to decide for themselves. This decision was reviewed on appeal by the Court of Appeal which found that the judge had taken into account all the relevant factors and that his ruling could not be faulted. At each step of the procedure, the applicant had therefore been given an opportunity to challenge the reliability and significance of the recording evidence.[48]

In relation to the conversations with H, however, there had been a violation of Article 6(1):

> In contrast to the position in the *Khan* case, the admissions allegedly made by the applicant to H, and which formed the main or decisive evidence against him at trial, were not spontaneous and unprompted statements volunteered by the applicant, but were induced by the persistent questioning of H, who, at the instance of the police, channelled their conversations into discussions of the murder in circumstances which can be regarded as the functional equivalent of interrogation, without any of the safeguards which would attach to a formal police interview, including the attendance of a solicitor and the issuing of the usual caution. While it is true that there was no special relationship between the applicant and H and that no factors of direct coercion have been identified, the Court considers that the applicant would have been subject to psychological pressures which impinged on the 'voluntariness' of the disclosures allegedly made by the applicant to H: he was a suspect in a murder case, in detention and under direct pressure from the police in interrogations about the murder, and would have been susceptible to persuasion to take H, with whom he shared a cell for some weeks, into his confidence. In those circumstances, the information gained by the use of H in this way may be regarded as

---

[47] (2002) 36 EHRR 12 (p 143) (judgment of 2002). See generally S Nash, 'Surreptitious Interrogation and Notions of Fairness: *Allan v United Kingdom*' (2003) 7 *International Journal of Evidence and Proof* 137.

[48] (2002) 36 EHRR 12 (p 143), [48] (judgment of 2002).

having been obtained in defiance of the will of the applicant and its use at trial impinged on the applicant's right to silence and privilege against self-incrimination.[49]

It is no surprise that the admission of evidence of undisputed reliability was considered not to violate Article 6, while Article 6 was held to have been violated by the admission of evidence of questionable reliability.

Consistently with its general approach, the European Court declared inadmissible under Article 6(1) the application of Chalkley, whose appeal to the Court of Appeal was discussed in detail earlier. Relying on *Khan v UK*, the European Court held that the proceedings had not been unfair.[50]

1.3 Article 6: The Domestic Jurisprudence

A few illustrations from recent English case law of the courts' approach to the exclusion of improperly obtained evidence in the light of Articles 8 and 6 may now be provided. In a decision on evidence of telephone intercepts, the House of Lords held, referring to *Khan v UK*, that 'the direct operation of articles 8 and 6 does not ... alter the vital role of section 78 as the means by which questions of the use of evidence obtained in breach of article 8 are to be resolved at a criminal trial. The criterion to be applied is the criterion of fairness in article 6 which is likewise the criterion to be applied by the judge under section 78.'[51]

In *R v Sanghera* the search of the defendant's premises had been conducted in breach of paragraph 1.3 of Code B of the Codes of Practice in that his consent to the search had not been obtained. The Court of Appeal held that appropriate consideration of section 78(1) was sufficient to ensure compliance with the Convention. The Court was of the view, however, that the trial judge had exercised his discretion appropriately in not excluding the evidence:

> It is important to note that ... the appellant did not challenge the fact of the discovery of the money. ... There was no issue as to the reliability of the evidence. ... In addition, there is the fact that there is no suggestion that the police were acting other than bona fide. ... The money was in the box above the safe. ... If the judge had acceded to the submissions that were made to him, the result of the failure to obtain formal written consent ... would have had the consequence of interfering with the achievement of justice.[52]

Once again, the commitment to accurate fact-finding is immediately apparent.

In *R v Loveridge*, the Court of Appeal held the secret filming by police of defendants in the cell area of a magistrates' court to be in contravention of section 41 of the Criminal Justice Act 1925 and a breach of Article 8.

> However, so far as the outcome of this appeal is concerned, the breach of Article 8 is only relevant if it interferes with the right of the applicants to a fair hearing. Giving full weight to

---

[49] (2002) 36 EHRR 12 (p 143), [52].

[50] *Chalkley v UK (Admissibility)*, Application no 63831/00, 26 Sep 2002.

[51] *R v P* [2001] 2 WLR 463, 475. See also *A-G's Reference (No 3 of 1999)* [2001] 2 WLR 56 (DNA evidence); *R v Sargent* [2001] UKHL 54, [2001] 3 WLR 992.   [52] [2001] 1 Cr App R 20 (p 299), [15]–[17].

the breach of the Convention, we are satisfied that the contravention of Article 8 did not interfere with the fairness of the hearing. The judge was entitled to rule as he did. The position is the same so far as section 78 of the Police and Criminal Evidence Act 1984 is concerned. We would here refer to the judgment of Swinton Thomas LJ in the case of *Perry* . . .[53]

The remarks of Swinton Thomas LJ in *R v Perry*,[54] a decision on video identification evidence obtained in consequence of breaches of Code D, probably represent the high-water mark of judicial antagonism to the idea that the law on the exclusion of improperly obtained evidence may be altered by the Human Rights Act 1998:

The purpose underlying the [Human Rights] Act is to protect citizens from a true abuse of human rights. If, as it seems to us has happened in this case, it is utilised by lawyers to jump on a bandwagon and to attempt to suggest that there has been a breach of the Act or of the Convention when either it is quite plain that there has not or alternatively the matter is amply covered by domestic law, then not only will the lawyers, but the Act itself (which is capable of doing a great deal of good to the citizens of this country) will be brought into disrepute. . . . In our judgment questions of breaches of the European Convention on Human Rights or the Act should not have formed any part of this appeal. All the submissions which have been made can properly and readily be dealt with under the provisions of our national law. It is devoutly to be hoped that the court's time will not be utilised in the future in this way.[55]

The European Court of Human Rights declared Perry's application inadmissible under Article 6(1), pointing out that he had been given every 'opportunity to challenge the reliability and quality of the identification evidence based on the videotape'. The Court reiterated:

that the use at trial of material obtained without a proper legal basis or through unlawful means will not generally offend the standard of fairness imposed by Article 6 § 1 where proper procedural safeguards are in place and the nature and source of the material is not tainted, for example, by any oppression, coercion or entrapment which would render reliance on it unfair in the determination of a criminal charge . . . The obtaining of such information is rather a matter which calls into play the Contracting State's responsibility under Article 8 to secure the right to respect for private life in due form.[56]

In *R v Mason*,[57] the police, having difficulty in obtaining evidence against those they thought were involved in a number of robberies, obtained permission from the Chief Constable to launch a covert operation. This involved arresting, interviewing, and charging the appellants in respect of different robberies, and detaining them in the custody suite of a police station in which was installed covert audio equipment. The appellants' conversations were tape recorded, and these recordings played a fundamental role in the prosecution case against the appellants. The appellants appealed

---

53 [2001] EWCA Crim 973, [2001] 2 Cr App R 29 (p 591), [33]. See also *R v Lawrence* [2002] Crim LR 584.
54 *The Times*, 28 April 2000.   55 Quotation from transcript from Smith Bernal.
56 *Perry v UK (Admissibility)*, Application no 63737/00, 26 Sep 2002.
57 [2002] EWCA Crim 385, [2002] 2 Cr App R 38 (p 628). See generally D Ormerod, 'Police Cells and Unwanted Bugs' (2003) 67 *Journal of Criminal Law* 37.

against their convictions on the basis, *inter alia*, that the evidence of the recordings ought not to have been admitted in evidence.

The Court of Appeal acknowledged, in familiar fashion, that there had been a breach of Article 8 but that the admission of the resulting evidence did not breach Article 6:

> ...what occurred does infringe Article 8(1). Furthermore it is now clear that the prosecution cannot rely on Article 8(2) to justify what took place because the surveillance was not conducted according to law.... This is because of the lack of any legal structure to which the public have access authorising the infringement. If there had been such authorisation there would have been no breach.[58]

> The fault is not having legislation like RIPA which clearly establishes what is the legal position.[59] It is the responsibility of the Government to provide remedies against this violation of Article 8. However, the remedy does not have to be the exclusion of the evidence. The remedy can be the finding, which we have now made, that there has been a breach of Article 8 or it can be an award of compensation. The European Court of Human Rights recognises that to insist on the exclusion of evidence could in itself result in a greater injustice to the public than the infringement of Article 8 creates for the appellants. The infringement is, however, a matter which the trial judge was required to take into account when exercising his discretion under section 78 of PACE.[60]

> ...everyone charged with a criminal offence is entitled to remain silent and not to incriminate himself but this right is not contravened if a person chooses to volunteer information as to the offences which he has committed. The police did no more than arrange a situation which was likely to result in the appellants volunteering confessions. The appellants were not tricked into saying what they did even though they were placed in a position where they were likely to do so. If evidence of a satisfactory nature could be obtained by other means, it is preferable that it is obtained by those means rather than covertly. Here, it was not unreasonably considered by the Chief Constable that the evidence would not be obtained by more conventional means. In so far as we need to do so, we would here rely upon the judgment of this court in *R v Perry*...[61]

The appellants' attempt to distinguish *Khan v UK* on the basis that the evidence here, unlike that in *Khan*, was not reliable and of very questionable quality was also rejected.[62]

In sum, therefore, the approach taken is that a court's 'powers to regulate the admission of evidence, pursuant inter alia to s 78 and its inherent jurisdiction, represent means of ensuring that Article 6 is not infringed.... unlawfully obtained evidence may be inadmissible but is not *ipso facto* so. Nor is a trial in which it is relied upon necessarily unfair.'[63]

---

[58] [2002] EWCA Crim 385, [2002] 2 Cr App R 38 (p 628), [65].

[59] See now the 'intrusive surveillance' provisions of the Regulation of Investigatory Powers Act 2000, discussed below. Para 5.4 of the Covert Surveillance: Code of Practice places a police cell within the definition of residential premises.   [60] [2002] EWCA Crim 385, [2002] 2 Cr App R 38 (p 628), [67].

[61] Ibid, [69].   [62] Ibid, [70]–[73].

[63] *R v Hardy* [2002] EWCA Crim 3012, [2003] 1 Cr App R 30 (p 494), [18]–[19].

1.4 The Regulation of Investigatory Powers Act 2000

The Regulation of Investigatory Powers Act 2000 ('RIPA')[64] has introduced a regime for the authorization of 'directed surveillance' and 'intrusive surveillance' operations. The accompanying Code of Practice provides optimistically that 'the proper authorisation of surveillance should ensure the admissibility of such evidence under the common law, section 78 of the Police and Criminal Evidence Act 1984 and the Human Rights Act 1998'.[65] 'Directed surveillance' is surveillance that is covert but not intrusive.[66] 'Intrusive surveillance' is covert surveillance that '(a) is carried out in relation to anything taking place on any residential premises or in any private vehicle; and (b) involves the presence of an individual on the premises or in the vehicle or is carried out by means of a surveillance device'.[67] Covert surveillance is surveillance 'carried out in a manner that is calculated to ensure that persons who are subject to the surveillance are unaware that it is or may be taking place'.[68]

The authorizing officer may grant authorization for direct surveillance to be carried out if it is believed that:

- the surveillance is proportionate to what is sought to be achieved; *and*
- the authorization is necessary in the interests of national security; or
- the authorization is necessary for the purpose of preventing or detecting crime or of preventing disorder; or
- the authorization is necessary in the interests of the economic well-being of the United Kingdom; or
- the authorization is necessary in the interests of public safety; or
- the authorization is necessary for the purpose of protecting public health; or
- the authorization is necessary for the purpose of assessing or collecting any tax, duty, levy or other imposition, contribution, or charge payable to a government department; or
- the authorization is necessary for any other purpose specified in an order made by the Secretary of State.[69]

All authorizations of intrusive surveillance must be made by the Secretary of State or a senior authorizing officer. Authorization may be granted if it is believed that:

- the surveillance is proportionate to what is sought to be achieved; *and*
- the authorization is necessary in the interests of national security; or

---

[64] See generally E Cape, 'The Right to Privacy—RIP?' [Jan 2001] *Legal Action* 21; G Ferguson and J Wadham, 'Privacy and Surveillance: A Review of the Regulation of Investigatory Powers Act 2000' [2003] *European Human Rights Law Review (Special Issue: Privacy 2003)* 101; P Mirfield, 'Regulation of Investigatory Powers Act 2000—(2): Evidential Aspects' [2001] *Criminal Law Review* 91.

[65] Covert Surveillance: Code of Practice, para 1.8.   [66] RIPA, s 26(2).   [67] RIPA, s 26(3).

[68] RIPA, s 26(9)(a). See generally H Fenwick, 'Covert Surveillance Under the Regulation of Investigatory Powers Act 2000, Part II' (2001) 65 *Journal of Criminal Law* 521; S Sharpe, 'Covert Surveillance and the Use of Informants' in M McConville and G Wilson (eds), *The Handbook of the Criminal Justice Process* (2002).

[69] RIPA, s 28.

- the authorization is necessary for the purpose of preventing or detecting serious crime; or

- the authorization is necessary in the interests of the economic well-being of the United Kingdom.[70]

Authorizations of intrusive surveillance, but not authorizations of directed surveillance, must generally be approved by a Surveillance Commissioner.[71]

1.5 Civil Proceedings

Case law dealing with improperly obtained evidence in civil proceedings is rarely encountered. In this context the decision of the Civil Division of the Court of Appeal in *Jones v University of Warwick*[72] is significant for two reasons. First, it appears to establish that the approach in civil cases to evidence obtained in violation of Article 8 should be fundamentally similar to that taken in criminal cases. Secondly, it suggests, interestingly, that this approach should be a flexible one involving the balancing of competing public interests. Jones, the claimant, injured her hand in an accident at work and sought damages from the defendant, her employer. The defendant admitted liability but did not accept the claimant's alleged continuing disability. Posing as a market researcher, an inquiry agent acting for the defendant's insurers gained access on two occasions to her home and, using a hidden camera, videotaped her without her knowledge. On viewing the films the defendant's medical expert concluded that the claimant's hand functioned entirely satisfactorily. The defendant sought to adduce the video in evidence, but the claimant argued for exclusion on the ground that her right to privacy under Article 8(1) had been violated.

The Court of Appeal considered that 'in both criminal and civil proceedings, courts can now adopt a less rigid approach to that adopted hitherto which gives recognition to the fact that there are conflicting public interests which have to be reconciled as far as this is possible'.[73] In this case:

> The court must try to give effect to what are here the two conflicting public interests. The weight to be attached to each will vary according to the circumstances. The significance of the evidence will differ as will the gravity of the breach of Article 8, according to the facts of the particular case. The decision will depend on all the circumstances. Here, the court cannot ignore the reality of the situation. This is not a case where the conduct of the defendant's insurers is so outrageous that the defence should be struck out. The case, therefore, has to be tried. It would be artificial and undesirable for the actual evidence, which is relevant and admissible, not to be placed before the judge who has the task of trying the case. . . . to exclude the use of the evidence would create a wholly undesirable situation. Fresh medical experts would have to be instructed on both sides. Evidence which is relevant would have to be concealed from

---

[70] RIPA, s 32.   [71] RIPA, s 36.
[72] [2003] EWCA Civ 151, [2003] 1 WLR 954. See generally C Foster, 'Section 6, Spies and Videotape' (2003) 147 *Solicitors' Journal* 466.   [73] [2003] EWCA Civ 151, [2003] 1 WLR 954, [24].

them, perhaps resulting in a misdiagnosis; and it would not be possible to cross-examine the claimant appropriately. For these reasons we do not consider it would be right to interfere with the judge's decision not to exclude the evidence.[74]

The Court proceeded, however, to add:

> While not excluding the evidence it is appropriate to make clear that the conduct of the insurers was improper and not justified.[75] . . . Excluding the evidence is not, moreover, the only weapon in the court's armoury. The court has other steps it can take to discourage conduct of the type of which complaint is made. In particular it can reflect its disapproval in the orders for costs which it makes. In this appeal, we therefore propose, because the conduct of the insurers gave rise to the litigation over admissibility of the evidence which has followed upon their conduct, to order the defendant to pay the costs of these proceedings to resolve this issue . . .[76]

It is noteworthy that, while it was acknowledged that a flexible 'balancing' approach should be taken to such problems in civil (and criminal) proceedings, it was held in the final analysis that, in the absence of especially outrageous conduct in this case, the public interest in the admission of relevant and reliable evidence should prevail.

1.6 A Way Forward?

The issue of the exclusion of improperly obtained evidence remains largely unresolved in English law. The unwillingness of the courts to provide any general guidance on the exercise of the section 78(1) discretion makes the comment of Lord Nicholls of Birkenhead in *R v Khan* that 'English law relating to the ingredients of a fair trial is highly developed'[77]

---

[74] Ibid, [28]. See also the decision of the Scottish Court of Session in *Martin v McGuiness* [2003] SLT 1424. The pursuer (claimant) brought an action against the defender (defendant) in respect of a road accident. The defender admitted liability but there remained the issue of the assessment of damages, with the defender contending that the pursuer exaggerated the effects of the accident. The defender sought to rely upon evidence obtained by private investigators through inquiries and surveillance carried out at the pursuer's home. Lord Bonomy held (ibid, [16]): 'In striking a fair balance between the interest of the pursuer in the security and integrity of his home as part of his right to respect for his private and family life and the competing interest of the defender in protecting his assets and the interests of the wider community in protecting theirs, I have had particular regard to the degree of intrusion into the pursuer's privacy (subterfuge in a conversation with the pursuer's wife at the door of her home and long-range video recording of the activities of the pursuer in the open area within the curtilage of his property capable of being viewed by a passer-by) on the one hand, and the requirement in an adversarial system of litigation that the defender should himself investigate the case against him with a view to defending himself and his assets from a false claim together with the general threat to the assets of the wider community from the impact of successful fraudulent claims on insurance premiums on the other hand. I have come to the conclusion that such inquiries and surveillance as could conceivably be proved as having been carried out in this case were reasonable and proportionate steps to be taken on behalf of the defender to protect his rights and as a contribution to the protection of the wider rights of the community, and were, therefore, necessary in a democratic society. The Court would not, in my opinion, be acting incompatibly with the pursuer's Article 8 right in admitting the evidence gathered by these inquiries and surveillance. The pursuer was bound to anticipate that his conduct might be scrutinised.'

[75] [2003] EWCA Civ 151, [2003] 1 WLR 954, [29].   [76] Ibid, [30].   [77] [1996] 3 All ER 289, 302.

seem wildly exaggerated.[78] An empirical study[79] has revealed virtually no consensus among judges on precisely what the section 78(1) discretion entails. The exercise of the discretion is typically approached on the basis that it would be patently obvious whether exclusion is justified in a given case. No particular enthusiasm is displayed for considering the principles justifying exclusion which have been identified by academic comment-ators. More worryingly, even strong statements by the Court of Appeal would appear to be ignored on occasion, with one judge reporting that if he ever found any evidence of bad faith on the part of the police, he would *invariably* exclude the evidence.

The narrowness of the discretion to exclude improperly obtained evidence in England and Wales is clearly due in no small measure to the restrictive interpretation accorded by appellate courts to the concept of trial fairness, which remains the sole criterion on which the issue of exclusion is to be determined. This stands in contrast to the position in a number of other Commonwealth jurisdictions, where it is openly acknowledged that improperly obtained evidence may be excluded even where its admission would not endanger the possibility of a fair trial. An excellent example is provided by the South African Bill of Rights, which provides: 'Evidence obtained in a manner that violates any right in the Bill of Rights must be excluded if the admission of that evidence would render the trial unfair *or otherwise be detrimental to the adminis-tration of justice.*'[80]

Nonetheless, the concept of trial fairness in England, while interpreted narrowly by appellate courts, is sufficiently nebulous to enable trial courts, if so minded, to achieve exclusion in a wider range of circumstances than might appear to be sanctioned by appellate decisions. Thus in *R v Veneroso*[81] the Crown Court at Inner London excluded evidence of the finding of drugs on the basis that the police officers, although acting in good faith, had not acted lawfully under section 17(1)(e) of the Police and Criminal Evidence Act 1984 because there was no evidence that they needed to enter the premises to save life or limb or prevent serious damage to property. This, the Court considered, constituted a clear breach of Article 8, and as the public interest in bringing the defendant to trial did not outweigh the need to protect his rights under Article 8 (although it might have been different if, for example, Semtex had been found), the evidence should be excluded under section 78(1).

What is clear, however, is that the reliability principle is at the forefront of the appellate courts' thinking. The relative frequency with which confessions are excluded from evidence is justified, in cases like *Cooke* and *Chalkley*, on the basis that confession

[78] See generally D Mathias, 'Probative Value, Illegitimate Prejudice and the Accused's Right to a Fair Trial' (2005) 29 *Criminal Law Journal* 8; J J Spigelman, 'The Truth Can Cost Too Much: The Principle of a Fair Trial' (2004) 78 *Australian Law Journal* 29; N Walker, 'What Does Fairness Mean in a Criminal Trial?' (2001) 151 *New Law Journal* 1240.

[79] M Hunter, 'Judicial Discretion: Section 78 in Practice' [1994] *Criminal Law Review* 558, 562–3.

[80] Constitution of the Republic of South Africa, s 35(5) (italics added). See generally P J Schwikkard and S E van der Merwe, *Principles of Evidence* (2nd ed 2002) Ch 12. See also the interpretation of s 24(2) of the Canadian Charter of Rights and Freedoms by the Supreme Court of Canada: *R v Collins* [1987] 1 SCR 265; *R v Stillman* [1997] 1 SCR 607; *R v Law* [2002] 1 SCR 227; *R v Fliss* [2002] 1 SCR 535; *R v Buhay* [2003] 1 SCR 631.

[81] [2002] Crim LR 306.

evidence is of questionable reliability. It is doubtless true that such evidence may well be of questionable reliability; that the reliability of confession evidence is notoriously sensitive to the manner in which it was obtained is, as has been seen in Chapter 2, well documented.[82] Non-confession evidence, on the other hand, is typically inherently reliable, its quality being unaffected by the manner or circumstances of its acquisition. Yet, as seen in Chapter 2, reliability is hardly the only consideration supporting the exclusion of confession evidence. Section 76 renders a confession obtained by oppression or in circumstances conducive to unreliability inadmissible in evidence *even if it is in fact reliable*. Section 78(1), too, may be said to encompass more than considerations of reliability: the strong statements made in decisions on the exclusion of confession evidence under section 78(1), referred to above, demonstrate that the Court of Appeal was focusing rather more on the police breaches themselves than on the nature of the evidence yielded by those breaches. Such statements suggest that the Court considered the breaches to be capable of leading to exclusion *regardless of the type of evidence in question*. It is therefore inappropriate for the Court of Appeal in cases like *Chalkley* to attempt to explain away the discretionary exclusion of confession evidence solely in terms of exclusion *because of* potential unreliability.

In the United States, an avowedly disciplinary principle is adopted. An exclusionary rule prohibits the introduction, in a criminal trial,[83] of evidence obtained in violation of a defendant's rights under the Fourth Amendment, which prohibits illegal searches and seizures. The Fourth Amendment exclusionary rule is 'a judicially created means of deterring illegal searches and seizures'.[84] It will be inapplicable, however, where its deterrence benefits would be outweighed by its costs, and it has been held on this basis that the rule does not apply where the defendant seeks to assert another person's Fourth Amendment rights;[85] or where the evidence is used to impeach a defendant's testimony;[86] or where the officer reasonably relied on a search warrant later deemed invalid;[87] or where the officer reasonably relied on a statute later deemed unconstitutional.[88]

The disciplinary principle has, however, been expressly rejected in England and Wales as the basis for exclusion of improperly obtained evidence.[89] Furthermore, a pure protective principle would treat as irrelevant the important consideration of whether the police acted in bad faith: the focus would be solely on whether a right of the defendant has been infringed.[90] Far more flexible is the integrity principle, which permits a court to take into account all relevant factors in determining whether to admit the evidence would compromise the integrity of the criminal justice system (and, perhaps,

---

[82] See generally, on the possible causes of false confessions, G H Gudjonsson, *The Psychology of Interrogations and Confessions: A Handbook* (2003) Ch 8; G H Gudjonsson, *The Psychology of Interrogations, Confessions and Testimony* (1992) 226–8; A Memon, A Vrij, and R Bull, *Psychology and Law: Truthfulness, Accuracy and Credibility* (2nd ed 2003) 77–81.

[83] See *US v Calandra* 414 US 338 (1974); *US v Janis* 428 US 433 (1976); *INS v Lopez-Mendoza* 468 US 1032 (1984).

[84] *Pennsylvania Bd of Probation and Parole v Scott* 524 US 357 (1998).

[85] *Alderman v US* 394 US 165 (1969).

[86] *Walder v US* 347 US 62 (1954); *US v Havens* 446 US 620 (1980).   [87] *US v Leon* 468 US 897 (1984).

[88] *Illinois v Krull* 480 US 340 (1987).   [89] See Ch 2.

[90] See generally I H Dennis, 'Reconstructing the Law of Criminal Evidence' (1989) 42 *Current Legal Problems* 21.

bring it into disrepute in the eyes of the public) to such an extent that it should be excluded. Thus bad faith is relevant because to tolerate an impropriety committed in bad faith would compromise integrity to a greater extent than to tolerate one committed in good faith. It is therefore entirely possible that, in relation to the exclusion of improperly obtained confession evidence, the English courts have—inasmuch as they treat bad faith as a relevant consideration—already moved some way towards a *sub silentio* adoption of the integrity principle.[91]

The Rome Statute of the International Criminal Court clearly adopts the integrity principle in relation to improperly obtained evidence. Article 69(7) provides:

> Evidence obtained by means of a violation of this Statute or internationally recognized human rights shall not be admissible if:
>
> (a) The violation casts substantial doubt on the reliability of the evidence; or
>
> (b) The admission of the evidence would be antithetical to and would seriously damage the integrity of the proceedings.

Provisions virtually identical to this appear in the Rules of Procedure and Evidence of the International Criminal Tribunals for Rwanda and the Former Yugoslavia.[92] In Canada and Australia, approaches based broadly on the integrity principle have also been expressly adopted.[93] In pursuance of these approaches, courts in these countries

---

[91]   Bad faith would also, of course, be a relevant consideration under the disciplinary principle.

[92]   Rule 95 of the Rules of Procedure and Evidence of both Tribunals provides: 'No evidence shall be admissible if obtained by methods which cast substantial doubt on its reliability or if its admission is antithetical to, and would seriously damage, the integrity of the proceedings.'

[93]   In Canada, the approach was developed by the Supreme Court of Canada in interpreting s 24(2) of the Canadian Charter of Rights and Freedoms, which provides: 'Where . . . a court concludes that evidence was obtained in a manner that infringed or denied any rights or freedoms guaranteed by this Charter, the evidence shall be excluded if it is established that, having regard to all the circumstances, the admission of it in the proceedings would bring the administration of justice into disrepute.' See the seminal case of *R v Collins* [1987] 1 SCR 265, and, more recently, *R v Stillman* [1997] 1 SCR 607, *R v Law* [2002] 1 SCR 227, *R v Fliss* [2002] 1 SCR 535, and *R v Buhay* [2003] 1 SCR 631. See generally P Cory, 'General Principles of *Charter* Exclusion (Exclusion of Conscriptive and Non-Conscriptive Evidence)' (1998) 47 *UNB Law Journal* 229; W D Delaney, 'Exclusion of Evidence Under the *Charter*: Stillman v The Queen' (1997) 76 *Canadian Bar Review* 521; R C Fraser and J A I Addison, 'What's Truth Got to Do with It? The Supreme Court of Canada and Section 24(2)' (2004) 29 *Queen's Law Journal* 823; N J S Gorham, 'Eight Plus Twenty-Four Two Equals Zero-Point-Five' (2003) 6 *Criminal Reports (6th)* 257; J Parfett, 'A Triumph of Liberalism: The Supreme Court of Canada and the Exclusion of Evidence' (2002) 40 *Alberta Law Review* 299; D M Paciocco, 'Evidence About Guilt: Balancing the Rights of the Individual and Society in Matters of Truth and Proof' (2001) 80 *Canadian Bar Review* 433; S Penney, 'Taking Deterrence Seriously: Excluding Unconstitutionally Obtained Evidence Under Section 24(2) of the Charter' (2004) 49 *McGill Law Journal* 105; M C Plaxton, 'Who Needs Section 24(2)? Or: Common Law Sleight-of-Hand' (2003) 10 *Criminal Reports (6th)* 236; D Stuart, '*Buhay*: No Automatic Inclusionary Rule Under Section 24(2) When Evidence is Non-Conscripted and Essential to Crown's Case' (2003) 10 *Criminal Reports (6th)* 233; D Stuart, 'Eight Plus Twenty-Four Two Equals Zero' (1998) 13 *Criminal Reports (5th)* 50; D Stuart, '*Stillman*: Limiting Search Incident to Arrest, Consent Searches and Refining the Section 24(2) Test' (1997) 5 *Criminal Reports (5th)* 99. See also L Barmes, 'Adjudication and Public Opinion' (2002) 118 *Law Quarterly Review* 600. In Australia, the approach was developed at common law (*R v Ireland* (1970) 126 CLR 321; *Bunning v Cross* (1978) 141 CLR 54), and is also encapsulated in s 138 of the Uniform Evidence Acts. See generally B Selway, 'Principle, Public Policy and Unfairness—Exclusion of Evidence on Discretionary Grounds' (2002) 23 *Adelaide Law Review* 1. Despite the fact that its heading refers to a discretion to *exclude*, s 138 also reverses the common law

have provided, in contrast to the position in England and Wales, a far clearer indication of the factors which may inform a decision on whether improperly obtained evidence should be admitted or excluded in a particular case. The following are the main factors considered relevant to such a decision. The first of these concerns the evidence in question, the subsequent five relate to the impropriety, and the final factor concerns the offence for which the defendant is being prosecuted. The factors are as follows:

1. *The nature of the evidence.* The more cogent the evidence the more it would weigh on the side of the public interest in bringing offenders to conviction.

2. *Whether the impropriety consisted of an infringement of an important right.* It would compromise integrity to a greater degree to excuse the infringement of an important right than to excuse the infringement of a more minor right.

3. *Whether the impropriety was deliberate or reckless, or simply inadvertent.* For a court effectively to turn a blind eye to deliberate or reckless impropriety would compromise integrity to a greater extent than would be the case if the impropriety was simply inadvertently committed.

4. *Whether the impropriety was committed in bad faith or in good faith.* The fact that the impropriety was committed in bad faith would weigh in favour of exclusion as courts should be slow to become complicit in attempts to profit from such conduct.

5. *Whether the impropriety occurred in circumstances of urgency or necessity.* Courts might be readier to excuse improprieties that were prompted by considerations of urgency or necessity since to do so might be less likely to compromise integrity than would otherwise be the case.

6. *Whether any other proceedings (in a court or otherwise) have been, or are likely to be, taken in relation to the impropriety.* A court might justifiably feel more comfortable about excusing impropriety in relation to which action has been or is likely to be taken.

7. *The seriousness of the offence charged.* The more serious the offence the greater the public interest in bringing its perpetrator to conviction and thus the greater the case for admission.

What is notable is that this 'balancing' approach is precisely that which found favour with the House of Lords in the context of the abuse of process doctrine. The narrowness of the discretion to exclude an item of 'tainted' prosecution evidence stands uneasily alongside the width of the discretion to discontinue a 'tainted' prosecution. The House of Lords has acknowledged in at least three decisions in the past decade or so[94] that the judicial

position by requiring the prosecution to satisfy the court that the evidence should be admitted. It would seem that the reversal of the onus has resulted in a slight increase in the incidence of exclusion: B Presser, 'Public Policy, Police Interest: A Re-Evaluation of the Judicial Discretion to Exclude Improperly or Illegally Obtained Evidence' (2001) 25 *Melbourne University Law Review* 757. On the Scottish position see P Duff, 'Irregularly Obtained Real Evidence: The Scottish Solution?' (2004) 8 *International Journal of Evidence and Proof* 77.

[94] *R v Horseferry Road Magistrates' Court, ex p Bennett* [1994] 1 AC 42; *R v Latif; R v Shahzad* [1996] 1 WLR 104; *R v Looseley; A-G's Reference (No 3 of 2000)* [2001] UKHL 53, [2001] 1 WLR 2060.

discretion to stay proceedings which amount to an abuse of the process of the court is in no way limited to situations where a stay is necessary to protect an innocent person from wrongful conviction. Even where there can be no doubt about the ability of a trial to determine guilt or innocence reliably, a stay should be ordered if the balance of public interest considerations makes it inappropriate that the prosecution should continue: 'the judge must weigh in the balance the public interest in ensuring that those that are charged with grave crimes should be tried and the competing public interest in not conveying the impression that the court will adopt the approach that the end justified any means'.[95]

The Court of Appeal, too, has not been hesitant to embrace the abuse of process doctrine. In *R v Mullen*,[96] the appellant was convicted of conspiracy to cause explosions and sentenced to 30 years' imprisonment. In the Court of Appeal it was argued that his trial should not have proceeded, primarily on the basis that 'the British authorities initiated and subsequently assisted in and procured the deportation of the appellant, by unlawful means, in circumstances in which there were specific extradition facilities between this country and Zimbabwe. In so acting they were not only encouraging unlawful conduct in Zimbabwe, but they were also acting in breach of public international law.'[97] The Court acknowledged that this was not a case in which there had been any danger of an unfair trial:

> ... it seems to us that *Bennett*-type abuse, where it would be offensive to justice and propriety to try the defendant at all, is different... from the type of abuse which renders a fair trial impossible... It arises not from the relationship between the prosecution and the defendant, but from the relationship between the prosecution and the Court. It arises from the Court's need to exercise control over executive involvement in the whole prosecution process, not limited to the trial itself.[98]

Significantly, the Court noted that 'certainty of guilt cannot displace the essential feature of this kind of abuse of process, namely the degradation of the lawful administration of justice'.[99] On the facts of the case:

> This Court recognises the immense degree of public revulsion which has, quite properly, attached to the activities of those who have assisted and furthered the violent operations of the IRA and other terrorist organisations. In the discretionary exercise, great weight must therefore be attached to the nature of the offence involved in this case. Against that, however, the conduct of the security services and police in procuring the unlawful deportation of the appellant in the manner which has been described, represents, in the view of this Court, a blatant and extremely serious failure to adhere to the rule of law with regard to the production of a defendant for prosecution in the English courts. The need to discourage such conduct on the part of those who are responsible for criminal prosecutions is a matter of public policy, to which... very considerable weight must be attached.[100]

---

[95]   *R v Latif; R v Shahzad* [1996] 1 WLR 104, 113.

[96]   [1999] 2 Cr App R 143. See generally L Davidson, 'Quashing Convictions for Pre-Trial Abuse of Process: Breaching Public International Law and Human Rights' [1999] *Cambridge Law Journal* 466; C Warbrick, 'Judicial Jurisdiction and Abuse of Process' (2000) 49 *International and Comparative Law Quarterly* 489.

[97]   [1999] 2 Cr App R 143, 156.   [98]   Ibid, 158.   [99]   Ibid, 155.   [100]   Ibid, 156–7.

The Court's conclusion was that 'we have no doubt that the discretionary balance comes down decisively against the prosecution of this offence'.[101] It is difficult to imagine a greater contrast between the approach taken here and the approach to section 78(1) in a case like *Chalkley*. Particularly notable is the acknowledgement in *Mullen* that the 'balance' came down in favour of a stay despite the seriousness of the offence in question.

Given the law's acceptance that proceedings may be stayed on account of pre-trial impropriety even if there is no danger of the trial being 'unreliable' in terms of its being unable to determine guilt or innocence accurately, consistency dictates that, by analogy, improperly obtained but reliable evidence should be capable of being excluded.[102] The peremptory dismissal in *Chalkley* of considerations drawn from the law of abuse of process is therefore particularly disappointing as it introduces a glaring anomaly into the law. Whether one is considering the possibility of excluding evidence on account of pre-trial police impropriety, or staying the proceedings on account of such impropriety, what is at stake is surely the same fundamental question: should the prosecution be deprived of the fruit of the pre-trial police impropriety, whether that fruit be an item of evidence or the case as a whole?[103] A further anomaly of the current situation is that the stricter approach is that which is to be applied in determining whether the potentially less drastic measure, exclusion, should be invoked. Considerations such as these have led Lord Justice Auld to call in his review for a proper investigation of the interplay between section 78(1) and the abuse of process doctrine.[104]

It is instructive to note that a deliberately flexible approach to exclusion was encapsulated in the original version of section 78(1), an amendment to the Police and Criminal Evidence Bill which was moved in the House of Lords by Lord Scarman and agreed to by the House. Indeed, this amendment was premised upon the presumption that improperly obtained evidence would be inadmissible, with the prosecution bearing the burden of satisfying the court that the evidence in question should be admitted. The amendment read:

> If it appears to the court in any proceedings that any evidence (other than a confession) proposed to be given by the prosecution may have been obtained improperly, the court shall not allow the evidence to be given unless—
>
> (a) the prosecution proves to the court beyond reasonable doubt that it was obtained lawfully and in accordance with a code of practice (where applicable) issued, approved, and in force, under Part VI of this Act; or

---

[101] Ibid, 157.

[102] See, eg, L Davidson, 'Quashing Convictions for Pre-Trial Abuse of Process: Breaching Public International Law and Human Rights' [1999] *Cambridge Law Journal* 466, 468: '...it is submitted that in the light of *Mullen* and the growing emphasis on human rights, law enforcement agencies would be wise to obtain evidence at home and abroad with the same care as is required when seeking the transfer of suspects'.

[103] See generally J Hunter, ' "Tainted" Proceedings: Censuring Police Illegalities' (1985) 59 *Australian Law Journal* 709.

[104] Lord Justice Auld, *A Review of the Criminal Courts of England and Wales* (2001) Ch 11 para 111, accessible via http://www.criminal-courts-review.org.uk. See also the arguments in A L-T Choo and S Nash, 'What's the Matter with Section 78?' [1999] *Criminal Law Review* 929.

(b) the court is satisfied that anything improperly done in obtaining it was of no material significance in all the circumstances of the case and ought, therefore, to be disregarded; or

(c) the court is satisfied that the probative value of the evidence, the gravity of the offence charged, and the circumstances in which the evidence was obtained are such that the public interest in the fair administration of the criminal law requires the evidence to be given, notwithstanding that it was obtained improperly.

When the Bill returned to the Commons, however, an amendment to replace the Lords' amendment was proposed by the Home Secretary. This was agreed to and now appears as section 78(1). The Home Secretary opined that it was inappropriate for improperly obtained evidence to be excluded to mark society's disapproval of improper police conduct.[105] A further objection to the Lords' amendment related to the heavy onus of proof which it placed upon the prosecution.[106] Finally, the criteria laid down in the Lords' amendment were considered to be too complex for a court to have to address in the course of ordinary criminal proceedings.[107] It is ironic that criteria of this kind are not considered too complex for Canadian and Australian courts. Notably, JUSTICE, the all-party legal human rights organization, has recommended that 'PACE should be amended to state specifically that the courts may exclude evidence that has been obtained in breach of a fundamental right guaranteed by the Human Rights Act 1998 if its admission would prejudice the integrity of the criminal justice system'.[108]

While an approach based broadly on the integrity principle, and involving a consideration of all relevant factors, has much to commend it, it is important that the exclusionary discretion be structured appropriately. Failure to do so might lead, for example, to the regular admission of improperly obtained evidence on the basis that, in a particular case, factors such as the seriousness of the offence charged outweigh all factors favouring exclusion. One commentator has noted in the Canadian context that 'it will be little comfort to an accused that he or she has established that the evidence was obtained in violation of a major *Charter* standard when it will nevertheless be used to convict because the violation wasn't in a home, the police were in good faith ignorance and/or the offence is considered serious'.[109] The following suggestion about how the discretion might be structured has been provided by Wasik, Gibbons, and Redmayne:

Judges might first look at two primary factors which reflect legitimacy considerations: (1) there should be a strong presumption of exclusion where evidence has been obtained because of deliberate breach of PACE or breach of the criminal law (whether deliberate or not); (2) there should be a strong presumption that credible evidence of guilt should be admitted. If these primary presumptions conflict, judges might then take the seriousness of the crime of which the defendant is accused into account. Judges might then consider a number of secondary factors which reflect the importance of protecting suspects.[110]

---

[105] See generally *Parliamentary Debates (Hansard): House of Commons (Vol 65)* (1984) col 1012.
[106] Ibid, col 1013.   [107] Ibid, col 1014.
[108] JUSTICE, *Under Surveillance: Covert Policing and Human Rights Standards* (1998) 76.
[109] D Stuart, 'Eight Plus Twenty-Four Two Equals Zero' (1998) 13 *Criminal Reports (5th)* 50, 63.
[110] M Wasik, T Gibbons, and M Redmayne, *Criminal Justice: Text and Materials* (1999) 450.

Consideration might also be given to according special treatment to Convention rights as far as evidence obtained in violation of such rights is concerned. A strategy of 'reading into' the Convention a rule requiring the mandatory exclusion of evidence obtained in breach of a Convention right, as Judge Loucaides apparently did in *Khan v UK*, is unlikely to gain widespread acceptance.[111] The best way forward may be to recognize a very strong presumption, rather than a rule, that section 78(1) should be invoked to exclude such evidence.[112] This approach would permit a degree of flexibility while treating breaches of Convention rights with the seriousness that they deserve.[113] Such a presumption could usefully be superimposed on the structured approach suggested by Wasik, Gibbons, and Redmayne. It would be a stronger presumption than the two strong presumptions that they identify in the passage quoted above. A party arguing for the admission of evidence obtained in violation of the Convention would have to satisfy the court that there are compelling considerations favouring admission. Realistically, there would probably need to be a number of factors all of which favour admission in order for the party to have any realistic prospect of success. Evidence obtained illegally or improperly, but not in breach of a Convention right, would not be subject to this 'primary' presumption of exclusion but would be treated in accordance with the general approach suggested by Wasik, Gibbons, and Redmayne.

2 Evidence Obtained in Undercover Police Operations

Criminal investigations were traditionally reactive in character, with the police 'reacting' to reports of offences by invoking the normal investigatory procedures of entry, search, and seizure, interviewing of suspects, and so on. Proactive methods of investigation,

---

[111] In *R v Button* [2005] EWCA Crim 516 the Court of Appeal made its feelings clear: 'What [counsel for the appellants] is saying is that the court is bound to exclude any evidence obtained in breach of Article 8 because otherwise it would be acting unlawfully. This is a startling proposition and one which we are pleased and relieved to be able to reject.' (Ibid, [24].) 'The intrusion or interference has already occurred, the evidence obtained is admissible under English law and so the court's obligation is confined to deciding whether or not, having regard to the way in which the evidence was obtained, it would be fair to admit it.' (Ibid, [23].)

[112] For a time New Zealand recognized a prima facie rule of exclusion, whereby there was a presumption that evidence obtained in breach of a right guaranteed by the New Zealand Bill of Rights Act 1990 would be excluded. This was abolished in *R v Shaheed* [2002] 2 NZLR 377 in favour of an approach whereby 'where there has been a breach of a right guaranteed to a suspect by the Bill of Rights, a Judge who is asked to exclude resulting evidence must determine whether that is a response which is proportionate to the character of such a breach of the right in question. The Judge must make that determination by means of a balancing process in which the starting point is to give *appropriate and significant weight* to the existence of that breach but which also takes proper account of the need for an effective and credible system of justice.' (Ibid, [156] (italics added).) See generally J Ip, 'The End of the Prima Facie Exclusionary Rule' (2002) 9 *Auckland University Law Review* 1016; R Mahoney, 'Abolition of New Zealand's Prima Facie Exclusionary Rule' [2003] *Criminal Law Review* 607. See also *R v Pou* [2002] 3 NZLR 637.

[113] See also D Ormerod, 'ECHR and the Exclusion of Evidence: Trial Remedies for Article 8 Breaches' [2003] *Criminal Law Review* 61, 78 ff. Cf the approach of Lord Steyn, speaking for the Privy Council in *Mohammed v The State* [1999] 2 WLR 552, who acknowledged that the breach of a constitutional right should be rather more likely to lead to exclusion than the breach of some other right.

'in which the reporting, observation and testimony can be done by the officials them-selves',[114] were traditionally far less common.[115] Proactive techniques may consist of the use of surveillance devices or the use of undercover police operations. Traditionally, under-cover police operations were mainly deployed in two scenarios: first, where a potential complainant might be unaware that a crime had been committed (in the case, for example, of regulatory offences), and, secondly, where potential complainants might be unwilling to report offences (for example, where 'victimless' crimes were concerned). In recent times, however, the use of undercover operations has been coming to light with greater frequency. Such operations raise a number of issues for consideration. First, there is a danger that an undercover officer might, in order to gain evidence of ongoing criminal activity, have to offer the opportunity for its commission, and in doing so, effectively create an offence which would not otherwise have been committed. Secondly, there is the issue of incrimin-ating statements made by a suspect to an undercover officer during an undercover opera-tion. These statements will have been obtained in a context far removed from an ordinary interview. Indeed, the well-publicized cases of Keith Hall and Colin Stagg in 1994[116] pro-vide evidence of undercover police operations being used in the investigation of serious offences such as murder, and apparently with a view to obtaining a confession from the suspect if at all possible. Thirdly, public attention has focused more recently on prosecu-tions launched on the basis of undercover operations for which journalists such as Mazher Mahmood of the *News of the World*, rather than police officers or agents, were responsible.[117] It will be seen below how issues pertaining to undercover operations have been dealt with in the English law of evidence.[118]

2.1 The European Court of Human Rights

In the major case of *Teixeira de Castro v Portugal*,[119] consideration was given by the European Court of Human Rights to issues pertaining to entrapment and undercover policing in the context of a conviction for drug-trafficking. Two plain-clothes police

---

[114] G Dworkin, 'The Serpent Beguiled Me and I Did Eat: Entrapment and the Creation of Crime' (1985) 4 *Law and Philosophy* 17, 18.

[115] See generally M Maguire and T John, 'Covert and Deceptive Policing in England and Wales: Issues in Regulation and Practice' (1996) 4 *European Journal of Crime, Criminal Law and Criminal Justice* 316, 316–19; P Gill, *Round Up the Usual Suspects? Developments in Contemporary Law Enforcement Intelligence* (2000) Ch 8.

[116] See A L-T Choo and M Mellors, 'Undercover Police Operations and What the Suspect Said (or Didn't Say)' in M Allen (ed), *Web Journal of Current Legal Issues Yearbook 1995* (1996) for a description of these cases.

[117] See *R v Shannon* [2001] 1 WLR 51.

[118] See generally D Birch, 'Excluding Evidence from Entrapment: What is a "Fair Cop"?' (1994) 47 *Current Legal Problems* 73; S Bronitt, 'The Law in Undercover Policing: A Comparative Study of Entrapment and Covert Interviewing in Australia, Canada and Europe' (2004) 33 *Common Law World Review* 35; A L-T Choo, 'The Legal Aspects of Undercover Police Operations in England and Wales' (1999) 2 *International Journal of Police Science and Management* 144; A L-T Choo and M Mellors, 'Undercover Police Operations and What the Suspect Said (or Didn't Say)' in M Allen (ed), *Web Journal of Current Legal Issues Yearbook 1995* (1996); G Robertson, 'Entrapment Evidence: Manna from Heaven, or Fruit of the Poisoned Tree?' [1994] *Criminal Law Review* 805; S Sharpe, 'Covert Police Operations and the Discretionary Exclusion of Evidence' [1994] *Criminal Law Review* 793; S Sharpe, 'Covert Policing: A Comparative View' (1996) 25 *Anglo-American Law Review* 163.

[119] (1999) 28 EHRR 101 (judgment of 1998).

officers approached one VS, saying that they were interested in purchasing heroin. VS mentioned Teixeira de Castro as someone who might be able to find some. VS did not, however, know Teixeira de Castro's address, which he had to obtain from FO. VS, FO, and the two officers then went to see Teixeira de Castro. The officers told him that they wished to buy 20 grams of heroin for 200,000 escudos, and produced a roll of banknotes. Teixeira de Castro agreed to procure the heroin and, accompanied by FO, went to the home of one JPO. JPO obtained heroin which he handed over in due course to Teixeira de Castro in exchange for payment. Teixeira de Castro then took the drugs to VS's home, where he was arrested.

The European Court accepted Teixeira de Castro's submission that his right to a fair trial under Article 6(1) of the European Convention on Human Rights had been violated. The Court noted:

> The use of undercover agents must be restricted and safeguards put in place even in cases concerning the fight against drug-trafficking. While the rise in organised crime undoubtedly requires that appropriate measures be taken, the right to a fair administration of justice nevertheless holds such a prominent place ... that it cannot be sacrificed for the sake of expedience. The general requirements of fairness embodied in Article 6 apply to proceedings concerning all types of criminal offence, from the most straightforward to the most complex. The public interest cannot justify the use of evidence obtained as a result of police incitement.[120]

The Court noted that the officers in the present case had gone beyond merely acting as undercover agents. There was no suggestion that the officers' intervention had taken place as part of an anti-drug-trafficking operation ordered and supervised by a judge, or that the competent authorities had had good reason to suspect that Teixeira de Castro was a drug-trafficker. On the contrary, he had no criminal record and no preliminary investigation had been opened about him. He was not even known to the police officers, who came into contact with him only through VS and FO. Additionally, the drugs were not at Teixeira de Castro's home but were obtained from a third party who had in turn obtained them from another person. There was no suggestion that Teixeira de Castro was predisposed to commit offences; it did not appear that at the time of his arrest, he had more drugs in his possession than the quantity requested by the police officers. What the police officers did was not to confine themselves to investigating his criminal activity in an essentially passive manner, but rather to exercise an influence such as to incite the commission of the offence. It was the statements of these officers which were to constitute the main basis of Teixeira de Castro's conviction.[121] In conclusion, therefore, the European Court observed 'that the two police officers' actions went beyond those of undercover agents because they instigated the offence and there is nothing to suggest that without their intervention it would have been committed'.[122]

In the light of the Human Rights Act 1998, the sentiments expressed by the European Court in *Teixeira de Castro*, and the actual decision of the Court, have assumed considerable significance in English law.

---

[120] Ibid, [36].   [121] Ibid, [38].   [122] Ibid, [39].

2.2 The Contemporary Approach in English Law

2.2.1 No Defence of Entrapment

In a strict sense, 'entrapment' refers to the enticement of a person, by an agent provocateur, to commit an offence which he or she would not otherwise have committed.[123] It has been well established for over two decades[124] that there is no defence of entrapment in English criminal law, but that entrapment can be taken into account in mitigation of sentence.[125] The absence in England and Wales of a substantive defence of entrapment stands in sharp contrast to the position in the Federal jurisdiction of the United States, which recognizes in its criminal law a defence of entrapment. In essence, where a sufficiently strong allegation of entrapment is made, the issue of entrapment must be left to the jury, who must acquit the defendant unless the prosecution proves to it beyond reasonable doubt that the defendant was not entrapped.[126]

2.2.2 Exclusion under Section 78(1) of the Police and Criminal Evidence Act 1984

It has been firmly established for over a decade that evidence obtained in undercover police operations *can* be excluded under section 78(1) if the circumstances warrant it, in the exercise of the court's discretion to exclude evidence that if admitted would affect the fairness of the proceedings to an unacceptable degree. The leading case is *R v Smurthwaite*,[127] in which the Court of Appeal provided a non-exhaustive list of factors which may be considered by a court in deciding whether to exercise its exclusionary discretion.[128] First, 'was the officer acting as an agent provocateur in the sense that he was enticing the defendant to commit an offence he would not otherwise have committed?'[129] Thus, the earlier uncertainty in English law about whether

---

[123] The term entrapment is also used in a broader sense to refer 'to activities taking place before or during the commission of an offence which may aid its commission or even influence the precise way in which it is carried out, but which do not "create" the crime': P Mirfield, *Silence, Confessions and Improperly Obtained Evidence* (1997) 201. See also S Bronitt and D Roche, 'Between Rhetoric and Reality: Sociolegal and Republican Perspectives on Entrapment' (2000) 4 *International Journal of Evidence and Proof* 77.

[124] *R v Sang* [1980] AC 402.

[125] See *R v Tonnessen* [1998] 2 Cr App R (S) 328; *R v Springer* [1999] 1 Cr App R (S) 217; *R v Shannon* [2001] 1 WLR 51, 73 (the trial judge 'imposed a lenient sentence having taken into account in the defendant's favour the full circumstances in which the offences were committed').

[126] *Sorrells v US* 287 US 435 (1932); *Sherman v US* 356 US 369 (1958); *Masciale v US* 356 US 386 (1958); *US v Russell* 411 US 423 (1973); *Hampton v US* 425 US 484 (1976); *Mathews v US* 108 S Ct 883 (1988); *Jacobson v US* 112 S Ct 1535 (1992). See generally R J Allen, M Luttrell, and A Kreeger, 'Clarifying Entrapment', *International Commentary on Evidence*, 1998, available via http://www.law.qub.ac.uk/ice; R C Park, 'Would a Market-Based Test Clarify Entrapment?', *International Commentary on Evidence*, 1999, available via http://www.law.qub.ac.uk/ice; K A Smith, 'Psychology, Factfinding, and Entrapment' (2005) 103 *Michigan Law Review* 759.

[127] [1994] 1 All ER 898. See also the earlier cases of *R v Harwood* [1989] Crim LR 285; *R v Gill* [1989] Crim LR 358; *R v Edwards* [1991] Crim LR 45; *Williams v DPP* [1993] 3 All ER 365.

[128] [1994] 1 All ER 898, 903. See also the discussion by P Mirfield, *Silence, Confessions and Improperly Obtained Evidence* (1997) 202–4.   [129] Cf *R v Kennedy* [1999] 1 Cr App R 54.

section 78(1) could be used at all to exclude evidence obtained by entrapment was resolved by *Smurthwaite*.[130] What is unclear, however, is the precise weight which *Smurthwaite* requires to be attached to this factor. Does the presence of entrapment weigh heavily in favour of exclusion, or is it a factor which carries no special weight and is merely to be balanced against all other relevant factors? The earlier case of *Williams v DPP* provides an illustration of failure to exercise the exclusionary discretion under section 78(1) despite the presence of entrapment. As part of 'Operation Rover', the police left an unattended and unsecured van containing dummy cartons of cigarettes in a busy street. The appellants came along, walked around the van, and then removed the cartons from the van. They were charged with interfering with a motor vehicle with intent to commit theft. The Divisional Court held that the justices had not erred in declining to exclude the evidence under section 78(1); the police had not, in the view of the Court, incited, counselled, or procured the commission of the offence.[131] Yet it is clear, as Mirfield points out, that 'the effect of the police conduct was certainly that an offence was committed which would not, without their intervention, have been committed'.[132]

Secondly, 'what was the nature of any entrapment?' This implies that certain types of entrapment may be acceptable, and that some types may be more acceptable than other types. Again, however, no guidance is provided on this vital issue.[133]

Thirdly, is what is at issue evidence of a *confession* to an offence, or is it evidence of the actual *commission* of an offence? What the Court of Appeal has in mind here is the legitimate uses of undercover police operations. Such an operation may legitimately be used, in appropriate circumstances, to obtain evidence of an offence while it is being committed, but may not be used as a means of deliberately circumventing Code C in order to obtain a confession. The extent to which incriminating statements made by an accused in the course of an undercover police operation may be excluded from evidence under section 78(1) was considered by the Court of Appeal in *R v Christou*.[134] The case arose from an undercover police operation which the Court of Appeal described as unique in the United Kingdom. A shop called 'Stardust Jewellers' was set up by the police for the purpose of combating burglary and robbery in parts of North London. This shop purported to conduct the business of buying and selling jewellery on a commercial basis, but was in reality an undercover operation and staffed solely by

---

[130] The argument that s 78(1) should not be able to be invoked to exclude evidence obtained by entrapment proceeded on the following (rather tenuous) basis. If entrapment evidence were excluded and the evidence were the only prosecution evidence, or perhaps a crucial part of the prosecution evidence, the case against the accused would collapse. This would be tantamount to a recognition of a defence of entrapment, which does not exist in England and Wales, through the back door.   [131] [1993] 3 All ER 365, 368.

[132] P Mirfield, *Silence, Confessions and Improperly Obtained Evidence* (1997) 202.

[133] Mirfield notes that of relevance to the second factor would probably be 'the way in which the intervention took place, as well, perhaps, as its culpability, both in terms of public danger and otherwise. For example, a police *agent* who joined in an already existing conspiracy would surely be more culpable if the conspiracy were one to cause explosions than if it were one to supply cannabis' (ibid).

[134] [1992] 1 QB 979. See A Ashworth, 'Should the Police Be Allowed to Use Deceptive Practices?' (1998) 114 *Law Quarterly Review* 108, 134–5.

two undercover officers. As a result of this operation, Christou and Wright were convicted of handling stolen goods. They argued that evidence of the conversations in the shop ought to have been excluded under section 78(1) on the basis, *inter alia*, that there had been a breach of Code C in that no cautions had been administered. The Court of Appeal held that Code C was inapplicable in this situation since the undercover officers had not been overtly acting as police officers. Having said this, however, the Court was careful to enter the following caveat: 'It would be wrong for police officers to adopt or use an undercover pose or disguise to enable themselves to ask questions about an offence uninhibited by the requirements of the Code and with the effect of circumventing it. . . . Were they to do so, it would be open to the judge to exclude the questions and answers under section 78 . . .'.[135] This caveat was actually applied by the Court in the later case of *R v Bryce*.[136]

Fourthly, 'how active or passive was the officer's role in obtaining the evidence?' This implies that to play an active role in an undercover operation may be less justifiable than to play a passive role, and thus the more active the officer's role, the more likely exclusion would be. No guidance is provided, however, on the question of what may constitute an active role and what may constitute a passive role.

Fifthly, is there strong corroboration of the prosecution version of what occurred during the undercover operation? Is there, for example, an 'unassailable record' of what occurred? The concern here is clearly with the possibility that evidence of what transpired in the course of the undercover operation may have been fabricated by the police.

Finally, the Court of Appeal in *Smurthwaite* thought that it would be necessary to consider whether the officer 'has abused his role to ask questions which ought properly to have been asked as a police officer and in accordance with the codes'. This is obviously linked to the third factor, as discussed above.

More recently, however, the Court of Appeal would appear to have embraced a much narrower approach to discretionary exclusion. In *R v Shannon*[137] the defendant was charged with supplying drugs to Mazher Mahmood of the *News of the World*, who was posing as an Arab sheikh in an elaborate operation. John Shannon was the real name of John Alford, an actor who appeared in the television programme *London's Burning*. Subsequent to the operation the *News of the World* published the front-page headline 'London's Burning Star is Cocaine Dealer', and the police took over investigative material from the *News of the World*. On the defendant's appeal against conviction the Court of Appeal held that the judge had 'found, rightly in our view, that the evidence fell short of establishing actual incitement or instigation of the offences concerned'.[138]

---

[135] [1992] 1 QB 979, 991. The High Court of Australia appears to have adopted the test of whether the statements were 'elicited' from the defendant by the undercover officer: *R v Swaffield* (1998) 72 ALJR 339; see generally L Martinez, 'Confessions and Admissions to Undercover Police and Police Agents' (2000) 74 *Australian Law Journal* 391; A Palmer, 'Applying *Swaffield*: Covertly Obtained Statements and the Public Policy Discretion' (2004) 28 *Criminal Law Journal* 217; A Palmer, 'Applying *Swaffield* Part II: Fake Gangs and Induced Confessions' (2005) 29 *Criminal Law Journal* 111; E Stone, 'The Law of Confessions in Theory and Practice: *Swaffield and Pavic*' (1999) 3 *International Journal of Evidence and Proof* 57. A similar approach is taken in Canada: *R v Liew* [1999] 3 SCR 227.   [136] [1992] 4 All ER 567.

[137] [2001] 1 WLR 51.   [138] Ibid, 70.

The Court, however, made observations suggesting that the discretion to exclude should be confined to situations where there were doubts about the *reliability* of the evidence—where, for example, the agent provocateur might not be a credible witness or there was no reliable recording of the undercover operation.[139] While these observations are strictly *obiter*, the focus on the quality of the evidence rather than its provenance would appear to be consistent with the prevailing approach of the courts to section 78(1), as discussed above, and to constitute a substantial narrowing of the approach in *Smurthwaite*. The *Shannon* approach to exclusion may, however, have gained some support in the House of Lords, as will be discussed below. It is also to be noted that the European Court of Human Rights[140] declared inadmissible Shannon's complaint 'under Article 6 of the Convention that the admission of and reliance upon the evidence obtained by entrapment by the journalist rendered his trial unfair':

> The Court finds no reason to question this assessment of the domestic courts or, on the basis of its own examination of the material before it, to reach a different conclusion. It further notes that the applicant did not at any stage, either in the domestic proceedings or in his application to the Court, allege that the audio or video evidence against him was not genuine or was otherwise unreliable. Had he done so, it has not been disputed that it would have been open to the applicant in the domestic proceedings to challenge its admission on this ground.
>
> In these circumstances, the Court finds that the admission of the evidence in question did not result in any unfairness and that no appearance of violation of Article 6 is disclosed in this respect.

2.2.3 The Abuse of Process Doctrine

Exclusion of evidence resulting from an undercover operation may or may not have the effect of preventing the trial from proceeding altogether. Whether it would have this effect would obviously be dependent on how important the evidence is to the prosecution case as a whole. The House of Lords has held, however, that in certain circumstances a court may, on account of improper conduct during an undercover operation, *directly* prevent the case from proceeding altogether. This would be achieved through the court's exercise of its judicial discretion to stay proceedings as an abuse of the process of the court. In *R v Latif; R v Shahzad*[141] the appeal to the House of Lords centred upon Shahzad, whose appeal was conjoined with that of Latif. Shahzad was accused of being knowingly concerned in the importation of heroin from Pakistan. He argued that the prosecution should have been stayed as an abuse of process because of the involvement and assistance of Honi, an informer, and officers of the Customs and Excise. Indeed, it was a Customs officer who actually imported the heroin. The House of Lords acknowledged[142] that 'Shahzad would probably not have committed the particular offence of which he was convicted, but for the conduct of Honi and customs

---

[139] See quotation at text accompanying footnote 146.

[140] *Shannon v UK (Admissibility)*, Application no 67537/01, 6 April 2004.

[141] [1996] 1 WLR 104. See generally A Ashworth, 'Should the Police Be Allowed to Use Deceptive Practices?' (1998) 114 *Law Quarterly Review* 108, 119–20; K Grevling, 'Undercover Operations: Balancing the Public Interest?' (1996) 112 *Law Quarterly Review* 401; S Sharpe, 'Judicial Discretion and Investigative Impropriety' (1997) 1(2) *International Journal of Evidence and Proof* 149.   [142] [1996] 1 WLR 104, 111–13.

officers, which included criminal conduct'. If, however, a court were always to stay the proceedings in such cases, it would 'incur the reproach that it is failing to protect the public from serious crime'. If, on the other hand, the proceedings were never to be stayed, 'the perception will be that the court condones criminal conduct and malpractice by law enforcement agencies. That would undermine public confidence in the criminal justice system and bring it into disrepute.' It would be inappropriate, therefore, to adopt either extreme position. The approach, rather, should be as follows. First, if the court concludes that the impugned conduct would make a fair trial impossible, the proceedings must automatically be stayed. What is envisaged here, clearly, is the unlikely possibility of the conduct affecting trial fairness in the sense of compromising the ability of the trial to determine guilt or innocence properly. In the present case, it was 'plain that a fair trial was possible and that such a trial took place'. In such a situation it would be necessary to proceed to the second question, which is whether, despite a fair trial being possible, the judge ought nevertheless to stay the proceedings on the basis that it would be contrary to the public interest in the integrity of the criminal justice system for the trial to proceed. In other words, 'it is for the judge in the exercise of his discretion to decide whether there has been an abuse of process, which amounts to an affront to the public conscience and requires the criminal proceedings to be stayed'. In exercising this discretion, the court must perform a balancing exercise: 'in a case such as the present the judge must weigh in the balance the public interest in ensuring that those that are charged with grave crimes should be tried and the competing public interest in not conveying the impression that the court will adopt the approach that the end justified any means'. In the circumstances of the present case the House of Lords concluded that the judge had not erred in declining to stay the proceedings: he had taken into account the relevant considerations placed before him and performed the balancing exercise. He had been entitled to take the view that Shahzad was an organizer in the heroin trade and had taken the initiative in proposing the importation. In addition, Shahzad was 37 years old at the time; he was not a vulnerable and unwilling person; he had made it clear from the beginning that he was ready and willing to arrange the export of heroin from Pakistan; the Customs and Excise had simply provided him with the opportunity to commit the offence if he was so minded, and he was so minded. Thus, 'the conduct of the customs officer was not so unworthy or shameful that it was an affront to the public conscience to allow the prosecution to proceed. Realistically, any criminal behaviour of the customs officer was venial compared to that of Shahzad.'

Latif; Shahzad established therefore that where undercover police operations are concerned, either the exclusion of evidence or a stay of the proceedings as a whole may be ordered by the trial judge in the exercise of his or her discretion. Unfortunately, the precise relationship between these alternative judicial measures was not properly clarified. *Latif; Shahzad* was followed, some years later, by the major decision of the House of Lords on entrapment in *R v Looseley; A-G's Reference (No 3 of 2000).*[143] The House

---

[143] [2001] UKHL 53, [2001] 1 WLR 2060. See generally A Ashworth, 'Re-Drawing the Boundaries of Entrapment' [2002] *Criminal Law Review* 161; B Lewin, 'Test Purchasing—The Impact of the Human Rights Act 1998

confirmed in *Looseley; A-G's Reference* that, while there is no substantive defence of entrapment in English criminal law,[144] proof that the defendant in a particular case was improperly entrapped should lead to a stay of the proceedings. Improper entrapment may occur where, for example, a person is induced to commit an offence by means of inducements which would not normally be associated with the commission of an offence of that type. In the words of Lord Nicholls of Birkenhead:

> . . . a useful guide is to consider whether the police did no more than present the defendant with an unexceptional opportunity to commit a crime. I emphasise the word unexceptional. The yardstick for the purpose of this test is, in general, whether the police conduct preceding the commission of the offence was no more than might have been expected from others in the circumstances. Police conduct of this nature is not to be regarded as inciting or instigating crime, or luring a person into committing a crime. The police did no more than others could be expected to do. The police did not create crime artificially.[145]

If, however, a stay is not ordered on the basis of improper entrapment, there remains the possibility that the evidence of the agent provocateur may be excluded under section 78(1). Reference has been made above to the narrow view on exclusion taken in *Shannon* in contrast to the somewhat broader view taken previously in *Smurthwaite*. The relevant passage in *Shannon* reads as follows:

> So, for instance, if there is good reason to question the *credibility* of evidence given by an agent provocateur, or which casts doubt on the *reliability* of other evidence procured by or resulting from his actions, and that question is not susceptible of being properly or fairly resolved in the course of the proceedings from available, admissible and 'untainted' evidence, then the judge may readily conclude that such evidence should be excluded. If, on the other hand, the unfairness complained of is no more than the visceral reaction that it is in principle unfair as a matter of policy, or wrong as a matter of law, for a person to be prosecuted for a crime which he would not have committed without the incitement or encouragement of others, then that is not itself sufficient . . .[146]

Of the three Law Lords in *Looseley; A-G's Reference* who considered the issue, two— Lord Hoffmann[147] and Lord Hutton[148]—would appear to have accepted that this passage correctly states the law. Rather confusingly, the third, Lord Nicholls of Birkenhead,

---

and the Regulation of Investigatory Powers Act 2000' (2001) 165 *Justice of the Peace* 956; S McKay, 'Entrapment: Competing Views on the Effect of the Human Rights Act on English Criminal Law' [2002] *European Human Rights Law Review* 764; S O'Doherty, 'Entrapment: From Mitigation to Abuse' (2002) 166 *Justice of the Peace* 984; D Ormerod and A Roberts, 'The Trouble with *Teixeira*: Developing a Principled Approach to Entrapment' (2002) 6 *International Journal of Evidence and Proof* 38; D Corker and D Young, *Abuse of Process in Criminal Proceedings* (2nd ed 2003) Ch 6. The appeals in the cases of Looseley and the Attorney-General's Reference were heard together by the House of Lords.

[144] Established previously in *R v Sang* [1980] AC 402.

[145] [2001] UKHL 53, [2001] 1 WLR 2060, [23]. For a press report of a case in which these principles were applied see J Bennetto, 'Ten Defendants Go Free After Decade-Long Police Sting Ends in Fiasco. Cost to the Taxpayer? £25m', *The Independent*, 29 July 2003, internet edition.

[146] *R v Shannon* [2001] 1 WLR 51, 68 (italics added).

[147] [2001] UKHL 53, [2001] 1 WLR 2060, [43].   [148] Ibid, [103].

stated without explanation that his interpretation of the judgment in *Shannon* was that it 'accepted that evidence may properly be excluded when the behaviour of the police or prosecuting authority has been such as to justify a stay on grounds of abuse of process'.[149] Thus Lord Hoffmann and Lord Hutton would appear implicitly to have endorsed a narrow approach to exclusion while Lord Nicholls, misinterpreting *Shannon*, has endorsed a broad approach. The result is that the scope of section 78(1) is no clearer in the light of *Looseley; A-G's Reference*.

One of the certified questions for the House of Lords in *Looseley; A-G's Reference* was as follows:

> In a case involving the commission of offences by an accused at the instigation of undercover police officers, to what extent, if any, have:
>
> (i)   the judicial discretion conferred by section 78 of the Police and Criminal Evidence Act 1984; and
>
> (ii) the power to stay the proceedings as an abuse of the court;
>
> been modified by article 6 of the European Convention on Human Rights and the jurisprudence of the European Court of Human Rights.

The House had no hesitation in holding that no modification had taken place. Appropriate use of exclusion and stays was, it was said, sufficient to ensure consistency between English law and *Teixeira de Castro v Portugal*.[150] Certainly, from a purely doctrinal standpoint, *R v Looseley; A-G's Reference (No 3 of 2000)* does no more than endorse the law prevailing prior to the Human Rights Act 1998; the 1996 decision of the House in *R v Latif; R v Shahzad*[151] had already made it clear that the abuse of process doctrine was available in entrapment cases alongside the section 78(1) discretion. What is notable about *Looseley; A-G's Reference*, however, is that we have, for the first time in England and Wales, an articulate, sustained, and authoritative judicial consideration of entrapment of the sort that comparable jurisdictions have had for some years.[152]

What is also novel about *Looseley; A-G's Reference* is that it provides a rare instance of a holding by an English appellate court that a stay on account of entrapment was the appropriate judicial response in a particular case. A clear majority of the House of Lords[153]

---

[149] [2001] UKHL 53, [2001] 1 WLR 2060, [12].

[150] (1999) 28 EHRR 101 (judgment of 1998); discussed above.   [151] [1996] 1 WLR 104.

[152] See, eg, *R v Mack* (1988) 44 CCC (3d) 513 in Canada and *Ridgeway v R* (1995) 184 CLR 19 in Australia.

[153] See Lord Hoffmann at [2001] UKHL 53, [2001] 1 WLR 2060, [81], and Lord Hutton at [116]. Lord Nicholls of Birkenhead ([32]) agreed with the reasoning of Lord Hoffmann and Lord Hutton. Lord Mackay of Clashfern ([33]) agreed with the reasoning of Lord Nicholls of Birkenhead, Lord Hoffmann, and Lord Hutton. The fifth Law Lord, Lord Scott of Foscote, was rather more cautious: 'I doubt whether the conduct of the police officers was out of the line of what might have been expected of many purchasers of contraband cigarettes. The inducements offered to the accused in order to persuade him to supply heroin do not seem to me to correspond with what would be necessary to cause the prosecution to be an affront to the public or to offend ordinary notions of fairness. This was, however, a matter for the discretion of the trial judge, and it may be that his value judgment was one that he was entitled to reach' ([127]).

considered that the trial judge in *A-G's Reference (No 3 of 2000)* had been right in staying the proceedings. In the words of Lord Hutton:

> In the case giving rise to the Attorney General's Reference I respectfully differ from the view taken by the Court of Appeal and I consider that the judge was right to rule that the prosecution should be stayed on the ground that the police officers had instigated the offence. It was clear on the facts that the reason why the acquitted person had supplied heroin to the officers was because they repeatedly offered to supply, and did supply to him, cut-price cigarettes and he wished to continue to benefit from that supply. When he was interviewed by the police after his arrest he said that he was not interested in heroin, but that he had become involved because two men had approached him offering to sell him cheap cigarettes. He said it was 'a favour for a favour'. Therefore the officers did more than give him the opportunity to commit the offence of supplying heroin—they instigated the offence because they offered him inducements that would not ordinarily be associated with the commission of such an offence.[154]

It is also noteworthy that the Court of Appeal in *R v Moon*, applying *Looseley; A-G's Reference*, allowed the appeal against conviction on the basis that:

> whether the matter is looked through the lens of the proper safeguards of authorisation, or through the lens of the appellant's absence of predisposition or antecedents, or through the lens of the actual nature of the police activities in relation to this appellant, the conclusion to which we are driven is that this appellant was lured into crime or was entrapped, and that it was a case of causing crime rather than merely providing an opportunity for it, and ultimately that it would be unfair for the State to prosecute her for this offending. In these circumstances, the application to stay for abuse should, we think, have been accepted.[155]

2.2.4 The Regulation of Investigatory Powers Act 2000

The Regulation of Investigatory Powers Act 2000 ('RIPA') has introduced a regime for the authorization of undercover operations, under the umbrella of 'covert human intelligence sources'.[156] The relevant Code of Practice is confident that 'the proper authorisation of a [covert human intelligence] source should ensure the suitability of such evidence under the common law, section 78 of the Police and Criminal Evidence Act 1984 and the Human Rights Act 1998'.[157] A 'source' includes an agent, an informant, and an undercover officer.[158] The authorizing officer may grant authorization for the use or conduct of a source if it is believed that:

- the use or conduct of the source is proportionate to what is sought to be achieved; *and*

- the authorization is necessary in the interests of national security; or

- the authorization is necessary for the purpose of preventing or detecting crime or of preventing disorder; or

---

[154] Ibid, [116].   [155] [2004] EWCA Crim 2872, [51].

[156] See generally S McKay, 'The Definition of the Covert Human Intelligence Source', *Archbold News*, 8 Mar 2004, 5.   [157] Covert Human Intelligence Sources: Code of Practice, para 1.9.

[158] Covert Human Intelligence Sources: Code of Practice, para 4.2.

- the authorization is necessary in the interests of the economic well-being of the United Kingdom; or
- the authorization is necessary in the interests of public safety; or
- the authorization is necessary for the purpose of protecting public health; or
- the authorization is necessary for the purpose of assessing or collecting any tax, duty, levy or other imposition, contribution, or charge payable to a government department; or
- the authorization is necessary for any other purpose specified in an order made by the Secretary of State.[159]

As in the case of directed surveillance, no approval by a Surveillance Commissioner is required.

2.2.5 Conclusion

The principle recognized by the House of Lords in *Looseley; A-G's Reference* is warmly to be welcomed. This principle, in a nutshell, with the fundamental 'test' italicized, is this: A defendant who *would not have committed an offence but for actions of agents of the State that were unreasonable in the circumstances* ought not to be convicted of the offence. Acceptance that such a defendant ought not to be convicted has led the House of Lords to adopt the principle, adopted over a decade earlier in Canada,[160] that such proceedings must automatically be stayed. To put it another way, the public interest in the integrity of the criminal justice system must, in such a case, automatically outweigh the public interest in bringing offenders to conviction. The difficulty lies, of course, in determining in the context of an individual case whether the italicized words above apply to the defendant. While courts must clearly be left with a degree of leeway in making such a determination, the factors identified by the Supreme Court of Canada as being relevant to the determination are worthy of consideration. The Court has stated:

> To determine whether the police have employed means which go further than providing an opportunity, it is useful to consider any or all of the following factors:
>
> - the type of crime being investigated and the availability of other techniques for the police detection of its commission;
> - whether an average person, with both strengths and weaknesses, in the position of the accused would be induced into the commission of a crime;
> - the persistence and number of attempts made by the police before the accused agreed to committing the offence;
> - the type of inducement used by the police including: deceit, fraud, trickery or reward;
> - the timing of the police conduct, in particular whether the police have instigated the offence or became involved in ongoing criminal activity;

---

[159] RIPA, s 29.
[160] *R v Mack* (1988) 44 CCC (3d) 513. See also, more recently, *R v Campbell* [1999] 1 SCR 565.

- whether the police conduct involves an exploitation of human characteristics such as the emotions of compassion, sympathy and friendship;

- whether the police appear to have exploited a particular vulnerability of a person such as a mental handicap or a substance addiction;

- the proportionality between the police involvement, as compared to the accused, including an assessment of the degree of harm caused or risked by the police, as compared to the accused, and the commission of any illegal acts by the police themselves;

- the existence of any threats, implied or express, made to the accused by the police or their agents;

- whether the police conduct is directed at undermining other constitutional values.[161]

One area of English law that remains unsettled concerns situations where the conduct of the undercover officer or agent falls short of conduct justifying a stay. The extent to which section 78(1) may be invoked in such a situation is, as we have seen, unclear, with *Smurthwaite* and *Shannon* pointing in different directions, and *Looseley; A-G's Reference* unhelpful. In 1998 JUSTICE issued a report on covert policing in which it recommended that, to ensure compliance with the fair trial rights of Article 6 of the European Convention, English law should contain a statutory defence of entrapment. By virtue of this defence, a defendant would not be liable to conviction if he or she would not have done the acts charged but for the incitement by an agent provocateur. It is arguable that, while not encapsulated in a statute, a reasonably coherent doctrine of entrapment that recognizes non-conviction of the defendant as the appropriate remedy is now, in the light of *Looseley; A-G's Reference*, recognized in English law. JUSTICE further recommended that, in cases falling short of the full defence, courts should give consideration to the possibility of exercising the section 78 discretion,[162] taking into account factors of the following kind:

THE SPECIFIC TYPE OF CRIME

- the type of crime being investigated
- by whom and on what grounds the police operation was authorised

THE LEVEL OF INDUCEMENT

- the persistence of the police
- the type of inducement used, and in particular, whether deceit, fraud or trickery was employed or whether some form of reward was offered
- the timing of the police conduct, and in particular, whether the police instigated the offence or became involved in on-going criminal activity
- whether the conduct exploited a particular vulnerability of a person, such as drug addiction or human emotions, such as friendship
- the existence of any threats implied or expressed

---

[161] (1988) 44 CCC (3d) 513, 560.
[162] JUSTICE, *Under Surveillance: Covert Policing and Human Rights Standards* (1998) 81.

OTHER CONSIDERATIONS

- the proportionality between the police conduct and the defendant's involvement in the criminal conduct
- the nature of the record of the operation or other corroborating evidence
- whether the conduct has implications for [the] defendant's enjoyment of other fundamental rights, such as the right to privacy
- whether there are broader considerations [implicating] the integrity of the criminal justice system[163]

Consistently with the arguments made above for taking a broad approach to section 78(1) that is analogous to the approach taken to abuse of process, it is submitted that this recommendation points the correct way forward for English law.

[163] JUSTICE, *Under Surveillance: Covert Policing and Human Rights Standards* (1998) 82.

6

Public Interest Immunity and Related Matters

It will have been seen from the examination of improperly obtained evidence in Chapter 5 that involved in that topic is a clash of two competing public interests: on the one hand, the public interest in allowing the admission of all relevant and reliable evidence, in order that those guilty of crimes may be brought to conviction, and, on the other hand, the public interest in maintaining the moral integrity of the criminal justice process. A similar clash of competing public interests underlies the doctrine of public interest immunity. The law takes the view that, in appropriate circumstances, material which would otherwise be disclosed in the course of litigation may be withheld on the basis that disclosure would undermine the public interest[1]—by, for example, compromising national security or the proper functioning of the public service. The issue of public interest immunity has been the subject of constant public attention for at least the past decade. It was subjected to intense scrutiny in the 1990s as a result of the Matrix Churchill case and the subsequent publication of the Scott Report. In the Matrix Churchill case, three directors of Matrix Churchill, a company manufacturing and exporting machine tools, were charged with supplying arms-making equipment to Iraq, in breach of the Government's published export guidelines. The directors' defence was that Government ministers were aware of, and authorized, the exporting, and that MI6 also knew. Four ministers signed public interest immunity certificates in relation to documents of which the defence sought disclosure. The trial judge ordered disclosure of some of these. The prosecution then discontinued the trial, because Alan Clark, the then Minister of State at the Department of Trade and Industry, admitted under cross-examination that the Government had been fully aware of the intended use of the equipment.[2] In the light of the Matrix Churchill case an inquiry by Sir Richard Scott, a High Court judge, was instituted. One of the issues into which he inquired was the use of public interest immunity certificates to restrict the availability of evidence at the criminal trial. The inquiry culminated in the publication of the Scott Report,[3] which

---

[1] See, eg, Criminal Procedure and Investigations Act 1996, ss 3(6), 7(5), 8(5), 9(8).

[2] See generally I Leigh, 'Matrix Churchill, Supergun and the Scott Inquiry' [1993] *Public Law* 630; I Leigh, 'Reforming Public Interest Immunity' in M J Allen (ed), *Web Journal of Current Legal Issues Yearbook 1995* (1996); A Tomkins, 'Public Interest Immunity After Matrix Churchill' [1993] *Public Law* 650.

[3] R Scott, *Report of the Inquiry into the Export of Defence Equipment and Dual-Use Goods to Iraq and Related Prosecutions* (1996).

made a number of important observations about the use of public interest immunity in criminal cases, in February 1996.

More recently, as will be seen in this chapter, debate has centred around the use in certain circumstances of *ex parte* hearings (that is, hearings at which the defence is not present) to determine public interest immunity issues in criminal cases.[4]

The focus of this chapter is on public interest immunity. The discussion of public interest immunity will be followed by a relatively brief account of two other types of information to which access may be restricted: information that is subject to an obligation of confidentiality and information relating to journalists' sources.

1 The Development of the Law

Public interest immunity was originally known as 'Crown privilege'. This reflected the fact that a claim to public interest immunity made by the Crown in proper form was considered to be final and could not be overridden by the court. The principle applied irrespective of whether the claim related to the contents of a particular document or to a class of documents.[5] In *Conway v Rimmer*,[6] however, the House of Lords discarded this old notion, holding that the court must be the final arbiter in relation to all public interest immunity claims. The approach to be adopted is as follows. The court must, in the context of the particular case, balance the considerations underlying public interest immunity against the public interest in the fair administration of justice. If the latter outweighs the former disclosure must be ordered.

What is at issue being *public* interest immunity rather than a private privilege, it is not necessary that the question be raised by a party to the proceedings: 'it must always be open to any person interested to raise the question and there may be cases where the trial judge should himself raise the question if no one else has done so'.[7] Relatedly, public interest immunity cannot be waived by a party to the proceedings.[8]

Subject to one possible exception,[9] the court has a general power to inspect a document that is subject to a public interest immunity claim in order to determine whether it should be disclosed or whether, instead, the claim should be upheld. While judges have expressed differing views on the basis on which the discretion to inspect is to be exercised,[10] the importance of inspection by the court in certain circumstances is

---

[4] See generally C Taylor, 'What Next for Public Interest Immunity?' (2005) 69 *Journal of Criminal Law* 75.

[5] *Duncan v Cammell, Laird & Co* [1942] AC 624.   [6] [1968] AC 910.

[7] *R v Lewes JJ, ex p Home Sec* [1973] AC 388, 400. See also *Duncan v Cammell, Laird & Co* [1942] AC 624, 642.

[8] *R v Lewes JJ, ex p Home Sec* [1973] AC 388; *D v NSPCC* [1978] AC 171.

[9] See *Balfour v Foreign Office* [1994] 1 WLR 681, discussed below.

[10] See, eg, *Air Canada v Secretary of State for Trade* [1983] 2 AC 394 in which Lord Fraser of Tullybelton, Lord Edmund-Davies, and Lord Wilberforce took the view that it would be appropriate to inspect only if the document was likely to support the case of the party seeking disclosure. Lords Scarman and Templeman, on the other hand, thought that it would be appropriate to inspect so long as the document was likely to be necessary for a fair determination of the case.

clear.[11] Indeed, as will be seen below, the House of Lords may have accepted in a decision in 2004[12] that inspection may be required in criminal cases.

Section 130 of the Uniform Evidence Acts in Australia is meant to reflect the common law on public interest immunity and as such may be regarded as providing a useful rationalization of the law applicable in England and Wales and, in particular, of the factors to be taken into account by a court:

(1) If the public interest in admitting into evidence information or a document that relates to matters of state is outweighed by the public interest in preserving secrecy or confidentiality in relation to the information or document, the court may direct that the information or document not be adduced as evidence.

(2) The court may give such a direction either on its own initiative or on the application of any person (whether or not the person is a party).

(3) In deciding whether to give such a direction, the court may inform itself in any way it thinks fit.

(4) . . .

(5) Without limiting the matters that the court may take into account for the purposes of subsection (1), it is to take into account the following matters:

(a) the importance of the information or the document in the proceeding;

(b) if the proceeding is a criminal proceeding—whether the party seeking to adduce evidence of the information or document is a defendant or the prosecutor;

(c) the nature of the offence, cause of action or defence to which the information or document relates, and the nature of the subject matter of the proceeding;

(d) the likely effect of adducing evidence of the information or document, and the means available to limit its publication;

(e) whether the substance of the information or document has already been published;

(f) if the proceeding is a criminal proceeding and the party seeking to adduce evidence of the information or document is a defendant—whether the direction is to be made subject to the condition that the prosecution be stayed.

(6) . . .

2 'Class' Claims and 'Contents' Claims

A 'class claim' to public interest immunity differs from a 'contents claim' in the sense that the claim is said to arise by virtue of the class to which the particular document belongs rather than the contents of the document. A class claim was at issue in *R v Lewes JJ, ex p Home Sec.*[13] The claim related to a letter to the Gaming Board about a

---

[11] See, eg, *R v K* (1993) 97 Cr App R 342 (decision of 1992) and *Wallace Smith Trust Co v Deloitte* [1996] 4 All ER 403, 413.   [12] *R v H* [2004] UKHL 3, [2004] 2 WLR 335.

[13] [1973] AC 388.

person who had applied to the Board for certificates of consent. The House of Lords noted: 'The claim in the present case is not based on the nature of the contents of this particular letter. It is based on the fact that the board cannot adequately perform their statutory duty unless they can preserve the confidentiality of all communications to them regarding the character, reputation or antecedents of applicants for their consent.'[14] Class claims can be somewhat controversial and it has been accepted that 'there is a heavy burden of proof on any authority which makes such a claim'.[15] It would also seem that there are certain circumstances in which class claims may not be made. In *Ex p Wiley*, all the parties in the House of Lords accepted, and the House agreed, that a class claim could not be made in respect of documents created in the course of investigating a complaint about police misconduct. The House left open the question, however, whether a class claim could be made in relation to the actual *reports* of the investigating officers. In *Taylor v Anderton*,[16] the Court of Appeal held that such a claim could indeed be made. The Court reached the same conclusion in the later case of *Kelly v Commissioner of Police of the Metropolis*,[17] where at issue were certain forms used by police forces and sent to the Crown Prosecution Service following an investigation into a suspected criminal offence. The question for the Court of Appeal was the extent to which public interest immunity attached to these forms so as to inhibit their disclosure for the purposes of civil proceedings against the police after the criminal proceedings had come to an end. It was held that the forms belonged to a class of documents to which public interest immunity attached.

The Government announced in late 1996 that class claims would no longer be made in relation to Government documents.[18] Rather, ministers would claim public interest immunity only where it is believed that disclosure of a document would cause real damage or harm to the public interest. This is very much to be welcomed, but the situation is now somewhat anomalous in that while ministers may no longer make class claims, non-Government bodies such as the police may continue to do so in certain circumstances, as the decisions in *Taylor* and *Kelly* illustrate. What is required now is legislation which makes the approach of the Government of general application.

We shall now examine a number of different contexts in which litigation concerning public interest immunity has arisen.

3 National Security and Analogous Concerns

Public interest immunity may be claimed on the basis of national security, or the maintenance of good diplomatic relations and international comity.[19] It has been seen earlier that courts have a general discretion to inspect documents to determine whether

---

[14] [1973] AC 400.   [15] Ibid.   [16] [1995] 1 WLR 447.   [17] *The Times*, 20 Aug 1997.
[18] See generally G Ganz, 'Volte-Face on Public Interest Immunity' (1997) 60 *Modern Law Review* 552; M Supperstone and J Coppel, 'A New Approach to Public Interest Immunity?' [1997] *Public Law* 211.
[19] The decision of the House of Lords in *Duncan v Cammell, Laird & Co* [1942] AC 624 provides a classic illustration of a claim based on national security concerns. See also *Hennessy v Wright* (1888) 21 QBD 509;

they should be disclosed or whether, instead, the claim to public interest immunity should be upheld. There may, however, be an exception to this in the case of claims to public interest immunity on the basis of risk to national security. The Court of Appeal held in *Balfour v Foreign Office* that 'once there is an actual or potential risk to national security demonstrated by an appropriate certificate the court should not exercise its right to inspect'.[20] Whether this is justifiable is debatable.

Public interest immunity may also be claimed in the interests of protection of good diplomatic relations and international comity. In *Buttes Oil Co v Hammer (No 3)*,[21] Brightman LJ said:

> In my view it is in the public interest of the United Kingdom that the contents of confidential documents addressed to, or emanating from sovereign states, or concerning the interests of sovereign states, arising in connection with an international territorial dispute between sovereign states, shall not be ordered by the courts of this country to be disclosed by a private litigant without the consent of the sovereign states concerned. I think that such an immunity is a public interest of the United Kingdom and I think that it outweighs the public interest that justice shall be administered on the basis of full disclosure of all relevant unprivileged documents. It is analogous to, but is clearly distinguishable from the public interest immunity which may attach to confidential documents of Her Majesty's Government. The resolution of a territorial dispute between sovereign states is a political question and it is undesirable that an English court should be seen to be forcing the disclosure of documents, prima facie of a confidential nature, for the ostensible purpose of pronouncing, albeit indirectly, on the merits of such a dispute.[22]

In a similar vein, inter-departmental memoranda between officials in a foreign embassy may also be subject to public interest immunity.[23]

4 Proper Functioning of the Public Service

The decision of the House of Lords in *Ex p Wiley*, as well as the earlier decisions of the House in *Conway v Rimmer*,[24] *Burmah Oil Co v Bank of England*,[25] and *Air Canada v Secretary of State for Trade*,[26] provide authoritative judicial acknowledgement that considerations pertaining to the proper functioning of departments of central government, or the police, may found a claim of public interest immunity in appropriate circumstances. But it is not just departments of central government or

---

Asiatic Petroleum Co Ltd v Anglo-Persian Oil Co Ltd [1916] 1 KB 822. Although the reasoning of the House of Lords in *Duncan* was subsequently disapproved by the House in *Conway v Rimmer*, the view was expressed in *Conway* that the actual result reached in *Duncan* was justifiable: [1968] AC 910, 938. See, however, M Spencer, 'Bureaucracy, National Security and Access to Justice: New Light on *Duncan v Cammell Laird*' (2004) 55 *Northern Ireland Legal Quarterly* 277.

[20] [1994] 1 WLR 681, 688.   [21] [1981] QB 223.
[22] Ibid, 265. The case was reversed on other grounds in [1982] AC 888.
[23] Cf *Fayed v Al-Tajir* [1987] 2 All ER 396.   [24] [1968] AC 910.   [25] [1980] AC 1090.
[26] [1983] 2 AC 394.

police departments which may be entitled to claim public interest immunity. In *D v NSPCC*,[27] the plaintiff claimed damages from the NSPCC for the injury to her health caused by the negligence of the NSPCC in pursuing the allegations of an informant that she had maltreated her child. These allegations had proved groundless. The NSPCC argued that documents which revealed the informant's identity were subject to public interest immunity. The House of Lords agreed, holding that the public interest in protecting the flow of information justified the refusal to order disclosure of the documents, since a consequence of disclosure might well be that the NSPCC's sources of information would dry up. The significance of this case, as Lord Woolf put it in *Ex p Wiley*, 'is that it made clear that the immunity does not only exist to protect the effective functioning of departments or organs of central government or the police, but also could protect the effective functioning of an organisation such as the NSPCC which was authorised under an Act of Parliament to bring legal proceedings for the welfare of children'.[28]

Other bodies which have been acknowledged by the courts as being able to claim public interest immunity in appropriate circumstances include local authorities,[29] the Gaming Board,[30] the Customs and Excise Commissioners,[31] and the Law Society.[32]

5 Criminal Cases

Traditionally, the issue of public interest immunity has tended to arise in non-criminal litigation. In more recent times, however, it has had to be considered in a number of criminal cases, of which the Matrix Churchill case is perhaps the best known. In the criminal sphere, the issue of public interest immunity acquires a special dimension. Where the defence is seeking disclosure of information held by the prosecution, a decision not to order disclosure may well result in the withholding of information which shows the defendant's innocence. The right of the defendant not to be convicted of an offence of which he or she is innocent may accordingly be compromised. Whether the approach of performing a 'balancing exercise' that is adopted by the civil courts is a meaningful approach in the criminal context may be questioned.

We shall examine now the two main contexts in which public interest immunity disputes in criminal cases have arisen: the disclosure of the identity of police informers, and the disclosure of the location of police observation points.

---

[27] [1978] AC 171.   [28] [1995] 1 AC 274, 291.

[29] *In re D (Infants)* [1970] 1 WLR 599; *Gaskin v Liverpool Council* [1980] 1 WLR 1549; *R v City of Birmingham DC, ex p O* [1982] 2 All ER 356; *Re M (A Minor) (Disclosure of Material)* [1990] 2 FLR 36.

[30] *R v Lewes JJ, ex p Home Sec* [1973] AC 388.

[31] *Norwich Pharmacal v Customs & Excise* [1974] AC 133; *A Crompton Ltd v Customs & Excise* [1974] AC 405.   [32] *Buckley v Law Society (No 2)* [1984] 3 All ER 313.

5.1 Disclosure of the Identity of Police Informers

The identity of police informers may be protected by public interest immunity.[33] The rationale for this long-established[34] principle was vividly described by McLachlin J in a decision of the Supreme Court of Canada:

[The principle] is an ancient and hallowed protection which plays a vital role in law enforcement. It is premised on the duty of all citizens to aid in enforcing the law. The discharge of this duty carries with it the risk of retribution from those involved in crime. The [principle] was developed to protect citizens who assist in law enforcement and to encourage others to do the same.[35]

In determining whether disclosure should be ordered the courts use the language of a balancing exercise but, as the following quotation indicates, where the material would clearly be helpful to the defence there is no question of this interest being counterbalanced by other asserted public interests. The judge has an important function in determining the potential effect of the material on the conduct of the defence case but if it is found that denial of access to the material would render any trial unfair the judge has no choice but to order disclosure:

If the disputed material may prove the defendant's innocence or avoid a miscarriage of justice, then the balance comes down resoundingly in favour of disclosing it. . . . the judge has to perform the balancing exercise by having regard on the one hand to the weight of the public interest in non-disclosure. On the other hand, he must consider the importance of the documents to the issues of interest to the defence, present and potential, so far as they have been disclosed to him or he can foresee them. Accordingly, the more full and specific the indication the defendant's lawyers give of the defence or issues they are likely to raise, the more accurately both prosecution and judge will be able to discuss the value to the defence of the material.[36]

The Court of Appeal has noted:

an increasing tendency for defendants to seek disclosure of informants' names and roles, alleging that those details are essential to the defence. Defences that the accused has been set up, and allegations of duress, which used at one time to be rare, have multiplied. We wish to alert judges to the need to scrutinise applications for disclosure of details about informants with very great care. They will need to be astute to see that assertions of a need to know such

---

[33] See generally H Mares, 'Balancing Public Interest and a Fair Trial in Police Informer Privilege: A Critical Australian Perspective' (2002) 6 *International Journal of Evidence and Proof* 94; C Taylor, 'In the Public Interest: Public Interest Immunity and Police Informants' (2001) 65 *Journal of Criminal Law* 435.

[34] See *A-G v Briant* (1846) 15 M & W 169, 185, 153 ER 808, 815: 'This has been a settled rule for fifty years . . .'.

[35] *R v Leipert* (1997) 143 DLR (4th) 38, 43–4. See also *D v NSPCC* [1978] AC 171; *R v Hennessey* (1979) 68 Cr App R 419, 426 (decision of 1978).

[36] *R v Keane* [1994] 1 WLR 746, 751–2. See also *Marks v Beyfus* (1890) 25 QBD 494, 499–500. A similar approach is taken in Canada: *R v Leipert* (1997) 143 DLR (4th) 38. Interestingly, the Supreme Court of Canada took the view that if a decision of non-disclosure was reached on the basis of an appropriate application of the balancing exercise, this would automatically mean that the accused's right to make full answer and defence under the Canadian Charter of Rights and Freedoms was not infringed.

details, because they are essential to the running of the defence, are justified. If they are not so justified, then the judge will need to adopt a robust approach in declining to order disclosure. Clearly, there is a distinction between cases in which the circumstances raise no reasonable possibility that information about the informant will bear upon the issues and cases where it will. Again, there will be cases where the informant is an informant and no more; other cases where he may have participated in the events constituting, surrounding, or following the crime. Even when the informant has participated, the judge will need to consider whether his role so impinges on an issue of interest to the defence, present or potential, as to make disclosure necessary.[37]

The Court of Appeal has held that a police informer wishing to sacrifice his or her anonymity is not automatically prevented by the doctrine of public interest immunity from doing so: 'if a police informer wishes personally to sacrifice his own anonymity, he is not precluded from doing so by the automatic application of the principle of public interest immunity... This follows, not from waiver of privilege attaching personally to the informer, but from the disappearance of the primary justification for the claim for public interest immunity.' It may, however, be possible to 'infer, for example, that disclosure might assist others involved in criminal activities, or reveal police methods of investigation, or hamper their operations, or indicate the state of their inquiries into any particular crime, or even that the police are in possession of information which suggests extreme and urgent danger to the informer if he were to proceed. Considerations such as these might, in an appropriate case, ultimately tip the balance in favour of preserving the informer's anonymity against his wishes in the public interest.'[38]

It should be noted that, in a criminal case, the Crown Prosecution Service may be able to disclose voluntarily to the defence, without obtaining a court order, documents in respect of which a class claim to public interest immunity can be made. However, the prior express written approval of the Treasury Solicitor to the voluntary disclosure must be obtained. To seek such approval the CPS should submit to the Treasury Solicitor copies of the relevant documents, identify the public interest immunity class into which they fall, and indicate the materiality of the documents to the proceedings.

> Before giving his approval, the Treasury Solicitor should consult any other relevant government department and satisfy himself that the balance in his view falls clearly in favour of disclosing the documents. In making that assessment he will inevitably have regard, inter alia, to (a) the particular class of documents involved, (b) their materiality to the proceedings and (c) the extent to which disclosure will damage the public interest in the integrity of the class claim. The Treasury Solicitor should be the readier to approve disclosure of documents likely to assist the defence case than those which the CPS wish to disclose with a view to furthering the interests of the prosecution.[39]

---

[37] *R v Turner* [1995] 1 WLR 264, 267.
[38] *Savage v Chief Constable of Hampshire* [1997] 2 All ER 631, 636.
[39] *R v Horseferry Road Magistrates' Court, ex p Bennett (No 2)* [1994] 1 All ER 289, 297.

5.2 Disclosure of the Location of Police Observation Points

The extent to which the police are required to disclose the location of premises used by them for surveillance purposes was considered in detail in *R v Johnson*:

> At the heart of this problem is the desirability, as far as that can properly be given, of re-assuring people who are asked to help the police that their identities will never be disclosed lest they become the victims of reprisals by wrongdoers for performing a public service.
>
> The minimum evidential requirements seem to us to be the following.
>
> (a) The police officer in charge of the observations to be conducted, no one of lower rank than a sergeant should usually be acceptable for this purpose, must be able to testify that beforehand he visited all observation places to be used and ascertained the attitude of occupiers of premises, not only to the use to be made of them, but to the possible disclosure thereafter of the use made and facts which could lead to the identification of the premises thereafter and of the occupiers. He may of course in addition inform the court of difficulties, if any, usually encountered in the particular locality of obtaining assistance from the public.
>
> (b) A police officer of no lower rank than a chief inspector must be able to testify that immediately prior to the trial he visited the places used for observations, the results of which it is proposed to give in evidence, and ascertained whether the occupiers are the same as when the observations took place and whether they are or are not, what the attitude of those occupiers is to the possible disclosure of the use previously made of the premises and of facts which could lead at the trial to identification of premises and occupiers.
>
> Such evidence will of course be given in the absence of the jury when the application to exclude the material evidence is made. The judge should explain to the jury . . . when summing up or at some appropriate time before that, the effect of his ruling to exclude, if he so rules.[40]

In *Blake v DPP*,[41] it was held that fear of harassment, as opposed to violence, by the occupiers of the premises is a sufficient basis for a public interest immunity claim.

5.3 The Scott Report

The Scott Report identified uncertainty about the scope of public interest immunity in criminal cases as one of the root causes of the miscarriage of justice in the Matrix Churchill case. With this in mind, Sir Richard Scott sought to set out the rules which he believed governed the issue. These include the following:

. . .

> (ii) PII claims on a class basis should not in future be made. PII contents claims should not be made in respect of documents which it is apparent are documents which might be of assistance to the defence.

. . .

---

[40] [1988] 1 WLR 1377, 1385–6. See also *R v Rankine* [1986] QB 861; *R v Hewitt* (1992) 95 Cr App R 81 (decision of 1991).   [41] (1993) 97 Cr App R 169 (decision of 1992).

(viii) ... the judge should be asked to decide whether the documents might be of assistance to the defence. If a document satisfies this test, the document ought not to be withheld from a defendant on PII grounds. There is no true balance to be struck. The weight of public interest factors underlying the PII claim is immaterial. However, existing authority, with its apparent endorsement of the 'balancing exercise' while at the same time requiring the disclosure of any document which 'may prove the defendant's innocence to avoid a miscarriage of justice', suffers, in my opinion, from some degree of ambiguity. It would be important, in my opinion, if disclosure of a material document is to be withheld, that the defendant should know whether the decision was based on the judge's conclusion that the document would not be of any assistance to the defence or on the judge's conclusion that, despite meeting that test, the weight of public interest factors precludes disclosure. The latter conclusion would, in my opinion, be wrong in principle and contrary to authority.

. . .

(x) If the documents, although relevant and *prima facie* disclosable, do not appear to be documents that might assist the defence, the judge may conclude that in view of the public interest factors underlying the PII claim, the documents need not be disclosed.[42]

There may be much to be said for Scott's argument that it is meaningless, in the context of criminal litigation, to speak in terms of a 'balancing exercise'. Scott's contention that class claims are inappropriate in criminal cases is echoed by Leigh,[43] who also argues that 'a mandatory statutory requirement of judicial inspection should apply to PII claims in criminal proceedings'.[44] It is disappointing that in its 2004 decision in *R v H* the House of Lords did not take the opportunity to dispel uncertainty in this area. A close reading of the itemized guidance provided in this decision[45] shows the House strongly implying, however, that in a criminal case the material in question must be inspected by the judge (it was said that the issue of what the material is that the prosecution seeks to withhold 'must be considered by the court in detail'), and also that the ultimate goal is to ensure that the trial process, viewed as a whole, is fair to the defendant.

6 Procedure

6.1 Civil Cases

Rule 31.19(1) of the Civil Procedure Rules provides: 'A person may apply, without notice, for an order permitting him to withhold disclosure of a document on the ground that disclosure would damage the public interest.' The application 'must be supported by evidence'.[46] For the purpose of determining the application the court may

---

[42] R Scott, *Report of the Inquiry into the Export of Defence Equipment and Dual-Use Goods to Iraq and Related Prosecutions* (1996) 1789–91. See also R Scott, 'The Acceptable and Unacceptable Use of Public Interest Immunity' [1996] *Public Law* 427.

[43] I Leigh, 'Reforming Public Interest Immunity' in M J Allen (ed), *Web Journal of Current Legal Issues Yearbook 1995* (1996).   [44] Ibid, 104.

[45] *R v H* [2004] UKHL 3, [2004] 2 WLR 335, [36]. Quoted at text accompanying footnote 66.

[46] Rule 31.19(7).

require the person seeking to withhold disclosure to produce the document to the court, and invite any person (whether a party or not) to make representations.[47]

6.2 Criminal Cases

Previously governed by the common law,[48] the approach in criminal cases was later encapsulated in the Crown Court (Criminal Procedure and Investigations Act 1996) (Disclosure) Rules 1997 and in the Magistrates' Courts (Criminal Procedure and Investigations Act 1996) (Disclosure) Rules 1997, and is now encapsulated in the Criminal Procedure Rules 2005.[49]

The general rule is that notice of any application by the prosecution to withhold material on the grounds of public interest immunity is to be given to the accused, with 'the nature of the material to which the application relates' being specified.[50] The hearing of the application is to be *inter partes*,[51] with the prosecutor and the accused being entitled to make representations to the court.[52] 'Where the prosecutor applies to the court for leave to make representations in the absence of the accused, the court may for that purpose sit in the absence of the accused and any legal representative of his.'[53]

'Where the prosecutor has reason to believe that to reveal to the accused the nature of the material to which the application relates would have the effect of disclosing that which the prosecutor contends should not in the public interest be disclosed', then the accused is still to be notified that an application has been made, but without the nature of the material to which the application relates being specified.[54] The hearing of the application is to be *ex parte*[55] with only the prosecutor being entitled to make representations to the court.[56] 'Where the prosecutor has reason to believe that to reveal to the accused the fact that an application is being made would have the effect of disclosing that which the prosecutor contends should not in the public interest be disclosed', the accused is not even to be notified that an application has been made.[57] The hearing of the application, again, is to be *ex parte*[58] with only the prosecutor being entitled to make representations to the court.[59]

Concern has been expressed about the inability of the defence to make representations to the court in certain circumstances. It has been suggested that a solution would be to appoint 'special counsel' to represent the interests of the defence. Such a person 'may not disclose to the subject of the proceedings the secret material disclosed to him,

---

[47] Rule 31.19(6).   [48] See *R v Davis* [1993] 1 WLR 613, 617–18.

[49] See also, on Crown Court trials, *R v Menga* [1998] Crim LR 58, and, on summary trials, F G Davies, 'Procedural Unfairness Arising from Public Interest Immunity Applications: Part I' (1997) 161 *Justice of the Peace* 951; F G Davies, 'Procedural Unfairness Arising from Public Interest Immunity Applications: Part II' (1997) 161 *Justice of the Peace* 971.   [50] Criminal Procedure Rules 2005, rule 25.1(2).

[51] Criminal Procedure Rules 2005, rule 25.2(3)(b).

[52] Criminal Procedure Rules 2005, rule 25.2(3)(c).   [53] Criminal Procedure Rules 2005, rule 25.2(4).

[54] Criminal Procedure Rules 2005, rule 25.1(4).   [55] Criminal Procedure Rules 2005, rule 25.2(5)(a).

[56] Criminal Procedure Rules 2005, rule 25.2(5)(b).   [57] Criminal Procedure Rules 2005, rule 25.1(5).

[58] Criminal Procedure Rules 2005, rule 25.2(5)(a).

[59] Criminal Procedure Rules 2005, rule 25.2(5)(b).

and is not in the ordinary sense professionally responsible to that party, but ... , subject to those constraints, is charged to represent that party's interests'.[60] The use of special counsel has been permitted, for example, in proceedings concerning the exclusion or removal of a person as being conducive to the public good or in the interests of national security.[61] On the appropriateness of using special counsel in public interest immunity hearings in criminal cases, the House of Lords has authoritatively stated in *R v H*,[62] in a passage quoted by the Grand Chamber of the European Court of Human Rights in *Edwards and Lewis v UK*:[63]

> There is as yet little express sanction in domestic legislation or domestic legal authority for the appointment of a special advocate or special counsel to represent, as an advocate in PII matters, a defendant in an ordinary criminal trial ... But ... cases will arise in which the appointment of an approved advocate as special counsel is necessary, in the interests of justice, to secure protection of a criminal defendant's right to a fair trial. Such an appointment does however raise ethical problems, since a lawyer who cannot take full instructions from his client, nor report to his client, who is not responsible to his client and whose relationship with the client lacks the quality of confidence inherent in any ordinary lawyer-client relationship, is acting in a way hitherto unknown to the legal profession. While not insuperable, these problems should not be ignored, since neither the defendant nor the public will be fully aware of what is being done. The appointment is also likely to cause practical problems: of delay, while the special counsel familiarises himself with the detail of what is likely to be a complex case; of expense, since the introduction of an additional, high-quality advocate must add significantly to the cost of the case; and of continuing review, since it will not be easy for a special counsel to assist the court in its continuing duty to review disclosure, unless the special counsel is present throughout or is instructed from time to time when need arises. Defendants facing serious charges frequently have little inclination to co-operate in a process likely to culminate in their conviction, and any new procedure can offer opportunities capable of exploitation to obstruct and delay. None of these problems should deter the court from appointing special counsel where the interests of justice are shown to require it. But the need must be shown. Such an appointment will always be exceptional, never automatic; a course of last and never first resort. It should not be ordered unless and until the trial judge is satisfied that no other course will adequately meet the overriding requirement of fairness to the defendant.[64]

The House of Lords also made the following observation: 'The occasions on which it will be appropriate to appoint special counsel in the magistrates' court will be even rarer than in the crown court.'[65]

---

[60] *R v H* [2004] UKHL 3, [2004] 2 WLR 335, [21].

[61] Pursuant to the Special Immigration Appeals Commission Act 1997, s 6; Special Immigration Appeals Commission (Procedure) Rules 2003, rule 34. See also *R (Roberts) v Parole Board* [2005] UKHL 45, [2005] 3 WLR 152.

[62] *R v H* [2004] UKHL 3, [2004] 2 WLR 335. See generally N Blake, 'Special Advocates in Criminal Trials' (2004) 154 *New Law Journal* 233; M Caplan and S Parkinson, 'Testing the PII Template' (2004) 154 *New Law Journal* 238; M Rea, 'Golden Rules' (2004) 148 *Solicitors' Journal* 314; C Taylor, 'The Courts and Applications for Public Interest Immunity: *R v H and C*' (2004) 8 *International Journal of Evidence and Proof* 179.

[63] (2005) 40 EHRR 24 (p 593) (judgment of 2004), [45].

[64] *R v H* [2004] UKHL 3, [2004] 2 WLR 335, [22].   [65] Ibid, [44].

More generally, the House of Lords has made it clear that, properly implemented, the established procedures for dealing with public interest immunity applications made by the prosecution are compliant with the right to a fair trial under Article 6. The following detailed guidance is provided in *R v H*:

When any issue of derogation from the golden rule of full disclosure comes before it, the court must address a series of questions:

(1) What is the material which the prosecution seek to withhold? This must be considered by the court in detail.

(2) Is the material such as may weaken the prosecution case or strengthen that of the defence? If No, disclosure should not be ordered. If Yes, full disclosure should (subject to (3), (4) and (5) below) be ordered.

(3) Is there a real risk of serious prejudice to an important public interest (and, if so, what) if full disclosure of the material is ordered? If No, full disclosure should be ordered.

(4) If the answer to (2) and (3) is Yes, can the defendant's interest be protected without disclosure or disclosure be ordered to an extent or in a way which will give adequate protection to the public interest in question and also afford adequate protection to the interests of the defence?

This question requires the court to consider, with specific reference to the material which the prosecution seek to withhold and the facts of the case and the defence as disclosed, whether the prosecution should formally admit what the defence seek to establish or whether disclosure short of full disclosure may be ordered. This may be done in appropriate cases by the preparation of summaries or extracts of evidence, or the provision of documents in an edited or anonymised form, provided the documents supplied are in each instance approved by the judge. In appropriate cases the appointment of special counsel may be a necessary step to ensure that the contentions of the prosecution are tested and the interests of the defendant protected ... In cases of exceptional difficulty the court may require the appointment of special counsel to ensure a correct answer to questions (2) and (3) as well as (4).

(5) Do the measures proposed in answer to (4) represent the minimum derogation necessary to protect the public interest in question? If No, the court should order such greater disclosure as will represent the minimum derogation from the golden rule of full disclosure.

(6) If limited disclosure is ordered pursuant to (4) or (5), may the effect be to render the trial process, viewed as a whole, unfair to the defendant? If Yes, then fuller disclosure should be ordered even if this leads or may lead the prosecution to discontinue the proceedings so as to avoid having to make disclosure.

(7) If the answer to (6) when first given is No, does that remain the correct answer as the trial unfolds, evidence is adduced and the defence advanced?

It is important that the answer to (6) should not be treated as a final, once-and-for-all, answer but as a provisional answer which the court must keep under review.[66]

Significantly, the House of Lords takes the view that in a case where the defence is not even permitted to be informed that a public interest immunity application is being

[66] Ibid, [36].

made, and 'the material to be withheld is of significant help to the defendant, there must be a very serious question whether the prosecution should proceed, since special counsel, even if appointed, cannot then receive any instructions from the defence at all'.[67]

The Court of Appeal has clarified its approach to appeals relating to public interest immunity hearings in the Crown Court:

> . . . it seems to us that the following principles should, generally speaking, guide the conduct of appeals to this Court which raise issues as to the trial judge's conduct of a Public Interest Immunity hearing:
>
> 1. The approach should be the same whether the ex parte PII hearing before the judge was or was not on notice. The principles in relation to the appointment of Special Counsel, or the need for the judge to recuse himself or herself are the same in both cases.
>
> 2. The Court of Appeal (Criminal Division) will have to review ex parte with the prosecution present all the material which was before the trial judge. A prosecution summary will not usually suffice, but is always desirable and, in a complex case, essential.
>
> 3. It will be necessary for that review to be carried out by the same constitution which is to hear the appeal.
>
> 4. The review will have to take place sufficiently in advance of the substantive appeal hearing to permit, in those exceptional cases where this is necessary, Special Counsel to be appointed and suitably prepared.
>
> 5. In the majority of cases, where the Public Interest Immunity material can be read in an hour or two, this should present no listing difficulty and the Public Interest Immunity hearing can take place . . . in the first week of a constitution sitting with the appeal being heard in the third week.
>
> 6. In the minority of cases, where the PII material is unusually voluminous, special listing arrangements will have to be made over a longer time scale.[68]

7 The Freedom of Information Act 2000

The doctrine of public interest immunity stands alongside, and probably overlaps substantially with, the operation of the Freedom of Information Act 2000.[69] In essence, the Act provides a general right of access to information held by public authorities.[70] There are, however, a number of exemptions from the general duty to disclose information. Many of these closely mirror the circumstances in which it may be possible for public interest immunity to be claimed. A few of the exemptions in the Act are specified to be absolute exemptions. In the case of all the other exemptions disclosure must not be made

---

[67] R v H [2004] UKHL 3, [2004] 2 WLR 335, [37].   [68] R v McDonald [2004] EWCA Crim 2614, [25].

[69] See generally D Basu, 'Freedom of Information—Part 1' (2004) 154 New Law Journal 1624; P Birkinshaw, 'Open All Hours: The Impact of the Labour Government's Legislation on Freedom of Information' (2001) 54 Current Legal Problems 179; T Cornford, 'The Freedom of Information Act 2000: Genuine or Sham?' [2001] 3 Web Journal of Current Legal Issues, available at http://webjcli.ncl.ac.uk/2001/issue3/cornford3. html; G Vassall-Adams, 'The Freedom of Information Act 2000 Explained' [Jan 2005] Legal Action 15; J Macdonald and C H Jones, The Law of Freedom of Information (2003). Useful guidance on the Act is accessible via http://www.dca.gov.uk/foi/guidance/index.htm.   [70] S 1.

if 'in all the circumstances of the case, the public interest in maintaining the exemption outweighs the public interest in disclosing the information'.[71] It will be seen that this is in essence the balancing test applied in determining public interest immunity claims.

Some of the relevant exemptions in the Act are, briefly, as follows:

• Information directly or indirectly supplied by, or relating to, certain bodies dealing with security matters.[72] This is an absolute exemption.[73]

• Any other information in relation to which an exemption is required to safeguard national security.[74]

• Information the disclosure of which would, or would be likely to, prejudice the defence of the British Islands or any colony, or the capability, effectiveness, or security of any relevant forces.[75]

• Information the disclosure of which would, or would be likely to, prejudice relations between the United Kingdom and any other State, international organization, or international court; the interests of the United Kingdom abroad; or the promotion or protection by the United Kingdom of those interests.[76]

• Confidential information obtained from a State other than the United Kingdom or from an international organization or international court.[77]

• Information the disclosure of which would, or would be likely to, prejudice relations between any of the administrations in the United Kingdom.[78]

• Information the disclosure of which would, or would be likely to, prejudice the economic interests of the United Kingdom or any part thereof, or the financial interests of any administration in the United Kingdom.[79]

• Information held by a public authority if it has at any time been held by the authority for the purposes of a criminal investigation or criminal proceedings.[80]

• Information held by a public authority and relating to the obtaining of information from confidential sources (informers) if the information held was obtained or recorded by the authority for the purposes of its functions relating to certain investigations or proceedings.[81]

• Information the disclosure of which would, or would be likely to, prejudice certain law enforcement matters.[82]

• Information contained in certain court and analogous records.[83] This is an absolute exemption.[84]

• Information held by a public authority with audit functions, the disclosure of which would, or would be likely to, prejudice the exercise by the authority of any of these functions.[85]

• Information in relation to which an exemption is required to avoid an infringement of the privileges of either House of Parliament.[86] This is an absolute exemption.[87]

---

[71] S 2(2)(b).   [72] S 23.   [73] S 2(3)(b).   [74] S 24.   [75] S 26.   [76] S 27(1).
[77] S 27(2).   [78] S 28.   [79] S 29.   [80] S 30(1).   [81] S 30(2).   [82] S 31.
[83] S 32.   [84] S 2(3)(c).   [85] S 33.   [86] S 34.   [87] S 2(3)(d).

• Information held by a Government department or by the National Assembly for Wales and relating to the formulation or development of Government policy, ministerial communications, law officers' advice, or the operation of any ministerial private office.[88]

• Information held by a public authority the disclosure of which, in the reasonable opinion of a qualified person, would, or would be likely to, prejudice the effective conduct of public affairs.[89] In relation to information held by the House of Commons or the House of Lords the exemption is absolute.[90]

• Information relating to communications with members of the Royal Family or with the Royal Household, or the conferring by the Crown of any honour or dignity.[91]

• Information the disclosure of which would, or would be likely to, endanger the physical or mental health or safety of any individual.[92]

• Information constituting a trade secret.[93]

• Information the disclosure of which 'would, or would be likely to, prejudice the commercial interests of any person (including the public authority holding it)'.[94]

• Information the disclosure of which 'would constitute or be punishable as a contempt of court'.[95] This is an absolute exemption.[96]

8 Confidentiality

Certain relationships—such as the relationship between doctor and patient, priest and penitent, banker and customer, or journalist and source—are carried on with the expectation that they are confidential relationships. It would appear that while such relationships are not protected by the doctrine of public interest immunity as such, a similar balancing test is to be applied in determining whether disclosure should be ordered:

1. There is no principle of public interest immunity ... protecting ... confidential documents ...

2. There is no principle in English law by which documents are protected from [disclosure] by reason of confidentiality alone. But there is no reason why, in the exercise of its discretion to order [disclosure], the tribunal should not have regard to the fact that documents are confidential, and that to order disclosure would involve a breach of confidence. ...

...

4. The ultimate test ... is whether [disclosure] is necessary for disposing fairly of the proceedings. If it is, then [disclosure] must be ordered notwithstanding confidentiality. But where the court is impressed with the need to preserve confidentiality in a particular case, it will consider carefully whether the necessary information has been or can be obtained by other means, not involving a breach of confidence.

---

[88] S 35.   [89] S 36.   [90] S 2(3)(e).   [91] S 37.   [92] S 38.   [93] S 43(1).
[94] S 43(2).   [95] S 44(1)(c).   [96] S 2(3)(h).

5. In order to reach a conclusion whether [disclosure] is necessary notwithstanding confidentiality the tribunal should inspect the documents. It will naturally consider whether justice can be done by special measures such as 'covering up', substituting anonymous references for specific names, or, in rare cases, hearing in camera.

6. The procedure by which this process is to be carried out is one for tribunals to work out in a manner which will avoid delay and unnecessary applications.[97]

9 The Contempt of Court Act 1981, Section 10

A specific statutory provision, section 10 of the Contempt of Court Act 1981, governs the disclosure of sources of information contained in *publications*:

No court may require a person to disclose, nor is any person guilty of contempt of court for refusing to disclose, the source of information contained in a publication for which he is responsible, unless it be established to the satisfaction of the court that disclosure is necessary in the interests of justice or national security or for the prevention of disorder or crime.

This provision was the subject of detailed consideration by the House of Lords in *X Ltd v Morgan-Grampian Ltd*.[98] Goodwin, a trainee journalist on the staff of *The Engineer*, which was published by Morgan-Grampian Ltd, was telephoned by a person who informed him that a company, Tetra Ltd, was in the process of raising a £5 million loan and had financial problems as a result of an expected loss of £2,100,000 for 1989 on a turnover of £20,300,000. This information came from a draft of Tetra Ltd's confidential corporate plan, a copy of which had been stolen. On application by Tetra Ltd, the High Court ordered that Goodwin disclose the identity of his source on the ground that such disclosure was 'necessary in the interests of justice' under section 10. The House of Lords agreed with the lower courts that disclosure in this case was 'necessary in the interests of justice'. Following the decision of the House of Lords, the High Court fined Goodwin £5,000 for contempt of court.

Goodwin took the case to the European Court of Human Rights,[99] alleging a breach of Article 10 of the European Convention on Human Rights, which provides:

1. Everyone has the right to freedom of expression. This right shall include freedom to hold opinions and to receive and impart information and ideas without interference by public authority and regardless of frontiers. This article shall not prevent States from requiring the licensing of broadcasting, television or cinema enterprises.

---

[97] *Science Research Council v Nassé* [1980] AC 1028, 1065–6. See also *Lonrho PLC v Fayed (No 4)* [1994] 2 WLR 209; *Wallace Smith Trust Co v Deloitte* [1996] 4 All ER 403, 412–13; *Pharaon v BCCI SA (in liquidation)* [1998] 4 All ER 455, 469 ('it is well settled that the public interest in upholding the duty of confidentiality existing between banker and customer, as well as the duty of confidentiality that can exist in other contexts, is subject to being overridden by a greater public interest').   [98] [1991] 1 AC 1.

[99] *Goodwin v UK* (1996) 22 EHRR 123 (judgment of 1996). See generally S Nash, 'Freedom of Expression, Disclosure of Journalists' Sources and the European Court of Human Rights: *Goodwin v United Kingdom*' (1997) 1 *International Journal of Evidence and Proof* 410.

2. The exercise of these freedoms, since it carries with it duties and responsibilities, may be subject to such formalities, conditions, restrictions or penalties as are prescribed by law and are necessary in a democratic society, in the interests of national security, territorial integrity or public safety, for the prevention of disorder or crime, for the protection of health or morals, for the protection of the reputation or rights of others, for preventing the disclosure of information received in confidence, or for maintaining the authority and impartiality of the judiciary.

Thus the purport of Article 10 is that even if there is a prima facie violation of the right to freedom of expression under paragraph 1, this violation may be justified under paragraph 2, with the result that Article 10 will not ultimately be breached.

The European Court found a breach of Article 10 in *Goodwin*, taking the view that the violation of his right could not be justified under paragraph 2:

As a matter of general principle, the 'necessity' for any restriction on freedom of expression must be convincingly established. . . . the interest of democratic society in ensuring and maintaining a free press . . . will weigh heavily in the balance in determining, as must be done under Article 10(2), whether the restriction was proportionate to the legitimate aim pursued. In sum, limitations on the confidentiality of journalistic sources call for the most careful scrutiny by the Court.[100]

On the facts of the present case, the Court cannot find that Tetra's interests in eliminating, by proceedings against the source, the residual threat of damage through dissemination of the confidential information otherwise than by the press, in obtaining compensation and in unmasking a disloyal employee or collaborator were, even if considered cumulatively, sufficient to outweigh the vital public interest in the protection of the applicant journalist's source.[101]

In sum, there was not, in the Court's view, a reasonable relationship of proportionality between the legitimate aim pursued by the disclosure order and the means deployed to achieve that aim. The restriction which the disclosure order entailed on the applicant journalist's exercise of his freedom of expression cannot therefore be regarded as having been necessary in a democratic society, within the meaning of Article 10(2), for the protection of Tetra's rights under English law . . .

    Accordingly, the Court concludes that both the order requiring the applicant to reveal his source and the fine imposed upon him for having refused to do so gave rise to a violation of his right to freedom of expression under Article 10.[102]

The issue has subsequently been considered by the Court of Appeal[103] in *Camelot Group v Centaur Ltd*.[104] The Court took the view that the fact that the European Court in *Goodwin* had reached a different *conclusion* from that reached by the House of Lords did not necessarily indicate that it had taken a different *approach*. In truth, 'the tests which the Court of Human Rights and the House of Lords applied were substantially the same', and the fact that different conclusions were reached 'is a no more surprising legal phenomenon than this court concluding that a particular course of conduct amounted to negligence when the court of first instance concluded that the very same course of conduct did *not* amount to negligence'.[105] In any event, 'there was a lapse of six years between

---

[100] *Goodwin v UK* (1996) 22 EHRR 123, [40] (judgment of 1996).   [101] Ibid, [45].   [102] Ibid, [46].

[103] See also the decision of the Chancery Division in *Michael O'Mara Books Ltd v Express Newspapers plc* [1999] FSR 49.

[104] [1998] 1 All ER 251. See generally T R S Allan, 'Journalists' Sources and Disloyal Employees: Discretion, Fact and Judgement' [1998] *Cambridge Law Journal* 235.

[105] [1998] 1 All ER 251, 259 (italics in original).

the performance of the balancing exercise in London and in Strasbourg. In such a period standards fundamental to the performance of the balancing exercise may change materially.'[106] In *Camelot* itself, the plaintiff company, which was authorized to run the National Lottery, had intended to publish final accounts on 3 June 1997. An unidentified employee had, however, leaked a copy of the draft accounts to a journalist employed by the defendant, which published an article disclosing their contents on 28 May 1997. In order to assist it in identifying the source of the leaked information, the plaintiff obtained an order requiring the defendant to deliver up to the plaintiff the draft accounts and any other confidential information of which it was in possession or to which it had access. The Court of Appeal held that this order had been correctly made. The Court noted that while the order was not in terms an order requiring disclosure of the source of information, it was clear that disclosure or facilitation of disclosure would be the effect of the order. Section 10 of the Contempt of Court Act 1981 was, therefore, applicable.[107] In considering section 10, 'a relevant but not conclusive factor is that an employer may wish to identify the employee so as to exclude him from future employment'. The Court considered this to be a factor which, even standing alone, could in some cases be strong enough to outweigh the important public interest in the ability of the press to protect the anonymity of its sources.[108] Also relevant in this case, however, was the existence of 'unease and suspicion amongst the employees of the company which inhibits good working relationships. Clearly there is a risk that an employee who has proved untrustworthy in one regard may be untrustworthy in a different respect and reveal the name of, say, a public figure who has won a huge lottery prize.'[109] In the result, therefore, 'the public interest in enabling the plaintiffs to discover a disloyal employee in their midst who leaked the confidential information which he did leak was greater than the public interest in enabling him to escape detection'.[110]

It would appear that another relevant factor in the determination of whether disclosure would be in the interests of justice is whether attempts have been made to identify the source by other means:

> To an extent, whether disclosure of a source is 'necessary' in the interests of justice can depend on whether the person seeking disclosure has made any attempt other than by applying to the court to find the source for himself and whether any such attempts, were they to be made, would have had any real prospects of making the compulsion of a court order unnecessary. . . . the making of such attempts is [not] a necessary precondition of the court's assistance, but its absence can be a powerful, even a decisive, factor against the intervention of the court . . .[111]

The House of Lords has now confirmed that the approach of the European Court to Article 10 in *Goodwin v UK* 'can be applied equally to section 10 now that article 10 is part of our domestic law'.[112]

---

[106] Ibid, 262.   [107] Ibid, 256.   [108] Ibid, 258.   [109] Ibid, 261.   [110] Ibid, 262.
[111] *Saunders v Punch Ltd* [1998] 1 All ER 234, 245.
[112] *Ashworth Hospital Authority v MGN Ltd* [2002] UKHL 29, [2002] 1 WLR 2033, [38]. See generally M Amos, 'A Storm Brewing' (2002) 152 *New Law Journal* 1230; J Schöpflin, 'Protection Racket' (2002) 146 *Solicitors' Journal* 628.

7

Legal Professional Privilege

1 The Concept of Privilege

'Privilege' is 'the right of a party to refuse to disclose a document or produce a document or to refuse to answer questions on the ground of some special interest recognised by law'.[1] Generally, therefore, a person entitled to claim privilege is not required to disclose the privileged material or to give evidence of that material. Such material is allowed to be withheld not because of its actual or potential unreliability, but rather, as in the case of material subject to public interest immunity, because of considerations of extrinsic policy. There are three main categories of privilege, sometimes termed the 'heads of privilege': (1) the privilege against self-incrimination; (2) 'without prejudice' negotiations; and (3) legal professional privilege. Detailed treatments of the privilege against self-incrimination and 'without prejudice' negotiations may be found in the standard textbooks. The focus of this chapter is on an examination of legal professional privilege. A few words will now be said, however, about the two other categories of privilege.

2 The Privilege against Self-Incrimination

The privilege against self-incrimination permits a witness in a trial to refuse to answer questions in certain circumstances. In *Blunt v Park Lane Hotel Ltd* Goddard LJ stated that 'the rule is that no one is bound to answer any question if the answer thereto would, in the opinion of the judge, have a tendency to expose the deponent to any criminal charge, penalty, or forfeiture which the judge regards as reasonably likely to be preferred or sued for'.[2] It is necessary:

> that before acceding to a claim to [the privilege against self-incrimination] the court should satisfy itself, from the circumstances of the case and the nature of the evidence which the witness is called to give, that there is a reasonable ground to apprehend real and appreciable danger to the witness with reference to the ordinary operation of the law in the ordinary course of things, and not a danger of an imaginary or insubstantial character. The duty imposed by the court is

---

[1] Civil Procedure Rules, glossary. See generally R Pattenden, *The Law of Professional-Client Confidentiality: Regulating the Disclosure of Confidential Personal Information* (2003) 16.05–16.64, as updated by http://www.uea.ac.uk/ law/resources/professional-client_index.htm. [2] [1942] 2 KB 253, 257.

non-delegable. It cannot simply adopt the conclusion of the solicitor advising the witness whose conclusion may or may not be correct...[3]

The role of the privilege in pre-trial criminal procedure, so far as the questioning of suspects at the pre-trial stage is concerned, has been discussed in some detail in Chapter 3. With respect to the questioning of a defendant in a criminal trial, the privilege has been affected by numerous statutory provisions such as section 1(2) of the Criminal Evidence Act 1898 and the provisions of the Criminal Justice Act 2003 on evidence of the defendant's bad character, discussed in Chapter 8. In civil trials, the privilege has been encapsulated in section 14(1) of the Civil Evidence Act 1968, which provides:

> The right of a person in any legal proceedings other than criminal proceedings to refuse to answer any question or produce any document or thing if to do so would tend to expose that person to proceedings for an offence or for the recovery of a penalty—
>
> (a) shall apply only as regards criminal offences under the law of any part of the United Kingdom and penalties provided for by such law; and
>
> (b) shall include a like right to refuse to answer any question or produce any document or thing if to do so would tend to expose the husband or wife of that person to proceedings for any such criminal offence or for the recovery of any such penalty.

It can be seen that only the law of some part of the United Kingdom[4] is relevant, and that the privilege extends to the witness's spouse. The privilege has, however, been subjected to criticism, with Lord Templeman stating in 1992 that 'I regard the privilege against self-incrimination exercisable in civil proceedings as an archaic and unjustifiable survival from the past'.[5]

3 'Without Prejudice' Negotiations

The position with respect to 'without prejudice' negotiations[6] is, in essence, that 'all negotiations genuinely aimed at settlement whether oral or in writing' are protected by privilege.[7] The application of 'without prejudice' privilege in a particular case may be justified on one of two bases. The first is 'the public policy of encouraging litigants to settle their differences rather than litigate them to a finish'.[8] Thus:

> There is a public policy benefit in helping parties who are attempting to negotiate settlements. It is always better if litigation can be avoided where there is some possibility of negotiations

---

[3] R (CPS) v Bolton Magistrates' Court [2003] EWHC 2697 (Admin), [2004] 1 Cr App R 33 (p 438), [25].

[4] This has been held to include EC law: In re Westinghouse Uranium Contract [1978] AC 547. Note that a court can in its discretion protect a person from self-incrimination in relation to foreign law: A-G for Gibraltar v May [1999] 1 WLR 998.   [5] A T & T Istel Ltd v Tully [1993] AC 45, 53.

[6] See generally K Awadalla, 'The Privileged Few' (2003) 147 Solicitors' Journal 43; D McGrath, 'Without Prejudice Privilege' (2001) 5 International Journal of Evidence and Proof 213; J Michaelson, 'Should This Be the End of "Without Prejudice"?' (2000) 150 New Law Journal 1850; C Mulcahy, 'Lifting the Veil on Without Prejudice Negotiations' (2000) 144 Solicitors' Journal 444; J Ross, 'The Without Prejudice Rule' (2002) 152 New Law Journal 1488; C Passmore, Privilege (1998) Ch 10.   [7] Rush & Tompkins v GLC [1989] AC 1280, 1299.

[8] Ibid.

resolving a dispute. The privilege attaching to without prejudice documents is there to support that policy.[9]

The second basis is the existence of an implied contract:

... there are circumstances in which the rule operates to defeat, not to promote, the underlying policy of encouraging parties to settle their disputes without resort to litigation. In those circumstances the rule has to be justified, if at all, on the basis of an agreement that negotiations will be conducted on terms that, if the negotiations fail, they will not be relied upon in subsequent litigation. In those cases the court does not have recourse to an implied contract as the mechanism by which effect is given to an underlying public policy; it recognises that effect must be given to a contract (which, if not expressed, may fall to be implied from the circumstances in which negotiations took place) notwithstanding that, by giving effect to that contract, the public interest in encouraging parties to accept realistic offers of settlement is frustrated.... And there are cases where the rule can only be justified on the basis of public policy; that is to say, where it cannot be justified on the basis of implied contract because the person against whom it is invoked was not party or privy to the negotiations ...[10]

The test for determining whether the privilege applies is as follows:

The court has to determine whether or not a communication is bona fide intended to be part of or to promote negotiations. To determine that, the court has to work out what, on a reasonable basis, the intention of the author was and how it would be understood by a reasonable recipient. If a document is marked 'without prejudice', that is some indication that the author intended the document so to be treated as part of a negotiating process, and in many cases a recipient would receive it understanding that that marking indicated that that was the author's intention.[11]

... the heading 'without prejudice' is not conclusive, but it may be one of the factors which indicates how one should assess the document itself.[12]

Even 'the opening shot in negotiations can, depending upon the circumstances, amount to bona fide without prejudice correspondence and be privileged accordingly'.[13]

The privilege extends beyond the protection of actual *admissions* made in the course of the negotiations:

... the protection of admissions against interest is the most important practical effect of the rule. But to dissect out identifiable admissions and withhold protection from the rest of without prejudice communications (except for a special reason) would not only create huge practical difficulties but would be contrary to the underlying objective of giving protection to the parties [to enable them to speak freely]. Parties cannot speak freely at a without prejudice meeting if they must constantly monitor every sentence, with lawyers or patent agents sitting at their shoulders as minders.[14]

---

[9] *Schering Corp v Cipla Ltd* [2004] EWHC 2587 (Ch), [2005] FSR 25 (p 575), [12].

[10] *Prudential Insurance Co of America v Prudential Assurance Co Ltd* [2003] EWCA Civ 1154, [21].

[11] *Schering Corp v Cipla Ltd* [2004] EWHC 2587 (Ch), [2005] FSR 25 (p 575), [14].

[12] Ibid, [15]. See generally J Levy, 'Misuse of the Magic Words', *The Times*, 15 Feb 2005, Law, 8; S Partington, 'Which Prejudice?' (2005) 149 *Solicitors' Journal* 255.

[13] *Schering Corp v Cipla Ltd* [2004] EWHC 2587 (Ch), [2005] FSR 25 (p 575), [18].

[14] *Unilever Plc v Procter & Gamble Co* [2000] 1 WLR 2436, 2448–9.

Negotiations on the issue of costs are disclosable and admissible in evidence if these negotiations have been expressly excluded from the scope of the privilege:

> Negotiations or offers which have taken place expressly on the 'without prejudice save as to costs' basis are of course admissible on that question. So much was decided in the family law context in *Calderbank v Calderbank* [1976] Fam 93 and in the general civil litigation context by *Cutts v Head* [1984] Ch 290. Such offers go by the name *'Calderbank offers'*.[15]

The Court of Appeal has noted that 'even in situations to which the without prejudice rule undoubtedly applies, the veil imposed by public policy may have to be pulled aside, even so as to disclose admissions, in cases where the protection afforded by the rule has been unequivocally abused'.[16] However, 'the expansion of exceptions should not be encouraged when an important ingredient of Lord Woolf's reforms of civil justice is to encourage those who are in dispute to engage in frank discussions before they resort to litigation'.[17]

4 Legal Professional Privilege

4.1 What is Legal Professional Privilege?[18]

When proceeding through this chapter, the following questions should be borne in mind. What exactly are the extrinsic policy considerations underlying the doctrine of legal professional privilege? Does the current state of the law reflect these considerations in a coherent manner?

Two types of communications may be subject to legal professional privilege:

1. Confidential[19] communications between *client and legal adviser* for the purpose of obtaining and giving legal advice may be subject to *legal advice privilege*. (Legal advice privilege also extends to certain related documents, or certain related items, that were created or brought into existence for the purpose of obtaining or giving legal

---

[15] *Reed Executive plc v Reed Business Information Ltd* [2004] EWCA Civ 887, [2004] 1 WLR 3026, [20].

[16] *Unilever Plc v Procter & Gamble Co* [2000] 1 WLR 2436, 2449. See generally C Passmore, 'Privilege Update' (1999) 149 *New Law Journal* 1865. See also *Savings & Investment Bank Ltd v Fincken* [2003] EWCA Civ 1630, [2004] 1 WLR 667, [57]: 'the mere inconsistency between an admission and a pleaded case or a stated position, with the mere possibility that such a case or position, if persisted in, may lead to perjury', does not amount to unequivocal abuse.

[17] *Unilever Plc v Procter & Gamble Co* [2000] 1 WLR 2436, 2449–50. See also *Berry Trade Ltd v Moussavi* [2003] EWCA Civ 715; I R Scott, 'Exceptions to Without Prejudice Rule' (2003) 22 *Civil Justice Quarterly* 316.

[18] See generally C Passmore, 'The Future of Legal Professional Privilege' (1999) 3 *International Journal of Evidence and Proof* 71; J Auburn, *Legal Professional Privilege: Law and Theory* (2000).

[19] *Three Rivers District Council v Bank of England (No 6)* [2004] UKHL 48, [2004] 3 WLR 1274, [24] per Lord Scott of Foscote: '. . . legal advice privilege arises out of a relationship of confidence between lawyer and client. Unless the communication or document for which privilege is sought is a confidential one, there can be no question of legal advice privilege arising. The confidential character of the communication or document is not by itself enough to enable privilege to be claimed but is an essential requirement.'

advice.) The rationale for legal advice privilege[20] has been authoritatively explained in the following terms:

> It is obviously true that in very many cases clients would have no inhibitions in providing their lawyers with all the facts and information the lawyers might need whether or not there were the absolute assurance of non-disclosure that the present law of privilege provides. But . . . it is necessary in our society, a society in which the restraining and controlling framework is built upon a belief in the rule of law, that communications between clients and lawyers, whereby the clients are hoping for the assistance of the lawyers' legal skills in the management of their (the clients') affairs, should be secure against the possibility of any scrutiny from others, whether the police, the executive, business competitors, inquisitive busybodies or anyone else . . . this idea . . . justifies . . . the retention of legal advice privilege in our law, notwithstanding that as a result cases may sometimes have to be decided in ignorance of relevant probative material.[21]

2. Confidential communications between *client or legal adviser and third parties* which have preparation for litigation as their sole or dominant purpose may be subject to *litigation privilege*. Thus,

> communications between parties or their solicitors and third parties for the purpose of obtaining information or advice in connection with existing or contemplated litigation are privileged, but only when the following conditions are satisfied: (a) litigation must be in progress or in contemplation; (b) the communications must have been made for the sole or dominant purpose of conducting that litigation; (c) the litigation must be adversarial, not investigative or inquisitorial.[22]

(Litigation privilege also extends to certain related documents, or certain related items, that were created or brought into existence for the sole or dominant purpose of preparing for litigation.)

These principles are also articulated in section 10 of the Police and Criminal Evidence Act 1984, which has been held[23] to encapsulate the common law:

> (1) Subject to subsection (2) below, in this Act 'items subject to legal privilege' means—
>
>   (a) communications between a professional legal adviser and his client or any person representing his client made in connection with the giving of legal advice to the client;
>
>   (b) communications between a professional legal adviser and his client or any person representing his client or between such an adviser or his client or any such representative and any other person made in connection with or in contemplation of legal proceedings and for the purposes of such proceedings; and

---

[20] For a discussion of legal advice privilege, see G C Hazard, Jr, 'An Historical Perspective on the Attorney-Client Privilege' (1978) 66 *California Law Review* 1061.

[21] *Three Rivers District Council v Bank of England (No 6)* [2004] UKHL 48, [2004] 3 WLR 1274, [34] per Lord Scott of Foscote. See also *R v Derby Magistrates' Court, ex p B* [1996] AC 487, 507, 508; *B v Auckland District Law Society* [2003] UKPC 38, [2003] 3 WLR 859, [37].

[22] *Three Rivers District Council v Bank of England (No 6)* [2004] UKHL 48, [2004] 3 WLR 1274, [102] per Lord Carswell.

[23] *R v CCC, ex p Francis & Francis* [1989] AC 346, 382, 384–5 per Lord Griffiths; 395 per Lord Goff of Chieveley.

(c) items enclosed with or referred to in such communications and made—

   (i) in connection with the giving of legal advice; or

   (ii) in connection with or in contemplation of legal proceedings and for the purposes of such proceedings,

when they are in the possession of a person who is entitled to possession of them.

(2) Items held with the intention of furthering a criminal purpose are not items subject to legal privilege.

The privilege is that of the client, and of the client's successors in title. Thus it has been acknowledged 'that legal professional privilege survives the death of a lawyer's client and vests in his or her personal representatives or, once administration is complete, in the person entitled to the deceased's estate'.[24] A similar approach is taken by the US Supreme Court, which has commented: 'Knowing that communications will remain confidential even after death encourages the client to communicate fully and frankly with counsel'.[25] There is, additionally, a principle that 'once privileged, always privileged'.[26] It may be possible, therefore, for privilege to be claimed in subsequent proceedings. Privilege may be invoked in subsequent litigation by the client or his or her successor in title if the subject matter of the second action is sufficiently connected with that of the first action for the document to be relevant in the second action.[27]

It is possible that, to be privileged, a document created for the purpose of obtaining legal advice must have been created by the client him- or herself, so that a document created by an *employee* of the client in order that the client may obtain legal advice is not privileged.[28] The House of Lords has declined to express a view on this.[29]

4.2 Collateral Facts and Pre-Existing Documents

Privilege does not extend to what may be termed 'collateral facts', and, thus, evidence of such facts is admissible.[30] A legal adviser is permitted, for example, to give evidence that he or she had a meeting with the client;[31] to give evidence about the physical or mental state of the client;[32] and to give evidence about the client's handwriting.[33] Equally, it is clear that pre-existing documents—that is, documents not actually brought into existence for the purpose either of obtaining/giving legal advice or of preparing for litigation—are

---

[24] *R v Molloy (Deceased)* [1997] 2 Cr App R 283, 284.

[25] *Swidler & Berlin v US* 524 US 399 (1998). See generally H L Ho, 'Legal Professional Privilege After Death of Client' (1999) 115 *Law Quarterly Review* 27; R C Wydick, 'The Attorney-Client Privilege: Does It Really Have Life Everlasting?' (1999) 87 *Kentucky Law Journal* 1165.

[26] *R v Derby Magistrates' Court, ex p B* [1996] AC 487, 503; *B v Auckland District Law Society* [2003] UKPC 38, [2003] 3 WLR 859, [44].   [27] *The 'Aegis Blaze'* [1986] 1 Lloyd's Rep 203, 209–10.

[28] *Three Rivers District Council v Bank of England (No 5)* [2003] EWCA Civ 474, [2003] 3 WLR 667.

[29] *Three Rivers District Council v Bank of England (No 6)* [2004] UKHL 48, [2004] 3 WLR 1274, [46]–[48] per Lord Scott of Foscote; [49] per Lord Rodger of Earlsferry; [63] per Baroness Hale of Richmond; [118] per Lord Carswell.

[30] See generally A Keane, *The Modern Law of Evidence* (5th ed 2000) 576, for a fuller discussion.

[31] *R (Howe) v South Durham Magistrates' Court* [2004] EWHC 362 (Admin), (2004) 168 JP 424.

[32] *Jones v Godrich* (1845) 5 Moo PC 16, 13 ER 394.   [33] *Dwyer v Collins* (1852) 21 LJ Ex 225, 227.

not privileged.[34] Section 10(1)(c) of the Police and Criminal Evidence Act 1984, as seen above, extends privilege to certain items 'made' in connection with the relevant purposes. The Court of Appeal held that the word 'made' is:

> certainly wide enough to include 'brought into existence,' and a sample of blood obtained and held in a particular container does constitute an 'item…made' for the purposes of legal proceedings etc. … (Documents are communications within section 10(1)(a) and (b)). The significance of 'made,' meaning 'brought into existence,' in our judgment, is that the privilege does not extend to objects which did not come into existence for the purpose of obtaining legal advice, etc. … [35]

A pre-existing document *will*, however, be privileged if to disclose it would have the effect of revealing the nature of the legal advice given to the client.[36]

4.3 'Legal Adviser'

At issue in *New Victoria Hospital v Ryan*[37] was correspondence between the hospital and a firm of personnel consultants which at the time did not employ any legally qualified staff. The Employment Appeal Tribunal held that privilege did not attach to the documents:

> because in our opinion the privilege should be strictly confined to legal advisers such as solicitors and counsel, who are professionally qualified, who are members of professional bodies, who are subject to the rules and etiquette of their professions, and who owe a duty to the court. This is a clearly defined and easily identifiable qualification for the attachment of privilege. To extend the privilege to unqualified advisers such as personnel consultants is in our opinion unnecessary and undesirable.[38]

The general position is, however, affected by a number of specific statutory provisions. For example, the effect of section 33 of the Administration of Justice Act 1985 is that licensed conveyancers are to be treated as solicitors for the purposes of legal professional privilege. To be noted also is section 280 of the Copyright, Designs and Patents Act 1988:

> (1) This section applies to communications as to any matter relating to the protection of any invention, design, technical information, or trade mark, or as to any matter involving passing off.
>
> (2) Any such communication—
>
>   (a) between a person and his patent agent, or
>
>   (b) for the purpose of obtaining, or in response to a request for, information which a person is seeking for the purpose of instructing his patent agent,
>
> is privileged from disclosure in legal proceedings in England, Wales or Northern Ireland in the same way as a communication between a person and his solicitor or, as the case may be,

---

[34] *Brown v Foster* (1857) 1 H & N 736, 156 ER 1397; *R v Peterborough Justice, ex p Hicks* [1977] 1 WLR 1371; *R v King* [1983] 1 WLR 411; *Ventouris v Mountain* [1991] 1 WLR 607.   [35] *R v R* [1994] 1 WLR 758, 763.
[36] *Dubai Bank Ltd v Galadari (No 7)* [1992] 1 WLR 106, 110. See also *Lyell v Kennedy* (1884) 27 Ch D 1, 26.
[37] [1993] ICR 201.   [38] Ibid, 203–4.

a communication for the purpose of obtaining, or in response to a request for, information which a person seeks for the purpose of instructing his solicitor.

...

Where the lawyer is an employee of the client the following considerations are relevant:

Lawyers do not cease to be regarded as professional legal advisers simply because they are employed by their clients, for example in a company's legal department, but in the nature of things those who are employed in that capacity are more likely than independent practitioners to become involved in aspects of the business that are essentially managerial or administrative in nature. To that extent it is less easy to maintain that all communications passing between them and the company's management attract privilege.[39]

Similar considerations apply where a legal adviser gives legal advice to a body of which he or she happens to be a member, such as a board of trustees:

Trustees are entitled to consult a solicitor with reference to the affairs of the trust, and the communications between them and their legal adviser are privileged if for the purpose of obtaining legal advice. Why should such communications be less privileged because the solicitor is himself one of the trustees? There is no valid distinction between such communications with the solicitor who is himself a trustee, and such communications with a solicitor who is outside the trust altogether. Of course the privilege is confined to communications genuinely for the purpose of getting legal advice. It would not extend to mere business communications with reference to the trust, not for the purpose of getting legal advice.[40]

4.4 'Legal Advice'

Clearly, 'legal advice is not confined to telling the client the law; it must include advice as to what should prudently and sensibly be done in the relevant legal context'.[41] After a brief period of uncertainty, it is now clear that what constitutes 'advice as to what should prudently and sensibly be done in the relevant legal context' is to be construed broadly:

The work of advising a client on the most suitable approach to adopt, assembling material for presentation of his case and taking statements which set out the relevant material in an orderly fashion and omit the irrelevant is to my mind the classic exercise of one of the lawyer's skills. [There is] no valid reason why that should cease to be so because the forum is an inquiry or other tribunal which is not a court of law, provided that the advice is given in a legal context . . . The skills of a lawyer in assembling the facts and handling the evidence are of importance in that forum as well as a court of law. The availability of competent legal advice will materially assist an inquiry by reducing irrelevance and encouraging the making of proper admissions.[42]

---

[39] *USA v Philip Morris Inc* [2003] EWHC 3028 (Comm), [64]. See also the decision of the Supreme Court of Canada in *Pritchard v Ontario (Human Rights Commission)* [2004] 1 SCR 809.

[40] *O'Rourke v Darbishire* [1920] AC 581, 602.   [41] *Balabel v Air India* [1988] Ch 317, 330.

[42] *Three Rivers District Council v Bank of England (No 6)* [2004] UKHL 48, [2004] 3 WLR 1274, [114] per Lord Carswell. See generally N Andrews, 'Legal Advice Privilege's Broad Protection—The House of Lords in *Three Rivers (No 6)*' (2005) 24 *Civil Justice Quarterly* 185; D Burrows, 'Legal Advice: Privilege Revisited' [2005] *Family Law* 491; J Fortnam and J Lobo, '*Three Rivers*: Comfort or Missed Opportunity?' (2004) 154 *New Law*

By a similar token, 'advice given by lawyers to objectors [at a planning inquiry] for the purpose of enhancing the prospects of a successful outcome, from their point of view, to the inquiry would be advice given in a relevant legal context and would qualify for legal advice privilege'. 'Every objector has the right under public law to present his case to the inquiry.'[43] Equally, 'advice and assistance given by lawyers to promoters of private Bills, although often, perhaps usually, presentational in character, would qualify for legal advice privilege. The relevant legal context seems...clear. The same would apply to advice by lawyers given to opponents of the proposed Bill.'[44] Again, 'advice given by parliamentary counsel to the Government in relation to the drafting and preparation of public Bills...should qualify for legal advice privilege....here too, the relevant legal context is unmistakable and...legal advice privilege should apply.'[45] Whether 'advice sought from and given by a lawyer as to how to set about joining a private club' would attract legal advice privilege would depend on the existence of a relevant legal context:

> Suppose the applicant for membership of the club had previously made an unsuccessful application to join the club, believed that his rejection had been inconsistent with the club's admission rules and wanted to make a fresh application with a view to testing the legality of his rejection if he were again to be blackballed....in those circumstances the communications between the lawyer and the applicant would be protected by legal advice privilege. It would be protected because the communication would have a relevant legal context. It would relate to the legal remedies that might be available if the applicant's application were again unsuccessful.[46]

4.5 Communications between Client and Legal Adviser

The extent to which communications between client and legal adviser must relate to the giving or obtaining of legal advice in order to be covered by legal advice privilege was explained by the House of Lords in *Minter v Priest*:

> The relationship of solicitor and client being once established, it is not a necessary conclusion that whatever conversation ensued was protected from disclosure. The conversation to secure this privilege must be such as, within a very wide and generous ambit of interpretation,

Journal 1750; N Jamieson and I Wilkinson, 'Privileged Position' (2004) 148 *Solicitors' Journal* 1329; C Pearson, 'Psst, Here's a Bit of Legal Advice', *The Times*, 16 Nov 2004, Law, 9; R Preston-Jones and J Paterson, 'Three Rivers Run Deep?' (2004) 154 *New Law Journal* 1709; J Seymour, 'Legal Advice Privilege and Presentational Advice' [2005] *Cambridge Law Journal* 54; C F H Tapper, 'Privilege, Policy and Principle' (2005) 121 *Law Quarterly Review* 181.

[43] *Three Rivers District Council v Bank of England (No 6)* [2004] UKHL 48, [2004] 3 WLR 1274, [39] per Lord Scott of Foscote.   [44] Ibid, [40] per Lord Scott of Foscote.

[45] Ibid, [41] per Lord Scott of Foscote.

[46] Ibid, [42] per Lord Scott of Foscote. See also C Pearson, 'Psst, Here's a Bit of Legal Advice', *The Times*, 16 Nov 2004, Law, 9: 'If I ask my lawyer how to place a bet on a horse in the Grand National that advice will not be privileged because the only consequences will be for my bank balance. If I ask for advice on how to set up a sweepstake that advice will be privileged, since it will involve perhaps my own legal rights and certainly those of others.'

must be fairly referable to the relationship, but outside that boundary the mere fact that a person speaking is a solicitor, and the person to whom he speaks is his client affords no protection.[47]

... communications between solicitor and client which do not pass for the purpose of giving or receiving professional advice are not protected. It follows that client and solicitor may meet for the purpose of legal advice and exchange protected communications, and may yet in the course of the same interview make statements to each other not for the purpose of giving or receiving professional advice but for some other purpose. Such statements are not within the rule . . .[48]

It is not necessary that the relations should have reached the definite status of solicitor and client. The solicitor may not be willing to be employed as a solicitor by the person with whom he may be communicating. If a person goes to a professional legal adviser for the purpose of seeing whether the professional person will give him professional advice, communications made for the purpose of indicating the advice required will be protected.[49]

Communications or documents passing between client and legal adviser may be privileged even if they do not actually contain legal advice or a request for legal advice. A pragmatic, purposive approach is to be taken to the issue:

... the test is whether the communication or other document was made confidentially for the purposes of legal advice. Those purposes have to be construed broadly. Privilege obviously attaches to a document conveying legal advice from solicitor to client and to a specific request from the client for such advice. But it does not follow that all other communications between them lack privilege. In most solicitor and client relationships, especially where a transaction involves protracted dealings, advice may be required or appropriate on matters great or small at various stages. There will be a continuum of communication and meetings between the solicitor and client. . . . Where information is passed by the solicitor or client to the other as part of the continuum aimed at keeping both informed so that advice may be sought and given as required, privilege will attach. A letter from the client containing information may end with such words as 'please advise me what I should do.' But, even if it does not, there will usually be implied in the relationship an overall expectation that the solicitor will at each stage, whether asked specifically or not, tender appropriate advice.[50]

Privilege would still attach where a relevant communication was not in fact received; 'if, for example, the sender of the communication had died before the communication had been sent to his legal adviser or the document concerned had been lost the privilege would still exist'.[51]

It has been held that 'if legal advice obtained by one person is passed on to another person for the sake of informing that other person in confidence of legal advice which that person needs to know by reason of a *sufficient common interest* between them', the legal advice remains privileged.[52]

---

[47] [1930] AC 558, 568 per Lord Buckmaster.   [48] Ibid, 581 per Lord Atkin.
[49] Ibid, 584 per Lord Atkin.   [50] *Balabel v Air India* [1988] Ch 317, 330.
[51] *Three Rivers District Council v Bank of England (No 5)* [2003] EWCA Civ 474, [2003] 3 WLR 667, [21].
[52] *Svenska v Sun Alliance* [1995] 2 Lloyd's Rep 84, 88 (italics added).

4.6 Communications with Third Parties

Communications with third parties are privileged only if they have preparation for litigation involving the client[53] as their sole or dominant purpose. In *Wheeler v Le Marchant*,[54] the question arose whether certain reports made to the defendant's solicitor by a surveyor were privileged. It was held that they were not, because although the reports did relate to the subject matter of the litigation, they had been made at a time when no litigation was actually contemplated.[55] It is necessary for privilege to attach that litigation be reasonably in prospect:

> It has been recognised on many occasions that there is a conflict between the need to enable clients to communicate freely with their legal advisers in relation to litigation and the need to ensure that all relevant material is before the court ... The point at which litigation should be regarded as sufficiently likely for confidential communications between client and his lawyer to attract privilege on this ground therefore involves striking an appropriate balance between these two factors. The requirement that litigation be 'reasonably in prospect' is not ... satisfied unless the party seeking to claim privilege can show that he was aware of circumstances which rendered litigation between himself and a particular person or class of persons a real likelihood rather than a mere possibility.[56]

But even if litigation were contemplated, preparation for the litigation must have been the sole or at least the dominant purpose of the communications. In *Woolley v North London Railway Co*,[57] it was held that even though litigation was contemplated, certain reports to the general manager of the railway company were not privileged, because they were made simply for the purpose of conveying information. In some situations communications may be made both for the purpose of preparation for contemplated litigation as well as for a different purpose—for example, the improvement of the safety of a railway. Unless the former purpose is at least the dominant purpose of the communications, privilege will not apply.[58] The 'dominant purpose' may be that of either the actual author of the document or anyone under whose direction it was brought into existence.[59]

As an alternative to a 'dominant purpose' test it might be possible to apply a 'sole purpose' test. In 1976 Australia adopted a 'sole purpose' test in preference to a 'dominant purpose' one.[60] The House of Lords in *Waugh v British Railways Board* was, however, unpersuaded by this approach, Lord Wilberforce commenting that 'to hold that the purpose ... must be the sole purpose would, apart from difficulties of proof, in my opinion, be too strict a requirement, and would confine the privilege too narrowly'.[61] It is notable that the 'sole purpose' test has now been abandoned in favour of a 'dominant purpose' one in Australia.[62]

---

[53] *USA v Philip Morris Inc* [2003] EWHC 3028 (Comm), [48].   [54] (1881) 17 Ch D 675.

[55] See also *Gotha City v Sotheby's* [1998] 1 WLR 114.

[56] *USA v Philip Morris Inc* [2003] EWHC 3028 (Comm), [46]; approved by the Court of Appeal in *USA v Philip Morris Inc* [2004] EWCA Civ 330, [2004] 1 CLC 811, [68].   [57] (1869) LR 4 CP 602.

[58] *Waugh v British Railways Board* [1980] AC 521. See also *Melik & Co v Norwich Union* [1980] 1 Lloyd's Rep 523; *Sec of State for Trade v Baker* [1998] 2 WLR 667.

[59] *Guinness Peat Ltd v Fitzroy Robinson* [1987] 1 WLR 1027.   [60] *Grant v Downs* (1976) 135 CLR 674.

[61] [1980] AC 521, 533.

[62] S 119 of the Uniform Evidence Acts in Australia; *Esso Australia Resources Ltd v Commissioner of Taxation* [1999] HCA 67.

4.7 Statutory Abrogation

Legal professional privilege may be abrogated by statute either expressly or by necessary implication:

> A necessary implication is not the same as a reasonable implication . . . A *necessary* implication is one which necessarily follows from the express provisions of the statute construed in their context. It distinguishes between what it would have been sensible or reasonable for Parliament to have included or what Parliament would, if it had thought about it, probably have included and what it is clear that the express language of the statute shows that the statute must have included. A necessary implication is a matter of express language and logic not interpretation.[63]

Thus in *R (Morgan Grenfell Ltd) v Special Comr*[64] the House of Lords held that legal professional privilege had not been abrogated by a statutory provision to the effect that 'an inspector may by notice in writing require a person—(a) to deliver to him such documents as are in the person's possession or power and as (in the inspector's reasonable opinion) contain, or may contain, information relevant to— (i) any tax liability to which the person is or may be subject, or (ii) the amount of any such liability . . . '.[65] The Law Lords rejected 'the argument that a general public interest in collecting revenue for the executive suffices (in peace-time) implicitly to override the basic right and public interest represented by legal professional privilege'.[66]

4.8 Waiver

As the privilege is that of the client, he or she may waive it, either expressly or impliedly.[67] 'A client expressly waives his legal professional privilege when he elects to disclose communications which the privilege would entitle him not to disclose.'[68] In relation to documents, 'the test is whether the *contents* of the document are being relied on, rather than its *effect*'.[69] A reference to the effect of a document does not constitute waiver, but deployment of the document (reliance on its contents) does. 'It must be right that a bare reference to a document in a pleading does not waive any privilege attaching

---

[63] *R (Morgan Grenfell Ltd) v Special Comr* [2002] UKHL 21, [2003] 1 AC 563, [45] (italics in original), approved in *B v Auckland District Law Society* [2003] UKPC 38, [2003] 3 WLR 859, [58].

[64] [2002] UKHL 21, [2003] 1 AC 563.   [65] Taxes Management Act 1970, s 20(1).

[66] [2002] UKHL 21, [2003] 1 AC 563, [46] per Lord Hobhouse of Woodborough. See generally E Brown, 'Legal Professional Privilege and the Inland Revenue' (2002) 152 *New Law Journal* 1020; S McNicol, 'Implications of the Human Right Rationale for Legal Professional Privilege—The Demise of Implied Statutory Abrogation?' in P Mirfield and R Smith (eds), *Essays for Colin Tapper* (2003); J Tiley, 'Professional Privilege and the Tax Man' [2002] *Cambridge Law Journal* 540.

[67] See generally *British American Tobacco (Investments) Ltd v USA* [2004] EWCA Civ 1064.

[68] *Paragon Finance v Freshfields* [1999] 1 WLR 1183, 1188.

[69] P Matthews and H M Malek, *Disclosure* (2nd ed 2001) 10.17 (italics in original), quoted in *Dunlop Slazenger International Ltd v Joe Bloggs Sports Ltd* [2003] EWCA Civ 901, [11]; *Lucas v Barking, Havering and Redbridge Hospitals NHS Trust* [2003] EWCA Civ 1102, [2003] 4 All ER 720, [19].

to it... If, on the other hand, a document is reproduced in full in the pleading, its confidentiality is gone and no question of privilege could arise. Where the line is drawn between these two extremes may be a matter of some nicety...'.[70]

It is not permissible to 'cherry-pick' by waiving privilege in relation to part of a communication or document but not in relation to other parts of the same communication or document that relate to the same subject matter. It has been said that 'waiver of part of a document is bound to lead to grave difficulties for all parties and to many unjustified suspicions';[71] 'to allow an individual item to be plucked out of context would be to risk injustice through its real weight or meaning being misunderstood'.[72] Waiver in relation to part of a document is possible, however, where the remainder of the document relates to such a distinct subject matter that severance is possible:

> The second question is whether, the whole of the memorandum being a privileged communication between legal adviser and client, the plaintiffs may waive the privilege with regard to the first two paragraphs of the memorandum but assert privilege over the additional matter. In my judgment, severance would be possible if the memorandum dealt with entirely different subject matters or different incidents and could in effect be divided into two separate memoranda each dealing with a separate subject matter.[73]

Waiver of privilege in relation to a communication or document does not automatically constitute waiver of privilege in relation to *other* communications or documents dealing with the same subject matter.[74] Whether it does constitute waiver would appear to be dependent on the circumstances: 'While there is no rule that a party who waives privilege in relation to one communication is taken to waive privilege in relation to all, a party may not waive privilege in such a partial and selective manner that unfairness or misunderstanding may result.'[75]

A client may impliedly waive privilege by bringing an action against his or her solicitor. The rationale for this has been explained as follows:

> When a client sues a solicitor who has formerly acted for him, complaining that the solicitor has acted negligently, he invites the court to adjudicate on questions directly arising from the confidential relationship which formerly subsisted between them. Since court proceedings are public, the client brings that formerly confidential relationship into the public domain. He thereby waives any right to claim the protection of legal professional privilege in relation to any communication between them so far as necessary for the just determination of his claim; or, putting the same proposition in different terms, he releases the solicitor to that extent from the obligation of confidence by which he was formerly bound. This is an implication of law,

---

[70] *Buttes Gas and Oil Co v Hammer (No 3)* [1981] QB 223, 252, revd in [1982] AC 888 on different grounds.

[71] *Great Atlantic Insurance v Home Insurance* [1981] 1 WLR 529, 537 per Templeman LJ.

[72] *Nea Karteria Maritime Co Ltd v Atlantic and Great Lakes Steamship Corporation* [1981] Com LR 138, 139, quoted in P Matthews and H M Malek, *Disclosure* (2nd ed 2001) 10.17 and in *Dunlop Slazenger International Ltd v Joe Bloggs Sports Ltd* [2003] EWCA Civ 901, [11]; *Lucas v Barking, Havering and Redbridge Hospitals NHS Trust* [2003] EWCA Civ 1102, [2003] 4 All ER 720, [19].

[73] *Great Atlantic Insurance v Home Insurance* [1981] 1 WLR 529, 536.

[74] *General Accident Corpn v Tanter* [1984] 1 WLR 100, 114–15. See also *Balkanbank v Taher, The Times*, 19 Feb 1994.   [75] *Paragon Finance v Freshfields* [1999] 1 WLR 1183, 1188.

the rationale of which is plain. A party cannot deliberately subject a relationship to public scrutiny and at the same time seek to preserve its confidentiality. He cannot pick and choose, disclosing such incidents of the relationship as strengthen his claim for damages and conceal- ing from forensic scrutiny such incidents as weaken it. He cannot attack his former solicitor and deny the solicitor the use of materials relevant to his defence. But, since the implied waiver applies to communications between client and solicitor, it will cover no communication to which the solicitor was not privy and so will disclose to the solicitor nothing of which he is not already aware.[76]

In *Lillicrap v Nalder & Son*,[77] the plaintiffs were property developers who engaged the defendants, a firm of solicitors, to act for them in a series of transactions. The plaintiffs brought an action against the defendants in respect of one of those transactions, alleg- ing negligence on the part of the defendants in failing to provide proper advice. The Court of Appeal held that the institution by a client of civil proceedings against his or her solicitor constitutes an implied waiver of legal professional privilege to the extent necessary to enable the court to adjudicate the dispute fully and fairly. Such waiver would extend only to documents relevant to an issue in the action. The waiver must extend sufficiently far, however, not only to enable the plaintiff to establish his or her cause of action, but also to enable the defendant to establish a defence to the cause of action if one exists. Here, the issue between the parties concerned causation of loss; the defendants admitted negligence but denied that this had caused the loss, and thus the plaintiffs had to establish such causation before they could be awarded substantial damages. It would be a defence for the defendants to establish, with reference to earlier transactions, that the plaintiffs would have proceeded with the transaction in question whatever advice they received. The documents in the other transactions were therefore relevant. Accordingly, the plaintiffs' implied waiver of privilege extended to the docu- ments in the other transactions.

Privilege would appear not to be waived where one defendant discloses legal advice to another in circumstances where confidentiality is assumed.[78]

It has been held that, if X makes a privileged document available to the police for the limited purpose of assisting in the conduct of criminal proceedings against Y, this cannot properly be construed as waiver of privilege for the purposes of X's subsequent civil action against Y. 'Indeed, it would...be contrary to public policy if the plaintiff's action in making the documents available in the criminal proceedings had the effect of automatically removing the cloak of privilege which would otherwise be available to it in the civil litigation for which the cloak was designed.'[79]

Specific provisions relating to instructions on which experts' reports are based are contained in the Civil Procedure Rules. Rule 35.10(3) provides: 'The expert's report

---

[76] *Paragon Finance v Freshfields* [1999] 1 WLR 1183, 1188. See generally J Auburn, 'Generalised Rules of Fairness in Evidence Law' (2000) 63 *Modern Law Review* 104. A petition for leave to appeal to the House of Lords was dismissed: [1999] 1 WLR 1463. See also *Nederlandse Reassurantie Groep Holding NV v Bacon & Woodrow* [1995] 1 All ER 976, 986.   [77] [1993] 1 WLR 94.

[78] *Gotha City v Sotheby's* [1998] 1 WLR 114.

[79] *British Coal Corpn v Dennis Rye Ltd* [1988] 1 WLR 1113, 1122.

must state the substance of all material instructions, whether written or oral, on the basis of which the report was written.' Rule 35.10(4) provides:

The instructions referred to in paragraph (3) shall not be privileged against disclosure but the court will not, in relation to those instructions—

(a) order disclosure of any specific document; or

(b) permit any questioning in court, other than by the party who instructed the expert,

unless it is satisfied that there are reasonable grounds to consider the statement of instructions given under paragraph (3) to be inaccurate or incomplete.

According to the Court of Appeal, 'CPR 35.10(4) is designed primarily to give protection to a party who would otherwise have waived privilege by being compelled to set out matters in an expert's report'.[80] It is:

a premise of the arrangements constituted by 35.10(3) and (4) that in the ordinary way the expert is to be trusted to comply with 35.10(3): the effect of the 35.10(4) restrictions is that the party on the other side may not as a matter of course call for disclosure of documents constituting the expert's instructions as a check to see that 35.10(3) has been fulfilled. There must be some concrete fact giving rise to 'reasonable grounds' within the closing words of 35.10(4). It is unsurprising that the expert is thus to be trusted; it is of a piece with his overriding duty to help the court (CPR 35.3). Overall, 35.10(4) ... strikes an important balance between on the one hand the protection of the party whose privilege is lost, and on the other the vindication of 35.10(3) where there is a real question-mark as to its fulfilment.[81]

As one commentator has written:

This is a pragmatic approach, avoiding satellite litigation and tactical warfare, but providing a remedy where there is obvious sharp or dishonest practice. Solicitors should though be aware that whenever they supply documentation to an expert, there is a risk that the court may at some stage in the future order disclosure of any document sent to the expert.[82]

'A wide reading of the term "instructions" ' [83] is to be taken: 'Material supplied by the instructing party to the expert as the basis on which the expert is being asked to advise should ... be considered as part of the instructions and thus subject to CPR 35.10(4).'[84]

The issue of waiver of legal professional privilege in the context of section 34 of the Criminal Justice and Public Order Act 1994 is discussed in detail in Chapter 3.

[80] *Lucas v Barking, Havering and Redbridge Hospitals NHS Trust* [2003] EWCA Civ 1102, [2003] 4 All ER 720, [31]. See D Hall, 'The Pitfall of Unintended Loss of Privilege' (2004) 154 *New Law Journal* 290; C Thomas, 'Disclosure of Privileged Documentation' (2003) 153 *New Law Journal* 1735.

[81] *Lucas v Barking, Havering and Redbridge Hospitals NHS Trust* [2003] EWCA Civ 1102, [2003] 4 All ER 720, [43].   [82] N Madge, 'Expert Privilege' (2003) 147 *Solicitors' Journal* 1226, 1227.

[83] *Lucas v Barking, Havering and Redbridge Hospitals NHS Trust* [2003] EWCA Civ 1102, [2003] 4 All ER 720, [42].   [84] Ibid, [34].

4.9 Facilitation of Crime or Fraud

'A well recognised exception to the right to assert legal professional privilege is where the document or documents in question came into existence in furtherance of some criminal or fraudulent purpose',[85] or 'where the privileged communication is itself the means of carrying out a fraud'[86] or crime. It has been held that 'what has to be shown prima facie is not merely that there is a bona fide and reasonably tenable charge of crime or fraud but a prima facie case that the communications in question were made in preparation for or in furtherance or as part of it'.[87] The law takes the view that, while there is a strong public interest in legal professional privilege, there is an equally strong public interest in combating crime or fraud and in protecting the victims or potential victims of it.[88] It has been emphasized that it is inappropriate to attempt an all-embracing definition of the necessary 'criminal or fraudulent' purpose. However, it would seem that:

> a deliberate misrepresentation made by a borrower to a building society for the purpose of procuring an advance is within the scope of the exception . . . Deceiving a person into lending money in circumstances where, if no deception had been practised, no loan might well have been forthcoming is . . . at least as iniquitous as entering into a transaction for the purpose of putting one's assets beyond the reach of one's creditors or otherwise prejudicing the interests of those creditors. The fact that the motive was to relieve financial pressure does not seem . . . to matter.[89]

It is inappropriate, in an attempt to invoke the 'facilitation of crime or fraud' exception, to seek to analyse issues likely to arise in the trial in question:

> In order to defeat a claim to legal professional privilege, it will not be appropriate . . . to seek to analyse the issues which are likely to arise in the . . . trial which gives rise to the initial privilege. To do so . . . would be to put the cart, in the form of analysis of the issues, before the horse, that is the trial. Where, however, there is evidence of specific agreement to pervert the course of justice, which is freestanding and independent, in the sense that it does not require any judgment to be reached in relation to the issues to be tried, the court may well be in a position to evaluate whether what has occurred falls within or outwith the protection of legal professional privilege . . .[90]

On the relevance of the solicitor's role in the context of a consideration of whether legal advice privilege has been defeated by the exception, it would appear that:

> provided the solicitor's *advice and assistance is employed in furtherance of 'the iniquity'* the exception comes into play in relation to confidential communications between the solicitor and client which would otherwise be protected by the client's privilege. It matters not whether the

[85] *Nationwide Building Society v Various Solicitors* [1999] PNLR 52, 72.
[86] *B v Auckland District Law Society* [2003] UKPC 38, [2003] 3 WLR 859, [44].
[87] *Butler v Board of Trade* [1971] Ch 680, 689.
[88] *Dubai Aluminium Co Ltd v Al Alawi* [1999] 1 WLR 1964,1969.
[89] *Nationwide Building Society v Various Solicitors* [1999] PNLR 52, 73.
[90] *R (Hallinan Blackburn Gittings & Nott) v Crown Court at Middlesex Guildhall* [2004] EWHC 2726 (Admin), [2005] 1 WLR 766, [25].

solicitor was engaged to advise in relation to the misrepresentation or whether he was aware that his involvement was in furthering the iniquity.[91]

The exception is clearly applicable to either type of legal professional privilege:

(1) the fraud exception can apply where there is a claim to litigation privilege as much as where there is a claim to legal advice privilege;

(2) nevertheless it can only be used in cases in which the issue of fraud is one of the issues in the action where there is a strong ... prima facie case of fraud ... ;

(3) where the issue of fraud is not one of the issues in the action, a prima facie case of fraud may be enough ...[92]

In *Dubai Aluminium Co Ltd v Al Alawi* it was held that where investigative agents employed by solicitors have engaged in criminal or fraudulent conduct for the purposes of acquiring evidence for litigation, 'any documents generated by or reporting on such conduct and which are relevant to the issues in the case ... fall outside the legitimate area of legal professional privilege'.[93] It was said that, ultimately, 'criminal or fraudulent conduct undertaken for the purposes of litigation falls on the same side of the line as advising on or setting up criminal or fraudulent transactions yet to be undertaken, as distinct from the entirely legitimate professional business of advising and assisting clients on their past conduct, however iniquitous'.[94]

Section 10(2) of the Police and Criminal Evidence Act 1984, which, as seen above, provides that 'items held with the intention of furthering a criminal purpose' are not subject to legal professional privilege, was considered in *R v CCC, ex p Francis & Francis.*[95] The majority of the House of Lords[96] held that as the holder of any items would normally be a solicitor,[97] and 'because cases of solicitors having the intention of furthering a criminal purpose are happily rare', 'intention' in section 10(2) must mean the intention of the holder *or any other person.* This interpretation, it was thought, 'would materially assist in achieving the purpose of [the legislation], and would prevent the principle of legal privilege being used to protect the perpetrators of serious crimes'.[98] It has the potential, however, of eroding the protection afforded by legal professional

---

[91] *Nationwide Building Society v Various Solicitors* [1999] PNLR 52, 74 (italics added). See also *R v Cox* (1884) 14 QBD 153, 165–6: 'The question ... is, whether, if a client applies to a legal adviser for advice intended to facilitate or to guide the client in the commission of a crime or fraud, the legal adviser being ignorant of the purpose for which his advice is wanted, the communication between the two is privileged? We expressed our opinion at the end of the argument that no such privilege existed. If it did, the result would be that a man intending to commit treason or murder might safely take legal advice for the purpose of enabling himself to do so with impunity, and that the solicitor to whom the application was made would not be at liberty to give information against his client for the purpose of frustrating his criminal purpose. Consequences so monstrous reduce to an absurdity any principle or rule in which they are involved.'

[92] *Kuwait Airways Corporation v Iraqi Airways Co* [2005] EWCA Civ 286, [42].

[93] [1999] 1 WLR 1964, 1969.   [94] Ibid, 1970.   [95] [1989] AC 346.

[96] Lord Brandon of Oakbrook, Lord Griffiths, and Lord Goff of Chieveley. Lord Bridge of Harwich and Lord Oliver of Aylmerton dissented.   [97] Ibid, 380.

[98] Ibid, 381 per Lord Brandon of Oakbrook.

privilege to a very significant degree.[99] As has been pointed out: 'A lawyer must now say to a client that nothing the client says will be protected from disclosure if anyone else in the world has a dishonest intention in relation to the subject matter and is using the client as an innocent tool.'[100]

4.10 An 'Absolute' Doctrine?

The question whether legal professional privilege constitutes an 'absolute' doctrine, or whether, instead, it is subject to a 'balancing' exercise, was considered by the House of Lords in two cases. The first of these, *R v Derby Magistrates' Court, ex p B*,[101] concerned legal advice privilege. A person was accused of a murder which his stepson B had earlier confessed to and been charged with. B was later acquitted when he retracted his confession and blamed his stepfather. The stepfather sought production of the instructions that B had initially given to his solicitors when admitting to the murder. The House of Lords held that it was inappropriate to balance the public interest underlying legal advice privilege against the public interest in ensuring that all relevant evidence was made available to the defence.[102] To acknowledge that such a balancing exercise may be performed would mean that:

> the client's confidence is necessarily lost. The solicitor, instead of being able to tell his client that anything which the client might say would never in any circumstances be revealed without his consent, would have to qualify his assurance. He would have to tell the client that his confidence might be broken if in some future case the court were to hold that he no longer had 'any recognisable interest' in asserting his privilege. One can see at once that the purpose of the privilege would thereby be undermined.[103]

Moreover, the House of Lords did not consider that the doctrine of public interest immunity, requiring as it does a balancing exercise, provided an appropriate analogy:

> As for the analogy with public interest immunity, . . . it by no means follows that because a balancing exercise is called for in one class of case, it may also be allowed in another. Legal professional privilege and public interest immunity are as different in their origin as they are in their scope. Putting it another way, if a balancing exercise was ever required in the case of legal professional privilege, it was performed once and for all in the 16th century, and since then has applied across the board in every case, irrespective of the client's individual merits.[104]

This decision is open to criticism on the ground that it overlooks the importance of the need to protect the innocent from wrongful conviction. Indeed, as the Privy Council has

---

[99] The interpretation might 'open the door to a spate of applications to obtain access to privileged material on the ground that the privilege is vitiated by a criminal intention on the part of some third party': ibid, 379 per Lord Bridge of Harwich.

[100] A L E Newbold, 'The Crime/Fraud Exception to Legal Professional Privilege' (1990) 53 *Modern Law Review* 472, 483. Cf C Passmore, *Privilege* (1998) 226.

[101] [1996] AC 487. See generally M Bowes, 'The Supremacy of Legal Professional Privilege: The *Derby Magistrates* Case', *Archbold News*, 3 May 1996, 5; C Tapper, 'Prosecution and Privilege' (1996) 1 *International Journal of Evidence and Proof* 5; A A S Zuckerman, 'Legal Professional Privilege—The Cost of Absolutism' (1996) 112 *Law Quarterly Review* 535.

[102] *R v Barton* [1973] 1 WLR 115 and *R v Ataou* [1988] QB 798 were overruled.

[103] [1996] AC 487, 508.   [104] Ibid.

subsequently observed, 'the public interest in overriding the privilege could scarcely have been higher than it was in ... *Ex p B*'.[105] To distinguish legal professional privilege from public interest immunity is not convincing, since in both cases the issue is whether the need to ensure that a defendant is able to establish his or her innocence may be overridden by extrinsic policy considerations. The fact that in the sixteenth century the balance may have come down in favour of upholding the privilege whatever the circumstances does not dictate that this should still be the case in the twenty-first century. Lord Taylor's fear that 'once any exception to the general rule is allowed, the client's confidence is necessarily lost', and that clients 'might ... be deterred from telling the whole truth to their solicitors', is based merely on an assumption which lacks empirical support.

In Canada, the right of an accused under section 7 of the Canadian Charter of Rights and Freedoms to make full answer and defence has provided the basis for a different approach. Given 'Canadians' abhorrence at the possibility of a faulty conviction',[106] 'solicitor–client privilege is not absolute and may, in rare circumstances, be required to yield in order to permit an accused to make full answer and defence to a criminal charge'.[107] The approach to be taken is as follows:

The ... test comprises a threshold question and a two-stage innocence at stake test, which proceed as follows:

- To satisfy the threshold test, the accused must establish that:
  - the information he seeks from the solicitor–client communication is not available from any other source; and
  - he is otherwise unable to raise a reasonable doubt.
- If the threshold has been satisfied, the judge should proceed to the innocence at stake test, which has two stages.
  - Stage #1: The accused seeking production of the solicitor–client communication has to demonstrate an evidentiary basis to conclude that a communication exists that could raise a reasonable doubt as to his guilt.
  - Stage #2: If such an evidentiary basis exists, the trial judge should examine the communication to determine whether, in fact, it is likely to raise a reasonable doubt as to the guilt of the accused.
- It is important to distinguish that the burden in the second stage of the innocence at stake test (likely to raise a reasonable doubt) is stricter than that in the first stage (could raise a reasonable doubt).
- If the innocence at stake test is satisfied, the judge should order disclosure of the communications that are likely to raise a reasonable doubt ...[108]

---

[105] *B v Auckland District Law Society* [2003] UKPC 38, [2003] 3 WLR 859, [48]. See generally M D J Conaglen, 'Disciplinary Investigations and Legal Professional Privilege' [2003] *Cambridge Law Journal* 580.

[106] *R v Brown* [2002] 2 SCR 185, [2].   [107] Ibid, [1].

[108] Ibid, [4]. See generally D Layton, '*R v Brown*: Protecting Legal-Professional Privilege' (2002) 50 *Criminal Reports (5th)* 37. See also *Smith v Jones* [1999] 1 SCR 455 (see generally R I Barrett, 'Legal Professional Privilege: A "Public Safety" Exception?' (1999) 73 *Australian Law Journal* 629; D Layton, 'The Public Safety Exception: Confusing Confidentiality, Privilege and Ethics' (2001) 6 *Canadian Criminal Law Review* 217; W N Renke,

Interestingly, the Privy Council, while confirming that *Ex p B* correctly represented English law,[109] did 'not overlook the fact that a different approach has been adopted in Canada, where the courts do conduct a balancing exercise by reference to the facts of the particular case. The common law is no longer monolithic...'.[110] As Pattenden has noted, however, consideration of the adoption in English law of an approach akin to the Canadian one would raise a number of questions:

- Should it apply to all criminal offences, or only serious crimes?
- Is the right confined to the defence?...
- What happens if the protected material to which the accused seeks access is simultaneously subject to the privilege against self-incrimination?
- To what extent, if at all, should the exception to LPP apply in circumstances where two persons are jointly standing trial and a communication by one co-defendant to his lawyer would materially assist the other?
- If, in the interests of avoiding a miscarriage of justice, a privileged communication has to be disclosed, what practical steps should the court take to protect the confidentiality of the disclosed material?[111]

The second relevant decision of the House of Lords concerns litigation privilege. At issue in *In re L (A Minor)*[112] was the extent to which litigation privilege was applicable in care proceedings under Part IV of the Children Act 1989. *Ex p B* was distinguished on the basis that what was decided in that case about the absolute nature of legal professional privilege was confined to legal advice privilege. Litigation privilege, the House of Lords reasoned:

is an essential component of adversarial procedure.... This raises the question of whether proceedings under Part IV of the Act are essentially adversarial in their nature. If they are, litigation privilege must continue to play its normal part. If they are not, different considerations may apply.[113]

'Secrets and Lives—The Public Safety Exception to Solicitor-Client Privilege: *Smith v Jones*' (1999) 37 *Alberta Law Review* 1045; B M Sheldrick, 'Administering Public Safety: Solicitor-Client Privilege, Medical Experts and the Adversarial Process: *Smith v Jones*' (2000) 4 *International Journal of Evidence and Proof* 119); *R v McClure* [2001] 1 SCR 445 (see generally D Layton, '*R v McClure*: The Privilege on the Pea' (2001) 40 *Criminal Reports (5th)* 19; G Murphy, 'The Innocence at Stake Test and Legal Professional Privilege: A Logical Progression for the Law... but Not in England' [2001] *Criminal Law Review* 728).

[109] *B v Auckland District Law Society* [2003] UKPC 38, [2003] 3 WLR 859, [54]: 'Their Lordships consider that the rationale of the doctrine compels this conclusion. If the lawyer is to be able to give his client an absolute and unqualified assurance that what he tells him will not be disclosed without his consent in any circumstances, the assurance must follow and not precede the undertaking of any balancing exercise.'

[110] Ibid, [55]. See also *Three Rivers District Council v Bank of England (No 6)* [2004] UKHL 48, [2004] 3 WLR 1274, [25] per Lord Scott of Foscote.

[111] R Pattenden, *The Law of Professional-Client Confidentiality: Regulating the Disclosure of Confidential Personal Information* (2003) 552–3.

[112] [1996] 2 WLR 395. See generally D Burrows, 'Privilege and Disclosure After *Re L*' (1996) 140 *Solicitors' Journal* 560; J McEwan, 'The Uncertain Status of Privilege in Children Act Cases: *Re L*' (1996) 1 *International Journal of Evidence and Proof* 80; R Mahoney, 'Reforming Litigation Privilege' (2001) 30 *Common Law World Review* 66; C Passmore, 'Privilege in the Lords' (1996) 146 *New Law Journal* 921.

[113] [1996] 2 WLR 395, 400–1.

The House of Lords considered that care proceedings under Part IV of the 1989 Act were 'essentially non-adversarial in their nature'.[114] Support for this view was gained from section 1(1) of the Act, which provides in part: 'When a court determines any question with respect to...the upbringing of a child...the child's welfare shall be the court's paramount consideration.' Thus, in view of the fact that litigation privilege arose essentially in an adversarial context and the fact that care proceedings were essentially non-adversarial, litigation privilege did not automatically apply in care proceedings and the House of Lords was at liberty to determine whether it should apply. The House considered 'that care proceedings under Part IV of the Act are so far removed from normal actions' that litigation privilege should have no application in such proceedings.[115]

This decision, then, makes much of the supposed distinction between legal advice privilege and litigation privilege. Whether this distinction is convincing, or whether legal advice privilege and litigation privilege are in reality, as Lord Nicholls of Birkenhead thought in his dissenting speech,[116] 'integral parts of a single privilege'[117] is debatable. It is at least arguable that the House of Lords in *In re L (A Minor)* should have taken the bold step of declaring *Ex p B* to have been wrongly decided, and not simply have confined the decision to cases of legal advice privilege. After all, 'if the House of Lords places child welfare above the litigant's interest why should the removal of legal professional privilege be confined to its litigation limb? In other words, should not communications between client and lawyer also be disclosable for the sake of protecting children from harm?'[118]

4.11 Non-Availability of Privilege in Another Jurisdiction

The fact that the privilege cannot, for whatever reason, be invoked in another jurisdiction is irrelevant to its availability in this one: 'privilege is not lost under English law because it cannot be claimed in another country'.[119] 'To suggest otherwise would mean that a court, when deciding whether to uphold a claim for privilege, would need to be informed as to whether privilege could be claimed in all the countries of the world.... The fact that under foreign law the document is not privileged or that the privilege that existed is deemed to have been waived is irrelevant.'[120]

4.12 Secondary Evidence

The general principle, affirmed in *Calcraft v Guest*,[121] is that where privileged information has become known to a person not entitled to it (that is, a person other than the client,

---

[114] Ibid, 401.

[115] Ibid, 402. See also *Three Rivers District Council v Bank of England (No 5)* [2003] EWCA Civ 474, [2003] 3 WLR 667, [2]: because 'litigation' means adversarial litigation, litigation privilege cannot be claimed in the context of a private non-statutory inquiry.   [116] [1996] 2 WLR 395, 408.

[117] See also C Passmore, *Privilege* (1998) 17–18.

[118] A A S Zuckerman, 'Legal Professional Privilege—The Cost of Absolutism' (1996) 112 *Law Quarterly Review* 535, 538.   [119] *British American Tobacco (Investments) Ltd v USA* [2004] EWCA Civ 1064, [38].

[120] *Bourns Inc v Raychem Corp* [1999] 3 All ER 154, 167.   [121] [1898] 1 QB 759.

the legal adviser, any relevant third parties, or any agents for communication such as clerks and secretaries), then it may be used by that person in evidence. It is irrelevant how that person came by this information. If the information became known as a result of an *inadvertent* disclosure (in contrast, for example, to a situation where the document was stolen), the effect of *Calcraft* has been reversed by rule 31.20 of the Civil Procedure Rules, which provides: 'Where a party inadvertently allows a privileged document to be inspected, the party who has inspected the document may use it or its contents only with the permission of the court.'

Even where the rule in *Calcraft* continues to apply, however, equity has stepped in to ameliorate the harshness of that rule. If the information has not already been used in evidence, an injunction may be able to be obtained to prevent its use.[122] It has been held that the same principles that govern a determination of whether an injunction should be granted are to apply to a determination under rule 31.20 of whether permission should be granted for the privileged document or its contents to be used: 'Whether the question is whether to grant an injunction or to make an order under that rule, the court should do what is just and equitable in all the circumstances of the case.'[123] For example, the fact that a document has been made available as a result of an obvious mistake is a consideration weighing in favour of preventing its use. A comprehensive summary of the relevant principles to be derived from the case law has been provided by the Court of Appeal:

(i) A party giving inspection of documents must decide before doing so what privileged documents he wishes to allow the other party to see and what he does not.

(ii) Although the privilege is that of the client and not the solicitor, a party clothes his solicitor with ostensible authority (if not implied or express authority) to waive privilege in respect of relevant documents.

(iii) A solicitor considering documents made available by the other party to litigation owes no duty of care to that party and is in general entitled to assume that any privilege which might otherwise have been claimed for such documents has been waived.

(iv) In these circumstances, where a party has given inspection of documents, including privileged documents which he has allowed the other party to inspect by mistake, it will in general be too late for him to claim privilege in order to attempt to correct the mistake by obtaining injunctive relief.

(v) However, the court has jurisdiction to intervene to prevent the use of documents made available for inspection by mistake where justice requires, as for example in the case of inspection procured by fraud.

(vi) In the absence of fraud, all will depend upon the circumstances, but the court may grant an injunction if the documents have been made available for inspection as a result of an obvious mistake.

---

[122] See generally *Lord Ashburton v Pape* [1913] 2 Ch 469; *Goddard v Nationwide* [1986] 3 WLR 734; *English & American Insurance Co Ltd v Herbert Smith* [1988] FSR 232; *Guinness Peat Ltd v Fitzroy Robinson* [1987] 1 WLR 1027; *Webster v James Chapman & Co* [1989] 3 All ER 939; *Derby & Co Ltd v Weldon (No 8)* [1990] 3 All ER 762; *IBM Corp v Phoenix International* [1995] 1 All ER 413.

[123] *Al Fayed v Commissioner of the Police of the Metropolis* [2002] EWCA Civ 780, [18].

(vii) A mistake is likely to be held to be obvious and an injunction granted where the documents are received by a solicitor and:

    (a) the solicitor appreciates that a mistake has been made before making some use of the documents; or

    (b) it would be obvious to a reasonable solicitor in his position that a mistake has been made;

and, in either case, there are no other circumstances which would make it unjust or inequitable to grant relief.

(viii) Where a solicitor gives detailed consideration to the question whether the documents have been made available for inspection by mistake and honestly concludes that they have not, that fact will be a relevant (and in many cases an important) pointer to the conclusion that it would not be obvious to the reasonable solicitor that a mistake had been made, but is not conclusive; the decision remains a matter for the court.

(ix) In both the cases identified in (vii) (a) and (b) above there are many circumstances in which it may nevertheless be held to be inequitable or unjust to grant relief, but all will depend upon the particular circumstances.

(x) Since the court is exercising an equitable jurisdiction, there are no rigid rules.[124]

While this summary specifically addresses the issue of obtaining injunctions, analogous considerations are to be applied, as we have seen earlier, to making determinations under rule 31.20.

It would appear that an injunction cannot be granted to an accused in a public prosecution to prevent the Crown from adducing admissible evidence relevant to the offence charged.[125] This is a controversial principle which, as Nourse LJ noted approvingly[126] in *Goddard v Nationwide*, has not been followed in New Zealand.[127]

Apart from an injunction and the protection afforded by rule 31.20, one other possible remedy may be available. The availability of this exclusionary remedy would appear to be limited to situations in which the privileged document was improperly obtained within the four walls of the courtroom. The view is taken that 'for a party to litigation to take possession by stealth or by a trick of documents belonging to the other side within the precincts of the court is probably contempt of court' which 'the court should not countenance . . . by admitting such documents in evidence'.[128]

4.13 The Relevance of Section 10 of the Contempt of Court Act 1981

Section 10 of the Contempt of Court Act 1981 has been examined in some detail in the preceding chapter. Its relevance in the field of legal professional privilege has been

---

[124] Ibid, [16]. See generally A Zuckerman, *Civil Procedure* (2003) 517–22, 550–3.
[125] *Butler v Board of Trade* [1971] Ch 680, 690; *R v Tompkins* (1978) 67 Cr App R 181 (decision of 1977).
[126] [1986] 3 WLR 734, 746.   [127] *R v Uljee* [1982] 1 NZLR 561.
[128] *ITC Ltd v Video Exchange Ltd* [1982] Ch 431, 441. See also *Goddard v Nationwide* [1986] 3 WLR 734, 745.

considered in *Saunders v Punch Ltd.*[129] The defendant published an article referring to meetings between the plaintiff and his former solicitors. The plaintiff obtained an injunction restraining further publication. He also sought an order for disclosure of the source of the information under section 10 of the Contempt of Court Act 1981, on the basis that such disclosure was necessary in the interests of justice. The court did not doubt that the interest in the preservation and protection of legal professional privilege was a 'towering public interest'.[130] In the present case, however, the injunction obtained by the plaintiff against the defendant already provided a high degree of protection, and thus the interests of justice did not require that disclosure of the source of the information should also be made.

5 Other Professional Privileges?

English law has steadfastly declined to acknowledge the existence of professional privilege in the context of professions other than the legal profession.[131] Rather, as was seen in Chapter 6, the determination of whether confidential communications occurring in the context of other professional relationships should be disclosed involves a balancing exercise:

> In relation to all other confidential communications, whether between doctor and patient, accountant and client, husband and wife, parent and child, priest and penitent, the common law recognises the confidentiality of the communication, will protect the confidentiality up to a point, but declines to allow the communication the absolute protection allowed to communications between lawyer and client giving or seeking legal advice. In relation to all these other confidential communications the law requires the public interest in the preservation of confidences and the private interest of the parties in maintaining the confidentiality of their communications to be balanced against the administration of justice reasons for requiring disclosure of the confidential material. There is a strong public interest that in criminal cases the innocent should be acquitted and the guilty convicted, that in civil cases the claimant should succeed if he is entitled to do so and should fail if he is not, that every trial should be a fair trial and that to provide the best chance of these desiderata being achieved all relevant material should be available to be taken into account. These are the administration of justice reasons to be placed in the balance. They will usually prevail.[132]

---

[129] [1998] 1 All ER 234. See generally C Passmore, 'Journalists and Privilege' (1998) 148 *New Law Journal* 519.

[130] [1998] 1 All ER 234, 246.

[131] On the US position see E J Imwinkelried, 'The Paradox of Privilege Law' in C M Breur, M M Kommer, J F Nijboer, and J M Reijntjes, *New Trends in Criminal Investigation and Evidence—Volume II* (2000); E Imwinkelried, 'The Rivalry Between Truth and Privilege: The Weakness of the Supreme Court's Instrumental Reasoning in *Jaffee v Redmond*, 518 US 1 (1996)' (1998) 49 *Hastings Law Journal* 969.

[132] *Three Rivers District Council v Bank of England (No 6)* [2004] UKHL 48, [2004] 3 WLR 1274, [28] per Lord Scott of Foscote.

8

Character Evidence

1 The Relevance of Evidence of Character

There are particular assumptions that underlie the treatment of evidence of character. In very simple terms, it is assumed that such evidence is relevant to propensity as well as to credit. Thus evidence that a person is of good character is considered relevant to her propensity to act in a manner consistent with that good character, and relevant to her credibility. Conversely, evidence of a person's bad character is considered relevant[1] to her propensity to act in a manner consistent with that bad character,[2] as well as relevant to lack of credit.[3] The treatment of character evidence as being relevant to propensity means that, in a criminal case, evidence of a defendant's bad character may be regarded as relevant to the issue of his guilt of the offence with which he is currently charged.

Such assumptions, however, overlook a number of important points. In the first place, the prejudicial effect of bad character evidence admitted on the issue of guilt in a jury trial may be considerable.[4] In very broad terms, the risk of prejudice may arise in one of two ways. First, the jury may overestimate the probative value of the evidence in question: they 'may reason that because the accused stole a bottle of whisky from a supermarket five years earlier he must also have been guilty of the theft of the car with which he is now charged'.[5] Secondly, even if not in fact satisfied beyond reasonable doubt of the accused's guilt, the jury may return a guilty verdict because he or she is thought to deserve punishment for the previous misconduct. This misconduct may not have led to a criminal prosecution, or a prosecution in respect of the conduct may have resulted either in an acquittal or in what the jury regard as unduly lenient punishment. The first

---

[1] See generally M Redmayne, 'The Relevance of Bad Character' [2002] *Cambridge Law Journal* 684.

[2] Empirical research 'has revealed that convictions for certain types of offence appear to increase the relative risk for subsequent convictions for very serious offences. In particular, the study has highlighted a number of "unusual" offences which appear to significantly increase the likelihood of a subsequent criminal conviction of murder or serious sexual assault': K Soothill, B Francis, E Ackerley, and R Fligelstone, *Murder and Serious Sexual Assault: What Criminal Histories Can Reveal About Future Serious Offending* (Police Research Series Paper 144) (2002) vii, available at http://www.homeoffice.gov.uk/rds/prgpdfs/prs144.pdf.

[3] For example, 'a past conviction for dishonesty could be said to be directly relevant to credit, a fortiori if the conviction was for giving perjured evidence in court':*Thomas v Comr of Police* [1997] 1 All ER 747, 763.

[4] See generally Law Commission (Consultation Paper No 141), *Criminal Law—Evidence in Criminal Proceedings: Previous Misconduct of a Defendant—A Consultation Paper* (1996) [7.1]–[7.41], available at http://www.lawcom. gov.uk/docs/cp141.pdf.   [5] A A S Zuckerman, *The Principles of Criminal Evidence* (1989) 222.

type of prejudice may be termed 'reasoning prejudice' and the second 'moral prejudice'.[6] It is notable that, in answer to the question '[if] a defendant has any similar previous convictions, do you think the jury should always be told about them before they go to consider their verdict?', 58 per cent of the jurors in the *Crown Court Study* said no, while 42 per cent said yes.[7] Mock jury research conducted at Oxford revealed that[8] 'after deliberation, participants who were told of a recent similar conviction rated the defendant as significantly more likely to have committed the crime with which he was charged than when they were told that he had a dissimilar conviction or no convictions'. Interestingly, the mock jurors regarded the defendant as *less* likely to have committed the crime if they were told that he had a recent dissimilar conviction, than if they were told nothing about his criminal record. 'A possible explanation for this finding', according to the Law Commission, 'is that a previous conviction for a specific offence evokes a stereo-type of a person who commits that type of offence *rather than* the different one charged. Another possible explanation... [is] that participants felt it was unfair on the defendant to introduce potentially prejudicial evidence of marginal relevance.' These results broadly followed the findings of the LSE Jury Project[9] over twenty years previously.[10]

Furthermore, another important assumption underlying this area of the law—that bad character provides a good indication that a person is not worthy of belief—'contrasts sharply with the tentative judgements of the psychologists in the matter of credibility assessment'.[11] As the Law Commission notes, psychological research has failed generally to demonstrate a significant link between bad character evidence and lack of veracity as a witness.[12] This is supported by the finding of the Oxford mock jury research that a defendant with a previous conviction (even one for an offence of dishonesty) was not rated as a less credible witness. Only a previous conviction for an indecent assault (especially an indecent assault on a child) adversely affected his credibility as a witness in the eyes of the participants.[13]

[6] A Palmer, 'The Scope of the Similar Fact Rule' (1994) 16 *Adelaide Law Review* 161, 169–72.

[7] M Zander and P Henderson, *The Royal Commission on Criminal Justice: Crown Court Study* (1993) 210.

[8] Law Commission (Consultation Paper No 141), *Criminal Law—Evidence in Criminal Proceedings: Previous Misconduct of a Defendant—A Consultation Paper* (1996) [D.21]–[D.23] (italics in original), available at http://www.lawcom.gov.uk/docs/cp141.pdf. See also S Lloyd-Bostock, 'The Effects on Juries of Hearing About the Defendant's Previous Criminal Record: A Simulation Study' [2000] *Criminal Law Review* 734.

[9] LSE Jury Project, 'Juries and the Rules of Evidence' [1973] *Criminal Law Review* 208.

[10] See also J McEwan, *The Verdict of the Court: Passing Judgment in Law and Psychology* (2003) 168–9.

[11] R Munday, 'The Paradox of Cross-Examination to Credit—Simply Too Close for Comfort' [1994] *Cambridge Law Journal* 303, 308.

[12] Law Commission (Consultation Paper No 141), *Criminal Law—Evidence in Criminal Proceedings: Previous Misconduct of a Defendant—A Consultation Paper* (1996) [6.16]–[6.17], available at http://www.lawcom.gov.uk/docs/cp141.pdf. J Endres, 'The Suggestibility of the Child Witness: The Role of Individual Differences and Their Assessment' (1997) 1 *Journal of Credibility Assessment and Witness Psychology* 44, 45 notes: 'The general credibility of a witness, a concept widely favored by the legal profession, does not enjoy great respectability in the eyes of empirical psychologists.... knowledge of a person's previous behavior in different circumstances certainly does not by itself provide sufficient reason to accept his or her testimony as truthful or to reject it as dishonest. Almost everyone would lie when their most vital interests are at stake, and even a person with a bad reputation for frequent lying may become the victim of a crime and give a truthful report about it.'

[13] Law Commission (Consultation Paper No 141), *Criminal Law—Evidence in Criminal Proceedings: Previous Misconduct of a Defendant—A Consultation Paper* (1996) App D, available at http://www.lawcom.gov.uk/docs/cp141.pdf.

2 Civil Proceedings

In *O'Brien v Chief Constable of South Wales Police*[14] the House of Lords gave thorough consideration to the issue of the admissibility of bad character evidence in civil cases, subjecting previous case law to scrutiny. The case concerned a claim for damages for malicious prosecution and misfeasance in public office. It was alleged by the claimant that two police officers had been guilty of malpractice in the investigation that led to his conviction. The House of Lords agreed with the Court of Appeal that evidence of the same officers' conduct in two other investigations was admissible. In the words of Lord Phillips of Worth Matravers:

> I would simply apply the test of relevance as the test of admissibility of similar fact evidence in a civil suit. Such evidence is admissible if it is potentially probative of an issue in the action.[15]
>
> This is not to say that ... policy considerations ... have no part to play in the conduct of civil litigation. . . . CPR 1.2 requires the court to give effect to the overriding objective of dealing with cases justly. This includes dealing with the case in a way which is proportionate to what is involved in the case, and in a manner which is expeditious and fair. CPR 1.4 requires the court actively to manage the case in order to further the overriding objective. CPR 32.1 gives the court the power to control the evidence. This power expressly enables the court to exclude evidence that would otherwise be admissible and to limit cross-examination.[16]
>
> Similar fact evidence will not necessarily risk causing any unfair prejudice to the party against whom it is directed. . . . It may, however, carry such a risk. Evidence of impropriety which reflects adversely on the character of a party may risk causing prejudice that is disproportionate to its relevance, particularly where the trial is taking place before a jury. In such a case the judge will be astute to see that the probative cogency of the evidence justifies this risk of prejudice in the interests of a fair trial.[17]
>
> Equally, when considering whether to admit evidence, or permit cross-examination, on matters that are collateral to the central issues, the judge will have regard to the need for proportionality and expedition. He will consider whether the evidence in question is likely to be relatively uncontroversial, or whether its admission is likely to create side issues which will unbalance the trial and make it harder to see the wood from the trees.[18]

The Court of Appeal's decision on the facts of the case, endorsed by the House of Lords, was as follows:

> Mr O'Brien has been in prison for 11 years, convicted of a murder which he says he did not commit and in respect of which his conviction has now been quashed. In order to succeed in his claim against the police who initiated his prosecution he wishes to adduce the relevant and logically probative evidence ... It is notoriously difficult for a claimant in his position to attract credence to his account if it is merely his word against that of a number of police officers.

---

[14] [2005] UKHL 26, [2005] 2 WLR 1038. See generally P Keleher, 'Admissible Evidence' (2005) 149 *Solicitors' Journal* 731.   [15] [2005] UKHL 26, [2005] 2 WLR 1038, [53].

[16] Ibid, [54].   [17] Ibid, [55].   [18] Ibid, [56].

If, however, ... evidence is also given of a number of incidents of similar malpractice by the same police officer(s), the position may be changed, and the evidence of malpractice may be overwhelming.[19]

3 Criminal Proceedings

3.1 The Defendant: Putting Character in Issue

An accused is entitled to introduce evidence of his good character. This may be achieved by cross-examining prosecution witnesses with a view to establishing his good character, or by adducing good-character evidence in chief (in the form of evidence given by the accused himself or by other defence witnesses). Where an accused has put his or her character in issue, section 101(1)(f) of the Criminal Justice Act 2003 may come into play to permit the court to admit evidence of bad character to correct any false impression that may have been created.

The following cases provide illustrations of actions which have been held to amount to putting character in issue:

• In *R v Ferguson*, even though 'he never intended to put his character in issue', the defendant effectively did so by introducing evidence that 'he had attended mass and service for over thirty-six years' and 'was a member of several religious societies'.[20]

• The defendant in *R v Baker* 'gave evidence that for four years he had been earning an honest living, and in our opinion this was evidence of good character ... '.[21]

• It was stated in *R v Coulman:* 'If you ask a man whether he is a married man with a family, in regular work, and has a wife and three children, you are setting up his character ... '.[22]

• In *R v Samuel* the Court of Criminal Appeal observed that the effect of a certain line of questioning had been 'to induce the jury to say: "This man is one of those people who, if he finds property, gives it up; in other words, he is an honest man." ... it is clear that those questions did put the appellant's character in issue. He was asking the jury to assume that he was a man who dealt honestly with property which he found.'[23]

• In *R v Anderson* the New Zealand Court of Appeal considered that mounting a defence to the effect 'that the accused would not have lost his temper and caused the injuries to the complainants because of the self-control developed through his martial arts training' would have been tantamount to putting character in issue.[24]

---

[19] [2003] EWCA Civ 1085, [2004] CP Rep 5, [80].   [20] (1909) 2 Cr App R 250, 251.
[21] (1912) 7 Cr App R 252, 253.   [22] (1927) 20 Cr App R 106, 108.
[23] (1956) 40 Cr App R 8, 10–11 (decision of 1956).   [24] [2000] 1 NZLR 667, [31].

By contrast, 'mere assertions of innocence or repudiation of guilt on the part of the prisoner' and 'reasons given by him for such assertion or repudiation'[25] have been held not to constitute putting character in issue. Further, in *R v Lee*, the Court of Appeal held that:

> this court finds it impossible to hold that the questions which were put to the prosecution witness... as to the convictions of the other men, were with a view to establishing the defendant's own good character. The questions were put with a view to establishing the bad character of the two other men and nothing else and the answer 'Yes' to the question 'Had they previous convictions?' had nothing whatever to do with the character of the defendant.... *it is not implicit in an accusation of dishonesty that the accuser himself is an honest man.*[26]

Finally, in *R v Redd* it was held that the appellant 'was not endeavouring to establish a good character merely because a witness whom he called, voluntarily and probably against the appellant's own desire, made a statement as to the appellant's good character...'.[27]

3.2 The Relevance of Evidence of the Defendant's Good Character

The precise relevance of evidence of the defendant's good character[28] was considered in detail by the Court of Appeal in *R v Vye*.[29] It was confirmed that such evidence is relevant to both credit and propensity (or, more specifically, the lack of propensity). Thus the fact that a defendant is of good character is thought to indicate that he or she is a person worthy of belief, and a person unlikely to have committed the offence with which he or she is charged.

So-called *Vye* directions are required[30] to be given to the jury on evidence of a defendant's good character.[31] The Privy Council noted in 2005:

> The principles to be applied regarding good character directions have been much more clearly settled by a number of decisions in recent years, and what might have been properly regarded at one time as a question of discretion for the trial judge has crystallised into an obligation as a matter of law.... The standard [*Vye*] direction should contain two limbs, the credibility direction, that a person of good character is more likely to be truthful than one of bad character, and the propensity direction, that he is less likely to commit a crime, especially one of the nature with which he is charged.[32]

---

[25] *R v Ellis* [1910] 2 KB 746, 763.   [26] [1976] 1 WLR 71, 73 (italics added).

[27] [1923] 1 KB 104, 107.

[28] See generally R Munday, 'What Constitutes a Good Character?' [1997] *Criminal Law Review* 247.

[29] [1993] 1 WLR 471.

[30] Contrast the position in Australia, where good-character directions are not mandatory: *Melbourne v R* [1999] HCA 32.

[31] On the position in magistrates' courts see G Woodward, 'The Good Character Direction and the Magistrates' Court' (2000) 164 *Justice of the Peace* 496.

[32] *Teeluck v The State* [2005] UKPC 14, [2005] 1 WLR 2421, [33].

The first limb of the direction, concerning credit, is required to be given where the defendant (1) has given evidence or (2) has not given evidence but relies at trial on exculpatory pre-trial statements made to the police or to others. The second limb of the direction, concerning propensity, is always to be given. 'It is a necessary part of counsel's duty to his client to ensure that a good character direction is obtained where the defendant is entitled to it and likely to benefit from it. The duty of raising the issue is to be discharged by the defence, not by the judge, and if it is not raised by the defence the judge is under no duty to raise it himself.'[33]

The Court of Appeal has emphasized that 'what is mandatory is to give both limbs of the direction, not to use any particular form of words',[34] and that:

> it must be for the trial judge in each case to decide how he tailors his direction to the particular circumstances. He would probably wish to indicate, as is commonly done, that good character cannot amount to a defence. . . . Provided that the judge indicates to the jury the two respects in which good character may be relevant, ie, credibility and propensity, this court will be slow to criticise any qualifying remarks he may make based on the facts of the individual case.[35]

However, 'character directions should not be given in the form of a question, but in the form of an affirmative statement. That applies even if the question is a leading question . . .'. Thus it is 'far from sufficient' to give a first-limb direction by merely asking the question: 'Is it more likely that he is telling the truth because he is a man of clean character?'[36]

Where a defendant of good character is tried jointly with one of bad character, a *Vye* direction in respect of the former is still required.[37]

---

[33] *Teeluck v The State* [2005] UKPC 14, [2005] 1 WLR 2421, [33].

[34] *R v Miah* [1997] 2 Cr App R 12, 22.   [35] *R v Vye* [1993] 1 WLR 471, 477.

[36] *R v Lloyd* [2000] 2 Cr App R 355, 360. *Lloyd* is discussed in R Munday, 'Judicial Studies Board Specimen Directions and the Enforcement of Orthodoxy: A Modest Case Study' (2002) 66 *Journal of Criminal Law* 158.

[37] *R v Vye* [1993] 1 WLR 471, 479; *R v Cain* [1994] 1 WLR 1449. The question 'whether defendants of disparate characters might require separate trials . . . is a matter for the judge and is to be decided in accordance with well-established principles. Problems such as . . . disparate characters are to be considered and weighed on a case by case basis. There can certainly be no rule in favour of separate trials for defendants of good and bad character. Generally, those jointly indicted should be jointly tried': *R v Vye* [1993] 1 WLR 471, 479. The presumption in favour of joint trials for those jointly indicted was also emphasized by Lord Steyn in *R v Hayter* [2005] UKHL 6, [2005] 1 WLR 605, [6]: 'The practice favouring joint criminal trials is clear. It has been accepted for a long time in English practice that, subject to a judge's discretion to order separate trials in the interests of justice, there are powerful public reasons why joint offences should be tried jointly . . . While considerations of the avoidance of delay, costs and convenience, can be cited in favour of joint trials this is not the prime basis of the practice. Instead it is founded principally on the perception that a just outcome is more likely to be established in a joint trial than in separate trials. The topic is intimately connected with public confidence in jury trials. Subject to a judge's discretion to order otherwise, joint trials of those involved in a joint criminal case are in the public interest and are the norm.' In *Pereira v UK (Admissibility)*, Application no 40741/02, 8 April 2003, the European Court of Human Rights stated: 'The Court notes the presumption applied by the domestic courts that the defendants involved in an offence should be tried together and considers that this is an unexceptionable approach, based on common sense principles attaching to the administration of justice.' See also, generally, A Samuels, 'Separate Trial for Co-Defendant?' (2003) 167 *Justice of the Peace* 209.

Clearly 'good character' is not an absolute concept and there may arise situations in which it is uncertain whether an unqualified *Vye* direction should be given. In *R v Gray* the Court of Appeal, after a consideration of the relevant case law, including the decision of the House of Lords in *R v Aziz*,[38] usefully summarized the applicable principles as follows:

(1) The primary rule is that a person of previous good character must be given a full direction covering both credibility and propensity. Where there are no further facts to complicate the position, such a direction is mandatory and should be unqualified . . .

(2) If a defendant has a previous conviction which, either because of its age or its nature, may entitle him to be treated as of effective good character, the trial judge has a discretion so to treat him, and if he does so the defendant is entitled to a *Vye* direction . . .; but

(3) Where the previous conviction can only be regarded as irrelevant or of no significance in relation to the offence charged, that discretion ought to be exercised in favour of treating the defendant as of good character . . . In such a case the defendant is again entitled to a *Vye* direction. It would seem to be consistent with principle (4) below that, where there is room for uncertainty as to how a defendant of effective good character should be treated, a judge would be entitled to give an appropriately modified *Vye* direction.

(4) Where a defendant of previous good character, whether absolute or . . . effective, has been shown at trial, whether by admission or otherwise, to be guilty of criminal conduct, the prima facie rule of practice is to deal with this by qualifying a *Vye* direction rather than by withholding it . . .; but

(5) In such a case, there remains a narrowly circumscribed residual discretion to withhold a good character direction in whole, or presumably in part, where it would make no sense, or would be meaningless or absurd or an insult to common sense, to do otherwise . . .

(6) Approved examples of the exercise of such a residual discretion are not common. . . . Lord Steyn in *Aziz* appears to have considered that a person of previous good character who is shown beyond doubt to have been guilty of serious criminal behaviour similar to the offence charged would forfeit his right to any direction . . .

(7) A direction should never be misleading. Where therefore a defendant has withheld something of his record so that otherwise a trial judge is not in a position to refer to it, the defendant may forfeit the more ample, if qualified, direction which the judge might have been able to give . . .[39]

It is considered that a *Vye* direction 'will have some value and will therefore be capable of having some effect in every case in which it is appropriate for such a direction to be given . . . If it is omitted in such a case it will rarely be possible for an appellate court to say that the giving of a good character direction could not have affected the outcome of the trial.'[40]

---

[38] [1995] 3 WLR 53.   [39] [2004] EWCA Crim 1074, [2004] 2 Cr App R 30 (p 498), [57].
[40] *Teeluck v The State* [2005] UKPC 14, [2005] 1 WLR 2421, [33].

3.3 Bad Character

The Criminal Justice Act 2003[41] replaces the old common law principles on the admissibility of evidence of bad character.[42] The relevant provisions of the Act had a tortuous journey through Parliament,[43] with the Government essentially presenting them as tilting the balance in criminal justice away from defendants and back in favour of victims and the community. For critics, however, the provisions create an unacceptable risk of prejudice to accused persons and the potential for miscarriages of justice. It is notable that the Court of Appeal has commented scathingly on the provisions in the following terms:

> It is more than a decade since the late Lord Taylor of Gosforth CJ called for a reduction in the torrent of legislation affecting criminal justice. Regrettably, that call has gone unheeded by successive governments. Indeed, the quantity of such legislation has increased and its quality has, if anything, diminished. The 2003 Act has 339 sections and 38 schedules and runs to 453 pages. It is, in pre-metric terms, an inch thick. The provisions [on evidence of bad character] have been brought into force prematurely, before appropriate training could be given by the Judicial Studies Board or otherwise to approximately 2,000 Crown Court and Supreme Court judges and 30,000 magistrates. In the meantime, the judiciary and, no doubt, the many criminal justice agencies for which this Court cannot speak, must, in the phrase familiar during the Second World War 'make do and mend'.[44]

3.3.1 Specific Statutory Provisions Admitting Bad Character Evidence

The provisions of the Criminal Justice Act 2003 stand alongside any specific statutory provisions that may have the effect of rendering admissible, in specific circumstances,

---

[41] See generally G Durston, 'Bad Character Evidence and Non-Party Witnesses Under the Criminal Justice Act 2003' (2004) 8 *International Journal of Evidence and Proof* 233; G Durston, 'Co-Defendants' Bad Character Evidence Under the Criminal Justice Act 2003' (2004) 168 *Justice of the Peace* 979; G Durston, 'The Impact of the Criminal Justice Act 2003 on Prosecution Evidence of Defendant Bad Character Adduced to "Undermine Credit" ' (2004) 168 *Justice of the Peace* 610; G Durston, 'The Impact of the Criminal Justice Act 2003 on Similar Fact Evidence' (2004) 68 *Journal of Criminal Law* 307; G Durston, 'The Usual Suspects?' (2004) 154 *New Law Journal* 1692; A Edwards, 'Gazette in Practice: Criminal Law' (2005) 102(24) *Law Society's Gazette* 30; J Heenan and S Heenan, 'The Criminal Justice Act 2003—Promoting or Undermining Public Confidence?' (2005) 169 *Justice of the Peace* 273; J Mackie, 'Dress Nonsense' (2004) 148 *Solicitors' Journal* 214; R Munday, 'Bad Character Rules and Riddles: "Explanatory Notes" and True Meanings of S 103(1) of the Criminal Justice Act 2003' [2005] *Criminal Law Review* 337; R Munday, 'What Constitutes "Other Reprehensible Behaviour" Under the Bad Character Provisions of the Criminal Justice Act 2003?' [2005] *Criminal Law Review* 24; S O'Neill, ' "Bad Character": Trying to Obtain Convictions at All Costs', *The Times*, 18 Jan 2005, Law, 3; P Plowden, 'Making Sense of Character Evidence' (2005) 155 *New Law Journal* 47; M Sikand, 'Defendants Have Lost Their Shields', *Archbold News*, 19 Jan 2005, 6; P Tain, 'Bad Character' (2004) 148 *Solicitors' Journal* 1449; C Tapper, 'Criminal Justice Act 2003: Part 3: Evidence of Bad Character' [2004] *Criminal Law Review* 533; P Wilcock and J Bennathan, 'The New Meaning of Bad Character' (2004) 154 *New Law Journal* 1054; *Criminal Justice Act 2003: A Current Law Statute Guide* (2004) 44-110–44-131; B Gibson, *Criminal Justice Act 2003: A Guide to the New Procedures and Sentencing* (2004) 60–6; A Keogh, *Criminal Justice Act 2003: A Guide to the New Law* (2004) Ch 7; R Taylor, M Wasik, and R Leng, *Blackstone's Guide to the Criminal Justice Act 2003* (2004) Ch 8; R Ward and O M Davies, *The Criminal Justice Act 2003: A Practitioner's Guide* (2004) Ch 5.

[42] 'The common law rules governing the admissibility of evidence of bad character in criminal proceedings are abolished': Criminal Justice Act 2003, s 99(1).

[43] See M Zander, 'The Criminal Justice Bill Gets Royal Assent' (2003) 153 *New Law Journal* 1778, 1779.

[44] *R v Bradley* [2005] EWCA Crim 20, (2005) 169 JP 73, [39]. See generally G Durston, 'Recent Developments in Bad Character Evidence' (2005) 169 *Justice of the Peace* 378; K Hossein-Bor, 'Life in Crime' (2005) 149 *Solicitors' Journal* 172.

evidence of an accused's previous misconduct. For example, section 1(2) of the Official Secrets Act 1911 provides:

> On a prosecution under this section, it shall not be necessary to show that the accused person was guilty of any particular act tending to show a purpose prejudicial to the safety or interests of the State, and, notwithstanding that no such act is proved against him, he may be convicted if, from the circumstances of the case, or his conduct, or *his known character as proved*, it appears that his purpose was a purpose prejudicial to the safety or interests of the State . . . [45]

Section 27(3) of the Theft Act 1968 provides:

> Where a person is being proceeded against for handling stolen goods (but not for any offence other than handling stolen goods), then at any stage of the proceedings, if evidence has been given of his having or arranging to have in his possession the goods the subject of the charge, or of his undertaking or assisting in, or arranging to undertake or assist in, their retention, removal, disposal or realisation, the following evidence shall be admissible for the purpose of proving that he knew or believed the goods to be stolen goods—
>
> (a) evidence that he has had in his possession, or has undertaken or assisted in the retention, removal, disposal or realisation of, stolen goods from any theft taking place not earlier than twelve months before the offence charged; and
>
> (b) (provided that seven days' notice in writing has been given to him of the intention to prove the conviction) evidence that he has within the five years preceding the date of the offence charged been convicted of theft or of handling stolen goods. [46]

The rationale for section 27(3) is a practical one:

> Guilty knowledge in handling cases is notoriously difficult to prove . . . People do from time to time acquire or deal with stolen goods without knowing or believing them to be stolen, and this possibility can make it difficult for the fact-finders to know whether a defence of lack of knowledge or belief might be true in the case before them. Their doubts in such cases can be resolved if they learn that the accused had dealt with other stolen property in the past, or has previous convictions for handling or theft. [47]

The provision may, however, be criticized on a number of bases:

> In the first place, the subsection relates not only to *previous* misconduct, but also to misconduct *after* the time of the alleged offence. Second, paragraph (a) allows evidence to be given of any act of handling even though no charge has been brought. This is likely to lead to disputes as to whether the defendant *was* in possession of stolen goods on a previous occasion. Further,

---

[45] Italics added.

[46] The House of Lords held in *R v Hacker* [1994] 1 WLR 1659 that, under s 27(3)(b), it is permissible for the goods in question to be identified: the prosecution is not restricted to identifying the fact, date, and place of conviction. This decision has been the subject of criticism: R Munday, 'Handling Convictions Admissible Under S 27(3) of the Theft Act 1968: Part 1' (1995) 159 *Justice of the Peace* 223; R Munday, 'Handling Convictions Admissible under s 27 (3) of the Theft Act 1968: Part 2' (1995) 159 *Justice of the Peace* 261.

[47] Law Commission (Law Com No 273), *Evidence of Bad Character in Criminal Proceedings* (2001) [4.13], available at http://www.lawcom.gov.uk/docs/lc273.pdf.

paragraph (a) applies only if the goods were stolen not more than 12 months before the alleged handling: it is irrelevant when the alleged handler dealt with those goods. This can lead to bizarre results.[48]

There have therefore been a number of calls for the repeal of section 27(3), including a recommendation to that effect from the Law Commission.[49]

3.3.2 The Criminal Justice Act 2003

Under the Criminal Justice Act 2003, evidence of a person's bad character is 'evidence of, or of a disposition towards, misconduct on his part, other than evidence which—(a) has to do with the alleged facts of the offence with which the defendant is charged, or (b) is evidence of misconduct in connection with the investigation or prosecution of that offence'.[50] 'Misconduct' is defined as 'the commission of an offence or other reprehensible behaviour'.[51]

3.3.2.1 Defendants

Evidence of a defendant's bad character is admissible in any one of seven situations. Section 101(1) of the Criminal Justice Act 2003 provides:

In criminal proceedings evidence of the defendant's bad character is admissible if, but only if—

(a) all parties to the proceedings agree to the evidence being admissible,

(b) the evidence is adduced by the defendant himself or is given in answer to a question asked by him in cross-examination and intended to elicit it,

(c) it is important explanatory evidence,

(d) it is relevant to an important matter in issue between the defendant and the prosecution,

(e) it has substantial probative value in relation to an important matter in issue between the defendant and a co-defendant,

(f) it is evidence to correct a false impression given by the defendant, or

(g) the defendant has made an attack on another person's character.

The five that require closer examination ((c)–(g)) will be considered below. In relation to offences committed by the defendant as a child, section 108(2) provides:

In proceedings for an offence committed or alleged to have been committed by the defendant when aged 21 or over, evidence of his conviction for an offence when under the age of 14 is not admissible unless—

(a) both of the offences are triable only on indictment, and

(b) the court is satisfied that the interests of justice require the evidence to be admissible.

---

[48] Law Commission (Law Com No 273), *Evidence of Bad Character in Criminal Proceedings* (2001) [4.21] (italics in original). [49] Ibid, [11.55].
[50] S 98.   [51] S 112.

In *R v Hanson*[52] the Court of Appeal gave detailed consideration to the provisions of the Criminal Justice Act 2003 in the specific context of evidence of a defendant's previous convictions.[53] Extensive reference will be made throughout the chapter to the judgment in *Hanson*. The basic approach to be taken to the provisions was expressed by the Court in the following terms:

> The starting point should be for judges and practitioners to bear in mind that Parliament's purpose in the legislation, as we divine it from the terms of the Act, was to assist in the evidence based conviction of the guilty, without putting those who are not guilty at risk of conviction by prejudice. It is accordingly to be hoped that prosecution applications to adduce such evidence will not be made routinely, simply because a defendant has previous convictions, but will be based on the particular circumstances of each case.[54]

3.3.2.1.1 *Important Explanatory Evidence: S 101(1)(c)*

Evidence is important explanatory evidence if '(a) without it, the court or jury would find it impossible or difficult properly to understand other evidence in the case, and (b) its value for understanding the case as a whole is substantial'.[55] Thus in a trial in which the defendant is charged with an assault on a prison officer it may be necessary to admit evidence that the defendant was serving a prison sentence at the time, in order that the jury can understand what he was doing inside the prison. 'Important explanatory evidence' is probably the same as what was termed 'background evidence' at common law. It is notable, however, that the Law Commission had recommended that, in addition to the two conditions that now feature in section 101(1)(c), there be a third condition: that 'the evidence carries no risk of prejudice to the defendant', or regardless of such a risk 'the interests of justice nevertheless require the evidence to be admissible'.[56]

3.3.2.1.2 *Relevance to Important Issue between Defendant and Prosecution: S 101(1)(d)*

Prosecution evidence[57] of a defendant's bad character is admissible on the basis of its relevance to an important matter in issue between the defendant and the prosecution. By virtue of section 103(1)(a), whether the defendant has 'a propensity to commit offences of the kind with which he is charged' constitutes a matter in issue between the defendant and the prosecution if such propensity is relevant to guilt of the offence charged. Such propensity may be established by evidence of a conviction of an offence of the same description[58] or an offence of the same category,[59] so long as section 103(3) is satisfied. Section 103(3) requires that the court be satisfied that establishing propensity in such a manner would not be unjust 'by reason of the length of time since the conviction or for any other reason'. It is provided that 'two offences are of the same description as each other if the statement of the offence in a written charge or indictment would,

---

52 [2005] EWCA Crim 824, (2005) 169 JP 250. See generally R Munday, ' "Round Up the Usual Suspects!" or What We Have to Fear from Part 11 of the Criminal Justice Act 2003' (2005) 169 *Justice of the Peace* 328 (taking a somewhat negative view of the decision); J R Spencer, 'Bad Character Gateways' (2005) 155 *New Law Journal* 650 (taking a more sympathetic view of the decision).   53 See also *R v Bovell* [2005] EWCA Crim 1091.
54 [2005] EWCA Crim 824, (2005) 169 JP 250, [4].   55 S 102.
56 Draft Criminal Evidence Bill, art 7(4), accessible via http://www.lawcom.gov.uk/docs/lcr273bill.pdf.
57 S 103(6).   58 S 103(2)(a).   59 S 103(2)(b).

in each case, be in the same terms',[60] and that 'two offences are of the same category as each other if they belong to the same category of offences prescribed for the purposes of this section by an order made by the Secretary of State'.[61] Such an order may be made only in respect of offences of the same type.[62] An order has been made prescribing two categories of offences: a category of theft offences and a category of sexual offences involving persons under the age of 16.[63]

The Court of Appeal made detailed comments in *Hanson* about the way in which propensity to commit offences of the kind charged may be demonstrated by evidence of previous convictions:

> There is no minimum number of events necessary to demonstrate such a propensity. The fewer the number of convictions the weaker is likely to be the evidence of propensity. A single previous conviction for an offence of the same description or category will often not show propensity. But it may do so where, for example, it shows a tendency to unusual behaviour or where its circumstances demonstrate probative force in relation to the offence charged... Child sexual abuse or fire setting are comparatively clear examples of such unusual behaviour but we attempt no exhaustive list. Circumstances demonstrating probative force are not confined to those sharing striking similarity. So, a single conviction for shoplifting, will not, without more, be admissible to show propensity to steal. But if the modus operandi has significant features shared by the offence charged it may show propensity.[64]

There is, however, a need for caution: 'It will often be necessary, before determining admissibility and even when considering offences of the same description or category, to examine each individual conviction rather than merely to look at the name of the offence or at the defendant's record as a whole.'[65] 'For example, convictions for handling and aggravated vehicle taking, although within the theft category, do not...show, without more pertinent information, propensity to burgle...or to steal...'.[66] 'The sentence passed will not normally be probative or admissible at the behest of the Crown, though it may be at the behest of the defence. Where past events are disputed the judge must take care not to permit the trial unreasonably to be diverted into an investigation of matters not charged on the indictment.'[67]

By virtue of section 103(1)(b), a matter in issue between the defendant and the prosecution will also include 'the question whether the defendant has a propensity to be untruthful, except where it is not suggested that the defendant's case is untruthful in any respect'. The Court of Appeal in *Hanson* observed that 'propensity to untruthfulness'

> is not the same as propensity to dishonesty. It is to be assumed, bearing in mind the frequency with which the words honest and dishonest appear in the criminal law, that Parliament deliberately chose the word 'untruthful' to convey a different meaning, reflecting a defendant's account of his behaviour, or lies told when committing an offence. Previous convictions, whether for offences of dishonesty or otherwise, are therefore only likely to be capable of

---

[60] S 103(4)(a).   [61] S 103(4)(b).   [62] S 103(5).
[63] Criminal Justice Act 2003 (Categories of Offences) Order 2004.
[64] [2005] EWCA Crim 824, (2005) 169 JP 250, [9].   [65] Ibid, [12].   [66] Ibid, [27].
[67] Ibid, [12].

showing a propensity to be untruthful where . . . truthfulness is an issue and, in the earlier case, either there was a plea of not guilty and the defendant gave an account, on arrest, in interview, or in evidence, which the jury must have disbelieved, or the way in which the offence was committed shows a propensity for untruthfulness, for example, by the making of false representations. The observations made [in relation to propensity to commit offences of the kind charged] as to the number of convictions apply equally here.[68]

Section 101(3) provides, however, that evidence admissible under section 101(1)(d) must not be admitted 'if, on an application by the defendant to exclude it, it appears to the court that the admission of the evidence would have such an adverse effect on the fairness of the proceedings that the court ought not to admit it'. In considering the exercise of this discretion 'the court must have regard, in particular, to the length of time between the matters to which that evidence relates and the matters which form the subject of the offence charged'.[69]

The change in the law brought about by section 101(1)(d) is a radical and fundamental one. Previously, the law, as explained in the decision of the House of Lords in *DPP v P*,[70] recognized a rule whereby relevant evidence of an accused's misconduct on other occasions was inadmissible on the issue of guilt at the behest of the prosecution. As an exception to this rule, such evidence was admissible, as so-called 'similar fact evidence', only if its probative value was sufficiently high to justify its admission, notwithstanding its prejudicial effect. Although a determination of whether such evidence was admissible was required as a matter of law, the 'probative value versus prejudicial effect' test was a 'discretionary' one in the sense that it was flexible and open-textured. Whether the test was satisfied necessarily depended on the circumstances of the particular case.

The Law Commission recommended little change to the existing law, essentially advocating that a test of heightened probative value be retained for the admissibility, for the prosecution, of evidence of bad character on the issue of guilt.[71] By contrast, Lord Justice Auld expressed some sympathy for the view, put forward by Professor John Spencer and others, that if no good character evidence emerged in the course of a trial then the jury might well suspect anyway that the defendant was probably of bad character. Such speculation might actually cause prejudice to the defendant. It would therefore be simpler and more honest to have a system involving more routine disclosure of a defendant's record, for example by informing the jury at the beginning of the trial whether the defendant had a record and if so what it was.[72] As McEwan has written:

To reveal criminal record in some cases and not others may create the worst of all worlds. Fact-finders may assume that defendants who do not raise evidence of their own good character are trying to conceal their previous convictions. Leaving courts to guess what these previous convictions might be could cause more harm than the truth would have done. . . . To eliminate

---

[68] Ibid, [13].   [69] S 101(4).   [70] [1991] 2 AC 447.

[71] Law Commission (Law Com No 273), *Evidence of Bad Character in Criminal Proceedings* (2001), available at http://www.lawcom.gov.uk/docs/lc273.pdf.

[72] Lord Justice Auld, *A Review of the Criminal Courts of England and Wales* (2001) Ch 11 paras 118–20, accessible via http://www.criminal-courts-review.org.uk.

uncertainty and arbitrariness, a rational system might routinely mention the defendant's previous convictions at the outset of a trial in as unsensational a fashion as possible.[73]

Section 101(1)(d) certainly represents an attempt to achieve more routine disclosure to the jury of evidence of a defendant's bad character that is adduced by the prosecution for its relevance to guilt. The extent to which the provision actually achieves this aim remains to be seen. It is true that the test for the admissibility, for the prosecution, of evidence of bad character on the issue of guilt appears to have been reduced to one of mere relevance. However, it may be possible for courts not enamoured of the radical change in the law to water down the effect of the provision, in the guise for example of avoiding unjustness under section 103(3) or of protecting the fairness of the proceedings under section 101(3). In the words of Dennis: 'It would not be surprising, for example, if judges had recourse to the substance of the old law on similar fact evidence in deciding on the admissibility of prosecution evidence of propensity…'.[74] Indeed, Lord Phillips of Worth Matravers remarked obiter in *O'Brien v Chief Constable of South Wales Police* that:

[the relevant sections] of the 2003 Act… preserve…, by rules of some complexity, the requirement that the similar fact evidence should have an enhanced probative value.[75]

The test of admissibility of similar facts against a defendant in criminal proceedings, as propounded in *DPP v P* and in the 2003 Act, requires an enhanced relevance or substantial probative value because, if the evidence is not cogent, the prejudice that it will cause to the defendant may render the proceedings unfair. The test of admissibility builds in protection for the defendant in the interests of justice. It leads to the exclusion of evidence which is relevant on the ground that it is not *sufficiently* probative.[76]

The Court of Appeal in *Hanson* had the following to say about the use of sections 101(3) and 103(3):

In a conviction case, the decisions required of the trial judge under section 101(3) and section 103(3), though not identical, are closely related. It is to be noted that [the] wording of section 101(3)—'must not admit'—is stronger than the comparable provision in section 78 of the Police and Criminal Evidence Act 1984—'may refuse to allow'. When considering what is just under section 103(3), and the fairness of the proceedings under section 101(3), the judge may, among other factors, take into consideration the degree of similarity between the previous conviction and the offence charged, albeit they are both within the same description or prescribed category. For example, theft and assault occasioning actual bodily harm may each embrace a wide spectrum of conduct. This does not however mean that what used to be referred [to] as striking similarity must be shown before convictions become admissible. The judge may also take into consideration the respective gravity of the past and present offences. He or she must always consider the strength of the prosecution case. If there is no or very little other evidence against a defendant, it is unlikely to be just to admit his previous convictions, whatever they are.[77]

[73] J McEwan, *The Verdict of the Court: Passing Judgment in Law and Psychology* (2003) 169–70.
[74] I Dennis, 'The Criminal Justice Act 2003: Part 2' [2004] *Criminal Law Review* 251, 252.
[75] [2005] UKHL 26, [2005] 2 WLR 1038, [33] (underlining added).
[76] Ibid, [52] (italics in original; underlining added).
[77] [2005] EWCA Crim 824, (2005) 169 JP 250, [10].

In principle, if there is a substantial gap between the dates of commission of and conviction for the earlier offences, we would regard the date of commission as generally being of more significance than the date of conviction when assessing admissibility. Old convictions, with no special feature shared with the offence charged, are likely seriously to affect the fairness of proceedings adversely, unless, despite their age, it can properly be said that they show a continuing propensity.[78]

Munday would advocate a stronger approach:

The writer would feel easier were propensity evidence not admitted unless the Judge was satisfied that the accused could be convicted solely on the other evidence in the case. This would encourage the police to investigate crimes thoroughly and the CPS to prosecute properly substantiated allegations. It would deter Judges from allowing weak cases to proceed to final verdict and, who knows, a few years down the track might avert the humiliation of a succession of character-driven miscarriages of justice.[79]

The obligation to issue a warning to the jury, where evidence is admitted under section 101(1)(d), was expressed by the Court of Appeal in *Hanson* as follows:

. . . in any case in which evidence of bad character is admitted to show propensity, whether to commit offences or to be untruthful the judge in summing-up should warn the jury clearly against placing undue reliance on previous convictions. Evidence of bad character cannot be used simply to bolster a weak case, or to prejudice the minds of a jury against a defendant. In particular, the jury should be directed; that they should not conclude that the defendant is guilty or untruthful merely because he has these convictions. That, although the convictions may show a propensity, this does not mean that he has committed this offence or been untruthful in this case; that whether they in fact show a propensity is for them to decide; that they must take into account what the defendant has said about his previous convictions; and that, although they are entitled, if they find propensity as shown, to take this into account when determining guilt, propensity is only one relevant factor and they must assess its significance in the light of all the other evidence in the case.[80]

3.3.2.1.3 Substantial Probative Value in Relation to Important Issue between Defendant and Co-Defendant: S 101(1)(e)

Where evidence of a defendant's bad character is of substantial probative value in relation to an important matter in issue between the defendant and a co-defendant, the evidence may be adduced by the co-defendant[81] or elicited by the co-defendant from a witness in cross-examination.[82] The matter in issue may be propensity: for example, in running a 'cut-throat defence', the co-defendant may, in an attempt to cast blame on the defendant, wish to rely on evidence of the defendant's bad character

---

[78] Ibid, [11].

[79] R Munday, ' "Round Up the Usual Suspects!" or What We Have to Fear from Part 11 of the Criminal Justice Act 2003' (2005) 169 *Justice of the Peace* 328, 335.

[80] [2005] EWCA Crim 824, (2005) 169 JP 250, [18].   [81] S 104(2)(a).   [82] S 104(2)(b).

in order to demonstrate propensity and hence the likelihood that the defendant is the sole guilty party.[83] Equally, credit may constitute a matter in issue between a defendant and co-defendant. Thus if, for example, 'the nature or conduct of [a defendant's] defence is such as to undermine [a] co-defendant's defence', evidence that is 'relevant to the question whether the defendant has a propensity to be untruthful' will be admissible at the behest of the co-defendant.[84]

3.3.2.1.4 Correction of False Impression: S 101(1)(f)

Where the defendant gives a false impression 'evidence which has probative value in correcting it'[85] is admissible at the behest of the prosecution,[86] but 'only if it goes no further than is necessary to correct the false impression'.[87]

What is meant by the concept of giving a false impression? It is provided that 'the defendant gives a false impression if he is responsible for the making of an express or implied assertion which is apt to give the court or jury a false or misleading impression about the defendant'.[88] Unless the defendant withdraws it or dissociates himself from it,[89] he is to be:

treated as being responsible for the making of an assertion if—

(a) the assertion is made by the defendant in the proceedings (whether or not in evidence given by him),

(b) the assertion was made by the defendant—

(i) on being questioned under caution, before charge, about the offence with which he is charged, or

(ii) on being charged with the offence or officially informed that he might be prosecuted for it,

and evidence of the assertion is given in the proceedings,

(c) the assertion is made by a witness called by the defendant,

(d) the assertion is made by any witness in cross-examination in response to a question asked by the defendant that is intended to elicit it, or is likely to do so, or

(e) the assertion was made by any person out of court, and the defendant adduces evidence of it in the proceedings.[90]

The defendant's conduct in the proceedings (including the defendant's appearance or dress[91]) may also be relevant: 'Where it appears to the court that a defendant, by means of his conduct (other than the giving of evidence) in the proceedings, is seeking to give the court or jury an impression about himself that is false or misleading, the court may if it appears just to do so treat the defendant as being responsible for the making of an assertion which is apt to give that impression.'[92]

---

[83] *R v Randall* [2003] UKHL 69, [2004] 1 WLR 56. See also *R v B (C)* [2004] EWCA Crim 1254, [2004] 2 Cr App R 34 (p 570); *R v Price* [2004] EWCA Crim 1359; *R v Murrell* [2005] EWCA Crim 382; *R v Rafiq* [2005] EWCA Crim 1423.   [84] S 104(1).
[85] S 105(1)(b).   [86] S 105(7).   [87] S 105(6).   [88] S 105(1)(a).   [89] S 105(3).
[90] S 105(2).   [91] S 105(5).   [92] S 105(4).

It is apparently intended that evidence admitted under section 101(1)(f) 'will primarily go to the credit of the defendant'.[93]

3.3.2.1.5 Attack on Character of Another: S 101(1)(g)

Where the defendant has made an attack on the character of another, evidence of the defendant's bad character becomes admissible on behalf of the prosecution.[94] There are three ways in which such an attack can be made:[95]

1. The defendant adduces evidence to the effect that that person 'has committed an offence (whether a different offence from the one with which the defendant is charged or the same one)'[96] or 'has behaved, or is disposed to behave, in a reprehensible way'.[97]

2. The defendant, or a legal representative appointed under section 38(4) of the Youth Justice and Criminal Evidence Act 1999, 'asks questions in cross-examination that are intended to elicit such evidence, or are likely to do so'.

3. Evidence is given that the defendant, on being questioned about the offence under caution or on being charged with it or officially informed that he or she might be prosecuted for it, made 'an imputation about the other person'. This is an assertion to the effect that the other person 'has committed an offence (whether a different offence from the one with which the defendant is charged or the same one)', or 'has behaved, or is disposed to behave, in a reprehensible way'.

The concept of 'attacking another person's character' in section 101(1)(g) mirrors the concept of casting 'imputations on the character of the prosecutor or the witnesses for the prosecution, or the deceased victim of the alleged crime', that was utilized in the previous legislation.[98] The Court in *Hanson* considered that 'pre-2003 Act authorities will continue to apply when assessing whether an attack has been made on another person's character, to the extent that they are compatible with [the new legislation]'.[99] The following guidelines which emerge from the decision of the House of Lords in *R v Selvey*[100] will presumably continue to be applicable:

• '... cross-examination of the accused as to character [is permitted] both when imputations on the character of the prosecutor and his witness are cast to show their unreliability as witnesses independently of the evidence given by them and also when the casting of such imputations is necessary to enable the accused to establish his defence ...'.

• 'In rape cases the accused can allege consent without placing himself in peril of such cross-examination ... This may be because such cases are sui generis ..., or on the ground that the issue is one raised by the prosecution.'

---

[93] See para 382 of the Explanatory Notes to the Act, accessible via http://www.hmso.gov.uk/acts/en2003/03en44-f.htm.   [94] S 106(3).

[95] These are set out in s 106(1)(a), s 106(1)(b), and s 106(1)(c).   [96] S 106(2)(a).

[97] S 106(2)(b).

[98] Criminal Evidence Act 1898, s 1(3)(ii), which replaced the Criminal Evidence Act 1898, s 1(f)(ii).

[99] [2005] EWCA Crim 824, (2005) 169 JP 250, [14].   [100] [1970] AC 304, 339.

• 'If what is said amounts in reality to no more than a denial of the charge, expressed, it may be, in emphatic language, it should not be regarded as coming within the section . . . '.

Evidence admissible under section 101(1)(g) is not, however, to be admitted 'if, on an application by the defendant to exclude it, it appears to the court that the admission of the evidence would have such an adverse effect on the fairness of the proceedings that the court ought not to admit it'.[101] In considering the exercise of this discretion 'the court must have regard, in particular, to the length of time between the matters to which that evidence relates and the matters which form the subject of the offence charged'.[102] It would appear, however, that the defendant's motive for doing what amounted to attacking the character of another is not a factor to be taken into account in considering the exercise of the discretion.[103]

The Explanatory Notes to the Criminal Justice Act 2003 state somewhat tentatively:

> Evidence admissible under section 101(1)(g) . . . will primarily go to the credit of the defendant. Currently a jury would be directed that evidence admitted in similar circumstances, under the [Criminal Evidence Act 1898], goes only to credibility and is not relevant to the issue of guilt. Such directions have been criticised and the new statutory scheme does not specify that this evidence is to be treated in such a way. However, it is expected that judges will explain the purpose for which the evidence is being put forward and direct the jury about the sort of weight that can be placed on it.[104]

3.3.2.1.6 Appeals

The Court of Appeal in *Hanson* made the following observations in relation to appeals based on the admission of evidence of a defendant's bad character:

> . . . this Court will be very slow to interfere with a ruling . . . as to admissibility . . . It will not interfere unless the judge's judgment as to the capacity of prior events to establish propensity is plainly wrong, or discretion has been exercised unreasonably in the *Wednesbury* sense . . .[105]
>
> Furthermore, if, following a ruling that evidence of bad character is admissible, a defendant pleads guilty, it is highly unlikely that this Court will entertain an appeal against conviction . . .[106]

3.3.2.1.7 Cross-Admissibility and Contamination

Where the prosecution adduces bad character evidence in its case in chief under section 101(1)(d) and section 103(1)(a), this evidence may consist of evidence of another alleged offence for which the defendant is being tried at the same trial. Thus where the defendant is being tried for offences A and B at the same trial, the prosecution may in seeking to prove offence A adduce evidence of alleged offence B, and in seeking to prove offence B adduce evidence of alleged offence A, if the evidence of each alleged offence is relevant, on the charge of the other, to the issue of propensity to commit offences of the kind in question. In such a situation of cross-admissibility there is potentially a danger

---

[101] S 101(3).   [102] S 101(4).   [103] *R v Bovell* [2005] EWCA Crim 1091, [31]–[32].
[104] http://www.hmso.gov.uk/acts/en2003/03en44-f.htm.
[105] [2005] EWCA Crim 824, (2005) 169 JP 250, [15].   [106] Ibid, [16].

that the evidence of the complainants in respect of offences A and B may have become 'contaminated' in some way. Such contamination may well be the result of collusion between the complainants, who may have put their heads together to concoct a story against the accused. Alternatively, there may be a more innocent explanation for the contamination: distortions may have crept in over time as the complainants repeatedly discussed the incidents amongst themselves. And contamination 'may happen without the witnesses even communicating directly with each other, eg where the witnesses are inexpertly questioned by the same investigative team'.[107]

Following the approach previously taken at common law,[108] the Criminal Justice Act 2003 makes it clear that the admissibility of bad character evidence is to be determined on the assumption that it is true.[109] Thus, even where it is alleged that two separate rape complaints are the result of collusion between the complainants, the court must assume that the evidence which they will give is true for the purpose of admissibility, and leave it to the jury to decide what, if any, weight should be given to the evidence. This is subject, however, to the following qualification: 'In assessing the relevance or probative value of an item of evidence for any purpose of this Chapter, a court need not assume that the evidence is true if it appears, on the basis of any material before the court (including any evidence it decides to hear on the matter), that no court or jury could reasonably find it to be true.'[110] Further, section 107 provides:

(1) If on a defendant's trial before a judge and jury for an offence—

  (a) evidence of his bad character has been admitted under any of paragraphs (c) to (g) of section 101(1), and

  (b) the court is satisfied at any time after the close of the case for the prosecution that—

    (i) the evidence is contaminated, and

    (ii) the contamination is such that, considering the importance of the evidence to the case against the defendant, his conviction of the offence would be unsafe,

  the court must either direct the jury to acquit the defendant of the offence or, if it considers that there ought to be a retrial, discharge the jury.

. . .

(5) For the purposes of this section a person's evidence is contaminated where—

  (a) as a result of an agreement or understanding between the person and one or more others, or

  (b) as a result of the person being aware of anything alleged by one or more others whose evidence may be, or has been, given in the proceedings,

  the evidence is false or misleading in any respect, or is different from what it would otherwise have been.

---

[107] Law Commission (Consultation Paper No 141), *Criminal Law—Evidence in Criminal Proceedings: Previous Misconduct of a Defendant—A Consultation Paper* (1996) [10.86] n 105, available at http://www.lawcom.gov.uk/docs/cp141.pdf.　　　　　　　　　　　　　　　　　　　[108] *R v H* [1995] 2 AC 596.

[109] S 109(1).　　　　[110] S 109(2).

3.3.2.1.8 Cross-Admissibility and Disputed Identification

Suppose that a defendant is charged with two offences which are alleged to bear a number of similarities. These similarities are such that the evidence of the offences would be potentially cross-admissible. Suppose, however, that there is disputed identification evidence in relation to each offence. Must the jury be satisfied of the defendant's guilt of each individual offence before it can use evidence of this offence under section 101(1)(d) and section 103(1)(a) in determining whether the defendant also committed the other offence?

If the position prior to the Criminal Justice Act 2003 is any indication, the answer to this question would appear to depend on whether the *only* evidence that is adduced to prove each offence is the evidence of the other offence. If this is the case, then the jury must be satisfied that the defendant committed each offence before it can use the evidence of the offence in deciding whether the defendant also committed the other offence. In all other cases, it is appropriate to invite the jury to decide whether, in the light of the similarities between them, the offences were committed by the same person, and, if so satisfied, to use the identification evidence in relation to both offences *cumulatively* to determine whether the defendant was responsible for both offences.[111]

3.3.2.1.9 Trials in which Evidence Is not Cross-Admissible

What of the situation where a defendant is charged with more than one offence at the same trial, and it is determined that the evidence is *not* cross-admissible? In such a case there is obviously a substantial danger of prejudice to the defendant if the trial were to proceed, as the jury would be hearing inadmissible evidence. The defence may wish therefore to apply for separate trials. Section 5(3) of the Indictments Act 1915 gives the court a discretion to sever the indictment and order separate trials:

> Where, before trial, or at any stage of a trial, the court is of opinion that a person accused may be prejudiced or embarrassed in his defence by reason of being charged with more than one offence in the same indictment, or that for any other reason it is desirable to direct that the person should be tried separately for any one or more offences charged in an indictment, the court may order a separate trial of any count or counts of such indictment.

It would seem, however, that the fact that the evidence is not cross-admissible is merely one factor to be considered by the court in exercising the discretion to order separate trials; it is not in any way decisive. Lord Taylor of Gosforth CJ stated in *R v Christou*:

> . . . the factors a judge should consider . . . will vary from case to case, but the essential criterion is the achievement of a fair resolution of the issues. That requires fairness to the accused but also to the prosecution and those involved in it. Some, but by no means an exhaustive list, of the factors which may need to be considered are:—how discrete or inter-related are the facts giving rise to the counts; the impact of ordering two or more trials on the defendant and his

[111] *R v W* [1998] 2 Cr App R 289, 304.

family, on the victims and their families, on press publicity; and importantly, whether directions the judge can give to the jury will suffice to secure a fair trial if the counts are tried together. In regard to that last factor, jury trials are conducted on the basis that the judge's directions of law are to be applied faithfully. Experience shows ... that juries, where counts are jointly tried, do follow the judge's directions and consider the counts separately.

Approaching the question of severance as indicated above, judges will often consider it right to order separate trials. But I reject the argument that either generally or in respect of any class of case, the judge must so order.[112]

Inasmuch as section 5(3) of the Indictments Act 1915 gives the court a *discretion* as to whether to order separate trials, it is clearly right that the House of Lords has decided that this discretion cannot be fettered. Perhaps the appropriate solution lies, therefore, in amending the legislation so that 'where evidence of two complainants is inadmissible against each other, separate trials must be held, if the defence so apply. If this were to increase the number of trials, at a greater cost to the public, it would be an unfortunate but unavoidable result.'[113] Such an approach is taken in Australia: 'If the evidence admissible on each count is not admissible on the other counts and there is a consequent risk of impermissible prejudice to an accused in the conduct of a single trial on all counts—and there usually is such a risk in sexual cases—separate trials should be ordered ...'.[114] In the absence of reform of English law along these lines, it is pleasing to note that strong directions are to be given to the jury:

Where ... the charges are not severed, it is essential that the jury is directed in clear terms that the evidence on each set of allegations is to be treated separately and that the evidence in relation to an allegation in respect of one victim cannot be treated as proof of an allegation against the other victim. If such a warning in clear terms is not given there is the risk that the jury may wrongly regard the evidence as cross-admissible in respect of each separate set of allegations ...[115]

3.3.2.2 Non-Defendants

Section 100(1) provides:

In criminal proceedings evidence of the bad character of a person other than the defendant is admissible if and only if—

(a) it is important explanatory evidence,

(b) it has substantial probative value in relation to a matter which—

(i) is a matter in issue in the proceedings, and
(ii) is of substantial importance in the context of the case as a whole,

or

(c) all parties to the proceedings agree to the evidence being admissible.

---

[112] [1996] 2 WLR 620, 622, 623, 629–30.

[113] C Mortimore, 'Severance Revisited' (1996) 140 *Solicitors' Journal* 611, 611. See also R Munday, 'Vaguely Similar Facts and Severance of Counts' (1996) 160 *Justice of the Peace* 663.

[114] *Hoch v R* (1988) 165 CLR 292, 298 per Brennan and Dawson JJ.

[115] *R v D* [2003] EWCA Crim 2424, [2004] 1 Cr App R 19 (p 206), [26].

3.3.2.2.1 Important Explanatory Evidence

Evidence is important explanatory evidence if '(a) without it, the court or jury would find it impossible or difficult properly to understand other evidence in the case, and (b) its value for understanding the case as a whole is substantial'.[116] Leave of the court is required for evidence to be given on this basis.[117]

3.3.2.2.2 Substantial Probative Value in Relation to an Important Issue

The Act specifically provides that in assessing probative value the court is to have regard to any factors it considers relevant, but must have regard to these factors:

(a) the nature and number of the events, or other things, to which the evidence relates;

(b) when those events or things are alleged to have happened or existed;

(c) where—

    (i) the evidence is evidence of a person's misconduct, and

    (ii) it is suggested that the evidence has probative value by reason of similarity between that misconduct and other alleged misconduct,

the nature and extent of the similarities and the dissimilarities between each of the alleged instances of misconduct;

(d) where—

    (i) the evidence is evidence of a person's misconduct,

    (ii) it is suggested that that person is also responsible for the misconduct charged, and

    (iii) the identity of the person responsible for the misconduct charged is disputed,

the extent to which the evidence shows or tends to show that the same person was responsible each time.[118]

Leave of the court is required for evidence to be given on this basis.[119]

3.3.2.2.3 General Evaluation

The regulation by section 100 of the Criminal Justice Act 2003 of evidence of the bad character of non-defendants is novel. While the provision may well have the effect of preventing mud-slinging by defendants, it does apply to the prosecution as well as the defence. In some cases it may simply serve to add an extra procedural hurdle to a prosecution. For instance, where a charge arises out of a street disturbance, the prosecution may wish to describe incidents of misconduct by a number of persons not on trial. Under section 100 it will be necessary for the prosecution to justify the inclusion of each such item of evidence and to seek the leave of the court to adduce it.

3.3.2.3 Notice

It is mandatory for notice to be given by a party of its intention to adduce or to elicit in cross-examination evidence of bad character under the Criminal Justice Act 2003.

---

[116] S 100(2).   [117] S 100(4).   [118] S 100(3).   [119] S 100(4).

To this end Part 35 of the Criminal Procedure Rules 2005 provides as follows:

WHEN THIS PART APPLIES

35.1 This Part applies in a magistrates' court and in the Crown Court when a party wants to introduce evidence of bad character as defined in section 98 of the Criminal Justice Act 2003.

INTRODUCING EVIDENCE OF NON-DEFENDANT'S BAD CHARACTER

35.2 A party who wants to introduce evidence of a non-defendant's bad character or who wants to cross-examine a witness with a view to eliciting that evidence, under section 100 of the Criminal Justice Act 2003 must apply in the form set out in the Practice Direction[120] and the application must be received by the court officer and all other parties to the proceedings—

(a) not more than 14 days after the prosecutor has complied or purported to comply with section 3 of the Criminal Procedure and Investigations Act 1996 (disclosure by the prosecutor); or

(b) as soon as reasonably practicable, where the application concerns a non-defendant who is to be invited to give (or has given) evidence for a defendant.

OPPOSING INTRODUCTION OF EVIDENCE OF NON-DEFENDANT'S BAD CHARACTER

35.3 A party who receives a copy of an application under rule 35.2 may oppose that application by giving notice in writing to the court officer and all other parties to the proceedings not more than 14 days after receiving that application.

PROSECUTOR INTRODUCING EVIDENCE OF DEFENDANT'S BAD CHARACTER

35.4

(1) A prosecutor who wants to introduce evidence of a defendant's bad character or who wants to cross-examine a witness with a view to eliciting that evidence, under section 101 of the Criminal Justice Act 2003 must give notice in the form set out in the Practice Direction[121] to the court officer and all other parties to the proceedings.

(2) Notice under paragraph (1) must be given—

(a) in a case to be tried in a magistrates' court, at the same time as the prosecutor complies or purports to comply with section 3 of the Criminal Procedure and Investigations Act 1996; and

(b) in a case to be tried in the Crown Court, not more than 14 days after—

(i) the committal of the defendant, or

(ii) the consent to the preferment of a bill of indictment in relation to the case, or

(iii) the service of notice of transfer under section 4(1) of the Criminal Justice Act 1987 (notices of transfer) or under section 53(1) of the Criminal Justice Act 1991 (notices of transfer in certain cases involving children), or

---

[120] http://www.dca.gov.uk/criminal/procrules_fin/contents/pdf/f43page1.pdf or http://www.hmcourts-service.gov.uk/courtfinder/forms/6442_0405.doc.

[121] http://www.dca.gov.uk/criminal/procrules_fin/contents/pdf/f44page1.pdf or http://www.hmcourts-service.gov.uk/courtfinder/forms/6443_0405.doc.

(iv) where a person is sent for trial under section 51 of the Crime and Disorder Act 1998 (sending cases to the Crown Court) the service of copies of the documents containing the evidence on which the charge or charges are based under paragraph 1 of Schedule 3 to that Act.

CO-DEFENDANT INTRODUCING EVIDENCE OF DEFENDANT'S BAD CHARACTER

35.5 A co-defendant who wants to introduce evidence of a defendant's bad character or who wants to cross-examine a witness with a view to eliciting that evidence under section 101 of the Criminal Justice Act 2003 must give notice in the form set out in the Practice Direction[122] to the court officer and all other parties to the proceedings not more than 14 days after the prosecutor has complied or purported to comply with section 3 of the Criminal Procedure and Investigations Act 1996.

DEFENDANT APPLYING TO EXCLUDE EVIDENCE OF HIS OWN BAD CHARACTER

35.6 A defendant's application to exclude bad character evidence must be in the form set out in the Practice Direction[123] and received by the court officer and all other parties to the proceedings not more than 7 days after receiving a notice given under rules 35.4 or 35.5.

METHODS OF GIVING NOTICE

35.7 Where this rule requires a notice or application to be given or sent it may, with the consent of the addressee, be sent by fax or other means of electronic communication.

COURT'S POWER TO VARY REQUIREMENTS UNDER THIS PART

35.8 The court may—

(a) allow a notice or application required under this rule to be given in a different form, or orally; or

(b) shorten a time-limit under this rule or extend it even after it has expired.

DEFENDANT WAIVING RIGHT TO RECEIVE NOTICE

35.9 A defendant entitled to receive a notice under this Part may waive his entitlement by so informing the court and the party who would have given the notice.

The Court of Appeal in *Hanson* made the following comments in relation to the giving of notice:

. . . in a conviction case the Crown needs to decide, at the time of giving notice of the application, whether it proposes to rely simply upon the fact of conviction or also upon the circumstances of it. The former may be enough when the circumstances of the conviction are sufficiently apparent from its description, to justify a finding that it can establish propensity, either to commit an offence of the kind charged or to be untruthful and that the requirements of section 103(3) and 101(3) can, subject to any particular matter raised on behalf of the defendant, be satisfied. For example, a succession of convictions for dwelling-house burglary,

---

[122] http://www.dca.gov.uk/criminal/procrules_fin/contents/pdf/f44page1.pdf or http://www.hmcourts-service.gov.uk/courtfinder/forms/6443_0405.doc.

[123] http://www.dca.gov.uk/criminal/procrules_fin/contents/pdf/f45page1-2.pdf or http://www.hmcourts-service.gov.uk/courtfinder/forms/6444_0405.doc.

where the same is now charged, may well call for no further evidence than proof of the fact of the convictions. But where, as will often be the case, the Crown needs and proposes to rely on the circumstances of the previous convictions, those circumstances and the manner in which they are to be proved must be set out in the application. There is a similar obligation of frankness upon the defendant, which will be reinforced by the general obligation contained in the new Criminal Procedure Rules to give active assistance to the court in its case management (see rule 3.3). Routine applications by defendants for disclosure of the circumstances of previous convictions are likely to be met by a requirement that the request be justified by identification of the reason why it is said that those circumstances may show the convictions to be inadmissible. We would expect the relevant circumstances of previous convictions generally to be capable of agreement, and that, subject to the trial judge's ruling as to admissibility, they will be put before the jury by way of admission. Even where the circumstances are genuinely in dispute, we would expect the minimum indisputable facts to be thus admitted. It will be very rare indeed for it to be necessary for the judge to hear evidence before ruling on admissibility under this Act.[124]

[124]   [2005] EWCA Crim 824, (2005) 169 JP 250, [17].

9
Hearsay Evidence

1 The Hearsay Debate

Hearsay evidence is evidence of an out-of-court statement that is being adduced in court as evidence of a matter stated in the statement. The common law traditionally recognized a rule against hearsay. Thus hearsay evidence was inadmissible unless it fell under an exception to the rule. As will be explained below, the position of hearsay evidence in civil proceedings is now governed by the Civil Evidence Act 1995 and in criminal proceedings by the Criminal Justice Act 2003.[1]

The perceived unreliability of hearsay evidence constitutes the main justification for recognizing a rule against hearsay:

> [Hearsay evidence] is not the best evidence and it is not delivered on oath. The truthfulness and accuracy of the person whose words are spoken to by another witness cannot be tested by cross-examination, and the light which his demeanour would throw on his testimony is lost.[2]

Any statement may be unreliable because of defects in the *perception, memory, sincerity,* or *ability to narrate clearly,* of the maker of the statement. Suppose that a witness, W, states in his or her testimony that 'The car I saw driving away was red'. This statement may be unreliable because (1) W may have perceived the car to be red when it was in reality of some other colour; (2) W may have genuinely forgotten that the car was of some other colour; (3) W may be lying; or (4) W may be trying to say that the car was of some other colour, but be lacking in the ability to narrate this clearly. In this situation, because the statement has been made in court by the person who witnessed the event, it will have been possible to observe his or her demeanour at

---

[1] See generally D Birch, 'Criminal Justice Act 2003: (4) Hearsay—Same Old Story, Same Old Song?' [2004] *Criminal Law Review* 556; D Birch, 'The New Law of Hearsay: Criminal Justice Act 2003', *Archbold News*, 8 Apr 2005, 6; G Durston, 'The Evidence of "Unavailable" Witnesses Under the Criminal Justice Act 2003' (2005) 69 *Journal of Criminal Law* 256; A Edwards, 'Gazette in Practice: Criminal Law' (2005) 102(24) *Law Society's Gazette* 30; P Tain, 'On Hearsay' (2005) 149 *Solicitors' Journal* 77; S Uglow, 'Section 115(3) of the Criminal Justice Act 2003: How Not to Overturn *Kearley*', *Archbold News*, 23 May 2005, 6; P Wilcock and J Bennathan, 'The New Rules of Hearsay Evidence' (2004) 154 *New Law Journal* 1174; *Criminal Justice Act 2003: A Current Law Statute Guide* (2004) 44-131–44-158; B Gibson, *Criminal Justice Act 2003: A Guide to the New Procedures and Sentencing* (2004) 66–74; A Keogh, *Criminal Justice Act 2003: A Guide to the New Law* (2004) Ch 8; R Taylor, M Wasik, and R Leng, *Blackstone's Guide to the Criminal Justice Act 2003* (2004) Ch 9; R Ward and O M Davies, *The Criminal Justice Act 2003: A Practitioner's Guide* (2004) Ch 6. [2] *Teper v R* [1952] AC 480, 486 per Lord Normand.

the time of making the statement. Further, the statement is likely to have been a sworn statement. Finally, it would be possible to subject the witness to 'contemporaneous' cross-examination in relation to the statement. Such cross-examination would, it is said, assist in exposing any defects in the witness's perception, memory, sincerity, or clarity of narration. Suppose, however, that the situation is one in which W is reporting an out-of-court statement: 'X *said* that the car she saw driving away was red.' In such a situation, cross-examination of W would be of limited efficacy in exposing possible defects in the perception, memory, sincerity, or ability to narrate clearly, of X. It is for this reason, it is said, that a rule against hearsay should be recognized.[3]

These arguments are, however, far from insurmountable, for the following reasons:

• As discussed in greater detail in Chapter 14, the extent to which observation of a witness's demeanour actually provides a good indication of the reliability of his or her testimony is a matter of considerable speculation.

• It is uncertain whether, in modern times, the taking of an oath (or the making of a solemn affirmation) necessarily guarantees the reliability of testimony.

• The utility of contemporaneous cross-examination in ensuring the reliability of evidence is also uncertain. Cross-examination may well be of little use in exposing insincerity,[4] and it is also possible that the efficacy of cross-examination in exposing faulty perception may not be as high as may be assumed.[5] Additionally, it should be noted that suggesting facts to a witness in cross-examination may actually distort, rather than assist, his or her memory.[6]

• For what it is worth,[7] and despite evidence to the contrary,[8] there is empirical evidence suggesting that the assumption that juries are incapable of assessing the

---

[3] Excellent aids to understanding the reliability rationale for the hearsay rule are provided by L H Tribe, 'Triangulating Hearsay' (1974) 87 *Harvard Law Review* 957 and M H Graham, ' "Stickperson Hearsay": A Simplified Approach to Understanding the Rule Against Hearsay' [1982] *University of Illinois Law Review* 887.

[4] T Finman, 'Implied Assertions as Hearsay: Some Criticisms of the Uniform Rules of Evidence' (1962) 14 *Stanford Law Review* 682, 690; R C Park, 'A Subject Matter Approach to Hearsay Reform' (1987) 86 *Michigan Law Review* 51, 96; E Swift, 'A Foundation Fact Approach to Hearsay' (1987) 75 *California Law Review* 1339, 1357 n 50. See also J Allan, 'The Working and Rationale of the Hearsay Rule and the Implications of Modern Psychological Knowledge' (1991) 44 *Current Legal Problems* 217.

[5] E A Scallen, 'Constitutional Dimensions of Hearsay Reform: Toward a Three-Dimensional Confrontation Clause' (1992) 76 *Minnesota Law Review* 623, 627 n 15.

[6] Australian Law Reform Commission, *Evidence (Vol 1)* (Report No 26: Interim) (1985) [663], available at http://www.austlii.edu.au/au/other/alrc/publications/reports/26/26_vol1.pdf; Scottish Law Commission (Scot Law Com No 149), *Evidence: Report on Hearsay Evidence in Criminal Proceedings* (1995) [3.14], available at http://www.scotlawcom.gov.uk/downloads/rep149.pdf.

[7] The limitations of relying on simulated trials and mock juries are obvious: see C Tapper, 'Hearsay in Criminal Cases: An Overview of Law Commission Report No 245' [1997] *Criminal Law Review* 771, 773.

[8] For discussions of empirical evidence concerning the hearsay rule see generally R C Park, 'Empirical Evaluation of the Hearsay Rule' in P Mirfield and R Smith (eds), *Essays for Colin Tapper* (2003); R C Park, 'Visions of Applying the Scientific Method to the Hearsay Rule' [2003] *Michigan State Law Review* 1149.

reliability of hearsay evidence competently may well be questionable.[9] In any event, it must be remembered that 'although the jury retains a powerful symbolic influence in criminal proceedings, its role has been increasingly curtailed by legislative changes, with the result that magistrates' trials are increasingly the norm rather than judge and jury trials'.[10]

Additionally, the hearsay rule as applied to prosecution evidence in criminal proceedings may be justified by reference to considerations of extrinsic policy.[11] It may be argued that a legal system where, for example, observers of events testify directly to what they saw would be perceived as procedurally fairer than one where hearsay evidence is adduced. Further, the hearsay rule may be regarded as protecting the value of individual dignity in criminal proceedings. Unlike its civil counterpart, a criminal trial has a special moral dimension, with the weight of the State ranged against an individual, whose conviction and punishment are being sought. An important feature of criminal justice is, therefore, the notion that human dignity must be respected when the power of the State is ranged against an individual, as in a criminal prosecution.[12] The ability of an accused person to confront and cross-examine the maker of a statement against him or her, and not just a person reporting the statement, is consistent with the right of accused persons to be treated with dignity: 'The idea that one who accuses another of wrong ought to do so in a forum where he assumes the consequences of his statement has sufficient power that no amount of cynical sneering about the utility of the oath, incidence of perjury prosecutions, or the value of cross-examination will suffice to overcome it as an important symbol of fairness.'[13] Moreover, the dignity of prosecution witnesses generally is also respected: the phenomenon of witnesses testifying in court and being subject to cross-examination reinforces the moral significance of the role of witnesses in the trial process. This is particularly true in the case of a witness who is also the alleged victim, since the phenomenon of a victim 'accusing' the defendant in person, in the formal setting of a courtroom, is of considerable symbolic importance.[14]

[9] M B Kovera, R C Park, and S D Penrod, 'Jurors' Perceptions of Eyewitness and Hearsay Evidence' (1992) 76 *Minnesota Law Review* 703; S Landsman and R F Rakos, 'Research Essay: A Preliminary Empirical Enquiry Concerning the Prohibition of Hearsay Evidence in American Courts' (1991) 15 *Law and Psychology Review* 65; P Miene, R C Park, and E Borgida, 'Juror Decision Making and the Evaluation of Hearsay Evidence' (1992) 76 *Minnesota Law Review* 683; R F Rakos and S Landsman, 'Researching the Hearsay Rule: Emerging Findings, General Issues, and Future Directions' (1992) 76 *Minnesota Law Review* 655. See also R D Friedman, 'Thoughts from Across the Water on Hearsay and Confrontation' [1998] *Criminal Law Review* 697, 701.

[10] J D Jackson, 'Hearsay: The Sacred Cow That Won't Be Slaughtered?' (1998) 2 *International Journal of Evidence and Proof* 166, 179.

[11] For a much fuller discussion, see A L-T Choo, *Hearsay and Confrontation in Criminal Trials* (1996) 37–42.

[12] See generally H Gross, *A Theory of Criminal Justice* (1979) 32–3; P Stein and J Shand, *Legal Values in Western Society* (1974) 130 ff.

[13] K W Graham, jun, 'The Right of Confrontation and the Hearsay Rule: Sir Walter Raleigh Loses Another One' (1972) 8 *Criminal Law Bulletin* 99, 133.

[14] E Swift, 'Smoke and Mirrors: The Failure of the Supreme Court's Accuracy Rationale in *White v Illinois* Requires a New Look at Confrontation' (1993) 22 *Capital University Law Review* 145, 172–3.

2 Hearsay Evidence in Civil Proceedings

The admissibility of hearsay evidence in civil proceedings is now governed by the Civil Evidence Act 1995,[15] the effect of which is as follows.

2.1 The General Principle

The general principle, laid down by section 1, is that the hearsay rule has no application in civil proceedings. In other words, hearsay evidence, first-hand or otherwise, is admissible in civil proceedings.[16] There are, however, a number of conditions to be satisfied and other points to be noted:

(a) Any party proposing to adduce hearsay evidence is to give such *notice* of that fact to all other parties as is reasonable and practicable in the circumstances for the purpose of enabling them to deal with any matters arising from the evidence being hearsay.[17] Detailed provision on the duty to give notice of intention to rely on hearsay evidence is made in rules 33.2 and 33.3 of the Civil Procedure Rules. Failure to give notice does not affect the admissibility of the evidence, but may be taken into account by the court (i) in considering the exercise of its powers with respect to the *course of proceedings and costs*, and (ii) as a matter adversely affecting the *weight* to be accorded to the evidence.[18] The requirement to give notice may, however, be waived by any party to whom it is to be given.[19]

(b) Where hearsay evidence is adduced and the maker of the statement is not called as a witness, provision is made for any other party to the proceedings, with the leave of the court, to call that person as a witness in order to cross-examine him or her on the statement.[20] One commentator has identified a number of the factors

---

[15] See generally D Barnett, 'Civil Evidence Act' (1997) 147 *New Law Journal* 701; 'The Civil Evidence Act 1995' (1996) 160 *Justice of the Peace* 82; I Grainger, 'Hearsay Evidence Admissible' (1996) 140 *Solicitors' Journal* 536; I Grainger, 'New Rules on Hearsay Notices' (1997) 141 *Solicitors' Journal* 112; A Hogan, 'The Civil Evidence Act 1995' (1997) 147 *New Law Journal* 226; R Munday, 'The Civil Evidence Act 1995 and the Diverging Paths of Civil and Criminal Hearsay Rules' [1997] *Cambridge Law Journal* 272; D O'Brien, 'The Rule Against Hearsay RIP' (1996) 146 *New Law Journal* 153; J Peysner, 'Hearsay is Dead! Long Live Hearsay!' (1998) 2 *International Journal of Evidence and Proof* 232; S E Salako, 'The Hearsay Rule and the Civil Evidence Act 1995: Where Are We Now?' (2000) 19 *Civil Justice Quarterly* 371.

[16] The proceedings for the making of an anti-social behaviour order under the Crime and Disorder Act 1998 have been held to be civil proceedings: *R (McCann) v Manchester Crown Court* [2002] UKHL 39, [2002] 3 WLR 1313. See generally C Bakalis, 'Anti-Social Behaviour Orders—Criminal Penalties or Civil Injunctions?' [2003] *Cambridge Law Journal* 583; S Macdonald, 'The Nature of the Anti-Social Behaviour Order—*R (McCann & Others) v Crown Court at Manchester*' (2003) 66 *Modern Law Review* 630; P Tain, 'Civil or Criminal?' (2002) 146 *Solicitors' Journal* 1037.

[17] S 2(1). This requirement has been criticized by J Peysner, 'Hearsay is Dead! Long Live Hearsay!' (1998) 2 *International Journal of Evidence and Proof* 232.   [18] S 2(4).

[19] S 2(3).

[20] S 3. See also rule 33.4 of the Civil Procedure Rules and, generally, I R Scott, 'Cross-Examination and Witness Statements' (2003) 22 *Civil Justice Quarterly* 307. S 3 and rule 33.4 are discussed in *Cottrell v General Cologne Re UK Ltd* [2004] EWHC 2402 (Comm).

which would presumably be taken into account by a court in determining whether to grant leave:

- the witness's reason for not being able to attend; in particular if he is dead, ill or out of the jurisdiction;
- how central that witness's evidence is to the case;
- whether the party seeking to cross-examine him is able to produce evidence at the application, on affidavit, to show that the witness is likely to be mistaken or lying (for example, a previous inconsistent statement or a vested interest in the outcome);
- whether the witness can reasonably be expected to remember the incidents which he is referring to;
- whether the witness is simply reporting second-hand hearsay, which will likewise be admissible.[21]

(c) In *assessing the weight* to be accorded to hearsay evidence, the court is to have regard to any circumstances from which any inference can reasonably be drawn about the reliability or otherwise of the evidence. In particular, regard is to be had to the following factors:

- whether it would have been reasonable and practicable for the party adducing the evidence to have produced the maker of the original statement as a witness;
- whether the original statement was made contemporaneously with the occurrence or existence of the matters stated in the statement;
- whether the evidence involves multiple hearsay;
- whether any person involved had any motive to conceal or misrepresent matters;
- whether the original statement was an edited account, or was made in collaboration with another or for a particular purpose;
- whether the circumstances in which the hearsay evidence is adduced are such as to suggest an attempt to prevent proper evaluation of its weight.[22]

(d) Section 5(1) provides:

Hearsay evidence shall not be admitted in civil proceedings if or to the extent that it is shown to consist of, or to be proved by means of, a statement made by a person who at the time he made the statement was *not competent as a witness*.

For this purpose 'not competent as a witness' means suffering from such mental or physical infirmity, or lack of understanding, as would render a person incompetent as a witness in civil proceedings; but a child shall be treated as competent as a witness if he satisfies the requirements of section 96(2)(a) and (b) of the Children Act 1989 (conditions for reception of unsworn evidence of child).[23]

(e) Provision is also made, in section 5(2), for the admissibility of evidence *attacking or supporting the credibility* of the maker of a statement not called as a witness, provided that such evidence would be admissible if he or she were called as a witness.

[21] D Barnett, 'Civil Evidence Act' (1997) 147 *New Law Journal* 701, 701.   [22] S 4.   [23] Italics added.

2.2 Specific Situations

The general principle, we have seen, is that all hearsay evidence is admissible in civil proceedings, provided that the general provisions of the Civil Evidence Act 1995 are satisfied. In addition, however, there are some specific situations to be considered.[24]

(a) A number of common law exceptions to the hearsay rule are specifically preserved by the Civil Evidence Act 1995.[25] In relation to each of these exceptions, all that must be determined is whether the requirements laid down at common law for the application of the exception are satisfied. The general provisions of the Act (for example, that requiring notice of intention to adduce hearsay evidence to be given) do not apply in relation to these preserved common law exceptions. The preserved common law exceptions are:

- The exception which renders *published works dealing with matters of a public nature* (for example, histories, scientific works, dictionaries, and maps) admissible as evidence of facts of a public nature stated in them.

- The exception which renders *public documents* (for example, public registers and returns made under public authority with respect to matters of public interest) admissible as evidence of facts stated in them.

- The exception which renders *records* (for example, the records of certain courts, treaties, Crown grants, pardons, and commissions) admissible as evidence of facts stated in them.

- The exception which renders evidence of a *person's reputation* admissible for the purpose of proving his or her good or bad character.

- The exception which renders evidence of *reputation or family tradition* admissible for the purpose of proving or disproving pedigree or the existence of a marriage;[26] or for the purpose of proving or disproving the existence of any public or general right, or of identifying any person or thing.

(b) Section 10(1) of the Civil Evidence Act 1995 provides: 'The actuarial tables (together with explanatory notes) for use in personal injury and fatal accident cases issued from time to time by the Government Actuary's Department are admissible in evidence for the purpose of assessing, in an action for personal injury, the sum to be awarded as general damages for future pecuniary loss.' The general provisions of the Act have no application to such evidence.

(c) The Civil Evidence Act 1995 provides that the following provisions remain in force, and are unaffected by the general provisions of the Act:

- Documentary Evidence Act 1868, section 2 (mode of proving certain official documents);

---

[24] For more detail see M N Howard (ed), *Phipson on Evidence* (15th ed 2000) Ch 26 (and supplements).
[25] S 7.
[26] By virtue of s 84(5) of the Civil Partnership Act 2004 this 'is to be treated as applying in an equivalent way for the purpose of proving or disproving the existence of a civil partnership'.

• Documentary Evidence Act 1882, section 2 (documents printed under the superintendence of the Stationery Office);

• Evidence (Colonial Statutes) Act 1907, section 1 (proof of statutes of certain legislatures);

• Evidence (Foreign, Dominion and Colonial Documents) Act 1933, section 1 (proof and effect of registers and official certificates of certain countries);

• Oaths and Evidence (Overseas Authorities and Countries) Act 1963, section 5 (provision in respect of public registers of other countries).[27]

3 Other Proceedings in which the Hearsay Rule Is Inapplicable

There are a number of particular categories of proceedings in which the hearsay rule has no application. For example, article 2 of the Children (Admissibility of Hearsay Evidence) Order 1993 provides:

In—

(a) civil proceedings before the High Court or a county court; and

(b)

   (i) family proceedings, and

   (ii) civil proceedings under the Child Support Act 1991 in a magistrates' court,

evidence given in connection with the upbringing, maintenance or welfare of a child shall be admissible notwithstanding any rule of law relating to hearsay.[28]

Also noteworthy is the principle that where hearsay evidence has legitimately been taken into account in reaching an administrative decision, a court reviewing the decision is also entitled to take that evidence into account, and is not confined to considering strictly admissible evidence. The court could make appropriate allowance for the fact that the evidence is hearsay in the weight it attaches to that evidence.[29] In *McCool v Rushcliffe BC*,[30] the Divisional Court had occasion to consider section 51(1) of the Local Government (Miscellaneous Provisions) Act 1976, which states that 'a district council shall, on the receipt of an application from any person for the grant to that person of a licence to drive private hire vehicles, grant to that person a driver's licence: Provided that a district council shall not grant a licence—(a) unless they are satisfied that the applicant is a fit and proper person to hold a driver's licence...'. The Divisional Court held that, in determining whether a person is a fit and proper person, within the meaning of section 51(1), to hold a licence to drive a private hire vehicle, a district council

---

[27] S 14(3).   [28] See, eg, *R v Stratford Youth Court, ex p S* [1998] 1 WLR 1758.
[29] *R v Home Secretary, ex p Rahman* [1997] 3 WLR 990.   [30] [1998] 3 All ER 889.

and (on appeal) a magistrates' court are entitled to take hearsay evidence into account. The Court noted that:

> in reaching their respective decisions, the borough council and the justices were entitled to rely on any evidential material which might reasonably and properly influence the making of a responsible judgment in good faith on the question in issue. Some evidence such as gossip, speculation and unsubstantiated innuendo would be rightly disregarded. Other evidence, even if hearsay, might by its source, nature and inherent probability carry a greater degree of credibility. All would depend on the particular facts and circumstances.[31]

4 Criminal Proceedings

The hearsay provisions of the Criminal Justice Act 2003[32] are largely modelled on the recommendations of the Law Commission.[33] The Criminal Justice Act 2003 maintains a general rule whereby 'a statement not made in oral evidence in the proceedings' is inadmissible 'as evidence of any matter stated'.[34] 'A statement is any representation of fact or opinion made by a person by whatever means; and it includes a representation made in a sketch, photofit or other pictorial form.'[35] The exclusionary rule applies only if 'the purpose, or one of the purposes, of the person making the statement appears to the court to have been—(a) to cause another person to believe the matter, or (b) to cause another person to act or a machine to operate on the basis that the matter is as stated'.[36] The effect of this is that only intended assertions in out-of-court statements are caught by the hearsay rule.[37] This reverses the former common law position as applied in *R v Kearley*.[38] At common law, so-called implied assertions were caught by the hearsay rule. Thus, in a situation where there was no intended assertion (either by words or by conduct) of a particular matter, but it was possible to *infer* an assertion of that matter from words or conduct, evidence of the words or conduct was inadmissible under the hearsay rule to establish the relevant matter in the same way that it would have been had the assertion been intended. In *Kearley* the question arose whether evidence that a number of telephone callers had requested the defendant to supply them with drugs was admissible to prove that the defendant was a supplier of drugs. In holding the evidence to be inadmissible, the majority of the House of Lords reasoned as follows. The making of the requests for drugs indicated that the callers believed Kearley to be a drug supplier. Although the callers did not externalize this belief expressly (by, for example, saying over the telephone, 'You, Kearley, are a drug supplier'), they did

---

[31] [1998] 3 All ER 889, 893.

[32] Cf the position in Scotland: P Duff, 'Hearsay Issues: A Scottish Perspective' [2005] *Criminal Law Review* 525.

[33] Law Commission (Law Com No 245), *Evidence in Criminal Proceedings: Hearsay and Related Topics* (1997), available at http://www.lawcom.gov.uk/docs/lc245.pdf.   [34] S 114(1).

[35] S 115(2).

[36] S 115(3). See generally G Durston, 'Implied Assertions and Hearsay' (2004) 154 *New Law Journal* 528.

[37] Contra S Uglow, 'Section 115(3) of the Criminal Justice Act 2003: How Not to Overturn *Kearley*', *Archbold News*, 23 May 2005, 6.

[38] [1992] 2 AC 228. See also *R v O'Connell* [2003] EWCA Crim 502. See generally G Taylor, 'Two English Hearsay Heresies' (2005) 9 *International Journal of Evidence and Proof* 110.

so impliedly through their requests. The requests were relevant only inasmuch as they contained implied assertions that Kearley was a drug supplier, and because express assertions to that effect would have been subject to the hearsay rule, so too should be the implied assertions.

The rationale for an approach of confining the hearsay rule to intended assertions was explained succinctly in a US case, *US v Long*:

> One of the principal goals of the hearsay rule is to exclude declarations when their veracity cannot be tested through cross-examination. When a declarant does not intend to communicate anything, however, his sincerity is not in question and the need for cross-examination is sharply diminished. Thus, an unintentional message is presumptively more reliable.[39]

In other words, absence of intent to assert or communicate the fact that is sought to be established is considered to negate the danger of insincerity. This approach may be subjected to the criticism that, inasmuch as it is designed to weed out unreliable hearsay, it does so by addressing only one hearsay danger, insincerity, to the exclusion of the dangers of faulty perception, erroneous memory, and lack of clarity in narration.[40]

The general prohibition against hearsay evidence in the Criminal Justice Act 2003 is subject to important exceptions. We shall now consider the four categories of exception that apply where first-hand hearsay evidence is at issue. This is where the maker of the out-of-court statement actually had personal knowledge (first-hand knowledge) of the matter stated in his or her statement. Such a situation may arise where, for example, the colour of a car is at issue, and it is proposed that an in-court witness testify that 'X told me that the car that X saw was red'. Where multiple hearsay is at issue (for example, testimony by an in-court witness that 'X told me that Y told her that the car that Y saw was red' or that 'X told me that Y told her that the car that Z saw was red'), a different set of principles applies, as will be explained later.

The Criminal Justice Act 2003 provides that first-hand hearsay evidence is admissible where one of the following four categories of exception applies:

- any statutory exception makes it admissible (section 114(1)(a));
- any common law exception preserved by the Act makes it admissible (section 114(1)(b));
- 'all parties to the proceedings agree to it being admissible' (section 114(1)(c));
- 'the court is satisfied that it is in the interests of justice for it to be admissible' (section 114(1)(d)).

The first, second, and fourth of these categories will now be considered in turn.

---

[39] 905 F 2d 1572, 1580 (DC Cir 1990).

[40] See also D Birch, 'Criminal Justice Act 2003: (4) Hearsay—Same Old Story, Same Old Song?' [2004] *Criminal Law Review* 556, 564–6.

4.1 Statutory Exceptions

The Criminal Justice Act 2003 itself contains a number of specific statutory exceptions to the hearsay rule:

4.1.1 Unavailability of Maker of Out-of-Court Statement

Broadly speaking, section 116 of the Act is aimed at securing the admissibility in evidence of an out-of-court statement where its maker is unavailable to testify for one of a number of specified reasons. Section 116 provides in part:

> (1) In criminal proceedings a statement not made in oral evidence in the proceedings is admissible as evidence of any matter stated if—
>
> > (a) oral evidence given in the proceedings by the person who made the statement would be admissible as evidence of that matter,
> >
> > (b) the person who made the statement (the relevant person) is identified to the court's satisfaction, and
> >
> > (c) any of the five conditions mentioned in subsection (2) is satisfied.
>
> (2) The conditions are—
>
> > (a) that the relevant person is dead;
> >
> > (b) that the relevant person is unfit to be a witness because of his bodily or mental condition;
> >
> > (c) that the relevant person is outside the United Kingdom and it is not reasonably practicable to secure his attendance;
> >
> > (d) that the relevant person cannot be found although such steps as it is reasonably practicable to take to find him have been taken;
> >
> > (e) that through fear the relevant person does not give (or does not continue to give) oral evidence in the proceedings, either at all or in connection with the subject matter of the statement, and the court gives leave for the statement to be given in evidence.

The unavailability of the maker of the out-of-court statement for one of the five reasons specified in section 116(2) must not have been brought about by the party seeking to give the statement in evidence in order to prevent him or her from giving oral evidence.[41] For the purposes of section 116(2)(e), 'fear' 'is to be widely construed and (for example) includes fear of the death or injury of another person or of financial loss'.[42] Moreover, leave may be given under section 116(2)(e):

> only if the court considers that the statement ought to be admitted in the interests of justice, having regard—(a) to the statement's contents, (b) to any risk that its admission or exclusion will result in unfairness to any party to the proceedings (and in particular to how difficult it will be to challenge the statement if the relevant person does not give oral evidence), (c) in appropriate cases, to the fact that a direction under section 19 of the Youth Justice and Criminal Evidence

---

[41] S 116(5).   [42] S 116(3).

Act 1999 (c 23) (special measures for the giving of evidence by fearful witnesses etc) could be made in relation to the relevant person, and (d) to any other relevant circumstances.[43]

4.1.2 Business and Other Documents

Section 117 of the Act does not, unlike section 116, alter previous hearsay doctrine in any radical way. Essentially a revised version of an exception that was previously contained in section 24 of the Criminal Justice Act 1988, section 117 provides:

(1) In criminal proceedings a statement contained in a document is admissible as evidence of any matter stated if—

    (a) oral evidence given in the proceedings would be admissible as evidence of that matter,

    (b) the requirements of subsection (2) are satisfied, and

    (c) the requirements of subsection (5) are satisfied, in a case where subsection (4) requires them to be.

(2) The requirements of this subsection are satisfied if—

    (a) the document or the part containing the statement was created or received by a person in the course of a trade, business, profession or other occupation, or as the holder of a paid or unpaid office,

    (b) the person who supplied the information contained in the statement (the relevant person) had or may reasonably be supposed to have had personal knowledge of the matters dealt with, and

    (c) each person (if any) through whom the information was supplied from the relevant person to the person mentioned in paragraph (a) received the information in the course of a trade, business, profession or other occupation, or as the holder of a paid or unpaid office.

(3) The persons mentioned in paragraphs (a) and (b) of subsection (2) may be the same person.

(4) The additional requirements of subsection (5) must be satisfied if the statement—

    (a) was prepared for the purposes of pending or contemplated criminal proceedings, or for a criminal investigation, but

    (b) was not obtained pursuant to a request under section 7 of the Crime (International Co-operation) Act 2003 (c 32) or an order under paragraph 6 of Schedule 13 to the Criminal Justice Act 1988 (c 33) (which relate to overseas evidence).

(5) The requirements of this subsection are satisfied if—

    (a) any of the five conditions mentioned in section 116(2) is satisfied (absence of relevant person etc), or

    (b) the relevant person cannot reasonably be expected to have any recollection of the matters dealt with in the statement (having regard to the length of time since he supplied the information and all other circumstances).

---

[43] S 116(4). See generally G Durston, 'Frightened Witnesses and the Criminal Justice Act 2003' (2004) 154 *New Law Journal* 1626.

(6) A statement is not admissible under this section if the court makes a direction to that effect under subsection (7).

(7) The court may make a direction under this subsection if satisfied that the statement's reliability as evidence for the purpose for which it is tendered is doubtful in view of—

(a) its contents,

(b) the source of the information contained in it,

(c) the way in which or the circumstances in which the information was supplied or received, or

(d) the way in which or the circumstances in which the document concerned was created or received.

4.1.3 Previous Inconsistent Statements

In certain circumstances the law permits a witness's out-of-court statement that is inconsistent with his or her in-court testimony[44] to be used to discredit the witness's testimony.[45] Equally, an out-of-court statement that is inconsistent with a hearsay statement that is admitted in evidence may be used to 'discredit' the hearsay statement.[46] The general effect of section 119 is that all such previous inconsistent statements may not only be used for the purposes of 'discrediting', but also become evidence of any matters stated in them.

4.1.4 Previous Consistent Statements

Section 120 prescribes the situations in which a previous consistent statement[47] will be admissible as evidence of the truth of its contents. These situations are as follows:

• The 'previous statement by the witness is admitted as evidence to rebut a suggestion that his oral evidence has been fabricated'.[48]

• The statement is one 'made by the witness in a document—(a) which is used by him to refresh his memory while giving evidence, (b) on which he is cross-examined, and (c) which as a consequence is received in evidence in the proceedings'.[49]

• 'The statement identifies or describes a person, object or place',[50] and 'while giving evidence the witness indicates that to the best of his belief he made the statement, and that to the best of his belief it states the truth'.[51]

• 'The statement was made by the witness when the matters stated were fresh in his memory but he does not remember them, and cannot reasonably be expected to remember them, well enough to give oral evidence of them in the proceedings',[52] and

---

[44] See generally G Durston, 'Previous (In)consistent Statements After the Criminal Justice Act 2003' [2005] *Criminal Law Review* 206; A Samuels, 'Inconsistent Statements' (2004) 168 *Justice of the Peace* 873.

[45] See Ch 14.   [46] Criminal Justice Act 2003, s 124(2)(c).

[47] See generally G Durston, 'Previous (In)consistent Statements After the Criminal Justice Act 2003' [2005] *Criminal Law Review* 206.   [48] S 120(2).

[49] S 120(3). See further Ch 14.   [50] S 120(5).   [51] S 120(4)(b).   [52] S 120(6).

'while giving evidence the witness indicates that to the best of his belief he made the statement, and that to the best of his belief it states the truth'.[53]

• 'The statement consists of a complaint made by the witness (whether to a person in authority or not) about conduct which would, if proved, constitute the offence or part of the offence',[54] 'the complaint was made as soon as could reasonably be expected after the alleged conduct',[55] 'the complaint was not made as a result of a threat or a promise',[56] 'before the statement is adduced the witness gives oral evidence in connection with its subject matter',[57] and 'while giving evidence the witness indicates that to the best of his belief he made the statement, and that to the best of his belief it states the truth'.[58]

This approach may be criticized for being unduly narrow. Of course it is true that there appears to be little necessity for the admissibility in evidence for their truth of statements of witnesses which are, by definition, *consistent* with their present testimony. However, evidence of statements about an event made by a witness at an earlier time (and hence closer to the time of the event) may, if it exists, be just the type of evidence which a jury would expect to hear in addition to statements about the same event made in court. In an article about countering negative inferences associated with the absence of evidence,[59] it has been argued that when certain issues are raised in jury trials, juries often develop expectations about the evidence which will be adduced for their consideration. The failure of a party to satisfy these expectations may result in negative (and often unfair) inferences being drawn against that party by the jury.

Lord Justice Auld would have liked to see the introduction of a rather more radical approach, so that:

• where a witness has made a prior statement, in written or recorded form, it should be admissible as evidence of any matter stated in it of which his direct oral evidence in the proceedings would be admissible provided that he authenticates it as his statement;

• an integral part of the new rule should be that a defendant's previous statement should in principle be admissible whether it supports or damages his case and the fact that it may appear to be self-serving should go only to weight; and

• the witness should be permitted, where appropriate, to adopt the statement in the witness box as his evidence in chief.[60]

4.2 Common Law Exceptions

A number of common law exceptions to the hearsay rule are specifically preserved by section 118 of the Act. All other common law exceptions are abolished. Section 118(1)

---

[53] S 120(4)(b).   [54] S 120(7)(c).   [55] S 120(7)(d).   [56] S 120(7)(e).   [57] S 120(7)(f).
[58] S 120(4)(b).

[59] S A Saltzburg, 'A Special Aspect of Relevance: Countering Negative Inferences Associated with the Absence of Evidence' (1978) 66 *California Law Review* 1011.

[60] Lord Justice Auld, *A Review of the Criminal Courts of England and Wales* (2001) Ch 11 para 92, accessible via http://www.criminal-courts-review.org.uk. See also D Birch, 'Criminal Justice Act 2003: (4) Hearsay—Same Old Story, Same Old Song?' [2004] *Criminal Law Review* 556, 569–72.

provides a list and brief description of the common law exceptions preserved:

The following rules of law are preserved.

PUBLIC INFORMATION ETC

1 Any rule of law under which in criminal proceedings—

(a) published works dealing with matters of a public nature (such as histories, scientific works, dictionaries and maps) are admissible as evidence of facts of a public nature stated in them,

(b) public documents (such as public registers, and returns made under public authority with respect to matters of public interest) are admissible as evidence of facts stated in them,

(c) records (such as the records of certain courts, treaties, Crown grants, pardons and commissions) are admissible as evidence of facts stated in them, or

(d) evidence relating to a person's age or date or place of birth may be given by a person without personal knowledge of the matter.

REPUTATION AS TO CHARACTER

2 Any rule of law under which in criminal proceedings evidence of a person's reputation is admissible for the purpose of proving his good or bad character.

NOTE

The rule is preserved only so far as it allows the court to treat such evidence as proving the matter concerned.

REPUTATION OR FAMILY TRADITION

3 Any rule of law under which in criminal proceedings evidence of reputation or family tradition is admissible for the purpose of proving or disproving—

(a) pedigree or the existence of a marriage,[61]

(b) the existence of any public or general right, or

(c) the identity of any person or thing.

NOTE

The rule is preserved only so far as it allows the court to treat such evidence as proving or disproving the matter concerned.

RES GESTAE

4 Any rule of law under which in criminal proceedings a statement is admissible as evidence of any matter stated if—

(a) the statement was made by a person so emotionally overpowered by an event that the possibility of concoction or distortion can be disregarded,

---

61 By virtue of s 84(5) of the Civil Partnership Act 2004 this 'is to be treated as applying in an equivalent way for the purpose of proving or disproving the existence of a civil partnership'.

(b) the statement accompanied an act which can be properly evaluated as evidence only if considered in conjunction with the statement, or

(c) the statement relates to a physical sensation or a mental state (such as intention or emotion).

CONFESSIONS ETC

5 Any rule of law relating to the admissibility of confessions or mixed statements in criminal proceedings.

ADMISSIONS BY AGENTS ETC

6 Any rule of law under which in criminal proceedings—

(a) an admission made by an agent of a defendant is admissible against the defendant as evidence of any matter stated, or

(b) a statement made by a person to whom a defendant refers a person for information is admissible against the defendant as evidence of any matter stated.

COMMON ENTERPRISE

7 Any rule of law under which in criminal proceedings a statement made by a party to a common enterprise is admissible against another party to the enterprise as evidence of any matter stated.

EXPERT EVIDENCE

8 Any rule of law under which in criminal proceedings an expert witness may draw on the body of expertise relevant to his field.

It is desirable to make further comment on the following of the above exceptions:

4.2.1 *Res Gestae*

Literally, the term *res gestae* means 'the transaction'. In essence, evidence of facts may be admissible as part of the *res gestae* if these facts are so closely connected in time, place, and circumstances with some transaction which is at issue that they can be said to form a part of that transaction. The main contexts in which hearsay statements may be admissible in evidence as part of the *res gestae*, outlined in section 118(1), will now be examined briefly.

4.2.1.1 Spontaneous Statements

The law relating to spontaneous statements was authoritatively clarified by Lord Ackner in *R v Andrews (Donald)*:

My Lords, may I therefore summarise the position which confronts the trial judge when faced in a criminal case with an application under the res gestae doctrine to admit evidence of statements, with a view to establishing the truth of some fact thus narrated, such evidence being truly categorised as 'hearsay evidence?'

1. The primary question which the judge must ask himself is—can the possibility of concoction or distortion be disregarded?

2. To answer that question the judge must first consider the circumstances in which the particular statement was made, in order to satisfy himself that the event was so unusual or startling or dramatic as to dominate the thoughts of the victim, so that his utterance was an instinctive reaction to that event, thus giving no real opportunity for reasoned reflection. In such a situation the judge would be entitled to conclude that the involvement or the pressure of the event would exclude the possibility of concoction or distortion, providing that the statement was made in conditions of approximate but not exact contemporaneity.

3. In order for the statement to be sufficiently 'spontaneous' it must be so closely associated with the event which has excited the statement, that it can be fairly stated that the mind of the declarant was still dominated by the event. Thus the judge must be satisfied that the event, which provided the trigger mechanism for the statement, was still operative. The fact that the statement was made in answer to a question is but one factor to consider under this heading.

4. Quite apart from the time factor, there may be special features in the case, which relate to the possibility of concoction or distortion....

5. As to the possibility of error in the facts narrated in the statement, if only the ordinary fallibility of human recollection is relied upon, this goes to the weight to be attached to and not to the admissibility of the statement and is therefore a matter for the jury. However, here again there may be special features that may give rise to the possibility of error.... In such circumstances the trial judge must consider whether he can exclude the possibility of error.

. . .

...Of course, having ruled the statement admissible the judge must...make it clear to the jury that it is for them to decide what was said and to be sure that the witnesses were not mistaken in what they believed had been said to them. Further, they must be satisfied that the declarant did not concoct or distort to his advantage or the disadvantage of the accused the statement relied upon and where there is material to raise the issue, that he was not activated by any malice or ill-will. Further, where there are special features that bear on the possibility of mistake then the juries' attention must be invited to those matters.

...I wholly accept that the doctrine [of res gestae] admits the hearsay statements, not only where the declarant is dead or otherwise not available but when he is called as a witness.... I would...strongly deprecate any attempt in criminal prosecutions to use the doctrine as a device to avoid calling, when he is available, the maker of the statement. Thus to deprive the defence of the opportunity to cross-examine him, would not be consistent with the fundamental duty of the prosecution to place all the relevant material facts before the court, so as to ensure that justice is done.[62]

The modern-day flexibility of this exception may be illustrated by the fact that, in *R v Lawson*,[63] words spoken within an hour of the incident were held to fall within the exception. Of course, the exception is clearly inapplicable where the relevant statement is made 20 minutes *before* the incident in question.[64]

---

[62] [1987] AC 281, 295, 300–2. See also *Ratten v R* [1972] AC 378; *Mills v R* [1995] 1 WLR 511; *R v Lawson* [1998] Crim LR 883; *R v Jamieson* [2003] EWCA Crim 3755.   [63] [1998] Crim LR 883.

[64] *R v Newport* [1998] Crim LR 581.

4.2.1.2 Statements Accompanying and Explaining a Relevant Act

In *R v Kearley*, Lord Bridge of Harwich 'accept[ed] the proposition that, if an action is *of itself* relevant to an issue, the words which accompany and explain the action may be given in evidence, whether or not they would be relevant independently'.[65] Thus, a statement made at the time of performing an act which would be relevant in the absence of the statement is admissible in evidence so long as the statement explains the act,[66] and was made more or less contemporaneously with the act by the person performing the act. The fact 'that the declaration was by one person, and the accompanying act by another', would not suffice.[67] If the relevant act was a continuing one, it is immaterial that a considerable period of time elapsed before the making of the statement; what is crucial is that it must have been made during the continuance of the act.[68]

It is inappropriate for a defendant who exercised the right to silence at both the pre-trial and trial stages to invoke the 'statements accompanying and explaining relevant acts' exception to secure the admission of evidence of exculpatory statements made out of court by the defendant.[69]

4.2.1.3 Statements concerning Contemporaneous State of Mind

Out-of-court statements concerning contemporaneous state of mind (such as knowledge, emotion, or intention) are admissible in evidence in certain circumstances. The extent to which evidence of hearsay statements suggesting knowledge of particular facts is admissible[70] has been explained as follows:

> It is, of course, elementary that statements made to a witness by a third party are not excluded by the hearsay rule when they are put in evidence solely to prove the state of mind either of the maker of the statement or of the person to whom it was made. What a person said or heard said may well be the best and most direct evidence of that person's state of mind. This principle can only apply, however, when the state of mind evidenced by the statement is either itself directly in issue at the trial or of *direct and immediate relevance* to an issue which arises at the trial.[71]

What is apparently required, therefore, is a degree of probative value substantially above the bare minimum.

There appear to be conflicting authorities on whether evidence suggesting an intent to perform a particular act is admissible to establish that the intent was in fact carried out (that is, that the act in question was performed).[72] The main authority cited for the view that such evidence is admissible is *R v Buckley*.[73] The accused was

---

[65] [1992] 2 AC 228, 246 (italics added).   [66] *R v Bliss* (1837) 7 Ad & E 550, 112 ER 577.

[67] *Howe v Malkin* (1878) 40 LT 196, 196.

[68] *Rawson v Haigh* (1824) 2 Bing 99, 130 ER 242; *Homes v Newman* [1931] 2 Ch 112.

[69] *R v Callender* [1998] Crim LR 337.

[70] See generally P B Carter, 'Hearsay, Relevance and Admissibility: Declarations as to State of Mind and Declarations Against Penal Interest' (1987) 103 *Law Quarterly Review* 106.

[71] *R v Blastland* [1986] AC 41, 54 (italics added). See also *R v Williams (David)* [1998] Crim LR 494.

[72] See generally C F H Tapper, '*Hillmon* Rediscovered and Lord St Leonards Resurrected' (1990) 106 *Law Quarterly Review* 441.   [73] (1873) 13 Cox CC 293.

charged with murdering a police officer on a certain night. The deceased's superior officer was permitted to testify that, that morning, the deceased had told him that he intended to watch the movements of the accused that night. The superior officer had then said, 'I will send a man to assist you about nine o'clock', to which the deceased had responded, 'That will be too late, I will go about dusk, myself'. No reference was made to the hearsay rule, and it should be noted that the decision might well have been influenced by the fact that there was evidence that the victim was seen shortly after dark, possibly travelling in the direction of the accused's cottage. More recently, in *R v Moghal*,[74] the accused was charged with a murder which could have been committed only by him, his mistress, or both. The mistress had earlier been acquitted. To support his defence that the mistress had alone been responsible for the murder, the accused sought to adduce in evidence a tape recording by her in which she declared her intention to kill the victim. The Court of Appeal thought that, had the trial judge been asked to rule on the issue, this evidence should have been held admissible.

The main authority cited for the view that such evidence is inadmissible is *R v Wainwright*.[75] This was a murder case in which the prosecution sought to adduce evidence that the victim had said, on leaving her home, that she was going to the accused's premises. The evidence was held to be inadmissible on the basis that 'it was only a statement of intention which might or might not have been carried out'.[76] To a similar effect are *R v Pook*[77] and *R v Thomson*.[78] In *Thomson*, the accused was charged with using an instrument on a woman for the purpose of procuring an abortion. In support of his defence that the woman (who had later died from an unrelated cause) had operated on herself, the accused sought to ask a prosecution witness in cross-examination whether the woman had stated, some weeks before the operation, that she intended to operate on herself. The Court of Criminal Appeal held that this evidence had been correctly excluded, expressly rejecting the argument that cases such as this, where it was the defence which was seeking to introduce the evidence of intent, should be distinguished from cases where such evidence was sought to be introduced by the prosecution. Finally, it should be noted that Lord Bridge expressed doubts in *Blastland* about what the Court of Appeal had said in *Moghal*, remarking that, 'I cannot see how a threat by Sadiga against Rashid's life, made six months before the murder, however virulently the threat was expressed, was of any relevance to the issue whether Moghal was a willing accomplice or an unwilling spectator when the murder was committed'.[79]

The apparent conflict remains formally unresolved, but a sensible approach may be to adopt the view of Mason CJ, expressed in the decision of the High Court of Australia in *Walton v R*, that 'out-of-court statements which tend to prove a plan or intention of the author [should be admissible in evidence], subject to remoteness in time and indications of unreliability or lack of probative value'.[80]

---

[74] (1977) 65 Cr App R 56 (decision of 1977).   [75] (1875) 13 Cox CC 171.
[76] Ibid, 172 per Lord Cockburn CJ.   [77] (1871) 13 Cox CC 172n.   [78] [1912] 3 KB 19.
[79] [1986] AC 41, 60.   [80] (1989) 166 CLR 283, 290. See also *Kamleh v R* [2005] HCA 2.

4.2.1.4 Statements concerning Contemporaneous Physical State

Such statements are admissible in evidence:

> . . . statements made by a workman to his wife of his sensations at the time, about the pain in the side or head, or what not—whether the statements were made by groans or by actions or were verbal statements—would be admissible to prove the existence of those sensations.[81]

> If a man says to his surgeon, 'I have a pain in the head,' or a pain in such a part of the body, that is evidence; but, if he says to his surgeon, 'I have a wound'; and was to add, 'I met John Thomas, who had a sword, and ran me through the body with it,' that would be no evidence against John Thomas . . .[82]

However, 'the statements must be confined to contemporaneous symptoms, and nothing in the nature of a narrative is admissible as to who caused them, or how they were caused'.[83]

Furthermore, as explained by Sir Jocelyn Simon P in *Tickle v Tickle*: 'If what a patient says about her state of health to a doctor is admissible as part of the res gestae notwithstanding the hearsay rule, it seems to me that what the doctor says to the patient is no less admissible when its adduction is required in order that justice should be done.'[84]

4.2.1.5 Availability of Maker of Statement

It has been confirmed that the failure to call the maker of a *res gestae* statement as a witness, if he or she is available, does not affect the admissibility in evidence of the statement, but is a factor that may be considered in the exercise of the exclusionary discretion in section 78 of the Police and Criminal Evidence Act 1984:

> Once evidence is within the res gestae exception to the hearsay rule, it is admissible. There is no rider that, as a matter of law, it is not to be admitted merely because the maker of the statement is available and can give evidence.[85]

> If the purpose of the Crown was that the res gestae evidence should be given without any opportunity being given to the defence to cross-examine the maker of the statement, the court might well conclude that the admission of the evidence would indeed have an adverse effect on the fairness of the proceedings and refuse to allow it to be given. As a general principle, it cannot be right that the Crown should be permitted to rely only on such part of a victim's evidence as they consider reliable, without being prepared to tender the victim to the defence, so that the defence can challenge that part of the victim's evidence on which the Crown seeks to rely and, if so advised, elicit that part of her evidence on which the defence might seek to rely.[86]

4.2.2 Common Enterprise

Where a party to a common purpose makes a statement in the course of and in furtherance of that purpose, this statement is admissible in evidence against all other

---

[81] *Gilbey v Great Western Railway Co* (1910) 102 LT 202, 203.
[82] *R v Nicholas* (1846) 2 Car & K 246, 248, 175 ER 102, 102.   [83] *R v Gloster* (1888) 16 Cox CC 471, 473.
[84] [1968] 1 WLR 937, 942.
[85] *A-G's Reference (No 1 of 2003)* [2003] EWCA Crim 1286, [2003] 2 Cr App R 29 (p 453), [18].
[86] Ibid, [21].

parties to the common purpose.[87] This exception to the hearsay rule is of particular relevance to prosecutions for conspiracy, but its use is not necessarily confined to such prosecutions. It is essential that independent evidence be adduced of the existence of the common purpose and the involvement in it of all persons against whom the statement is to be used. The exception is inapplicable 'where individual defendants are charged with a number of separate substantive offences and the terms of a common enterprise are not proved or are ill-defined'.[88]

4.3 Admissibility in the Interests of Justice

Very radically by the standards of previous hearsay doctrine, hearsay evidence will now be admissible if 'the court is satisfied that it is in the interests of justice for it to be admissible'.[89] In deciding whether a statement should be admitted in evidence on this basis:

> the court must have regard to the following factors (and to any others it considers relevant)—
>
> (a) how much probative value the statement has (assuming it to be true) in relation to a matter in issue in the proceedings, or how valuable it is for the understanding of other evidence in the case;
>
> (b) what other evidence has been, or can be, given on the matter or evidence mentioned in paragraph (a);
>
> (c) how important the matter or evidence mentioned in paragraph (a) is in the context of the case as a whole;
>
> (d) the circumstances in which the statement was made;
>
> (e) how reliable the maker of the statement appears to be;
>
> (f) how reliable the evidence of the making of the statement appears to be;
>
> (g) whether oral evidence of the matter stated can be given and, if not, why it cannot;
>
> (h) the amount of difficulty involved in challenging the statement;
>
> (i) the extent to which that difficulty would be likely to prejudice the party facing it.[90]

This inclusionary power or 'safety valve' is clearly aimed at securing the admissibility of hearsay evidence considered sufficiently reliable. While such a power is now a feature of hearsay doctrine in several common law jurisdictions,[91] it is not

---

[87] See generally *R v Walters* (1979) 69 Cr App R 115 (decision of 1979); *R v Donat* (1986) 82 Cr App R 173 (decision of 1985); *R v Gray* [1995] 2 Cr App R 100; *R v Jones* [1997] 2 Cr App R 119; *R v Murray* [1997] 2 Cr App R 136.   [88] *R v Murray* [1997] 2 Cr App R 136, 148.

[89] S 114(1)(d). Birch describes this as the 'single most intriguing feature of the Act': D Birch, 'The New Law of Hearsay: Criminal Justice Act 2003', *Archbold News*, 8 April 2005, 6, 9.

[90] S 114(2). See generally G Durston, 'Hearsay Evidence and the New Inclusionary Discretion' (2004) 168 *Justice of the Peace* 788.

[91] See generally A L-T Choo, *Hearsay and Confrontation in Criminal Trials* (1996) Ch 7.

uncontroversial, for reasons vividly explained by the US Supreme Court in *Crawford v Washington*:[92]

> Reliability is an amorphous, if not entirely subjective, concept. There are countless factors bearing on whether a statement is reliable... Whether a statement is deemed reliable depends heavily on which factors the judge considers and how much weight he accords each of them. Some courts wind up attaching the same significance to opposite facts. For example, the Colorado Supreme Court held a statement more reliable because its inculpation of the defendant was 'detailed,'... while the Fourth Circuit found a statement more reliable because the portion implicating another was 'fleeting'... The Virginia Court of Appeals found a statement more reliable because the witness was in custody and charged with a crime (thus making the statement more obviously against her penal interest),... while the Wisconsin Court of Appeals found a statement more reliable because the witness was *not* in custody and *not* a suspect... Finally, the Colorado Supreme Court in one case found a statement more reliable because it was given 'immediately after' the events at issue,... while that same court, in another case, found a statement more reliable because two years had elapsed ...[93]

4.4 Multiple Hearsay

The preceding discussions apply only to the admissibility of first-hand hearsay. Multiple hearsay (second-hand hearsay, third-hand hearsay, etc.) is admissible only where one of the requirements in section 121(1) is satisfied. Section 121 provides:

> (1) A hearsay statement is not admissible to prove the fact that an earlier hearsay statement was made unless—
>
> (a) either of the statements is admissible under section 117, 119 or 120,
>
> (b) all parties to the proceedings so agree, or
>
> (c) the court is satisfied that the value of the evidence in question, taking into account how reliable the statements appear to be, is so high that the interests of justice require the later statement to be admissible for that purpose.
>
> (2) In this section 'hearsay statement' means a statement, not made in oral evidence, that is relied on as evidence of a matter stated in it.

4.5 Other Safeguards

There is a specific power to exclude hearsay evidence under section 126(1)(b) of the Criminal Justice Act 2003 if 'the court is satisfied that the case for excluding the statement, taking account of the danger that to admit it would result in undue waste of

---

[92] 124 S Ct 1354 (2004). See generally A Choo, '*Crawford v Washington*: A View from Across the Atlantic', http://www.bepress.com/ice/vol2/iss1/art4/.

[93] 124 S Ct 1354, 1371 (2004) (italics in original). Note, however, the comment by H L Ho that while 'there can be differences of opinion on the reliability of a statement', 'it is another thing altogether to suggest that it is *impossible* to make any objectively defensible assessment of reliability': H L Ho, 'Confrontation and Hearsay: A Critique of *Crawford*' (2004) 8 *International Journal of Evidence and Proof* 147, 160 (italics in original).

time, substantially outweighs the case for admitting it, taking account of the value of the evidence'. Additionally, section 125(1) provides:

> If on a defendant's trial before a judge and jury for an offence the court is satisfied at any time after the close of the case for the prosecution that—
>
> (a) the case against the defendant is based wholly or partly on a statement not made in oral evidence in the proceedings, and
>
> (b) the evidence provided by the statement is so unconvincing that, considering its importance to the case against the defendant, his conviction of the offence would be unsafe,
>
> the court must either direct the jury to acquit the defendant of the offence or, if it considers that there ought to be a retrial, discharge the jury.

4.6 Notice

Part 34 of the Criminal Procedure Rules 2005 makes it mandatory for notice to be given by a party of its intention to introduce certain hearsay evidence under the Criminal Justice Act 2003:

WHEN THIS PART APPLIES

34.1 This Part applies in a magistrates' court and in the Crown Court where a party wants to introduce evidence on one or more of the grounds set out in section 114(1)(a) to (d) of the Criminal Justice Act 2003, and in this Part that evidence is called 'hearsay evidence'.

NOTICE OF HEARSAY EVIDENCE

34.2 The party who wants to introduce hearsay evidence must give notice in the form set out in the Practice Direction[94] to the court officer and all other parties.

WHEN THE PROSECUTOR MUST GIVE NOTICE OF HEARSAY EVIDENCE

34.3 The prosecutor must give notice of hearsay evidence—

(a) in a magistrates' court, at the same time as he complies or purports to comply with section 3 of the Criminal Procedure and Investigations Act 1996 (disclosure by prosecutor); or

(b) in the Crown Court, not more than 14 days after—

    (i) the committal of the defendant, or

    (ii) the consent to the preferment of a bill of indictment in relation to the case, or

    (iii) the service of a notice of transfer under section 4 of the Criminal Justice Act 1987 (serious fraud cases) or under section 53 of the Criminal Justice Act 1991 (certain cases involving children), or

    (iv) where a person is sent for trial under section 51 of the Crime and Disorder Act 1998 (indictable-only offences sent for trial), the service of copies of the documents

---

[94] http://www.dca.gov.uk/criminal/procrules_fin/contents/pdf/f41page1-2.pdf or http://www.hmcourts-service.gov.uk/courtfinder/forms/6440_0405.doc.

containing the evidence on which the charge or charges are based under paragraph 1 of Schedule 3 to the 1998 Act.

WHEN A DEFENDANT MUST GIVE NOTICE OF HEARSAY EVIDENCE

34.4 A defendant must give notice of hearsay evidence not more than 14 days after the prosecutor has complied with or purported to comply with section 3 of the Criminal Procedure and Investigations Act 1996 (disclosure by prosecutor).

OPPOSING THE INTRODUCTION OF HEARSAY EVIDENCE

34.5 A party who receives a notice of hearsay evidence may oppose it by giving notice within 14 days in the form set out in the Practice Direction[95] to the court officer and all other parties.

METHODS OF GIVING NOTICE

34.6 Where this Part requires a notice to be given it may, with the consent of the addressee, be sent by fax or other means of electronic communication.

COURT'S POWER TO VARY REQUIREMENTS UNDER THIS PART

34.7 The court may—

(a) dispense with the requirement to give notice of hearsay evidence;

(b) allow notice to be given in a different form, or orally; or

(c) shorten a time limit or extend it (even after it has expired).

WAIVING THE REQUIREMENT TO GIVE A NOTICE OF HEARSAY EVIDENCE

34.8 A party entitled to receive a notice of hearsay evidence may waive his entitlement by so informing the court and the party who would have given the notice.

4.7 A Brief Evaluation

It has been seen that the provisions of the Criminal Justice Act 2003, largely following the recommendations of the Law Commission, maintain a 'rule and exceptions' approach to hearsay doctrine, albeit that the specific exceptions are broad and there is an interests-of-justice exception. Lord Justice Auld was critical in his Report of any approach to hearsay that continues to maintain a prima facie exclusionary rule, recommending 'further consideration of the reform of the rule against hearsay, in particular with a view to making hearsay generally admissible subject to the principle of best evidence, rather than generally inadmissible subject to specified exceptions as proposed by the Law Commission'.[96]

An alternative approach might have been to maintain a rule against hearsay but, instead of recognizing specific exceptions *and* an interests-of-justice exception, simply

---

[95] http://www.dca.gov.uk/criminal/procrules_fin/contents/pdf/f42page1-2.pdf or http://www.hmcourts-service. gov.uk/courtfinder/forms/6441_0405.doc.

[96] Lord Justice Auld, *A Review of the Criminal Courts of England and Wales* (2001) Ch 11 para 104, accessible via http://www.criminal-courts-review.org.uk.

to have recognized the interests-of-justice exception as the only exception. It is arguable that the availability of an interests-of-justice exception makes the existence of specific exceptions unnecessary. Dennis writes of the interests-of-justice exception: 'It will be interesting to see whether the discretion remains as intended, a marginal sweeping-up power operating outside the statutory and preserved common law exceptions in ss 116–118, or whether in practice it will be invoked in addition to, or even in substitution for, those exceptions.'[97] It has been questioned, for example, whether there was any real point to preserving the common law *res gestae* exception.[98] It seems clear that most of the hearsay evidence admissible under this exception would be caught in any event by the specific exceptions in the Act, with the remainder certainly able to be admitted under the interests-of-justice exception.

The Canadian experience is instructive in this context. In *R v Khan*[99] in 1990, the Supreme Court of Canada radically recognized the existence of a residual discretion to admit hearsay evidence where, in the context of the particular case, the evidence is necessary and sufficiently reliable. Technically, this residual exception stands alongside and does not replace the specific exceptions to the hearsay rule. The Supreme Court has stated, however, that all specific exceptions must be interpreted in the light of the necessity-and-reliability test. Thus the fact that a specific exception applies does not mean that the evidence will be admissible if the application of the necessity-and-reliability test requires otherwise.[100] It is, however, only in rare cases that 'evidence falling within an existing exception may be excluded because the indicia of necessity and reliability are lacking in the particular circumstances of the case'.[101]

4.8 The European Human Rights Dimension

Brief consideration should be given to the issue of the extent to which the admission in evidence for the prosecution of out-of-court statements may fall foul of the European

---

[97] I Dennis, 'The Criminal Justice Act 2003: Part 2' [2004] *Criminal Law Review* 251, 252. Similarly, Birch asks: 'if the "interests of justice" suggest admissibility, might a court now simply say so, and get on with the case, whether or not the evidence is equally admissible under another exception?' Birch does not consider that such an approach would be appropriate: 'Given that it must be sound practice to choose as the basis of admissibility an exception that requires as little as possible by way of supporting argument, the more straightforward automatic exceptions should surely be considered first. It would also be advisable, when formulating an argument under the safety valve, to brief oneself as to the grounds on which the evidence has fallen short of admissibility under one of the regular exceptions . . .'. See D Birch, 'The New Law of Hearsay: Criminal Justice Act 2003', *Archbold News*, 8 April 2005, 6, 9.

[98] See generally D Ormerod, 'Redundant Res Gestae?' [1998] *Criminal Law Review* 301.

[99] [1990] 2 SCR 531. See also *R v F (W J)* [1999] 3 SCR 569; *R v Parrott* [2001] 1 SCR 178. On the Canadian approach to hearsay, see, generally, S Akhtar, 'Hearsay: The Denial of Confirmation' (2005) 26 *Criminal Reports (6th)* 46; N Bala, 'The Supreme Court Sends a Clear Message (Again): Children Are Not Adults' (1999) 27 *Criminal Reports (5th)* 195; R Bessner, 'Sensitivity of the Supreme Court to the Plight of Child Victims of Sexual Abuse' (1999) 27 *Criminal Reports (5th)* 189; R J Delisle, '*B (K G)* and Its Progeny' (1998) 14 *Criminal Reports (5th)* 75; R Prithipaul, 'Observations on the Current Status of the Hearsay Rule' (1996) 39 *Criminal Law Quarterly* 84; H Stewart, 'Hearsay After *Starr*' (2001) 7 *Canadian Criminal Law Review* 5; D Stuart, '*Starr* and *Parrott*: Favouring Exclusion of Hearsay to Protect Rights of Accused' (2001) 39 *Criminal Reports (5th)* 284; L Stuesser, '*R v Starr* and Reform of the Hearsay Exceptions' (2001) 7 *Canadian Criminal Law Review* 55.

[100] *R v Starr* [2000] 2 SCR 144.   [101] *R v Mapara* [2005] SCC 23, [15].

Convention on Human Rights. Article 6(3)(d) of the Convention provides, *inter alia*, that everyone charged with a criminal offence has the right 'to examine or have examined witnesses against him...'. There have been a number of decisions of the European Court of Human Rights interpreting Article 6(3)(d) of the European Convention,[102] but there is little predictive value in these pronouncements. On issues of principle the Court tends to make bland statements like the following:

All the evidence must normally be produced in the presence of the accused at a public hearing with a view to adversarial argument. As a rule, a conviction should not be based on the testimony of a witness whom the accused has not had an opportunity to challenge and question. However, Article 6(3)(d) does not grant the accused an unlimited right to secure the appearance of witnesses in court. It is normally for the national courts to decide whether it is necessary or advisable to hear a particular witness.[103]

In *Unterpertinger v Austria*,[104] *Kostovski v Netherlands*,[105] *Windisch v Austria*,[106] *Delta v France*,[107] *Lüdi v Switzerland*,[108] *Saïdi v France*,[109] *Van Mechelen v Netherlands*,[110] *PS v Germany*,[111] and *Lucà v Italy*,[112] the Court upheld the applicants' arguments that they had been denied fair trials on the basis of violations of Article 6(3)(d). In all of these cases, the out-of-court statements constituted the only evidence, or an important part of the evidence, against the applicants. Illustrative is *Van Mechelen v Netherlands*, where the basis of the applicants' complaint was that they had been convicted essentially on the evidence of police officers whose identity had not been disclosed to them and who had not been heard either in public or in their presence. The European Court noted that the police officers in question had been with the investigating judge in a separate room, from which the accused and even their counsel were excluded. All communication was via a sound link. Thus, not only were the defence unaware of the identity of the police witnesses, but also they were deprived of the opportunity of testing the reliability of these witnesses by observing their demeanour under direct questioning. In the Court's view, there had been no satisfactory explanation of why it was necessary to resort to such extreme limitations on the right of the accused to have the evidence against them given in their presence, or of why less far-reaching measures were not considered.[113]

---

[102] See generally D J Birch, 'Hearsay-Logic and Hearsay-Fiddles: *Blastland* Revisited' in P Smith (ed), *Criminal Law: Essays in Honour of J C Smith* (1987) 35–6; A Brown, 'Hearsay and Human Rights' (1999) 143 *Solicitors' Journal* 314; W E O'Brian Jr, 'The Right of Confrontation: US and European Perspectives' (2005) 121 *Law Quarterly Review* 481; P O'Connor, 'Article 6 and Hearsay Under Sections 23 and 26 of the Criminal Justice Act 1988', *Archbold News*, 3 Nov 2003, 7; C Osborne, 'Hearsay and the European Court of Human Rights' [1993] *Criminal Law Review* 255; H Reiter, 'Hearsay Evidence and Criminal Process in Germany and Australia' (1984) 10 *Monash University Law Review* 51, 70–1; S J Summers, 'The Right to Confrontation After *Crawford v Washington*: A "Continental European" Perspective', http://www.bepress.com/ice/vol2/iss1/art3/; Law Commission (Law Com No 245), *Evidence in Criminal Proceedings: Hearsay and Related Topics* (1997) Part V, available at http://www.lawcom.gov.uk/docs/lc245.pdf.
[103] *Laukkanen v Finland*, Application no 50230/99, 3 Feb 2004, [35].
[104] (1991) 13 EHRR 175 (judgment of 1986).   [105] (1990) 12 EHRR 434 (judgment of 1989).
[106] (1991) 13 EHRR 281 (judgment of 1990).   [107] (1993) 16 EHRR 574 (judgment of 1990).
[108] (1993) 15 EHRR 173 (judgment of 1992).   [109] (1994) 17 EHRR 251 (judgment of 1993).
[110] (1998) 25 EHRR 647 (judgment of 1997).   [111] (2003) 36 EHRR 61 (p 1139) (judgment of 2001).
[112] (2003) 36 EHRR 46 (p 807) (judgment of 2001).
[113] *Van Mechelen v Netherlands* (1998) 25 EHRR 647 (judgment of 1997), 674.

The Court observed:

> It is true…that the anonymous police officers were interrogated before an investigating judge, who had himself ascertained their identity and had, in a very detailed official report of his findings, stated his opinion on their reliability and credibility as well as their reasons for remaining anonymous.
>
> However these measures cannot be considered a proper substitute for the possibility of the defence to question the witnesses in their presence and make their own judgment as to their demeanour and reliability. It thus cannot be said that the handicaps under which the defence laboured were counterbalanced by the above procedures.[114]

The Court concluded, therefore, that it could not be said that the proceedings taken as a whole had been fair.

In *Isgrò v Italy*,[115] *Asch v Austria*,[116] *Artner v Austria*,[117] *Doorson v Netherlands*,[118] *SN v Sweden*,[119] and *Laukkanen v Finland*,[120] however, the applicants' arguments failed in the European Court. Speaking in the context of a child complainant of sexual abuse, M, the Court said in *SN v Sweden*:

> Nor can it be said that the applicant was denied his rights under Art 6(3)(d) on the ground that he was unable to examine or have examined the evidence given by M during the trial and appeal proceedings. Having regard to the special features of criminal proceedings concerning sexual offences, this provision cannot be interpreted as requiring in all cases that questions be put directly by the accused or his or her defence counsel, through cross-examination or by other means. The Court notes that the videotape of the first police interview was shown during the trial and appeal hearings and that the record of the second interview was read out before the District Court and the audiotape of that interview was played back before the Court of Appeal. In the circumstances of the case, these measures must be considered sufficient to have enabled the applicant to challenge M's statements and his credibility in the course of the criminal proceedings. Indeed, that challenge resulted in the Court of Appeal reducing the applicant's sentence because it considered that part of the charges against him had not been proved.[121]

It is notable that in *SN v Sweden* a violation was not found notwithstanding that 'the statements made by M were virtually the sole evidence on which the courts' findings of guilt were based'.[122] Cases in which violations have not been found have, however, been typically those in which the impugned evidence did not constitute the only, or the main, evidence against the accused.[123]

The approach of the Court of Appeal for England and Wales to the hearsay provisions of the Criminal Justice Act 1988, which predated those of the Criminal Justice Act 2003,

---

[114] *Van Mechelen v Netherlands* (1998) 25 EHRR 647 (judgment of 1997), 675.   [115] 1/1990/192/252.
[116] (1993) 15 EHRR 597 (judgment of 1991).   [117] 39/1991/291/362.
[118] (1996) 22 EHRR 330 (judgment of 1996).   [119] (2004) 39 EHRR 13 (p 304) (judgment of 2002).
[120] Application no 50230/99, 3 Feb 2004.   [121] (2004) 39 EHRR 13 (p 304) (judgment of 2002), [52].
[122] Ibid, [46]. See generally L Ellison, 'The Right of Challenge in Sexual Offence Cases: *SN v Sweden*' (2003) 7 *International Journal of Evidence and Proof* 62.
[123] See, eg, *Isgrò v Italy*, 1/1990/192/252; *Asch v Austria* (1993) 15 EHRR 597 (judgment of 1991); *Artner v Austria*, 39/1991/291/362; *Doorson v Netherlands* (1996) 22 EHRR 330 (judgment of 1996). See also *Magnusson v Sweden (Admissibility)*, Application no 53972/00, 16 Dec 2003: '… it would appear that the boys' testimony was not the only primary evidence against the applicant in the trial'.

may be instructive, as it is highly likely that a similar approach will be taken to the provisions of the 2003 Act. The Court found the relevant provisions of the 1988 Act to be in themselves Convention-compliant on the basis, in essence, that they provided sufficient protection against unfairness to the accused.[124] The Court considered in one case that 'the proper application of the Convention coincides with the proper applica- tion of the statute'.[125] In another case the Court remarked in a similar vein: 'Since the whole basis of the exercise of the discretion conferred by section 26 [of the 1988 Act] is to assess the interests of justice by reference to the risk of unfairness to the accused, our procedures appear to us to accord fully with our treaty obligations.'[126] Thus the Court did not consider that the statutory provisions in themselves violated Article 6; what was required was that they could be seen, in the context of the case as a whole, to have been appropriately used. In *R v Sellick* the Court of Appeal summed up the relevant prin- ciples emerging from the European Court jurisprudence as follows:

i) The admissibility of evidence is primarily for the national law;

ii) Evidence must normally be produced at a public hearing and as a general rule Article 6(1) and (3)(d) require a defendant to be given a proper and adequate opportunity to challenge and question witnesses;

iii) It is not necessarily incompatible with Article 6(1) and (3)(d) for depositions to be read and that can be so even if there has been no opportunity to question the witness at any stage of the proceedings. Article 6(3)(d) is simply an illustration of matters to be taken into account in considering whether a fair trial has been held. The reasons for the court holding it necessary that statements should be read and the procedures to counterbalance any handicap to the defence will all be relevant to the issue, whether, where statements have been read, the trial was fair.

iv) The quality of the evidence and its inherent reliability, plus the degree of caution exercised in relation to reliance on it, will also be relevant to the question whether the trial was fair.

[v)] . . . it . . . cannot be right for there to be some absolute rule that, where compelling evidence is the sole or decisive evidence, an admission in evidence of a statement must then automatically lead to a defendant's Article 6 rights being infringed.[127]

The Court in *Sellick* also made specific observations on the possible use by the prosecution of the statements of persons allegedly kept away by fear:

Our view is that certainly care must be taken to see that sections 23 and 26, and indeed the new provisions in the Criminal Justice Act 2003, are not abused. Where intimidation of witnesses is alleged the court must examine with care the circumstances. Are the witnesses truly being kept away by fear? Has that fear been generated by the defendant, or by persons acting with the defendant's authority? Have reasonable steps been taken to trace the witnesses and bring them into court? Can anything be done to enable the witnesses to be brought to court to give

---

[124] See generally *R v Gokal* [1997] 2 Cr App R 266, 280; *R v Thomas*, *The Times*, 24 July 1998; *R v Radak* [1999] 1 Cr App R 187; *R v D* [2002] EWCA Crim 990, [2003] QB 90; *R v Sellick* [2005] EWCA Crim 651, [2005] 2 Cr App R 15 (p 211). See also *R v Rutherford* [1998] Crim LR 490.

[125] *R v Radak* [1999] 1 Cr App R 187, 202.   [126] *R v Gokal* [1997] 2 Cr App R 266, 280.

[127] [2005] EWCA Crim 651, [2005] 2 Cr App R 15 (p 211), [50], [53].

evidence and be there protected? It is obvious that the more 'decisive' the evidence in the statements, the greater the care will be needed to be sure why it is that a witness cannot come and give evidence. The court should be astute to examine the quality and reliability of the evidence in the statement . . . It will, as section 26 states, be looking at the interests of justice, which includes justice to the defendant and justice to the victims. The judge will give warnings to the jury stressing the disadvantage that the defendant is in, not being able to examine a witness.[128]

The direction given to the jury we accept is a delicate one. In the defendant's own interests he or she will not wish stress to be placed on the fact that the reason why a witness has not come to give evidence orally is because a judge has formed the view that the witness has been kept away by fear.[129]

[128] [2005] EWCA Crim 651, [2005] 2 Cr App R 15 (p 211), [57].   [129] Ibid, [58].

10

Expert Evidence

The admissibility in certain circumstances of expert opinion evidence constitutes an important exception to the general rule which prohibits the admission of evidence of a witness's opinion and allows only the admission of evidence of facts perceived by a witness. The issue of expert opinion evidence continues to generate considerable publicity, with the chairman of the Criminal Cases Review Commission reported as saying in late 2004 that there is a 'need to examine the whole law of admissibility of expert witnesses from first principles. The time has come to develop more stringent rules.'[1] Expert evidence in criminal cases[2] has been brought dramatically to public attention since 2003 by three high-profile cases. The Court of Appeal quashed the convictions of Sally Clark,[3] Angela Cannings,[4] and Donna Anthony,[5] each of whom had been convicted of murdering two of her infant children.[6] Crucially, in each case, expert evidence had been presented at trial with a view to highlighting the improbability that two (in the case of Clark and Anthony) or three (in the case of Cannings) infant deaths in the same family could be due to natural causes. In the aftermath of the judgment in the Cannings case, the Attorney-General Lord Goldsmith 'established a review of past cases where a parent or carer had been convicted of killing an infant under two in the past 10 years'. A total of 297 such cases were identified. The review of these cases revealed 28 cases in which there was a cause for concern. The defence solicitors, Criminal Cases Review Commission, and Court of Appeal were informed of this.[7] Furthermore, in March 2005 the House of Commons Science and Technology Committee published a report entitled *Forensic Science on Trial*.[8]

---

[1] R Cowan, 'Call for Overhaul of Expert Testimony', *Guardian*, 30 Nov 2004, 9.

[2] For general discussions see P Roberts, 'Science, Experts, and Criminal Justice' in M McConville and G Wilson (eds), *The Handbook of the Criminal Justice Process* (2002); A Samuels, 'The Expert in Criminal Cases', *Archbold News*, 6 Dec 2004, 7; M Redmayne, *Expert Evidence and Criminal Justice* (2001).

[3] [2003] EWCA Crim 1020, [2003] 2 FCR 447.   [4] [2004] EWCA Crim 01, [2004] 2 Cr App R 7 (p 63).

[5] [2005] EWCA Crim 952.

[6] See generally A Levy, 'Commentary: Value of Experts and Their Evidence Must Be Questioned If Justice Is to Be Done', *Guardian*, 20 Jan 2004, 3; B Mahendra, 'Crime and the Flawed Expert' (2003) 153 *New Law Journal* 296; B Mahendra, 'Justice—Tarnished, Tardy but Triumphant' (2003) 153 *New Law Journal* 162; B Mahendra, 'The Legacy of Roy Meadow' (2004) 154 *New Law Journal* 283; J Rowe, 'Expert Evidence and Sudden Infant Deaths: Where Next?' (2004) 154 *New Law Journal* 1757; M Smulian, 'On Good Authority?' (2004) 101(9) *Law Society's Gazette* 22; D Wheeler, 'The Far-Reaching Impact of *Cannings*' (2004) 154 *New Law Journal* 113; A Wilson, 'Expert Testimony in the Dock' (2005) 69 *Journal of Criminal Law* 330; G Wood, 'Equality of Arms' (2004) 148 *Solicitors' Journal* 7.

[7] House of Lords Hansard, 21 Dec 2004: Column 1658. See also *The Review of Infant Death Cases Following the Court of Appeal Decision in the Case of* R v Cannings *(2004)*, available at http://www.lslo.gov.uk/pdf/ Infant_death_report.pdf.

[8] House of Commons Science and Technology Committee, *Forensic Evidence on Trial* (Seventh Report of Session 2004–05) (HC 96-I) (2005), available at http://www.publications.parliament.uk/pa/cm200405/

In the previous decade, expert opinion evidence in criminal cases also had a high profile owing to its role in contributing to a number of major miscarriages of justice. Pre-eminent among these was the case of Judith Ward, whose conviction of the murder of a number of people by planting a bomb on a bus carrying service personnel and their families was quashed by the Court of Appeal in 1992. The Court 'identified the cause of the injustice done to the appellant on the scientific side of the case as stemming from the fact that three senior [government] forensic scientists...regarded their task as being to help the police. They became partisan.'[9]

The *Crown Court Study* found that there was probably prosecution scientific evidence in around a third of contested cases.[10] In only around a quarter of cases in which there was such evidence was it challenged by the defence. Overall, therefore, there was a challenge by the defence to prosecution scientific evidence in under a tenth of all contested cases.[11] According to prosecution barristers ('Pb'), defence barristers ('Db'), and the Crown Prosecution Service ('CPS') respectively, the types of scientific evidence involved, in order of frequency, were as follows:[12]

Types of scientific evidence

	Pb (%)	Db (%)	CPS (%)
Medical	47	52	44
Drugs	22	18	24
Fingerprints	12	12	10
Blood samples (person)	9	10	8
Handwriting (documents)	7	7	6
Contact evidence (person)	7	(not listed)	6
Blood samples (alcohol/drugs)	6	5	4
Firearms/ballistics	5	4	7
Contact evidence (property)	4	2	6
Other*	13	17	11
Total	132	127	126
	(N = 249)	(N = 269)	(N = 197)

Note
* 'Other' scientific evidence included DNA samples; footprints; evidence of cause of fire or impact of vehicle; evidence of speed of vehicle; facial mapping; meteorological evidence re weather on the day.

cmselect/cmsctech/96/96i.pdf. See generally B Mahendra, 'Parliament Tries Science' (2005) 155 *New Law Journal* 790.

[9] *R v Ward* [1993] 2 All ER 577, 628.

[10] See also the study of the provision of expert opinion to family courts by C A Kaplan et al, 'The Use of Expert Witnesses—Trials and Tribulations' [1997] *Family Law* 735.

[11] M Zander and P Henderson, *The Royal Commission on Criminal Justice: Crown Court Study* (1993) 83–4, 86.

[12] Ibid, 85.

In civil cases expert evidence is now specifically dealt with in Part 35 of the Civil Procedure Rules, as supplemented by the relevant Practice Direction.[13] It is common to hear calls for aspects of the practices and procedures applicable in civil cases to be adopted in criminal cases.[14] This will be explored in more detail later.

1 The Fact and Opinion Distinction

As indicated above, the significance of a witness being classified as an expert lies partly in the rule that an expert (unlike other witnesses) may give evidence of opinion as well as of fact. It is however noteworthy that, although treated in the law of evidence as fundamental, the distinction between 'fact' and 'opinion' may not withstand close scrutiny. Thayer wrote that 'in a sense all testimony to matter of fact is opinion evidence; *ie*, it is a conclusion formed from phenomena and mental impressions'.[15] To put it another way: 'In the very basic sense that everything we imagine we see, and everything we think we know, is our own personal reconstruction of sense-data, everything is a matter of "opinion."'[16] Wigmore observed:

> If ... our notion of the supposed firm distinction between 'opinion' and 'fact' is that the one is certain and sure, the other not, surely a just view of their psychological relations serves to demonstrate that in strict truth nothing is certain. Or if we prefer the suggestion of Sir G C Lewis that the test is whether 'doubt can reasonably exist,' then certainly it must be perceived that the multiple doubts which ought to exist would exclude vast masses of indubitably admissible testimony. Or if we prefer the idea that 'opinion' is inference and fact is 'original perception,' then it may be understood that no such distinction can scientifically be made, since the processes of knowledge and the sources of illusion are the same for both. It is impossible, then (supposing it were desirable), to confine witnesses to some fancied realm of 'knowledge' or 'fact' and to forbid them to enter the domain of 'opinions' or inferences. There are no such contrasted groups of certain and uncertain testimony, and there never can be.[17]

Although we may accept these powerful arguments, it is true to say that in practice, as will be seen below, lawyers and the courts have a working common understanding of matters of opinion on which only experts will be permitted to give evidence.

---

[13] See generally L Blom-Cooper, 'Experts and Assessors: Past, Present and Future' (2002) 21 *Civil Justice Quarterly* 341; G Edmond, 'After Objectivity: Expert Evidence and Procedural Reform' (2003) 25 *Sydney Law Review* 131; C Jackson, 'The Uses and Abuses of Experts and Their Evidence' [2000] *Journal of Personal Injury Litigation* 19.

[14] See, eg, G Wood, 'Medical Experts Are Usurping the Jury's Role', *The Times*, 13 July 2004, Law, 8.

[15] J B Thayer, *A Preliminary Treatise on Evidence at the Common Law* (1898) 524.

[16] P Roberts, 'Tyres with a "Y": An English Perspective on *Kumho Tire* and Its Implications for the Admissibility of Expert Evidence', accessible via http://www.law.qub.ac.uk/ice.

[17] J H Wigmore, *Evidence in Trials at Common Law (Vol 7)* (rev by J H Chadbourn, 1978) 16. See also C A G Jones, *Expert Witnesses: Science, Medicine, and the Practice of Law* (1994) 103: 'All statements of fact are, to some degree, statements of conclusion and judgement.'

2 Admissibility

The Court of Appeal has summarized the principles governing the admissibility of expert opinion evidence as follows:

> For expert evidence to be admissible, two conditions must be satisfied: first, that study or experience will give a witness's opinion an authority which the opinion of one not so qualified will lack; and secondly the witness must be so qualified to express the opinion.... If these two conditions are met the evidence of the witness is admissible, although the weight to be attached to his opinion must of course be assessed by the tribunal of fact...[18]

This quotation reflects the fact that, although not often well articulated in the cases, there are clearly two fundamental issues which underlie considerations of the admissibility of expert opinion evidence. These may be referred to, in short, as the issues of necessity and reliability. The first condition essentially encapsulates concerns relating to necessity and the second concerns relating to reliability. The role of expert witnesses is 'to furnish the Judge or jury with the necessary scientific criteria for testing the accuracy of their conclusions, so as to enable the Judge or jury to form their own independent judgment' by the application of these criteria to the facts proved in evidence'.[19] Thus expert opinion evidence is considered unnecessary where the trier of fact may be expected to have the ability to form its opinion on the issue in question without assistance. To treat the trier of fact to expert opinion evidence in such a situation would not only usurp the role of the trier of fact, but also create the danger that the trier of fact would be too readily influenced by that evidence and thus accord it undue weight.[20]

In civil proceedings expert evidence is specifically dealt with in Part 35 of the Civil Procedure Rules, as supplemented by the relevant Practice Direction. Rule 35.1 of the Civil Procedure Rules provides: 'Expert evidence shall be restricted to that which is reasonably required to resolve the proceedings.'[21] Rule 35.4(1) provides: 'No party may call an expert or put in evidence an expert's report without the court's permission.'

The potentially strong influence on a jury in a criminal trial of apparently cogent expert evidence adduced by the prosecution is undeniable.[22] It is, therefore, only in

---

[18] *R v Luttrell* [2004] EWCA Crim 1344, [2004] 2 Cr App R 31 (p 520), [32]–[33]. See generally M Redmayne, *Expert Evidence and Criminal Justice* (2001) Chs 5 and 6.

[19] *Davie v Edinburgh Magistrates* [1953] SC 34, 40.

[20] 'In the case of expert witnesses the court is likely to lower its guard': *Cala Homes (South) Ltd v Alfred McAlpine Homes East Ltd* [1995] FSR 818, 843.

[21] There is anecdotal evidence that this has been achieved (H Hallett, 'Expert Witnesses in the Courts of England and Wales' (2005) 79 *Australian Law Journal* 288, 294): 'As a civil trial judge I can say from my own experience that the CPR seem to have had the desired effect. Expert evidence is generally restricted to cases where it is essential and by the time a case comes on for trial the issues have usually narrowed significantly. The culture that Lord Woolf wished to foster [through the CPR] seems to be developing without draconian restrictions.'

[22] Notably, 90% of jurors in the *Crown Court Study* found scientific evidence presented by expert witnesses either 'not at all difficult' (56%) or 'not very difficult' (34%) to understand, with only 9% finding it 'fairly difficult', and 1% 'very difficult': M Zander and P Henderson, *The Royal Commission on Criminal Justice: Crown Court Study* (1993) 206.

those situations where the trier of fact may be expected to require the assistance of an expert that such evidence should be admissible.

While the notion of necessity in this context may appear superficially attractive, it may not withstand close scrutiny. As will be seen in the course of this chapter, whether the trier of fact may be expected to be able to form its opinion on a particular issue without the assistance of an expert is a question which is often inherently incapable of accurate determination. There is, furthermore, empirical evidence suggesting that the tendency of juries to accord undue weight to expert evidence may not be as strong as is popularly thought.[23] In any event, cogent expert testimony may be precisely the type of evidence on which considerable weight *should* be placed by the trier of fact. What is really to be guarded against, rather, is the placing of undue weight on expert evidence which may cause an incorrect result to be reached in the case. This is the concern of what appears to be the second criterion for admissibility, that of reliability. The law effectively requires that expert opinion evidence be demonstrated to be sufficiently reliable to be admitted. As has been stated by the Court of Appeal: 'In each case it must be for the judge to decide whether the issue is one on which the jury could be assisted by expert evidence, and whether the expert tendered has the expertise to provide such evidence.'[24] On the appropriateness of holding a voir dire hearing to determine the issue of expertise, the Court of Appeal has remarked:

> We were not shown any English authority on the question of holding a *voir dire* to decide whether a purported expert should be allowed to give evidence. In the vast majority of cases it seems to us the judge will be able to make the decision from the written material before him. There will be rare cases . . . where it will be necessary in order to do justice to hold a *voir dire* . . .[25]

> A judge should be astute to avoid unnecessary satellite litigation which is likely to increase expense and increase the length of the trial. This is perhaps particularly true of a serious fraud case, where the expense and length will already inevitably be considerable.[26]

The extent to which the twin issues of necessity and reliability are adequately accounted for in the law on the admissibility of expert opinion evidence is a question which ought to underlie any consideration of the law in this area.

---

[23] E J Imwinkelried, 'The Next Step in Conceptualizing the Presentation of Expert Evidence as Education: The Case for Didactic Trial Procedures' (1997) 1(2) *International Journal of Evidence and Proof* 128, 134–6. Cf, however, House of Commons Science and Technology Committee, *Forensic Evidence on Trial* (Seventh Report of Session 2004–05) (HC 96-I) (2005) [167] (bold font removed): 'Advancements in science and technology impact on both the techniques used by criminals and the approaches employed in fighting and detecting crime. It is, therefore, highly likely that the number of cases which depend on complex forensic evidence will increase. This is already happening with regard to digital evidence. The Home Office should undertake research to test whether there would be value in extending the arrangements for complex fraud trials to be tried without a jury to other serious cases that rest on highly complex scientific evidence. This research must also address public attitudes towards this possibility.' Available at http://www.publications.parliament.uk/pa/cm200405/cmselect/cmsctech/96/96i.pdf.   [24] *R v Stockwell* (1993) 97 Cr App R 260, 264 (decision of 1993).

[25] *R v G* [2004] EWCA Crim 1240, [2004] 2 Cr App R 38 (p 638), [30].   [26] Ibid, [31].

2.1 Statutory Provisions

Provision on the admissibility of expert opinion evidence is on occasion made expressly by Parliament. Section 4 of the Obscene Publications Act 1959, for example, expressly permits the admission of such evidence:

(1) Subject to subsection (1A) of this section a person shall not be convicted of an offence . . . if it is proved that publication of the article in question is justified as being for the public good on the ground that it is in the interests of science, literature, art or learning, or of other objects of general concern.

. . .

(2) It is hereby declared that the opinion of experts as to the literary, artistic, scientific or other merits of an article may be admitted in any proceedings under this Act either to establish or to negative the said ground.

. . .

Statutory provisions may also expressly declare the admission of expert opinion evidence to be essential in particular situations. For example, section 1(1) of the Criminal Procedure (Insanity and Unfitness to Plead) Act 1991 provides:

A jury shall not return a special verdict under section 2 of the Trial of Lunatics Act 1883 (acquittal on ground of insanity) except on the written or oral evidence of two or more registered medical practitioners at least one of whom is duly approved.

In a similar vein, section 4(6) of the Criminal Procedure (Insanity) Act 1964 provides that a court is not to make a finding of unfitness to plead 'except on the written or oral evidence of two or more registered medical practitioners at least one of whom is duly approved'.

Psychiatric injury may constitute 'actual bodily harm' for the purpose of the offence of assault occasioning actual bodily harm under section 47 of the Offences Against the Person Act 1861. Although not expressly required by section 47, it has been held that, if psychiatric injury were relied on as the basis of a section 47 prosecution, it is essential that expert evidence be adduced. The Court of Appeal stated in *R v Morris*: 'in the absence of psychiatric evidence supporting the prosecution case (1) that the victim's symptoms other than pain amounted to psychological illness or injury and (2) that the pains experienced were the result of the appellant's (non-physical) assault, the case should not have been allowed to go before the jury'.[27]

2.2 *Mens Rea*, Defences, and Credibility

To what extent is expert opinion evidence admissible on the issues of the *mens rea* of the accused, defences raised by the accused, and the credibility of witnesses?

---

[27] [1998] 1 Cr App R 386, 395.

2.2.1 *Mens Rea*

The relevant principle governing the admissibility of expert evidence on the issue of *mens rea* was stated in *R v Chard*:

> ... one purpose of jury trials is to bring into the jury box a body of men and women who are able to judge ordinary day-to-day questions by their own standards, that is, the standards in the eyes of the law of theoretically ordinary reasonable men and women. That is something which they are well able by their ordinary experience to judge for themselves. Where the matters in issue go outside that experience and they are invited to deal with someone supposedly abnormal, for example, supposedly suffering from insanity or diminished responsibility, then plainly in such a case they are entitled to the benefit of expert evidence. But where ... they are dealing with someone who by concession was on the medical evidence entirely normal, it seems to this Court abundantly plain, on first principles of the admissibility of expert evidence, that it is not permissible to call a witness, whatever his personal experience, merely to tell the jury how he thinks an accused man's mind—assumedly a normal mind—operated at the time of the alleged crime with reference to the crucial question of what that man's intention was.[28]

Chard was distinguished in *R v Toner* where it was considered that expert evidence on the possible effect of mild hypoglycemia on the ability to form an intent was admissible, just as medical evidence on the effect of a drug on the ability to form an intent would be: 'These are matters outside the ordinary experience of jurors. They cannot bring to bear their own judgment without the assistance of expert evidence ... '.[29]

In *R v Masih*,[30] the Court of Appeal considered that expert evidence would generally be admissible on the issue of *mens rea* in the case of defendants coming into the class of mental defective with an IQ of 69 and below. This was to enable the jury to be enlightened on a matter which was presumably outside their experience. The Court of Appeal in *R v Reynolds*[31] took a similar view.

2.2.2 Provocation

In the classic, if controversial, case of *R v Turner*, the Court of Appeal stated:

> Jurors do not need psychiatrists to tell them how ordinary folk who are not suffering from any mental illness are likely to react to the stresses and strains of life. It follows that the proposed evidence was not admissible to establish that the defendant was likely to have been provoked.[32]

Similar views on the admissibility of expert opinion evidence on the issue of provocation were expressed by Lord Simon of Glaisdale in *R v Camplin*.[33] In a similar vein, the

---

[28] (1972) 56 Cr App R 268, 270–1 (decision of 1971).

[29] (1991) 93 Cr App R 382, 387 (decision of 1991). See also *R v Coles* [1995] 1 Cr App R 157.

[30] [1986] Crim LR 395.   [31] [1989] Crim LR 220.

[32] [1975] QB 834, 841–2. See generally R D Mackay, A M Colman, and P Thornton, 'The Admissibility of Expert Psychological and Psychiatric Testimony' in A Heaton-Armstrong, E Shepherd, and D Wolchover (eds), *Analysing Witness Testimony: A Guide for Legal Practitioners and Other Professionals* (1999); M Redmayne, *Expert Evidence and Criminal Justice* (2001) Ch 6.

[33] [1978] AC 705, 727. Thus, 'problems can arise in directing the jury about the use of ... psychiatric evidence, when, as sometimes happens, both [the defences of diminished responsibility and provocation] are run

psychiatric evidence sought to be adduced in *R v Hurst*[34] to support the defence of duress by threats, in circumstances where the defendant did not suffer from psychiatric illness or disorder, was held to be inadmissible. It is important, however, that cases like *Turner* and *Hurst* should not be read as positing a rule requiring the automatic inadmissibility of all expert opinion evidence sought to be adduced in support of the defences of provocation and duress. Much must depend on the facts of the particular case, and the precise purpose for which it is proposed to adduce the evidence. It is notable that the Court of Appeal suggested in *R v Ahluwalia* that psychiatric evidence would be admissible where a condition such as post-traumatic stress disorder is relied upon as the basis for the defence of provocation.[35] In a similar vein, 'evidence of a disorder of a type properly to be regarded as a mental illness or condition such as might render the defendant peculiarly vulnerable to pressure or suggestibility' is admissible on the issue of duress.[36]

2.2.3 Credibility

Immediately after the two sentences quoted above, in the text accompanying footnote 32, the Court in *Turner* continued:

> The same reasoning applies to its suggested admissibility on the issue of credibility. The jury had to decide what reliance they could put upon the defendant's evidence. He had to be judged as someone who was not mentally disordered. This is what juries are empanelled to do. The law assumes they can perform their duties properly. The jury in this case did not need, and should not have been offered the evidence of a psychiatrist to help them decide whether the defendant's evidence was truthful.[37]

Thus expert opinion evidence is, in general, inadmissible on the issue of a witness's credibility.[38] As an application of this principle:

> . . . the Crown cannot call a witness of fact and then, without more, call a psychologist or psychiatrist to give reasons why the jury should regard that witness as reliable.

in tandem': G J Durston, 'Expert Opinion Evidence in Criminal Trials: A Review of the Current Position' (1996) 160 *Justice of the Peace* 837, 838.

[34] [1995] 1 Cr App R 82.

[35] [1992] 4 All ER 889, 898. See also the decision of the High Court of Australia in *Osland v R* [1998] HCA 75, which appears to permit expert evidence where 'battered woman syndrome' is relied upon as the basis of the defence of provocation or self-defence. See generally B A Hocking, 'A Tale of Two Experts: The Australian High Court Takes a Cautious Stand' (2000) 64 *Journal of Criminal Law* 245.

[36] *R v Huckerby* [2004] EWCA Crim 3251, [103].

[37] [1975] QB 834, 842. *Lowery v R* [1974] AC 85 was considered 'to have been decided on its special facts. We do not consider that it is an authority for the proposition that in all cases psychologists and psychiatrists can be called to prove the probability of the accused's veracity. If any such rule was applied in our courts, trial by psychiatrists would be likely to take the place of trial by jury and magistrates. We do not find that prospect attractive and the law does not at present provide for it' ([1975] QB 834, 842).

[38] And see generally *Re N (A Minor)* [1996] 4 All ER 225 and *Re M and R (Minors)* [1996] 4 All ER 239. It is interesting to note that the reluctance of English law to admit expert evidence on the issue of credibility is not mirrored in all jurisdictions; on the practice in Germany see J Hunter and K Cronin, *Evidence, Advocacy and Ethical Practice: A Criminal Trial Commentary* (1995) 363–4.

... if the defence propose to call an expert witness to say that a witness of fact for the Crown should be regarded as unreliable due to some mental abnormality outwith the jury's experience, then, depending on the precise issue, it may be open to the Crown to call an expert in rebuttal, or even (anticipating the defence expert) as part of the prosecution case. It may even be open to the Crown to rebut by expert evidence a case put only in cross-examination that a prosecution witness is unreliable in a particular respect arising from mental abnormality. Much may depend upon the nature of the abnormality and of the cross-examination. If such evidence is admitted, great care would need to be taken to restrict the expert opinion to meeting the specific challenge and not to allow it to extend to 'oath-helping'.[39]

Where, however, the suggestion is that a witness is *incapable* of telling the truth because of mental illness, *medical*[40] evidence may be permitted:

Human evidence ... is subject to many cross-currents such as partiality, prejudice, self-interest and, above all, imagination and inaccuracy. Those are matters with which the jury, helped by cross-examination and common sense, must do their best. But when a witness through physical (in which I include mental) disease or abnormality is not capable of giving a true or reliable account to the jury, it must surely be allowable for medical science to reveal this vital hidden fact to them. ... it must ... be allowable to call medical evidence of mental illness which makes a witness incapable of giving reliable evidence, whether through the existence of delusions or otherwise.[41]

It may be doubted whether there really is a clear-cut distinction between lack of credibility as a result of *incapacity* to tell the truth because of mental illness, and lack of credibility as a result of such factors as partiality, prejudice, self-interest, imagination, or inaccuracy.

The Court of Appeal has, however, noted that in recent times 'there has been a greater willingness to accept medical expert evidence on the issue of the credibility of a witness'. That said, it is 'necessary to take into account the importance of the evidence that the witness gives. If the evidence of the witness is of little significance to the issues at the trial, the admission of expert evidence is unlikely to be justified.'[42] It is not essential for the expert evidence to be based on an examination of the witness:

... while, of course, the court will carefully scrutinise medical evidence before deciding whether it should be admitted, the absence of an examination of a witness or defendant concerned cannot be decisive in determining the admissibility of the expert evidence. The Court has to determine whether the evidence could be considered credible evidence by the jury as to an abnormality from which the witness suffered at the time of giving evidence and which might mean that the jury would not attach the weight it would otherwise do to the witness's evidence. The absence of an examination by the expert goes to the weight to be attached to the expert's opinion and not to the admissibility of that opinion. What a court must be on its guard against is

---

39 *R v Robinson* [1994] 3 All ER 346, 352.

40 See also *R v MacKenney* (1983) 76 Cr App R 271 (decision of 1981).

41 *Toohey v Metropolitan Police Commissioner* [1965] AC 595, 608 per Lord Pearce.

42 *R v Pinfold* [2003] EWCA Crim 3643, [2004] 2 Cr App R 5 (p 32), [15]. See generally P Roberts, 'Towards the Principled Reception of Expert Evidence of Witness Credibility in Criminal Trials' (2004) 8 *International Journal of Evidence and Proof* 215.

any attempt to detract from the jury's task of finding for themselves what evidence to believe. The court should therefore not allow evidence to be placed before the jury which does not allege any medical abnormality as the basis for the evidence of a witness being approached with particular caution by the jury. Ultimately, it remains the jury's task to decide for themselves whether they believe a witness' testimony.[43]

2.2.4 Evaluation

The general approach of the courts to the admissibility of expert opinion evidence on the issues of the *mens rea* of the accused, defences raised by the accused, and the credibility of witnesses, may be easily criticized. As Mackay and Colman argue:

In decisions regarding admissibility, the crucial question ought to be whether or not the expert evidence could make a significant contribution to the jury's understanding of the accused's state of mind. This must depend, of course, on the judge's assessment of the probative value of the evidence. If the expert evidence points to an abnormal state of mind or personality *of any degree* on the defendant's part at the time of the alleged offence, then we submit that the court ought to exercise its discretion in favour of admitting the evidence. There are many abnormal states of mind brought about by situational forces . . . which, although they do not involve mental disorders in any medical sense, none the less lie demonstrably beyond the understanding of ordinary people, and in relation to which expert evidence could therefore contribute significantly to a jury's understanding. . . . evidence on such matters ought in our view to be admitted, for to exclude it might deprive the jury of evidence that could help them to understand the defendant's state of mind at the material time.[44]

That the orthodox approach of the English courts as encapsulated in *Turner* cannot withstand close scrutiny has been recognized in the High Court of Australia:

[The approach] assumes that 'ordinary' or 'normal' has some clearly understood meaning and, as a corollary, that the distinction between normal and abnormal is well recognized. Further, it assumes that the commonsense of jurors is an adequate guide to the conduct of people who are 'normal' even though they may suffer from some relevant disability. And it assumes that the expertise of psychiatrists (or, in the present case, psychologists) extends only to those who are 'abnormal'. None of these assumptions will stand close scrutiny.[45]

The view has been taken in the High Court of Australia that, while the possibility of *impaired memory* as a consequence of alcoholism or substance abuse 'is a matter well within the experience of ordinary persons', 'the experience of ordinary persons is not such that most will know the mental state of a person who suffers some *mental impairment* in consequence of alcoholism or substance abuse'.[46] Equally, while mere anti-social behaviour may well be within the experience of ordinary persons, this is not true

---

[43] *R v Pinfold* [2003] EWCA Crim 3643, [2004] 2 Cr App R 5 (p 32), [16].

[44] R D Mackay and A M Colman, 'Excluding Expert Evidence: A Tale of Ordinary Folk and Common Experience' [1991] *Criminal Law Review* 800, 809 (italics in original).

[45] *Murphy v R* (1989) 167 CLR 94, 111 per Mason CJ and Toohey J. See generally J Hunter and J Bargen, 'Diminished Responsibility: "Abnormal" Minds, Abnormal Murderers and What the Doctor Said' in S M H Yeo (ed), *Partial Excuses to Murder* (1990).   [46] *Farrell v R* [1998] HCA 50, [11] (italics added).

of an anti-social personality disorder which renders the person in question inherently less truthful than the average person.[47]

Even in England and Wales, however, there are signs that the Court of Appeal's questionable remarks in *Turner* are being gradually diluted. In *R v Strudwick*, for example, the Court of Appeal observed:

> It is not suggested here that the appellant is suffering from a mental illness, but that is not in itself conclusive against the admission of this evidence. The law is in a state of development in this area. There may well be other mental conditions about which a jury might require expert assistance in order to understand and evaluate their effect on the issues in a case.[48]

It is to be noted that the expert opinion evidence sought to be adduced on matters such as *mens rea*, defences, and credibility is often exculpatory evidence sought to be introduced by defendants in their defence. This ought, one might argue, to be a factor favouring the admissibility of the evidence.

2.3 Confessions

Similar principles are applied in determining whether the jury in a criminal case should be permitted to hear expert opinion evidence on the issue of the reliability of a confession. In *R v Weightman*, such evidence was held to be inadmissible on the basis that the defendant, although 'histrionic, theatrical and likely to say things to draw attention to herself', did not have a personality 'beyond the experience of normal non-medical people'. The jury, it was said, 'would not have been helped by having a psychiatrist talking about "emotional superficiality" and "impaired capacity to develop and sustain deep or enduring relationships"'.[49] Where, however, the evidence indicates a mental disorder, different considerations apply. The Court of Appeal noted in late 2004 that 'this court has long recognised an exception in the case of "out of court" confessions where there is evidence of a disorder of a type properly to be regarded as a mental illness or condition such as might render the defendant peculiarly vulnerable to pressure or suggestibility'.[50] Thus:

> ... the expert evidence of a psychiatrist or a psychologist may properly be admitted if it is to the effect that a defendant is suffering from a condition not properly described as mental illness, but from a personality disorder so severe as properly to be categorised as mental disorder. ... such evidence is admissible on the issue whether what a defendant has said in a confession or admission was reliable and therefore likely to have been true.
>
> We emphasise that the occasions on which such evidence will properly be admissible will probably be rare. This decision is not to be construed as an open invitation to every defendant who repents of having confessed and seeks to challenge the truth of his confession to seek the aid of a psychiatrist.[51]

---

[47] Ibid, [12].   [48] (1994) 99 Cr App R 326, 332 (decision of 1993).
[49] (1991) 92 Cr App R 291, 297 (decision of 1990).   [50] *R v Huckerby* [2004] EWCA Crim 3251, [103].
[51] *R v Ward* [1993] 2 All ER 577, 641.

In *R v O'Brien*[52] the Court of Appeal gave detailed consideration to the admissibility of expert evidence on the issue of whether a mental disorder might render a confession unreliable. The Court noted that 'an anti social personality disorder does not necessarily mean that the defendant is a compulsive liar or fantasist or that his confession . . . might be unreliable'. There must be

> defined limits for the case in which expert evidence . . . may be used. First the abnormal disorder must not only be of the type which might render a confession . . . unreliable, there must also be a very significant deviation from the norm shown. . . . Second, there should be a history pre-dating the making of the admissions . . . which is not based solely on a history given by the subject, which points to or explains the abnormality or abnormalities.
>
> If such evidence is admitted, the jury must be directed that they are not obliged to accept such evidence. They should consider it if they think it right to do so, as throwing light on the personality of the defendant and bringing to their attention aspects of that personality of which they might otherwise have been unaware.

Similar principles apply in relation to the admissibility of expert opinion evidence in a voir dire hearing held to determine whether a confession should be excluded from evidence.[53]

2.4 Psychological Autopsies

R v Gilfoyle concerned the admissibility of evidence of a 'psychological autopsy' in a prosecution for murder in which the defendant contended that the victim, his wife, had committed suicide. The evidence consisted of the opinion of a psychologist who, after considering, *inter alia*, the 'suicide note', diary, and other documents written by the deceased, and the views of the defendant and his family, concluded that there was 'convincing support for the deceased having taken her own life'.[54] Holding this evidence to be inadmissible, the Court noted:

> The use of psychological profiling as an aid to police investigation is one thing, but its use as a means of proof in court is another. Psychiatric evidence as to the state of mind of a defendant, witness or deceased falling short of mental illness may . . . be admissible in some cases when based for example, on medical records and/or recognised criteria . . . But the present academic status of psychological autopsies is not . . . such as to permit them to be admitted as a basis for expert opinion before a jury.

The Court 'very much doubt[ed] whether assessing levels of happiness or unhappiness is a task for an expert rather than jurors and none of the points which he makes about the "suicide" notes is outwith the experience of a jury'.[55]

---

[52]   *The Times*, 16 Feb 2000 (transcript from Smith Bernal).

[53]   See *R v Everett* [1988] Crim LR 826; *R v Silcott, The Times*, 9 Dec 1991; *R v Heaton* [1993] Crim LR 593 (expert opinion evidence inadmissible because there was no suggestion of mental handicap or retardation, and the defendant was within the normal range of intelligence albeit towards the lower end of it); *R v Walker* [1998] Crim LR 211.   [54]   [2001] 2 Cr App R 5 (p 57), [23].

[55]   Ibid, [25].

2.5 Obscenity

In *R v Stamford*, where the defendant was charged with posting packets containing indecent articles, the Court of Appeal held that 'evidence is not admissible on the issue whether a particular article is indecent or not, or whether it is obscene or not. That issue is a matter entirely for the jury, and it is one which they must decide without ... the assistance of persons who may have views on the matter, or might be able to speak as to the effect on them of the article in question.'[56] This may be compared, however, with the earlier case of *DPP v A & BC Chewing Gum Ltd*,[57] where the defendant was charged with publishing for gain some obscene cards, which were sold with packets of bubble gum. Evidence of experts in child psychiatry about what effect the cards would be likely to have on children was held by the Divisional Court to be admissible. The Court thought that, if adults had been at issue, expert opinion evidence might have been unnecessary, but in the case of children, such evidence was admissible, because the trier of fact would require all the assistance which it could get in considering the effect of the publication on children. The authority of this case is perhaps somewhat doubtful: the Court of Appeal in *Stamford* described it as 'a very special case',[58] and doubts about it were expressed by Viscount Dilhorne in *DPP v Jordan*.[59] More recently, however, it has been referred to seemingly approvingly by the Court of Appeal:

> In cases involving children, expert medical and psychiatric evidence from paediatricians and allied disciplines is often quite indispensable to the court. As Lord Parker CJ said in *DPP v A & BC Chewing Gum Ltd* [1967] 2 All ER 504 at 506, [1968] 1 QB 159 at 165, when dealing with children, the court needs 'all the help [it] can get'. But that dependence in no way compromises the fact that the final decision in the case is the judge's and his alone.[60]

2.6 Age

At issue in *R v Land*[61] was a prosecution under section 1(1)(c) of the Protection of Children Act 1978 for possessing indecent photographs of children. At the time, a 'child' for the purposes of this provision was either a person under 16 or a person who appeared, from the evidence as a whole, to have been under 16 at the material time. The Court of Appeal held expert evidence to be inadmissible on the question whether the prosecution had established that the person in the photograph was under 16:

> The purpose of expert evidence is to assist the court with information which is outside the normal experience and knowledge of the judge or jury. Perhaps the only certainty which applies to

---

[56] [1972] 2 QB 391, 398.   [57] [1968] 1 QB 159.   [58] [1972] 2 QB 391, 397.

[59] [1977] AC 699, 722. See also F E Raitt, 'A New Criterion for the Admissibility of Scientific Evidence: The Metamorphosis of Helpfulness' (1998) 1 *Current Legal Issues* 153, 159: 'The judicial reasoning [in *A & BC Chewing Gum Ltd*] is fallacious. If adult jurors are deemed not to need expert assistance in relation to the effects of obscene pictures on adults on the grounds that, as adults themselves, they are fully cognizant with the effects of obscenity on all adults, then it is illogical to argue for an exception in the case of children. For indeed all adult jurors have also experienced childhood.'   [60] *Re M and R (Minors)* [1996] 4 All ER 239, 249.

[61] [1998] 1 Cr App R 301.

the problem in this case is that each individual reaches puberty in his or her own time. For each the process is unique and the jury is as well placed as an expert to assess any argument addressed to the question whether the prosecution has established as it must before there can be a conviction, that the person depicted in the photograph is under 16 years old.[62]

It has been noted that when 'assessing a child's age, . . . it is surely not inconceivable that in a difficult case, perhaps involving children of backgrounds unfamiliar to the jury, an expert's evidence might prove of assistance, and it is perhaps questionable whether the court should have expressed its view on the inadmissibility of such evidence in quite such categorical terms'.[63]

2.7 DNA Evidence and Evidence of Probabilities

DNA evidence[64] can be an extremely powerful tool in the prosecutorial armoury. The potential that such evidence may be misused is however (or perhaps consequently) very considerable. In *R v Doheny* the Court of Appeal provided detailed guidance on the issue of DNA evidence. It is worth quoting extensively from the judgment:

When a criminal leaves a stain of blood or semen at the scene of the crime it may prove possible to extract from that crime stain sufficient sections of DNA to enable a comparison to be made with the same sections extracted from a sample of blood provided by the suspect. . . .

. . .

It is easy, if one eschews rigorous analysis, to draw [a conclusion like the following]:

1. Only one person in a million will have a DNA profile which matches that of the crime stain.

2. The defendant has a DNA profile which matches the crime stain.

3. Ergo there is a million to one probability that the defendant left the crime stain and is guilty of the crime.

Such reasoning . . . is fallacious and it has earned the title of 'The Prosecutor's Fallacy'. . . .

Taking our example, the prosecutor's fallacy can be simply demonstrated. If one person in a million has a DNA profile which matches that obtained from the crime stain, then the suspect will be 1 of perhaps 26 men in the United Kingdom who share that characteristic. If no fact is known about the Defendant, other than that he was in the United Kingdom at the time of the crime the DNA evidence tells us no more than that there is a statistical probability that he was the criminal of 1 in 26.

The significance of the DNA evidence will depend critically upon what else is known about the suspect. If he has a convincing alibi at the other end of England at the time of the crime, it will appear highly improbable that he can have been responsible for the crime, despite his matching

---

[62] [1998] 1 Cr App R 301, 306.

[63] S Doran, J Jackson, and K Quinn, 'Evidence' [1998] *All ER Annual Review* 225, 232.

[64] See generally G Cooke, 'Are We Still Mis-Using DNA Evidence?', *Archbold News*, 13 Apr 2000, 4; I W Evett, L A Foreman, G Jackson, and J A Lambert, 'DNA Profiling: A Discussion of Issues Relating to the Reporting of Very Small Match Probabilities' [2000] *Criminal Law Review* 341; M Goode, 'Some Observations on Evidence of DNA Frequency' (2002) 23 *Adelaide Law Review* 45; B Mahendra, 'The Lawyer's Guide to DNA Evidence in Criminal Cases' (2002) 152 *New Law Journal* 1110; S Watson, 'One in a Billion' (2004) 148 *Solicitors' Journal* 335; *DNA: 21st Century Crime Fighting Tool* (2003), available at http://www.homeoffice.gov.uk/docs2/dnacrimefightingtool.pdf.

DNA profile. If, however, he was near the scene of the crime when it was committed, or has been identified as a suspect because of other evidence which suggests that he may have been responsible for the crime, the DNA evidence becomes very significant. The possibility that two of the only 26 men in the United Kingdom with the matching DNA should have been in the vicinity of the crime will seem almost incredible and a comparatively slight nexus between the defendant and the crime, independent of the DNA, is likely to suffice to present an overall picture to the jury that satisfies them of the defendant's guilt.

...

When the scientist gives evidence it is important that he should not overstep the line which separates his province from that of the jury.

He will properly explain to the jury the nature of the match ('the matching DNA characteristics') between the DNA in the crime stain and the DNA in the blood sample taken from the defendant. He will properly, on the basis of empirical statistical data, give the jury the random occurrence ratio—the frequency with which the matching DNA characteristics are likely to be found in the population at large. Provided that he has the necessary data, and the statistical expertise, it may be appropriate for him then to say how many people with the matching characteristics are likely to be found in the United Kingdom—or perhaps in a more limited relevant sub-group, such as, for instance, the caucasian, sexually active males in the Manchester area.

This will often be the limit of the evidence which he can properly and usefully give. It will then be for the jury to decide, having regard to all the relevant evidence, whether they are sure that it was the defendant who left the crime stain, or whether it is possible that it was left by someone else with the same matching DNA characteristics.

The scientist should not be asked his opinion on the likelihood that it was the defendant who left the crime stain, nor when giving evidence should he use terminology which may lead the jury to believe that he is expressing such an opinion.

...

When the judge comes to sum-up, the jury are likely to need careful directions in respect of any issues of expert evidence and guidance to dispel any obfuscation that may have been engendered in relation to areas of expert evidence where no real issue exists. The judge should explain to the jury the relevance of the random occurrence ratio in arriving at their verdict and draw attention to the extraneous evidence which provides the context which gives that ratio its significance, and that which conflicts with the conclusion that the defendant was responsible for the crime stain. In so far as the random occurrence ratio is concerned, a direction along these lines may be appropriate, although any direction must always be tailored to the facts of the particular case:

> 'Members of the jury, if you accept the scientific evidence called by the Crown, this indicates that there are probably only four or five white males in the United Kingdom from whom that semen stain could have come. The defendant is one of them. If that is the position, the decision you have to reach, on all the evidence, is whether you are sure that it was the defendant who left that stain or whether it is possible that it was one of that other small group of men who share the same DNA characteristics.'[65]

---

[65] [1997] 1 Cr App R 369, 371–5. See also *Pringle v R* [2003] UKPC 9, [19]. See the critique of *Doheny* by M Redmayne, 'Presenting Probabilities in Court: The DNA Experience' (1997) 1 *International Journal of Evidence and Proof* 187, 209 ff. See also K Hunter, 'A New Direction on DNA?' [1998] *Criminal Law Review* 478; M Redmayne, 'Appeals to Reason' (2002) 65 *Modern Law Review* 19; V Rondinelli, 'Three Card Monty: Presenting DNA Statistical Evidence to Juries' (2002) 3 *Criminal Reports (6th)* 52.

More recently the Court of Appeal has remarked that in the 'matter of DNA evidence, which is nearly always important, judges should consider with great care the way in which they present the scientific evidence to the jury. They should not present mere speculative possibilities which, although they cannot be scientifically eliminated, are not supported by any positive evidence in a way which goes far to destroy the common-sense force of scientific evidence which defendants can genuinely rely upon.'[66]

The Court of Appeal has disapproved of attempts to lead evidence of Bayes' Theorem[67] before a jury. Very briefly, this involves a jury being invited to assign a numerical value to the likelihood that each particular item of evidence suggests that the defendant is guilty, and by multiplying these individual figures together to determine the overall likelihood of guilt. In *R v Adams* the Court of Appeal remarked:

> ... the attempt to determine guilt or innocence on the basis of a mathematical formula, applied to each separate piece of evidence, is simply inappropriate to the jury's task. Jurors evaluate evidence and reach a conclusion not by means of a formula, mathematical or otherwise, but by the joint application of their individual common sense and knowledge of the world to the evidence before them. ... to introduce Bayes Theorem, or any similar method, into a criminal trial plunges the jury into inappropriate and unnecessary realms of theory and complexity deflecting them from their proper task.[68]

In *R v Clark*,[69] expert evidence was presented to the effect that, because there was a one in 8,543 chance of an infant within a family dying as a result of SIDS (sudden infant death syndrome, or 'cot death'), the probability of two infants in the same family dying as a result of SIDS was accordingly about one in 73 million.[70] It was also said that, with about 700,000 live births annually in Great Britain, this might be expected to occur about once every 100 years.[71] The presentation of this evidence was disapproved by the Court of Appeal:

> Inherent in the evidence were dangers. The jury were required to return separate verdicts on the two counts but the 1 in 73 million figure encouraged consideration of the two counts together as a package. If the jury concluded that one or other death was not a SIDS case (whether from natural causes or from unnatural causes), then the chance that the other child's death was a SIDS case was 1 in 8,543 and the 1 in 73 million figure was wholly irrelevant.

---

[66] *R v Mitchell* [2004] EWCA Crim 1928, [16]. See also K Squibb-Williams, 'The New DNA Guidance' (2004) 154 *New Law Journal* 1693.

[67] See generally D Hodgson, 'A Lawyer Looks at Bayes' Theorem' (2002) 76 *Australian Law Journal* 109; C Jowett, 'Sittin' in the Dock with the Bayes' (2001) 151 *New Law Journal* 201; A Ligertwood, 'Avoiding Bayes in DNA Cases' (2003) 77 *Australian Law Journal* 317; M Redmayne, 'Objective Probability and the Assessment of Evidence' (2003) 2 *Law, Probability and Risk* 275; R Allen and M Redmayne (eds), 'Bayesianism and Juridical Proof' (1997) 1 *International Journal of Evidence and Proof: Special Issue*.

[68] [1996] 2 Cr App R 467, 481, 482. See also *R v Doheny* [1997] 1 Cr App R 369, 374–5 and *R v Adams (No 2)* [1998] 1 Cr App R 377, 384–5. On *Adams* and *Adams (No 2)*, see generally D Balding, 'Probable Cause?', *The Times Higher Education Supplement*, 24 Oct 1997, 23; B Robertson and T Vignaux, 'Explaining Evidence Logically' (1998) 148 *New Law Journal* 159; B Steventon, 'Statistical Evidence and the Courts—Recent Developments' (1998) 62 *Journal of Criminal Law* 176.

[69] [2003] EWCA Crim 1020, [2003] 2 FCR 447. See generally C Aitken, 'Conviction by Probability?' (2003) 153 *New Law Journal* 1153; D Dwyer, 'The Duties of Expert Witnesses of Fact and Opinion: *R v Clark (Sally)*' (2003) 7 *International Journal of Evidence and Proof* 264.   [70] $1/8,543 \times 1/8,543 = 1/72,982,849$.

[71] $73,000,000 \div 700,000 = 104$ approximately.

In any event, juries know from their own experience that cot deaths are rare. The 1 in 8,543 figure can do nothing to identify whether or not an individual case is one of those rare cases.

Generally juries would not need evidence to tell them that two deaths in a family are much rarer still. Putting the evidence of 1 in 73 million before the jury with its related statistic that it was the equivalent of a single occurrence of two such deaths in the same family once in a century was tantamount to saying that without consideration of the rest of the evidence one could be just about sure that this was a case of murder.[72]

But this would be an erroneous conclusion because the particular facts which produce a first SIDS death in a family may also be an operative factor in relation to a second SIDS death. It would be quite wrong therefore to apply statistical findings relating to the population as a whole to a family which has already suffered one SIDS death.

Certainly, empirical research has demonstrated that the assessment of probabilities causes real problems for lawyers, even those who have received considerable amounts of formal mathematical education.[73]

More recently, in *R v Anthony*, the Court of Appeal made the following observations:

It is perhaps necessary to emphasise that we have no difficulty in understanding the proposition that nowadays two infant deaths from natural causes in the same family is a rare occurrence. The question is what safe inference, if any, may be drawn from that fact. It seems to us that no inference can safely be drawn without simultaneously giving full weight to the additional rarity that a mother would act so unnaturally as to smother two of her babies. We acknowledge that this catastrophe sometimes happens, but, unless that second fact is given equal weight with the first, any inference based on the first taken in isolation from the second is likely to be flawed.[74]

2.8 Foreign Law

Proof of the substance of foreign law is treated as a matter of expert evidence, in contrast with English law which is the subject of argument by counsel and which the judge is presumed to know. The Court of Appeal has noted:

In our judgment, the function of the expert witness on foreign law can be summarised as follows:—

(1) to inform the Court of the relevant contents of the foreign law; identifying statutes or other legislation and explaining where necessary the foreign Court's approach to their construction;

(2) to identify judgments or other authorities, explaining what status they have as sources of the foreign law; and

---

[72] [2003] EWCA Crim 1020, [2003] 2 FCR 447, [173]–[175].

[73] P Hawkins and A Hawkins, 'Lawyers' Probability Misconceptions and the Implications for Legal Education' (1998) 18 *Legal Studies* 316. The decisions of the Court of Appeal in *Adams* and *Adams (No 2)* may be compared with the classic Californian case of *People v Collins* 438 P 2d 33 (1968), where the Supreme Court of California was less dismissive than the English Court of Appeal of the concept of evidence of mathematical probability, but found on the facts of the case that such evidence had been improperly introduced.

[74] [2005] EWCA Crim 952, [77].

(3) where there is no authority directly in point, to assist the English judge in making a finding as to what the foreign Court's ruling would be if the issue was to arise for decision there.

The first and second of these require the exercise of judgment in deciding what the issues are and what statutes or precedents are relevant to them, but it is only the third which gives much scope in practice for opinion evidence, which is the basic role of the expert witness. And it is important, in our judgment, to note the purpose for which the evidence is given. This is to pre-dict the likely decision of a foreign court, not to press upon the English judge the witness's per-sonal views as to what the foreign law might be.[75]

2.9 Further Illustrations

Keeping in mind the twin issues of necessity and reliability, a number of further illus-trations of the courts' approach to the admissibility of expert evidence may now be pro-vided. In *R v Inch*[76] the defendant was accused of wounding the victim by striking him with a martial arts instrument. His defence was that the wound was caused when the victim head-butted him. At issue was the admissibility in evidence of the opinion of a medical orderly, who had attended the victim, that the wound, because of its depth and shape, had been caused by a blow from an instrument rather than by a collision of heads. The Courts-Martial Appeal Court held that this evidence was inadmissible: any evidence about the nature of the wound ought to have been given by someone qualified to express a professional opinion.

The Court of Appeal has noted 'that a court should be slow to find a professionally qualified man guilty of a breach of his duty of skill and care towards a client (or third party), without evidence from those within the same profession as to the standard expected on the facts of the case and the failure of the professionally qualified man to measure up to that standard. It is not an absolute rule ... but, unless it is an obvious case, in the absence of the relevant expert evidence the claim will not be proved.'[77]

At issue in *R v Theodosi*[78] was the opinion of a police officer who had attended an accident scene and carried out an investigation involving the observation of markings in the road and various measurements. The officer in question was qualified at an advanced level in the investigation and reconstruction of road accidents, and the inter-pretation of evidence found at the scenes of such accidents. The officer's opinion was as follows:

The onus for this accident lies wholly with Mr Theodosi, the driver of the Peugeot. We have a scen-ario of three young men, two of whom were driving very powerful cars. Mr Theodosi, who was the last vehicle of the three, may have allowed himself to be drawn into a manoeuvre beyond his limited driving experience in that he had to keep up with his friends, or he may have wanted to show off to the passengers that he had in his vehicle. Either way Mr Theodosi's actions in

---

[75] *MacMillan Inc v Bishopsgate Investment Trust Plc*, CA, 4 Nov 1998; transcript from Smith Bernal.
[76] (1990) 91 Cr App R 51 (decision of 1989).
[77] *Sansom v Metcalfe Hambleton & Co* [1998] PNLR 542, 549.   [78] [1993] RTR 179.

overtaking two other vehicles at a speed in the region of twice the legal speed limit for the road, amounts in my opinion to nothing less than a wanton act putting himself and others at risk.[79]

The Court of Appeal held that, because 'the reference by the officer to peer groups was wholly outside his expertise', and because to admit the evidence would be to usurp the function of the jury, the opinion evidence in question was inadmissible.[80] This may be compared with the earlier decision of the Court in *R v Oakley*,[81] where it was held that a police constable who had 15 years' experience in the traffic division, and had passed a qualifying examination as an accident investigator, had been rightly permitted to give expert opinion evidence on how a road accident had occurred. Similarly, in *R v Hodges*,[82] evidence of a police officer in relation to the normal manner of supply of heroin, the usual price, and the quantity of drugs that would constitute a supply for personal use was held to have been correctly admitted as expert evidence.[83]

The issue of expert evidence in the context of voice identification is noteworthy, with a distinction drawn between such identification and visual identification. 'Expert evidence is rarely, if ever, admitted in cases of visual identification. The tribunal of fact is considered to be in as good a position to assess CCTV footage or video tapes or photographs as witnesses...'. However, 'expert evidence is receivable in cases of voice identification'.[84] In *R v Robb*, a case concerning voice identification, the Court of Appeal held that the evidence of an expert was admissible even though the auditory technique employed by him to identify the defendant's voice was not supplemented by acoustic analysis:

We do not doubt that his judgment, based on close attention to voice quality, voice pitch and the pronunciation of vowels and consonants, would have a value significantly greater than that of the ordinary untutored layman, as the judgment of a hand-writing expert is superior to that of the man in the street. Dr Baldwin's reliance on the auditory technique must, on the evidence, be regarded as representing a minority view in his profession but he had reasons for his preference and on the facts of this case at least he was not shown to be wrong.[85]

More recently, in *R v O'Doherty*, the Court of Appeal of Northern Ireland has effectively sidelined *Robb*. The Court observed: 'Time has moved on.... prosecutors in the rest of Europe invariably present auditory analysis... and quantitative acoustic analysis...'.[86] Thus:

... in the present state of scientific knowledge no prosecution should be brought in Northern Ireland in which one of the planks is voice identification given by an expert which is solely confined to auditory analysis. There should also be expert evidence of acoustic analysis...[87]

We make three exceptions to this general statement. Where the voices of a known group are being listened to and the issue is, 'which voice has spoken which words' or where there are rare

[79] Ibid, 181.   [80] Ibid, 184.   [81] (1980) 70 Cr App R 7 (decision of 1979).

[82] [2003] EWCA Crim 290, [2003] 2 Cr App R 15 (p 247).

[83] In addition, it would appear permissible for a police officer to testify that items found at the defendant's premises are of a type frequently found in the home of drug dealers: *R v Jeffries* [1997] Crim LR 819.

[84] *R v O'Doherty* [2002] NI 263, [2003] 1 Cr App R 5 (p 77), [63].

[85] (1991) 93 Cr App R 161, 166 (decision of 1991).

[86] [2002] NI 263, [2003] 1 Cr App R 5 (p 77), [57].   [87] Ibid, [59].

characteristics which render a speaker identifiable—but this may beg the question—or the issue relates to the accent or dialect of the speaker . . . acoustic analysis is not necessary.[88]

. . . if evidence of voice recognition is relied on by the prosecution, the jury should be allowed to listen to a tape-recording on which the recognition is based, assuming that the jury have heard the accused giving evidence. It also seems to us that the jury may listen to a tape-recording of the voice of the suspect in order to assist them in evaluating expert evidence and in making up their own minds as to whether the voice on the tapes is the voice of the defendant.[89]

Evidence of 'facial mapping' sought to be adduced to assist the jury to determine whether the person shown on security photographs was the defendant was considered in *R v Stockwell*. The Court of Appeal held:

Where, for example, there is a clear photograph and no suggestion that the subject has changed his appearance, a jury could usually reach a conclusion without help. Where, as here, however, it is admitted that the appellant had grown a beard shortly before his arrest, and it is suggested further that the robber may have been wearing clear spectacles and a wig for disguise, a comparison of photograph and defendant may not be straightforward. In such circumstances we can see no reason why expert evidence, if it can provide the jury with information and assistance they would otherwise lack, should not be given.[90]

A similar approach was taken in *R v Clarke* to evidence of 'video superimposition mapping', which was described succinctly by the Court of Appeal as follows:

Photographs from the scene in the bank were transferred to high quality video tape. The same was done with police identification photos of the appellant. Each was blown-up to about the same size. The machine was set to display both the head of the robber and the head of the suspect in exactly the same position on the television screen. Dr Vanezis then wiped a line up and down the screen: above the line was the appellant's face, below it was the face of the robber. As the line moved up and down so more of the one face and less of the other would be seen. Then the process was repeated but with a vertical line from side to side. Having compared the two photographs in this way, Dr Vanezis concluded that the appellant and the robber were the same man.[91]

The Court concluded:

This is clearly a case like *Stockwell* where the comparison was not an entirely straightforward one. The process of enhancement that was used here enabled the jury to appreciate the similarity in configuration. . . . there was similarity of configuration between the ears, and the same point could be made in respect of the eyebrows. It is, therefore, not right to say that expert evidence could not have played a useful role here in assisting the jury in connection with the issue of identity.[92]

---

[88] [2002] NI 263, [2003] 1 Cr App R 5 (p 77), [60].

[89] Ibid, [63]. See generally W E O'Brian Jr, 'Court Scrutiny of Expert Evidence: Recent Decisions Highlight the Tensions' (2003) 7 *International Journal of Evidence and Proof* 172; D Ormerod, 'Sounding Out Expert Voice Identification' [2002] *Criminal Law Review* 771.   [90] (1993) 97 Cr App R 260, 263–4 (decision of 1993).

[91] [1995] 2 Cr App R 425, 428.

[92] Ibid, 431. See generally M C Bromby, 'At Face Value?' (2003) 153 *New Law Journal* 302. See also *R v Meads* [1996] Crim LR 519 on expert evidence as to handwriting.

Evidence from an expert with lip-reading skills was considered in *R v Luttrell*,[93] where the Court of Appeal said:

> Lip-reading is a well recognised skill and lip-reading from video footage is no more than an application of that skill. It may increase the difficulty of the task, as may the speaker's facial features and the angle of the observation, but the nature of the skill remains the same.... It does not of course follow that, in every case where lip-reading evidence is tendered, it will be admissible. The decision in each case is likely to be highly fact sensitive. For example, a video may be of such poor quality or the view of the speaker's face so poor that no reliable interpretation is possible. There may also be cases where the interpreting witness is not sufficiently skilled. A judge may properly take into account: whether consistency with extrinsic facts confirms or inconsistency casts doubt on the reliability of an interpretation; whether information provided to the lip-reader might have coloured the reading; and whether the probative effect of the evidence depends on the interpretation of a single word or phrase or on the whole thrust of the conversation. In the light of such considerations, (which are not intended to be exhaustive) a judge may well rule on the voire dire that any lip-reading evidence proffered should not be admitted before the jury. As to the skill of such a witness, we have been told that there are presently only four witnesses in this country ... who undertake this kind of forensic work. As and when new witnesses appear, it will be entirely appropriate, when they first give evidence, for their expertise to be challenged and tested by reference, in appropriate cases, to disclosed material bearing on their skill or lack of it.[94]

> ... lip reading evidence requires a warning from the judge as to its limitations and the concomitant risk of error, not least because it will usually be introduced through an expert who may not be completely accurate:... lip reading evidence will, on occasion, fall significantly short of perfection. That imperfection does not render the material inadmissible,... but it does necessitate a careful and detailed direction.... its precise terms will be fact-dependent, but in most, if not all cases, the judge should spell out to the jury the risk of mistakes as to the words that the lip reader believes were spoken; the reasons why the witness may be mistaken; and the way in which a convincing, authoritative and truthful witness may yet be a mistaken witness.

> Furthermore, the judge should deal with the particular strengths and weaknesses of the material in the instant case, carefully setting out the evidence, together with the criticisms that can properly be made of it because of other evidence. The jury should be reminded that the quality of the evidence will be affected by such matters as the lighting at the scene, the angle of the view in relation to those speaking, the distances involved, whether anything interfered with the observation, familiarity on the part of the lip-reader with the language spoken, the extent of the use of single syllable words, any awareness on the part of the expert witness of the context of the speech and whether the probative value of the evidence depends on isolated words or phrases or the general impact of long passages of conversation. However,... the precise terms of the direction will depend on the facts of the case, and the instruction to the jury in this [area] should never be given mechanistically.[95]

---

93 [2004] EWCA Crim 1344, [2004] 2 Cr App R 31 (p 520). See generally G Forlin and S Jackson, 'The Need to Test Expert Evidence', *Archbold News*, 24 July 2004, 5; S Jackson and G Forlin, 'Read My Lips' (2004) 154 *New Law Journal* 1146.   94 [2004] EWCA Crim 1344, [2004] 2 Cr App R 31 (p 520), [38].
95 Ibid, [44].

2.10 Other Jurisdictions

Extensive consideration was given to the issue of expert evidence in the landmark 1993 decision of the US Supreme Court in *Daubert v Merrell Dow Pharmaceuticals, Inc.*[96] *Daubert*, which was cited with apparent approval by the Court of Appeal in *R v Dallagher*,[97] contains valuable guidance on the sorts of considerations which may be taken into account in determining admissibility. At issue was rule 702 of the Federal Rules of Evidence, which prior to being amended in 2000 provided: 'If scientific, technical, or other specialized knowledge will assist the trier of fact to understand the evidence or to determine a fact in issue, a witness qualified as an expert by knowledge, skill, experience, training, or education, may testify thereto in the form of an opinion or otherwise.' The Supreme Court emphasized that a determination of admissibility under rule 702 was a flexible one;[98] many factors were relevant and thus the Court did 'not presume to set out a definitive checklist or test', but considered that 'some general observations' would be appropriate.[99]

First, can the theory or technique in question be, and has it been, tested?[100]

A second 'consideration is whether the theory or technique has been subjected to peer review and publication':

> Publication (which is but one element of peer review) is not a *sine qua non* of admissibility; it does not necessarily correlate with reliability, . . . and in some instances well-grounded but innovative theories will not have been published . . . Some propositions, moreover, are too particular, too new, or of too limited interest to be published. But submission to the scrutiny of the scientific community is a component of 'good science,' in part because it increases the likelihood that substantive flaws in methodology will be detected. . . . The fact of publication (or lack thereof) in a peer-reviewed journal thus will be a relevant, though not dispositive, consideration in assessing the scientific validity of a particular technique or methodology on which an opinion is premised.[101]

Thirdly, 'in the case of a particular scientific technique, the court ordinarily should consider the known or potential rate of error, . . . and the existence and maintenance of standards controlling the technique's operation'.[102]

Finally, has the theory or technique in question gained general acceptance? 'Widespread acceptance can be an important factor in ruling particular evidence admissible . . .'.[103]

It may be helpful to

> read the admissibility criteria set out in *Daubert* without unnecessary technicality and at a level of generality which brings out their good sense, along the following lines:
>
> 1. Is the science tried and tested in practice, or is it so far just a matter of speculation or hypothesis?

---

[96] 113 S Ct 2786 (1993).

[97] [2002] EWCA Crim 1903, [2003] 1 Cr App R 12 (p 195), [29]. See generally W E O'Brian Jr, 'Court Scrutiny of Expert Evidence: Recent Decisions Highlight the Tensions' (2003) 7 *International Journal of Evidence and Proof* 172.   [98] 113 S Ct 2786, 2797 (1993).

[99] Ibid, 2796.   [100] Ibid.   [101] Ibid, 2797.   [102] Ibid.   [103] Ibid.

2. Has the science been exposed to informed analysis and criticism, or has it been hidden away and insulated from critical scrutiny?

3. Where practical trials have been undertaken, how often do the empirical data bear out the theory, and, conversely, how often is the theory unconfirmed or even confounded when tested in practice?

4. How does the science rate in the expert opinion of other relevant practitioners?[104]

The Supreme Court confirmed in 1999 in a subsequent case, *Kumho Tire Co v Carmichael*, that the *Daubert* guidelines applied 'not only to testimony based on "scientific" knowledge, but also to testimony based on "technical" and "other specialized" knowledge'.[105] The Court reiterated that 'the trial judge must have considerable leeway in deciding in a particular case how to go about determining whether particular expert testimony is reliable'.[106]

As will have become clear from earlier discussion, it is a rule of English law that to be admitted, expert evidence must be necessary in the sense of addressing an issue which the jury is not competent to determine unaided. The usefulness of this rule may be questioned. The law may well make inaccurate assumptions about the ability of the trier of fact to cope without the expert evidence, an issue which is inherently incapable of accurate determination.[107] If that is the case, it is arguable that the admissibility test should focus on reliability rather than necessity. Indeed, this would appear to have been the approach taken to rule 702 of the US Federal Rules of Evidence even in its pre-2000 form, when it provided, in essence, for the admissibility of expert evidence *if it would assist the trier of fact* to understand the evidence in the case or to determine a fact in issue. In other words, expert evidence was admissible if it was considered to be necessary; if it would not

---

[104] P Roberts, 'Tyres with a "Y": An English Perspective on *Kumho Tire* and Its Implications for the Admissibility of Expert Evidence', accessible via http://www.law.qub.ac.uk/ice.   [105] 119 S Ct 1167, 1171 (1999).

[106] Ibid, 1176. See also *General Electric Co v Joiner* 522 US 136 (1997), where the US Supreme Court discussed the approach to be taken by an appellate court in reviewing a trial court's decision to admit or exclude expert testimony under *Daubert*. See generally, among numerous discussions of the post-*Daubert* position in the USA, D E Bernstein, 'Comment on *Kumho Tire*', available at http://www.law.umich.edu/thayer/berkumho.htm; E K Cheng and A H Yoon, 'Does *Frye* or *Daubert* Matter? A Study of Scientific Admissibility Standards' (2005) 91 *Virginia Law Review* 471; G Edmond, 'Deflating *Daubert*: *Kumho Tire Co v Carmichael* and the Inevitability of *General* Acceptance (*Frye*)' (2000) 23 *University of New South Wales Law Journal* 38; G Edmond, 'Judicial Representations of Scientific Evidence' (2000) 63 *Modern Law Review* 216, 227–33; S Ghosh, 'Comment on *Kumho Tire*', available at http://www.law.umich.edu/thayer/ghokumho.htm; M H Graham, 'The *Daubert* Dilemma: At Last a Viable Solution' (1998) 2 *International Journal of Evidence and Proof* 211 (which contains a discussion of the ambiguities inherent in the decision); C Nesson and J Demers, 'Gatekeeping: An Enhanced Foundational Approach to Determining the Admissibility of Scientific Evidence' (1998) 49 *Hastings Law Journal* 335; Note, 'Reliable Evaluation of Expert Testimony' (2003) 116 *Harvard Law Review* 2142; C Pamplin, 'Taking Experts out of the Court' (2004) 154 *New Law Journal* 1771; S Pearl and G Luxmoore, 'The Judge as Gatekeeper—A US Practice Worth Adopting' (1998) 148 *New Law Journal* 974; P Roberts, 'Tyres with a "Y": An English Perspective on *Kumho Tire* and Its Implications for the Admissibility of Expert Evidence', accessible via http://www.law.qub.ac.uk/ice; D G Savage, 'Putting the Brakes on Junk Analysis' [May 1999] *ABA Journal* 38; B M Sheldrick, 'Assessing Scientific Methodology in Toxic Tort Cases: *General Electric Co et al v Joiner*' (1999) 3 *International Journal of Evidence and Proof* 250; W C Smith, 'No Escape from Science' [Aug 2000] *ABA Journal* 60.

[107] See also F E Raitt, 'A New Criterion for the Admissibility of Scientific Evidence: The Metamorphosis of Helpfulness' (1998) 1 *Current Legal Issues* 153.

assist the trier of fact then it would be unnecessary. Despite this, the guidelines laid down in *Daubert* focused exclusively, as we have seen, on reliability concerns. Speculating about whether the trier of fact would be able to cope if the expert evidence were not adduced would appear not to have been a relevant consideration.

Subsequent to *Daubert* and *Kumho Tire*, rule 702 was expanded in 2000 to read:

> If scientific, technical, or other specialized knowledge will assist the trier of fact to understand the evidence or to determine a fact in issue, a witness qualified as an expert by knowledge, skill, experience, training, or education, may testify thereto in the form of an opinion or otherwise, if (1) the testimony is based upon sufficient facts or data, (2) the testimony is the product of reliable principles and methods, and (3) the witness has applied the principles and methods reliably to the facts of the case.

Thus reliability considerations are now formally incorporated within rule 702.

An approach involving an identification and consideration of all relevant factors clearly has more to commend it than an approach involving unclear or unarticulated reasoning. Odgers and Richardson have noted in the Australian[108] context:

> ... it may be more appropriate to see the issue as an exercise in balancing. There are recent decisions in Australia which suggest such an approach, one in which the test renders inadmissible an expert opinion if the benefits to be derived from the opinion are outweighed by the disadvantages associated with it. According to this approach, relevant considerations would include:
>
> • the reliability of the particular field of expertise;
> • the reliability of the application of that field of expertise to the particular issue;
> • the reliability of the expert's opinion (taking into account the expert's qualifications, experience, facilities and resources);
> • the likely capacity of the tribunal of fact to understand and assimilate the evidence, without being misled or simply deferring to the expert opinion;
> • the likely capacity of the tribunal of fact to properly determine the issue without the benefit of the expert opinion (thus, counter-intuitive expert testimony is more likely to be admitted than expert testimony which confirms common sense perceptions);

---

[108] See also *HG v R* [1999] HCA 2; *Velevski v R* [2002] HCA 4. On the position in Canada, see generally N Bala, 'R v D (D): The Supreme Court and Filtering of Social Science Knowledge About Children' (2001) 36 *Criminal Reports (5th)* 283; P Roberts, 'Expert Evidence in Canadian Criminal Proceedings: More Lessons from North America' (1998) 1 *Current Legal Issues* 175; B M Sheldrick, 'Expert Evidence, Sexual Assault, and the Testimony of Children: R v DD' (2001) 5 *International Journal of Evidence and Proof* 199. On South Africa see generally L Meintjes-Van der Walt, 'The Proof of the Pudding: The Presentation and Proof of Expert Evidence in South Africa' (2003) 47 *Journal of African Law* 88; L Meintjes-Van der Walt, 'Ruling on Expert Evidence in South Africa: A Comparative Analysis' (2001) 5 *International Journal of Evidence and Proof* 226. On Italy see D Dwyer, 'Changing Approaches to Expert Evidence in England and Italy', accessible via http://www.law.qub.ac.uk/ice. For a comparative study of England and Wales, the Netherlands, and South Africa, see L Meintjes-van der Walt, *Expert Evidence in the Criminal Justice Process: A Comparative Perspective* (2001). For a comparative study of the Netherlands and the USA see P van Kampen, 'Expert Evidence Compared' in M Malsch and J F Nijboer (eds), *Complex Cases: Perspectives on the Netherlands Criminal Justice System* (1999); P T C van Kampen, *Expert Evidence Compared: Rules and Practices in the Dutch and American Criminal Justice System* (1998).

- the importance of the issue to which the evidence relates;
- the likely court time utilised if the opinion is admitted;
- the danger that the focus of the trial will shift from the evidence of the facts in dispute to the conflict between the competing theories of the various expert witnesses; and
- whether the evidence is being led against a defendant in a criminal trial.[109]

In relation to the last consideration mentioned by Odgers and Richardson, one writer has gone so far as to argue that 'scientific evidence failing to satisfy [a standard of 'general acceptance'] should *always* be excluded when offered against the defendant in a criminal case'.[110]

3 Use of the Work of Others and the Rule against Hearsay

Suppose that a doctor seeks, in giving her opinion about a patient's condition, to base that opinion on accrued medical knowledge as well as on a questionnaire that was completed by the patient about his symptoms.[111] This scenario raises the following questions. To what extent may an expert base an opinion on the work of others? What are the implications of the rule against hearsay? These questions, previously governed by the common law,[112] are now addressed in the Criminal Justice Act 2003. Section 118(1) specifically preserves the 'rule of law under which in criminal proceedings an expert witness may draw on the body of expertise relevant to his field'. Furthermore, section 127 provides that an expert may base an opinion on a statement prepared by another[113] if the following four conditions are satisfied:

- the statement has been prepared for the purposes of the proceedings[114] or a criminal investigation from which the proceedings arise;[115]
- 'the person who prepared the statement had or may reasonably be supposed to have had personal knowledge of the matters stated';[116]
- appropriate notice is given that the expert will in evidence base an opinion on the statement;[117]

---

[109] S J Odgers and J T Richardson, 'Keeping Bad Science out of the Courtroom—Changes in American and Australian Expert Evidence Law' (1995) 18 *University of New South Wales Law Journal* 108, 126–7.

[110] A Stein, 'The Refoundation of Evidence Law' (1996) 9 *Canadian Journal of Law and Jurisprudence* 279, 331 (italics added). Contra R C Park, '*Daubert* on a Tilted Playing Field' (2003) 33 *Seton Hall Law Review* 1113.

[111] See R Taylor, M Wasik, and R Leng, *Blackstone's Guide to the Criminal Justice Act 2003* (2004) 161.

[112] *English Exporters v Eldonwall Ltd* [1973] Ch 415; *R v Abadom* [1983] 1 WLR 126; *H v Schering Chemicals* [1983] 1 WLR 143; *R v Hodges* [2003] EWCA Crim 290, [2003] 2 Cr App R 15 (p 247). See also *R v Jackson* [1996] 2 Cr App R 420. See generally A Ashworth and R Pattenden, 'Reliability, Hearsay Evidence and the English Criminal Trial' (1986) 102 *Law Quarterly Review* 292, 302–3.   [113] S 127(2).

[114] S 127(1)(a).   [115] S 127(6).   [116] S 127(1)(b).   [117] S 127(1)(c).

- 'the notice gives the name of the person who prepared the statement and the nature of the matters stated'.[118]

The statement is to be treated in the proceedings as evidence of what it states.[119]

Section 127 does not apply, however, 'if the court, on an application by a party to the proceedings, orders that it is not in the interests of justice that it should apply'.[120] The matters to be considered in deciding whether to make such an order include:

(a) the expense of calling as a witness the person who prepared the statement;

(b) whether relevant evidence could be given by that person which could not be given by the expert;

(c) whether that person can reasonably be expected to remember the matters stated well enough to give oral evidence of them.[121]

If section 127 were to be disapplied, the effect would be that the maker of the statement on which the expert relied would be required to be called as a witness as a precondition for the admissibility of the expert evidence.

4 'Ultimate Issues'

The common law may once have recognized a rule prohibiting an expert from giving an opinion on the very issue which the trier of fact is to determine. In civil proceedings the 'ultimate issue rule', as such a rule is known, has been expressly abolished by section 3 of the Civil Evidence Act 1972:

(1) Subject to any rules of court made in pursuance of this Act, where a person is called as a witness in any civil proceedings, his opinion on any relevant matter on which he is qualified to give expert evidence shall be admissible in evidence.

(2) ...

(3) In this section 'relevant matter' includes an issue in the proceedings in question.

In criminal cases the judiciary has tended to highlight the futility of an ultimate issue rule:

Whether an expert can give his opinion on what has been called the ultimate issue, has long been a vexed question. There is a school of opinion supported by some authority doubting whether he can ... On the other hand, if there is such a prohibition, it has long been more honoured in the breach than the observance ...

...

The rationale behind the supposed prohibition is that the expert should not usurp the functions of the jury. But since counsel can bring the witness so close to opining on the ultimate

---

[118] S 127(1)(d).   [119] S 127(3).   [120] S 127(4).   [121] S 127(5).

issue that the inference as to his view is obvious, the rule can only be . . . a matter of form rather than substance.[122]

Those who practise in the criminal courts see every day cases of experts being called on the question of diminished responsibility, and although technically the final question 'Do you think he was suffering from diminished responsibility?' is strictly inadmissible, it is allowed time and time again without any objection.[123]

The express abolition of any ultimate issue rule in criminal proceedings must be regarded as long overdue.

5. Expert Witnesses

5.1 Qualifications, Duties, and Responsibilities

The issue of determining whether expert witnesses are appropriately qualified was addressed by the Runciman Royal Commission:

75. Expert witnesses need to be identified as such by reference to their experience and qualifications. At present, this is a matter for the courts to assess and we think that it should continue to be so. The courts should be guided, where there is any doubt, by whether the witness possesses a professional qualification guaranteed by membership of the appropriate professional body or the possession of a relevant professional or vocational degree, diploma or certificate. We see no need for a system of statutory certification or accreditation of expert witnesses nor for the maintenance of a register of experts by a Government Department. We do, however, recommend that the professional bodies assist the courts in their task of assessment by maintaining a special register of their members who are suitably qualified to act as expert witness in particular areas of expertise. We do not see professional bodies as guaranteeing the competence of individuals. But they might be asked to give advice to legal representatives on the qualifications that witnesses should hold if they are to be considered expert in a particular field.[124]

In the light of evidence of dissatisfaction among solicitors with the competence of experts,[125] the attractiveness of this proposal cannot be doubted.

In view of the legal culture in which they operate, there are powerful reasons why an expert witness might choose to remain 'deferential' in court[126] or become partisan.[127]

---

[122] *R v Stockwell* (1993) 97 Cr App R 260, 265 (decision of 1993). See also, generally, *Re M and R (Minors)* [1996] 4 All ER 239, 251. The Supreme Court of Canada has stated that 'expert testimony is admissible even if it relates directly to the ultimate question which the trier of fact must answer': *R v R (D)* (1996) 107 CCC (3d) 289, 304.   [123] *DPP v A & BC Chewing Gum Ltd* [1968] 1 QB 159, 164.

[124] Royal Commission on Criminal Justice, *Report* (Cm 2263) (1993) 160–1. On the issue of accreditation see further P Cooper, 'Quality Checking the Experts' (2005) 155 *New Law Journal* 286; H Hallett, 'Expert Witnesses in the Courts of England and Wales' (2005) 79 *Australian Law Journal* 288, 294–5; A Keogh, 'Experts in the Dock' (2004) 154 *New Law Journal* 1762; M Solon, 'Experts: Amateurs or Accredited?' (2004) 154 *New Law Journal* 292.   [125] See 'Solicitors Condemn Failings of Expert Witnesses' (1998) 142 *Solicitors' Journal* 531.

[126] C A G Jones, *Expert Witnesses: Science, Medicine, and the Practice of Law* (1994) 126–7.

[127] *R v Ward* [1993] 2 All ER 577, 628: '. . . we have identified the cause of the injustice done to the appellant on the scientific side of the case as stemming from the fact that three senior forensic scientists at RARDE regarded

It is therefore important that the duties and responsibilities of expert witnesses are clearly appreciated. Rule 35.3 of the Civil Procedure Rules provides:

(1) It is the duty of an expert to help the court on the matters within his expertise.

(2) This duty overrides any obligation to the person from whom he has received instructions or by whom he is paid.

Further clarification of the duties of experts is provided in the Practice Direction:

1.2 Expert evidence should be the independent product of the expert uninfluenced by the pressures of litigation.

1.3 An expert should assist the court by providing objective, unbiased opinion on matters within his expertise, and should not assume the role of an advocate.

1.4 An expert should consider all material facts, including those which might detract from his opinion.

1.5 An expert should make it clear:

(a) when a question or issue falls outside his expertise; and

(b) when he is not able to reach a definite opinion, for example because he has insufficient information.

While the following observations on the duties and responsibilities of expert witnesses were made, prior to the Civil Procedure Rules, with civil cases in mind,[128] they are also clearly applicable, *mutatis mutandis*, in criminal cases:

The duties and responsibilities of expert witnesses . . . include the following:

1. Expert evidence presented to the court should be, and should be seen to be, the independent product of the expert uninfluenced as to form or content by the exigencies of litigation . . .

2. An expert witness should provide independent assistance to the court by way of objective, unbiased opinion in relation to matters within his expertise . . . An expert witness . . . should never assume the role of an advocate.

3. An expert witness should state the facts or assumptions upon which his opinion is based. He should not omit to consider material facts which could detract from his concluded opinion . . .

4. An expert witness should make it clear when a particular question or issue falls outside his expertise.

5. If an expert's opinion is not properly researched because he considers that insufficient data is available, then this must be stated with an indication that the opinion is no more than a provisional one . . . In cases where an expert witness, who has prepared a report, could not

their task as being to help the police. They became partisan. It is the clear duty of government forensic scientists to assist in a neutral and impartial way in criminal investigations. They must act in the cause of justice.' It has been argued, however, that ' "neutrality" is better understood as a social and representational achievement shaped by the ability of those supporting or defending a panel, expert, opinion or text to manage or sustain that appearance than as an intrinsic attribute manifested in a person(s) or their knowledge behaviour and methods': G Edmond, 'Judicial Representations of Scientific Evidence' (2000) 63 *Modern Law Review* 216, 248.

[128] These observations are considered to be encapsulated in the Civil Procedure Rules: *Stevens v Gullis* [2000] 1 All ER 527, 532–3.

assert that the report contained the truth, the whole truth and nothing but the truth without some qualification, that qualification should be stated in the report . . .

6. If, after exchange of reports, an expert witness changes his view on a material matter having read the other side's expert's report or for any other reason, such change of view should be communicated (through legal representatives) to the other side without delay and when appropriate to the court.

7. Where expert evidence refers to photographs, plans, calculations, analyses, measurements, survey reports or other similar documents, these must be provided to the opposite party at the same time as the exchange of reports . . .[129]

It may be inappropriate for an expert to give evidence if he or she is in some way an 'interested party':

It is not the existence of an interest or connection with the litigation or a party thereto, but the nature and extent of that interest or connection which determines whether an expert witness should be precluded from giving evidence. Hence, once such an interest or connection is ascertained a decision must be made promptly as a matter of case management as to whether the expert's evidence is precluded or not.[130]

Also requiring attention is the role played by solicitors in this area. There is evidence, for example, that solicitors may exert pressure on experts to modify their reports or opinions.[131] While there may be legitimate reasons for seeking such modification in some cases, the possibility of inappropriate pressure cannot be ignored. Further, the fact that many solicitors are apparently slow in paying expert witnesses their fees[132] is clearly a cause for concern.

Consistently with the idea of promoting consensualism over adversarialism, discussions between experts are actively encouraged in civil proceedings. Rule 35.12 of the Civil Procedure Rules provides:

(1) The court may, at any stage, direct a discussion between experts for the purpose of requiring the experts to—

(a) identify and discuss the expert issues in the proceedings; and

(b) where possible, reach an agreed opinion on those issues.

(2) The court may specify the issues which the experts must discuss.

(3) The court may direct that following a discussion between the experts they must prepare a statement for the court showing—

(a) those issues on which they agree; and

(b) those issues on which they disagree and a summary of their reasons for disagreeing.

---

[129] *The 'Ikarian Reefer'* [1993] FSR 563, 565–6. The position in care proceedings was addressed by the Family Division in *In re B (Minors) (Care Proceedings: Practice)* [1999] 1 WLR 238.

[130] *Armchair Passenger Transport Ltd v Helical Bar Plc* [2003] EWHC 367 (QB), [48].

[131] See generally 'Cash and Quibble for Experts' (1997) 147 *New Law Journal* 1718; N Hilborne, 'Survey Raises Concerns over Experts' Independence' (1997) 141 *Solicitors' Journal* 935; M Streeter, 'Pressure Put on Expert Witnesses', The Independent, 8 Nov 1997, 2.

[132] 'Cash and Quibble for Experts' (1997) 147 *New Law Journal* 1718, 1718.

(4) The content of the discussion between the experts shall not be referred to at the trial unless the parties agree.

(5) Where experts reach agreement on an issue during their discussions, the agreement shall not bind the parties unless the parties expressly agree to be bound by the agreement.[133]

5.2 Legal Protection for the Expert's Independence

The particular duties of the expert have been described above. It will be apparent that these duties, rooted in independence, impartiality, and scientific rigour, may be at odds with the expectations of the party paying the expert's fee. For this reason, the law has developed rules designed to restrict influences which may distract the expert from his or her duty.

An expert may not, to a large extent, be sued for negligence or breach of contract by the party retaining him or her. The position would appear to be as follows:[134]

• Expert witnesses *who give evidence* are immune from suit in relation to anything which they say in court, and in relation to anything stated in their report.

• Where the expert has been retained to advise on the merits of a claim, the immunity does not extend to protect the expert from a suit in relation to that advice. It is irrelevant that it may have been in contemplation, at the time of the advice, that the expert would be a witness if the litigation were to proceed.

• The immunity does, however, protect an expert from suit in relation to the contents of a report prepared for the purpose of exchange prior to a trial in which it is proposed to call the expert to give evidence, but in which the expert does not eventually testify, or which eventually never takes place. It is said that underlying this immunity is the importance of ensuring that court time is not taken up with matters not truly in issue, and the importance thus of encouraging experts to identify in advance of trial those parts of their evidence on which they are or are not in agreement. The public interest in facilitating full and frank discussion between experts prior to trial requires that each should be free to make proper concessions without fear of possible liability in negligence.

A costs order against an expert is, however, possible. In *Phillips v Symes (No 2)* Peter Smith J in the Chancery Division stated:

It seems to me that in the administration of justice, especially, in the light of the clearly defined duties now enshrined in CPR Pt 35 and the practice direction supplementing Part 35, it would be quite wrong of the court to remove from itself the power to make a costs order in appropriate circumstances against an expert who, by his evidence, causes significant expense to be incurred, and does so in flagrant reckless disregard of his duties to the court.[135]

I do not regard the other available sanctions as being either effective or anything other than blunt instruments. The proper sanction is the ability to compensate a person who has suffered loss by reason of that evidence. . . . I do not accept that experts will, by reason of this

---

[133] See generally B Thompson, 'Well Met?' (2003) 153 *New Law Journal* 1145.

[134] See *Stanton v Callaghan* [1998] 4 All ER 961, 983–4; discussed by C Passmore, 'Expert Witness Immunity' (1998) 148 *New Law Journal* 1758.   [135] [2004] EWHC 2330 (Ch), [2005] 1 WLR 2043.

potential exposure, be inhibited from fulfilling their duties. That is a cri de coeur often made by professionals, but I cannot believe that an expert would be deterred, because a costs order might be made against him in the event that his evidence is given recklessly in flagrant disregard for his duties. The high level of proof required to establish the breach cannot be ignored.[136]

5.3 Presence in Court

In contrast to the general rule, an expert witness may, exceptionally, be present during the evidence of other witnesses.[137] This exception rests upon an assumption that as a professional the expert will be impartial and unlikely to be swayed by hearing other witnesses. It is in part justified on the basis that an expert may be required to assess and advise the party on the quality and implications of the other party's case. It is arguable that this close involvement with the party and legal team in trial strategy may undermine the impartial role required of the witness in law.

5.4 'Blaming' Experts

Ultimately, it would be unfair to lay undue blame at the door of expert witnesses in all cases where problems have been uncovered. As the House of Commons Science and Technology Committee has acknowledged:

Expert witnesses have been penalised far more publicly than the judge or lawyers in cases where expert evidence has been called into question. These cases represent a *systems* failure. Focussing criticism on the expert has a detrimental effect on the willingness of other experts to serve as witnesses and detracts attention from the flaws in the court process and legal system which, if addressed, could help to prevent future miscarriages of justice.[138]

The Committee recommends mandatory training of barristers in the area of forensic evidence,[139] and also 'that judges be given an annual update on scientific developments of relevance to the courts'.[140] Indeed, the Committee goes so far as to

recommend that the Home Office issue a consultation on the development of a cadre of lawyers and judges with specialist understanding of specific areas of forensic evidence. An additional

---

[136] Ibid, [96]. See generally S Partington, 'The Risks of Professing an Opinion' (2004) 154 *New Law Journal* 1766.

[137] *Tomlinson v Tomlinson* [1980] 1 WLR 322, 328.

[138] House of Commons Science and Technology Committee, *Forensic Evidence on Trial* (Seventh Report of Session 2004–05) (HC 96-I) (2005) [170] (italics in original, bold font removed), available at http://www. publications.parliament.uk/pa/cm200405/cmselect/cmsctech/96/96i.pdf.

[139] Ibid, [180] (bold font removed): 'While we have no particular complaints about the quality of the guidance available to lawyers on the understanding and presentation of forensic evidence, it is of great concern that there is currently no mandatory training for lawyers in this area. In view of the increasingly important role played by DNA and other forensic evidence in criminal investigations, it is wholly inadequate to rely on the interest and self-motivation of the legal profession to take advantage of the training on offer. We recommend that the Bar make a minimum level of training and continuing professional development in forensic evidence compulsory.'   [140] Ibid, [182] (bold font removed).

benefit to this would be the creation of a small group of judges and prosecution and defence lawyers with the ability and current knowledge to act as mentors to their peers when required.[141]

6 'Battles of Experts' and the Presentation of Expert Evidence

Presentation of expert evidence[142] in the form of a written report is the norm in civil cases. Rule 35.5(1) of the Civil Procedure Rules provides: 'Expert evidence is to be given in a written report unless the court directs otherwise.' Rule 35.10 provides:

> . . .
>
> (2) At the end of an expert's report there must be a statement that—
>
> (a) the expert understands his duty to the court; and
>
> (b) he has complied with that duty.
>
> (3) The expert's report must state the substance of all material instructions, whether written or oral, on the basis of which the report was written.
>
> (4) The instructions referred to in paragraph (3) shall not be privileged against disclosure but the court will not, in relation to those instructions—
>
> (a) order disclosure of any specific document; or
>
> (b) permit any questioning in court, other than by the party who instructed the expert,
>
> unless it is satisfied that there are reasonable grounds to consider the statement of instructions given under paragraph (3) to be inaccurate or incomplete.[143]

In criminal cases reports by experts are admissible in evidence in accordance with section 30 of the Criminal Justice Act 1988:

> (1) An expert report shall be admissible as evidence in criminal proceedings, whether or not the person making it attends to give oral evidence in those proceedings.
>
> (2) If it is proposed that the person making the report shall not give oral evidence, the report shall only be admissible with the leave of the court.
>
> (3) For the purpose of determining whether to give leave the court shall have regard—
>
> (a) to the contents of the report;

---

[141] House of Commons Science and Technology Committee, *Forensic Evidence on Trial* (Seventh Report of Session 2004–05) (HC 96-I) (2005) [184] (bold font removed). See also A Wilson, 'Expert Testimony in the Dock' (2005) 69 *Journal of Criminal Law* 330, 346.

[142] See generally L Meintjes-Van der Walt, 'Expert Odyssey: Thoughts on the Presentation and Evaluation of Scientific Evidence' (2003) 120 *South African Law Journal* 352; L Meintjes-van der Walt, *Expert Evidence in the Criminal Justice Process: A Comparative Perspective* (2001) Ch 6.

[143] See generally P Creffield, 'Medical Evidence' (2003) 153 *New Law Journal* 1160; C Phipps, 'Being Frank with Experts' (2000) 144 *Solicitors' Journal* 90; B Thompson, 'How to Write an Expert Report' (2004) 154 *New Law Journal* 808.

(b) to the reasons why it is proposed that the person making the report shall not give oral evidence;

(c) to any risk, having regard in particular to whether it is likely to be possible to controvert statements in the report if the person making it does not attend to give oral evidence in the proceedings, that its admission or exclusion will result in unfairness to the accused or, if there is more than one, to any of them; and

(d) to any other circumstances that appear to the court to be relevant.

(4) An expert report, when admitted, shall be evidence of any fact or opinion of which the person making it could have given oral evidence.

(5) In this section 'expert report' means a written report by a person dealing wholly or mainly with matters on which he is (or would if living be) qualified to give expert evidence.

The use of single joint experts in civil cases is addressed in rule 35.7 of the Civil Procedure Rules:

(1) Where two or more parties wish to submit expert evidence on a particular issue, the court may direct that the evidence on that issue is to [be] given by one expert only.

(2) The parties wishing to submit the expert evidence are called 'the instructing parties'.

(3) Where the instructing parties cannot agree who should be the expert, the court may—

(a) select the expert from a list prepared or identified by the instructing parties; or

(b) direct that the expert be selected in such other manner as the court may direct.[144]

The Practice Direction provides:

6 Where the court has directed that the evidence on a particular issue is to be given by one expert only (rule 35.7) but there are a number of disciplines relevant to that issue, a leading expert in the dominant discipline should be identified as the single expert. He should prepare the general part of the report and be responsible for annexing or incorporating the contents of any reports from experts in other disciplines.

Each instructing party may give instructions to a single joint expert,[145] but 'must, at the same time, send a copy of the instructions to the other instructing parties'.[146]

The Runciman Royal Commission devoted considerable attention to the issue of expert evidence in criminal cases, making a large number of suggestions for reform. The following are some of the recommendations of the Commission pertaining to the presentation of expert evidence:

71. . . . we recommend that far more use is made of written summaries of such expert evidence as is not contested. All too often, expert evidence is given orally by witnesses in order, it would

---

[144] See generally B Braithwaite, 'A Case of Two Experts are Better Than One', *The Times*, 1 June 2004, Law, 4; M Cohen, 'Single Joint Experts: Surveying the Results' (2003) 153 *New Law Journal* 306; M Cohen, 'To Meet or Not to Meet?' (2001) 151 *New Law Journal* 761; G L Davies, 'Current Issues—Expert Evidence: Court Appointed Experts' (2004) 23 *Civil Justice Quarterly* 367; R Jacob, 'Court-Appointed Experts v Party Experts: Which is Better?' (2004) 23 *Civil Justice Quarterly* 400; J A Jolowicz, 'A Note on Experts' (2004) 23 *Civil Justice Quarterly* 408; B Thompson, 'The Problem with Single Joint Experts' (2004) 154 *New Law Journal* 1134.

[145] Rule 35.8(1).   [146] Rule 35.8(2).

seem, to enhance the value of the evidence in the eyes of the jury. But where the defence have agreed the evidence, there should be no question of cross-examination and the attendance of the witness and his or her appearance in the box is unnecessary. . . . We therefore recommend that, where the expert evidence is agreed, it should be presented to the jury as clearly as possible, normally by written statement. It would be for counsel to speak to such a statement in their opening and closing speeches.

72. Where the evidence is in dispute and the expert witness goes into the witness box, his or her evidence can often be greatly assisted by the use of visual and other technical aids and we recommend that these are used wherever possible. . . .

73. . . . many experts feel that they are not always given a proper opportunity to explain what the scientific evidence really means. This may be because counsel stop short of asking vital questions from lack of scientific knowledge or inadequate briefing or because they make inadequate use of the opportunity to re-examine after cross-examination or because they do not want the answer to be heard. We recommend that trial judges, where the evidence is disputed, ask expert witnesses before they leave the witness box whether there is anything else that they wish to say. To avoid inadmissible evidence being heard, the judge should put this question in the absence of the jury and, if the expert witness does indicate a wish to clarify the evidence, it should be heard before the jury returns. If the judge is satisfied that there can be no objection to the evidence, it should be put before the jury. Expert witnesses should on the same basis be readier to ask the judge to be allowed to add to what they have said in examination or cross-examination in order to make themselves clear. They might best do this by telling their solicitor on leaving the witness box that they wish to clarify the evidence just given. The solicitor would be under an obligation to inform counsel and counsel to tell the judge. The judge would then explore the admissibility of the evidence in the absence of the jury as we propose above and, if appropriate, the witness would be recalled to clarify the earlier evidence.[147]

It is arguable that the adversarial mode of trial is not well suited to the determination of questions pertaining to expert evidence.[148] Contrary to popular belief, there is often no objective 'truth' to be discovered in matters of science; it cannot be said that to choose between the evidence of two opposing expert witnesses is necessarily to choose between objectively 'correct' and objectively 'incorrect' evidence. 'Disagreement plays an inevitable role in science, just as it does in law.'[149] Partly for this reason, it has often been suggested that a system of court experts should be introduced in England and Wales. This is an idea which has precipitated considerable debate in recent times and which did not find favour with the Runciman Royal Commission:

74. . . . In [the] view [of some] expert evidence should be given by a court expert, either instead of or in addition to the experts who appear for the prosecution and the defence. Alternatively, some would recommend that judges should sit in the relevant cases with an expert assessor or

---

[147] Royal Commission on Criminal Justice, *Report* (Cm 2263) (1993) 159–60.

[148] See generally P Alldridge, 'Scientific Expertise and Comparative Criminal Procedure' (1999) 3 *International Journal of Evidence and Proof* 141.

[149] M Redmayne, 'Expert Evidence and Scientific Disagreement' (1997) 30 *UC Davis Law Review* 1027, 1080. It has been noted, in relation to medical evidence, that 'the law often stubbornly fails to recognise uncertainty in medical knowledge and practice', and that the validity even of honest medical disagreement may not be accepted: B Mahendra, 'When Experts Seem to Disagree' (1997) 147 *New Law Journal* 637, 638.

assessors. We have considered these suggestions but are not in favour of them. A court expert, even if subject to examination and cross-examination, would by implication carry more weight than an expert for the prosecution or the defence. There would, however, be no guarantee that he or she was any nearer to the truth of the matter than the expert witnesses for the parties. A court expert should not in our view be the only expert, since that would deprive the parties of the opportunity of leading their own expert evidence. But to have a court expert in addition to the experts for the parties would greatly extend the amount of time spent in examination and cross-examination of all three experts without making discovery of the truth any more certain. The worst solution of all, in our view, would be to have the expert sitting with the judge as an assessor, since his or her evidence would not be susceptible to examination or cross-examination by either side.[150]

Yet the Commission's fear that the use of court experts may result in great weight being placed by the jury on evidence which may be no more reliable than evidence given by experts called by the parties is unjustified. The point, as Alldridge succinctly puts it, is surely that 'court-appointed witnesses *should* carry more weight, because there is every reason to believe that their evidence will be better evidence'.[151] Court experts are common in Continental jurisdictions. The French system of court experts, for example, seeks to eliminate the 'battle of the experts' in the courtroom by emphasizing consensualism rather than confrontation. In order to be eligible to serve the court in a particular case, court experts have to be licensed. The *juge d'instruction* typically makes the decision about whether an expert is to be appointed, and if so which expert. In most cases, a single expert will be appointed, although there will often be a panel in difficult cases. On completion, the expert's report is delivered to the *juge d'instruction* for communication to the parties, who may ask the *juge d'instruction* to direct the expert to perform further tests or provide more information, or to appoint another expert for a second opinion.[152]

Significantly, the Court of Appeal appeared to suggest in *R v Cannings* that, in a case turning on a fundamental 'battle of the experts', it might be inappropriate for the prosecution to continue or even to have been brought:

... where a full investigation into two or more sudden unexplained infant deaths in the same family is followed by a serious disagreement between reputable experts about the cause of death, and a body of such expert opinion concludes that natural causes, whether explained or

---

[150]   Royal Commission on Criminal Justice, *Report* (Cm 2263) (1993) 160.

[151]   P Alldridge, 'Forensic Science and Expert Evidence' (1994) 21 *Journal of Law and Society* 136, 142 (italics added). Cf P Roberts, 'Forensic Science Evidence After Runciman' [1994] *Criminal Law Review* 780, 788–91.

[152]   The source of this information is J R Spencer, 'Court Experts and Expert Witnesses: Have We a Lesson to Learn from the French?' (1992) 45 *Current Legal Problems* 213, which may be consulted for a very readable account of the French system. Note also the interesting suggestion that procedures based on a 'didactic' approach to the presentation of expert evidence be introduced: E J Imwinkelried, 'The Next Step in Conceptualizing the Presentation of Expert Evidence as Education: The Case for Didactic Trial Procedures' (1997) 1(2) *International Journal of Evidence and Proof* 128, 132. For criticism, see G Edmond, 'The Next Step or *Moonwalking*? Expert Evidence, the Public Understanding of Science and the Case Against Imwinkelried's Didactic Trial Procedures' (1998) 2 *International Journal of Evidence and Proof* 13. See also Imwinkelried's response: E Imwinkelried, 'Didactic Trial Procedures' (1998) 2 *International Journal of Evidence and Proof* 205.

unexplained, cannot be excluded as a reasonable (and not a fanciful) possibility, the prosecution of a parent or parents for murder should not be started, or continued, unless there is additional cogent evidence, extraneous to the expert evidence, ... which tends to support the conclusion that the infant, or where there is more than one death, one of the infants, was deliberately harmed. In cases like the present, if the outcome of the trial depends exclusively or almost exclusively on a serious disagreement between distinguished and reputable experts, it will often be unwise, and therefore unsafe, to proceed.[153]

In its subsequent decision in *R v Anthony* the Court of Appeal was careful, however, to sound the following note of caution:

Properly understood *Cannings* is not authority for the bare proposition that a dispute between reputable experts in a specialist field should produce an acquittal. ... care must be taken not to transpose judicial comment on matters of evidence in the *Cannings* case into formal judicial precedent in a different case where the combined effect of the evidence, whether extraneous to or linked with or arising from the medical evidence, is different.[154]

Likewise, in *R v Kai-Whitewind*, the Court of Appeal emphatically dissociated itself from the view

that whenever there is a conflict between expert witnesses, the case for the prosecution must fail unless the conviction is justified by evidence independent of the expert witnesses. ... In *Cannings* there was essentially no evidence beyond the inferences based on coincidence which the experts for the Crown were prepared to draw. Other reputable experts in the same specialist field took a different view about the inferences, if any, which could or should be drawn. Hence the need for additional cogent evidence. With additional evidence, the jury would have been in a position to evaluate the respective arguments and counter-arguments: without it, in cases like *Cannings*, they would not.[155]

7 Disclosure of Expert Evidence

In civil cases, rule 35.13 of the Civil Procedure Rules provides: 'A party who fails to disclose an expert's report may not use the report at the trial or call the expert to give evidence orally unless the court gives permission.' Rule 35.11 provides: 'Where a party has disclosed an expert's report, any party may use that expert's report as evidence at the trial.'

The general requirement in criminal cases is that a party proposing to adduce expert evidence is, as soon as practicable, to 'furnish the other party or parties with a statement in writing of any finding or opinion which he proposes to adduce by way of such evidence',[156] and:

where a request in writing is made to him in that behalf by any other party, provide that party also with a copy of (or if it appears to the party proposing to adduce the evidence to be more

---

[153] [2004] EWCA Crim 01, [2004] 2 Cr App R 7 (p 63), [178].   [154] [2005] EWCA Crim 952, [81].
[155] [2005] EWCA Crim 1092, [84]–[85].   [156] Criminal Procedure Rules 2005, rule 24.1(1)(i).

practicable, a reasonable opportunity to examine) the record of any observation, test, calculation or other procedure on which such finding or opinion is based and any document or other thing or substance in respect of which any such procedure has been carried out.[157]

A party failing to comply with this may not adduce the evidence without the leave of the court.[158] In addition, there is a duty on a defendant who instructs an expert with a view to the expert's providing an expert opinion for possible use as evidence to give notice of the expert's name and address.[159]

8 Replacing Expert Witness

It may be appropriate, where a party in a civil case seeks to replace one expert witness with another, to require disclosure of the original witness's report:

> Expert shopping is undesirable and, wherever possible, the court will use its powers to prevent it. It needs to be emphasised that, if a party needs the permission of the court to rely on expert witness B in place of expert witness A, the court has the power to give permission on condition that A's report is disclosed to the other party or parties, and that such a condition will usually be imposed. In imposing such a condition, the court is not abrogating or emasculating legal professional privilege; it is merely saying that, if a party seeks the court's permission to rely on a substitute expert, it will be required to waive privilege in the first expert's report as a condition of being permitted to do so.[160]

> . . . the condition of disclosure . . . should not only apply to the first expert's 'final' report, if by that is meant the report signed by the first expert as his or her report for disclosure. It should apply at least to the first expert's report(s) containing the substance of his or her opinion.[161]

9 Evaluation of Expert Evidence

Evaluation of expert opinion evidence[162] is considered strictly to be within the province of the trier of fact. In *R v Stockwell* it was stressed that 'the judge should make clear to the jury that they are not bound by the expert's opinion, and that the issue is for them to decide',[163]

---

[157] Criminal Procedure Rules 2005, rule 24.1(1)(ii).   [158] Criminal Procedure Rules 2005, rule 24.3.

[159] Criminal Procedure and Investigations Act 1996, s 6D. See Ch 14.

[160] *Vasiliou v Hajigeorgiou* [2005] EWCA Civ 236, [2005] 1 WLR 2195, [29].

[161] Ibid, [30]. See generally S Partington and J-C Domaingue, 'Disclosure of Expert Reports' (2005) 155 *New Law Journal* 785, who advise (ibid, 788): 'If you are thinking of dispensing with your first expert, weigh up whether a credible reason can be advanced that might persuade the court against the precondition of disclosure, but bear in mind that the presumption seems to be in favour of the other side.' Legal professional privilege is discussed in Ch 7.

[162] See generally L Meintjes-Van der Walt, 'Expert Odyssey: Thoughts on the Presentation and Evaluation of Scientific Evidence' (2003) 120 *South African Law Journal* 352.

[163] (1993) 97 Cr App R 260, 266 (decision of 1993). There is a Judicial Studies Board Specimen Direction on expert evidence (Direction 33) but, as with all such directions, it is 'to be adapted to the facts of any particular case according to the judgment of the trial judge'; the fact that it has 'not slavishly been followed' does not automatically provide a good ground of appeal: *R v Fitzpatrick, The Times*, 19 Feb 1999 (transcript from Smith Bernal).

and in *Dover District Council v Sherred* that a county court judge 'is not bound to accept the evidence even of an expert witness, if there is a proper basis for rejecting it in the other evidence which he has heard, or the expert evidence is such that he does not believe it or for whatever reason is not convinced by it'.[164] Thus it has been held that a judge hearing a claim for damages for personal injury arising from an accident at work, where the sole issue turned on conflicting medical opinion, ought to have addressed and resolved that conflict. It was inappropriate for him simply to have decided the case without making any clear findings of fact or giving proper reasons.[165] In a similar vein, the House of Lords has noted that:

> [a] court is not bound to hold that a defendant doctor escapes liability for negligent treatment or diagnosis just because he leads evidence from a number of medical experts who are genuinely of opinion that the defendant's treatment or diagnosis accorded with sound medical practice. . . . the court has to be satisfied that the exponents of the body of opinion relied on can demonstrate that such opinion has a logical basis. In particular, in cases involving, as they so often do, the weighing of risks against benefits, the judge before accepting a body of opinion as being responsible, reasonable or respectable, will need to be satisfied that, in forming their views, the experts have directed their minds to the question of comparative risks and benefits and have reached a defensible conclusion on the matter.[166]

On the other hand, however, 'it will very seldom be right for a judge to reach the conclusion that views genuinely held by a competent medical expert are unreasonable. The assessment of medical risks and benefits is a matter of clinical judgment which a judge would not normally be able to make without expert evidence.'[167]

---

[164] (1997) 29 HLR 864, 867 (decision of 1997).   [165] *Sewell v Electrolux Ltd, The Times,* 7 Nov 1997.
[166] *Bolitho v City and Hackney HA* [1997] 4 All ER 771, 778. See also *Armstrong v First York* [2005] EWCA Civ 277, [27]: 'there is no principle of law that an expert's evidence in an unusual field . . . must be dispositive of liability in such a case'.   [167] *Bolitho v City and Hackney HA* [1997] 4 All ER 771, 779.

11

Witnesses

Growing attention is being paid by the law of evidence to the experiences of witnesses.[1] Three broad issues pertaining to witnesses are examined in this chapter. First, we consider whether certain categories of persons may be incompetent to testify, or, even if competent to testify, may not be compellable to do so. Secondly, we examine the relaxation of the rules on corroboration and the modern approach to possibly unreliable witnesses. Thirdly, we ask if there are any special measures or procedures for easing the burden on testifying witnesses, and whether these are adequate.

1 Competence

It has long been the general rule that any person is competent to testify (that is, is permitted to testify if he or she wishes to do so).[2]

1.1 Criminal Cases: General Principles

For criminal proceedings the general rule of universal competence is expressed in the Youth Justice and Criminal Evidence Act 1999,[3] but is specifically provided to be subject to two exceptions. First, a defendant is not competent to testify for the prosecution[4] unless he or she 'is not, or is no longer, liable to be convicted of any offence in the proceedings (whether as a result of pleading guilty or for any other reason)'.[5] Secondly, a person is not competent to testify if it appears to the court that he or she is unable to give intelligible testimony. The ability to give intelligible testimony is the ability to '(a) understand questions put to him as a witness, and (b) give answers to them which can be understood'.[6] Where a question is raised (either by a party[7] or by the court[8]) about the competence of a witness, section 54 makes a number of relevant provisions:

> (2) It is for the party calling the witness to satisfy the court that, on a balance of probabilities, the witness is competent to give evidence in the proceedings.

[1] See, eg, H Angle, S Malam, and C Carey, *Witness Satisfaction: Findings from the Witness Satisfaction Survey 2002* (Home Office Online Report 19/03), available at http://www.homeoffice.gov.uk/rds/pdfs2/rdsolr1903.pdf.
[2] This was not always the case: see generally C J W Allen, *The Law of Evidence in Victorian England* (1997) Chs 3, 4. [3] S 53(1).
[4] S 53(4). [5] S 53(5). [6] S 53(3). [7] S 54(1)(a). [8] S 54(1)(b).

(4) Any proceedings held for the determination of the question shall take place in the absence of the jury (if there is one).

(5) Expert evidence may be received on the question.

(6) Any questioning of the witness (where the court considers that necessary) shall be conducted by the court in the presence of the parties.

1.2 Sworn and Unsworn Evidence

The general expectation is that witnesses are to be sworn for the purpose of giving evidence on oath.[9] The manner in which an oath is administered and taken is prescribed by section 1 of the Oaths Act 1978. A person objecting to being sworn may instead make a solemn affirmation,[10] which will 'be of the same force and effect as an oath'.[11] Where an oath has been duly administered and taken, its validity will not be affected by the fact that the person taking it had no religious belief at the time.[12] Nor will an oath be invalid simply because, for example, it was taken by a Muslim on the New Testament: what matters is that the oath is one which appears to the court to be binding on the witness's conscience, and, more importantly, one 'which the witness himself considers to be binding upon his conscience'.[13] The offence of perjury is committed where a person sworn as a witness wilfully makes a statement which he or she knows to be false or does not believe to be true.[14]

In criminal proceedings, a witness under the age of 14 cannot be sworn.[15] A witness who has reached the age of 14 can be sworn if 'he has a sufficient appreciation of the solemnity of the occasion and of the particular responsibility to tell the truth which is involved in taking an oath'.[16] A witness who is able to give intelligible testimony is to 'be presumed to have a sufficient appreciation of those matters if no evidence tending to show the contrary is adduced (by any party)'.[17] If, however, such evidence were to be adduced, 'it is for the party seeking to have the witness sworn to satisfy the court that, on a balance of probabilities, the witness has attained the age of 14 and has a sufficient appreciation of the [relevant] matters'.[18] The determination of whether a witness may be sworn is to 'take place in the absence of the jury (if there is one)',[19] but where any questioning of the witness is considered necessary by the court this is to 'be conducted by the court in the presence of the parties'.[20] Expert evidence may be received on the question of whether a witness may be sworn.[21]

In a criminal case a person of whatever age who is competent to testify[22] but may not be sworn[23] is to give unsworn evidence,[24] which has the same effect as sworn

---

[9] For a critical view of oaths, see L James, 'Oaths and Religious Privilege' (1997) 161 *Justice of the Peace* 998.

[10] Oaths Act 1978, s 5(1).

[11] S 5(4). It may be argued that it may be more appropriate in contemporary society for all witnesses to make solemn affirmations: J Carter, 'Affirmation for All?' (2003) 167 *Justice of the Peace* 464. See also T Gleeson, 'I Swear by Almighty God—but I'm Not Sure Why' (2005) 169 *Justice of the Peace* 450.

[12] S 4(2).   [13] *R v Kemble* [1990] 1 WLR 1111, 1114.   [14] Perjury Act 1911, s 1.

[15] Youth Justice and Criminal Evidence Act 1999, s 55(2)(a).   [16] S 55(2)(b).   [17] S 55(3).

[18] S 55(4).   [19] S 55(5).   [20] S 55(7).   [21] S 55(6).   [22] S 56(1)(a).

[23] S 56(1)(b).   [24] S 56(2).

evidence: 'A deposition of unsworn evidence...may be taken for the purposes of criminal proceedings as if that evidence had been given on oath.'[25] It is an offence to give false unsworn evidence in circumstances in which, had the evidence been given on oath, the person would have been guilty of perjury.[26]

In civil cases, the effect of section 96 of the Children Act 1989 is as follows. A child (defined as someone under the age of 18[27]) who understands the nature of an oath must give sworn evidence. A child who does not understand the nature of an oath may give unsworn evidence if 'he understands that it is his duty to speak the truth'[28] and 'has sufficient understanding to justify his evidence being heard'.[29]

2 Compellability

Any person competent to testify is considered, as a general rule, to be compellable to do so. A number of exceptions to this will be considered below. A compellable witness's refusal to testify may constitute contempt of court:

> The role of the courts, in seeking to provide the public with protection against criminal conduct, can only properly be performed if members of the public co-operate with the courts. That co-operation includes participation in the trial process, sometimes as a juror, sometimes as a witness. Witnesses who may have important evidence to give must come to court if they are summoned, that is, formally directed to do so. If they choose to ignore a summons, they are in contempt of court and can expect to be punished because their failure to attend is likely to disrupt the trial process and, in some cases, to undermine it entirely.[30]

It is important to note, however, that the fact that a person is compell*able* to testify does not mean that he or she will necessarily be *compelled* to testify. A court has a discretion about whether to order the attendance of a potential witness, and may, in the exercise of this discretion, decline to authorize the issue of a witness summons if it would be oppressive to do so.[31]

2.1 The Accused in a Criminal Case

2.1.1 Testifying in his or her own Defence

The Criminal Evidence Act 1898 made accused persons competent to testify in their own defence for the first time.[32] The incompetence of accused persons as defence witnesses prior to this was premised on the specious assumption that they would only perjure themselves if permitted to testify.[33] By testifying,[34] an accused becomes liable to

---

[25] S 56(3).   [26] S 57.   [27] S 105(1).   [28] S 96(2)(a).   [29] S 96(2)(b).

[30] *R v Yusuf* [2003] EWCA Crim 1488, [2003] 2 Cr App R 32 (p 488), [16].

[31] *Re P (Witness Summons)* [1997] 2 FLR 447.

[32] S 1. See generally C J W Allen, *The Law of Evidence in Victorian England* (1997) Ch 5.

[33] See generally ibid, 167–71.

[34] Or simply by being sworn, even if no questions are then put by defence counsel: *R v Bingham* [1999] 1 WLR 598.

be cross-examined by the prosecution as well as by any co-accused, even if he or she has not actually given evidence against that co-accused.[35] It is also noteworthy that the prosecution may use evidence elicited from a testifying accused (both in evidence-in-chief[36] and in cross-examination[37]) against any co-accused.

The Criminal Evidence Act 1898 provides that a testifying accused 'shall, unless otherwise ordered by the court, give his evidence from the witness box or other place from which the other witnesses give their evidence'.[38] It has been held that there must be good reason for any departure from the general rule. 'There may be cases in which a prisoner is so infirm that he cannot walk from the dock to the witness box without inconvenience or pain. There may be cases where the prisoner exhibits violence which may be more easily quelled in the dock than in the witness box. But apart from cases of such a nature the right of the prisoner to give his evidence from the witness box should not be interfered with . . .'.[39]

While accused persons are competent to testify in their own defence, they are not compellable to do so.[40] The Criminal Justice and Public Order Act 1994 makes it clear that the changes in the law which it introduces[41] do *not* 'render the accused compellable to give evidence on his own behalf, and he shall accordingly not be guilty of contempt of court by reason of a failure to do so'.[42] This legislation provides, however, that 'the court or jury, in determining whether the accused is guilty of the offence charged, may draw such inferences as appear proper from the failure of the accused to give evidence or his refusal, without good cause, to answer any question'.[43] An accused will be taken to

---

[35] *R v Hilton* [1972] 1 QB 421.   [36] *R v Rudd* (1948) 32 Cr App R 138 (decision of 1948).

[37] *R v Paul* [1920] 2 KB 183.   [38] S 1(g).

[39] *R v Symonds* (1924) 18 Cr App R 100, 101. See also *R v Farnham JJ, ex p Gibson* (1991) 155 JP 792 (decision of 1991).   [40] S 1(a).

[41] See generally J S W Black, 'Inferences from Silence: Redressing the Balance? (1)' (1997) 141 *Solicitors' Journal* 741; J D Jackson, 'Interpreting the Silence Provisions: The Northern Ireland Cases' [1995] *Criminal Law Review* 587; A F Jennings, 'Resounding Silence' (1996) 146 *New Law Journal* 725; A F Jennings, 'Resounding Silence—2' (1996) 146 *New Law Journal* 764; A F Jennings, 'Resounding Silence—3' (1996) 146 *New Law Journal* 821; P Mirfield, 'Two Side-Effects of Sections 34 to 37 of the Criminal Justice and Public Order Act 1994' [1995] *Criminal Law Review* 612; S Nash, 'Silence as Evidence: A Commonsense Development or a Violation of a Basic Right?' (1997) 21 *Criminal Law Journal* 145; S Nash, 'Silence as Evidence: Inquisitorial Developments in England and Wales' [1996] *Scots Law Times* 69; M Nichols, 'Liberal Democracy and the Emergence of Law: The Right to Silence' [1997] *UCL Jurisprudence Review* 239; R Pattenden, 'Inferences from Silence' [1995] *Criminal Law Review* 602; R Pattenden, 'Silence: Lord Taylor's Legacy' (1998) 2 *International Journal of Evidence and Proof* 141; A Samuels, 'The Right of Silence and Adverse Inferences' (1998) 162 *Justice of the Peace* 201; S Easton, *The Case for the Right to Silence* (2nd ed 1998) 146–8.   [42] S 35(4).

[43] S 35(3). By contrast, greater commitment to the right to silence at trial is displayed by the Australian and Canadian courts: see *Weissensteiner v R* (1993) 178 CLR 217, *RPS v R* [2000] HCA 3, and *Azzopardi v R* [2001] HCA 25 (Australia); *R v Noble* (1997) 146 DLR (4th) 385 (Canada). See generally G L Davies, 'Application of *Weissensteiner* to Direct Evidence' (2000) 74 *Australian Law Journal* 371; C Eakin, '*RPS v R*: The Resilience of the Accused's Right to Silence' (2000) 22 *Sydney Law Review* 639; D Hamer, 'The Privilege of Silence and the Persistent Risk of Self-Incrimination: Part II' (2004) 28 *Criminal Law Journal* 200; P Healy, 'More Protection for the Silent Accused in Canada: *Noble*' (1998) 2 *International Journal of Evidence and Proof* 247; I Laing, '*R v Noble*: The Supreme Court and the Permissible Use of Silence' (1998) 43 *McGill Law Journal* 637; R Leng, 'Silence in Court: From Common Sense to Common Law: *Azzopardi*' (2002) 6 *International Journal of Evidence and Proof* 62; S Penney, 'What's Wrong with Self-Incrimination? The Wayward Path of Self-Incrimination Law in the Post-Charter Era—Part III: Compelled Communications, the Admissibility of Defendants' Previous

have refused to answer a question with good cause if '(a) he is entitled to refuse to answer the question by virtue of any enactment, whenever passed or made, or on the ground of privilege; or (b) the court in the exercise of its general discretion excuses him from answering it'.[44] An accused may not be convicted solely on an inference drawn from his or her silence in court.[45]

It is impermissible for inferences to be drawn if, in the words of section 35(1)(b), 'it appears to the court that the physical or mental condition of the accused makes it undesirable for him to give evidence'. Section 35(1)(b) is, however, of limited utility. It would appear that, should the defence not raise the issue, a court has no obligation to inquire of its own motion whether section 35(1)(b) may be applicable in the case at hand.[46] Further, the Court of Appeal held in *R v Friend*[47] that it could not be said that the judge had 'applied the wrong test' in determining the applicability of section 35(1)(b) 'if only because there is no right test'.[48] Friend, a 15-year-old, was charged with murder. The judge accepted psychological evidence that he had a mental age of around nine years, and that his comprehension and ability to give an account of himself were limited. It was concluded, however, that section 35(1)(b) was inapplicable since the accused was not abnormally suggestible and had provided an apparently coherent account of events during police interviews. This decision was upheld by the Court of Appeal. The Court thought that 'a physical condition might include a risk of an epileptic attack; a mental condition, latent schizophrenia where the experience of giving evidence might trigger a florid state'.[49] It will, however, 'only be in very rare cases that a judge will have to consider whether it is undesirable for an accused to give evidence on account of his *mental* condition', because such an accused is likely to have been found to be unfit to plead in the first place.[50] The Court also failed to be swayed by the argument that, because of the accused's mental age, he should have had the same immunity from adverse inference that the legislation provided at the time for persons under 14.[51] The trial judge's decision could not be impugned as it was not unreasonable in the *Wednesbury* sense; he had acted rationally in taking into account relevant factors and leaving irrelevant ones out of consideration.[52]

Given the manner in which section 35(1)(b) is drafted, it is unsurprising that the Court of Appeal is prepared to accord considerable leeway to trial judges in determining the applicability of the provision. Perhaps the solution lies, therefore, in amending

Testimony, and Inferences from Defendants' Silence' (2004) 48 *Criminal Law Quarterly* 474; E Stone, 'Calling a Spade a Spade: The Embarrassing Truth About the Right to Silence' (1998) 22 *Criminal Law Journal* 17. Cf G L Davies, 'The Prohibition Against Adverse Inferences from Silence: A Rule Without Reason?—Part I' (2000) 74 *Australian Law Journal* 26; G L Davies, 'The Prohibition Against Adverse Inferences from Silence: A Rule Without Reason?—Part II' (2000) 74 *Australian Law Journal* 99. The English position prior to the 1994 Act is discussed in S Nash, 'Silence as Evidence: A Commonsense Development or a Violation of a Basic Right?' (1997) 21 *Criminal Law Journal* 145.

[44] S 35(5).   [45] S 38(3).   [46] *R v A* [1997] Crim LR 883.

[47] [1997] 2 All ER 1011. See generally S Sharpe, 'Vulnerable Defendants and Inferences from Silence: Part 1' (1997) 147 *New Law Journal* 842; S Sharpe, 'Vulnerable Defendants and Inferences from Silence: Part 2' (1997) 147 *New Law Journal* 897.   [48] [1997] 2 All ER 1011, 1020.

[49] Ibid.   [50] Ibid, 1018 (italics added).   [51] Ibid, 1019.   [52] Ibid, 1021.

section 35(1)(b) by replacing the subjective test which it provides with a tighter and more objective test.

The issue of the drawing from silence in court of 'such inferences as appear proper' (section 35(1)(b)) was considered by the Court of Appeal in *R v Cowan*.[53] The Court held[54] that the use of the phrase 'such inferences as appear proper' was clearly 'intended to leave a broad discretion to a trial judge to decide in all the circumstances whether any proper inference is capable of being drawn by the jury. If not he should tell them so; otherwise it is for the jury to decide whether in fact an inference should properly be drawn.' But while a judge may 'direct or advise a jury against drawing such inference if the circumstances of the case justify such a course', 'in our view there would need either to be some evidential basis for doing so or some exceptional factors in the case making that a fair course to take'. It is clear that a judge *should not* direct a jury to draw no inferences merely on the basis that the defendant failed to testify through fear that his previous convictions would be put to him if he did so.[55]

The Court provided a brief catalogue of essential elements which should be contained in a direction to the jury. These are as follows:

• The jury must be directed that the burden of proof remains upon the prosecution throughout, and on what the required standard is.

• 'It is necessary for the judge to make clear to the jury that the defendant is entitled to remain silent. That is his right and his choice. The right of silence remains.'

• Given that an inference from silence cannot on its own prove guilt, the judge is required to direct the jury that they 'must be satisfied that the prosecution have established a case to answer before drawing any inferences from silence'. Rather confusingly,[56] as will be seen in Chapter 14, the concept of a 'case to answer' (or a 'prima facie case') is one which is also within the province of the judge: if a case to answer has not been established at the end of the prosecution evidence the judge is required to stop the case from proceeding. The Court in *Cowan* considered that to require the jury to make a second determination of whether there is a case to answer is not inappropriate since 'the jury may not believe the witnesses whose evidence the judge considered sufficient to raise a prima facie case. It must therefore be made clear to them that they must find there to be a case to answer on the prosecution evidence before drawing an adverse inference from the defendant's silence.' However, as Pattenden has observed:

> The accepted test of a *prima facie* case is whether there is prosecution evidence, assumed to be true and uncontradicted, upon which a reasonable jury could convict. What test is the jury to apply? The passage supposes that the jury, unlike the judge, will consider the credibility of the prosecution witnesses. If so, how does a finding of a *prima facie* case differ from a finding of

---

[53] [1995] 3 WLR 818. See generally K Browne, 'An Inference of Guilt?' (1997) 141 *Solicitors' Journal* 202; R Munday, '*Cum Tacent Clamant*: Drawing Proper Inferences from a Defendant's Failure to Testify' [1996] *Cambridge Law Journal* 32.   [54] [1995] 3 WLR 818, 823–4.

[55] Ibid, 823. See also *R v Taylor* [1999] Crim LR 77; *R v Becouarn* [2005] UKHL 55.

[56] See, eg, 'Inferences from a Defendant's Failure to Testify' (1997) 161 *Justice of the Peace* 1131, 1131.

guilt? Is it a case of concentrating exclusively on the prosecution evidence, other than any inferences arising from the accused's in-court silence? Are jurors capable of this?[57]

• The jury should be directed that 'if, despite any evidence relied upon to explain his silence or in the absence of any such evidence, the jury conclude the silence can only sensibly be attributed to the defendant's having no answer or none that would stand up to cross-examination, they may draw an adverse inference'. Notably, the Court was insistent that any reasons which defence counsel may wish to put forward to the jury to explain the accused's silence cannot simply take the form of assertions, but must be supported by evidence. Such an obligation may be considered to place an unduly onerous (and at times perhaps impossible) task on defence counsel, given the wide array of reasons which defendants may have for choosing to remain silent in court.

The Court stressed that it would 'not lightly interfere with a judge's exercise of discretion to direct or advise the jury as to the drawing of inferences from silence and as to the nature, extent and degree of such inferences. He is in the best position to have the feel of the case and so long as he gives the jury adequate directions of law as indicated above and leaves the decision to them, this court will be slow to substitute its view for his.' In a subsequent case this point was reiterated by the Court: 'we wish to repeat that we do not give any encouragement to appeals which are based upon the assertion that the Judge ought to have exercised his discretion differently or ought to have said more or less than he, in fact, said in the instant case'.[58] Such sentiments are not without merit and are in any event consistent with the trend of treating judges as the repository of large amounts of discretion where issues of evidence and procedure are concerned, with the role of the Court of Appeal being confined to interfering only where matters have gone obviously wrong. Notwithstanding this, it is certainly arguable that the Court of Appeal is leaving rather too much discretion in the hands of judges, and that one can reasonably expect more detailed guidelines to be provided on the issue of when precisely it would be appropriate for a jury to be advised *against* drawing adverse inferences. This would at least constitute one step towards the better protection of those who with good reason choose to exercise a right which after all still exists.

The Court of Appeal would appear, however, to take seriously a failure to direct the jury on one of the essential elements listed in *Cowan*. The conviction in *R v Birchall*[59] was quashed on account of the trial judge's failure to direct the jury that they had to be satisfied that the prosecution had established a case to answer before drawing any inference from the accused's silence. The fact that there may in fact have been a clear prima facie case was regarded as irrelevant. The Court commented that the drawing of inferences from silence was a particularly sensitive area, with many respected authorities having expressed concern that section 35 and analogous provisions might lead to wrongful convictions. Additionally, it seemed possible that the application of these provisions could lead to the United Kingdom being found in breach of

---

[57] R Pattenden, 'Silence: Lord Taylor's Legacy' (1998) 2 *International Journal of Evidence and Proof* 141, 149.

[58] *R v Napper* (1997) 161 JP 16, 22 (decision of 1995).   [59] *The Times*, 10 Feb 1998.

Articles 6(1) and 6(2) of the European Convention on Human Rights, unless the provisions were the subject of carefully framed directions to juries.[60]

Clearly it would be unfair for adverse inferences to be drawn from silence in court if the accused were not put on notice that it would be permissible for such inferences to be drawn. Hence the requirement that the court must:

> at the conclusion of the evidence for the prosecution, satisfy itself (in the case of proceedings on indictment, in the presence of the jury) that the accused is aware that the stage has been reached at which evidence can be given for the defence and that he can, if he wishes, give evidence and that, if he chooses not to give evidence, or having been sworn, without good cause refuses to answer any question, it will be permissible for the court or jury to draw such inferences as appear proper from his failure to give evidence or his refusal, without good cause, to answer any question.[61]

A practice direction spells out in detail the steps the judge should take to discharge this obligation, both in cases where the accused is legally represented and in cases where the accused is not legally represented.[62] This obligation to put the accused 'on notice' may be viewed as analogous to the obligation to caution suspects that it may be possible to draw adverse inferences from silence in the police station.[63]

Another aspect of a trial judge's duties when summing up in a case where the defendant had failed to testify was considered by the Court of Appeal in *R v Soames-Waring*.[64] The Court approved what an earlier Court of Appeal had said in *R v Curtin*:[65]

> When . . . the defendant was interviewed at length but did not give evidence, the judge, as in every other case, has to decide how fairly and conveniently he should place the defence case before the jury . . .

> When . . . the interviews were long, their terms had been rehearsed in evidence, reference to important parts had already no doubt been made more than once by counsel, and the jury had full transcripts of everything that had been said, it was not necessarily inappropriate in itself for the judge to deal with the interviews by specifically inviting the jury's attention to relevant passages by page numbers . . .

The Court of Appeal in *Soames-Waring* noted that while the appellant had not given evidence, the judge had invited the jury to read the whole of the summary of his interview with the police, and had then referred them to the salient parts in relation to each count. Thus the judge had done all that he could properly be expected to do in placing before the jury what was being advanced as giving rise to a defence.

---

[60] See also *R v El-Hannachi* [1998] 2 Cr App R 226.

[61] Criminal Justice and Public Order Act 1994, s 35(2). In *Radford v Kent County Council* (1998) 162 JP 697 (decision of 1998) it was held, however, that where justices omitted to give a 35(2) warning *but then* did not draw an inference, this omission did not render the convictions unsafe.

[62] *Consolidated Criminal Practice Direction*, IV.44, accessible via http://www.hmcourts-service.gov.uk/ cms/files/consolidated_criminal_practice_direction0405.pdf.   [63] See Ch 3.

[64] *The Times*, 20 July 1998, [1999] Crim LR 89.   [65] CA, unrep, 24 May 1996.

2.1.2 Testifying on behalf of a Co-Accused

It is clear that the same principles apply to testifying on behalf of a co-accused as apply to testifying on one's own behalf.[66] Thus an accused is competent, but not compellable, to give evidence on behalf of a co-accused. This can be justified on the basis that one accused may wish to give evidence *against*, rather than on behalf of, another. An accused, to be compellable to testify on behalf of a co-accused, must have ceased to be an accused in the same trial. He or she may, for example, have pleaded guilty,[67] been acquitted as a result of a direction to acquit by the trial judge,[68] or become liable to be tried separately as a result of the indictment being severed.[69]

2.2 The Accused's Spouse

Specific rules pertaining to the compellability of the spouse of an accused are provided in section 80 of the Police and Criminal Evidence Act 1984.[70] These rules apply only to a *current* spouse; it is expressly provided that 'a person who has been but is no longer married to the accused shall be compellable to give evidence as if that person and the accused had never been married'.[71] Further, they do not apply to an unmarried partner. The Court of Appeal has remarked that the words of the provision

> speak of the 'wife or husband of a person charged' being compellable only in certain circumstances. They do not speak of a person in the position of a wife...we do not accept the proposition...that proper respect for family life as envisaged by Article 8 [of the European Convention on Human Rights] requires that a co-habitee of a defendant, whether or not married to him, should not be required to give evidence or to answer questions about a statement which he has already made. This is plainly...an area where the interests of the family must be weighed against those of the community at large, and it is precisely the sort of area in which the European Court defers to the judgment of States in relation to their domestic courts. There may be much to be said for the view that with very limited exceptions all witnesses who are competent should also be compellable, and certainly the material before us does not enable us to conclude that because a concession has been made to husbands and wives proper respect for family life requires that a similar concession be made to those in the position of a husband or a wife....if the concession were to be widened it is not easy to see where, logically, the widening should end. That objection may not be insuperable but the possibility of serious limitations being placed upon society's power to enforce the criminal law is obvious.[72]

It is made clear by section 80A that the 'failure of the wife or husband of a person charged in any proceedings to give evidence in the proceedings shall not be made the subject of any comment by the prosecution'.[73] This prohibition does not extend to the

---

[66] S 1 of the Criminal Evidence Act 1898 makes provision as to the competence and compellability of an accused 'for the defence *at every stage of the proceedings*' (italics added).

[67] *R v Boal* [1965] 1 QB 402.   [68] *R v Conti* (1974) 58 Cr App R 387 (decision of 1973).

[69] *R v Richardson* (1967) 51 Cr App R 381 (decision of 1967).

[70] See generally P Creighton, 'Spouse Competence and Compellability' [1990] *Criminal Law Review* 34; S Edwards, 'Compelling a Reluctant Spouse' (1989) 139 *New Law Journal* 691.   [71] S 80(5).

[72] *R v Pearce* [2001] EWCA Crim 2834, [2002] 1 Cr App R 39 (p 551), [12].   [73] S 80(8).

trial judge, who may make such comment. A trial judge is thus able, by electing simply to make a comment him- or herself, to 'cure' a breach of section 80A by the prosecution. In *R v Whitton*,[74] the accused was charged with assault occasioning actual bodily harm. At issue was whether she had been acting in self-defence. In his closing speech prosecution counsel, in clear breach of the forerunner to section 80A, commented that the accused's husband, who had been present at the scene, had not been called as a witness. In his summing-up, the judge commented twice on the failure of the husband to testify. The Court of Appeal held that the appeal should be dismissed since counsel's error had been effectively 'subsumed' within the judge's summing-up and had not therefore undermined in any way the safety of the conviction.

2.2.1 Testifying for the Prosecution

If the accused's spouse ('S') happens to be an accused in the same trial, then obviously[75] he or she will not be competent, and therefore will not be compellable, to testify for the prosecution.[76] If S is not an accused in the same trial, then he or she will, if competent, be compellable to give prosecution evidence in respect *only* of any specified offence with which any person is charged.[77] An offence is a specified offence if:

(a) it involves an assault on, or injury or a threat of injury to, the wife or husband or a person who was at the material time under the age of 16;

(b) it is a sexual offence alleged to have been committed in respect of a person who was at the material time under that age; or

(c) it consists of attempting or conspiring to commit, or of aiding, abetting, counselling, procuring or inciting the commission of, an offence falling within paragraph (a) or (b) above.[78]

A 'sexual offence' is defined as 'an offence under the Sexual Offences Act 1956, the Indecency with Children Act 1960, the Protection of Children Act 1978 or Part 1 of the Sexual Offences Act 2003'.[79]

2.2.2 Testifying for the Accused

If the accused's spouse ('S') happens to be an accused in the same trial as the accused ('A'), then—consistently with the principle that one accused should not be compellable

---

[74] [1998] Crim LR 492.

[75] As seen above, an accused person is never competent to give prosecution evidence in the same trial.

[76] See also s 80(4).

[77] S 80(2A)(b). For an account of an unsuccessful attempt to prevent a marriage from taking place in order to maintain the compellability of a spouse to give prosecution evidence, see *R (CPS) v Registrar General of Births, Deaths and Marriages* [2002] EWCA Civ 1661, [2003] QB 1222. See generally D Dwyer, 'Can a Marriage Be Delayed in the Public Interest So As to Maintain the Compellability of a Prosecution Witness?: *R (on the application of the Crown Prosecution Service) v Registrar General of Births, Deaths and Marriages*' (2003) 7 *International Journal of Evidence and Proof* 191; J R Spencer, 'Spouses as Witnesses: Back to Brighton Rock?' [2003] *Cambridge Law Journal* 250.   [78] S 80(3).

[79] S 80(7).

to give evidence on behalf of another—S will not be compellable to testify on behalf of A.[80] If S is not an accused in the same trial, then he or she will be compellable to give evidence on behalf of A by virtue of section 80(2).

2.2.3 Testifying for a Co-Accused

If the accused's spouse ('S') happens to be an accused in the same trial as a co-accused ('C') of the accused, then—consistently with the principle that one accused should not be compellable to give evidence on behalf of another—S will not be compellable to testify on behalf of C.[81] If S is not an accused in the same trial, then he or she will be compellable to give evidence on behalf of C in respect of any specified offence with which C is charged.[82] The definition of a specified offence has been provided above.

2.2.4 An Evaluation

It would appear that considerations pertaining to the notions of the sanctity of marriage and the preservation of matrimonial harmony underlie the strategy of making an accused's spouse a non-compellable witness for the prosecution and a co-accused, except in the case of specific offences of violence or sexual offences.[83] It is doubtful, however, whether such notions hold as much sway today as they may once have done, and in particular whether they have sufficient force to outweigh the public interest in the conviction of the guilty. In any event, it is the principle of non-compellability itself which may well undermine marital harmony, given that it

> may tempt an accused to exert unedifying pressure on his or her spouse to refrain from testifying, to say nothing of the threat of reprisals. . . . Now, if a wife or husband succumbs to pressure from their accused partner, they are in effect made an unwilling accomplice to the offence in assisting their spouse to escape punishment (assuming, of course, that he is guilty). A spouse who thus becomes an instrument of their partner's wrongdoing suffers moral degradation, which itself could undermine the couple's relationship, as well as being detrimental to the innocent spouse.[84]

In this respect, an approach like that taken in the Uniform Evidence Acts in Australia to the compellability of an accused's spouse to testify as a prosecution witness may be preferable. The Act provides that an accused's spouse, de facto spouse, parent, or child is compellable to testify for the prosecution in the case of particular offences against children, and domestic violence offences.[85] In the case of all other offences, there is no *rule* of non-compellability. On the contrary, there is a presumption of compellability which is capable of being rebutted. A person who is the spouse, de facto spouse, parent, or child of the defendant is entitled to object to being required to testify for the prosecution.

---

[80] See also s 80(4).   [81] See also s 80(4).   [82] S 80(2A)(a).

[83] Criminal Law Revision Committee, *Eleventh Report: Evidence (General)* (Cmnd 4991) (1972) [147], [155].

[84] P Roberts and A Zuckerman, *Criminal Evidence* (2004) 232. For an alternative perspective, see R O Lempert, 'A Right to Every Woman's Evidence' (1981) 66 *Iowa Law Review* 725.   [85] S 19.

This objection will succeed if:

(a) there is a likelihood that harm would or might be caused (whether directly or indirectly) to the person, or to the relationship between the person and the defendant, if the person gives the evidence; and

(b) the nature and extent of that harm outweighs the desirability of having the evidence given.

In determining the issue all relevant factors may be considered, and the following *must* be considered:

(a) the nature and gravity of the offence for which the defendant is being prosecuted;

(b) the substance and importance of any evidence that the person might give and the weight that is likely to be attached to it;

(c) whether any other evidence concerning the matters to which the evidence of the person would relate is reasonably available to the prosecutor;

(d) the nature of the relationship between the defendant and the person;

(e) whether, in giving the evidence, the person would have to disclose matter that was received by the person in confidence from the defendant.[86]

2.3 The Accused's Civil Partner

Section 84(1) of the Civil Partnership Act 2004 provides: 'Any enactment or rule of law relating to the giving of evidence by a spouse applies in relation to a civil partner as it applies in relation to the spouse.'

2.4 Bankers

Section 6 of the Bankers' Books Evidence Act 1879 provides:

A banker or officer of a bank shall not, in any legal proceeding to which the bank is not a party, be compellable to produce any banker's book the contents of which can be proved under this Act, or to appear as a witness to prove the matters, transactions, and accounts therein recorded, unless by order of a judge made for special cause.

2.5 Judges

The rule is that a judge is *not compellable* 'to give evidence of those matters of which he became aware relating to and as a result of his performance of his judicial functions'. This rule does not, therefore, apply to 'collateral incidents' such as a murder witnessed by the judge in the courtroom. But since the judge remains *competent* to testify even as to matters which relate to and of which he became aware as a result of his performance of judicial functions, 'if a situation arises where his evidence is vital, the judge should be

---

[86] S 18.

able to be relied on not to allow the fact that he cannot be compelled to give evidence to stand in the way of his doing so'.[87]

2.6 The Sovereign

Not uncontroversially, the sovereign is not compellable to testify.[88]

3 Corroboration, Witness Unreliability, and Judicial Warnings

An indicator of the reliability of an item of prosecution evidence may be provided by the fact that it is supported by other evidence in the case. As discussed in Chapter 4, the concept of supporting evidence plays an important role in the law relating to identification evidence. Traditionally, English law placed considerable emphasis on a particular type of support known as 'corroboration'.[89] Corroborative evidence 'must be independent testimony which affects the accused by connecting or tending to connect him with the crime. In other words, it must be evidence which implicates him, that is, which confirms in some material particular not only the evidence that the crime has been committed, but also that the prisoner committed it.'[90]

There now remain only a few situations in which corroboration of evidence is a prerequisite to conviction.[91] Whether evidence is corroborated is ultimately a question for the trier of fact.

3.1 Speeding

A person may not be convicted of an offence of speeding under section 89(1) of the Road Traffic Regulation Act 1984 on the uncorroborated evidence of a witness 'to the effect that, in the opinion of the witness, the person prosecuted was driving the vehicle at a speed exceeding a specified limit'.[92] This has been interpreted as meaning that a defendant cannot be convicted on uncorroborated evidence given by a witness of his or her 'visual impression of a defendant's speed. That is so whether the witness is an untutored bystander or a police officer who may have considerable expertise in visually assessing

---

[87] *Warren v Warren* [1996] 4 All ER 664, 671.

[88] See generally D Pannick, 'The Queen Should Not Always Be Treated Like Royalty', *The Times*, 26 Nov 2002, Law, 4; D Pannick, 'Turning Queen's Evidence' [2003] *Public Law* 201.

[89] For a historical perspective see J H Langbein, *The Origins of Adversary Criminal Trial* (2003) Ch 4.

[90] *R v Baskerville* [1916] 2 KB 658, 667.

[91] This is in contrast to the position in Scotland, where evidence of all the essential ingredients of an offence must be corroborated: see generally A Brown, 'Two Cases on Corroboration' [1998] *Scots Law Times* 71; D Sheldon, 'Corroboration and Relevance: Some Further Thoughts on *Fox v HM Advocate* and *Smith v Lees*' [1998] *Scots Law Times* 115.   [92] Road Traffic Regulation Act 1984, s 89(2).

the speed of moving vehicles.'[93] A defendant can, however, be convicted on the uncorroborated evidence of an expert in post-accident reconstruction:

> to the effect that, having inspected damage to the vehicle driven by the person prosecuted following a collision and having inspected and measured marks on the road at the place of collision and inspected marks on such vehicle, and having carried out certain tests, and having made calculations based on the physical signs observed and the tests carried out (such damage, marks, tests and calculations being described in evidence), he was of opinion that the person prosecuted was driving the vehicle at a speed exceeding a specified limit before the collision.[94]

3.2 Perjury

A person charged

- with any offence against the Perjury Act 1911, or 'any offence declared by any other Act to be perjury or subornation of perjury, or to be punishable as perjury or subornation of perjury',
- may not be convicted on the uncorroborated evidence of a witness 'as to the falsity of any statement alleged to be false'.[95]

The actual falsity of the statement is not a prerequisite to a conviction for perjury; the offence can be committed so long as the defendant does not believe it to be true. Thus, because what is required is corroboration of *evidence of falsity*, there may well be perjury prosecutions in which the corroboration requirement will not apply. In practice, however, these are likely to be very rare, since the vast majority of perjury prosecutions do involve an allegation that the statement in question is false.[96]

3.3 Attempts to Commit the Above Offences

By virtue of section 2(2)(g) of the Criminal Attempts Act 1981, any statutory provision having the effect of requiring evidence to be corroborated as a prerequisite to conviction applies also to an *attempt* to commit the offence in question.

3.4 Criminal Justice and Public Order Act 1994, Section 32(1)

Immediately prior to the Criminal Justice and Public Order Act 1994, trial judges were obliged to issue a warning to the jury about convicting the accused on the uncorroborated evidence of (1) an alleged accomplice of the accused testifying for the prosecution; or (2) a complainant in a sexual case; or (3) a prosecution witness who was not in one of these two categories but fulfilled 'analogous criteria';[97] for example, a witness whose

---

[93] *Crossland v DPP* [1988] 3 All ER 712, 714.   [94] Ibid, 713.
[95] Perjury Act 1911, s 13. See *R v Hamid* (1979) 69 Cr App R 324 (decision of 1979); *R v Carroll* (1994) 99 Cr App R 381 (decision of 1993).   [96] *R v Rider* (1986) 83 Cr App R 207 (decision of 1986).
[97] *R v Spencer* [1987] AC 128.

evidence may have been tainted by an improper motive[98] or who was 'suspect' by reason of mental condition or criminal connection.[99] Section 32(1) abolishes the warning requirement in relation to alleged accomplices and complainants in sexual cases:[100]

> Any requirement whereby at a trial on indictment it is obligatory for the court to give the jury a warning about convicting the accused on the uncorroborated evidence of a person merely because that person is—
>
> (a) an alleged accomplice of the accused, or
>
> (b) where the offence charged is a sexual offence, the person in respect of whom it is alleged to have been committed,
>
> is hereby abrogated.

Analogous provision is made for summary trials in section 32(3).

Section 32(1) was the subject of detailed consideration by the Court of Appeal in *R v Makanjuola*.[101] The following key points emerge from this decision:[102]

• It would be inappropriate for judges to continue effectively to apply the old common law by giving, in the exercise of their 'discretion', precisely those warnings which were required at common law in relation to accomplices and complainants in sexual cases.

• Rather, the discretion about whether a warning in relation to *any* witness should be given, and, if so, in what terms, should be exercised by taking into account the following factors: the circumstances of the case, the issues raised, and the content and quality of the witness's evidence.

• It will often be considered that no special warning is required at all. But in some cases, it may be appropriate to warn the jury to exercise caution before acting upon the evidence of a particular witness. There will need to be an *evidential basis* for suggesting that the evidence of the witness may be unreliable. An evidential basis cannot be provided by mere suggestion by cross-examining counsel. In a more extreme case—for example, if the witness is shown to have lied, to have made previous false complaints, or to bear the defendant some grudge—a stronger warning may be thought appropriate and the judge may suggest that it would be wise to look for some supporting material before acting on the evidence.

• If a question arises about whether a special warning should be given in respect of a witness, it is desirable that the question be resolved by discussion with counsel in the absence of the jury before final speeches. The desirability of this was emphasized again by the Court in *R v Walker*.[103]

---

[98] *R v Beck* [1982] 1 WLR 461.   [99] *R v Spencer* [1987] AC 128.
[100] See generally D J Birch, 'Corroboration: Goodbye to All That?' [1995] *Criminal Law Review* 524; I Dennis, 'The Criminal Justice and Public Order Act 1994: The Evidence Provisions' [1995] *Criminal Law Review* 4; J Hartshorne, 'Corroboration and Care Warnings After *Makanjuola*' (1998) 2 *International Journal of Evidence and Proof* 1; P Lewis, 'Corroboration Reborn' (1996–7) 7 *King's College Law Journal* 140; P Mirfield, ' "Corroboration" After the 1994 Act' [1995] *Criminal Law Review* 448.   [101] [1995] 1 WLR 1348.
[102] Ibid, 1351–2.   [103] [1996] Crim LR 742.

• Where a warning *is* given in the exercise of discretion, it will be appropriate to do so as part of the judge's review of the evidence and comments on how the evidence should be evaluated. The strength and terms of the warning are matters for the judge to decide.

• The Court of Appeal would be reluctant to interfere with the exercise of discretion by the trial judge (who, after all, has had the advantage of assessing the manner and content of the witness's evidence), except in a case where that exercise is unreasonable in the *Wednesbury* sense. This point was emphasized again by the Court in *R v R*,[104] where the burden on an appellant of showing *Wednesbury* unreasonableness in this context was described as a heavy one. Thus in *R* the Court refused to interfere with the trial judge's exercise of discretion in relation to the strength of the warning given. One case in which the Court has been prepared to allow an appeal on the basis of failure to consider giving a warning is that of *R v Walker*.[105] The complainant had made a complaint of rape, later retracted the complaint, and later still withdrawn the retraction. The complainant's evidence was unsupported. It was held that the retraction of the complaint and the withdrawal of the retraction were important and relevant to the complainant's credibility. Thus it was not sufficient that the matter had been widely canvassed in counsel's speeches; a special warning of the type referred to in *Makanjuola* should also have been considered.

It is to be noted that section 32(1) abolishes the warning requirement in relation to just two of the three categories of witnesses attracting mandatory corroboration warnings immediately prior to the Criminal Justice and Public Order Act 1994. The third category, of which no mention was made in *Makanjuola*, would seem to remain unaffected. Given that this third category is merely a product of 'the overriding rule... that [the judge] must put the defence fairly and adequately'[106] to the jury, its survival is in no way inconsistent with *Makanjuola*. The discretionary warnings, tailored to the circumstances of the particular case, which *Makanjuola* advocates are clearly themselves a product of the same overriding rule.

The exhortation in *Makanjuola* that it is inappropriate for trial judges to continue to apply the old law in the exercise of their 'discretion' is very much to be welcomed. Despite this, there is a danger that trial judges may in fact be continuing to give strong warnings in relation to alleged accomplices testifying for the prosecution and complainants in sexual cases, even if a warning is not warranted in the circumstances of the particular case. 'Although the Court of Appeal has dealt with the issue in a perfectly satisfactory way, research is required into whether its pronouncements are being followed by trial judges.'[107] As the prosecution cannot appeal against an acquittal, it would effectively be unable to bring such a practice to the attention of the Court of Appeal except by means of an Attorney-General's reference. It is strongly arguable, therefore, that section 32(1) should have been couched in stronger terms, actively *prohibiting* warnings in relation to these two categories of witnesses except in exceptional circumstances.[108]

---

[104] [1996] Crim LR 815.   [105] [1996] Crim LR 742.   [106] *R v Spencer* [1987] AC 128, 142.
[107] J Temkin, *Rape and the Legal Process* (2nd ed 2002) 263.   [108] Ibid, 263–7.

The further development of education programmes which seek to dispel the myth that women are prone to making false accusations of rape should also be encouraged. Further, as Mack suggests, consideration could be given to the possibility of providing juries with information about the reality of rape and the effects of rape on victims, so that women's testimony can be placed in the appropriate context; to the possibility of calling expert witnesses to dispel misconceptions which the jury may hold and which may prevent them from evaluating the complainant's testimony properly; and even to the possibility of admitting statistical or expert evidence demonstrating the falsity of rape myths which were once actively endorsed by the law and are still accepted by many jurors.[109]

A situation where an appellate court may consider it appropriate for the discretion to give a care warning to have been exercised in favour of giving one is in relation to 'cell confessions'. The Privy Council has explained that it is

> not possible to lay down any fixed rules about the directions which the judge should give to a jury about the evidence which one prisoner gives against another prisoner about things done or said while they are both together in custody. But . . . a judge must always be alert to the possibility that the evidence by one prisoner against another is tainted by an improper motive, and the possibility that this may be so has to be regarded with particular care where a prisoner who has yet to face trial gives evidence that the other prisoner has confessed to the very crime for which he is being held in custody.[110]

> . . . there are two steps which the judge must follow . . . , and . . . they are both equally important. The first is to draw the jury's attention to the indications that may justify the inference that the prisoner's evidence is tainted. The second is to advise the jury to be cautious before accepting his evidence. Some of the indications that the evidence may be tainted may have been referred to by counsel, but it is the responsibility of the judge to examine the evidence for himself so that he can instruct the jury fully as to where these indications are to be found and as to their significance. Counsel may well have suggested to the jury that the evidence is unreliable, but it is the responsibility of the judge to add his own authority to these submissions by explaining to the jury that they must be cautious before accepting and acting upon that evidence.[111]

Taking into account previous authorities on the issue, the Court of Appeal provided in *R v Stone*[112] in early 2005 a summary of what it regarded as the applicable principles:

> Any case involving a cell confession will prompt the most careful consideration by the judge.[113]

> But the judge's consideration is not trammelled by fixed rules . . . there will generally be a need for the judge to point out to the jury that such confessions are often easy to concoct and difficult to prove and that experience has shown that prisoners may have many motives to lie. If the prison informant has a significant criminal record or a history of lying then usually the judge should point this out to the jury and explain that it gives rise to a need for great care and why.

---

[109] K Mack, 'Continuing Barriers to Women's Credibility: A Feminist Perspective on the Proof Process' (1993) 4 *Criminal Law Forum* 327, 350–1.   [110] *Benedetto v R* [2003] UKPC 27, [2003] 1 WLR 1545, [34].

[111] Ibid, [35]. See generally P Tain, 'Confessions of a Cellmate' (2003) 147 *Solicitors' Journal* 566. See also *R v Causley* [1999] Crim LR 572; *R v Price* [2004] EWCA Crim 1359.

[112] [2005] EWCA Crim 105. See generally C Wells and M Stevenson, 'Cell Confessions—No Stone Left Unturned' (2005) 155 *New Law Journal* 550; D Wolchover and A Heaton-Armstrong, 'Confessors of the (Prison) Cloth', *Archbold News*, 23 May 2005, 8.   [113] [2005] EWCA Crim 105, [82].

The trial judge will be best placed to decide the strength of such warnings and the necessary extent of the accompanying analysis.[114]

But not every case requires such a warning. This Court has said repeatedly that a summing-up should be tailored by the judge to the circumstances of the particular case. That principle bears repetition. If an alleged confession, for whatever reason, would not have been easy to invent, it would be absurd to require the judge to tell the jury that confessions are often easy to concoct. Similarly, ... in a case where the defence has deliberately not cross-examined the informant as to motive of hope of advantage, the law does not require the judge to tell the jury that, merely because the informant was a prisoner, there may have been such a motive.[115]

The Court of Appeal has acknowledged that 'a judge, in exercising his discretion as to what to say to the jury should at least warn them, where one defendant has given evidence adverse to another, to examine the evidence of each with care because each has or may have an interest of his own to serve'.[116]

The unpredictability generated by the discretionary nature of care warnings and their effect is well illustrated by the decision of the Supreme Court of Canada in *R v Brooks*.[117] Of the seven judges who sat on the Supreme Court in this case, three[118] held that on the facts of the case a care warning about the evidence of two 'jailhouse informants' should have been given in the exercise of discretion. Three judges[119] thought that the trial judge had not erred in failing to give a care warning. The seventh judge[120] thought that a care warning should have been given, but held that the prosecution's appeal should be allowed because there was no reasonable possibility that the verdict would have been different if the warning had been given. Thus the result was that the prosecution's appeal was allowed and the conviction restored, even though four of the seven judges thought that a care warning should have been given in the exercise of discretion on the facts of the case.

Rather than rely on a care warning it may be appropriate in some cases for section 78 of the Police and Criminal Evidence Act 1984 to be utilized to exclude totally from the jury's consideration the evidence of the impugned witness. The courts are cautious about such a strategy, with the Court of Appeal remarking that the possibility of using section 78 in this way 'could only even arguably arise if it was thought, first, that no reasonable jury could accept the witness's evidence; but second, for some reason the grounds for demonstrating that that was so could not be put before the jury'.[121]

3.5 Evidence of Accused's Lies

Before leaving the subject of warnings, it would seem appropriate to address briefly the issue of evidence of lies told by an accused, either in or out of court. The prosecution

[114] [2005] EWCA Crim 105, [83].   [115] Ibid, [84].

[116] *R v Jones* [2003] EWCA Crim 1966, [2004] 1 Cr App R 5 (p 60), [41].

[117] [2000] 1 SCR 237. See generally G T G Seniuk, 'Liars, Scoundrels and the Search for Truth' (2000) 30 *Criminal Reports (5th)* 244.   [118] Iacobucci, Major, and Arbour JJ.

[119] Gonthier, McLachlin, and Bastarache JJ.   [120] Binnie J.

[121] *R v Smith* [2003] EWCA Crim 3847, [46]. Reversed by the House of Lords on other grounds: *R v Smith* [2005] UKHL 12, [2005] 1 WLR 704.

may wish to adduce this evidence since, in the words of the Court of Appeal in *R v Lucas*, 'it accords with good sense that a lie told by a defendant about a material issue may show that the liar knew if he told the truth he would be sealing his fate'.[122] The telling of lies need not *necessarily*, however, indicate a consciousness of guilt:

People do not always tell the truth. Laudable as it may be to do so, whatever the circumstances, they do not, or cannot, always bring themselves to face up to reality. Innocent people sometimes tell lies even when by doing so they create or reinforce the suspicion of guilt. In short, therefore, while lying is often resorted to by the guilty to hide and conceal the truth, the innocent can sometimes misguidedly react to a problem, or postpone facing up to it or attempt to deflect ill-founded suspicion, or fortify their defence by telling lies. For example, a married man who has had consensual sexual intercourse with a woman and is then faced with an allegation of raping her will sometimes untruthfully deny the act of sexual intercourse at all, in order selfishly to avoid embarrassment to him of his wife's discovery of his infidelity or, less selfishly perhaps, the consequent anguish that the knowledge may cause to her and to their children.[123]

Thus evidence of lies must be treated with caution, and there are therefore circumstances in which a judicial direction concerning a defendant's lies (or a *Lucas* direction, as it is known) may be required.[124] The purpose of the direction is to avoid the risk that the jury may adopt the reasoning 'that lying demonstrates, and is consistent only with, a desire to conceal guilt, or, putting it another way, ... jump from the conclusion that the defendant has lied to the further conclusion that he must therefore be guilty'.[125] In *R v Burge*, the Court of Appeal undertook the task of

summarising the circumstances in which, in our judgment, a *Lucas* direction is usually required. There are four such circumstances but they may overlap:

1. Where the defence relies on an alibi.

2. Where the judge considers it desirable or necessary to suggest that the jury should look for support or corroboration of one piece of evidence from other evidence in the case, and amongst that other evidence draws attention to lies told, or allegedly told, by the defendant.

3. Where the prosecution seek to show that something said, either in or out of the court, in relation to a separate and distinct issue was a lie, and to rely on that lie as evidence of guilt in relation to the charge which is sought to be proved.

4. Where although the prosecution have not adopted the approach to which we have just referred, the judge reasonably envisages that there is a real danger that the jury may do so.

...a judge would be wise always, before speeches and summing-up in circumstance number four, and perhaps also in other circumstances, to consider with counsel whether, in the instant

---

[122] [1981] QB 720, 724.   [123] *R v Middleton, The Times*, 12 April 2000, transcript [18].

[124] See generally 'Conduct or Behaviour After the Offence (Alleged): The *Lucas* Direction' (2000) 164 *Justice of the Peace* 760; L Connor, 'Lies, Lying, and *Lucas*' (2004) 168 *Justice of the Peace* 168; K Grevling, 'Silence, Lies and Vicious Circularity' in P Mirfield and R Smith (eds), *Essays for Colin Tapper* (2003).

[125] *R v Middleton, The Times*, 12 April 2000, transcript [20].

case, such a direction is in fact required, and, if so, how it should be formulated. If the matter is dealt with in that way, this court will be very slow to interfere with the exercise of the judge's discretion. Further, the judge should, of course, be assisted by counsel in identifying cases where a direction is called for.[126]

On the *content* of a *Lucas* direction, the Court said:

The direction should, if given, so far as possible, be tailored to the circumstances of the case, but it will normally be sufficient if it makes the two basic points:

1. that the lie must be admitted or proved beyond reasonable doubt, and;
2. that the mere fact that the defendant lied is not in itself evidence of guilt since defendants may lie for innocent reasons, so only if the jury is sure that the defendant did not lie for an innocent reason can a lie support the prosecution case.[127]

The Court has emphasized more recently that:

the four situations outlined in *Burge* . . . were an attempt by the Court to identify common instances where a *Lucas* direction is required, but without seeking to reduce the force of the general principle that such a direction is required if there is a danger that the jury may regard the fact, if it be a fact, that a defendant has told lies as probative of his guilt on the charge. . . . the purpose of a *Lucas* direction is to guard against the forbidden line of reasoning that the telling of lies equals guilt. That may be true whether the lie is told in or out of court.[128]

R v Nash is a case in which it was held that a *Lucas* direction ought to have been given. The defendant was convicted of criminal damage with an air rifle. He had initially lied to the police when he denied owning an air weapon. The Court of Appeal considered that 'the absence of the conventional *Lucas* direction in the present case amounted to a misdirection rendering the verdict of the jury unsafe':[129]

. . . a *Lucas* direction is necessary where a lie is relied upon by the prosecution or might be used by the jury to support evidence of guilt as opposed to merely reflecting on the defendant's credibility. . . . whether or not counsel specifically relied upon that lie (the denial of owning an air rifle) in support of guilt, it was a matter which the jury may well have taken into account in support of guilt and may perhaps have regarded . . . as establishing guilt. In the absence of direct evidence implicating the appellant, it is likely to have featured strongly in their thinking.[130]

In Chapter 3 consideration was given to the directions to the jury that are required in relation to prosecution evidence that the defendant failed to mention during police questioning a fact later relied on in court. The Court of Appeal has clarified that 'where the same response is relied upon both as a lie and a failure to mention a fact relied upon by the defence then both directions should be given'.[131]

---

[126] [1996] 1 Cr App R 163, 173–4.

[127] Ibid, 174. See also *R v Hill* [1996] Crim LR 419; *R v Robinson* [1996] Crim LR 417; *R v Genus* [1996] Crim LR 502; *R v Harron* [1996] 2 Cr App R 457; *R v Jefford* [2003] EWCA Crim 1987, [23].

[128] *R v Jefford* [2003] EWCA Crim 1987, [19].   [129] [2004] EWCA Crim 164, [17].

[130] Ibid, [15].   [131] *R v O (A)* [2000] Crim LR 617, transcript [11].

4 Measures Designed to Ease the Burden on Witnesses

In recent times greater attention has been accorded to the treatment of witnesses in general and vulnerable witnesses in particular. Child witnesses, for example, were traditionally regarded with great suspicion. However, it may be demonstrated by reference to psychological and other evidence that this suspicion is largely unwarranted.[132] First, the notion that children's memories are unreliable is a misleading generalization. The significant point, rather, is that the reliability of a child's memory is dependent to a great extent upon the manner in which he or she was questioned. Secondly, it has traditionally been suggested that children are egocentric in the sense that they have no concern about the impact of their actions (for example, lying) on others, and in the sense that they cannot remember details which do not interest them directly. Now while there is evidence that very young children may be egocentric in the first sense, it is unclear whether this kind of egocentrism actually has any effect on a child's veracity. Furthermore, there is no evidence that egocentrism in the second sense is more peculiar to children than to adults. Thirdly, children have traditionally been regarded as particularly suggestible, but Spencer and Flin point out that 'the psychological research shows that children, like adults, can be suggestible but that this risk can be minimised by the use of sensitive questioning techniques in the hands of a skilled interviewer'.[133] Fourthly, it is often thought that children cannot distinguish fact from fantasy, but the reality is that there is no evidence suggesting that children routinely fantasize about the sort of incidents which might result in court proceedings. Children's fantasies are characterized instead by their daily experience and personal knowledge. Finally, there is the notion that children are prone to making false allegations. In fact, however, there is no evidence to support the assumption that children are more inclined to lie than adults.

Some relatively simple and straightforward steps can obviously be taken to ease the ordeal endured by child witnesses, such as 'reducing the chances of distressing postponements, ensuring barristers use simple language, encouraging children to say whether there is something they do not understand and arranging for the child to have regular breaks'.[134] The question to be considered is what further measures are, or should be, available.

In civil cases rule 32.3 of the Civil Procedure Rules very simply provides: 'The court may allow a witness to give evidence through a video link or by other means.'

---

[132] See J R Spencer and R H Flin, *The Evidence of Children: The Law and the Psychology* (2nd ed 1993) Ch 11. See also A Mortimer and E Shepherd, 'The Frailty of Children's Testimony' in A Heaton-Armstrong, E Shepherd, and D Wolchover, *Analysing Witness Testimony: A Guide for Legal Practitioners and Other Professionals* (1999); G Sattar and R Bull, 'Child Witnesses in Court: Psycho-Legal Issues' (1996) 140 *Solicitors' Journal* 401; C Stern and W Stern (J T Lamiell, translator), *Recollection, Testimony, and Lying in Early Childhood* (1999); H L Westcott, G M Davies, and R H C Bull (eds), *Children's Testimony: A Handbook of Psychological Research and Forensic Practice* (2002).

[133] J R Spencer and R H Flin, *The Evidence of Children: The Law and the Psychology* (2nd ed 1993) 307.

[134] Ibid. See also M Bowes, 'Children Who Deserve a Fair Hearing', *The Times*, 15 Feb 2005, Law, 7.

In *Polanski v Condé Nast Publications Ltd* the House of Lords considered the applicability of rule 32.3 in the case of a fugitive who sought to bring a libel action. In the words of Lord Nicholls of Birkenhead:

> Despite his fugitive status, a fugitive from justice is entitled to invoke the assistance of the court and its procedures in protection of his civil rights. He can bring or defend proceedings even though he is, and remains, a fugitive. If the administration of justice is not brought into disrepute by a fugitive's ability to have recourse to the court to protect his civil rights even though he is and remains a fugitive, it is difficult to see why the administration of justice should be regarded as brought into disrepute by permitting the fugitive to have recourse to one of the court's current procedures which will enable him in a particular case to pursue his proceedings while remaining a fugitive. To regard the one as acceptable and the other as not smacks of inconsistency. If a fugitive is entitled to bring his proceedings in this country there can be little rhyme or reason in withholding from him a procedural facility flowing from a modern technological development which is now readily available to all litigants. For obvious reasons, it is not a facility claimants normally seek to use, but it is available to them. To withhold this facility from a fugitive would be to penalise him because of his status.[135]
>
> That would lack coherence. It would be to give with one hand and take away with the other: a fugitive may bring proceedings here, but his position as a fugitive will tell against him when the court is exercising its discretionary powers. It would also be arbitrary in its practical effect today. A fugitive may bring proceedings here but not if it should chance that his own oral evidence is needed. Then, despite the current availability of VCF [video conferencing], he cannot use that facility and a civil wrong suffered by him will pass unremedied.[136]
>
> No doubt special cases may arise. But the general rule should be that in respect of proceedings properly brought in this country, a claimant's unwillingness to come to this country because he is a fugitive from justice is a valid reason, and can be a sufficient reason, for making a VCF order.[137]

The Court of Appeal has acknowledged that there is a general responsibility on the part of trial judges to ensure the appropriate treatment of witnesses in criminal cases:

> The trial judge is . . . obliged to have regard not only to the need to ensure a fair trial for the defendant but also to the reasonable interests of other parties to the court process, in particular witnesses, and among witnesses particularly those who are obliged to relive by describing in the witness box an ordeal to which they say they have been subject. It is the clear duty of the trial judge to do everything he can, consistently with giving the defendant a fair trial, to minimise the trauma suffered by other participants.[138]

In addition, a number of more substantial measures have been adopted in legislation in an attempt to assist witnesses, including in particular child witnesses.[139] These measures

---

[135] [2005] UKHL 10, [2005] 1 WLR 637, [31].   [136] Ibid, [32].

[137] Ibid, [33]. See generally A Melville-Brown, 'Screen Test' (2005) 102(10) *Law Society's Gazette* 27.

[138] *R v Brown* [1998] 2 Cr App R 364, 371.

[139] See generally V Baird, 'Youth Justice and Criminal Evidence Act 1999: Part 2' [Dec 1999] *Legal Action* 15; P Bates, 'The Youth Justice and Criminal Evidence Act—The Evidence of Children and Vulnerable Adults' (1999) 11 *Child and Family Law Quarterly* 289; D Birch, 'A Better Deal for Vulnerable Witnesses?' [2000] *Criminal Law Review* 223; J McEwan, 'In Defence of Vulnerable Witnesses: The Youth Justice and Criminal Evidence

will now be examined. As will be seen, the statutory provisions in question have been promulgated with the laudable but sometimes apparently elusive goal in mind of enhancing the quality of evidence and protecting witnesses, while at the same time protecting the right of the defendant to a fair trial.[140]

4.1 The Criminal Justice Act 2003

4.1.1 Live Links

A live link[141] is:

a live television link or other arrangement by which a witness, while at a place in the United Kingdom which is outside the building where the proceedings are being held, is able to see and hear a person at the place where the proceedings are being held and to be seen and heard by ... [:]

(a) the defendant or defendants,

(b) the judge or justices (or both) and the jury (if there is one),

(c) legal representatives acting in the proceedings, and

(d) any interpreter or other person appointed by the court to assist the witness.[142]

The effect of section 51 of the Criminal Justice Act 2003 is that a witness, other than the defendant, may give evidence through a live link if the court so directs.[143] Such a direction is to be given only if 'the court is satisfied that it is in the interests of the efficient or effective administration of justice for the person concerned to give evidence in the proceedings through a live link'.[144] 'In deciding whether to give a direction ... the court must consider all the circumstances of the case'[145] including in particular the following:

(a) the availability of the witness,

(b) the need for the witness to attend in person,

(c) the importance of the witness's evidence to the proceedings,

(d) the views of the witness,

Act 1999' (2000) 4 *International Journal of Evidence and Proof* 1; J McEwan, 'Special Measures for Witnesses and Victims' in M McConville and G Wilson, *The Handbook of the Criminal Justice Process* (2002); J R Spencer, 'The Youth Justice and Criminal Evidence Act 1999: The Evidence Provisions', *Archbold News*, 28 Jan 2000, 5; P Tain, 'Youth Justice (1)' (2000) 144 *Solicitors' Journal* 140; D Wurtzel, 'Special Measures Directions', *Archbold News*, 19 Sep 2002, 5. For a comparative perspective see Reid Howie Associates, *Vulnerable and Intimidated Witnesses: Review of Provisions in Other Jurisdictions* (2002), available at http://www.scotland.gov.uk/cru/resfinds/viwp.pdf.

[140] The Director of Public Prosecutions optimistically considers this to be an attainable goal: 'It is possible to find a balance that improves the respect with which victims and witnesses are treated, while at the same time upholding defendant rights and fair trial principles': K Macdonald, 'Our System of Justice Must Enjoy Public Confidence', *Independent*, 1 Feb 2005, 27.

[141] See generally R Taylor, M Wasik, and R Leng, *Blackstone's Guide to the Criminal Justice Act 2003* (2004) 75–7.   [142] Criminal Justice Act 2003, s 56(2), s 56(3).

[143] S 51(1).   [144] S 51(4)(a).   [145] S 51(6).

(e) the suitability of the facilities at the place where the witness would give evidence through a live link,

(f) whether a direction might tend to inhibit any party to the proceedings from effectively testing the witness's evidence.[146]

Where a direction is given by the court the witness may not give evidence otherwise than through a live link.[147] The court may, however, rescind the direction 'if it appears to the court to be in the interests of justice to do so'.[148]

In relation to proceedings in the Crown Court the following specific provision is made: 'The judge may give the jury (if there is one) such direction as he thinks necessary to ensure that the jury gives the same weight to the evidence as if it had been given by the witness in the courtroom or other place where the proceedings are held.'[149]

4.1.2 Video Recordings

The effect of section 137 of the Criminal Justice Act 2003 is that the court may direct that a video recording of an account given by a witness, other than the defendant,[150] may be admitted as the witness's evidence-in-chief[151] if:

- the proceedings are 'for an offence triable only on indictment, or for a prescribed offence triable either way';[152]

- the events claimed to have been witnessed include conduct constituting the whole or part of the offence charged,[153] or 'events closely connected with such events';[154] and

- 'the account was given at a time when those events were fresh in the person's memory';[155] and

- it appears to the court that 'the witness's recollection of the events in question is likely to have been significantly better when he gave the recorded account than it will be when he gives oral evidence in the proceedings';[156] and

- it appears to the court that 'it is in the interests of justice for the recording to be admitted, having regard in particular to . . . (a) the interval between the time of the events in question and the time when the recorded account was made; (b) any other factors that might affect the reliability of what the witness said in that account; (c) the quality of the recording; (d) any views of the witness as to whether his evidence in chief should be given orally or by means of the recording'.[157]

Section 138(1) provides: 'Where a video recording is admitted under section 137, the witness may not give evidence in chief otherwise than by means of the recording as

---

[146] S 51(7). [147] S 52(2). [148] S 52(3). [149] S 54(2). [150] S 137(3)(a).
[151] S 137(1)(f). [152] S 137(1)(a). [153] S 137(1)(b)(i). [154] S 137(1)(b)(ii).
[155] S 137(1)(d). [156] S 137(3)(b)(i). [157] S 137(3)(b)(ii), s 137(4).

to any matter which, in the opinion of the court, has been dealt with adequately in the recorded account.' In relation to a part of a recording, section 138(3) provides:

In considering whether any part of a recording should be not admitted under section 137, the court must consider—

(a) whether admitting that part would carry a risk of prejudice to the defendant, and

(b) if so, whether the interests of justice nevertheless require it to be admitted in view of the desirability of showing the whole, or substantially the whole, of the recorded interview.

4.2 The Youth Justice and Criminal Evidence Act 1999

4.2.1 Special Measures Directions for Vulnerable and Intimidated Witnesses

Section 19 of the 1999 Act makes provision for special measures directions to be given. The provisions of the Act relating to special measures have been described by Lord Justice Auld in his Review as 'extraordinarily complicated and prescriptive'.[158]

4.2.1.1 Eligible Witnesses

There are essentially four categories of witnesses, not including the defendant, who are eligible for consideration for 'special measures'. The following are the four categories of eligible witness:

- *Category 1*: A witness 'under the age of 17 at the time of the hearing'.[159]
- *Category 2*: It is considered by the court 'that the quality of evidence given by the witness is likely to be diminished by reason of'[160] mental disorder[161] or 'a significant impairment of intelligence and social functioning'.[162]
- *Category 3*: It is considered by the court 'that the quality of evidence given by the witness is likely to be diminished by reason of'[163] the fact 'that the witness has a physical disability or is suffering from a physical disorder'.[164]
- *Category 4*: The witness is one in respect of whom 'the court is satisfied that the quality of evidence given by the witness is likely to be diminished by reason of fear or distress on the part of the witness in connection with testifying in the proceedings'.[165] In determining whether a witness falls within the fourth category:

the court must take into account, in particular—

(a) the nature and alleged circumstances of the offence to which the proceedings relate;

(b) the age of the witness;

---

[158] Lord Justice Auld, *Review of the Criminal Courts of England and Wales* (2001) Ch 11 para 126, accessible via http://www.criminal-courts-review.org.uk/.   [159] S 16(1)(a).
[160] S 16(1)(b).   [161] S 16(2)(a)(i).   [162] S 16(2)(a)(ii).   [163] S 16(1)(b).
[164] S 16(2)(b).   [165] S 17(1).

    (c) such of the following matters as appear to the court to be relevant, namely—
        (i)   the social and cultural background and ethnic origins of the witness,
        (ii) the domestic and employment circumstances of the witness, and
        (iii) any religious beliefs or political opinions of the witness;

    (d) any behaviour towards the witness on the part of—
        (i)   the accused,
        (ii) members of the family or associates of the accused, or
        (iii) any other person who is likely to be an accused or a witness in the proceedings.[166]

A witness who is a complainant of a sexual offence is automatically an eligible witness under the fourth category 'unless the witness has informed the court of the witness' wish not to be so eligible'.[167]

The quality of evidence means 'its quality in terms of completeness, coherence and accuracy; and for this purpose "coherence" refers to a witness's ability in giving evidence to give answers which address the questions put to the witness and [which] can be understood both individually and collectively'.[168]

There is evidence suggesting that practical difficulties have been encountered in ensuring that all eligible witnesses are identified as such: 'In 2004, the Witness Service received 20,146 referrals of people who were identified as vulnerable or intimidated and therefore eligible for special measures, [but] Witness Service personnel subsequently identified a further 18,466 whom we found had slipped through the net.'[169]

The Act makes provision for eight different special measures. These will be outlined below. Of these measures, two are unavailable to a witness who is eligible only under category 4.[170]

Having determined that a witness is an eligible witness:

the court must then—

    (a) determine whether any of the special measures available in relation to the witness (or any combination of them) would, in its opinion, be likely to improve the quality of evidence given by the witness; and

    (b) if so—
        (i)   determine which of those measures (or combination of them) would, in its opinion, be likely to maximise so far as practicable the quality of such evidence; and
        (ii) give a direction under this section providing for the measure or measures so determined to apply to evidence given by the witness.[171]

In determining whether any measure or measures would be likely to improve, or to maximize so far as practicable, the quality of evidence:

the court must consider all the circumstances of the case, including in particular—

    (a) any views expressed by the witness; and

    (b) whether the measure or measures might tend to inhibit such evidence being effectively tested by a party to the proceedings.[172]

Special additional rules apply to child witnesses, as will be explained later.

---

[166] S 17(2).   [167] S 17(4).   [168] S 16(5).
[169] H Reeves, 'Witness Support' [June 2005] *Counsel* 18, 19.   [170] S 18(1).   [171] S 19(2).
[172] S 19(3).

4.2.1.2 The Special Measures

The following are the measures in relation to which special measures directions may be made.

4.2.1.2.1 Screens

This is a measure, prescribed by section 23, whereby 'the witness, while giving testimony or being sworn in court, [is] prevented by means of a screen or other arrangement from seeing the accused'.[173] Such an arrangement must not, however:

prevent the witness from being able to see, and to be seen by—

(a) the judge or justices (or both) and the jury (if there is one);

(b) legal representatives acting in the proceedings; and

(c) any interpreter or other person appointed (in pursuance of the direction or otherwise) to assist the witness.[174]

'Provided the jury [are] correctly instructed as to the implications of the use of screens, ... it cannot possibly be the case ... that the fact that a witness gives evidence without screens requires all the rest to do so as well.'[175]

4.2.1.2.2 Live Links

This measure, which allows 'the witness to give evidence by means of a live link',[176] stands alongside the provisions on live links contained in the Criminal Justice Act 2003, examined above. An important difference is that a live link under the Youth Justice and Criminal Evidence Act 1999 allows a witness not to be seen and heard by the defendant.[177] Where a direction has been made, 'the witness may not give evidence in any other way without the permission of the court'.[178] Such permission may be given 'if it appears to the court to be in the interests of justice to do so'.[179]

4.2.1.2.3 Evidence in Private

The following provisions of section 25 of the Youth Justice and Criminal Evidence Act 1999 are self-explanatory:

(1) A special measures direction may provide for the exclusion from the court, during the giving of the witness's evidence, of persons of any description specified in the direction.

(2) The persons who may be so excluded do not include—

(a) the accused,

(b) legal representatives acting in the proceedings, or

(c) any interpreter or other person appointed (in pursuance of the direction or otherwise) to assist the witness.

---

[173] S 23(1).

[174] S 23(2). In *A-G for the Sovereign Base Areas of Akrotiri and Dhekelia v Steinhoff* [2005] UKPC 30 the Privy Council held that, in the circumstances of the case, the requirements of a fair trial had not been compromised by the breach of s 23 arising from the fact that (ibid, [2]) 'the arrangement of the courtroom and screen were such that the witness could not be seen by both counsel at once. Accordingly, it was decided that counsel should change places, so that each could see the witness while questioning her. Both could, of course, hear her throughout ...'.   [175] *R v Brown* [2004] EWCA Crim 1620, [12].

[176] S 24(1).   [177] S 24(8).   [178] S 24(2).   [179] S 24(3).

(3) A special measures direction providing for representatives of news gathering or reporting organisations to be so excluded shall be expressed not to apply to one named person who—

    (a) is a representative of such an organisation, and

    (b) has been nominated for the purpose by one or more such organisations,

unless it appears to the court that no such nomination has been made.

(4) A special measures direction may only provide for the exclusion of persons under this section where—

    (a) the proceedings relate to a sexual offence; or

    (b) it appears to the court that there are reasonable grounds for believing that any person other than the accused has sought, or will seek, to intimidate the witness in connection with testifying in the proceedings.

4.2.1.2.4 No Wigs or Gowns

This is a measure whereby 'the wearing of wigs or gowns [may] be dispensed with during the giving of the witness's evidence'.[180]

4.2.1.2.5 Video-Recorded Evidence-in-Chief

This measure,[181] which allows 'a video recording of an interview of the witness to be admitted as evidence in chief of the witness',[182] stands alongside the provisions on video recordings in the Criminal Justice Act 2003, examined above. A direction is not, however, to be made in respect of the admission of a recording or a part of a recording 'if the court is of the opinion, having regard to all the circumstances of the case, that in the interests of justice the recording, or that part of it, should not be so admitted'.[183] In considering whether any *part* of a recording should not be admitted 'the court must consider whether any prejudice to the accused which might result from that part being so admitted is outweighed by the desirability of showing the whole, or substantially the whole, of the recorded interview'.[184] Even where a direction has provided for a recording to be admitted, the court may subsequently direct that it not be admitted if it appears to the court that the witness, without the agreement of the parties,[185] will be unavailable for cross-examination,[186] or if 'any rules of court requiring disclosure of the circumstances in which the recording was made have not been complied with to the satisfaction of the court'.[187] Where a matter has, in the opinion of the court, been *dealt with adequately* in the recorded testimony, no further evidence-in-chief in relation to that matter is allowed.[188] Where some other matter is, in the opinion of the court, *dealt with* in the recorded testimony, no further evidence-in-chief in relation to that matter is allowed without the permission of the court.[189] Such permission may be given 'if it appears to the court to be in the interests of justice to do so'.[190]

---

[180] S 26.
[181] See generally D Heraghty, 'Gearing Up for Greater Use of Video Evidence' (2003) 153 *New Law Journal* 460.
[182] S 27(1).　　　[183] S 27(2).　　　[184] S 27(3).　　　[185] S 27(4)(a)(ii).　　　[186] S 27(4)(a)(i).
[187] S 27(4)(b).　　　[188] S 27(5)(b)(i).　　　[189] S 27(5)(b)(ii).　　　[190] S 27(7).

To what extent is it permissible to accede to a request from the jury for a video recording to be replayed? The Court of Appeal has observed that:

> the replaying of video evidence is a departure from the normal method of conducting a criminal trial and that this should only take place where there are exceptional reasons. That is, of course, because the replaying of such evidence disturbs the traditional balance of a trial and may be seen as giving the prosecution a second bite at the evidential cherry. However, ... that general observation does not derogate from the propriety of such a course being followed when a jury has requested to review the evidence of a complainant for the purpose of seeing *how* the complainant gave his or her evidence, as opposed simply to being reminded of the *content* of that evidence, the judge being well able to remedy the latter position without resort to a re-run of the video film, always provided that he gives an appropriate 'balancing' direction to the jury [that is, one in which the jury is reminded of the cross-examination and re-examination of the complainant].[191]

It is clear that:

> the principal benefit of pre-trial evidence-taking would be to remove the ... witness from the formal and intimidating environment of the court room. An additional benefit credited to pre-recorded examination-in-chief is that the testimony is likely to be more reliable when it is taken much closer to the event in question.[192]

4.2.1.2.6 Video-Recorded Cross-Examination and Re-Examination

A direction providing for a video recording to be admitted as evidence-in-chief may also provide for any cross-examination and re-examination to be video recorded,[193] and for the recording to be admitted as the witness's evidence under cross-examination or on re-examination.[194] Further:

> Such a recording must be made in the presence of such persons as rules of court or the direction may provide and in the absence of the accused, but in circumstances in which—
>
> (a) the judge or justices (or both) and legal representatives acting in the proceedings are able to see and hear the examination of the witness and to communicate with the persons in whose presence the recording is being made, and
>
> (b) the accused is able to see and hear any such examination and to communicate with any legal representative acting for him.[195]

No further cross-examination or re-examination is to be permitted unless the court gives a further direction providing for another video-recorded cross-examination or re-examination.[196] Such a further direction may be given only:

> if it appears to the court—
>
> (a) that the proposed cross-examination is sought by a party to the proceedings as a result of that party having become aware, since the time when the original recording was

191 *R v Mullen* [2004] EWCA Crim 602, [2004] 2 Cr App R 18 (p 290), [63] (italics in original).
192 D Cooper, 'Pigot Unfulfilled: Video-Recorded Cross-Examination Under Section 28 of the Youth Justice and Criminal Evidence Act 1999' [2005] *Criminal Law Review* 456, 463.   193 S 28(1)(a).
194 S 28(1)(b).   195 S 28(2).   196 S 28(5).

made . . . , of a matter which that party could not with reasonable diligence have ascertained by then, or

(b) that for any other reason it is in the interests of justice to give the further direction.[197]

While the possibility of video-recorded cross-examination is very much to be welcomed for its potential in reducing the trauma that might be inflicted by the criminal justice process, there is a need for caution: 'It would be very unfortunate if the new provision led to an *increase* in cross-examination of children, for example in those cases in which the defendant decides to plead guilty when the trial begins, *after* the child's cross-examination has been conducted.'[198] There also remains the fundamental issue that the witness *is* still subjected to the process of cross-examination, with all that this entails:

> The experience of being cross-examined, rather than the environment in which cross-examination occurs, seems now to be the main 'unresolved' problem for child witnesses. Taking cross-examination out of the main trial proceedings will undoubtedly bring some benefits for the administration of justice, but a temporal relocation will not alter the basic character of sceptical questioning by opposing counsel. Although no jury will be present to observe counsel's pre-trial cross-examination of a child witness, counsel will proceed in the knowledge that the process is being video-recorded and will be scrutinised by a jury at a later date. There is no reason to suppose that counsel's tactics in cross-examining a child witness will change in any substantial way merely to accommodate the prospect of a technologically engineered time-delay between cross-examination and final adjudication. The unresolved issue is whether cross-examination is the best procedural mechanism for testing the evidence of children.[199]

4.2.1.2.7 Intermediaries

The following provisions of section 29 of the Youth Justice and Criminal Evidence Act 1999 are self-explanatory:

(1) A special measures direction may provide for any examination of the witness (however and wherever conducted) to be conducted through an interpreter or other person approved by the court for the purposes of this section ('an intermediary').

(2) The function of an intermediary is to communicate—

   (a) to the witness, questions put to the witness, and

   (b) to any person asking such questions, the answers given by the witness in reply to them,

and to explain such questions or answers so far as necessary to enable them to be understood by the witness or person in question.

(3) Any examination of the witness in pursuance of subsection (1) must take place in the presence of such persons as rules of court or the direction may provide, but in circumstances in which—

   (a) the judge or justices (or both) and legal representatives acting in the proceedings are able to see and hear the examination of the witness and to communicate with the intermediary, and

---

[197] S 28(6).

[198] P Bates, 'The Youth Justice and Criminal Evidence Act—The Evidence of Children and Vulnerable Adults' (1999) 11 *Child and Family Law Quarterly* 289, 300 (italics in original).

[199] D Cooper, 'Pigot Unfulfilled: Video-Recorded Cross-Examination Under Section 28 of the Youth Justice and Criminal Evidence Act 1999' [2005] *Criminal Law Review* 456, 464.

(b) (except in the case of a video recorded examination) the jury (if there is one) are able to see and hear the examination of the witness.

. . .

(5) A person may not act as an intermediary in a particular case except after making a declaration, in such form as may be prescribed by rules of court, that he will faithfully perform his function as intermediary.[200]

This measure is not available in respect of a witness who is eligible only under category 4.[201]

4.2.1.2.8 Aids to Communication

Section 30 provides: 'A special measures direction may provide for the witness, while giving evidence (whether by testimony in court or otherwise), to be provided with such device as the court considers appropriate with a view to enabling questions or answers to be communicated to or by the witness despite any disability or disorder or other impairment which the witness has or suffers from.'

This measure is not available in respect of a witness who is eligible only under category 4.[202]

4.2.1.3 Child Witnesses

There is a specific set of rules that is applicable to a witness, other than the defendant, who is under 17 at the time of the hearing (or, where the admissibility of a video recording is at issue, under 17 when the recording was made[203]). These important rules are additional to the general rules on eligible witnesses examined above.[204] In essence, three different categories of child witness are recognized:

1. A witness in a case concerning one of the sexual offences specified in section 35(3)(a).

2. A witness in a case concerning one of the offences specified in section 35(3)(b), (c), or (d). These include offences involving kidnapping, false imprisonment, abduction, cruelty, or violence.

3. A witness in a case concerning any other offence.

The first two categories of child witnesses are those who, in the words of section 21(1)(b), are 'in need of special protection'.

The highest level of protection is prescribed for witnesses in the first category, and the lowest level for witnesses in the third. Where a witness falls under the third ('any other offence') category, the rule is that the court is to direct (1) that any relevant video

---

[200] See generally L Ellison, 'Cross-Examination and the Intermediary: Bridging the Language Divide?' [2002] *Criminal Law Review* 114. Ellison argues: 'The use of intermediaries may facilitate more effective communication but . . . fundamental obstacles to truly empathic communication will remain' (ibid, 127). See also, generally, the material on 'Intermediaries' accessible via http://www.homeoffice.gov.uk/justice/legalprocess/witnesses/ and D Wurtzel, 'Intermediaries', *Archbold News*, 1 July 2003, 6.   [201] S 18(1).
[202] S 18(1).   [203] S 21(9), s 22.
[204] See generally L C H Hoyano, 'Variations on a Theme by Pigot: Special Measures Directions for Child Witnesses' [2000] *Criminal Law Review* 250.

recording must be admitted as evidence-in-chief[205] unless the court is of the opinion, having regard to all the circumstances of the case, that the interests of justice require otherwise;[206] and (2) that 'any evidence given by the witness in the proceedings which is not given by means of a video recording (whether in chief or otherwise) [is] to be given by means of a live link'.[207] This rule does not, however, apply if 'the court is satisfied that compliance with it would not be likely to maximise the quality of the witness's evidence so far as practicable (whether because the application to that evidence of one or more other special measures available in relation to the witness would have that result or for any other reason)'.[208]

Where a witness falls under the second category, the rule is that the court is to direct (1) that any relevant video recording must be admitted as evidence-in-chief[209] unless the court is of the opinion, having regard to all the circumstances of the case, that the interests of justice require otherwise;[210] and (2) that 'any evidence given by the witness in the proceedings which is not given by means of a video recording (whether in chief or otherwise) [is] to be given by means of a live link'.[211] The rule is not subject to the 'quality' proviso that applies in relation to the third category.

Where a witness falls under the first category, the rule is that the court is to direct (1) that any relevant video recording must be admitted as evidence-in-chief[212] unless the court is of the opinion, having regard to all the circumstances of the case, that the interests of justice require otherwise;[213] and (2) that any cross-examination[214] and re-examination[215] are to be video recorded, unless the witness has informed the court that he or she does not want this.[216] Again, this rule is not subject to the 'quality' proviso that applies in relation to the third category.

In *R (D) v Camberwell Green Youth Court*[217] it was argued in effect that the fact that the 'quality' proviso does not apply in relation to child witnesses in need of special protection, thus precluding the individual consideration of the neccessity for special measures directions for those witnesses at the stage at which the direction is made, constituted a violation of the general fair trial guarantee of Article 6 and of Article 6(3)(d).[218] This argument was rejected by the House of Lords. In the words of Baroness Hale of Richmond:

> It is very difficult, and counsel found it difficult, to think of reasons which might make a live link or the admission of a recording unjust which were unrelated either to the quality of the equipment on the day, to the content and quality of the video recording, or the unavailability of the recorded witness for cross-examination (express power to exclude the video recording in these circumstances is preserved by section 27(4)).[219]

> All the evidence is produced at the trial in the presence of the accused, some of it in pre-recorded form and some of it by contemporaneous television transmission. The accused can

---

[205] S 21(3)(a).   [206] S 21(4)(b).   [207] S 21(3)(b).   [208] S 21(4)(c).   [209] S 21(3)(a).
[210] S 21(4)(b).   [211] S 21(3)(b).   [212] S 21(3)(a).   [213] S 21(4)(b).   [214] S 21(6)(a).
[215] S 21(6)(b).   [216] S 21(7)(b).

[217] [2005] UKHL 4, [2005] 1 WLR 393. See generally G Stewart, G Carter Stephenson, and M Hardie, 'Child Witnesses' (2005) 149 *Solicitors' Journal* 194.   [218] Art 6(3)(d) is considered in Ch 9.

[219] [2005] UKHL 4, [2005] 1 WLR 393, [46].

see and hear it all. The accused has every opportunity to challenge and question the witnesses against him at the trial itself. The only thing missing is a face to face confrontation, but . . . the Convention does not guarantee a right to face to face confrontation.[220]

The measures with which we are concerned do give the accused the opportunity of challenging the witness directly at the time when the trial is taking place. The court also has the opportunity to scrutinise the video-recorded interview at the outset and exclude all or part of it. At the trial, it has the fall-back of allowing the witness to give evidence in the court room or to expand upon the video recording if the interests of justice require this. There is nothing in the case law cited to suggest that this procedure violates the rights of the accused under [A]rticle 6.[221]

. . . the Strasbourg Court would [not] regard our domestic legal system as so set in stone that Parliament is not entitled to modify or adapt it to meet modern conditions, provided that those adaptations comply with the essential requirements of [A]rticle 6. In this case, the modification is simply the use of modern equipment to put the best evidence before the court while preserving the essential rights of the accused to know and to challenge all the evidence against him. There are excellent policy reasons for doing this. Parliament having decided that this is justified, the domestic legal system is entitled to adopt the general practice without the need to show special justification in every case.[222]

In a similar vein, the jurisprudence of the Supreme Court of Canada[223] and the US Supreme Court[224] suggests a tendency to find measures designed to ease the burden on witnesses to be compliant with human rights guarantees.[225]

4.2.1.4 Warnings

Section 32 provides:

Where on a trial on indictment evidence has been given in accordance with a special measures direction, the judge must give the jury such warning (if any) as the judge considers necessary to ensure that the fact that the direction was given in relation to the witness does not prejudice the accused.

There is no requirement, where such a warning has been given at the time of the evidence being given, for it to be repeated in the summing-up. The Court of Appeal observed in the context of a consideration of the use of screens:

The question is whether effectively the judge has got across to the jury the essential matter of the use of screens and the conclusions that they should draw and not draw from it. That is much more likely to impress itself on the jury if it is given at the time that the witnesses give evidence than if it is repeated at a later date in the summing-up. Indeed, for the judge to revert to it might in some circumstances give the matter more emphasis, derogatory to the defendants, than it deserves.[226]

---

[220] Ibid, [49].   [221] Ibid, [51].   [222] Ibid, [53].

[223] *R v L (D O)* [1993] 4 SCR 419; *R v Levogiannis* [1993] 4 SCR 475.

[224] *Maryland v Craig* 497 US 836 (1990).

[225] See generally L C H Hoyano, 'Striking a Balance Between the Rights of Defendants and Vulnerable Witnesses: Will Special Measures Directions Contravene Guarantees of a Fair Trial?' [2001] *Criminal Law Review* 948.   [226] *R v Brown* [2004] EWCA Crim 1620, [21].

4.2.1.5 Surveys of Vulnerable and Intimidated Witnesses

Research into the views of vulnerable and intimidated witnesses ('VIWs') on their experiences has been undertaken with a view to assessing the effect of the special measures provisions of the Youth Justice and Criminal Evidence Act 1999. The research consisted of surveys undertaken with samples of VIWs. Phase 1 was conducted before the implementation of the relevant provisions, and phase 2 after the majority of special measures had been introduced in the Crown Court and had had time to 'bed in'.

On the general experience of being a witness, some of the findings of the research were as follows:[227]

- Most vulnerable victims and witnesses found their experience stressful, although there was a reduction in these feelings between phases 1 and 2, both overall (from 77% to 70%) and specifically relating to the court environment (from 27% to 17%). VIWs using special measures in phase 2 were less likely than those not using measures to experience anxiety.

- The most commonly reported causes of anxiety were seeing the defendant in court, (mentioned by 24%) and not knowing what would happen (mentioned by 17%).

  . . .

- There has been a small . . . increase in the proportion of VIWs who said that they were satisfied overall with their experience, from 64 per cent to 69 per cent. . . . There has been a corresponding . . . decrease in the proportion expressing that they were 'very dissatisfied' overall, from 22 per cent to 17 per cent.

- In phase 2, VIWs using special measures were more likely to be satisfied overall compared with those not using these measures.

- Overall satisfaction has increased mostly among women and intimidated witnesses.

- Dissatisfaction was strongly associated with whether witnesses felt intimidated.

- 61 per cent of VIWs said that if they were asked to be a witness again, they would be likely to agree to this. However, only 44 per cent of VIWs said they would be 'happy' to be a witness again.

- There was a strong correlation between overall satisfaction and likelihood to agree to being a witness again, with 70 per cent of those satisfied saying they would be likely compared with only 33 per cent of those dissatisfied.

- VIWs receiving special measures were more likely to consider that the CJS meets the needs of victims, is effective in bringing criminals to justice and treats witnesses fairly and with respect.

---

[227] B Hamlyn, A Phelps, J Turtle, and G Sattar, *Are Special Measures Working? Evidence from Surveys of Vulnerable and Intimidated Witnesses* (Home Office Research Study 283) (2004) 102–3, available at http://www. homeoffice. gov.uk/rds/pdfs04/hors283.pdf. For discussions of the position prior to the 1999 Act see J Cherryman, N King, and R Bull, 'Child Witness Investigative Interviews: An Analysis of the Use of Children's Video-Recorded Evidence in North Yorkshire' (1999) 2 *International Journal of Police Science and Management* 50; G M Davies and H L Westcott, *Interviewing Child Witnesses Under the* Memorandum of Good Practice: *A Research Review* (Police Research Series Paper 115) (1999), available at http://www.homeoffice.gov.uk/rds/prgpdfs/fprs115.pdf; G Davis, L Hoyano, C Keenan, L Maitland, and R Morgan, *An Assessment of the Admissibility and Sufficiency of Evidence in Child Abuse Prosecutions* (1999), available at http://www.homeoffice.gov.uk/rds/pdfs/occ-childabuse.pdf.

A number of the findings of the research that were of specific relevance to the issue of the use of special measures were as follows:[228]

- The use of interpreters, signers and other intermediaries was negligible.

- The use of video-recorded statements among witnesses aged under 17 rose from 30 per cent in phase 1 to 42 per cent in phase 2. In phase 2, nine in ten using this found it helpful.

- In phase 1, almost three-quarters of VIWs thought that it would have been helpful to have been cross-examined on videotape before the trial.

- In phase 1, 43 per cent of witnesses under 17 who gave evidence said they were offered use of a live TV link, this doubling to 83 per cent in phase 2. A further 15 per cent of adult witnesses in phase 2 were offered this facility. At phase 2, 90 per cent of all witnesses using this facility found it helpful.

- In phase 2, one in eight (13%) reported use of screens in court, up from only 3 per cent in phase 1. Sixty per cent of VIWs in phase 2 who did not have access to this facility or a live TV link thought they would have been helpful.

- Removal of wigs and gowns at Crown Court was relatively rare, although it increased from 8 per cent to 15 per cent between survey phases.

- Most of the VIWs for whom the public gallery had been cleared, thought this special measure was helpful.

- In phase 1, only 12 per cent of VIWs said they had been consulted about the use of measures currently available, although this rose nearly three-fold to 32 per cent in phase 2. Half (51%) of sex offence victims said they were consulted. At phase 2, 87 per cent of witnesses who were consulted about the use of measures said that their views had been acted upon at least to some extent.

- A third of VIWs in phase 2 who used special measures said that these enabled them to give evidence they would not otherwise have been willing or able to give. This figure was particularly high for sex offence victims (44%).

- Overall, the use of special measures had increased, in particular for live television link, video-recorded evidence-in-chief, and removal of wigs and gowns.

- The highest level of unmet need was for measures that resulted in the witness avoiding seeing the defendant such as screens and live TV link. However, the level of unmet need among VIWs giving evidence has reduced significantly from 50 per cent to 31 per cent between the survey phases.

It is undeniable in the light of the above findings that the relevant provisions of the Youth Justice and Criminal Evidence Act 1999 have proved to be a qualified success. There is, however, no room for complacency. A joint NSPCC and Victim Support report published in late 2004 and detailing 'the experiences of 50 young witnesses aged between seven and seventeen giving evidence in criminal court proceedings[,] ... the majority giving evidence in sexual offence cases', revealed that 39 per cent of those

---

[228] B Hamlyn, A Phelps, J Turtle, and G Sattar, *Are Special Measures Working? Evidence from Surveys of Vulnerable and Intimidated Witnesses* (Home Office Research Study 283) (2004) 80–1, available at http://www. homeoffice.gov.uk/rds/pdfs04/hors283.pdf.

giving their evidence by means of a live link 'were upset that the defendant could still watch them'.[229] Attention also needs to be paid to relevant pre-trial practices and procedures such as the techniques employed in interviewing witnesses, preparation of witnesses for court, and the provision of appropriate therapy to witnesses.[230]

4.2.2 No Cross-Examination by Defendant in Person

4.2.2.1 Complainants in Sexual Offence Trials

Section 34 provides that a person charged with a sexual offence may not cross-examine in person a complainant of that offence, either about that offence or about any other offence with which he or she is charged.[231]

4.2.2.2 'Protected Witnesses'

Section 35 provides that a person charged with one of a number of specified offences may not cross-examine in person an alleged witness (who may be the complainant) who is a 'protected witness', either about that offence or about any other offence with which he or she is charged. This applies to alleged witnesses who are co-defendants. The specified offences fall, in essence, into two categories:

1. The first category consists of the sexual offences listed in section 35(3)(a). In relation to offences in this category, a 'protected witness' is one who is under 17, *or* was under 17 when a video recording later admitted as evidence-in-chief was made, *or* was under 17 when his or her evidence-in-chief was given.

---

[229] http://www.nspcc.org.uk/html/home/informationresources/courtfailings.htm. See also http://www.nspcc. org.uk/html/home/informationresources/childvictims.htm; B Esam, 'Caring for Children in Court: Making a Difference for Child Witnesses' (2005) 169 *Justice of the Peace* 271; H Reeves, 'Witness Support' [June 2005] *Counsel* 18.

[230] See B Boulter, 'Treading Carefully' (2001) 145 *Solicitors' Journal* 412; M Bowes, 'Children Who Deserve a Fair Hearing', *The Times*, 15 Feb 2005, Law, 7; R Bull and E Corran, 'Interviewing Child Witnesses: Past and Future' (2002) 4 *International Journal of Police Science and Management* 315; D Heraghty, 'Gearing Up for Greater Use of Video Evidence' (2003) 153 *New Law Journal* 460; Home Office, Crown Prosecution Service, and Department of Health, *Provision of Therapy for Child Witnesses Prior to a Criminal Trial: Practice Guidance* (2001), available at http://www.cps.gov.uk/publications/docs/therapychild.pdf or http://www.homeoffice. gov.uk/docs/therapybook.pdf; Home Office, Crown Prosecution Service, and Department of Health, *Provision of Therapy for Vulnerable or Intimidated Adult Witnesses Prior to a Criminal Trial: Practice Guidance* (2001), available at http://www.cps.gov.uk/publications/prosecution/pretrialadult.html or http://www.homeoffice. gov.uk/docs/provisionoftherapy.pdf; Home Office, Lord Chancellor, Crown Prosecution Service, and Department of Health, *Achieving Best Evidence in Criminal Proceedings: Guidance for Vulnerable or Intimidated Witnesses, Including Children (Vols 1, 2, and 3)* (2002), accessible via http://www.cps.gov.uk/publications/prosecution/ index.html or http://www.homeoffice.gov.uk/justice/legalprocess/witnesses/index.html.

[231] See generally L A Iding, 'Crossing the Line: The Case for Limiting Personal Cross-Examination by an Accused in Sexual Assault Trials' (2004) 49 *Criminal Law Quarterly* 69. On whether claimants alleging sexual misconduct in civil trials should have the same protection against cross-examination by the defendant in person, see B Hewson, 'Cross-Examination in Civil Actions for Assault' (2002) 146 *Solicitors' Journal* 54. Hewson argues (ibid): 'There is a fundamental difference between the criminal and civil process. In a prosecution, the state controls the process. . . . The complainant is a witness, and not represented. By contrast, in a civil claim, what is at stake is a private dispute about money. . . . An experienced civil judge, who decides facts as well as law, can be expected to control proceedings effectively, even where a defendant appears in person. He can also compensate any deserving claimant, whose feelings are outraged by a defendant's offensive conduct in court.'

2. The second category consists of the offences listed in section 35(3)(b), (c), and (d). These include offences involving kidnapping, false imprisonment, abduction, cruelty, or violence. In relation to offences in this category, a 'protected witness' is one who is under 14, *or* was under 14 when a video recording later admitted as evidence-in-chief was made, *or* was under 14 when his or her evidence-in-chief was given.

4.2.2.3 Discretion

Where neither section 34 nor section 35 is applicable, section 36 gives courts an over-riding discretion:

(2) If it appears to the court—

(a) that the quality of evidence given by the witness on cross-examination—

(i) is likely to be diminished if the cross-examination (or further cross-examination) is conducted by the accused in person, and

(ii) would be likely to be improved if a direction were given under this section, and

(b) that it would not be contrary to the interests of justice to give such a direction,

the court may give a direction prohibiting the accused from cross-examining (or further cross-examining) the witness in person.

(3) In determining whether subsection (2)(a) applies in the case of a witness the court must have regard, in particular, to—

(a) any views expressed by the witness as to whether or not the witness is content to be cross-examined by the accused in person;

(b) the nature of the questions likely to be asked, having regard to the issues in the proceedings and the defence case advanced so far (if any);

(c) any behaviour on the part of the accused at any stage of the proceedings, both generally and in relation to the witness;

(d) any relationship (of whatever nature) between the witness and the accused;

(e) whether any person (other than the accused) is or has at any time been charged in the proceedings with a sexual offence or an offence to which section 35 applies, and (if so) whether section 34 or 35 operates or would have operated to prevent that person from cross-examining the witness in person;

(f) any direction under section 19 which the court has given, or proposes to give, in relation to the witness.

Section 36 does not apply to a witness who is a co-defendant.[232]

4.2.2.4 Legal Representation

If an accused who is prohibited from cross-examining a witness in person has no legal representative to conduct the cross-examination on his or her behalf,[233] and if the court considers it necessary in the interests of justice for the witness to be cross-examined by a legal representative appointed to represent the interests of the accused, the court must

---

[232] S 36(4)(a).   [233] S 38(3).

choose and appoint a qualified legal representative to cross-examine the witness in the interests of the accused.[234]

4.2.2.5 Warnings

Section 39(1) provides:

> Where on a trial on indictment an accused is prevented from cross-examining a witness in person by virtue of section 34, 35 or 36, the judge must give the jury such warning (if any) as the judge considers necessary to ensure that the accused is not prejudiced—
>
> (a) by any inferences that might be drawn from the fact that the accused has been prevented from cross-examining the witness in person;
>
> (b) where the witness has been cross-examined by a legal representative appointed under section 38(4), by the fact that the cross-examination was carried out by such a legal representative and not by a person acting as the accused's own legal representative.

4.2.3 Restriction on Sexual History Evidence

The long-overdue abolition of mandatory warnings to juries about convicting on the uncorroborated evidence of a complainant in a sexual case has been discussed above. The extent to which evidence of a complainant's sexual conduct on other occasions is admissible in a rape trial is another issue which for a long time has sparked controversy and which seems likely to continue to do so. Traditionally, in rape trials, the defence would be permitted to present evidence or cross-examine the complainant concerning her sexual history. Notwithstanding the normal rule that evidence must be relevant, such evidence was admitted routinely without inquiry as to its possible relevance to either the issues in the case or credibility.[235] This was not an acceptable state of affairs and the issue was referred to a special committee chaired by Heilbron J. The report of that committee noted that the admission of sexual history evidence was humiliating for rape complainants and led to a significant number of complainants either not report- ing or withdrawing complaints of rape.[236] Following recommendations in the Heilbron report, restrictions on the admission of sexual history evidence were first imposed by section 2 of the Sexual Offences (Amendment) Act 1976. This provision was rightly criticized for investing too much discretion in trial judges in determining whether the defence should be permitted to introduce such evidence.[237]

Looking further afield, we find that other jurisdictions face similar difficulties in crafting 'rape shield laws' in an attempt to regulate the admissibility of sexual history evidence.[238] Notable is the experience of Canada, where the rape shield provisions then

---

[234] S 38(4).

[235] D W Elliott, 'Rape Complainants' Sexual Experience with Third Parties' [1984] *Criminal Law Review* 4.

[236] Home Office, *Report of the Advisory Group on the Law of Rape* (Cmnd 6352) (1975).

[237] See generally N Kibble, 'The Sexual History Provisions: Charting a Course Between Inflexible Legislative Rules and Wholly Untrammelled Judicial Discretion?' [2000] *Criminal Law Review* 274; J Temkin, 'Sexual History Evidence—The Ravishment of Section 2' [1993] *Criminal Law Review* 3.

[238] See generally N Kibble, 'Judicial Discretion and the Admissibility of Prior Sexual History Evidence Under Section 41 of the Youth Justice and Criminal Evidence Act 1999: Sometimes Sticking to Your Guns Means Shooting Yourself in the Foot: Part 2' [2005] *Criminal Law Review* 263.

in operation were declared unconstitutional by the Supreme Court of Canada in *R v Seaboyer*,[239] on the basis that they violated the fundamental principle, enshrined in the Canadian Charter of Rights and Freedoms, that the innocent should not be punished. As a result of the decision in *Seaboyer* new provisions were enacted. These are less tightly drafted, according trial judges much greater latitude in admitting sexual history evidence.[240]

New rape shield provisions were introduced in England and Wales in section 41 of the Youth Justice and Criminal Evidence Act 1999. In essence, section 41 imposes a prima facie prohibition on the introduction of evidence of the complainant's sexual behaviour: in a sexual offence trial no evidence may be adduced, and no question may be asked in cross-examination, about the complainant's sexual behaviour without the leave of the court.[241] 'Sexual behaviour' includes 'sexual experience'.[242] The concept of sexual behaviour has been explained as follows:

> In many cases it will be very easy to say what is or is not sexual behaviour, but there are obviously borderline cases in which the sexuality of what happens may be not so apparent as to lead on to the conclusion that the behaviour under examination is sexual. It would not be possible to try to define sexual behaviour further. Indeed, it probably would be foolish to do so. It is really a matter of impression and common sense.[243]

It is unnecessary for a sexual experience to have been perceived as one by the complainant: 'if the application of the Act did depend on the perception of the patient, then many vulnerable people, not just young children but also persons with learning difficulties... would lose its protection'.[244]

Section 41 makes no distinction between sexual behaviour of the complainant with the accused and sexual behaviour with third parties. This is controversial because, for some commentators, it appears obvious that a jury would not be able to understand a case of alleged sexual assault without knowing of a pre-existing sexual relationship between the parties. Leave to introduce evidence of the complainant's sexual behaviour may be granted only if its refusal 'might have the result of rendering unsafe a conclusion of the jury or (as the case may be) the court on any relevant issue in the case'.[245] Additionally, there are only four specific situations in which leave may be granted. These are as follows:

1. The evidence or question relates to a relevant issue in the case and that issue is not an issue of consent: section 41(3)(a). Clearly contemplated here is relevance to *belief* in

---

[239] (1991) 83 DLR (4th) 193.

[240] See generally N Kibble, 'Judicial Discretion and the Admissibility of Prior Sexual History Evidence Under Section 41 of the Youth Justice and Criminal Evidence Act 1999: Sometimes Sticking to Your Guns Means Shooting Yourself in the Foot: Part 2' [2005] *Criminal Law Review* 263, 266–8; N Kibble, 'The Sexual History Provisions: Charting a Course Between Inflexible Legislative Rules and Wholly Untrammelled Judicial Discretion?' [2000] *Criminal Law Review* 274, 282–3; J Temkin, 'Sexual History Evidence—The Ravishment of Section 2' [1993] *Criminal Law Review* 3, 17–19. Note that the new Canadian provisions survived a Charter challenge in *R v Darrach* [2000] 2 SCR 443. See generally R J Delisle, 'Adoption, Sub-Silentio, of the Paciocco Solution to Rape Shield Laws' (2001) 36 *Criminal Reports (5th)* 254.   [241] S 41(1).

[242] S 42(1)(c).   [243] *R v Mukadi* [2003] EWCA Crim 3765, [14].

[244] *R v E* [2004] EWCA Crim 1313, [6].   [245] S 41(2)(b).

consent. It is notable that the new substantive law on sexual offences, contained in the Sexual Offences Act 2003, permits the defendant to escape liability only if his belief in consent was reasonable rather than simply honest. The extent to which sexual history evidence may be regarded as relevant in establishing a reasonable belief in consent may be expected to be rather more limited than the extent to which it is relevant in establishing a merely honest belief.[246]

2. The evidence or question relates to an issue of consent and the relevant sexual behaviour 'is alleged to have taken place at or about the same time as the event which is the subject matter of the charge against the accused': section 41(3)(b).

3. The evidence or question relates to an issue of consent and the relevant sexual behaviour 'is alleged to have been, in any respect, so similar . . . to any sexual behaviour of the complainant which (according to evidence adduced or to be adduced by or on behalf of the accused) took place as part of the event which is the subject matter of the charge against the accused, or . . . to any other sexual behaviour of the complainant which (according to such evidence) took place at or about the same time as that event, that the similarity cannot reasonably be explained as a coincidence': section 41(3)(c).

4. 'The evidence or question . . . relates to any evidence adduced by the prosecution about any sexual behaviour of the complainant; and . . . in the opinion of the court, would go no further than is necessary to enable the evidence adduced by the prosecution to be rebutted or explained by or on behalf of the accused': section 41(5).

In each case, 'the evidence or question must relate to a specific instance (or specific instances) of alleged sexual behaviour on the part of the complainant'.[247] In relation to the first three situations outlined above, section 41(4) provides that, 'no evidence or question shall be regarded as relating to a relevant issue in the case if it appears to the court to be reasonable to assume that the purpose (or main purpose) for which it would be adduced or asked is to establish or elicit material for impugning the credibility of the complainant as a witness'.[248]

Within a few months of coming into force section 41 was the subject of detailed consideration by the House of Lords in *R v A (No 2)*.[249] The question certified for the

---

[246] See generally J McEwan, 'Proving Consent in Sexual Cases: Legislative Change and Cultural Evolution' (2005) 9 *International Journal of Evidence and Proof* 1.

[247] S 41(6). See *R v White* [2004] EWCA Crim 946.

[248] See *R v Abdelrahman* [2005] EWCA Crim 1367, [26]: '. . . the sole purpose of the proposed questions in the present case . . . was to establish [the complainant] as a maker of false allegations of rape. That, in our judgment, is undoubtedly a matter of credibility rather than being related to any substantive issue between the prosecution and the defence in this case.' Cf *R v Martin* [2004] EWCA 916, [2004] 2 Cr App R 22 (p 354), [37]: 'We conclude that, on ordinary principles of interpretation, it was one purpose but not "the purpose" or "the main purpose" of the questions to impugn the credibility of the complainant.'

[249] [2001] UKHL 25, [2001] 2 WLR 1546. See generally D Birch, 'Rethinking Sexual History Evidence: Proposals for Fairer Trials' [2002] *Criminal Law Review* 531; D Birch, 'Untangling Sexual History Evidence: A Rejoinder to Professor Temkin' [2003] *Criminal Law Review* 370; G Brennan, 'Sexual History Evidence: The Youth Justice and Criminal Evidence Act 1999' (2002) 8 *Queen Mary Law Journal* 7; K Cook, 'Sexual History Evidence: The Defendant Fights Back' (2001) 151 *New Law Journal* 1133; A Kavanagh, 'Unlocking the Human Rights Act: The "Radical" Approach to Section 3(1) Revisited' [2005] *European Human Rights Law*

House was as follows: 'May a sexual relationship between a defendant and complainant be relevant to the issue of consent so as to render its exclusion under section 41 of the Youth Justice and Criminal Evidence Act 1999 a contravention of the defendant's right to a fair trial?' At issue in this case was evidence of instances of sexual behaviour involving the defendant and the complainant that had taken place between one week and three weeks before the alleged rape. The House of Lords held that section 41(3)(b) was clearly inapplicable since it would be artificial to stretch the phrase 'at or about the same time' to encompass sexual behaviour taking place a week or more previously. The case was, however, remitted to the trial judge to consider whether section 41(3)(c) might be applicable. The House considered section 3 of the Human Rights Act 1998, which requires legislation to be interpreted compatibly with the Convention if possible, to be applicable here. Section 3

> requires the court to subordinate the niceties of the language of section 41(3)(c), and in particu-
> lar the touchstone of coincidence, to broader considerations of relevance judged by logical and
> common sense criteria of time and circumstances. After all, it is realistic to proceed on the basis
> that the legislature would not, if alerted to the problem, have wished to deny the right to an
> accused to put forward a full and complete defence by advancing truly probative material. It is
> therefore possible under section 3 to read section 41, and in particular section 41(3)(c), as sub-
> ject to the implied provision that evidence or questioning which is required to ensure a fair trial
> under [A]rticle 6 of the Convention should not be treated as inadmissible. The result of such a
> reading would be that sometimes logically relevant sexual experiences between a complainant
> and an accused may be admitted under section 41(3)(c). On the other hand, there will be cases
> where previous sexual experience between a complainant and an accused will be irrelevant, eg
> an isolated episode distant in time and circumstances. Where the line is to be drawn must be left
> to the judgment of trial judges. On this basis a declaration of incompatibility can be avoided. If
> this approach is adopted, section 41 will have achieved a major part of its objective but its
> excessive reach will have been attenuated in accordance with the will of Parliament as reflected
> in section 3 of the 1998 Act.[250]

Thus, in summary:

> the effect of the decision today is that under section 41(3)(c) of the 1999 Act, construed
> where necessary by applying the interpretative obligation under section 3 of the Human Rights
> Act 1998, and due regard always being paid to the importance of seeking to protect the
> complainant from indignity and from humiliating questions, the test of admissibility is whether
> the evidence (and questioning in relation to it) is nevertheless so relevant to the issue of consent

Review 259; J McEwan, 'The Rape Shield Askew? *R v A*' (2001) 5 *International Journal of Evidence and Proof* 257; P Mirfield, 'Human Wrongs?' (2002) 118 *Law Quarterly Review* 20; M Redmayne, 'Myths, Relationships and Coincidences: The New Problems of Sexual History' (2003) 7 *International Journal of Evidence and Proof* 75; P Rook, 'Restrictions on Evidence or Questions About the Complainant's Sexual History', *Criminal Bar Association Newsletter*, June 2004, 10, accessible via http://www.criminalbar.com; D Sandy, '*R v A*: The Death of the Declaration of Incompatibility?' (2001) 151 *New Law Journal* 1615; J R Spencer, ' "Rape Shields" and the Right to a Fair Trial' [2001] *Cambridge Law Journal* 452; J Temkin, 'Sexual History Evidence—Beware the Backlash' [2003] *Criminal Law Review* 217; L Ellison, *The Adversarial Process and the Vulnerable Witness* (2001) 120–1; S Lees, *Carnal Knowledge: Rape on Trial* (2002) xxvi–xxxiii; J Temkin, *Rape and the Legal Process* (2nd ed 2002) Ch 4.

[250] [2001] UKHL 25, [2001] 2 WLR 1546, [45].

that to exclude it would endanger the fairness of the trial under [A]rticle 6 of the [C]onvention. If this test is satisfied the evidence should not be excluded.[251]

This decision represents another valiant attempt on the part of the House of Lords to find some part of English law—in this instance a legislative scheme designed to *restrict* rather than to increase the amount of information available to a court—to be Convention compliant. This has been achieved, as Dennis puts it, by 'suppl[ying] the residual inclusionary discretion which is so conspicuously lacking in the text of section 41'.[252] The use of section 3 is not, however, to be resorted to lightly, as the Court of Appeal has cautioned:

> In our judgment *R v A* is not authority for any wider reading of section 41 by force of section 3 of the Human Rights Act in a case where sexual acts of the complainant with men other than the appellant are sought to be adduced than is justified by the application of conventional canons of construction. At the least it would take a very special case to accommodate evidence of such acts in circumstances in which they would not be accommodated by an ordinary reading of the section.[253]

In an important decision, the Court of Appeal managed to avoid altogether the use of section 3 of the Human Rights Act, by holding section 41 of the 1999 Act to be inapplicable in the first place:

> It seems to this court that normally questions or evidence about false statements in the past by a complainant about sexual assaults or such questions or evidence about a failure to complain about the alleged assault which is the subject matter of the charge, while complaining about other sexual assaults, are not ones 'about' any sexual behaviour of the complainant. They relate not to her sexual behaviour but to her statements in the past or to her failure to complain. . . . It is, therefore, unnecessary to invoke s 3 of the 1998 Act.[254]

Being defence evidence, evidence found to be admissible under section 41 may not be excluded in the exercise of discretion:

> It is sometimes loosely suggested that the operation of s 41 involves the exercise of judicial discretion. In reality, the trial judge is making a judgment whether to admit, or refuse to admit evidence which is relevant, or asserted by the defence to be relevant. If the evidence is not relevant, on elementary principles, it is not admissible. If it is relevant, then subject to s 41(4) and assuming that the criteria for admitting the evidence are established, in our judgment the court lacks any discretion to refuse to admit it, or to limit relevant evidence which is properly admissible. In short, once the criteria for admissibility are established, all the evidence relevant to the issues may be adduced. As part of his control over the case, the judge is required to ensure that a complainant is not unnecessarily humiliated or cross-examined with inappropriate aggression, or treated otherwise than with proper courtesy. All that is elementary, but his

---

[251] [2001] UKHL 25, [2001] 2 WLR 1546, [46]. See also *R v T* [2004] EWCA Crim 1220, [2004] 2 Cr App R 32 (p 551).

[252] I H Dennis, *The Law of Evidence* (2nd ed 2002) 512. See the use of s 3 in *R v R* [2003] EWCA Crim 2754.

[253] *R v White* [2004] EWCA Crim 946, [35].

[254] *R v T* [2001] EWCA Crim 1877, [2002] 1 All ER 683, [33], [37]. See also *R v Davies* [2004] EWCA Crim 1389.

obligation to see that the complainant's interests are protected throughout the trial process does not permit him, by way of a general discretion, to prevent the proper deployment of evidence which falls within the ambit permitted by the statute merely because . . . it comes in a stark, uncompromising form.[255]

Given the failure of its predecessor to protect complainants adequately from inappropriate questioning in court, it is pleasing that the new rape shield legislation has, for all its difficulties, been found to be Convention complaint. A structured statutory scheme like that encapsulated in section 41, which prescribes specific situations in which sexual history evidence that is relevant to consent will be admissible, certainly has more to commend it than the highly discretionary approach that was encapsulated in section 2(2) of the Sexual Offences (Amendment) Act 1976. Under that approach, a successful argument that sexual experience evidence was of relevance to the issue of consent, rather than merely to credit, was treated by the courts as a good ground for allowing the introduction of the evidence. There was little proper analysis by the courts of the extent to which sexual experience evidence may have appropriately been regarded as relevant to the issue of consent.[256] It is easy for such 'relevance' to be simply assumed in a situation where such an assumption may in fact be highly questionable, as McColgan succinctly explains:

. . . are women who are or have been sexually active more likely to have consented to sexual activity they characterize as rape than women who are or have not been so active? Is it more likely that a man with a reputation for generosity consented to the appropriation of his possessions, in a case where he alleges theft by the appropriator, than a man who has a reputation for meanness? Of course it is not. Neither his generosity nor her other sexual activities render it more likely that they consented to the activity of which they now complain. It is perhaps more likely, in fact, that the mean man and sexually conservative woman would repent their uncharacteristic behaviour and re-define it subsequently to themselves and others than that the generous man and sexually active woman would re-define behaviour which was not unusual for them.[257]

It would be naïve to assume, however, that the introduction of tighter legislation alone would result in a substantial improvement in the treatment of complainants.[258]

---

[255] *R v F* [2005] EWCA Crim 493, [2005] 2 Cr App R 13 (p 187), [29].

[256] See generally J Temkin, 'Sexual History Evidence—The Ravishment of Section 2' [1993] *Criminal Law Review* 3. See also A J Turner, 'The Law of Rape: The Previous Sexual Experience of the Complainant' (1998) 162 *Justice of the Peace* 396; A A S Zuckerman, *The Principles of Criminal Evidence* (1989) 248 n 5. For an alternative view, see G Durston, 'Cross-Examination of Rape Complainants: Ongoing Tensions Between Conflicting Priorities in the Criminal Justice System' (1998) 62 *Journal of Criminal Law* 91.

[257] A McColgan, 'Common Law and the Relevance of Sexual History Evidence' (1996) 16 *Oxford Journal of Legal Studies* 275, 285.

[258] On the obstacles encountered by complainants of rape see generally J Bennetto, 'Juries Letting Rapists off the Hook "Despite Clear Evidence" ', *Independent*, 30 June 2004, 19; D Orr, 'Women, Rape and the Blame Game', *Independent*, 7 June 2005, 27; Y Roberts, 'A New Myth: Women Play Dirty on Rape', *Independent on Sunday*, 12 June 2005, 25; T Shaikh, 'Police Review Handling of Rape Investigations', *Independent*, 6 June 2005, 8; J Temkin, 'Prosecuting and Defending Rape: Perspectives from the Bar' (2000) 27 *Journal of Law and Society* 219; R Verkaik, 'Rape Trials Still Hit by "She Asked for It" Culture', *Independent*, 7 Jan 2003, 2; J Harris and S Grace, *A Question of Evidence? Investigating and Prosecuting Rape in the 1990s* (Home Office Research Study

What is also required is a change in judicial attitudes, possibly through better judicial training, as well as a change in the attitudes of other lawyers involved in the system.[259] Ultimately, the treatment of rape complainants in court may be viewed as being 'rooted in the inadequate regulation of cross-examination not only in rape cases but across the board and in the nature of cross-examination itself. The focus of the current debate on rape trials must therefore be widened to include the conduct of cross-examination in general in adversarial criminal proceedings.'[260] It is also to be hoped that the practice of 'reading down' the new provisions to ensure Convention compliance will—in the face of apparent judicial discontent with the provisions[261]—be kept within proper limits and not be permitted to dilute the impact of the provisions. In this connection it is pleasing to note that the results of one study of the effect of section 41 have suggested 'that judges are generally far more thoughtful in relation to sexual history evidence than is supposed, and that they take great care when making decisions to allow questioning or evidence and how much to allow'.[262]

4.3 Child Defendants

The provisions on live links and video recordings in the Criminal Justice Act 2003, and the provisions on special measures in the Youth Justice and Criminal Evidence Act 1999, do not apply to defendants.[263] In *R (S) v Waltham Forest Youth Court*[264] it was confirmed that a special measures direction could not be given in respect of a 13-year-old defendant even if she was intending to give evidence against her co-defendants. This state of affairs was not thought to constitute a violation of the defendant's right to a fair trial under

196) (1999), available at http://www.homeoffice.gov.uk/rds/pdfs/hors196.pdf; HM Crown Prosecution Service Inspectorate and HM Inspectorate of Constabulary, *A Report on the Joint Inspection into the Investigation and Prosecution of Cases Involving Allegations of Rape* (2002), available at http://www.homeoffice.gov.uk/hmic/ CPSI_HMIC_Rape_Thematic.pdf; L Kelly, J Lovett, and L Regan, *A Gap or a Chasm? Attrition in Reported Rape Cases* (Home Office Research Study 293) (2005), available at http://www.homeoffice.gov.uk/rds/pdfs05/ hors293.pdf.

[259] 'Speaking Up for Justice', *Archbold News*, 13 July 1998, 4, 5. There is evidence that judicial training may have proved effective: N Kibble, 'Judicial Perspectives on the Operation of S 41 and the Relevance and Admissibility of Prior Sexual History Evidence: Four Scenarios: Part 1' [2005] *Criminal Law Review* 190, 205.

[260] L Ellison, 'Cross-Examination in Rape Trials' [1998] *Criminal Law Review* 605, 614. See also L Ellison, 'The Mosaic Art?: Cross-Examination and the Vulnerable Witness' (2001) 21 *Legal Studies* 353; L Ellison, 'Rape and the Adversarial Culture of the Courtroom' in M Childs and L Ellison (eds), *Feminist Perspectives on Evidence* (2000); L Ellison, *The Adversarial Process and the Vulnerable Witness* (2001).

[261] See N Kibble, 'Section 41 Youth Justice and Criminal Evidence Act 1999: Fundamentally Flawed or Fair and Balanced?', *Archbold News*, 20 Sep 2004, 6.

[262] Ibid, 9. See also N Kibble, 'Judicial Perspectives on the Operation of S 41 and the Relevance and Admissibility of Prior Sexual History Evidence: Four Scenarios: Part 1' [2005] *Criminal Law Review* 190, 204: 'The judges' responses suggest that far from allowing questioning and evidence in relation to sexual history to be admitted as a matter of course, many judges approach the question of relevance and admissibility thoughtfully and with an awareness of the dangers of admitting irrelevant evidence.'

[263] See generally I Harris, 'Special Measures for Defendants?', *Archbold News*, 7 Apr 2003, 7. This is in contrast to the position in Scotland under the Criminal Procedure (Scotland) Act 1995 (as amended by the Vulnerable Witnesses (Scotland) Act 2004).

[264] [2004] EWHC 715 (Admin), [2004] 2 Cr App R 21 (p 335).

Article 6.[265] Controversially in the view of some, the protection of child defendants who testify in the Crown Court is not regulated under any particular statutory régime. Lord Justice Auld in his Review noted 'a striking difference between the care for children as witnesses in [the provisions of the Youth Justice and Criminal Evidence Act 1999] and the lack of any corresponding provision for them when they are accused of grave crime in the Crown Court, a disparity that concerns many judges'.[266] Rather, the protection of child defendants testifying in the Crown Court is simply the subject of a practice direction handed down by the Lord Chief Justice in the aftermath of the decision of the European Court of Human Rights in *T v UK*,[267] where the trial of two boys for the murder of the toddler James Bulger was found to have breached Article 6. The practice direction provides in part:

THE OVERRIDING PRINCIPLE

IV.39.3   . . . The trial process should not itself expose the young defendant to avoidable intimidation, humiliation or distress. All possible steps should be taken to assist the young defendant to understand and participate in the proceedings. The ordinary trial process should, so far as necessary, be adapted to meet those ends. Regard should be had to the welfare of the young defendant as required by section 44 of the Children and Young Persons Act 1933.

THE TRIAL

IV.39.9   The trial should, if practicable, be held in a courtroom in which all the participants are on the same or almost the same level.

IV.39.10   A young defendant should normally, if he wishes, be free to sit with members of his family or others in a like relationship and in a place which permits easy, informal communication with his legal representatives and others with whom he wants or needs to communicate.

IV.39.11   The court should explain the course of proceedings to a young defendant in terms he can understand, should remind those representing a young defendant of their continuing duty to explain each step of the trial to him and should ensure, so far as practicable, that the trial is conducted in language which the young defendant can understand.

IV.39.12   The trial should be conducted according to a timetable which takes full account of a young defendant's inability to concentrate for long periods. Frequent and regular breaks will often be appropriate.

IV.39.13   Robes and wigs should not be worn unless the young defendant asks that they should or the court for good reason orders that they should. Any person responsible for the security of a young defendant who is in custody should not be in uniform.

---

[265] In *R (D) v Camberwell Green Youth Court* [2005] UKHL 4, [2005] 1 WLR 393, [63], Baroness Hale of Richmond reserved her position on whether the *Waltham Forest* case was correctly decided.

[266] Lord Justice Auld, *Review of the Criminal Courts of England and Wales* (2001) Ch 11 para 126, accessible via http://www.criminal-courts-review.org.uk/.

[267] (2000) 30 EHRR 121 (judgment of 1999). See generally A A Gillespie, 'Practice Direction on Child Defendants and the Case of *T v UK*' (2000) 150 *New Law Journal* 320; E Henderson, 'The European Convention and Child Defendants' [2000] *Cambridge Law Journal* 235.

There should be no recognisable police presence in the courtroom save for good reason.

IV.39.14   The court should be prepared to restrict attendance at the trial to a small number, perhaps limited to some of those with an immediate and direct interest in the outcome of the trial. The court should rule on any challenged claim to attend.

IV.39.15   . . . the court may restrict the number of those attending in the courtroom to report the trial to such number as is judged practicable and desirable. In ruling on any challenged claim to attend the courtroom for the purpose of reporting the trial the court should be mindful of the public's general right to be informed about the administration of justice in the Crown Court. Where access to the courtroom by reporters is restricted, arrangements should be made for the proceedings to be relayed, audibly and if possible visually, to another room in the same court complex to which the media have free access if it appears that there will be a need for such additional facilities.

IV.39.16   Where the court is called upon to exercise its discretion in relation to any procedural matter falling within the scope of this practice direction but not the subject of specific reference, such discretion should be exercised having regard to the principles in paragraph IV.39.3.[268]

More recently, in its decision in *SC v UK* in 2004, the European Court of Human Rights found a breach of Article 6(1) in circumstances where:

. . . the applicant seems to have had little comprehension of the role of the jury in the proceedings or of the importance of making a good impression on them. Even more strikingly, he does not seem to have grasped the fact that he risked a custodial sentence and, even once sentence had been passed and he had been taken down to the holding cells, he appeared confused and expected to be able to go home with his foster father.[269]

The Court observed that:

. . . when the decision is taken to deal with a child, such as the applicant, who risks not being able to participate effectively because of his young age and limited intellectual capacity, by way of criminal proceedings rather than some other form of disposal directed primarily at determining the child's best interests and those of the community, it is essential that he be tried in a specialist tribunal which is able to give full consideration to and make proper allowance for the handicaps under which he labours, and adapt its procedure accordingly.[270]

It is to be hoped that such sentiments are heeded.

4.4 Witness Familiarization Arrangements

The usefulness of witness familiarization arrangements, in the interest of ensuring that witnesses are treated appropriately, is increasingly being emphasized. In *R v Momodou*

---

[268] *Consolidated Criminal Practice Direction*, available at http://www.hmcourts-service.gov.uk/cms/files/consolidated_criminal_practice_direction0405.pdf. See also Lord Woolf, 'Rights of Child Defendants', Keynote Speech, Michael Sieff Foundation Conference, 25 April 2002, available at http://www.dca.gov.uk/judicial/speeches/lcj250402.htm.   [269] (2005) 40 EHRR 10 (p 226) (judgment of 2004), [33].

[270] Ibid, [35]. See generally P Tain, 'Children in the Dock' (2004) 148 *Solicitors' Journal* 841.

the Court of Appeal provided detailed guidance on the issue. The relevant passages of the judgment are worth quoting in full:

> There is a dramatic distinction between witness training or coaching, and witness familiarisation. Training or coaching for witnesses in criminal proceedings (whether for prosecution or defence) is not permitted. This is the logical consequence of the well-known principle that discussions between witnesses should not take place, and that the statements and proofs of one witness should not be disclosed to any other witness. . . . The witness should give his or her own evidence, so far as practicable uninfluenced by what anyone else has said, whether in formal discussions or informal conversations. The rule reduces, indeed hopefully avoids, any possibility that one witness may tailor his evidence in the light of what anyone else said, and equally avoids any unfounded perception that he may have done so. These risks are inherent in witness training. Even if the training takes place one-to-one with someone completely remote from the facts of the case itself, the witness may come, even unconsciously, to appreciate which aspects of his evidence are perhaps not quite consistent with what others are saying, or indeed not quite what is required of him. An honest witness may alter the emphasis of his evidence to accommodate what he thinks may be a different, more accurate, or simply better remembered perception of events. A dishonest witness will very rapidly calculate how his testimony may be 'improved'. These dangers are present in one-to-one witness training. Where however the witness is jointly trained with other witnesses to the same events, the dangers dramatically increase. Recollections change. Memories are contaminated. Witnesses may bring their respective accounts into what they believe to be better alignment with others. They may be encouraged to do so, consciously or unconsciously. They may collude deliberately. They may be inadvertently contaminated. Whether deliberately or inadvertently, the evidence may no longer be their own. Although none of this is inevitable, the risk that training or coaching may adversely affect the accuracy of the evidence of the individual witness is constant. So we repeat, witness training for criminal trials is prohibited.[271]

> This principle does not preclude pre-trial arrangements to familiarise the witness with the layout of the court, the likely sequence of events when the witness is giving evidence, and a balanced appraisal of the different responsibilities of the various participants. Indeed such arrangements, usually in the form of a pre-trial visit to the court, are generally to be welcomed. Witnesses should not be disadvantaged by ignorance of the process, nor, when they come to give evidence, taken by surprise at the way it works. None of this however involves discussions about proposed or intended evidence. Sensible preparation for the experience of giving evidence, which assists the witness to give of his or her best at the forthcoming trial, is permissible. Such experience can also be provided by out of court familiarisation techniques. The process may improve the manner in which the witness gives evidence by, for example, reducing the nervous tension arising from inexperience of the process. Nevertheless the evidence remains the witness's own uncontaminated evidence. Equally, the principle does not prohibit training of expert and similar witnesses in, for example, the technique of giving comprehensive evidence of a specialist kind to a jury, both during evidence-in-chief and in cross-examination, and, another example, developing the ability to resist the inevitable pressure of going further in evidence than matters covered by the witnesses' specific expertise. The critical feature of training of this kind is that it should not be arranged in the context of nor related to any forthcoming trial, and it can therefore have no impact whatever on it.[272]

[271] [2005] EWCA Crim 177, [2005] 2 Cr App R 6 (p 85), [61].   [272] Ibid, [62].

In the context of an anticipated criminal trial, if arrangements are made for witness familiar-isation by outside agencies, not, for example, that routinely performed by or through the Witness Service, the following broad guidance should be followed. In relation to prosecution witnesses, the Crown Prosecution Service should be informed in advance of any proposal for familiarisation. If appropriate after obtaining police input, the Crown Prosecution Service should be invited to comment in advance on the proposals. If relevant information comes to the police, the police should inform the Crown Prosecution Service. The proposals for the intended familiarisation programme should be reduced into writing, rather than left to informal conversa-tions. If, having examined them, the Crown Prosecution Service suggests that the programme may be breaching the permitted limits, it should be amended. If the defence engages in the process, it would in our judgment be extremely wise for counsel's advice to be sought, again in advance, and again with written information about the nature and extent of the training. In any event, it is in our judgment a matter of professional duty on counsel and solicitors to ensure that the trial judge is informed of any familiarisation process organised by the defence using outside agencies, and it will follow that the Crown Prosecution Service will be made aware of what has happened.[273]

This familiarisation process should normally be supervised or conducted by a solicitor or barrister, or someone who is responsible to a solicitor or barrister with experience of the criminal justice process, and preferably by an organisation accredited for the purpose by the Bar Council and Law Society. None of those involved should have any personal knowledge of the matters in issue. Records should be maintained of all those present and the identity of those responsible for the familiarisation process, whenever it takes place. The programme should be retained, together with all the written material (or appropriate copies) used during the familiarisation sessions. None of the material should bear any similarity whatever to the issues in the criminal proceedings to be attended by the witnesses, and nothing in it should play on or trigger the witness's recollection of events. . . . If discussion of the instant criminal proceedings begins, as it almost inevitably will, it must be stopped. And advice given about precisely why it is impermissible, with a warning against the danger of evidence contamination and the risk that the course of justice may be perverted. Note should be made if and when any such warning is given.[274]

All documents used in the process should be retained, and if relevant to prosecution witnesses, handed to the Crown Prosecution Service as a matter of course, and in relation to defence witnesses, produced to the court. None should be destroyed. It should be a matter of profes-sional obligation for barristers and solicitors involved in these processes, or indeed the trial itself, to see that this guidance is followed.[275]

[273] [2005] EWCA Crim 177, [2005] 2 Cr App R 6 (p 85), [63].   [274] Ibid, [64].
[275] Ibid, [65]. See generally G Langdon-Down, 'Witness Training Is in the Dock', *The Times*, 15 Feb 2005, Law, 6.

12

Burden and Standard of Proof

This chapter is divided into two parts. The first part is concerned with the manner in which a dispute as to which party bears the burden of proving a particular issue in a trial should be resolved. The question may arise in a criminal trial as to whether it is the prosecution or defence which bears the burden of proving a certain issue, and in a civil trial as to whether it is the claimant or defendant who bears the burden of proving a certain issue. Another question which may arise concerns the standard to which the burden of proving a particular issue requires to be discharged. This is the subject of the second part of the chapter.

1 Burden of Proof

1.1 The Legal Burden and the Evidential Burden

The *legal burden of proof* is the probative burden, and relates to the duty of a party to prove a particular fact to the trier of fact by the end of the trial. Failure to discharge this burden means that the issue will be decided in favour of the other party. The legal burden of proof, which is most commonly known simply as the 'burden of proof',[1] is therefore the final, or ultimate, burden of proving a particular fact.[2] The *evidential burden of proof*, by contrast, is merely a provisional burden.[3] It relates to the duty of a party to make a matter a 'live issue' at the trial—in other words, to adduce sufficient evidence of a particular issue to satisfy the judge that the issue should be left to the trier of fact for its consideration. As the Supreme Court of Canada has explained:

> An 'evidential burden' is not a burden of proof. It determines whether an issue should be left to the trier of fact, while the 'persuasive burden' determines how the issue should be decided.[4]

> These are fundamentally different questions. The first is a matter of law; the second, a question of fact. Accordingly, on a trial before judge and jury, the judge decides whether the evidential burden has been met. In answering that question, the judge does not evaluate the quality,

---

[1] It is also known as the 'risk of non-persuasion', the 'fixed burden of proof', and the 'persuasive burden'.
[2] See generally S Wexler, 'Burden of Proof, Writ Large' (1999) 33 *University of British Columbia Law Review* 75.
[3] It is also known as the 'burden of adducing evidence' and the 'burden of passing the judge'.
[4] *R v Fontaine* [2004] 1 SCR 702, [11] (underlining in original).

weight or reliability of the evidence. The judge simply decides whether there is evidence upon which a properly instructed jury could reasonably decide the issue.[5]

1.2 Incidence of Legal Burden

1.2.1 Criminal Trials

1.2.1.1 The *Woolmington* Rule

In *Woolmington v DPP*, the House of Lords had to consider the summing-up by a trial judge to the effect that if, on a charge of murder, the prosecution satisfied the jury that the defendant had caused the victim's death, and the defendant wished to argue that it was a pure accident, then the defence bore the legal burden of proving this. It would appear that some earlier authorities had suggested that this represented the law. The House of Lords held, however, that inasmuch as they suggested this, those authorities were incorrect. Viscount Sankey LC stated:

> Throughout the web of the English Criminal Law one golden thread is always to be seen, that it is the duty of the prosecution to prove the prisoner's guilt subject to what I have already said as to the defence of insanity and subject also to any statutory exception.[6]

The position, then, may be stated simply. In a criminal trial, the prosecution generally bears the legal burden of proving every issue. In general, therefore, *actus reus, mens rea*, and the lack of a defence must all be proved by the prosecution. This reflects the principle of the presumption of innocence. In a criminal trial, the might of a 'strong' state is ranged against a 'weak' individual. If a conviction results, serious consequences may flow from this, including the possible deprivation of liberty. It is appropriate, therefore, for the prosecution to have to prove the defendant's guilt, rather than for the defendant to have to prove his or her own innocence. Roberts has identified three broad reasons for the presumption of innocence.[7] First, to place the burden of proof in relation to a particular issue on the defence would mean that the trier of fact must convict if it remains undecided about facts material to that issue. Secondly, 'for as long as criminal proceedings are initiated and structured by the prosecutor's presentation of a prima facie case to answer on specified charges—as opposed, say, to requiring each of us to undergo monthly confessionals before an inquisitor—placing the burden of proof on a defendant will often deprive him of a fair opportunity to answer the allegations against him'. Finally, in most cases, the investigative resources to which the prosecution has access are greatly superior to those to which the defence has access.

The 'Woolmington rule' is, however, subject to two broad exceptions. First, there is the defence of insanity. An accused who raises insanity or insane automatism as a defence

---

[5] *R v Fontaine* [2004] 1 SCR 702, [12]. See generally D Stuart, '*Fontaine*: Lowering the Bar for Evidentiary Burdens for Defences to Be Put to Juries' (2004) 18 *Criminal Reports (6th)* 238.   [6] [1935] AC 462, 481.
[7] P Roberts, 'Taking the Burden of Proof Seriously' [1995] *Criminal Law Review* 783, 785–7.

(or who argues unfitness to plead) bears the legal burden of proving it. What have become known as the *M'Naghten* rules were promulgated in *M'Naghten's Case*:

> we have to submit our opinion to be, that the jurors ought to be told in all cases that every man is to be presumed to be sane, and to possess a sufficient degree of reason to be responsible for his crimes, *until the contrary be proved to their satisfaction*; and that to establish a defence on the ground of insanity, *it must be clearly proved that*, at the time of the committing of the act, the party accused was labouring under such a defect of reason, from disease of the mind, as not to know the nature and quality of the act he was doing; or, if he did know it, that he did not know he was doing what was wrong.[8]

The Supreme Court of Canada has held that the presumption of sanity embodied in the Canadian Criminal Code violated the presumption of innocence guaranteed by section 11(d) of the Canadian Charter of Rights and Freedoms, but that the placing of the legal burden on the accused constituted a reasonable limit within the meaning of section 1[9] of the Charter.[10] A number of arguments have been advanced to justify treating the defence of insanity differently from the other common law defences in English law where burden of proof is concerned. It has been argued, for example, that, there being a presumption of sanity (as made clear in *M'Naghten* itself), it must be for the accused to prove his or her insanity. This, however, is a non sequitur. All the word 'presumption' means in this context is that insanity will not be an issue in a trial until the evidential burden in relation to the issue is discharged—that is, until sufficient evidence is adduced to make it a 'live issue'. In this sense, there is surely equally a 'presumption' that the accused was not acting in self-defence, under duress, as a result of provocation, or in a state of non-insane automatism, yet the legal burden of proof in relation to these defences lies on the prosecution. Secondly, it has been argued that to place the legal burden on the prosecution would be to impose a burden which would be very difficult to discharge, thus making it easy for the defence to make false claims of insanity. Again, however, there are other common law defences in relation to which the prosecution bears legal burdens which may be similarly difficult to discharge. Thirdly, it is said that to place the legal burden on the defence would not cause unfairness, since insanity is a matter which would be peculiarly within the knowledge of the accused. But so is *mens rea*, which must be proved by the prosecution.[11]

Where an accused charged with murder raises the defence *either* of insanity or of diminished responsibility, section 6 of the Criminal Procedure (Insanity) Act 1964 permits the prosecution to adduce evidence to prove the *other* defence. In this situation, the legal burden of proof falls on the prosecution. In a similar vein, section 4 of the same

---

[8] (1843) 10 Cl & F 200, 210, 8 ER 718, 722 (italics added).

[9] 'The *Canadian Charter of Rights and Freedoms* guarantees the rights and freedoms set out in it subject only to such reasonable limits prescribed by law as can be demonstrably justified in a free and democratic society.'

[10] *R v Chaulk* (1990) 62 CCC (3d) 193.

[11] For a much fuller discussion of these, and related, issues, see T H Jones, 'Insanity, Automatism, and the Burden of Proof on the Accused' (1995) 111 *Law Quarterly Review* 475. See also T H Jones, 'Insanity and the Burden of Proof on the Accused: A Human Rights Approach' in J F Nijboer and J M Reijntjes (eds), *Proceedings of the First World Conference on New Trends in Criminal Investigation and Evidence* (1997).

Act allows the issue of unfitness to plead and stand trial to be raised either by the defence or by the prosecution, and where raised by the prosecution, the legal burden of proving the issue falls on the prosecution.[12]

The second broad exception to the *Woolmington* rule arises where a statutory provision places the legal burden of proving a particular issue on the defendant. As Ashworth and Blake found in their empirical study, there is no shortage of examples of legislation which places the legal burden of proving particular issues on the defendant. They remark:

> It is a fair conclusion from the evidence presented here that many of those who prepare, draft and enact criminal legislation for England and Wales either fail to recognise these violations of the presumption of innocence, or disagree with the presumption of innocence or its application in this sphere, or fail to appreciate what can be achieved by placing only an evidential burden (rather than the legal burden) on defendants in respect of defences.[13]

1.2.1.2 Express Statutory Exceptions

1.2.1.2.1 Reverse-Onus Provisions

On occasion, the legal burden of proving a particular issue is placed *expressly* on the defendant by statute, as the following examples[14] illustrate.

Prevention of Crime Act 1953, section 1(1):

> Any person who without lawful authority or reasonable excuse, *the proof whereof shall lie on him*, has with him in any public place any offensive weapon shall be guilty of an offence . . .

Homicide Act 1957, section 2(2):

> On a charge of murder, *it shall be for the defence to prove* that the person charged is by virtue of this section not liable to be convicted of murder.

Homicide Act 1957, section 4(2):

> Where it is shown that a person charged with the murder of another killed the other or was a party to his being killed, *it shall be for the defence to prove* that the person charged was acting in pursuance of a suicide pact between him and the other.

Criminal Justice Act 1988, section 139(4):

> *It shall be a defence for a person charged* with an offence under this section *to prove* that he had good reason or lawful authority for having the article with him in a public place.

Fireworks Act 2003, section 11(8):

> In proceedings against any person for an offence of contravening a prohibition imposed by fireworks regulations made by virtue of section 3(1) *it is a defence for that person to show that*

---

[12] *R v Robertson* [1968] 1 WLR 1767.

[13] A Ashworth and M Blake, 'The Presumption of Innocence in English Criminal Law' [1996] *Criminal Law Review* 306, 315.

[14] Italics added in all cases. See also Prevention of Corruption Act 1916, s 2; Criminal Justice Act 1925, s 47; Misuse of Drugs Act 1971, s 28(2); Vehicle Excise and Registration Act 1994, s 53; Serious Organised Crime and Police Act 2005, s 128(4).

he had no reason to suspect that the person to whom he supplied, offered to supply or agreed to supply the fireworks was below the age specified in the regulations.

Gangmasters (Licensing) Act 2004, section 13(2):

In proceedings against a person for an offence under subsection (1) [the offence of entering into arrangements with gangmasters in relation to unlicensed activities] *it is a defence for him to prove* that he—(a) took all reasonable steps to satisfy himself that the gangmaster was acting under the authority of a valid licence, and (b) did not know, and had no reasonable grounds for suspecting that the gangmaster was not the holder of a valid licence.

Hunting Act 2004, section 4:

It is a defence for a person charged with an offence under section 1 in respect of hunting *to show* that he reasonably believed that the hunting was exempt.

Serious Organised Crime and Police Act 2005, section 135:

(3) A person taking part in or organising the demonstration who knowingly fails to comply with a condition which is applicable to him and which is imposed or varied by a direction under this section is guilty of an offence.

(4) *It is a defence for him to show* that the failure to comply arose from circumstances beyond his control.

1.2.1.2.2 The Effect of the Human Rights Act 1998

One of the major ongoing debates in the law of evidence relates to the extent to which reverse-onus clauses in statutory provisions may conflict with Article 6(2) of the European Convention on Human Rights.[15] In addressing the question the courts have made skilful use of section 3 of the Human Rights Act 1998, which provides: '(1) So far as it is possible to do so, primary legislation and subordinate legislation must be read and given effect in a way which is compatible with the Convention rights.' In their quest to avoid making a declaration of incompatibility under section 4, the courts have been prepared, using section 3, to 'read down' legislation in a manner that has not proved uncontroversial.

European Court jurisprudence establishes that Article 6(2), which provides that everyone charged with a criminal offence shall be presumed innocent until proven guilty, is not an absolute and unqualified right. Presumptions of fact and law are permissible provided that they are confined within reasonable limits and strike a fair balance between the interests of the community and the rights of the individual.[16] Thus in appropriate circumstances criminal statutes can transfer the burden of proof to the

---

[15] For a discussion of some of the earlier developments see A L-T Choo and S Nash, 'Evidence Law in England and Wales: The Impact of the Human Rights Act 1998' (2003) 7 *International Journal of Evidence and Proof* 31, 56–60 (on which I have drawn in this section); V Tadros and S Tierney, 'The Presumption of Innocence and the Human Rights Act' (2004) 67 *Modern Law Review* 402.

[16] *Salabiaku v France* (1991) 13 EHRR 379 (judgment of 1988); *Hoang v France* (1993) 16 EHRR 53 (judgment of 1992); *Telfner v Austria* (2002) 34 EHRR 7 (p 207) (judgment of 2001); *Janosevic v Sweden* (2004) 38 EHRR 22 (p 473) (judgment of 2002); *Västberga Taxi Aktiebolag v Sweden*, Application no 36985/97, 23 July 2002.

accused without violating the presumption of innocence. The current dilemma for English courts[17] is whether, and in what circumstances, it is justifiable and proportionate to impose not only an evidential but also a legal or persuasive burden on the accused.

In *R v DPP, ex p Kebilene*[18] the House of Lords did not accept the Divisional Court's observation that reverse-onus provisions in section 16A of the Prevention of Terrorism (Temporary Provisions) Act 1989 would inevitably lead to a finding of incompatibility with the Convention. Noting that Convention case law indicated that each case should be examined on its merits, Lord Hobhouse of Woodborough accepted that in appropriate circumstances a reverse-onus provision could be justified even though it appeared 'on its face' to be contrary to the Convention.[19] Lord Hope of Craighead emphasized the importance of achieving an appropriate balance between competing interests and observed that Article 6(2):

> is not regarded as imposing an absolute prohibition on reverse onus clauses, whether they be evidential (presumptions of fact) or persuasive (presumptions of law). In each case the question will be whether the presumption is within reasonable limits.[20]

In *R v Lambert*,[21] however, the majority of the House of Lords took the view that interpreting reverse-onus provisions as imposing more than an evidential burden on the accused would require a high level of justification to be Convention compliant. Following his conviction for a drugs offence under section 5(3) of the Misuse of Drugs Act 1971, the appellant submitted that reverse-onus provisions in this statute were incompatible with Article 6(2). Under section 28 of the 1971 Act, a person found in possession of a controlled drug is required to 'prove' that he or she did not know that it was a controlled drug. Lambert argued that requiring him to prove lack of knowledge was inconsistent with the presumption of innocence. Although this case was primarily concerned with the retrospective application of the Human Rights Act 1998, the House went on to consider the interpretation of reverse-onus clauses. The majority considered in the context of this case that placing the persuasive burden on the accused was disproportionate and unjustified and would be inconsistent with Article 6(2). Lord Steyn observed[22] that the principle of proportionality required the House to assess whether

---

[17] For discussions of English law prior to the Human Rights Act 1998, see A Ashworth and M Blake, 'The Presumption of Innocence in English Criminal Law' [1996] *Criminal Law Review* 306; D J Birch, 'Hunting the Snark: The Elusive Statutory Exception' [1988] *Criminal Law Review* 221; P Mirfield, 'An Ungrateful Reply' [1988] *Criminal Law Review* 233; P Roberts, 'Taking the Burden of Proof Seriously' [1995] *Criminal Law Review* 783; A A S Zuckerman, 'The Third Exception to the *Woolmington* Rule' (1976) 92 *Law Quarterly Review* 402.

[18] [1999] 3 WLR 972. See generally I Hare, 'Placing the Onus Back on the Trial' [2000] *Cambridge Law Journal* 1; P Lewis, 'The Human Rights Act 1998: Shifting the Burden' [2000] *Criminal Law Review* 667; P Roberts, 'The Presumption of Innocence Brought Home? *Kebilene* Deconstructed' (2002) 118 *Law Quarterly Review* 41.

[19] [1999] 3 WLR 972, 1009.   [20] Ibid, 997.

[21] [2001] UKHL 37, [2001] 3 WLR 206. See generally G Dingwall, 'Statutory Exceptions, Burdens of Proof and the Human Rights Act 1998' (2002) 65 *Modern Law Review* 450; P Roberts, 'Drug Dealing and the Presumption of Innocence: The Human Rights Act (Almost) Bites' (2002) 6 *International Journal of Evidence and Proof* 17; P Tain, 'Transferred Burden' (2001) 145 *Solicitors' Journal* 855.

[22] [2001] UKHL 37, [2001] 3 WLR 206, [38].

there was a 'pressing necessity to impose a legal rather than evidential burden on the accused'. He expressed concern that imposing a persuasive burden could lead to a conviction even though the jury considered it reasonably possible that the defendant had been 'duped'. Noting that a guilty verdict could result in life imprisonment, he considered that:

> the transfer of the legal burden in section 28 does not satisfy the criterion of proportionality. Viewed in its place in the current legal system section 28 of the 1971 Act is a disproportionate reaction to perceived difficulties facing the prosecution in drugs cases.[23]

Notwithstanding the public interest in combating drug trafficking, Lord Clyde was also concerned that a consequence of imposing the legal burden on the accused was that:

> it would be possible for an accused person to be convicted where the jury believed he might well be innocent but have not been persuaded that he probably did not know the nature of what he possessed. The jury may have a reasonable doubt as to his guilt in respect of his knowledge of the nature of what he possessed but still be required to convict. Looking to the potentially serious consequences of a conviction at least in respect of class A drugs it does not seem to me that such a burden is acceptable.[24]

Disagreeing with the other Law Lords, Lord Hutton considered that the social threat posed by drugs was sufficiently grave to justify the imposition of a persuasive burden.[25]

Applying section 3 of the Human Rights Act 1998, the majority of the House of Lords was satisfied that a conflict with the Convention could be avoided by reading down section 28, a task that could be achieved 'without doing violence to the language or to the objective of that section'.[26] Thus, references to 'prove' and 'proves' in this provision should be construed as meaning 'giving sufficient evidence', thereby imposing only an evidential burden on the accused and not a persuasive one.[27]

The House of Lords returned to the issue of reverse-onus provisions in *R v Johnstone*,[28] in the context of section 92(5) of the Trade Marks Act 1994, which provides that it is a defence to a charge under section 92 of the Act for the defendant 'to *show* that he believed on reasonable grounds that the use of the sign in the manner in which it was used, or was to be used, was not an infringement of the registered trade mark'.[29] Lord Nicholls of Birkenhead, with whom the other Law Lords agreed on this point, remarked:

> I turn to section 92. (1) Counterfeiting is fraudulent trading. It is a serious contemporary problem. Counterfeiting has adverse economic effects on genuine trade. It also has adverse effects on consumers, in terms of quality of goods and, sometimes, on the health or safety of consumers. The Commission of the European Communities has noted the scale of this 'widespread phenomenon with a global impact'... Urgent steps are needed to combat counterfeiting and piracy... Protection of consumers and honest manufacturers and traders from counterfeiting is

---

[23] Ibid, [41].   [24] Ibid, [156].   [25] Ibid, [198].   [26] Ibid, [17] per Lord Slynn of Hadley.
[27] Ibid, [42] per Lord Steyn. *Lambert* was followed by the Court of Appeal in *R v Carrera* [2002] EWCA Crim 2527.   [28] [2003] UKHL 28, [2003] 1 WLR 1736.
[29] Italics added.

an important policy consideration. (2) The offences created by section 92 have rightly been described as offences of 'near absolute liability'. The prosecution is not required to prove intent to infringe a registered trade mark. (3) The offences attract a serious level of punishment: a maximum penalty on indictment of an unlimited fine or imprisonment for up to 10 years or both, together with the possibility of confiscation and deprivation orders. (4) Those who trade in brand products are aware of the need to be on guard against counterfeit goods. They are aware of the need to deal with reputable suppliers and keep records and of the risks they take if they do not. (5) The section 92(5) defence relates to facts within the accused person's own knowledge: his state of mind, and the reasons why he held the belief in question. His sources of supply are known to him. (6) Conversely, by and large it is to be expected that those who supply traders with counterfeit products, if traceable at all by outside investigators, are unlikely to be co-operative. So, in practice, if the prosecution must prove that a trader acted dishonestly, fewer investigations will be undertaken and fewer prosecutions will take place.[30]

In my view factors (4) and (6) constitute compelling reasons why the section 92(5) defence should place a persuasive burden on the accused person. Taking all the factors mentioned above into account, these reasons justify the loss of protection which will be suffered by the individual. Given the importance and difficulty of combating counterfeiting, and given the comparative ease with which an accused can raise an issue about his honesty, overall it is fair and reasonable to require a trader, should need arise, to prove on the balance of probability that he honestly and reasonably believed the goods were genuine.[31]

The decision in late 2004 of the House of Lords in *Sheldrake v DPP; A-G's Reference (No 4 of 2002)*[32] may be regarded as providing for the time being the most authoritative judicial consideration of the relevant legal principles. This decision involved two conjoined cases. *Sheldrake* concerned section 5(2) of the Road Traffic Act 1988, which provides a defence to a charge, under section 5(1)(b), of being in charge of a motor vehicle after consuming excess alcohol. Section 5(2) provides that it would be a defence to *prove* that the circumstances at the time were such that there was no likelihood of the vehicle being driven whilst the proportion of alcohol remained likely to exceed the prescribed limit. The House of Lords held unanimously that section 5(2) should not be read down. In the words of Lord Bingham of Cornhill:

It may not be very profitable to debate whether section 5(2) infringes the presumption of innocence. It may be assumed that it does. Plainly the provision is directed to a legitimate object: the prevention of death, injury and damage caused by unfit drivers. Does the provision meet the tests of acceptability identified in the Strasbourg jurisprudence? In my view, it plainly does. I do not regard the burden placed on the defendant as beyond reasonable limits or in any way arbitrary. It is not objectionable to criminalise a defendant's conduct in these circumstances without requiring a prosecutor to prove criminal intent. The defendant has a full opportunity to

---

[30]   [2003] UKHL 28, [2003] 1 WLR 1736, [52].   [31]   Ibid, [53].

[32]   [2004] UKHL 43, [2004] 3 WLR 976. See generally P W Ferguson, 'Proof of Innocence' [2004] *Scots Law Times* 223; J Hodivala, 'Lost Innocence' (2004) 148 *Solicitors' Journal* 1336; N Padfield, 'The Burden of Proof Unresolved' [2005] *Cambridge Law Journal* 17; D Rhodes, 'Life in Crime' (2004) 148 *Solicitors' Journal* 1307; J R Spencer, '*Attorney-General's Reference (No 4 of 2002)* and *Sheldrake v DPP* [2004] 3 WLR 976', *Archbold News*, 11 Nov 2004, 5; C Wells, 'Reversing the Burden' (2005) 155 *New Law Journal* 183.

show that there was no likelihood of his driving, a matter so closely conditioned by his own knowledge and state of mind at the material time as to make it much more appropriate for him to prove on the balance of probabilities that he would not have been likely to drive than for the prosecutor to prove, beyond reasonable doubt, that he would. I do not think that imposition of a legal burden went beyond what was necessary. If a driver tries and fails to establish a defence under section 5(2), I would not regard the resulting conviction as unfair . . .[33]

A-G's Reference (No 4 of 2002) concerned section 11(2) of the Terrorism Act 2000, which provides a defence to a charge, under section 11(1), of belonging or professing to belong to a proscribed organization. Section 11(2) provides that it would be a defence to *prove* that (a) the organization was not proscribed when the defendant became a member or began to profess being a member, and (b) he or she did not take part in the activities of the organization at any time while it was proscribed. The majority of the House of Lords held that 'section 11(2) of the Act should be read and given effect as imposing on the defendant an evidential burden only'.[34] The following considerations were said to support this conclusion:

(1) . . . a person who is innocent of any blameworthy or properly criminal conduct may fall within section 11(1). There would be a clear breach of the presumption of innocence, and a real risk of unfair conviction, if such persons could exonerate themselves only by establishing the defence provided on the balance of probabilities. It is the clear duty of the courts, entrusted to them by Parliament, to protect defendants against such a risk. It is relevant to note that a defendant who tried and failed to establish a defence under section 11(2) might in effect be convicted on the basis of conduct which was not criminal at the date of commission.

(2) While a defendant might reasonably be expected to show that the organisation was not proscribed on the last or only occasion on which he became a member or professed to be a member, so as to satisfy subsection (2)(a), it might well be all but impossible for him to show that he had not taken part in the activities of the organisation at any time while it was proscribed, so as to satisfy subsection (2)(b). Terrorist organisations do not generate minutes, records or documents on which he could rely. Other members would for obvious reasons be unlikely to come forward and testify on his behalf. If the defendant's involvement . . . had been abroad, any evidence might also be abroad and hard to adduce. While the defendant himself could assert that he had been inactive, his evidence might well be discounted as unreliable. . . . Thus although section 11(2) preserves the rights of the defence, those rights would be very hard to exercise effectively.

(3) If section 11(2) were held to impose a legal burden, the court would retain a power to assess the evidence, on which it would have to exercise a judgment. But the subsection would provide no flexibility and there would be no room for the exercise of discretion. If the defendant failed to prove the matters specified in subsection (2), the court would have no choice but to convict him.

(4) The potential consequence for a defendant of failing to establish a subsection (2) defence is severe: imprisonment for up to ten years.

(5) While security considerations must always carry weight, they do not absolve member states from their duty to ensure that basic standards of fairness are observed.

[33] [2004] UKHL 43, [2004] 3 WLR 976, [41].   [34] Ibid, [53].

(6) Little significance can be attached to the requirement in section 117 of the Act that the Director of Public Prosecutions give his consent to a prosecution . . .[35]

The omission of section 11(2) from the provisions deemed by section 118(2) of the Act to be subject to an evidential burden of proof was regarded as irrelevant: section 11(2) 'should be treated as if section 118(2) applied to it. Such was not the intention of Parliament when enacting the 2000 Act, but it was the intention of Parliament when enacting section 3 of the 1998 Act.'[36]

The difficulties inherent in an approach involving case-by-case determinations of whether section 3 should be used to 'read down' statutory provisions requiring the defendant to 'prove' or 'show' an issue are obvious. Lord Nicholls of Birkenhead acknowledges openly: 'Identifying the requirements of a reasonable balance is not as easy as might seem. One is seeking to balance incommensurables.'[37] Nonetheless, the acknowledgment that it is *possible* in the post-Human Rights Act era for such words to be 'read down' represents a major advance in the law. Any prospect of a substantial reduction in the uncertainty and lack of predictive value of the current approach has not, however, materialized notwithstanding successive considerations of the issue by the House of Lords. As Ashworth has noted in his commentary on *Sheldrake v DPP*; *A-G's Reference (No 4 of 2002)*: 'The least satisfactory aspect of this decision is that it furnishes courts with no clear guidance on how to interpret statutes that impose a burden of proof on the defendant.'[38] Indeed, it can be said that the decision of the House in relation to the *A-G's Reference (No 4 of 2002)* has served to bring the problem of uncertainty and unpredictability into even sharper focus. The decision of the House in this case was reached by a slender 3 : 2 majority, with the two dissenting Law Lords agreeing with the conclusion of the Court of Appeal that the provision should not be 'read down'. Of the total of eight appellate judges who considered the case, therefore, only three reached the conclusion that ultimately prevailed.

In the final analysis, the most appropriate solution to the problem of reverse-onus provisions may well be that encapsulated in the following comment:

> The time has come for a category of 'administrative regulations' which would carry little stigma and no possibility of imprisonment. Only for such 'non-crimes' should . . . reverse burdens be acceptable.[39]

1.2.1.3 Implied Statutory Exceptions

In summary trials, the issue of how it is to be determined whether the legislature has impliedly placed the legal burden of proof in relation to a particular issue on the defendant

---

[35] [2004] UKHL 43, [2004] 3 WLR 976, [51].   [36] Ibid, [53].

[37] *R v Johnstone* [2003] UKHL 28, [2003] 1 WLR 1736, [49].

[38] A J Ashworth, 'Commentary' [2005] *Criminal Law Review* 218, 219. See also J R Spencer, '*Attorney-General's Reference (No 4 of 2002)* and *Sheldrake v DPP* [2004] 3 WLR 976', *Archbold News*, 11 Nov 2004, 5, 6: 'The law that results from the majority decision in this case is clearer than before: but regrettably, the legal waters are still a little murky. Although the majority said that the maximum penalty is a relevant factor, they seem to accept that "reverse burdens" can properly apply in at least some cases where the penalty is heavy.'

[39] N Padfield, 'The Burden of Proof Unresolved' [2005] *Cambridge Law Journal* 17, 19–20.

is governed by section 101 of the Magistrates' Courts Act 1980 (formerly section 81 of the Magistrates' Courts Act 1952):

> Where the defendant to an information or complaint relies for his defence on any exception, exemption, proviso, excuse or qualification, whether or not it accompanies the description of the offence or matter of complaint in the enactment creating the offence or on which the complaint is founded, the burden of proving the exception, exemption, proviso, excuse or qualification shall be on him; and this notwithstanding that the information or complaint contains an allegation negativing the exception, exemption, proviso, excuse or qualification.

The crucial issue, therefore, is to determine whether the defendant is relying for his or her defence on an *exception, exemption, proviso, excuse,* or *qualification*. If so, then the legal burden of proof in relation to the particular issue falls on the defendant. Whether the wording of the provision is such that the exception, exemption, proviso, excuse, or qualification accompanies the description of the offence is irrelevant. It is clear that in trials on indictment, too, legal burdens may be placed on the defence impliedly as well as expressly.[40] Section 101 has been held to encapsulate the common law, and, accordingly, the same approach to determining whether the legislature has impliedly placed the legal burden of proof in relation to a particular issue on the defendant is to be taken in trials on indictment as is taken in summary trials.

The seminal case on implied statutory exceptions to the *Woolmington* rule is the decision of the House of Lords in *R v Hunt*.[41] The fundamental consideration was taken to be that 'Parliament can never lightly be taken to have intended to impose an onerous duty on a defendant to prove his innocence in a criminal case, and a court should be very slow to draw any such inference from the language of a statute'. The House of Lords considered that a useful starting point was the decision of the Court of Appeal in *R v Edwards*. The Court of Appeal had stated that any exception to the general rule that the prosecution bears the legal burden of proving all elements of an offence 'is limited to offences arising under enactments which prohibit the doing of an act save in *specified circumstances* or by persons of *specified classes* or with *specified qualifications* or with the *licence or permission of specified authorities*'.[42] Thus, if the statutory enactment were of this kind, the legal burden would fall on the defence to prove that the act had been done in one of the specified circumstances, or that the defendant belonged to a specified class, or that he or she had a specified qualification, or that he or she had the necessary licence or permission. If the enactment were not of this kind, then the *Woolmington* principle would apply and the prosecution would bear the legal burden of proving all elements of the offence. The House of Lords in *Hunt* considered this formula, however, to be an 'excellent guide to construction' rather than a fixed rule.

---

[40] *R v Hunt* [1987] AC 352.

[41] Ibid. See generally F Bennion, 'Statutory Exceptions: A Third Knot in the Golden Thread?' [1988] *Criminal Law Review* 31; D J Birch, 'Hunting the Snark: The Elusive Statutory Exception' [1988] *Criminal Law Review* 221; P Healy, 'Proof and Policy: No Golden Threads' [1987] *Criminal Law Review* 355; P Mirfield, 'The Legacy of *Hunt*' [1988] *Criminal Law Review* 19; P Mirfield, 'An Ungrateful Reply' [1988] *Criminal Law Review* 233; P Roberts, 'Taking the Burden of Proof Seriously' [1995] *Criminal Law Review* 783; J C Smith, 'The Presumption of Innocence' (1987) 38 *Northern Ireland Legal Quarterly* 223; A A S Zuckerman, 'No Third Exception to the *Woolmington* Rule' (1987) 103 *Law Quarterly Review* 170.   [42] [1975] QB 27, 40 (italics added).

It is also necessary to take into account other considerations, and especially considerations of policy, to determine legislative intent: 'the court should look to other considerations to determine the intention of Parliament such as the mischief at which the Act was aimed and practical considerations affecting the burden of proof and, in particular, the ease or difficulty that the respective parties would encounter in discharging the burden'.[43] Attention was drawn to the earlier decision of the House in *Nimmo v Alexander Cowan & Sons Ltd*.[44] This concerned a now-repealed statutory provision that 'every place at which any person has at any time to work…shall, *so far as is reasonably practicable*, be made…safe for any person working there'.[45] An application of the *Edwards* formula would suggest that, in a criminal prosecution under this provision, the legal burden in relation to the issue of reasonable practicability would fall on the prosecution: the prosecution would have the legal burden of proving that it was reasonably practicable to make the working place safe. It was held in *Nimmo*, however, that the defence bore the legal burden of proving that it was *not* reasonably practicable to make the working place safe. This was explained in *Hunt* on the basis that it would be easier for the defence than the prosecution to bear the appropriate legal burden.

The House of Lords also explained the results reached in two decisions of the Court of Criminal Appeal. The first case, *R v Oliver*,[46] concerned a prosecution for selling sugar without a licence in contravention of the following article: 'Subject to any directions given or except under and in accordance with the terms of a *licence, permit or other authority* granted by or on behalf of the Ministry no…wholesaler shall by way of trade…supply…any sugar.'[47] It was held that the legal burden lay on the defendant to prove that he had the necessary licence to sell sugar. The second case, *R v Putland*,[48] concerned a prosecution for acquiring silk stockings without surrendering clothing coupons, in contravention of an article providing that 'a person shall not acquire rationed goods…without *surrendering…coupons*….'[49] It was held that the legal burden lay on the prosecution to prove that the stockings had been bought without the surrender of coupons. The House of Lords in *Hunt* considered that 'the real distinction between these two cases lies in the comparative difficulty which would face a defendant in discharging the burden of proof'; in *Oliver*:

> it would have been a simple matter for the defendant to prove that he had a licence if such was the case but in the case of purchase of casual articles of clothing it might, as the court pointed out in *Putland's* case, be a matter of the utmost difficulty for a defendant to establish that he had given the appropriate number of coupons for them. It appears … that it was this consideration that led the court to construe that particular regulation as imposing the burden of proving that coupons had not been surrendered upon the prosecution.[50]

R v Hunt itself concerned a prosecution for the unlawful possession of morphine under section 5 of the Misuse of Drugs Act 1971. The accused wanted to rely in his

---

[43] [1987] AC 352, 374.   [44] [1968] AC 107.   [45] Factories Act 1961, s 29(1) (italics added).
[46] [1944] KB 68.   [47] Sugar (Control) Order 1940, art 2 (italics added).   [48] [1946] 1 All ER 85.
[49] Consumer Rationing (Consolidation) Order 1944 (SR & O 1944 No 800), Art 4 (italics added).
[50] [1987] AC 352, 375.

defence on the Misuse of Drugs Regulations 1973, which provided that section 5 did not apply to any preparation of morphine containing 0.2 per cent of morphine or less. The question for the House of Lords was which party bore the legal burden of proof in relation to the issue of the percentage of morphine. It was held that this burden was borne by the prosecution. In so deciding, the House of Lords placed emphasis on the fact that, as it would be extremely rare for a prosecution under the 1971 Act to be brought without the substance in question having been analysed, there would be no difficulty for the prosecution to produce evidence to show that it did not fall within the provision in the Regulations on which the defendant sought to rely. 'On the other hand if the burden of proof is placed upon the defendant he may be faced with very real practical difficulties in discharging it. The suspected substance is usually seized by the police for the purposes of analysis and there is no statutory provision entitling the defendant to a proportion of it. Often there is very little of the substance and if it has already been analysed by the prosecution it may have been destroyed in the process.'[51] It was also considered appropriate to 'have regard to the fact that offences involving the misuse of hard drugs are among the most serious in the criminal calendar', and thus 'to resolve any ambiguity in favour of the defendant and to place the burden of proving the nature of the substance involved in so serious an offence upon the prosecution'.[52]

The issue was considered by the Divisional Court in *Polychronakis v Richards and Jerrom Ltd*.[53] At issue was section 80(4) of the Environmental Protection Act 1990, which provides that 'if a person on whom an abatement notice is served, *without reasonable excuse*, contravenes or fails to comply with any requirement or prohibition imposed by the notice, he shall be guilty of an offence'.[54] The Court drew attention to the fact that section 80(7) and section 80(9) of the same Act create defences by providing that 'it shall be a defence to prove', in the case of section 80(7), 'that the best practicable means were used to prevent, or to counteract the effects of, the nuisance', and, in the case of section 80(9), that one of the conditions specified was satisfied. Because there are statutory defences expressly placing the legal burden of proof on the defendant, Parliament must have intended that the legal burden of proving the absence of reasonable excuse under section 80(4) would fall on the prosecution.[55]

Of course, an approach permitting courts to go beyond even the clear wording of a statutory provision is sufficiently flexible to be used to 'explain' decisions reached in previous cases which may be more appropriately regarded as wrongly decided.

---

[51] Ibid, 377.   [52] Ibid, 378.   [53] [1998] JPL 588.   [54] Italics added.

[55] [1998] JPL 588, 591–2. See also *DPP v Kavaz* [1999] RTR 40: prosecution for using a motor vehicle without a Test Certificate—defendant bears legal burden of proving possession of a certificate; prosecution for using a motor vehicle without insurance—defendant bears legal burden of proving possession of a policy. The relevant statutory provisions are to be found in ss 47 and 143 of the Road Traffic Act 1988. S 47(1) provides: 'A person who uses on a road at any time, or causes or permits to be so used, a motor vehicle to which this section applies, and as respects which no test certificate has been issued within the appropriate period before that time, is guilty of an offence.' S 143 provides: 'Subject to the provisions of this Part of this Act—(a) a person must not use a motor vehicle on a road . . . unless there is in force in relation to the use of the vehicle by that person such a policy of insurance or such a security in respect of third party risks as complies with the requirements of this Part of this Act . . .'.

This may be illustrated by way of an example.[56] Section 161(1) of the Highways Act 1980[57] provides that it is an offence 'if a person, without lawful authority or excuse, deposits any thing whatsoever on a highway...'. Section 137(1) of the same Act[58] provides that it is an offence 'if a person, without lawful authority or excuse, in any way wilfully obstructs...a highway...'. The former provision has been held to place the legal burden of proof in relation to the issue of lawful authority or excuse on the defence; it would be for the defendant to prove the existence of lawful authority or excuse to the trier of fact.[59] The latter provision, however, has been construed as placing the legal burden on the prosecution; the prosecution would bear the legal burden of proving the absence of lawful authority or excuse.[60] It would be possible to explain this difference in outcomes by reference to *Hunt*-type policy reasoning: we could argue, in the words of Smith, that:

> the obstruction section is the more important one in practice and its interpretation has serious implications for civil liberties because those taking part in demonstrations or picketing are likely to find themselves charged with an offence under this section. To impose on such persons the burden of proving that every obstruction of the highway which they might have caused was done with lawful authority or excuse would be a grave step.

Yet this reasoning, as Smith goes on to point out, seems unconvincing when viewed alongside the fact that the two provisions are contained in the same statute and couched in identical terms.[61]

As for the consideration of the relative ease or difficulty of discharging the legal burden, there is no reason why the mere fact that the defendant holds the relevant information or has better or even exclusive access to it should justify placing the *legal* burden on the defence. Surely, if it is considered that this should justify placing *some* burden on the defence, it would be sufficient to place on the defence the evidential burden of putting forward sufficient evidence to put the relevant matter in issue; once the defendant does this, 'his advantage evaporates'.[62] It is notable that the consideration that the defendant in a particular case can supposedly discharge the legal burden with relative ease probably remains the single most important factor influencing the courts. *Environment Agency v M E Foley Contractors Ltd*[63] concerned section 33(1)(a) of the Environmental Protection Act 1990, which provides that a person shall not 'deposit controlled waste, or knowingly cause or knowingly permit controlled waste to be deposited in or on any land unless a waste management licence authorising the deposit is in force and the deposit is in accordance with the licence'. The Administrative Court

---

[56] Adapted from J C Smith, 'The Presumption of Innocence' (1987) 38 *Northern Ireland Legal Quarterly* 223.
[57] Formerly Highways Act 1959, s 140(1).   [58] Formerly Highways Act 1959, s 121(1).
[59] *Gatland v Metropolitan Police Commissioner* [1968] 2 QB 279.
[60] *Nagy v Weston* [1965] 1 All ER 78; *Hubbard v Pitt* [1975] 3 All ER 1; *Hirst v Chief Constable of West Yorkshire* (1987) 85 Cr App R 143 (decision of 1986).
[61] J C Smith, 'The Presumption of Innocence' (1987) 38 *Northern Ireland Legal Quarterly* 223, 232–3.
[62] A Stein, 'After *Hunt*: The Burden of Proof, Risk of Non-Persuasion and Judicial Pragmatism' (1991) 54 *Modern Law Review* 570, 572.   [63] [2002] EWHC 258 (Admin), [2002] 1 WLR 1754.

held: 'In the case of the first defendant ... it was for the prosecution to prove that it had delivered special waste, namely contaminated soil, but not that it had done so without prior written approval. The latter negative averment was of a matter peculiarly within the first defendant's knowledge and it was for it to establish the requisite approval on a balance of probabilities if it sought to challenge the prosecution case in that respect.'[64]

The Administrative Court took a similar approach shortly afterwards in *R (Grundy & Co Excavations Ltd) v Halton Division Magistrates' Court*,[65] which concerned provisions of the Forestry Act 1967. Section 17(1) of the Act provides: 'Anyone who fells a tree without the authority of a felling licence, the case being one in which section 9(1) of this Act applies so as to require such a licence, shall be guilty of an offence ... '. Section 9(1) provides in essence that a felling licence is required, with subsections (2), (3), and (4) then listing situations where subsection (1) does not apply. The Court held that the factual situations in subsections (2), (3), and (4) were exceptions within the meaning of section 101 of the Magistrates' Courts Act 1980 and thus the legal burden of proving that one of them applied fell on the defendant. This conclusion, the Court thought, was prompted by (1) the fact that the factual situations were described as exceptions in the Act itself ('in section 9(5)(a) the [Forestry] Commissioners are given power to make regulations which provide for "additional *exceptions* from the application of subsection (1)" and in section 9(5)(c) the power extends to restricting or suspending "the *exception* in subsection 3(b)" '[66]); (2) the general terms of the statute;[67] and (3) practical considerations:

> If no burden were imposed on the accused, the [Forestry] Commission would have to negative all factual situations provided for both in subsections (2) to (4) and in the not insignificant number of regulations which have been made. That would, quite simply, be impossible.[68]

> On the other hand, if a burden is imposed on the accused, the facts should be within his knowledge. If the accused is the person who would obtain the licence under section 10, there will be no difficulty in his proving all the facts in any of the subsections upon which he can rely. If the accused is a contractor, there should again be no real difficulty in establishing the relevant facts.[69]

The Court added that while 'the reverse onus of proof provisions in sections 9 and 17 of the 1967 Act, read together, derogate from the presumption of innocence in [A]rticle 6(2)',[70] 'when all the relevant circumstances are taken into account, the Commission have shown that it is necessary to impose a legal burden on the defence ... to do so is entirely proportionate':[71]

> A key consideration in determining the question whether it was necessary to impose a legal as opposed to an evidential burden seems ... to be the efficacy of the former and the unworkability of the latter. There is ... no difficulty in an accused proving any particular set of facts upon which he wishes to rely in order to establish one of the exceptions. On the other hand it would

---

[64] Ibid, [28].   [65] [2003] EWHC 272 (Admin), (2003) 167 JP 387.   [66] Ibid, [27] (italics added).
[67] Ibid, [28].   [68] Ibid, [29].   [69] Ibid, [30].   [70] Ibid, [61].   [71] Ibid, [70].

not be easy for the Commission to prove that the facts did not establish an exception once it had been identified by way of evidence by the accused. For example in many cases it will no longer be possible for the Commission to identify the size of the trees once they have been felled without a licence. . . . the scheme will only really work if the burden is on the accused.[72]

Such an approach may well be appropriate for summary trials. There is much to be said, however, for adopting a separate approach in relation to trials on indictment. Trials on indictment differ from summary trials in a number of important respects: they are inherently more 'serious' and formal affairs, and have the potential to lead to far more drastic consequences for those found guilty. It would arguably be more consistent with the presumption of innocence, therefore, for the law to embrace a principle whereby, in trials on indictment, legal burdens can be placed on defendants by the legislature *expressly* only, and not by implication. On such an approach, where in a trial on indictment a statutory provision is construed as impliedly placing a burden on the defence, that burden can only be an evidential burden.[73] If Parliament wishes to place a legal burden upon the defence in a trial on indictment, it must do so expressly. The House of Lords considered that adoption of this principle would represent 'such a fundamental change' that it must be a matter for Parliament rather than the House of Lords.[74] Furthermore, the adoption of such a principle would mean, of course, that, in the case of offences triable either way, the location of the burden of proof may differ according to whether the offence is being tried summarily or on indictment. Lord Griffiths commented that 'the law would have developed on absurd lines if in respect of the same offence the burden of proof today differed according to whether the case was being heard by the magistrates or on indictment'.[75] It is unclear, however, why this should be regarded as a matter of such concern. After all, for the reasons just stated, a Crown Court prosecution would by its nature be of a completely different dimension from a prosecution in the magistrates' court for precisely the same offence.

1.2.1.4 Effect of Misdirection

A misdirection (or failure to give a direction) to the jury in a criminal trial on burden of proof can lead to the quashing of a conviction on appeal. In *R v Zarrabi*,[76] the trial judge informed the jury that he was going to deal with the burden of proof, but in fact directed them on the standard of proof. The Court of Appeal held that this constituted a misdirection and quashed the conviction. The conviction in *R v Moon*[77] was quashed because the jury had been directed that the legal burden of proof in relation to self-defence fell on the accused. In *R v O'Brien*, where 'nowhere in the whole of his summing-up did the judge direct the jury that it was for the prosecution to prove that the defendant was not acting in lawful self-defence',[78] the Court of Appeal held: 'This was undoubtedly an important misdirection in relation

---

[72] [2003] EWHC 272 (Admin), (2003) 167 JP 387, [67]. See also *DPP v Barker* [2004] EWHC 2502 (Admin), (2004) 168 JP 617.

[73] Cf Criminal Law Revision Committee, *Eleventh Report: Evidence (General)* (Cmnd 4991) (1972) 88–90.

[74] *R v Hunt* [1987] AC 352, 376.   [75] Ibid, 373.   [76] *The Times*, 23 Feb 1985.

[77] [1969] 1 WLR 1705.   [78] [2004] EWCA Crim 2900, [23].

to a very significant aspect of the law of self-defence. It would not be just, in our judgment, to dismiss this appeal on the basis that, notwithstanding a misdirection, these convictions were safe.'[79]

1.2.2 Civil Trials

The principle in civil trials[80] is that the party asserting an issue essential to his or her case bears the legal burden of proof in relation to that issue. Unlike the position in criminal trials, there is no presumption in civil trials, where in theory the parties are 'equals', that the party bringing the action bears the legal burden of proof in relation to every issue. Thus in a tort action for negligence, the claimant bears the legal burden of proving the existence of a duty of care, breach of that duty, and the consequential loss. If the defendant wishes to raise a defence such as *volenti non fit injuria* or contributory negligence, then he or she bears the legal burden of proving that defence. In a similar vein, the claimant in a contract action bears the legal burden of proving the existence of a contract, breach of that contract, and the consequential loss. The legal burden of proving a defence such as discharge by agreement or frustration falls on the defendant.

In *Munro, Brice & Co v War Risks Association*,[81] it was held that in an action on a policy insuring against loss by perils of the sea, with a clause excepting loss by capture, seizure, and consequences of hostilities, a plaintiff whose ship had been lost at sea did not bear the legal burden of proving that it had not been lost by the excepted causes. The legal burden of proving that it *had* been so lost fell on the defendant. The court took the view 'that ... when in an action upon a policy of marine insurance the assured has proved that his ship was sunk at sea, he has made out a prima facie case against his underwriters on that policy, and that it is for them to set up the free of capture and seizure exception and to bring themselves within it if they can'.[82] This decision may be compared with that reached in *The Glendarroch*.[83] The plaintiffs brought an action for the non-delivery of goods shipped under a bill of lading. The goods had been damaged by sea water through the stranding of the vessel. The bill of lading exempted the defendants from liability for loss or damage occasioned by perils of the sea, provided that the defendants were not negligent. The Court of Appeal held that the legal burden of proving the contract, and the non-delivery of the goods, was borne by the plaintiffs. If the defendants relied on the exemption clause, then the legal burden fell on them to prove that the damage was caused by a peril of the sea. But if the plaintiffs then relied on the proviso, they bore the legal burden of proving that the damage was caused by the defendants' negligence.[84]

Where it is clear that an issue asserted by a party is one which is essential to his or her case, then that party bears the legal burden in relation to the issue even if this means having to 'prove a negative'. In *Abrath v North Eastern Railway Co* it was held that, in an action for malicious prosecution, the plaintiff has the legal burden of

---

[79] Ibid, [35].

[80] See generally C R Williams, 'Burdens and Standards in Civil Litigation' (2003) 25 *Sydney Law Review* 165.

[81] [1918] 2 KB 78.   [82] Ibid, 88.   [83] [1894] P 226.   [84] Ibid, 231.

proving *absence of reasonable or probable cause* for institution of the prosecution. The court noted that:

> in one sense that is the assertion of a negative, and we have been pressed with the proposition that when a negative is to be made out the onus of proof shifts. That is not so. If the assertion of a negative is an essential part of the plaintiff's case, the proof of the assertion still rests upon the plaintiff. The terms 'negative' and 'affirmative' are after all relative and not absolute.[85]

Whether a particular issue is one which is essential to a party's case is dependent on the substantive law. If the substantive law is not clear on the issue—for example, if there is no applicable precedent—then the matter may be decided in accordance with considerations of policy. The consideration that it is easier to 'prove a positive' than to 'prove a negative' may then assume significance. In *Joseph Constantine Steamship Line Ltd v Imperial Smelting Corpn Ltd*, a ship on charter was destroyed by an explosion. The charterers brought an action claiming damages from the owners for failure to load. The owners raised the defence of frustration. The issue arose whether the owners bore the legal burden of proving that the explosion (the frustrating event) was *not* their fault, or whether the charterers bore the legal burden of proving that the explosion *was* the fault of the owners. The House of Lords held that the burden was borne by the charterers. Lord Russell of Killowen remarked that 'the proving of a negative, a task always difficult and often impossible, would be a most exceptional burden to impose on a litigant'.[86] Stone has pointed out in his analysis of the case that, even in a situation where proof of fault or absence of fault is in fact practically impossible, the holding of the House of Lords can be justified from the viewpoint of policy. This is because the assumption can be made that the vast majority of frustration cases involve no human fault. Thus, to require a defendant pleading frustration to prove absence of fault will necessarily do injustice to the vast majority of defendants, while to require the plaintiff to prove fault will necessarily do injustice to only a small minority of plaintiffs.[87]

The Privy Council has taken the view that it is preferable that the burden of proof in relation to the issue of mitigation of damage should lie with the defendant than with the claimant. Thus it should not be for a claimant who has refused medical treatment to prove that this refusal was reasonable, but rather for the defendant to prove that it was unreasonable.[88]

1.3 Incidence of Evidential Burden

Generally, the party which bears the legal burden of proving a particular issue also bears the evidential burden in relation to that issue. In criminal trials, however, this is not always the case. It is true that both the legal and the evidential burden in relation to

---

[85] (1883) 11 QBD 440, 457. See also ibid, 462.   [86] [1942] AC 154, 177.

[87] J Stone, 'Burden of Proof and the Judicial Process: A Commentary on *Joseph Constantine Steamship, Ltd v Imperial Smelting Corporation, Ltd*' (1944) 60 *Law Quarterly Review* 262, 278.

[88] *Geest plc v Lansiquot* [2002] UKPC 48, [2002] 1 WLR 3111, [14].

actus reus and *mens rea* fall on the prosecution. The fact that the prosecution bears the evidential burden in relation to *actus reus* and *mens rea* means that any failure on its part to discharge this burden by the close of its case will entitle the defence to a ruling that there is no case for it to answer. Similarly, where the defence bears the legal burden of proof in relation to a particular issue (either pursuant to the *M'Naghten* rules or pursuant to an express or implied statutory exception to the *Woolmington* rule), the evidential burden in relation to that issue is also borne by the defence.

An exception to the general principle arises where the legal burden of disproving a common law defence falls on the prosecution. This is the position with respect to the common law defences of self-defence,[89] duress,[90] provocation,[91] and non-insane automatism.[92] If the defendant seeks to rely on one of these defences, then, unless sufficient evidence to put the defence in issue has already emerged during the trial, the defence (rather than the prosecution) bears an evidential burden. To discharge this, it must introduce sufficient evidence to satisfy the trial judge that the defence in question should be left to the jury for its consideration. The legal burden of proving to the jury that the defendant was not acting in self-defence, under duress, as a result of provocation, or in a state of non-insane automatism (as the case may be) then falls on the prosecution.

The same approach is taken to statutory defences in relation to which the prosecution bears the burden of proof, but the details of which the prosecution would require notice. For example, section 1(1)(a) of the Sexual Offences Act 1967 (now repealed) provided that 'a homosexual act in private shall not be an offence provided that the parties consent thereto and have attained the age of sixteen years'. Section 1(6) of the same Act provided that 'where in any proceedings it is charged that a homosexual act is an offence the prosecutor shall have the burden of proving that the act was done otherwise than in private or otherwise than with the consent of the parties or that any of the parties had not attained the age of sixteen years'. It was held that privacy, consent, or age was to be put in issue by the defence, and if this evidential burden was discharged, the legal burden then fell on the prosecution.[93] *Polychronakis v Richards and Jerrom Ltd*, as seen above, concerns a statutory provision construed by the Divisional Court as placing the legal burden of disproving a defence on the prosecution. The Court held, however, that while the legal burden of proof in relation to the issue of reasonable excuse fell on the prosecution, the evidential burden fell on the defence: 'once the defendant has laid the proper evidential basis for a contention that he has a reasonable excuse, it is for the prosecution to satisfy the court . . . that the excuse is not a reasonable one'.[94] Referring to *R v Clarke*,[95] the Court noted that it had similarly been decided in the context of the drink-driving legislation that 'once there was some evidence of a reasonable excuse for failing to provide a specimen it was for the prosecution to eliminate the existence of such a defence to the satisfaction of the jury'.[96] A similar

---

[89] *R v Lobell* [1957] 1 QB 547.   [90] *R v Gill* [1963] 1 WLR 841.   [91] *Mancini v DPP* [1942] AC 1.
[92] *Bratty v A-G for NI* [1963] AC 386.   [93] *R v Spight* [1986] Crim LR 817.
[94] [1998] JPL 588, 592.   [95] [1969] 1 WLR 1109.   [96] [1998] JPL 588, 591.

approach has also been taken to section 95(1) of the Public Health Act 1936 in relation to the existence of a reasonable excuse for failure to comply with a nuisance order.[97]

2 Standard of Proof

If a party bears the legal burden of proving a particular issue, to what standard does that party need to discharge the burden? 'The function of a standard of proof', the US Supreme Court has noted succinctly, 'is to "instruct the factfinder concerning the degree of confidence our society thinks he should have in the correctness of factual conclusions for a particular type of adjudication."[98] . . . The standard serves to allocate the risk of error between the litigants and to indicate the relative importance attached to the ultimate decision.'[99]

2.1 Criminal Trials

2.1.1 Where the Prosecution Bears the Legal Burden

Where the prosecution bears the legal burden of proving a particular issue, it must be proved 'beyond reasonable doubt'.[100]

> . . . the standard of proof beyond a reasonable doubt is . . . inextricably linked to that basic premise which is fundamental to all criminal trials: the presumption of innocence. The two concepts are forever as closely linked as Romeo with Juliet or Oberon with Titania . . . If the presumption of innocence is the golden thread of criminal justice then proof beyond a reasonable doubt is the silver and these two threads are forever intertwined in the fabric of criminal law.[101]

What the requirement of proof beyond reasonable doubt means is that, if the trier of fact is left with *at least reasonable doubt* about the defendant's guilt, an acquittal must follow. The degree of probability required by the beyond-reasonable-doubt standard is thus a high one,[102] but the standard does not, by definition, require that the prosecution's case be proved beyond *all* doubt.[103] 'The law would fail to protect the community if it admitted fanciful possibilities to deflect the course of justice. If the evidence is so

---

[97] *Saddleworth Urban District Council v Aggregate and Sand Ltd* (1970) 69 LGR 103, 107.

[98] Quoting from *In re Winship* 397 US 358, 370 (1970).

[99] *Addington v Texas* 441 US 418, 423 (1979). Lord Bingham CJ stated that 'the standard of proof required must in my judgment always depend on the nature of the proceeding and the potential consequences of an adverse finding': *McCool v Rushcliffe BC* [1998] 3 All ER 889, 894.

[100] See generally J C Smith, 'Satisfying the Jury' [1988] *Criminal Law Review* 335.

[101] *R v Lifchus* [1997] 3 SCR 320, [27]. See generally R Pattenden, 'Explaining a "Reasonable Doubt" to Juries: *R v Lifchus*' (1998) 2 *International Journal of Evidence and Proof* 253.

[102] Note the comment of the US Supreme Court in *Addington v Texas* 441 US 418, 428 (1979) that 'the heavy standard applied in criminal cases manifests our concern that the risk of error to the individual must be minimized even at the risk that some who are guilty might go free'.

[103] See ibid, 430: 'If the state was required to guarantee error-free convictions, it would be required to prove guilt beyond all doubt.'

strong against a man as to leave only a remote possibility in his favour which can be dismissed with the sentence "of course it is possible, but not in the least probable," the case is proved beyond reasonable doubt, but nothing short of that will suffice.'[104]

It is important that the jury in a trial on indictment be directed on the appropriate standard of proof:

> The jury must be clearly and unambiguously instructed that the burden of proving the guilt of the accused lies and lies only on the Crown, that (subject to [certain] exceptions . . .) there is no burden on the accused to prove anything and that if, on reviewing all the evidence, the jury are unsure of or are left in any reasonable doubt as to the guilt of the accused that doubt must be resolved in favour of the accused. Such an instruction has for very many years been regarded as a cardinal requirement of a properly conducted trial. The courts have not been willing to countenance departures from it.[105]

In giving such a direction, it is not incumbent on the judge to use any particular form of words, so long as the correct message is conveyed.[106] 'It is the effect of the summing-up as a whole that matters.'[107] Clearly, a direction that the jury must simply be 'satisfied' of guilt is inadequate.[108] But while proof beyond reasonable doubt clearly does not require that the jury be sure or certain of guilt,[109] it would appear that English law is prepared to err on the side of the defence by acknowledging that 'one would be on safe ground if one said in a criminal case to a jury: "You must be satisfied beyond reasonable doubt" and one could also say: "You, the jury, must be completely satisfied," or better still: "You must feel sure of the prisoner's guilt." '[110] This is to be contrasted with the position in Canada, where it has been observed:

> In the United Kingdom juries are instructed that they may convict if they are 'sure' or 'certain' of the accused's guilt. Yet . . . that instruction standing alone is both insufficient and potentially misleading. Being 'certain' is a conclusion which a juror may reach but, it does not indicate the route the juror should take in order to arrive at the conclusion. . . . It is only after proper instructions

---

[104] *Miller v Minister of Pensions* [1947] 2 All ER 372, 373.

[105] *R v Bentley* [2001] 1 Cr App R 21 (p 307), [49].

[106] *R v Kritz* [1950] 1 KB 82, 89; *R v Hepworth* [1955] 2 QB 600, 603–4; *Ferguson v R* [1979] 1 WLR 94, 99.

[107] *Walters v R* [1969] 2 AC 26, 31. A similar approach is taken in Canada: *R v Rhee* [2001] 3 SCR 364, [32] ('When reviewing a pre-*Lifchus* reasonable doubt charge, there is no particular mistake or omission that will automatically constitute a reversible error in and of itself, nor is there an additional instruction that will immediately cure a particular shortcoming. Ultimately, the focus must be on whether there is a reasonable likelihood that the jury misunderstood the criminal standard of proof'). See also *R v Beauchamp* [2000] 2 SCR 720; *R v Russell* [2000] 2 SCR 731; *R v Avetysan* [2000] 2 SCR 745; *R v Pan* [2001] 2 SCR 344. See generally P Healy, 'Direction and Guidance on Reasonable Doubt in the Charge to the Jury' (2001) 6 *Canadian Criminal Law Review* 161.   [108] *R v Bentley* [2001] 1 Cr App R 21 (p 307), [42].

[109] W Young, 'Summing-Up to Juries in Criminal Cases—What Jury Research Says About Current Rules and Practice' [2003] *Criminal Law Review* 665, 674: 'The certainty implied by the words "satisfied so that you are sure" or even just "sure" does not fit altogether easily with the uncertainties implicit in the phrase "reasonable doubt".'

[110] *R v Hepworth* [1955] 2 QB 600, 603. An empirical study found 'that three-quarters of both the general public sample and of the magistrates' sample said they would need to be at least 90 per cent sure before convicting. That suggests that most people, whatever their role and experience of the system, take the business of convicting very seriously' (M Zander, 'The Criminal Standard of Proof—How Sure Is Sure?' (2000) 150 *New Law Journal* 1517, 1519).

have been given as to the meaning of the expression 'beyond a reasonable doubt' that a jury may be advised that they can convict if they are 'certain' or 'sure' that the accused is guilty.[111]

As has been noted:

> The concept of proof beyond reasonable doubt does not require the prosecution to establish its case as a matter of absolute or scientific certainty. However the 'satisfied so that you are sure' or 'are sure' formulations are likely to be taken by many (and perhaps most) jurors as conveying just that. So there is a gap between the message that judges try to give and the message as understood by many or most jurors.[112]

It would appear to be permissible in English law for a jury to be told that a reasonable doubt is 'that quality and kind of doubt which, when you are dealing with *matters of importance in your own affairs*, you allow to influence you one way or the other'.[113] In *R v Ching*,[114] the jury were directed as follows:

> ...A reasonable doubt, it has been said, is a doubt to which you can give a reason as opposed to a mere fanciful sort of speculation such as 'Well, nothing in this world is certain nothing in this world can be proved.' ...It is sometimes said the sort of matter which might influence you if you were to consider some business matter. A matter, for example, of a mortgage concerning your house, or something of that nature.[115]

The Court of Appeal held that while the trial judge had not stressed that the relevant doubts were those which had to be overcome in *important* business affairs, he had not fallen in error since 'what he did was to pick an example, which for sensible people would be an important matter'.[116] This case may be contrasted with *R v Gray*.[117] The trial judge defined a 'reasonable doubt' as 'a doubt based upon good reason and not a fanciful doubt', and as 'the sort of doubt which might affect you in the conduct of your *everyday affairs*'. The Court of Appeal held that if the trial judge had referred to *important affairs* then the direction would have been unobjectionable, but 'everyday affairs' might have suggested to the jury a standard of proof which was too low.

In Canada, by contrast, the view is taken that 'to invite jurors to apply to a criminal trial the standard of proof used for even the important decisions in life runs the risk of significantly reducing the standard to which the prosecution must be held'.[118]

In *R v Stafford*[119] the trial judge told the jury to 'remember that a reasonable doubt is one for which you could give reasons if you were asked'. On appeal, the Court of Appeal

---

[111] *R v Lifchus* [1997] 3 SCR 320, [33]–[34] (underlining in original). See also the empirical research which found that defining the standard of proof only in terms of being 'sure' of guilt 'encourages a disproportionate number of potential jurors to refuse convictions on less than an (impossible!) requirement of 100% certainty': J W Montgomery, 'The Criminal Standard of Proof' (1998) 148 *New Law Journal* 582, 584.

[112] W Young, 'Summing-Up to Juries in Criminal Cases—What Jury Research Says About Current Rules and Practice' [2003] *Criminal Law Review* 665, 675.   [113] *Walters v R* [1969] 2 AC 26.

[114] (1976) 63 Cr App R 7 (decision of 1976).   [115] Ibid, 8.   [116] Ibid, 10.

[117] (1974) 58 Cr App R 177 (decision of 1973).

[118] *R v Lifchus* [1997] 3 SCR 320, [24]. See also *R v Bisson* [1998] 1 SCR 306. On the other hand, 'to advise jurors that a "reasonable doubt" is a doubt which is so serious as to prevent them from eating or sleeping is manifestly misleading . . . These words would lead a juror to set an unacceptably *high* standard of certainty': *R v Lifchus* [1997] 3 SCR 320, [26] (italics added).   [119] [1968] 3 All ER 752.

disapproved of this definition. In *McGreevy v DPP*,[120] the House of Lords expressed the view that 'it would be undesirable to lay it down as a rule which would bind judges that a direction to a jury in cases where circumstantial evidence is the basis of the prosecution case must be given in some special form, provided always that in suitable terms it is made plain to a jury that they must not convict unless they are satisfied of guilt beyond all reasonable doubt'.[121]

2.1.2 Where the Defence Bears the Legal Burden

Where the defence bears the legal burden of proving a particular issue, it need only be proved on the 'preponderance of probability', or, as it is more commonly termed, on the 'balance of probability'.[122] This is the civil standard of proof, which will be considered in detail shortly.

2.1.3 Effect of Misdirection

While a misdirection (or failure to give a direction) to the jury in a criminal trial on standard of proof can lead to the quashing of a conviction on appeal, 'a conviction may be regarded as safe despite the absence of an adequate direction even on a matter as fundamental as the standard of proof. But that could only be an appropriate conclusion where the case against the defendant was properly held to be overwhelming...'.[123]

2.2 Civil Trials

2.2.1 The General Rule

Where a legal burden requires to be discharged in civil proceedings,[124] the relevant standard of proof is proof on the balance (or preponderance) of probability,[125] which is lower than the beyond-reasonable-doubt standard. Thus, 'if the evidence is such that the tribunal can say: "We think it more probable than not," the burden is discharged, but, if the probabilities are equal, it is not'.[126] In other words, 'the balance of probability standard means that a court is satisfied an event occurred if the court considers that, on the evidence, the occurrence of the event was more likely than not'.[127] This standard is

---

[120] [1973] 1 WLR 276.   [121] Ibid, 285.

[122] See, eg, *R v Carr-Briant* [1943] KB 607, *R v Dunbar* [1958] 1 QB 1, and *Public Prosecutor v Yuvaraj* [1970] 2 WLR 226 (cases where the burden was placed on the defence expressly by statute); *Sodeman v R* [1936] 2 All ER 1138 (insanity); *R v Podola* [1960] 1 QB 325 (unfitness to plead).

[123] *R v Bentley* [2001] 1 Cr App R 21 (p 307), [43]. See also *R v Edwards* (1983) 77 Cr App R 5 (decision of 1983).

[124] See generally C R Williams, 'Burdens and Standards in Civil Litigation' (2003) 25 *Sydney Law Review* 165.

[125] See generally D Hamer, 'The Civil Standard of Proof Uncertainty: Probability, Belief and Justice' (1994) 16 *Sydney Law Review* 506; M Redmayne, 'Standards of Proof in Civil Litigation' (1999) 62 *Modern Law Review* 167; A Stein, 'An Essay on Uncertainty and Fact-Finding in Civil Litigation, with Special Reference to Contract Cases' (1998) 48 *University of Toronto Law Journal* 299.

[126] *Miller v Minister of Pensions* [1947] 2 All ER 372, 374.   [127] *In re H (Minors)* [1996] 2 WLR 8, 23.

often described as a flexible one the application of which is dependent upon the subject matter of the proceedings and particularly the seriousness of the allegation.[128] What precisely this flexibility entails has been explained by the House of Lords:

> When assessing the probabilities the court will have in mind as a factor, to whatever extent is appropriate in the particular case, that the more serious the allegation the less likely it is that the event occurred and, hence, the stronger should be the evidence before the court concludes that the allegation is established on the balance of probability. Fraud is usually less likely than negligence. Deliberate physical injury is usually less likely than accidental physical injury. A step-father is usually less likely to have repeatedly raped and had non-consensual oral sex with his under age stepdaughter than on some occasion to have lost his temper and slapped her. Built into the preponderance of probability standard is a generous degree of flexibility in respect of the seriousness of the allegation.
>
> Although the result is much the same, this does not mean that where a serious allegation is in issue the standard of proof required is higher. It means only that the inherent probability or improbability of an event is itself a matter to be taken into account when weighing the probabilities and deciding whether, on balance, the event occurred. The more improbable the event, the stronger must be the evidence that it did occur before, on the balance of probability, its occurrence will be established.[129]

The notion of the inherent probability or improbability of an event would appear, therefore, to underlie the entire determination of whether sufficient evidence has been adduced to prove that the event occurred. The desirability of reliance upon such a vague and imprecise notion may be questioned. As has been argued:

> . . . we simply do not know very much about the general prevalence of fraud, negligence, arson or child abuse, and this makes the claim that serious forms of behaviour are rarer than less serious ones problematic. Even if there is a general correlation between gravity and frequency of wrongdoing, it beggars belief to presume that the correlation always holds.[130]

Until relatively recently, there was considerable uncertainty about the relevant standard of proof where allegations of sexual abuse were made in care proceedings, with suggestions made in some cases that such allegations had to be proved to a standard higher than proof on the balance of probability. The House of Lords affirmed in *In re H (Minors)*, however, that the relevant 'standard of proof is the ordinary civil standard of balance of probability'.[131] 'Despite their special features, family proceedings remain

---

[128] *Bater v Bater* [1951] P 35, 37.

[129] *In re H (Minors)* [1996] 2 WLR 8, 23–4. Note that the Court of Appeal held in *Lawrence v Chester Chronicle, The Times*, 8 Feb 1986, that, in trials of defamation actions (civil actions tried with a jury), it was not generally necessary for the jury to be directed about the flexibility inherent in the civil standard of proof and the relevance of the seriousness of the alleged defamatory statement; in most cases this was a matter for the jury's common sense. Interestingly, empirical research suggests that, even in criminal cases, juries may apply a higher standard of proof where a more serious offence is involved: R J Simon and L Mahan, 'Quantifying Burdens of Proof: A View from the Bench, the Jury, and the Classroom' (1971) 5 *Law and Society Review* 319, 328. See also J McEwan, *The Verdict of the Court: Passing Judgment in Law and Psychology* (2003) 135.

[130] M Redmayne, 'Standards of Proof in Civil Litigation' (1999) 62 *Modern Law Review* 167, 184–5.

[131] [1996] 2 WLR 8, 24, approving *H v H (Minors) (Child Abuse: Evidence)* [1990] Fam 86, 94, 100, *In re M (A Minor) (Appeal) (No 2)* [1994] 1 FLR 59, 67, and *In re W (Minors) (Sexual Abuse: Standard of Proof)* [1994]

essentially a form of civil proceedings. Family proceedings often raise very serious issues, but so do other forms of civil proceedings.'[132] The House of Lords was not keen on the idea of adopting a third standard of proof, lying between the balance-of-probability and beyond-reasonable-doubt standards, for some civil cases. Not only would there be a danger, it was thought, that a third standard would cause uncertainty and inconsistency, but it would in any event add little to the 'flexible' balance-of-probability standard currently applied.[133]

The Court of Appeal has confirmed that these observations remain valid:

> We understand that in many applications for care orders counsel are now submitting that the correct approach to the standard of proof is to treat the distinction between criminal and civil standards as 'largely illusory'. In our judgment this approach is mistaken. The standard of proof to be applied . . . is the balance of probabilities and the approach to these difficult cases was laid down . . . in *In re H (Minors)* . . . There would appear to be no good reason to leap across a division, on the one hand, between crime and preventative measures taken to restrain defendants for the benefit of the community and, on the other hand, wholly different considerations of child protection and child welfare . . . The strict rules of evidence applicable in a criminal trial which is adversarial in nature is to be contrasted with the partly inquisitorial approach of the court dealing with children cases in which the rules of evidence are considerably relaxed.[134]

2.2.2 Contempt of Court

It is well established that contempt of court must be proved beyond reasonable doubt, even if the alleged contempt was of a civil court. In *In re Bramblevale Ltd*, Lord Denning MR remarked:

> A contempt of court is an offence of a criminal character. A man may be sent to prison for it. It must be satisfactorily proved. To use the time-honoured phrase, it must be proved beyond reasonable doubt.[135]

2.2.3 Allegations of Criminal Conduct

It has generally been held that allegations of criminal conduct in civil proceedings need be proved on the balance of probability only, and not beyond reasonable doubt. This is, of course, consistent with the view of the House of Lords in *In re H (Minors)* that the

---

1 FLR 419, 424 per Balcombe LJ; and disapproving *In re G (A Minor) (Child Abuse: Standard of Proof)* [1987] 1 WLR 1461, 1466, and *In re W (Minors) (Sexual Abuse: Standard of Proof)* [1994] 1 FLR 419, 429. See generally A Bainham, 'Sexual Abuse in the Lords' [1996] *Cambridge Law Journal* 209; D Burrows, 'Care Proceedings After *Re H*' (1996) 140 *Solicitors' Journal* 94; C Keenan, 'Finding That a Child Is at Risk from Sexual Abuse: *Re H (Minors) (Sexual Abuse: Standard of Proof)*' (1997) 60 *Modern Law Review* 857; R Stevens, 'Getting over the Threshold—An Exegesis of Section 31(2) of the Children Act 1989' (1996) 160 *Justice of the Peace* 111. *In re H (Minors)* was applied in *Re M and R (Minors)* [1996] 4 All ER 239.

[132] *In re H (Minors)* [1996] 2 WLR 8, 23.   [133] Ibid, 24.

[134] *In re U (A Child)* [2004] EWCA Civ 567, [2004] 3 WLR 753, [13]. A petition for leave to appeal to the House of Lords was refused: [2004] 1 WLR 2854.

[135] [1970] Ch 128, 137. See also the decision of the High Court of Australia in *Witham v Holloway* (1995) 69 ALJR 847 and C J Miller, 'Proof of Civil Contempt' (1996) 112 *Law Quarterly Review* 539.

only standard of proof applicable in civil proceedings is the balance-of-probability standard. Thus this standard was applied in *In re Dellow's Will Trusts*,[136] where the issue arose in civil proceedings of whether a wife had killed her husband, and *Post Office v Estuary Radio Ltd*,[137] where in an application for an injunction under the Wireless Telegraphy Act 1949, an allegation of a criminal offence under the same Act was made. More recently, in *Francisco v Diedrick*,[138] it was held that the appropriate standard of proof in a civil action for damages for assault and battery causing death was the civil standard, but it had to be borne in mind that the allegation (effectively an allegation of murder) was one of utmost gravity. Noteworthy, too, is Lord Bingham CJ's interesting observation in *McCool v Rushcliffe BC* that 'where in civil proceedings it is sought to prove conduct amounting to or analogous to a criminal offence, the standard of proof must be *analogous, at least, to that appropriate in criminal proceedings*'.[139]

In *Halford v Brookes*,[140] by contrast, a different approach was taken. The plaintiff brought a tort action for damages in respect of the murder of her daughter, whom she alleged had been murdered by the defendants. It was held that the allegation of murder had to be proved beyond reasonable doubt: the court considered that nobody, whether in a civil or criminal court, should be declared guilty of murder unless the tribunal was sure that there was no other sensible conclusion. In the light of *In re H (Minors)*, *Halford v Brookes* is perhaps most appropriately regarded as wrongly decided. There may, however, be some merit in the *Halford* approach. It is certainly arguable that it is justifiable for such serious allegations as murder to have to be proved beyond reasonable doubt, even if they are made in civil proceedings. A necessary (but perhaps ultimately insurmountably difficult) task would be to delineate clearly those allegations which would be regarded as sufficiently 'serious' as to warrant application of the beyond-reasonable-doubt standard.

2.2.4 Quasi-Criminal Proceedings

General principles would require application of the civil standard even where important matters such as a person's liberty or livelihood are at stake in a non-criminal case. In *R v Home Secretary, ex p Khawaja*, the applicant was detained as an illegal entrant and applied for judicial review of the order detaining him. The House of Lords had to consider the issue of the standard to which the executive was to prove that an individual had obtained leave to enter the United Kingdom by deception. It was held that the appropriate standard of proof was:

> the civil standard flexibly applied in the way set forth in the cases . . . Liberty is at stake: that is . . . a grave matter. The reviewing court will therefore require to be satisfied that the facts which are required for the justification of the restraint put upon liberty do exist. The flexibility of the civil standard of proof suffices to ensure that the court will require the high degree of probability which is appropriate to what is at stake. . . . The strictness of the criminal formula is unnecessary to enable justice to be done . . .[141]

---

[136] [1964] 1 WLR 451.   [137] [1967] 1 WLR 1396.   [138] *The Times*, 3 April 1998.
[139] [1998] 3 All ER 889, 894 (italics added).   [140] *The Times*, 3 Oct 1991.
[141] [1984] AC 74, 113–14. Applied by the Court of Appeal in *R v Home Secretary, ex p Rahman* [1997] 3 WLR 990.

In a similar vein, the Court of Appeal has held that, in disciplinary proceedings under the Fire Services (Discipline) Regulations 1948, a disciplinary offence need only be proved on the balance of probability. Despite the fact that the Regulations used 'the language of the criminal law' by speaking of 'offences', 'the accused', 'charges', and 'punishments', the Court did not regard these proceedings as criminal proceedings.[142]

The Privy Council has given consideration to issues raised by proceedings in a particular committee of the General Medical Council known as the Committee on Professional Performance ('CPP'), apparently endorsing a flexible approach to the issue of the standard of proof applicable in CPP proceedings:

> The function of the CPP is not penal. It is to protect the public and to rehabilitate (if possible) practitioners whose professional standards have fallen too low. In the first of its tasks (that is deciding whether the standard of a practitioner's performance has been seriously deficient) the CPP has to ascertain the primary facts (which in many cases may not be seriously in doubt) and then to exercise their judgment (in the case of some but not all the members of the CPP, their professional judgment as experienced doctors). In this exercise the standard of proof of the primary facts ought not, in the generality of cases, to be an issue which gives rise to much difficulty. So far as it is a material issue the standard should in their Lordships' view, in the generality of cases, be the ordinary civil standard of proof. There may be exceptional cases (probably cases in which the practitioner is fortunate to be facing the CPP rather than the Professional Conduct Committee) in which a heightened civil standard might be appropriate, as explained by the House of Lords in re H (minors) . . .[143]

In *R v Milk Marketing Board, ex p Austin*,[144] however, it was held that when a person's livelihood was at stake the standard of proof should be no lower than that applicable in criminal proceedings. A similar approach was taken in *In re a Solicitor*,[145] where the issue was the standard of proof which had to be applied by a disciplinary tribunal in determining an allegation of misconduct. The Divisional Court stated that 'at least in cases such as the present, where what is alleged is *tantamount to a criminal offence*, the tribunal should apply the criminal standard of proof, that is to say proof to the point where they feel sure that the charges are proved or, put in another way, proof beyond reasonable doubt'.[146] Like *Halford v Brookes*, therefore, *Austin* and *In re a Solicitor* seem to be out of step with the general approach of speaking in terms of a 'flexible' balance-of-probability standard of proof in civil proceedings.

It is certainly arguable that, where the livelihood or liberty of a person is at stake, proof beyond reasonable doubt should be required. After all, as has been seen above, the justification for the adoption of the criminal standard in proceedings for contempt of court is that such proceedings are 'of a criminal character'. Arguably, the same reasoning should apply in the case of other quasi-criminal proceedings.[147] This, indeed, is the view that would appear to have been endorsed by the House of Lords in *R (McCann) v Manchester*

---

[142] *R v Hants CC, ex p Ellerton* [1985] 1 WLR 749.   [143] *Sadler v GMC* [2003] UKPC 59, [73].

[144] *The Times*, 21 March 1983.   [145] [1993] QB 69.   [146] Ibid, 81 (italics added).

[147] See generally A A S Zuckerman, 'Evidence' [1985] *All ER Review* 155, 156–7.

Crown Court.[148] Lord Hope of Craighead commented that 'it is not an invariable rule that the lower standard of proof must be applied in civil proceedings. I think that there are good reasons, in the interests of fairness, for applying the higher standard when allegations are made of criminal or quasi-criminal conduct which, if proved, would have serious consequences for the person against whom they are made.'[149] In this case the House thought that, even though the proceedings for the making of an anti-social behaviour order under the Crime and Disorder Act 1998 were civil rather than criminal, the court should, before making such an order, be satisfied to the criminal standard of proof that a defendant had, in the words of section 1(1)(a) of the Act, 'acted . . . in an anti-social manner, that is to say, in a manner that caused or was likely to cause harassment, alarm or distress to one or more persons not of the same household as himself'. Given that 'the condition in section 1(1)(a) that the defendant has acted in an anti-social manner raises serious questions of fact, and the implications for him of proving that he has acted in this way are also serious',[150] 'pragmatism dictates that the task of magistrates should be made more straightforward by ruling that they must in all cases under section 1 apply the criminal standard'.[151]

2.3 The United States: An Intermediate Standard

It has been seen that the prevailing view in English law is that there are only two standards of proof, one applicable in criminal proceedings and the other applicable in non-criminal proceedings. In preference to applying the criminal standard where quasi-criminal proceedings, or very serious allegations such as murder, are involved, or recognizing the existence of a third standard of proof, the courts have traditionally made much of the inherent flexibility of the civil standard. In the United States, by contrast, the existence of a third standard, lying in between the civil and criminal standards, is acknowledged. This intermediate standard[152] is typically expressed in terms of a requirement of 'clear and convincing evidence',[153] and has been applied in civil cases involving allegations of fraud or some other quasi-criminal wrongdoing; in civil cases where particularly important individual interests are at stake, such as deportation[154] and denaturalization[155] proceedings; and in civil proceedings brought under state law to commit an individual involuntarily to a state mental hospital for an indefinite period.[156] Perhaps it is time, in the interests of achieving greater certainty and consistency

---

[148] [2002] UKHL 39, [2002] 3 WLR 1313. See generally C Bakalis, 'Anti-Social Behaviour Orders—Criminal Penalties or Civil Injunctions?' [2003] *Cambridge Law Journal* 583; S Macdonald, 'The Nature of the Anti-Social Behaviour Order—*R (McCann & Others) v Crown Court at Manchester*' (2003) 66 *Modern Law Review* 630; P Tain, 'Civil or Criminal?' (2002) 146 *Solicitors' Journal* 1037.

[149] [2002] UKHL 39, [2002] 3 WLR 1313, [82].   [150] Ibid, [83].

[151] Ibid, [37]. See also *B v Chief Constable* [2001] 1 All ER 562; *Chief Constable of Lancashire v Potter* [2003] EWHC 2272 (Admin).   [152] See the general discussion in *Addington v Texas* 441 US 418 (1979).

[153] Although any combination of the adjectives 'clear', 'cogent', 'unequivocal', and 'convincing' may be encountered.   [154] *Woodby v INS* 385 US 276, 285 (1966).

[155] *Schneiderman v US* 320 US 118, 125, 159 (1943); *Chaunt v US* 364 US 350, 353 (1960).

[156] *Addington v Texas* 441 US 418 (1979).

in the longer term, for the English law on the standard of proof in non-criminal proceedings to be subjected to a fundamental reconsideration. The way forward may be to acknowledge openly the existence of an intermediate standard of proof, identifying carefully the types of civil proceedings in which this standard should be applied. As a corollary of this, consideration could also be given to the possibility of identifying clearly the types of civil proceedings in which application of the criminal standard may be appropriate.

13

Proof without Evidence

To require evidence to be called to prove every single matter requiring proof in a trial would serve no useful purpose and lead to the unnecessary prolongation of trials. On occasion, therefore, a matter may be regarded as proved even though no evidence has been adduced to prove it in the normal way. In this chapter, three devices used in the law of evidence to achieve this are examined.

1 Formal Admissions

A *formal admission* by a party of the existence of a particular fact absolves the party who would otherwise bear the burden of proving that fact of the responsibility of doing so. Formal admissions are to be distinguished from informal admissions, which in civil cases are typically simply called 'admissions' and in criminal cases confessions (discussed in Chapter 2).[1] Whereas an informal admission constitutes *evidence* which is adduced to prove a particular fact, a formal admission abrogates the need for evidence to be adduced.

1.1 Criminal Cases

The position in criminal cases is governed by section 10 of the Criminal Justice Act 1967:

(1) Subject to the provisions of this section, any fact of which oral evidence may be given in any criminal proceedings may be admitted for the purpose of those proceedings by or on behalf of the prosecutor or defendant, and the admission by any party of any such fact under this section shall as against that party be conclusive evidence in those proceedings of the fact admitted.

(2) An admission under this section—

(a) may be made before or at the proceedings;

(b) if made otherwise than in court, shall be in writing;

---

[1] See *DPP v Mooney* [1997] RTR 434, in which it was made clear that proof of disqualification on a charge of driving while disqualified could be provided by an informal admission by the defendant that he was disqualified; the admission did not have to be a formal admission under s 10 of the Criminal Justice Act 1967.

(c) if made in writing by an individual, shall purport to be signed by the person making it and, if so made by a body corporate, shall purport to be signed by a director or manager, or the secretary or clerk, or some other similar officer of the body corporate;

(d) if made on behalf of a defendant who is an individual, shall be made by his counsel or solicitor;

(e) if made at any stage before the trial by a defendant who is an individual, must be approved by his counsel or solicitor (whether at the time it was made or subsequently) before or at the proceedings in question.

(3) An admission under this section for the purpose of proceedings relating to any matter shall be treated as an admission for the purpose of any subsequent criminal proceedings relating to that matter (including any appeal or retrial).

(4) An admission under this section may with the leave of the court be withdrawn in the proceedings for the purpose of which it is made or any subsequent criminal proceedings relating to the same matter.

1.2 Civil Cases

For civil cases, Part 14.1(1) of the Civil Procedure Rules provides: 'A party may admit the truth of the whole or any part of another party's case.' Part 14.1(2) continues: 'He may do this by giving notice in writing (such as in a statement of case or by letter).'

2 Judicial Notice

Judicial notice refers to facts, which a judge can be called upon to receive and to act upon, either from his general knowledge of them, or from inquiries to be made by himself for his own information from sources to which it is proper for him to refer.[2]

As this statement implies, judicial notice may be taken of facts either pursuant to the judge's general knowledge of them, or pursuant to proper inquiries made by him or her. It seems accepted that the concept of judicial notice is 'in large measure an application of common sense'.[3]

2.1 Judicial Notice pursuant to General Knowledge

It is well established that courts may take judicial notice of various matters when they are so notorious, or clearly established, or susceptible of demonstration by reference to a readily

---

[2] *Commonwealth Shipping Representative v P & O Branch Service* [1923] AC 191, 212. Cf the position under the Uniform Evidence Acts in Australia: *Gattellaro v Westpac Banking Corporation* [2004] HCA 6; R I Barrett, 'Judicial Notice' (2004) 78 *Australian Law Journal* 445.

[3] *DPP v Hynde* (1997) 161 JP 671, 678 (decision of 1997), approving *Andrews and Hirst on Criminal Evidence* (2nd ed) 5-02. For discussion by a US commentator, see R Slovenko, 'The Superfluous Rule of Evidence on Judicial Notice' (1998) 2 *International Journal of Evidence and Proof* 51.

obtainable and authoritative source, that evidence of their existence is unnecessary . . . Generally, matters directed by statute, or which have been so notified by the well established practice or precedents of the court, must be recognised by the judges; but beyond this, they have a wide discretion and may notice much which they cannot be required to notice. The matters notice-able may include facts which are in issue or relevant to the issue; and the notice is in some cases conclusive and in others merely prima facie and rebuttable . . .[4]

For example, judicial notice has been (or may be) taken of the fact that a fortnight is too short a period for human gestation, so that a 'husband, who had no access [to his wife] till within a fortnight of his wife's delivery, could not be the actual father of the child';[5] of the fact 'that cats belong to a genus or class of animals that are ordinarily kept for domestic purposes';[6] of the fact that people other than the addressee will read and have in fact read what is written on a postcard;[7] of the fact that 'a boy employed to ride a bicy-cle through London traffic runs the risk of injury by collision with other vehicles';[8] and of the fact that a butterfly knife is an article made for use in causing injury to a person.[9]

It is clear that in certain circumstances judicial notice may be taken of matters of *local* knowledge. The Court of Appeal has held that:

a judge may rely on his own local knowledge where he does so 'properly and within reasonable limits.' This judicial function appears to be acceptable where 'the type of knowledge is of a quite general character and is not liable to be varied by specific individual characteristics of the indi-vidual case.' This test allows a judge to use what might be called 'special (or local) general knowledge:' see *Phipson on Evidence*, ch 2/09.

On this basis it was held that a judge had been 'entitled to take judicial notice of his "special (or local) knowledge" of how [a] council had conducted themselves in relation to undertakings given to the court in similar cases'.[10]

The position of justices in magistrates' courts is governed by principles similar to those applicable to trials on indictment and County Court trials.[11] Indeed, the very essence of summary justice may suggest that it would be inappropriate to prohibit the use of 'actual local knowledge gained by justices as ordinary citizens of the place in which they live and in which they from time to time dispense justice'.[12] 'It must be recognised in cases . . . which involve local knowledge that justices simply cannot turn out of their minds knowledge which they acquire locally nor is it desirable that they should.'[13] But it

---

[4] *Mullen v Hackney LBC* [1997] 1 WLR 1103, 1105.

[5] *R v Luffe* (1807) 8 East 193, 202, 103 ER 316, 319.   [6] *Nye v Niblett* [1918] 1 KB 23, 25.

[7] *Huth v Huth* [1915] 3 KB 32.

[8] *Dennis v A J White and Company* [1917] AC 479, 491.

[9] *DPP v Hynde* (1997) 161 JP 671 (decision of 1997). 'This decision is to be welcomed, as judicial notice of the dangerousness of such a weapon can only result in the acceleration of cases through the courts and in greater consistency in the prosecution of offences related to the use or possession of butterfly knives': S Doran, J Jackson, and K Quinn, 'Evidence' [1998] *All ER Annual Review* 225, 236.

[10] *Mullen v Hackney LBC* [1997] 1 WLR 1103, 1105. For criticism, see C Allen, 'Judicial Notice Extended: *Mullen v Hackney London Borough Council*' (1998) 2 *International Journal of Evidence and Proof* 37.

[11] *Ingram v Percival* [1969] 1 QB 548; *Wetherall v Harrison* [1976] QB 773; *Norbrook Laboratories (GB) Ltd v Health and Safety Executive, The Times*, 23 Feb 1998.   [12] *Bowman v DPP* [1991] RTR 263, 269.

[13] Ibid, 270.

has been emphasized that, although 'Justices are fully entitled to take into account their own knowledge in relation to matters which are well known in the locality',[14] they must be 'extremely circumspect' in doing so, and 'it is always wise ... to make the fact that local knowledge is going to be used known to the defence and the prosecution so as to give those representing those parties the opportunity of commenting upon the knowledge which the justice or justices claim to have and which they aim to use for the purpose of aiding them in reaching a determination'.[15]

Thus it has been held, for example, that justices were entitled to use their local knowledge about whether particular water was tidal,[16] and 'to use their own local knowledge of what ha[d] been going on as to the use of a particular piece of land'.[17] In *Paul v DPP* the appellant was convicted of kerb-crawling on an information alleging that he solicited a woman for the purpose of prostitution from a motor vehicle, in such a manner or in such circumstances as to be likely to cause a nuisance to other persons in the neighbourhood. The Divisional Court held that:

> the justices, who did not have any evidence that anyone had actually been caused nuisance, took into account their local knowledge. In particular they took into account the fact that the area of Studley Road and Biscot Road is an area often frequented by prostitutes and there is a constant procession of cars driving around the area at night. Secondly, and perhaps most importantly of all, they took into account that it was a heavily populated residential area.
>
> Both the matters to which I have just referred are matters which justices, in my view, are entitled to take into account in considering an offence of this sort and deciding whether or not the circumstances are such as likely to cause a nuisance. They are matters within their local knowledge; and they are matters which make[] it peculiarly appropriate that offences of this sort should be determined by magistrates who have that local knowledge for the very reason that enables them to take account of their knowledge of the area[,] the people who are likely to be about and the people who are likely to be affected by what takes place.[18]

In appropriate circumstances justices may also take notice of any relevant specialized or technical knowledge that they may possess. In *R v Field, ex p White* the justices considered 'that it was a matter of common knowledge that cocoa, as an article of commerce, must necessarily contain a large proportion of other ingredients'. The justices had served in the Navy where cocoa with very large percentages of foreign matter was a regular article of food. Wills J held: 'I do not say that the Justices pursued an altogether prudent course; and perhaps if the occasion arose again they would be wiser to hear evidence, and keep themselves technically right. However, they decided the case as they did upon their own knowledge; and in the nature of things, no one in determining a case of this kind can discard his own particular knowledge of a subject of this kind.'[19] More recently, in *Wetherall v Harrison*, the Divisional Court held[20] that it had been proper to

---

[14] *Norbrook Laboratories (GB) Ltd v Health and Safety Executive, The Times*, 23 Feb 1998; transcript from Smith Bernal.   [15] *Bowman v DPP* [1991] RTR 263, 269.

[16] *Ingram v Percival* [1969] 1 QB 548.   [17] *Bowman v DPP* [1991] RTR 263, 269.

[18] (1990) 90 Cr App R 173, 176–7 (decision of 1989).   [19] (1895) 64 LJMC 158, 158–60.

[20] [1976] QB 773, 777–8.

have regard to the views of one of the justices on the bench, a practising registered medical practitioner, on whether a fit had been simulated or genuine.

> If the justice is a specialist, be he a doctor, or an engineer or an accountant, or what you will, it is not possible for him to approach the decision in the case as though he had not got that training, and indeed I think it would be a very bad thing if he had to. In a sense, the bench of justices are like a jury, they are a cross-section of people, and one of the advantages which they have is that they bring a lot of varied experience into the court room and use it.

Special knowledge may only be drawn upon, however, to *interpret* evidence which has been heard; it may not be used to *contradict* such evidence. Additionally, the justice with the relevant knowledge 'ought really to ... wait[ ] until asked to make a contribution on his specialist subject', and 'should not press his views unduly on the rest of the bench'.

In *Carter v Eastbourne Borough Council* it was held that the justices had not been entitled to rely on their knowledge 'from our own experience in our own gardens and woodlands that the trees in the photographs must have been over four years of age'.[21]

2.2 Judicial Notice pursuant to Proper Inquiry

2.2.1 Facts of a Political or Diplomatic Nature

A court may take judicial notice, after having recourse to any proper source of information, of facts of a political or diplomatic nature. Thus a court is permitted, for example, 'to take judicial notice of the sovereignty of a State, and for that purpose (in any case of uncertainty) to seek information from a Secretary of State; and when information is so obtained the Court does not permit it to be questioned by the parties';[22] or to take judicial notice of the status of a person claiming diplomatic privilege, treating as conclusive a statement made to the court by the Attorney-General on the instructions of the Foreign Office.[23] In 1946 the Court of Appeal held that 'there can, on the authorities, be no question but that the certificate of the Foreign Secretary given on behalf of the Crown as to the existence of a state of war involving His Majesty is conclusive and binding on this court, and this is so whether questions of fact or law are involved therein'.[24]

2.2.2 Historical Facts

Judicial notice may be taken of facts gleaned from historical works dealing with ancient facts of a public nature.[25]

2.2.3 Customs

Judicial notice may be taken, after appropriate inquiry, of the customs and practices of particular organizations and professions. Thus judicial notice has been taken of such

---

[21] (2000) 164 JP 273, 276 (decision of 2000).
[22] *Duff Development Co v Kelantan Government* [1924] AC 797, 805–6.
[23] *Engelke v Musmann* [1928] AC 433.
[24] *R v Bottrill, ex p Kuechenmeister* [1947] KB 41, 53.   [25] *Read v Bishop of Lincoln* [1892] AC 644.

matters as the practices of the accountancy profession,[26] and (on the evidence of an official from the Ordnance Survey Office) of the fact that a line on a map indicated the centre of an existing hedge.[27]

2.2.4 Foreign Law?

In relation to the possibility of judicial notice being taken of foreign law, the Court of Appeal has said:

> Foreign law must be proved strictly. It should be proved . . . by calling a properly qualified expert in that law, who will give evidence himself unless his testimony is agreed or no issue is taken. . . . in criminal cases foreign law cannot be the subject of judicial notice . . .[28]

2.3 Statutory Provisions

Statutory provisions may have the effect of requiring judicial notice to be taken of particular matters. The Interpretation Act 1978,[29] for example, requires judicial notice to be taken of all Acts passed after 1850, unless the contrary is expressly provided by the Act in question. While there is no statutory provision requiring judicial notice to be taken of statutory instruments, the Court of Appeal in *R v Jones* endorsed the actions of the trial court in effectively taking judicial notice of the relevant statutory instrument which provided that the Alcotest R 80 breath-testing device was of a type approved by the Secretary of State. The Court of Appeal held that 'the number of decided cases in which it has been proved that the Alcotest R 80 device is of an approved type has by now become so large and so widely reported that, in our judgment, a court (including the jury) is entitled to take judicial notice of that fact, and its formal proof is accordingly no longer necessary.'[30]

2.4 The Consequences of Taking Judicial Notice

The consequences of taking judicial notice would seem to differ according to the subject matter of the inquiry. For example, by their very nature, the results of inquiries into facts of a political or diplomatic character are treated as binding on the court. By contrast, in *Heather v P-E Consulting Group* it was held: 'Skilled accountants may well be much better qualified than most judges to formulate and explain [sound accountancy principles]. But nevertheless . . . it is the judge and not the witness who must decide whether a witness's evidence in fact exemplifies sound accountancy principles.'[31]

---

[26] *Heather v P-E Consulting Group* [1973] Ch 189.   [27] *Davey v Harrow Corporation* [1958] 1 QB 60.
[28] *R v Okolie, The Times,* 16 June 2000; transcript, [11].   [29] S 3, s 22(1), Sch 2 para 2.
[30] [1970] 1 WLR 16, 20.   [31] [1973] Ch 189, 218.

3 Presumptions

A presumption operates to cause a particular fact to be treated as proved unless the presumption is rebutted. A *persuasive* presumption is one which operates unless the party seeking to rebut it discharges the legal burden of disproving the fact in question. An *evidential* presumption is a weaker one: the party seeking to rebut it bears only an evidential burden and thus has merely to adduce sufficient evidence to put in issue the existence of the fact in question. The legal burden then falls on the party relying upon the presumption to prove that fact.

The word presumption is also used loosely in other senses. The word may amount simply to a shorthand way of referring to a particular principle or rule of law. The 'presumption of innocence', for example, refers to the principle that the prosecution in a criminal case generally bears the legal burden of proving every issue. Equally, the 'presumption of sanity' signifies that the legal burden of proving insanity lies on a defendant seeking to invoke the defence.[32] There is also, for example, an 'irrebuttable' or 'conclusive' presumption that a child under 10 cannot be guilty of an offence. Section 50 of the Children and Young Persons Act 1933 provides: 'It shall be conclusively presumed that no child under the age of ten years can be guilty of any offence.' This differs from a true presumption in that it cannot be rebutted, and is thus in reality a rule of law. The possible human rights implications of the irrebuttable presumption in section 15(2) of the Road Traffic Offenders Act 1988 that an alleged drink-driver's blood alcohol level at the time of the alleged offence was not less than at the time of the specimen were considered in *Griffiths v DPP*:

> ... section 15(2) ... is a fair compromise between the considerations, first, that anyone who takes any alcohol before driving will to some extent expose the public to risk and that the level at which an offence is created (which is of a quantitative rather than a qualitative basis) is fixed is artificial [*sic*]. Parliament, while preserving the right of any person to take a drink before driving, expressed itself in such a way that if such a person is then subjected to a breath, blood or urine test which shows an excess proportion of alcohol the person who has provided that specimen is, by section 15(2), assumed to have had no less a proportion of alcohol in his breath at the time when he was driving. ... that is a proportionate response to what is generally perceived to be, and is, reprehensible conduct on the part of any person who takes a car on to the road having consumed alcohol. ... it was not competent to the court to receive evidence from an expert which would have undermined or contradicted the statutory assumption created by section 15(2). Moreover, that statutory assumption ... [is] wholly proportionate to the situation where a person having taken drink then proceeds to drive a motor vehicle on a road. There is, therefore, no infringement of a defendant's right to a fair trial under Article 6.1 and 6.2.[33]

Further, the word presumption may simply signify a *permissible* inference. The 'presumption of intention', for example, permits the inference to be drawn that a person

---

[32] See Ch 12.   [33] [2002] EWHC 792 (Admin), (2002) 166 JP 629, [30].

intended the natural consequences of his or her actions. Section 8 of the Criminal Justice Act 1967 provides:

> A court or jury, in determining whether a person has committed an offence,—
>
> (a) shall not be bound in law to infer that he intended or foresaw a result of his actions by reason only of its being a natural and probable consequence of those actions; but
>
> (b) shall decide whether he did intend or foresee that result by reference to all the evidence, drawing such inferences from the evidence as appear proper in the circumstances.[34]

In a similar vein, the 'presumption of the continuance of life' allows an inference to be drawn, from the fact that a person was alive on a certain date, that he or she was still alive on a subsequent date.[35] Such inferences do not amount to presumptions which must stand unless rebutted.

A brief review will now be undertaken of a number of true (that is, rebuttable) presumptions.

3.1 Presumption of Marriage[36]

'Where there is a ceremony followed by cohabitation as husband and wife, a strong presumption arises that the parties are lawfully married.'[37] Both the *formal* validity of the ceremony (for example, that the appropriate licence was issued[38]) and the *essential* validity of the ceremony (for example, that the parties had capacity to marry[39]) are presumed. Additionally, the presumption of marriage arises from evidence that the parties cohabited and were reputed to be married.[40] It would appear that the presumption of marriage is a persuasive one[41] which 'can only be displaced by what I would call positive, not merely "clear", evidence . . . How positive, and how clear, must depend among other things upon the strength of the evidence which gives rise to the presumption—primarily, the length of cohabitation and evidence that the parties regarded themselves and were treated by others as man and wife.'[42] The presumption cannot be relied upon

---

[34] See also *R v Woollin* [1999] AC 82.

[35] *MacDarmaid v A-G* [1950] P 218; *Re Peete* [1952] 2 All ER 599.

[36] See generally A H Borkowski, 'The Presumption of Marriage' (2002) 14 *Child and Family Law Quarterly* 251; R Probert, 'When Are We Married? Void, Non-Existent and Presumed Marriages' (2002) 22 *Legal Studies* 398.

[37] *Mahadervan v Mahadervan* [1964] P 233, 244.   [38] *Piers v Piers* (1849) 2 HL Cas 331, 9 ER 1118.

[39] *Re Peete* [1952] 2 All ER 599; *Taylor v Taylor* [1967] P 25.   [40] *In re Taylor, decd* [1961] 1 WLR 9.

[41] *Mahadervan v Mahadervan* [1964] P 233; *Taylor v Taylor* [1967] P 25 (where the presumption in favour of a marriage (arising from a ceremony and subsequent cohabitation) was held to be incapable of being rebutted by a presumption in favour of an *earlier* marriage (also arising from a ceremony and subsequent cohabitation), because of doubts about the validity of the earlier ceremony. But 'if no reason could be shown for doubting the validity of the earlier ceremony and if no question arose as to the ending of the earlier marriage by death or divorce, then evidence of the earlier marriage would displace the original presumption in favour of the later one' (ibid, 35)).

[42] *Chief Adjudication Officer v Bath* [2000] 1 FLR 8, 18 per Evans LJ. In *Mahadervan v Mahadervan*, however, it was stated 'that where a ceremony of marriage is proved followed by cohabitation as husband and wife, a presumption is raised which cannot be rebutted by evidence which merely goes to show on a balance of probabilities that there was no valid marriage: it must be evidence which satisfies *beyond reasonable doubt* that there was no valid marriage': [1964] P 233, 246 (italics added). This older view may now be regarded as having been superseded.

where there is positive evidence that the statutory requirements for a marriage ceremony were not complied with.[43]

3.2 Presumption of Legitimacy

There is undoubtedly a presumption . . . that a child born in wedlock to a married woman is the child of her husband. That presumption applies not only to a child born during wedlock but also to a child clearly conceived during wedlock. . . . The presumption that a child conceived during wedlock is a legitimate child of the husband applies just as much whether the husband and wife are living together in the ordinary way or whether they are separated by agreement, or by a deed, or simply separated . . . The presumption ceases to operate if the parties are separated under an order of the court such as, for example, a decree of judicial separation, which does away with the duty of the spouses to live together. . . . the presumption that a child conceived during wedlock is legitimate continues to operate after the presentation of a petition for divorce or nullity, or even the pronunciation of a decree nisi either for nullity or for divorce.[44]

It is clear that this is a persuasive presumption; a party wishing to rebut it bears the legal burden of proving illegitimacy. Section 26 of the Family Law Reform Act 1969 provides: 'Any presumption of law as to the legitimacy . . . of any person may in any civil proceedings be rebutted by evidence which shows that it is more probable than not that that person is illegitimate . . .'.

3.3 Presumption of Death

By virtue of a long sequence of judicial statements, which either assert or assume such a rule, it appears accepted that there is a convenient presumption of law applicable to certain cases of seven years' absence where no statute applies. That presumption in its modern shape takes effect (without examining its terms too exactly) substantially as follows. Where as regards 'AB' there is no acceptable affirmative evidence that he was alive at some time during a continuous period of seven years or more, then if it can be proved first, that there are persons who would be likely to have heard of him over that period, secondly that those persons have not heard of him, and thirdly that all due inquiries have been made appropriate to the circumstances, 'AB' will be presumed to have died at some time within that period.[45]

It would seem that the presumption of death is an evidential presumption.[46]

The common law presumption of death exists alongside the following statutory provisions:

• Section 57 of the Offences Against the Person Act 1861, which provides for the offence of bigamy, makes it clear that 'nothing in this section contained shall extend . . . to any person marrying a second time whose husband or wife shall have been continually absent from such person for the space of seven years then

---

[43] *Chief Adjudication Officer v Bath* [2000] 1 FLR 8, 18.   [44] *Knowles v Knowles* [1962] P 161, 166–7.
[45] *Chard v Chard* [1956] P 259, 272 per Sachs J.
[46] *Prudential Assurance Co v Edmonds* (1877) 2 App Cas 487, 511.

last past, and shall not have been known by such person to be living within that time ... '.

• Section 184 of the Law of Property Act 1925 provides: 'In all cases where ... two or more persons have died in circumstances rendering it uncertain which of them survived the other or others, such deaths shall (subject to any order of the court), for all purposes affecting the title to property, be presumed to have occurred in order of seniority, and accordingly the younger shall be deemed to have survived the elder.'

• Section 19(3) of the Matrimonial Causes Act 1973 provides that in proceedings relating to the dissolution of marriage, 'the fact that for a period of seven years or more the other party to the marriage has been continually absent from the petitioner and the petitioner has no reason to believe that the other party has been living within that time shall be evidence that the other party is dead until the contrary is proved'.

3.4 Presumption of Regularity

The presumption of regularity in reality refers to two different presumptions. First, there is an evidential presumption that a mechanical instrument which is usually in working order was indeed in working order at a particular time. Thus, 'if evidence is given that a mechanical device such as a watch or speedometer ... recorded a particular time or a particular speed, which is the purpose of that instrument to record, that can by itself be prima facie evidence, on which a court can act, of that time or speed'.[47] It has been said of traffic lights that 'when you have a device of this kind set up for public use in active operation, ... the presumption should be that it is in proper working order unless there is evidence to the contrary ... '.[48]

Secondly, it is presumed that a person acting in an official or public capacity was acting properly and was properly appointed: *omnia praesumuntur rite esse acta*. This presumption is probably a persuasive one.[49] It may not, however, be relied upon by the prosecution in a criminal case in establishing an essential element of an offence.[50]

3.5 *Res Ipsa Loquitur*

What is considered the classic statement of the doctrine of *res ipsa loquitur* ('the thing speaks for itself')[51] was provided in *Scott v London and St Katherine Docks Co*:

... where the thing is shewn to be under the management of the defendant or his servants, and the accident is such as in the ordinary course of things does not happen if those who have the

---

[47] *Nicholas v Penny* [1950] 2 KB 466, 473.   [48] *Tingle Jacobs & Co v Kennedy* [1964] 1 WLR 638, 639.
[49] *R v Verelst* (1813) 3 Camp 432, 170 ER 1435.   [50] *Dillon v R* [1982] AC 484.
[51] See generally R Munday, 'Does Latin Impede Legal Understanding? The Case of "Res Ipsa Loquitur" ... Apparently' (2000) 164 *Justice of the Peace* 995.

management use proper care, it affords reasonable evidence, in the absence of explanation by the defendants, that the accident arose from want of care.[52]

In other words, if an accident is one which in the normal course of events will not have occurred in the absence of negligence on the part of the defendant, the doctrine of *res ipsa loquitur* applies to create a presumption of negligence. An application of the doctrine may be found in the decision of the Court of Appeal in *Widdowson v Newgate Meat Corporation*. The plaintiff's claim for damages for personal injuries arose from an accident which took place when the plaintiff, a pedestrian, was knocked down by a van being driven by a Mr Scullion on behalf of the defendants, his employers. The Court of Appeal held that, 'although it is not common for liability to be established in a road traffic accident on the application of the maxim "*res ipsa loquitur*",[53] the trial judge had been wrong not to invoke that maxim. 'In the present case the van was in the control of Mr Scullion, who was under a duty to drive it with due care and attention for other road users . . . That having been Mr Scullion's duty, it can fairly be said, in the terms of the authorities, that the accident would not have happened *in the ordinary course of things* (*ie* on the footing that the plaintiff was behaving as an ordinary, prudent pedestrian) if Mr Scullion had used proper care . . . '.[54] Thus the maxim applied, and, 'as the defendant called no evidence to rebut the inference that he had been negligent',[55] the plaintiff's appeal was allowed. The Court of Appeal acknowledged that 'if a defendant does adduce evidence, that evidence must be evaluated to see if it is still reasonable to draw the inference of negligence from the mere fact of the accident', and thus 'the situation might have been very different if Mr Scullion had given evidence'.[56]

But what is the strength of the presumption of *res ipsa loquitur*? In *Scott* itself it was stated vaguely that the presumption would afford 'reasonable evidence' of negligence which would stand in the absence of explanation by the defendant. The House of Lords in *Thomson v Kvaerner Govan Ltd* was similarly vague. Lord Hope of Craighead, with whom the other Law Lords agreed, remarked as follows:

> There is no doubt that cases do arise from time to time where the onus passes to the defenders [defendants] to *provide an explanation* for an accident which does not point to fault on their part. But if that is to happen the evidence must first raise a presumption that they were to blame for the accident. The paradigm case is where the pursuer [claimant] shows that he is entitled to the benefit of the maxim *res ipsa loquitur* . . . This requires circumstances to be established which afford reasonable evidence, in the absence of *explanation by the defenders*, that the accident arose from their negligence.[57]

The question remains, however, whether the presumption is a persuasive or evidential one. Does the defendant, in providing an explanation for the accident, need to *prove* the absence of negligence? Or is the defendant required merely to adduce sufficient

---

[52] (1865) 3 H & C 596, 601, 159 ER 665, 667. See also *Lloyde v West Midlands Gas Board* [1971] 1 WLR 749, 755–6.
[53] [1998] PIQR P 138, p 140.   [54] Ibid, p 143 (italics in original).   [55] Ibid, p 142.
[56] Ibid, p 141.   [57] [2003] UKHL 45, [26] (italics added).

evidence of absence of negligence to make it a 'live issue', with the burden of proving negligence resting ultimately with the claimant? *Barkway v South Wales Transport Co Ltd*, which concerned a burst tyre, would appear to endorse the view that the presumption is persuasive:

> To displace the presumption, the defendants must go further and prove (or it must emerge from the evidence as a whole) either *(a)* that the burst itself was due to a specific cause which does not connote negligence on their part but points to its absence as more probable, or *(b)*, if they can point to no such specific cause, that they used all reasonable care in and about the management of their tyres . . .[58]

More recently, however, the Privy Council took the view in *Ng Chun Pui v Lee Chuen Tat* that the presumption is merely evidential.[59]

There is yet a further view, which is that the doctrine of *res ipsa loquitur* does not constitute a true presumption at all. On this view it is neither a persuasive nor an evidential presumption, but merely gives rise to an *inference* of negligence. This inference of negligence is to be considered by the trier of fact alongside all the other evidence in the case to determine whether the claimant has discharged the legal burden of proving negligence on the part of the defendant. This less rigid, and more principled, approach has been adopted by the Supreme Court of Canada:

> It would appear that the law would be better served if the maxim was treated as expired and no longer used as a separate component in negligence actions. After all, it was nothing more than an attempt to deal with circumstantial evidence. That evidence is more sensibly dealt with by the trier of fact, who should weigh the circumstantial evidence with the direct evidence, if any, to determine whether the plaintiff has established on a balance of probabilities a *prima facie* case of negligence against the defendant.[60]

The High Court of Australia, too, has adopted a similar approach:

> In Australia, the invocation of the maxim creates no presumption and shifts no burden of proof to the defendant. All that it does, when applicable, is to raise an inference of the existence of negligence. In days when jury trials of factual contests in civil causes were more common in Australia than they are today, the maxim was an occasional friend to a plaintiff to ensure that the plaintiff got to the jury. It did not, however, ensure a verdict from the jury in the plaintiff's favour. It still remained for the judge to instruct the jury that the plaintiff bore the onus of proving the case on the balance of probabilities and for the jury to conclude whether they should draw the inference which the plaintiff invited.[61]

---

[58] [1948] 2 All ER 460, 470.

[59] [1988] RTR 298, 301. Referred to approvingly by the Court of Appeal in *Widdowson v Newgate Meat Corporation* [1998] PIQR P 138.

[60] *Fontaine v British Columbia (Official Administrator)* [1998] 1 SCR 424, [27]. See generally M McInnes, 'The Death of *Res Ipsa Loquitur* in Canada' (1998) 114 *Law Quarterly Review* 547.

[61] *Schellenberg v Tunnel Holdings Pty Ltd* [2000] HCA 18, [111] per Kirby J. See generally L Schulz, '*Res Ipsa Loquitur* in Australia—The Maxim Remains' (2000) 26 *Monash University Law Review* 379; S Smith, 'Another Look at Res Ipsa Loquitur' (2000) 74 *Australian Law Journal* 506.

Support for such an approach can also be found in the judgment of May LJ in *Fryer v Pearson:*

> It is not, I hope, just affectation which leads to me to believe that we should stop using unhelpful Latin phrases. It troubles me that we still tend to fall into the habit of talking about maxims or doctrines which go under labels in Latin whose meaning does not express a defined principle, and which those for whose benefit we operate will probably not understand.[62]

> I do not myself find it particularly helpful to try to define in the abstract what a so-called doctrine of 'it speaks for itself' embraces and then to wonder whether it applies to the facts of a particular case.[63]

3.6 Conflicting Presumptions

If two different presumptions of equal strength (for example, two persuasive presumptions) apply to a particular issue, but lead to conflicting results, the presumptions effectively 'neutralize' each other and the issue is to be determined without recourse to the presumptions.[64]

3.7 Conviction as Evidence of Commission of Offence

In *Hollington v F Hewthorn & Co Ltd,*[65] which concerned an action for damages arising from a road traffic accident, evidence of the defendant's conviction for careless driving was held to be inadmissible. Lord Goddard LJ's judgment is commonly regarded as authority for the proposition that evidence of the determination of a jury at an earlier trial is inadmissible to prove the facts on which that determination was based, as it is merely evidence of the opinion of the jury. As was seen in Chapter 10, opinion evidence, in contrast to evidence of facts, is generally considered inadmissible.[66]

The rule in *Hollington* has, however, been modified by legislation in both civil and criminal cases.

3.7.1 Civil Cases

Section 11 of the Civil Evidence Act 1968 provides:

> (1) In any civil proceedings the fact that a person has been convicted of an offence by or before any court in the United Kingdom or by a court-martial there or elsewhere shall (subject to subsection (3) below) be admissible in evidence for the purpose of proving, where to do so is relevant to any issue in those proceedings, that he committed that offence, whether he was so convicted upon a plea of guilty or otherwise and whether or not he is a party to the civil

---

[62] *The Times,* 4 April 2000; transcript, [18].   [63] Ibid, [19]. See generally C Witting, '*Res Ipsa Loquitur:* Some Last Words?' (2001) 117 *Law Quarterly Review* 392.

[64] *Monckton v Tarr* (1930) 23 BWCC 504.   [65] [1943] KB 587.

[66] In *Hollington v F Hewthorn & Co Ltd* [1943] KB 587, Lord Goddard LJ said (ibid, 595): 'It frequently happens that a bystander has a complete and full view of an accident. It is beyond question that, while he may inform the court of everything that he saw, he may not express any opinion on whether either or both of the parties were negligent.'

proceedings; but no conviction other than a subsisting one shall be admissible in evidence by virtue of this section.

(2) In any civil proceedings in which by virtue of this section a person is proved to have been convicted of an offence by or before any court in the United Kingdom or by a court-martial there or elsewhere—

(a) he shall be taken to have committed that offence unless the contrary is proved; and

(b) without prejudice to the reception of any other admissible evidence for the purpose of identifying the facts on which the conviction was based, the contents of any document which is admissible as evidence of the conviction, and the contents of the information, complaint, indictment or charge-sheet on which the person in question was convicted, shall be admissible in evidence for that purpose.

(3) Nothing in this section shall prejudice the operation of section 13 of this Act or any other enactment whereby a conviction or a finding of fact in any criminal proceedings is for the purpose of any other proceedings made conclusive evidence of any fact.

Thus a conviction is to be regarded as evidence that the offence was committed unless the contrary is proved. In order to 'prove his innocence in a subsequent civil action' a person can, in the words of Lord Denning MR, 'call his previous witnesses and hope that the judge will believe them now, even if they were disbelieved before. He can also call any fresh witnesses whom he thinks will help his case. In addition, I think he can show that the witnesses against him in the criminal trial were mistaken. For instance, in a traffic accident he could prove that a witness who claimed to have seen it was miles away and committed perjury.'[67] In *J v Oyston* the plaintiff brought a civil action against the defendant, who had previously been convicted of indecently assaulting and raping the plaintiff. The defendant sought to call evidence to discredit the plaintiff, and in doing so challenge the convictions. It was held that it was not an abuse of process for the defendant to seek to have the issue of his guilt reheard with such new evidence as he sought to adduce; the public policy considerations preventing a *plaintiff* in civil proceedings from reopening the issue of a conviction once it was finally determined did not apply to a *defendant* in civil proceedings.[68]

In determining whether the party seeking to prove his or her innocence has discharged the burden of doing so, is it permissible effectively to attach different *weights* to different types of convictions? If so, then it may be possible to argue, for example, that a conviction pursuant to a guilty plea should be accorded less weight than one resulting from a trial and verdict; or that a conviction resulting from a majority verdict should be accorded less weight than one resulting from a unanimous verdict; or that a conviction against which no appeal has been taken should not be accorded as much weight as one confirmed on appeal. Two conflicting approaches to the question have emerged in the case law. According to one approach, it is impermissible to inquire into the weight which the criminal conviction may carry.[69] The contrary view, however, is that it is

---

[67] *Stupple v Royal Insurance Co* [1971] 1 QB 50, 72.   [68] [1999] 1 WLR 694, 700.

[69] See, eg, *Stupple v Royal Insurance Co* [1971] 1 QB 50, 75–6 per Buckley LJ. See also *Wright v Wright, The Times*, 15 Feb 1971.

permissible to look behind the fact of conviction at considerations which may throw light on the weight to be attached to the conviction:

> Take a plea of guilty. Sometimes a defendant pleads guilty in error: or in a minor offence he may plead guilty to save time and expense, or to avoid some embarrassing fact coming out. Afterwards, in the civil action, he can, I think, explain how he came to plead guilty.
>
> Take next a case in the magistrates' court when a man is convicted and bound over or fined a trifling sum, but had a good ground of appeal, and did not exercise it because it was not worth while. Can he not explain this in a civil court? I think he can. He can offer any explanation in his effort to show that the conviction was erroneous ...[70]

The latter approach would seem to have more to commend it, being more sensitive to the notion of a conviction being merely *presumptive* of guilt. There is no reason in principle why the party seeking to rebut the presumption, or the party seeking to uphold it, should be restricted in any way. While, as indicated in the quotation just presented, the circumstances of the conviction may be such that the person seeking to rebut the presumption may be able to explain it away, there may equally be situations at the other end of the spectrum: 'it ... is obvious that, when a man has been convicted by 12 of his fellow countrymen and countrywomen at a criminal trial, the verdict of the jury is a matter which is entitled to very great weight when the convicted person is seeking, in the words of the statute, to prove the contrary'.[71]

In defamation actions, there is an *irrebuttable* presumption that a conviction is evidence of the commission of the offence. Section 13(1) of the Civil Evidence Act 1968 provides:

> In an action for libel or slander in which the question whether the plaintiff did or did not commit a criminal offence is relevant to an issue arising in the action, proof that, at the time when that issue falls to be determined, he stands convicted of that offence shall be conclusive evidence that he committed that offence; and his conviction thereof shall be admissible in evidence accordingly.

A succinct summary of the relevant principles in this area has been provided by the Court of Appeal:

> (a) A collateral attack on an earlier decision of a court of competent jurisdiction may be but is not necessarily an abuse of the process of the court. (b) If the earlier decision is that of a court exercising a criminal jurisdiction then, because of the terms of sections 11 to 13 of the Civil Evidence Act 1968, the conviction will be conclusive in the case of later defamation proceedings but will constitute prima facie evidence only in the case of other civil proceedings.... (c) If the earlier decision is that of a court exercising a civil jurisdiction then it is binding on the parties to that action and their privies in any later civil proceedings. (d) If the parties to the later civil proceedings were not parties to or privies of those who were parties to the earlier proceedings then it will only be an abuse of the process of the court to challenge the factual findings and conclusions of the judge or jury in the earlier action if (i) it would be manifestly unfair to a party to the

---

[70] *Stupple v Royal Insurance Co* [1971] 1 QB 50, 72–3 per Lord Denning MR. See also *Taylor v Taylor* [1970] 1 WLR 1148.   [71] *Taylor v Taylor* [1970] 1 WLR 1148, 1152.

later proceedings that the same issues should be relitigated or (ii) to permit such relitigation would bring the administration of justice into disrepute.[72]

3.7.2 Criminal Cases

Section 74 of the Police and Criminal Evidence Act 1984 provides:

> (1) In any proceedings the fact that a person other than the accused has been convicted of an offence by or before any court in the United Kingdom or by a Service court outside the United Kingdom shall be admissible in evidence for the purpose of proving, where to do so is relevant to any issue in those proceedings, that that person committed that offence, whether or not any other evidence of his having committed that offence is given.

> (2) In any proceedings in which by virtue of this section a person other than the accused is proved to have been convicted of an offence by or before any court in the United Kingdom or by a Service court outside the United Kingdom, he shall be taken to have committed that offence unless the contrary is proved.

> (3) In any proceedings where evidence is admissible of the fact that the accused has committed an offence, in so far as that evidence is relevant to any matter in issue in the proceedings for a reason other than a tendency to show in the accused a disposition to commit the kind of offence with which he is charged, if the accused is proved to have been convicted of the offence—

> (a) by or before any court in the United Kingdom; or

> (b) by a Service court outside the United Kingdom,

> he shall be taken to have committed that offence unless the contrary is proved.

> (4) Nothing in this section shall prejudice—

> (a) the admissibility in evidence of any conviction which would be admissible apart from this section; or

> (b) the operation of any enactment whereby a conviction or a finding of fact in any proceedings is for the purposes of any other proceedings made conclusive evidence of any fact.

3.7.2.1 Convictions of Persons other than the Accused

The effect of section 74(1) is that where proof that a person other than the accused committed an offence is relevant, that person's conviction of the offence is admissible in evidence to prove that he or she committed the offence. By virtue of section 74(2), proof of the person's conviction of the offence means that he or she is to be taken to have committed that offence unless the contrary is proved.

The Court of Appeal has held that section 74(1) should be used sparingly.[73] Its purpose is to allow the fact that a person other than the accused has committed an offence

---

[72] *Secretary of State for Trade and Industry v Bairstow* [2003] EWCA Civ 321, [2003] 3 WLR 841, [38].

[73] *R v Robertson* [1987] QB 920, 928. See also *R v Kempster* [1989] 1 WLR 1125; *R v Mahmood* [1997] 1 Cr App R 414; *R v Dixon* (2000) 164 JP 721 (decision of 2000).

to be placed before the jury, where this fact is relevant[74] to an issue in the case. The phrase 'issue in the proceedings' is to be given a broad interpretation:

> The word 'issue' in relation to a trial is apt to cover not only an issue which is an essential ingredient in the offence charged, for instance in a handling case the fact that the goods were stolen (that is the restricted meaning), but also less fundamental issues, for instance evidential issues arising during the course of the proceedings (that is the extended meaning). Section 74 by using the words 'any issue in those proceedings' does not seek to limit the word 'issue' to the restricted meaning indicated above.

The Court has also rejected the contention 'that the section applies only to proof of conviction of offences in which the defendant on trial played no part'.[75] The judge must consider, however, whether evidence admissible under section 74(1) should nevertheless be excluded in the exercise of discretion. In addition, the jury must be clearly told why the evidence is before them and to what issue it is relevant (as well as to what issues it is *not* relevant).[76] It would appear that a trial in which section 74(1) has been used will be regarded as complying with Article 6 if there has been appropriate consideration of the possibility of discretionary exclusion and appropriate directions have been given to the jury.[77]

An indication of what may be regarded as sufficient grounds for the exercise of an exclusionary discretion has emerged from a number of decisions of the Court of Appeal. It would seem that where the evidence admissible under section 74(1) 'expressly or by necessary inference imports the complicity' of the accused it should be excluded under section 78.[78] This is because it would be inappropriate for such evidence to be admitted in the absence of an opportunity for the accused to cross-examine the person convicted, particularly in relation to the complicity of the accused. It is, of course, entirely possible that even if the person convicted were to testify at the accused's trial, the defence would not exercise its right to cross-examine, or that such cross-examination if conducted would 'turn out to be a disaster' for the defence. This cannot, however, be assumed. It has also been made clear that 'whilst evidence which of itself establishes complicity should be excluded under section 78, evidence which does not of itself show complicity but is used as a basis for other evidence to that end need not necessarily be excluded'.[79]

---

[74] See *R v Wardell* [1997] Crim LR 450.   [75] *R v Robertson* [1987] QB 920, 927.   [76] Ibid, 928.

[77] *MH v UK (Admissibility)*, Application no 28572/95, 17 Jan 1997: 'An application was made by the prosecution, under section 74 of the Police and Criminal Evidence Act 1984, to use the guilty plea of FS in the trial of the applicant. Whilst under section 78 of the Police and Criminal Evidence Act 1984, the judge had a discretion not to admit the guilty plea, the judge, having heard the point argued by counsel for the applicant and for the prosecution, chose not to exercise this discretion applying the test of whether the prejudicial effect outweighed the probative value, and thus the plea was admitted. . . . the admission of the guilty plea must be looked at in conjunction with the warning given to the jury about the relevance of the guilty plea. In these circumstances . . . the judge's ruling that the guilty plea be admitted as the probative value of the guilty plea outweighed the prejudicial effect, does not disclose an arbitrary or unreasonable exercise of the discretion conferred upon him. . . . the admission of the guilty plea of FS [did not render] the trial of the applicant unfair.'

[78] *R v Curry* [1988] Crim LR 527; LEXIS transcript.

[79] *R v Kempster* [1989] 1 WLR 1125, 1134. It may be permissible, therefore, for the prosecution to adduce the evidence to prevent mystification of the jury.

An illustration of the application of section 74(1) may be found in the decision of the Court of Appeal in *R v Robertson*. Robertson was charged with conspiring with Poole and Long to commit burglaries. Poole and Long pleaded guilty to relevant *substantive* counts of burglary, with which Robertson was not charged. At Robertson's trial, evidence of Poole and Long's convictions was admitted pursuant to section 74(1), and this was upheld by the Court of Appeal. An issue in the case was 'whether there was a conspiracy between Poole and Long', given that the prosecution was seeking to prove that Robertson was a party to such a conspiracy. Evidence of Poole and Long's convictions of burglary was clearly highly relevant to the issue of whether there had been a conspiracy between the two of them to commit the burglaries.[80] The Court of Appeal also rejected the argument that the evidence should have been excluded under section 78. In doing so, it distinguished its earlier decision in *R v O'Connor*.[81] In that case, O'Connor was charged with conspiring with Beck to commit an offence. Beck pleaded guilty to the conspiracy. It was held that evidence of Beck's conviction of conspiring with O'Connor should not have been admitted in O'Connor's trial. The Court of Appeal in *Robertson* acknowledged that this decision was correct: Beck's conviction of the very conspiracy offence with which O'Connor was being tried might well have led the jury to infer that O'Connor must have conspired with Beck. In *Robertson*, however, the convictions of Poole and Long for the *substantive* offences did not on their face incriminate Robertson at all. Indeed, even if Poole and Long had testified at Robertson's trial, the defence would probably not have exercised its right to cross-examine them, since such cross-examination would probably have produced disastrous results for the defence.[82]

By contrast, section 74(1) was held to be inapplicable in *R v Mahmood*. Mahmood, Manzur, and Linton were charged with rape. Linton pleaded guilty. At issue in the trial of Mahmood and Manzur was whether, as the defendants contended, the complainant had consented or alternatively they had believed that she was consenting, or whether, as the prosecution contended, she was incapable of consenting by reason of drink. The Court of Appeal held section 74(1) to be inapplicable on the basis that it was impossible, without knowing the reason for Linton's guilty plea, to identify the precise *issue* in the trial to which evidence of this plea was relevant. Linton could have pleaded guilty because he had known that the complainant *could not* consent by reason of drink; or because he had known that she *was not* consenting; or because he had been reckless about whether she was consenting. Given the prosecution's contention that the complainant could not consent by reason of her drunken state, 'there was a very real danger that the jury would assume that Linton's plea meant that he knew full well she could not consent, and conclude therefore these appellants must have known that also'.[83]

3.7.2.2 Convictions of the Accused

Section 74(3) makes analogous provision in relation to the accused: where the fact that the accused committed an offence constitutes admissible evidence,[84] proof of his or her

---

[80] [1987] QB 920, 927.   [81] (1987) 85 Cr App R 298 (decision of 1986).   [82] [1987] QB 920, 928.
[83] [1997] 1 Cr App R 414, 419.   [84] See especially Ch 8.

conviction of the offence means that the offence is to be taken to have been committed by him or her unless the contrary is proved.

3.7.2.3 Ancillary Matters

Section 75(1) makes it clear that where a conviction is admissible in evidence, evidence of the contents of certain documents is admissible for the purpose of identifying the facts on which the conviction was based:

> Where evidence that a person has been convicted of an offence is admissible by virtue of section 74 above, then without prejudice to the reception of any other admissible evidence for the purpose of identifying the facts on which the conviction was based—
>
> (a) the contents of any document which is admissible as evidence of the conviction; and
>
> (b) the contents of the information, complaint, indictment or charge-sheet on which the person in question was convicted,
>
> shall be admissible in evidence for that purpose.

Section 75(4) provides:

> Nothing in section 74 above shall be construed as rendering admissible in any proceedings evidence of any conviction other than a subsisting one.

What constitutes a subsisting conviction has been explained by the Court of Appeal:

> The purpose which lies behind the enactment of section 74 was to enable proof of the commission of an offence by X to be proved by the record without the necessity of calling X to admit the truth of what appears on the record. Therefore, what is important is either that a jury has found X's offence proved, or that X himself has before a court formally admitted that he has committed the offence. Provided that his plea has not been withdrawn nor the verdict of the jury, where there has been one, has been quashed on appeal, the conviction subsists. Whether or not X has been sentenced is irrelevant on the issue of whether he has committed the offence.[85]

---

[85] *R v Robertson* [1987] QB 920, 931.

14

The Course of Evidence

1 The Adversarial Tradition

This chapter examines the principles relating to the presentation of evidence in court. The English trial process is based on the adversarial tradition. This is to be distinguished from the inquisitorial model which is typically associated with Continental European jurisdictions. The adversarial model in its paradigmatic form views the presentation of evidence as the responsibility of the parties, with the judge playing the role of a 'neutral' umpire. Adversarialism connotes 'a system of adjudication in which procedural action is controlled by the parties and the adjudicator remains essentially passive'.[1] By contrast, a pure inquisitorial model sees the judge playing a major role in the presentation of evidence by calling and examining witnesses to whom the parties may put supplementary questions.[2] Trials in adversarial jurisdictions are also said to be characterized by greater formality and theatricality than those in inquisitorial jurisdictions.[3] Of course, no jurisdiction conforms fully to either a pure adversarial or inquisitorial model, and it must not be thought that the two models are in any event diametrically opposed.[4] Later we examine two fundamental features of the adversarial model—the principle of orality and the notion of a neutral judge—to determine the extent to which English law has remained committed to

---

[1] M R Damaška, *Evidence Law Adrift* (1997) 74.

[2] See generally N Jörg, S Field, and C Brants, 'Are Inquisitorial and Adversarial Systems Converging?' in P Fennell, C Harding, N Jörg, and B Swart (eds), *Criminal Justice in Europe: A Comparative Study* (1995); J H Langbein, 'Historical Foundations of the Law of Evidence: A View from the Ryder Sources' (1996) 96 *Columbia Law Review* 1168, 1168–9; J F Nijboer, 'Common Law Tradition in Evidence Scholarship Observed from a Continental Perspective' (1993) 41 *American Journal of Comparative Law* 299; S Wesley, 'A Glimpse of French Criminal Justice—1' (1998) 148 *New Law Journal* 326; S Wesley, 'A Glimpse of French Criminal Justice—2' (1998) 148 *New Law Journal* 669; J McEwan, *Evidence and the Adversarial Process: The Modern Law* (2nd ed 1998) Ch 1; Royal Commission on Criminal Justice, *Report* (Cm 2263) (1993) 3; M Zander, *Cases and Materials on the English Legal System* (7th ed 1996) 283–300. See also M R Damaška, *The Faces of Justice and State Authority: A Comparative Approach to the Legal Process* (1986).

[3] See generally J McEwan, *Evidence and the Adversarial Process: The Modern Law* (2nd ed 1998) 11–12. As has been noted, 'trial procedure plays an important ceremonial part in the public ritual of judging an offender and setting him apart from law-abiding members of society': L Re, 'Oral v Written Evidence: The Myth of the "Impressive Witness" ' (1983) 57 *Australian Law Journal* 679, 689.

[4] See A Eser, 'Collection and Evaluation of Evidence in Comparative Perspective' (1997) 31 *Israel Law Review* 429, 429.

these ideals. First, however, the principles relating to pre-trial disclosure by the parties to litigation will be considered.

1.1 Disclosure

There are two broad rationales for disclosure, applicable to both civil and criminal proceedings. First, disclosure serves the basic requirement of adversarial trial, that the defendant must be in a position to answer the case against him or her. This rationale explains the requirement of disclosure of the prosecution case in criminal proceedings, and, in civil proceedings, the requirement to disclose the documents on which the claimant relies. The second rationale is that parties in both types of proceedings are placed under a duty to see that justice is done.

The duty to do justice has long been recognized in criminal proceedings, in which the prosecutor is conceived as a 'minister of justice' (a person who administers or dispenses justice) rather than a partisan actor whose only interest lies in securing a conviction. The justification for this duty in criminal proceedings is that the prosecutor represents the state, and the state's interest is in getting the right or just result, whatever that may be. It follows therefore that while effectively prosecuting a case, the prosecutor must also lend necessary aid to the defence and in particular should make available evidence or other material which might assist the defence. It is arguable that a similar duty to do justice is now extended to both the defendant and his or her representatives by virtue of the Criminal Procedure and Investigations Act 1996 (as amended) which (as will be discussed below) places the defendant under extensive pre-trial disclosure duties in favour of the prosecution. It should be noted that this involves a substantial departure from pure adversarialism in criminal procedure. Some commentators feel that it is wrong in principle for the defendant to be burdened with duties to assist the prosecution, and that rather the defendant should be fully entitled to devote all his energies to his own defence.[5]

In civil procedure, the notion that a defendant owes a duty to secure justice is new (and equally controversial in that it derogates from the adversarial ideal). The duty was introduced by Lord Woolf's civil procedure reforms and is expressed in Part 1 of the Civil Procedure Rules, which establishes 'enabling the court to deal with cases justly' as the overriding objective of the civil process[6] and places both parties under a corresponding duty to help the court to further that overriding objective.[7]

1.1.1 Civil

The disclosure of documents in civil proceedings is governed by the Civil Procedure Rules. Disclosing a document means 'stating that the document exists or has existed'.[8] Only documents which are or have been in a party's control are subject to disclosure by that party.[9] A document is or has been in a party's control if '(a) it is or was in his physical possession; (b) he has or has had a right to possession of it; or

---

[5] See Note of Dissent by M Zander in Royal Commission on Criminal Justice, *Report* (Cm 2263) (1993) 221–3.
[6] Rule 1.1(1).   [7] Rule 1.3.   [8] Rule 31.2.   [9] Rule 31.8(1).

(c) he has or has had a right to inspect or take copies of it'.[10] A party is generally required to disclose:

(a) the documents on which he relies; and

(b) the documents which—

    (i) adversely affect his own case;

    (ii) adversely affect another party's case; or

    (iii) support another party's case; and

(c) the documents which he is required to disclose by a relevant practice direction.[11]

The party is required to make a reasonable search for such documents.[12] The factors relevant in deciding the reasonableness of the search include '(a) the number of documents involved; (b) the nature and complexity of the proceedings; (c) the ease and expense of retrieval of any particular document; and (d) the significance of any document which is likely to be located during the search'.[13] 'Any duty of disclosure continues until the proceedings are concluded.'[14]

Specific provision is made in rule 31.17 in relation to disclosure by third parties:

(1) This rule applies where an application is made to the court under any Act for disclosure by a person who is not a party to the proceedings.

. . .

(3) The court may make an order under this rule only where—

    (a) the documents of which disclosure is sought are likely to support the case of the applicant or adversely affect the case of one of the other parties to the proceedings; and

    (b) disclosure is necessary in order to dispose fairly of the claim or to save costs.

. . .

Rule 31.19(1) provides: 'A person may apply, without notice, for an order permitting him to withhold disclosure of a document on the ground that disclosure would damage the public interest.' More has been said about the procedure for claiming public interest immunity in Chapter 6.

A document which a party fails to disclose may not be relied on by that party 'unless the court gives permission'.[15] The use by a party of a document which has been disclosed to that party is governed by rule 31.22(1):

A party to whom a document has been disclosed may use the document only for the purpose of the proceedings in which it is disclosed, except where—

(a) the document has been read to or by the court, or referred to, at a hearing which has been held in public;

(b) the court gives permission; or

(c) the party who disclosed the document and the person to whom the document belongs agree.[16]

---

[10] Rule 31.8(2).   [11] Rule 31.6.   [12] Rule 31.7(1).   [13] Rule 31.7(2).   [14] Rule 31.11(1).
[15] Rule 31.21.   [16] See *Marlwood Commercial Inc v Kozeny* [2004] EWCA Civ 798, [2004] 3 All ER 648.

1.1.2 Criminal

1.1.2.1 Prosecution

The rationale for prosecution disclosure has been neatly summarized as follows:

> Advance disclosure by the prosecution serves two main purposes. The first is its contribution to a fair trial looked at as a whole. The second is its contribution to the efficiency, including the speed, of the pre-trial and trial process and to considerate treatment of all involved in it. There are two categories of material held by the prosecution: the first is 'evidence', ie that upon which the prosecution will rely to prove its case. The second is 'unused material' which encompasses all other information and material that the prosecution has seen or collected. Early and full disclosure of all material in the first category and of relevant material in the second is vital for good preparation for trial, narrowing disputed issues, and most importantly to ensuring a fair trial. If the prosecution knows of or has information in its possession which it is not using but which may help the defence secure an acquittal, justice obviously demands disclosure. Failure of the prosecution to disclose such material has been a major factor in overturning convictions, often after the defendant has spent many years in jail, so it is imperative that the right decision on disclosure is made by the prosecution.[17]

As the quotation suggests, the possible duties on the prosecution to disclose material to the defence fall into two categories. First, the prosecution has a duty in certain cases to disclose its case. The position has been succinctly summarized by Leng:

> For the most serious cases which are tried before a judge and jury in the Crown Court, disclosure of the prosecution case [must] take[] place . . . Disclosure is made of written versions of all witness statements or other evidence which the prosecution intends to adduce at court.
>
> For less serious cases, in which a choice is made to hold the trial in the local magistrates' court, the prosecution must disclose its case but may choose whether to provide full copies of the evidence or a summary of the case. For the least serious category of offences which may be tried only in the magistrates' court, there is no duty on the prosecution to disclose the case prior to trial.[18]

Secondly, the Criminal Procedure and Investigations Act 1996 as amended, most particularly by the Criminal Justice Act 2003,[19] contains complex provisions on prosecution disclosure of unused material. These will be dealt with here in brief outline only.

The test of disclosure of unused prosecution material is contained in section 3 of the Criminal Procedure and Investigations Act 1996. The prosecutor must 'disclose to the

---

[17] Lord Justice Auld, *A Review of the Criminal Courts of England and Wales* (2001) Ch 10 para 115, accessible via http://www.criminal-courts-review.org.uk/.

[18] R Leng, 'The Exchange of Information and Disclosure' in M McConville and G Wilson (eds), *The Handbook of the Criminal Justice Process* (2002) 208.

[19] See generally D Corker, 'Disclosure Stripped Bare', *Archbold News*, 11 Nov 2004, 6; P Keleher, 'Showing Your Hand', *Criminal Bar Association News*, Dec 2004, 10, accessible via http://www.criminalbar.com; M Redmayne, 'Criminal Justice Act 2003: (1) Disclosure and Its Discontents' [2004] *Criminal Law Review* 441; V Smith, 'Defence by Ambush' (2004) 168 *Justice of the Peace* 24; P Wilcock and J Bennathan, 'New Disclosure Rules for 2005' (2004) 154 *New Law Journal* 918; R Taylor, M Wasik, and R Leng, *Blackstone's Guide to the Criminal Justice Act 2003* (2004) Ch 3.

accused any prosecution material which has not previously been disclosed to the accused and which might reasonably be considered capable of undermining the case for the prosecution against the accused or of assisting the case for the accused'.[20] 'Material must not be disclosed under this section to the extent that the court, on an application by the prosecutor, concludes it is not in the public interest to disclose it and orders accordingly.'[21]

'The prosecutor must keep under review the question whether at any given time (and, in particular, following the giving of a defence statement) there is prosecution material which' ought to be disclosed under the test of disclosure.[22]

1.1.2.2 Defence

The Criminal Procedure and Investigations Act 1996 (as amended) also contains complex provisions on defence disclosure. The issue of defence disclosure has proved somewhat controversial. Despite evidence that, prior to the introduction of defence disclosure obligations, 'ambush defences' that were sprung at a late stage were by no means widespread,[23] justifications have continued to be put forward for the recognition by the law of such obligations. As stated by Lord Justice Auld in the Criminal Courts Review:

> ...some contributors to the Review argued...that the interests of justice justify a right of defence by ambush as a protection against abuse of public authority. In particular, they suggested that a defendant may be justified in holding back his defence since it may give the prosecution an opportunity before trial to strengthen or change a weak case or to fabricate or falsify evidence to overcome it. To the extent that the prosecution may legitimately wish to fill possible holes in its case once issues have been identified by [defence disclosure], I can understand why, as a matter of tactics, a defendant might prefer to keep his case close to his chest. But that is not a valid reason for preventing a full and fair hearing on the issues canvassed at the trial. A criminal trial is not a game under which a guilty defendant should be provided with a sporting chance. It is a search for truth in accordance with the twin principles that the prosecution must prove its case and that a defendant is not obliged to inculpate himself, the object being to convict the guilty and acquit the innocent. Requiring a defendant to indicate in advance what he disputes about the prosecution case offends neither of those principles. Equally untenable is the suggestion that defence by ambush is a permissible protection against the possibility of dishonesty of police and/or prosecutors in the conduct of the prosecution....a criminal justice process cannot sensibly be designed on a general premise that those responsible for law are likely to break it. In those cases where, unfortunately, the police or other public officers are dishonest, the criminal trial process itself is the medium for protection and exposure.[24]

In cases which are to be tried on indictment, where 'the prosecutor complies with section 3 or purports to comply with it',[25] 'the accused must give a defence statement to the court and the prosecutor'.[26] It is notable therefore that this obligation arises even

---

[20] S 3(1)(a).   [21] S 3(6).   [22] S 7A(2).

[23] Royal Commission on Criminal Justice, *Report* (Cm 2263) (1993) 98 n 29.

[24] Lord Justice Auld, *A Review of the Criminal Courts of England and Wales* (2001) Ch 10 para 154, accessible via http://www.criminal-courts-review.org.uk/.   [25] S 5(1)(b).

[26] S 5(5).

where the prosecution simply *purports* to comply with its obligation to make disclosure. What constitutes a 'defence statement' is clarified in section 6A:

> (1) ... a defence statement is a written statement—
>
>> (a) setting out the nature of the accused's defence, including any particular defences on which he intends to rely,
>>
>> (b) indicating the matters of fact on which he takes issue with the prosecution,
>>
>> (c) setting out, in the case of each such matter, why he takes issue with the prosecution, and
>>
>> (d) indicating any point of law (including any point as to the admissibility of evidence or an abuse of process) which he wishes to take, and any authority on which he intends to rely for that purpose.
>
> (2) A defence statement that discloses an alibi must give particulars of it, including—
>
>> (a) the name, address and date of birth of any witness the accused believes is able to give evidence in support of the alibi, or as many of those details as are known to the accused when the statement is given;
>>
>> (b) any information in the accused's possession which might be of material assistance in identifying or finding any such witness in whose case any of the details mentioned in paragraph (a) are not known to the accused when the statement is given.
>
> (3) For the purposes of this section evidence in support of an alibi is evidence tending to show that by reason of the presence of the accused at a particular place or in a particular area at a particular time he was not, or was unlikely to have been, at the place where the offence is alleged to have been committed at the time of its alleged commission.
>
> ...

Defence obligations in relation to any possible witnesses are prescribed in section 6C:

> (1) The accused must give to the court and the prosecutor a notice indicating whether he intends to call any persons (other than himself) as witnesses at his trial and, if so—
>
>> (a) giving the name, address and date of birth of each such proposed witness, or as many of those details as are known to the accused when the notice is given;
>>
>> (b) providing any information in the accused's possession which might be of material assistance in identifying or finding any such proposed witness in whose case any of the details mentioned in paragraph (a) are not known to the accused when the notice is given.
>
> (2) Details do not have to be given under this section to the extent that they have already been given under section 6A(2).
>
> ...
>
> (4) If, following the giving of a notice under this section, the accused—
>
>> (a) decides to call a person (other than himself) who is not included in the notice as a proposed witness, or decides not to call a person who is so included, or

(b) discovers any information which, under subsection (1), he would have had to include in the notice if he had been aware of it when giving the notice,

he must give an appropriately amended notice to the court and the prosecutor.

Section 6D imposes obligations on the defence in relation to any possible expert evidence:

(1) If the accused instructs a person with a view to his providing any expert opinion for possible use as evidence at the trial of the accused, he must give to the court and the prosecutor a notice specifying the person's name and address.

(2) A notice does not have to be given under this section specifying the name and address of a person whose name and address have already been given under section 6C.

. . .

Where one of a number of specified failures in relation to disclosure by the accused has occurred or where the accused at trial acts inconsistently in some way with the defence disclosure, it is possible that 'the court or any other party may make such comment as appears appropriate',[27] and that 'the court or jury may draw such inferences as appear proper in deciding whether the accused is guilty of the offence concerned'.[28] The accused is not to be convicted solely on such an inference.[29]

1.2 Orality

Orality is one principal feature of the adversarial model. Heavy reliance is placed in the Anglo-American trial process, and particularly in criminal trials, on the oral testimony of witnesses. There are said to be substantial benefits associated with having witnesses testify publicly in open court. It is said, in particular, that observation of a witness's demeanour[30] provides a good indication of the reliability of his or her testimony:

All of us know that, in every-day life, the way a man behaves when he tells a story—his intonations, his fidgetings or composure, his yawns, the use of his eyes, his air of candor or of evasiveness—may furnish valuable clues to his reliability. Such clues are by no means impeccable guides, but they are often immensely helpful.[31]

The assumption, then, is that a person's demeanour while stating a fact provides valuable clues about whether he or she is being truthful, whether he or she perceived the fact correctly, and whether his or her memory is functioning effectively. The extent, however, to which this assumption actually reflects reality is a matter of considerable speculation. Wellborn has reviewed a considerable body of experimental evidence relating to the utility of demeanour in indicating unreliability.[32] By and large, the experimental

---

[27] S 11(5)(a).   [28] S 11(5)(b).   [29] S 11(10).

[30] On evidence of *out-of-court* demeanour, see *R v Keast* [1998] Crim LR 748.

[31] J Frank, *Courts on Trial: Myth and Reality in American Justice* (1950) 21.

[32] O G Wellborn III, 'Demeanor' (1991) 76 *Cornell Law Review* 1075. See also J Allan, 'The Working and Rationale of the Hearsay Rule and the Implications of Modern Psychological Knowledge' (1991) 44 *Current*

research has revealed that demeanour is of little benefit to ordinary observers in assessing whether a person is untruthful. First, observation of facial behaviour appears to be of little value, and there is indeed some evidence which suggests that such observation actually *decreases* the accuracy of lie detection. Secondly, little assistance would appear to be gained from listening to the voice of the respondent, as subjects who merely read transcripts performed just as well as, or even better than, those who heard recordings of the respondent's voice. Finally, there is no compelling evidence that lying is accompanied by distinctive body behaviour which can be discerned by observers.[33] The experimental research has also revealed that demeanour may be of even less assistance in the assessment of the accuracy of a person's perceptions and memory.[34] Thus Wellborn concludes that, consistently, the experiments have demonstrated that the capacity of ordinary people to detect unreliability by observing demeanour is simply a myth.[35]

In the light of such considerations, the question arises whether the reliance currently placed on oral testimony is misplaced, and whether more emphasis should be placed instead on preparation of evidence in advance of trial. Detailed discussion of this is beyond the scope of a book of this nature. It is certainly possible, however, to argue that allowing freer admissibility in evidence of written statements prepared prior to trial would have the advantage of addressing the problem of overawed witnesses who do not 'give their best' in the courtroom. It has been noted[36] that although court proceedings are generally becoming increasingly user-friendly, 'every barrister has had the problem of the witness who gave his or her statement confidently in the barrister's chambers, forgetting vital aspects in the witness box'. And while it is usually possible to elicit these aspects from the witness eventually, the experience of doing so may be a time-consuming and unpleasant one. On the other hand, concern has been expressed that written statements, because of the involvement of lawyers in their preparation, are likely to be 'adulterated' by such involvement. A misleading sense of structure and order, and hence a misleading sense of respectability and persuasiveness, might be brought to the evidence.[37] Of course, it may be possible to conceive of proposals for reform which ensure that a new set of problems is not introduced. For example, it may be possible to introduce a pre-trial procedure whereby a neutral official has the duty, as soon as possible

---

Legal Problems 217, 225–6; L Re, 'Oral v Written Evidence: The Myth of the "Impressive Witness" ' (1983) 57 Australian Law Journal 679; J R Spencer, 'Orality and the Evidence of Absent Witnesses' [1994] Criminal Law Review 628, 637.

[33] See the summary in O G Wellborn III, 'Demeanor' (1991) 76 Cornell Law Review 1075, 1088. For details see ibid, 1078–88. See also M Stone, 'Instant Lie Detection? Demeanour and Credibility in Criminal Trials' [1991] Criminal Law Review 821; P Ekman, Telling Lies: Clues to Deceit in the Marketplace, Politics, and Marriage (1992) 291–2; J McEwan, Evidence and the Adversarial Process: The Modern Law (2nd ed 1998) 107; A Vrij, Detecting Lies and Deceit: The Psychology of Lying and the Implications for Professional Practice (2000).

[34] O G Wellborn III, 'Demeanor' (1991) 76 Cornell Law Review 1075, 1088–91.

[35] Ibid, 1104. See also J McEwan, The Verdict of the Court: Passing Judgment in Law and Psychology (2003) 105: 'Although laboratory studies . . . have limited generalisability to court proceedings, there has emerged sufficient data on lying behaviour severely to undermine belief in demeanour as a clue to honesty. "Body language" appears to mislead as much as it informs.'

[36] P W Young and C D Curtis, 'Oral or Written Evidence?' (1997) 71 Australian Law Journal 459, 460.

[37] Ibid, 461–5.

after the event in question, to elicit the story of a witness and record it, preferably on audio or video tape.[38]

In civil proceedings the principle of orality may be regarded as having been substantially eroded. Rule 32.2(1)(a) of the Civil Procedure Rules pays lip-service to the principle of orality by prescribing a 'general rule' that, at trial, 'any fact which needs to be proved by the evidence of witnesses is to be proved . . . by their oral evidence given in public'. This is subject, however, to the importance that is accorded to the use of witness statements.[39] 'A witness statement is a written statement signed by a person which contains the evidence which that person would be allowed to give orally.'[40] 'The court will order a party to serve on the other parties any witness statement of the oral evidence which the party serving the statement intends to rely on in relation to any issues of fact to be decided at the trial.'[41] A party who has served a witness statement and wishes to rely on the evidence of the witness 'must call the witness to give oral evidence unless the court orders otherwise or he puts the statement in as hearsay evidence'.[42] Significantly, however, the witness's witness statement is to stand as his or her evidence-in-chief unless the court orders otherwise.[43] The witness 'may with the permission of the court—(a) amplify his witness statement; and (b) give evidence in relation to new matters which have arisen since the witness statement was served on the other parties'.[44] Permission will be given only if the court 'considers that there is good reason not to confine the evidence of the witness to the contents of his witness statement'.[45]

1.3 A 'Neutral' Judge

1.3.1 Calling Witnesses

1.3.1.1 Civil Proceedings

In civil proceedings the principle that it is the responsibility of the parties to decide what witnesses to call would appear to be adhered to strictly. Thus it has been held that 'it is certainly not the law, that a judge, or any person in a judicial position, such as an arbitrator, has any power himself to call witnesses to fact against the will of either of the parties'.[46] The order in which witnesses are called would also appear to be completely within the discretion of the parties.[47]

1.3.1.2 Criminal Proceedings

In criminal trials,[48] the responsibility for calling witnesses rests primarily with the parties. Generally speaking, the prosecution should secure the attendance of all witnesses

---

[38] L Re, 'Oral v Written Evidence: The Myth of the "Impressive Witness" ' (1983) 57 *Australian Law Journal* 679, 689.   [39] See generally G Exall, 'Civil Litigation Brief' (2001) 145 *Solicitors' Journal* 578.

[40] Rule 32.4(1).   [41] Rule 32.4(2).   [42] Rule 32.5(1). On hearsay evidence see Ch 9.

[43] Rule 32.5(2).   [44] Rule 32.5(3).   [45] Rule 32.5(4).

[46] *In re Enoch and Zaretzky, Bock & Co* [1910] 1 KB 327, 333. See also *Briscoe v Briscoe* [1968] P 501, 505.

[47] *Briscoe v Briscoe* [1968] P 501, 505.

[48] See generally *R v Russell-Jones* [1995] 1 Cr App R 538; *R v Brown* [1997] 1 Cr App R 112. See also *R v Gunden* [1997] Crim LR 903.

whose statements have been served upon the defence as part of the prosecution case and whose evidence would not be admissible by way of an exception to the hearsay rule.[49] These witnesses should then be called to testify (or at least called and tendered for cross-examination[50]), unless it is considered that the witness's evidence would be unworthy of belief. This would be the case if the evidence is inconsistent with, or contrary to, the prosecution case. The prosecution should not refrain from calling a witness merely because his or her evidence would not fit in exactly with the case that the prosecution is seeking to prove.[51] In the *Crown Court Study*, the judges stated that they were aware in 19 per cent of cases of at least one important witness who was not called by either the prosecution or the defence.[52]

Unlike the position in civil trials, the judge in a criminal trial does have a limited power to call witnesses in the interests of justice. The Court of Appeal has stated:

> It is well established that the judge in a criminal trial has power to call a witness. It is, however, a power which should be used most sparingly and rarely exercised . . . Where the power is exercised, it should be for achieving the ends of justice and fairness.[53]

Similar principles apply in summary trials.[54]

As in civil trials, the order in which witnesses are to be called in a criminal trial is generally a matter within the discretion of the parties. Where the defendant testifies, however, he or she is to be called before the other defence witnesses, unless the court in its discretion directs otherwise.[55]

1.3.2 Questioning Witnesses

The power of a judge to question witnesses is heavily circumscribed. The particular importance of ensuring that the judge in a criminal trial is not seen by the jury to be 'descending into the arena' was emphasized by the Court of Appeal in a passage worth quoting in full:

> The judge is not an advocate. Under the English and Welsh system of criminal trials he is much more like the umpire at a cricket match. He is certainly not the bowler, whose business it is to get the batsman out. If a judge, without any conscious intention to be unfair, descends into the forum and asks great numbers of pointed questions of the accused when he is giving his evidence in-chief, the jury may very well get the impression that the judge does not believe a word that the witness is saying and by putting these pointed questions, to which there is sometimes

---

[49] See the discussion of the hearsay rule in Ch 9.

[50] This process involves the witness being called and asked no substantive questions by the prosecution, but instead 'tendered' for cross-examination by the defence. This option may be taken if it is felt, for example, that the witness's evidence would not add much to the prosecution case.

[51] See generally A Samuels, 'The Prosecution Refuse to Call the Witness', *Archbold News*, 11 Mar 1999, 7.

[52] M Zander and P Henderson, *The Royal Commission on Criminal Justice: Crown Court Study* (1993) 110–11.

[53] *R v Grafton* [1993] QB 101, 107. See also *R v Tregear* [1967] 2 QB 574; *R v Roberts* (1985) 80 Cr App R 89 (decision of 1984).   [54] *R v Haringey JJ, ex p DPP* [1996] 2 WLR 114.

[55] Police and Criminal Evidence Act 1984, s 79.

only a lame answer, blows the evidence out of the water during the stage that counsel ought to be having the opportunity to bring the evidence of the accused to the attention of the jury in its most impressive pattern and shape. The importance of counsel having that opportunity is not diminished—indeed it is enhanced—if the evidence emerging in-chief is a story that takes a bit of swallowing. If the judge, when the witness is skating over thin ice, asks pointed questions so that the ice seems to crack, the jury may well get the impression, however perfectly the judge may later sum up the case, that the judge has seen through the evidence in-chief so that the jury do not take it very seriously either.[56]

In *R v Frixou*,[57] the defendant was asked 189 questions in examination-in-chief, of which 106 were asked by the Recorder. A substantial number of the Recorder's questions were in the form of cross-examination and appeared hostile. The defendant appealed successfully against conviction on the ground that the Recorder's frequent and apparently hostile interventions denied him a fair trial. The Court of Appeal considered that the defendant had not been treated fairly in the witness box and had been effectively deprived of the opportunity to put his whole case before the jury in an ordered and structured form prior to that case being tested by the rigours of cross-examination; the cross-examination by the judge during the defendant's examination-in-chief made it virtually impossible for him to appear to best advantage before the jury. Accordingly, the conviction was unsafe.

To a similar effect is *R v Roncoli*,[58] in which the appeal to the Court of Appeal was allowed on the basis that, after the defendant had been examined in chief, the trial judge effectively cross-examined him, asking hostile questions which when transcribed ran to six pages of text. In these questions, the judge set out the law and pressed the defendant on whether he still maintained that he had acted in self-defence, in terms which would be expected from prosecution counsel ('I am putting to you quite simply that the danger [said to have been presented by the victim] had gone'). The Court of Appeal considered that the impression the jury would have been left with was that the judge considered the defendant to have no defence.

The question ultimately is whether the judicial conduct has rendered the trial unfair. In *CG v UK* the European Court of Human Rights held:

The Court observes in the first place that, although the evidence of S and of the applicant herself in which the interventions occurred was doubtless the most important oral evidence given in the trial, it made up only a part of the trial proceedings which occupied three days. Further, while certain of these interventions of the trial judge were found by the Court of Appeal to be without justification, others were found to be justified. While the Court accepts the assessment of the Court of Appeal that the applicant's counsel found himself incommoded and disconcerted by these interruptions, it also agrees with the Court of Appeal, from its own examination of the transcript of the evidence, that the applicant's counsel was never prevented from continuing with the line of defence that he was attempting to develop either in cross-examination or through his own witness. In addition, the Court attaches importance to the fact that the

---

[56] *R v Gunning* (1994) 98 Cr App R 303, 306 (decision of 1980).   [57] [1998] Crim LR 352.
[58] [1998] Crim LR 584.

applicant's counsel was able to address the jury in a final speech which lasted for 45 minutes without interruption, apart from a brief intervention which was found to be justified, and that the substance of the applicant's defence was reiterated in the trial judge's summing-up, albeit in a very abbreviated form.[59]

In these circumstances, the Court does not find that the judicial interventions in the present case, although excessive and undesirable, rendered the trial proceedings as a whole unfair.[60]

2 The Course of the Trial

In a trial, the case for the prosecution (in a criminal trial) or claimant (in a civil trial) is presented first. Thus, the claimant or prosecution calls its witnesses and questions them. This process of questioning one's own witnesses is known as *examination-in-chief*. After a particular witness has been examined in chief, he or she may then be questioned by any of the other parties in the case. This process of questioning witnesses called by another party is known as *cross-examination*. After cross-examination, the witness may be subjected to a *re-examination* by the party calling him or her. Questioning in re-examination is generally limited to matters arising from the evidence given by the witness in cross-examination.[61]

After all the witnesses for the claimant/prosecution have been called, the case for the claimant/prosecution is closed, and the defence then presents its case by calling its own witnesses. In the same way, each witness is examined in chief, and may then be cross-examined and re-examined. After the defence case is closed, closing speeches are made by counsel for all the parties in the case, and, in a criminal trial on indictment, the trial judge then sums up the case to the jury. In the course of the summing-up, the jury may have to be instructed about a number of the evidential issues which have arisen in the case. As seen in the course of this book, alleged misdirections to the jury on such issues constitute a frequent ground of appeal.

2.1 Submissions of 'No Case to Answer'

In a criminal trial, after the closure of the case for the prosecution and before the defence has started to call its witnesses, a submission of no case to answer[62] may be made by the defence. If this submission is successful, the case will be dismissed and an acquittal directed. In considering a no-case submission in a trial on indictment, it must be borne in mind that, paradoxically, a holding that there is no case to answer may constitute a usurpation of the role of the jury and, at the same time, protection of the accused from the danger of an unjust conviction. The relevant principles to be applied

---

[59] (2002) 34 EHRR 31 (p 789) (judgment of 2001), [41].   [60] Ibid, [42].

[61] *Prince v Samo* (1838) 7 Ad & E 627, 112 ER 606.

[62] See generally R Pattenden, 'The Submission of No Case—Some Recent Developments' [1982] *Criminal Law Review* 558.

in considering a no-case submission were clarified by the Court of Appeal in *R v Galbraith*:

> How then should the judge approach a submission of 'no case'? (1) If there is no evidence that the crime alleged has been committed by the defendant, there is no difficulty. The judge will of course stop the case. (2) The difficulty arises where there is some evidence but it is of a tenuous character, for example because of inherent weakness or vagueness or because it is inconsistent with other evidence. (a) Where the judge comes to the conclusion that the prosecution evidence, taken at its highest, is such that a jury properly directed could not properly convict upon it, it is his duty, upon a submission being made, to stop the case. (b) Where however the prosecution evidence is such that its strength or weakness depends on the view to be taken of a witness's reliability, or other matters which are generally speaking within the province of the jury and where on one possible view of the facts there *is* evidence upon which a jury could properly come to the conclusion that the defendant is guilty, then the judge should allow the matter to be tried by the jury.[63]

It is to be noted that the *Crown Court Study* found that submissions of no case to answer were made in just under one-third of cases, and that 27 per cent of these submissions were successful.[64] The fact that the judicial power to withdraw cases needs to be exercised in a small but significant minority of cases raises questions about the extent to which the Crown Prosecution Service may be failing, in the exercise of its prosecutorial discretion, to weed out cases unworthy of prosecution.[65]

The importance of the existence of such a judicial controlling power is well illustrated by the decision of the Court of Appeal in *R v McKenzie*[66] on confession evidence, examined in Chapter 2. It is arguable, however, that the test in *Galbraith* is insufficiently wide. There is no reason why it should be impermissible for a trial judge to withdraw a case from the jury in circumstances where, if the defendant were to be convicted and were to appeal, the Court of Appeal would be bound to quash the conviction.[67] Thus the Runciman Royal Commission 'recommend[ed] that the Court of Appeal's decision in *Galbraith* be reversed so that a judge may stop any case if he or she takes the view that the prosecution evidence is demonstrably unsafe or unsatisfactory or too weak to be allowed to go to the jury'.[68]

It would appear that a trial judge has a responsibility to consider whether there is evidence on which the jury can safely convict even in the absence of a no-case submission.

---

[63] [1981] 1 WLR 1039, 1042 (italics in original). Clearly, a no-case submission should be heard in the absence of the jury, although there may well be exceptional circumstances in which it would be appropriate to accede to a defence request that it be heard in the jury's presence. If the judge rules in favour of a no-case submission on some charges but not on others, or rules in favour of the submission in respect of some defendants but not others, the jury need simply be told that the decision was taken for legal reasons. See generally *Crosdale v R* [1995] 1 WLR 864.

[64] M Zander and P Henderson, *The Royal Commission on Criminal Justice: Crown Court Study* (1993) 124–5.

[65] See P E Lewis, 'The CPS and Acquittals by Judge: Finding the Balance' [1997] *Criminal Law Review* 653.

[66] [1993] 1 WLR 453.

[67] See generally A A S Zuckerman, *The Principles of Criminal Evidence* (1989) 56–8.

[68] Royal Commission on Criminal Justice, *Report* (Cm 2263) (1993) 59. This is also advocated by A Ashworth and M Redmayne, *The Criminal Process* (3rd ed 2005) 314. Cf J D Jackson and S Doran, 'Judge and Jury: Towards a New Division of Labour in Criminal Trials' (1997) 60 *Modern Law Review* 759, 768–9.

Thus, if at the conclusion of all the evidence in the case the judge is of the view that no reasonable jury properly directed can safely convict, he or she should generally raise that view for discussion with counsel in the jury's absence, whether or not a no-case submission was made at the conclusion of the prosecution case. If, having heard submissions, the judge remains of that view, then the case should be withdrawn from the jury.[69]

The Court of Appeal would appear to take the view that the erroneous rejection of a submission of no case to answer should lead to a conviction being quashed irrespective of what transpired during the remainder of the trial:

> What if a submission is wrongly rejected but the defendant is cross-examined into admitting his guilt? Should the conviction be said to be unsafe? We think it should. The defendant was entitled to be acquitted after the evidence against him had been heard. To allow the trial to continue beyond the end of the prosecution case would be an abuse of process and fundamentally unfair.[70]

In civil trials without a jury, the position would appear to be different. The view is taken that, because a judge acts as both trier of law and trier of fact, it would be inappropriate for him or her to express an opinion about the evidence unless *all* the evidence in the case has been called. Thus:

> The disadvantages of entertaining a submission of no case to answer are plain and obvious . . . Essentially they are twofold. First, . . . the submission interrupts the trial process and requires the judge to make up his mind as to the facts on the basis of one side's evidence only and applying the lower test of a *prima facie* case with the result that, if he rejects the submission, he must then make up his mind afresh in the light of whatever further evidence has been called and on the application of a different test. This, to say the least, is not a very satisfactory procedure. The second disadvantage . . . is that if the judge both entertains and accedes to a submission of no case, his judgment may be reversed on appeal with all the expense and inconvenience resulting from the need to resume the hearing or, more probably, retry the action.[71]

'Rarely, if ever', therefore, 'should a judge trying a civil action without a jury entertain a submission of no case to answer.'[72]

2.2 Adducing Evidence after Closure of Case

The claimant or prosecution may wish, after closing its case, to adduce further evidence because of the emergence of defence evidence which contradicts its case. There is a discretion to permit the claimant/prosecution to adduce further evidence in such a manner.[73]

---

[69] *R v Brown, The Times*, 13 Dec 1997.

[70] *R v Smith* [1999] 2 Cr App R 238, 242. See generally V Tunkel, 'When Safe Convictions Are Unsafely Quashed' (1999) 149 *New Law Journal* 1089.

[71] *Benham Ltd v Kythira Investments Ltd* [2003] EWCA Civ 1794, [2004] CP Rep 17, [31]. See generally I R Scott, 'Submission of No Case to Answer' (2004) 23 *Civil Justice Quarterly* 96.

[72] *Benham Ltd v Kythira Investments Ltd* [2003] EWCA Civ 1794, [2004] CP Rep 17, [32]. See also *Alexander v Rayson* [1936] 1 KB 169, 178; *Laurie v Raglan Building Co* [1942] 1 KB 152; *Young v Rank* [1950] 2 KB 510. On the position in tribunals see *Logan v Commissioners of Customs & Excise* [2003] EWCA Civ 1068, [2004] ICR 1.

[73] *R v Frost* (1839) 9 Car & P 129, 159, 173 ER 771, 784; *R v Scott* (1984) 79 Cr App R 49, 51–2 (decision of 1984); *R v Hutchinson* (1986) 82 Cr App R 51, 58–9 (decision of 1985).

This may be permitted if the claimant/prosecution could not, before closing its case, have reasonably anticipated or foreseen the need to call that evidence. In determining the issue, a court should take into account any pre-trial notice which the claimant/prosecution may have received of defence evidence likely to be given which would call for denial beforehand by way of adduction of evidence by the claimant/prosecution. Equally, account should also be taken of the extent to which the claimant/prosecution may have been put 'on notice' of the need to call the evidence by the nature of the cross-examination of its witnesses. Because the test is one of *reasonable* anticipation, however, it is unnecessary for the claimant/prosecution 'to take notice of fanciful and unreal statements no matter from what source they emanate'.[74] Presumably, the imposition by the Criminal Procedure and Investigations Act 1996 of a general obligation on the defence to disclose its case prior to trial will have reduced the scope for the exercise of the discretion to permit the prosecution to adduce further evidence after closing its case.

3 Questioning one's own Witnesses: Examination-in-Chief and Re-Examination

To be examined now are the principles which govern the questioning of one's own witnesses, whether in the course of examination-in-chief or re-examination.

3.1 No Leading Questions

Generally speaking, it is impermissible to ask leading questions when examining one's own witness.[75] A leading question is one which directly or indirectly suggests to the witness the answer to be given. A question is not a leading question merely because it is susceptible of a 'yes' or 'no' answer. There are a number of exceptions to the rule against leading questions, the more important of which are as follows. First, it is permissible, and indeed probably desirable, to lead one's own witness in relation to introductory and uncontentious matters such as the witness's name and address. Secondly, as will be seen below, leading questions may be put to one's own witness if he or she has been declared 'hostile'. Thirdly, leading questions may be put to a witness to draw his or her attention to something which, or someone whom, he or she is being asked to identify. Fourthly, the witness may be led if his or her inability to answer questions put in the usual way arises from the complicated nature of the subject matter. Fifthly, where the witness has apparently forgotten something, and all other attempts to jog his or her

---

[74] *R v Hutchinson* (1986) 82 Cr App R 51, 59 (decision of 1985).
[75] See generally *Maves v Grand Trunk Pacific R Co* (1913) 14 DLR 70, which contains a detailed treatment of the issue, on which this section is based.

memory have failed, a leading question may be put. The procedure to be followed in such a situation has been described thus:

> A case which not infrequently arises in practice is that of a witness who recounts a conversation and in doing so omits one or more statements which counsel examining him is instructed formed part of it. The common and proper practice is to ask the witness to repeat the conversation from the beginning. It is often found that in his repetition he gives the lacking statement—possibly omitting one given the first time. This method may be tried more than once, and as a matter of expediency—so as to have the advantage of getting the whole story on the witness' own unaided recollection—counsel might pass on to some other subject and later revert to the conversation, asking him to again state it. But when this method fails, the trial Judge undoubtedly ought to permit a question containing a reference to the subject-matter of the statement which it is supposed has been omitted by the witness. If this method fails, then and not till then—that is when his memory appears to be entirely exhausted, the trial Judge should allow a question to be put to him containing the supposedly omitted matter.[76]

It is said that, if leading questions were permitted on matters of substance, a questioner would be tempted to question in such a manner as to elicit only such information as would be favourable to his or her own side. In particular, witnesses who are suggestible or inexperienced could be easily led into providing the testimony which the questioner wishes to elicit.

It would seem that evidence elicited by means of an improper leading question is not inadmissible per se, but will carry little or no weight.[77]

3.2 No 'Oath-Helping'

As a general rule, it is impermissible for a party to lead evidence for the sole purpose of bolstering the creditworthiness of its own witness.[78] The adduction of such evidence may be permitted, however, if there has been a challenge to the creditworthiness of the witness by the opposing party. As will be seen later, this may occur where the other party introduces evidence of the witness's general reputation for lack of veracity.

3.3 Hostile Witnesses

An *unfavourable witness* is one who fails to 'come up to proof' or who gives evidence which is unfavourable to the case of the party calling him or her. Where this has occurred, the party calling the witness may not call evidence specifically to discredit the witness, but may call evidence which is inconsistent with or which contradicts the evidence given by this witness.[79] The Uniform Evidence Acts in Australia go further by

---

[76] *Maves v Grand Trunk Pacific R Co* (1913) 14 DLR 70, 77.   [77] *Moor v Moor* [1954] 1 WLR 927, 928.

[78] *R v Hamilton, The Times,* 25 July 1998.

[79] *Ewer v Ambrose* (1825) 3 B & C 746, 750, 107 ER 910, 911–12.

permitting the party calling an unfavourable witness to cross-examine that witness with the leave of the court.[80]

A *hostile witness*,[81] on the other hand, is one who shows no desire to tell the truth. The question of whether a witness is hostile is a question of law. Hostility:

> may be demonstrated by the witness's manner and demeanour alone. Thus a witness who declines to answer questions at all, or repeatedly says 'I can't remember' . . . may be treated as hostile . . . On the other hand, the hostility may be demonstrated by inconsistency between the witness's evidence and a prior statement . . . The inconsistency need not take the form of a flat contradiction.[82]

Such factors as the witness's demeanour or the fact that the evidence being given by the witness is inconsistent with an earlier statement made out of court by the witness, considered in isolation or even together, do not, however, *automatically* signify hostility.[83] For example, the witness may be able to provide a legitimate explanation for the inconsistency.

Once a witness has been declared hostile, the party calling the witness has a common law right to cross-examine that witness,[84] in accordance with the rules of cross-examination to be examined below.[85] In addition, section 3 of the Criminal Procedure Act 1865 ('Lord Denman's Act'), which applies to both criminal and civil proceedings, provides:

> A party producing a witness shall not be allowed to impeach his credit by general evidence of bad character; but he may, in case the witness shall in the opinion of the judge prove adverse, *contradict him by other evidence*, or, *by leave of the judge, prove that he has made at other times a statement inconsistent with his present testimony*; but before such last-mentioned proof can be given the circumstances of the supposed statement, sufficient to designate the particular occasion, must be mentioned to the witness, and he must be asked whether or not he has made such statement.[86]

'Adverse' in section 3 'means "hostile" rather than merely "unfavourable" '.[87] Thus, section 3 permits the party calling the hostile witness to contradict that witness by other evidence—a strategy which, we have seen, is also available in relation to unfavourable witnesses. More importantly, section 3 also permits the party, with the leave of the judge, to prove to the trier of fact that a previous inconsistent statement[88] was made. The circumstances of the supposed statement must first be put carefully[89] to the witness in

---

[80] S 38(1)(a). See generally T H Smith and O P Holdenson, 'Comparative Evidence: The Unhelpful Witness' (1998) 72 *Australian Law Journal* 720.

[81] See generally M Newark, 'The Hostile Witness and the Adversary System' [1986] *Criminal Law Review* 441; R Pattenden, 'The Hostile Witness' (1992) 56 *Journal of Criminal Law* 414.

[82] *R v Jobe* [2004] EWCA Crim 3155, [66].   [83] *R v Maw* [1994] Crim LR 841.

[84] *R v Thompson* (1977) 64 Cr App R 96, 99 (decision of 1976).

[85] As will be seen, one of the features of cross-examination is that leading questions may be asked of the witness.   [86] Italics added.

[87] *R v Jobe* [2004] EWCA Crim 3155, [66]. See also *Greenough v Eccles* (1859) 5 CB (NS) 786, 141 ER 315, discussing the forerunner to s 3.

[88] See generally A Samuels, 'Inconsistent Statements' (2004) 168 *Justice of the Peace* 873.

[89] *R v Dat* [1998] Crim LR 488.

cross-examination, and the witness asked whether he or she made such a statement. If the witness admits to having done so, and adopts the contents of the whole or part of the previous statement, then whatever is adopted will effectively become part of the witness's in-court testimony.[90] If, however, the witness denies having made the statement, then the making of the statement may be proved to the trier of fact under section 3.

The general effect of section 119 of the Criminal Justice Act 2003 is that all such previous inconsistent statements may now not only be used for the purposes of 'discrediting' the witness, but also become evidence of any matters stated in them. In civil proceedings, the Civil Evidence Act 1995 permits such statements to be admitted as evidence of the facts contained in them, so long as the requirements of the Act (discussed in Chapter 9) are satisfied.

3.4 Refreshing Memory in Criminal Cases

3.4.1 In Court

At common law it was permissible for a witness to refresh his or her memory, while giving evidence in court, by referring to a document either made or verified by him- or herself 'contemporaneously', that is at the same time as or soon after the events described. The most significant application of the rule related to police officers' notebooks. The rule was criticized for excluding other similarly reliable sources which failed the test of contemporaneity because witnesses in general, unlike police officers, are not trained to note down the details of significant events at the earliest opportunity. The common law rule is now reformed and replaced by section 139 of the Criminal Justice Act 2003.[91] Section 139 provides:

(1) A person giving oral evidence in criminal proceedings about any matter may, at any stage in the course of doing so, refresh his memory of it from a document made or verified by him at an earlier time if—

   (a) he states in his oral evidence that the document records his recollection of the matter at that earlier time, and

   (b) his recollection of the matter is likely to have been significantly better at that time than it is at the time of his oral evidence.

(2) Where—

   (a) a person giving oral evidence in criminal proceedings about any matter has previously given an oral account, of which a sound recording was made, and he states in that evidence that the account represented his recollection of the matter at that time,

   (b) his recollection of the matter is likely to have been significantly better at the time of the previous account than it is at the time of his oral evidence, and

---

[90] *R v Maw* [1994] Crim LR 841.
[91] See generally R Taylor, M Wasik, and R Leng, *Blackstone's Guide to the Criminal Justice Act 2003* (2004) 167–70.

(c) a transcript has been made of the sound recording,

he may, at any stage in the course of giving his evidence, refresh his memory of the matter from that transcript.

This represents a substantial loosening of the (admittedly liberally interpreted[92]) common law position, as it no longer requires the making or verification of the document to have been *contemporaneous* with the occurrence of the relevant matter.

3.4.2 Status of the Memory-Refreshing Document

There are a number of situations in which a memory-refreshing document may become evidence in the case and therefore an exhibit. The more important of these are the following.

• Where a witness has 'refreshed memory' from a document, the opposing party may ask to inspect the document and may cross-examine the witness on the document. The judge may let the jury have copies of the document if this would assist them in following the cross-examination.[93] If in the course of cross-examining on the memory-refreshing document, the cross-examiner confines him- or herself to the parts of the document which the witness has used to refresh memory, then the party calling the witness cannot require the document to be treated as evidence in the case. If, however, the cross-examiner strays into parts of the document which the witness has not used to refresh memory, this entitles the party calling the witness to insist that these parts of the document be treated as evidence in the case.[94] In criminal cases such evidence would now, by virtue of section 120(3) of the Criminal Justice Act 2003,[95] not only go to the creditworthiness of the witness (to demonstrate consistency) but also be admissible to establish the truth of those parts of the document. It would be admissible for this purpose in civil cases, provided that the relevant requirements of the Civil Evidence Act 1995 (examined in Chapter 9) are satisfied. Of course, even though parts of a memory-refreshing document may become liable to be treated as evidence as a result of cross-examination by the opposing party, the judge retains a discretion not to allow the document to go before the jury if this could result in prejudice to the defendant.[96]

• A record in a memory-refreshing document may also be treated as evidence in the case if the cross-examining party adduces this in evidence to discredit the witness by demonstrating its inconsistency with the witness's testimony.[97]

• Where an allegation is made that a record in a document which a witness has used to refresh memory was concocted, the party calling the witness is entitled to put the

---

[92] *R v Gordon* [2002] EWCA Crim 01.   [93] *R v Sekhon* (1987) 85 Cr App R 19, 22–3 (decision of 1986).

[94] *R v Britton* [1987] 1 WLR 539, 541–2. See also *Gregory v Tavernor* (1833) 6 Car & P 280, 281, 172 ER 1241, 1242; *Senat v Senat* [1965] P 172, 177.   [95] See Ch 9 and section 3.5 below.

[96] See *R v Virgo* (1978) 67 Cr App R 323 (decision of 1978).

[97] *R v Sekhon* (1987) 85 Cr App R 19, 23 (decision of 1986).

record in evidence, in order to rebut the allegation by establishing the record's genuineness through demonstrating that it appears to be a contemporaneous record which has not been altered subsequently.[98]

3.4.3 Out of Court

The courts take a very permissive attitude to the practice of allowing witnesses to refresh memory out of court.[99] It is reasoned that if this were to be forbidden, the experience of testifying would, especially if there has been a long time lapse between the alleged offence and the trial, become more a test of memory than one of truthfulness, and difficulties would be placed in the way of honest witnesses.[100] In any event, a ban on refreshing memory out of court is considered to be one which would be impossible for the courts to enforce. The Court of Appeal has noted that:

> obviously it would be wrong if several witnesses were handed statements in circumstances which enabled one to compare with another what each had said. But there can be no general rule . . . that witnesses may not before trial see the statements which they made at some period reasonably close to the time of the event which is the subject of the trial. Indeed, one can imagine many cases, particularly those of a complex nature, where such a rule would militate very greatly against the interests of justice.[101]

The fact that a witness has refreshed memory out of court is relevant, however, to the weight to be accorded to that witness's testimony. Thus:

> if the prosecution is aware that statements have been seen by witnesses it will be appropriate to inform the defence. But if, for any reason, this is not done, the omission cannot of itself be a ground for acquittal. . . . If the mere fact that the prosecution had not volunteered the information were a bar to conviction, this would be an artificial and arbitrary rule more appropriate to a game or a sporting contest than to a judicial process. The question for the court is whether, in the event, the trial can be continued without prejudice or risk of injustice to the defendant.[102]

While the willingness of the courts to permit refreshing memory out of court is understandable and, indeed, to be applauded, there is a danger that practice in the area may become too unregulated. Perhaps the introduction of a Code of Practice governing practices and procedures in the area may be a desirable way forward.

[98] *R v Sekhon* (1987) 85 Cr App R 19, 22.

[99] See *Lau Pak Ngam v R* [1966] Crim LR 443; *R v Richardson* [1971] 2 QB 484; *R v Westwell* [1976] 2 All ER 812. See generally M N Howard, 'Refreshment of Memory out of Court' [1972] *Criminal Law Review* 351.

[100] The Court of Appeal has noted (*R v Westwell* [1976] 2 All ER 812, 814): 'We have all, from time to time, seen the plight of an apparently honest witness, subjected to captious questioning about minor differences between his evidence in the witness box and the statement he made long ago and has never seen since, although his tormentor has it in his hand and has studied it in detail. Although such cross-examination frequently generates in the jury obvious sympathy with the witness and obvious irritation with the cross-examiner, it must leave a witness who has come to court to do his honest best with a smarting sense of having been treated unfairly.'   [101] *R v Richardson* [1971] 2 QB 484, 490.

[102] *R v Westwell* [1976] 2 All ER 812, 814–15.

3.5 Evidence of Previous Consistent Statements in Criminal Trials

The rule against previous consistent statements[103] (also known as the rule against narrative or the rule against self-corroboration) renders out-of-court statements by a witness which are consistent with his or her present testimony in court inadmissible in evidence.[104] It is said that, were this not the case, potential witnesses would be tempted to prepare to boost their creditworthiness at trial by mentioning relevant facts to as many people as possible prior to trial.[105] A number of exceptions to the rule against previous consistent statements are, however, recognized in criminal trials. First, there are a number of situations in which a previous consistent statement will be admissible as evidence of consistency and hence credit, and also admissible, by virtue of section 120 of the Criminal Justice Act 2003, as evidence of the truth of its contents. These situations are as follows:

• The 'previous statement by the witness is admitted as evidence to rebut a suggestion that his oral evidence has been fabricated'.[106]

• The statement is one 'made by the witness in a document—(a) which is used by him to refresh his memory while giving evidence, (b) on which he is cross-examined, and (c) which as a consequence is received in evidence in the proceedings'.[107]

• 'The statement identifies or describes a person, object or place',[108] and 'while giving evidence the witness indicates that to the best of his belief he made the statement, and that to the best of his belief it states the truth'.[109]

• 'The statement was made by the witness when the matters stated were fresh in his memory but he does not remember them, and cannot reasonably be expected to remember them, well enough to give oral evidence of them in the proceedings';[110] and 'while giving evidence the witness indicates that to the best of his belief he made the statement, and that to the best of his belief it states the truth'.[111]

• 'The statement consists of a complaint made by the witness (whether to a person in authority or not) about conduct which would, if proved, constitute the offence or part of the offence',[112] 'the complaint was made as soon as could reasonably be expected after the alleged conduct',[113] 'the complaint was not made as a result of a threat or a promise',[114] 'before the statement is adduced the witness gives oral evidence in connection with its subject matter',[115] and 'while giving evidence the witness indicates that to

---

[103] See generally R N Gooderson, 'Previous Consistent Statements' [1968] *Cambridge Law Journal* 64.

[104] *R v Roberts* [1942] 1 All ER 187; *R v P (G R)* [1998] Crim LR 663.

[105] See also *Fox v GMC* [1960] 1 WLR 1017, 1024–5: 'All trials, civil and criminal, must be conducted with an effort to concentrate evidence upon what is capable of being cogent and ... it does not help to support the evidence of a witness, who is the accused person, to know that he has frequently told other persons before the trial what his defence was. Evidence to that effect is therefore in a proper sense immaterial.'   [106] S 120(2).

[107] S 120(3).   [108] S 120(5).   [109] S 120(4)(b).   [110] S 120(6).   [111] S 120(4)(b).

[112] S 120(7)(c).   [113] S 120(7)(d).   [114] S 120(7)(e).   [115] S 120(7)(f).

the best of his belief he made the statement, and that to the best of his belief it states the truth'.[116]

There is a further situation in which a previous consistent statement will be admissible as evidence of both consistency and the truth of its contents, that is, when it was made at about the same time that the event occurred.

3.5.1 Statements Admissible as Part of the *Res Gestae*

A previous consistent statement of a witness is admissible in evidence of the witness's consistency if it was made contemporaneously, or roughly contemporaneously, with a relevant event.[117] Such a statement is said to be admissible as part of the *res gestae*. It would also be admissible as evidence of the truth of its contents, since, as seen in Chapter 9, statements forming part of the *res gestae* are admissible in evidence as an exception to the hearsay rule.

Finally, there are two situations in which a previous consistent statement will be admissible as evidence of consistency, but not necessarily as evidence of the truth of its contents, that is, when the statement is made on accusation or on discovery of incriminating articles.

3.5.2 Statements Made on Accusation

A purely inculpatory statement, or a partly inculpatory and partly exculpatory statement, made by a suspect in response to an accusation may be admissible in evidence, under the confession exception to the hearsay rule, for the truth of its facts.[118] Where the statement is purely exculpatory, however, it may be admissible, as an exception to the rule against previous consistent statements, to prove consistency and hence support the witness's creditworthiness. The statement need not have been made on the witness's first encounter with the police, but the longer the time lapse between the first encounter and the making of the statement, the less weight it carries, and the jury may be directed accordingly. A 'carefully prepared written statement to the police' would be inadmissible in evidence.[119]

It would appear that a statement made on accusation will be inadmissible in evidence if the accused's reaction has already been adequately proved by other evidence.[120]

A statement made on accusation that is admissible as evidence of consistency will also be admissible as evidence of the truth of its contents if the 'interests of justice' test in section 114(1)(d) of the Criminal Justice Act 2003[121] is satisfied.

---

[116] S 120(4)(b). For a comparative perspective on the admission of evidence of such complaints, see T H Smith and O P Holdenson, 'Comparative Evidence: Admission of Evidence of Recent Complaint in Sexual Offence Prosecutions—Part I' (2001) 75 *Australian Law Journal* 623; T H Smith and O P Holdenson, 'Comparative Evidence: Admission of Evidence of Recent Complaint in Sexual Offence Prosecutions—Part II' (2001) 75 *Australian Law Journal* 694.   [117] *R v Fowkes, The Times,* 8 March 1856.

[118] See Ch 2.

[119] *R v Pearce* (1979) 69 Cr App R 365, 369–70 (decision of 1979). See also *R v Storey* (1968) 52 Cr App R 334 (decision of 1968); *R v Donaldson* (1977) 64 Cr App R 59 (decision of 1976).

[120] *R v Tooke* (1990) 90 Cr App R 417 (decision of 1989).   [121] See Ch 9.

3.5.3 Statements Made on Discovery of Incriminating Articles

Exculpatory statements made by an accused when incriminating articles were found in his or her possession would be admissible in evidence, if the accused testifies to the same effect at trial, of his or her consistency. They would also be admissible as evidence of the truth of their contents if the 'interests of justice' test in section 114(1)(d) of the Criminal Justice Act 2003[122] is satisfied. In *R v Abraham*,[123] it was argued at trial that some glass jars which were found unconcealed in the defendant's house, and which had been taken from a shop, had been found by the defendant in a field. It was held that evidence was admissible that the defendant had said to his neighbours, before suspicion existed or a search for the property had been made, that the property had been found in a field.

3.6 Evidence of Previous Consistent Statements in Civil Trials

The position with respect to evidence of previous consistent statements in civil trials is governed by the Civil Evidence Act 1995. Section 6(2) provides that such statements are admissible in evidence either with the leave of the court or for the purpose of rebutting an allegation of fabrication. Because the Civil Evidence Act 1995 has effectively abolished the hearsay rule in civil proceedings, such statements will be admissible in evidence for their truth,[124] subject to the relevant provisions of the Act, discussed in Chapter 9, being satisfied.

4. Cross-Examination

4.1 The Purposes of Cross-Examination

Cross-examination, described by Wigmore as 'beyond any doubt the greatest legal engine ever invented for the discovery of truth',[125] is said to constitute a powerful weapon in exposing the possible unreliability of that witness's testimony. The purpose of cross-examination is twofold: first, to elicit evidence supporting the cross-examining party's version of the facts, and, secondly, to discredit the evidence of the witness. Evidence which is otherwise inadmissible does not become admissible by being put to a witness in cross-examination.[126]

The two essential restrictions which apply to examination-in-chief do not apply to cross-examination. In *Parkin v Moon*, Alderson B observed: 'I apprehend you may put

---

[122] See Ch 9.   [123] (1848) 3 Cox CC 430.   [124] See s 6(1).

[125] J H Wigmore (rev J H Chadbourn), *Evidence in Trials at Common Law (Vol 5)* (1974) 32.

[126] In *R v Gray*, *The Times*, 9 March 1998, the Court of Appeal held that it was not appropriate to ask a defendant in cross-examination to explain statements made against him by a co-defendant in a document which, although admissible in evidence against the co-defendant, was inadmissible in evidence against him. Any practice of conducting such cross-examination should not be continued.

a leading question to an unwilling witness on the examination in chief at the discretion of the Judge; but you may *always* put a leading question in cross-examination, whether a witness be unwilling or not.'[127] Secondly, questions may be asked in cross-examination which go solely to the creditworthiness of the witness.

Contrary to popular belief, the utility of cross-examination in ensuring the reliability of evidence may be limited. Cross-examination may well be of little use in exposing a witness's insincerity;[128] 'it is, in truth, quite doubtful whether it is not the honest but weak or timid witness, rather than the rogue, who most often goes down under the fire of a cross-examination'.[129] It is also possible that the efficacy of cross-examination in exposing the faulty perception by a witness of the events supposedly 'witnessed' may not be as high as may be assumed.[130] Additionally, suggesting facts to a witness in cross-examination may actually distort, rather than assist, his or her memory.[131]

Where it is not possible to complete, or even commence, the cross-examination of a witness who has been examined in-chief, the trial judge would appear to have a discretion to prevent the trial from proceeding altogether. In considering the issue, all relevant factors would need to be considered. Thus, where there has in fact been substantial cross-examination of the witness, and the evidence of the witness is strongly supported, then it may be appropriate to let the trial proceed, especially if the jury is warned against placing undue weight on the witness's evidence.[132] On the other hand, even a strong warning may not suffice if there has been no cross-examination at all, and the witness's evidence is unsupported.[133]

4.2 Limitations on Cross-Examination

The right to cross-examine is, naturally, subject to some limitations. As has been noted in the House of Lords:

> It is right to make due allowance for the irritation caused by the strain and stress of a long and complicated case, but a protracted and irrelevant cross-examination not only adds to the cost of litigation, but is a waste of public time. Such a cross-examination becomes indefensible when

---

[127] (1836) 7 Car & P 408, 409, 173 ER 181, 181–2 (italics added).

[128] T Finman, 'Implied Assertions as Hearsay: Some Criticisms of the Uniform Rules of Evidence' (1962) 14 *Stanford Law Review* 682, 690; R C Park, 'A Subject Matter Approach to Hearsay Reform' (1987) 86 *Michigan Law Review* 51, 96; E Swift, 'A Foundation Fact Approach to Hearsay' (1987) 75 *California Law Review* 1339, 1357 n 50. See also J Allan, 'The Working and Rationale of the Hearsay Rule and the Implications of Modern Psychological Knowledge' (1991) 44 *Current Legal Problems* 217.

[129] J W Strong (ed), *McCormick on Evidence* (4th ed 1992) 41.

[130] E A Scallen, 'Constitutional Dimensions of Hearsay Reform: Toward a Three-Dimensional Confrontation Clause' (1992) 76 *Minnesota Law Review* 623, 627 n 15.

[131] Australian Law Reform Commission, *Evidence (Vol 1)* (Report No 26: Interim) (1985) [663], available at http://www.austlii.edu.au/au/other/alrc/publications/reports/26/26_vol1.pdf; Scottish Law Commission (Scot Law Com No 149), *Evidence: Report on Hearsay Evidence in Criminal Proceedings* (1995) [3.14], available at http://www.scotlawcom.gov.uk/downloads/rep149.pdf.

[132] See *R v Stretton* (1988) 86 Cr App R 7 (decision of 1986); *R v Wyatt* [1990] Crim LR 343.

[133] See *R v Lawless* (1994) 98 Cr App R 342 (decision of 1993).

it is conducted . . . without restraint and without the courtesy and consideration which a witness is entitled to expect in a Court of law.[134]

In cross-examining a witness as to credit, what must be borne in mind is that the concern is with the witness's 'likely standing after cross-examination with the tribunal which is trying him or listening to his evidence'.[135] There is an important difference, it has been said, between eliciting material which sheds light on the background and general attitude of a witness, and eliciting material which shows the witness actually not to have told the truth.[136] Thus cross-examination as to credit should be of such a nature that the imputation conveyed by the questions would, if true, seriously affect the opinion of the trier of fact of the witness's creditworthiness. Such questions would be improper if the imputation which they convey relates to matters which are so remote in time, or of such a character, that the imputation, if true, would not affect, or would affect only slightly, the opinion of the trier of fact of the witness's creditworthiness. The questioning would also be improper if the importance of the imputation made against the witness is grossly disproportionate to the importance of his or her evidence.[137]

Where cross-examination of a complainant of a sexual offence is concerned, section 41 of the Youth Justice and Criminal Evidence Act 1999 (examined in Chapter 11), which places very substantial limitations on cross-examination as to credit (and indeed also places restrictions on cross-examination as to facts in issue), must be borne in mind.

It is considered permissible to cross-examine a defendant in a criminal trial about whether the defendant has any knowledge of why the complainant may have a motive to lie: 'The question permitted by the judge was, as it seems to us, admissible because it was relevant. If there was anything known to the defendant which provided a reason for a complainant to lie, this would tend to undermine her credibility.'[138] This is to be contrasted with the position in Australia, where the High Court of Australia has held that 'it is necessary to distinguish between cross-examination of a witness as to the motive of that witness to lie and cross-examination of another witness designed to show that that witness does not know of any fact from which to infer that the first witness had a motive to lie'.[139] Thus, in Australia, while it is permissible for the defence to cross-examine a complainant with a view to eliciting a motive to lie, it is generally impermissible for the prosecution to cross-examine the accused to establish that the accused has no knowledge of any fact from which it may be inferred that the complainant has a motive to lie. This is because the fact that the accused has no such knowledge is considered to be typically of no relevance. 'To ask an accused the question: "Why would the complainant lie?" is to invite the jury to accept the complainant's evidence unless some positive answer to that question is given by the accused.'[140]

---

[134] *Mechanical and General Inventions Co and Lehwess v Austin and the Austin Motor Co* [1935] AC 346, 360.

[135] *R v Sweet-Escott* (1971) 55 Cr App R 316, 320 (decision of 1971).

[136] *R v Ellis* [1998] Crim LR 660.　　　　[137] See *Hobbs v Tinling* [1929] 2 KB 1, 50–1.

[138] *R v B* [2003] EWCA Crim 951, [2003] 1 WLR 2809, [41]. Leave to appeal to the House of Lords was refused: [2004] 1 WLR 13.　　　　[139] *Palmer v R* [1998] HCA 2, [26].

[140] Ibid, [21].

4.3 The Rule in *Browne v Dunn*

As a general rule, a party which fails to put a particular issue to a witness in cross-examination of that witness cannot later invite the jury to reject the witness's evidence-in-chief on that issue, and to accept the cross-examining party's version of the issue.[141] The rule, known as the rule in *Browne v Dunn*,[142] has been referred to by the Privy Council in the following terms:

> Their Lordships have been referred to a number of authorities relating to the need, where the court is invited to reject the testimony of a witness, and to accept evidence to a contrary effect, to put the conflicting evidence to the witness whose testimony is attacked. *Browne v Dunn* . . . is cited as authority for [the] proposition which is stated thus in the headnote:
>
>> 'If in the course of a case it is intended to suggest that a witness is not speaking the truth upon a particular point, his attention must be directed to the fact by cross-examination showing that that imputation is intended to be made, so that he may have an opportunity of making any explanation which is open to him, unless it is otherwise perfectly clear that he has had full notice beforehand that there is an intention to impeach the credibility of his story, or (per Lord Morris) the story is of an incredible and romancing character.'
>
> The principle, is of course, of particular importance in criminal cases . . .[143]

4.4 The Collateral-Finality Rule

4.4.1 The Rule

Subject to certain exceptions, the *collateral-finality rule* provides that where cross-examination goes solely to a collateral matter (typically, the creditworthiness of a witness), the witness's answers are to be treated as final. The cross-examining party may not therefore adduce evidence to rebut these answers.[144] It is only where cross-examination goes to a fact in issue that the cross-examining party may call rebuttal evidence. Considerations of convenience and practicality underlie this rule: in the interest of keeping the length of trials within proper limits, there must obviously be some limit on the extent to which exploration of answers given to questions asked in cross-examination on collateral matters should be permitted.[145] 'If we lived for a thousand years' then unlimited exploration might be possible, but as we do not, 'some line must be drawn'.[146]

The crucial issue, therefore, is to determine whether the cross-examination goes to facts in issue, with the result that the collateral-finality rule has no application. That

---

[141] See *Browne v Dunn* (1893) 6 R 67; *R v Hart* (1932) 23 Cr App R 202; *R v Fenlon* (1980) 71 Cr App R 307 (decision of 1980); *Wharf Properties Ltd v Eric Cumine Associates* (1991) 29 Con LR 84.

[142] (1893) 6 R 67.   [143] *Wharf Properties Ltd v Eric Cumine Associates* (1991) 29 Con LR 84, 97–8.

[144] 'Where cross-examination is directed at collateral issues such as the credibility of the witness, as a rule the answers of the witness are final and evidence to contradict them will not be permitted': *R v Edwards* [1991] 1 WLR 207, 215. See also *R v Neale* [1998] Crim LR 737.

[145] 'The rule is necessary to confine the ambit of a trial within proper limits and to prevent the true issue from becoming submerged in a welter of detail': *R v Edwards* [1991] 1 WLR 207, 215. See also *R v Neale* [1998] Crim LR 737.   [146] *A-G v Hitchcock* (1847) 1 Ex 91, 105, 154 ER 38, 44.

determination is not, however, a straightforward one, as the distinction between relevance to facts in issue and relevance to credit 'is often difficult to draw'.[147] *R v Busby*[148] may be regarded as an illustration of the non-applicability of the collateral-finality rule on the basis that the cross-examination went to a fact in issue. The appellant was alleged to have made very damaging remarks to the police when interviewed about his alleged offences. Two police officers were cross-examined to establish that one of them, in the presence of the other, had threatened a potential defence witness to prevent him from giving evidence. Both officers denied threatening this witness. The issue arose of whether this witness could be called to testify about the officers' visit to him. The Court of Appeal held:

> We are of the opinion that the learned judge was wrong to refuse to admit the evidence. If true, it would have shown that the police were prepared to go to improper lengths in order to secure the accused's conviction. It was the accused's case that the statement attributed to him had been fabricated, a suggestion which could not be accepted by the jury unless they thought that the officers concerned were prepared to go to improper lengths to secure a conviction. . . . In the present case, the evidence, if true, would have indicated that the officers were prepared to cheat in furtherance of the prosecution.[149]

There is considerable uncertainty, however, about whether the true basis of the decision in *Busby* was that the cross-examination went to facts in issue, with the result that the collateral-finality rule was inapplicable. Can the question whether the officers were prepared to go to improper lengths to secure the accused's conviction really have been regarded as a *fact in issue*? The decision in *Busby* has also been interpreted in the following ways:

• The cross-examination did go to credit, but the 'bias' exception to the collateral-finality rule (examined below) applied.[150]

• The cross-examination did go to credit, but there is a new exception to the collateral-finality rule which allows evidence to be adduced showing the improper lengths to which the police are prepared to resort to secure a conviction.[151]

R v Nagrecha is a decision in which the Court of Appeal clearly, though not unquestionably, held the collateral-finality rule to be inapplicable on the basis that the cross-examination went to a fact in issue. The appellant was accused of indecent assault. The defence cross-examined the complainant about allegations of sexual impropriety she had made against other men. She denied having made these complaints. The Court of Appeal held that the trial judge had erred in not permitting the defence to call evidence of the making of the complaints: 'Such evidence went not merely to credit, but to the heart of the case, in that it bore on the crucial issue as to whether or not there had been any indecent assault.'[152] No explanation was provided of how evidence that *complaints*

---

[147] *R v Edwards* [1991] 1 WLR 207, 215. See also *R v Busby* (1982) 75 Cr App R 79, 82 (decision of 1981); *R v Fahy* [2002] EWCA Crim 525.   [148] (1982) 75 Cr App R 79 (decision of 1981).
[149] Ibid, 82.   [150] See *R v Edwards* [1991] 1 WLR 207.
[151] See *R v Funderburk* [1990] 1 WLR 587.   [152] [1997] 2 Cr App R 401, 410.

had been made *previously* would be of relevance to the issue of whether there had been *any indecent assault* in *this case*.

The law has recognized that injustice would result if the collateral-finality rule were to be applied rigidly in all circumstances. Accordingly, there are five established exceptions to the rule.

4.4.2 The Exceptions

4.4.2.1 Proof of Previous Inconsistent Statements

A cross-examiner may seek to discredit a witness by exposing the fact that the witness has made a previous inconsistent statement.[153] The usual principles relating to cross-examination as to credit, examined earlier, govern the question whether a witness may be cross-examined on a previous inconsistent statement with a view to discrediting that witness.[154] If the witness denies having made the statement, then, as an exception to the collateral-finality rule, it may be possible to lead evidence in rebuttal to prove that the statement was in fact made. It is here that section 4 and, perhaps, section 5 of the Criminal Procedure Act 1865 come into play. Section 4 provides:

> If a witness, upon cross-examination as to a former statement made by him relative to the subject matter of the indictment or proceeding, and inconsistent with his present testimony, does not distinctly admit that he has made such statement, proof may be given that he did in fact make it; but before such proof can be given the circumstances of the supposed statement, sufficient to designate the particular occasion, must be mentioned to the witness, and he must be asked whether or not he has made such statement.

Section 5 provides:

> A witness may be cross-examined as to previous statements made by him in writing, or reduced into writing, relative to the subject matter of the indictment or proceeding, without such writing being shown to him; but if it is intended to contradict such witness by the writing, his attention must, before such contradictory proof can be given, be called to those parts of the writing which are to be used for the purpose of so contradicting him: Provided always, that it shall be competent for the judge, at any time during the trial, to require the production of the writing for his inspection, and he may thereupon make such use of it for the purposes of the trial as he may think fit.

These provisions apply to both civil and criminal proceedings. Section 4 applies to statements made either orally or in writing, while section 5 applies only to statements made in writing. As can be seen, both sections 4 and 5 require that the previous statement, in order to be able to be proved, must be 'relative to the subject matter of the indictment or proceeding'.

The Court of Appeal considered these principles relating to cross-examination on a previous inconsistent statement in *R v Funderburk*.[155] The appellant was accused of

---

[153] See generally A Samuels, 'Inconsistent Statements' (2004) 168 *Justice of the Peace* 873.
[154] *R v Funderburk* [1990] 1 WLR 587.   [155] [1990] 1 WLR 587.

unlawful sexual intercourse with a 13-year-old girl. The girl described the first incident in terms which clearly amounted to an account of the loss of her virginity. The defence applied (1) to put to her that, prior to that incident, she had told a potential witness that she had had intercourse with two other men and, if she denied this, (2) to call that witness to testify to the contrary. The trial judge refused both applications. The Court of Appeal held, first, that the complainant could have been cross-examined on her previous inconsistent statements:

> It seems to us that the jury, having heard a graphic account from the child's evidence-in-chief as to how she had lost her virginity, might reasonably have wished to re-appraise her evidence and her credibility if they had heard that on other occasions she had spoken of experiences which, if true, would indicate that she could not have been a virgin at the time of the incident she so vividly described. Her standing as a witness might have been reduced.

Secondly, the Court of Appeal held that, 'on the likely scenario that the child had denied making the inconsistent statements', these statements could have been proved pursuant to section 4. 'It seems to us that on the way the prosecution presented the evidence the challenge to the loss of virginity was a challenge that not only did the jury deserve to know about on the basis that it might have affected their view on the central question of credit, but was *sufficiently closely related to the subject matter of the indictment* for justice to require investigation for the basis of such a challenge.'[156]

Where a previous inconsistent statement is given in evidence in *criminal* proceedings under section 4 or section 5, it may now be used not only to discredit the witness but also, by virtue of section 119 of the Criminal Justice Act 2003,[157] as evidence of the truth of its contents. In *civil* proceedings, the Civil Evidence Act 1995 permits such a statement to be admitted as evidence of the facts contained in it, so long as the requirements of the Act, discussed in Chapter 9, are satisfied.

Since section 5 provides that it is open to the judge to 'make such use of that statement for the purposes of the trial as he may think fit', he or she is able, strictly speaking, to allow the entire statement to go before the jury. It may, however, be preferable in appropriate cases to permit the jury to see only that portion of the statement which relates to the matter on which the witness has been cross-examined.[158]

4.4.2.2 Previous Convictions

It is settled 'that a conviction for any offence could be put to a witness by way of cross-examination as to credit, even though the offence was not one of dishonesty'.[159] Section 6 of the Criminal Procedure Act 1865, which applies to both civil and criminal proceedings, provides that if, on being questioned as to whether he or she has any previous convictions, a witness 'either denies or does not admit the fact, or refuses to answer, it shall be lawful for the cross-examining party to prove such conviction'.

---

[156] Ibid, 598 (italics added).   [157] See Ch 9.
[158] See *R v Beattie* (1989) 89 Cr App R 302, 306 (decision of 1989).
[159] *Clifford v Clifford* [1961] 1 WLR 1274, 1276.

The extent to which a witness can be discredited by means of his or her previous convictions is subject to limitations. In the case of civil trials, section 4(1) of the Rehabilitation of Offenders Act 1974 provides that evidence of 'spent' convictions is inadmissible. Under section 7(3) of the same Act, however, such evidence is permissible where justice cannot be done in the case without the evidence being admitted. Section 7(3) has been interpreted as giving judges a wide discretion in determining whether the strong presumption against permitting cross-examination on 'spent' convictions, or admitting evidence of such convictions, is rebutted. Thus where it is sought to use a witness's 'spent' convictions to discredit that witness, the court should be satisfied that the witness's creditworthiness cannot be fairly assessed unless the evidence is admitted.[160] It has also been noted that in a civil case where:

> the judge is himself the tribunal of fact . . . , if he rules that the evidence should not be admitted, he has to put it out of his mind and decide the case without reference to it. This is never an easy exercise, and . . . a considerable responsibility rests upon counsel, not to seek leave to refer to previous convictions except in a case where it is clearly arguable that they should be admitted under s 7(3). It would be wrong even to make an application which had no realistic prospect of success.[161]

The most important limitation in criminal cases is provided by sections 100 and 101 of the Criminal Justice Act 2003, which, as has been seen in detail in Chapter 8, place restrictions on the extent to which a witness in a criminal case may be cross-examined on his or her previous convictions. It is to be noted that section 4(1) of the Rehabilitation of Offenders Act 1974 has no application in criminal proceedings,[162] but a Practice Direction recommends that a spent conviction should never be referred to in criminal proceedings 'when such reference can reasonably be avoided'.[163] Further, 'no one should refer in open court to a spent conviction without the authority of the judge, which authority should not be given unless the interests of justice so require'.[164]

4.4.2.3 Bias

As an exception to the collateral-finality rule, it is possible for evidence to be adduced that a witness holds a bias against or in favour of a party or the cause of action. Such bias must actually be demonstrated by the evidence. Thus, if in cross-examination a witness denies having been *offered* a bribe by someone acting on behalf of one of the parties, rebuttal evidence cannot be led to show that the witness was offered the bribe, since being offered a bribe does not necessarily indicate bias. But a witness's denial in cross-examination that he or she *took* a bribe can be rebutted, since proof of the taking of the bribe would indicate bias.[165]

---

[160] *Thomas v Comr of Police* [1997] 1 All ER 747. See C Manchester, 'Admissibility of Spent Convictions in Civil Cases: *Thomas v Commissioner of Police for the Metropolis*' (1997) 1(3) *International Journal of Evidence and Proof* 152.   [161] *Thomas v Comr of Police* [1997] 1 All ER 747, 765.

[162] S 7(2)(a).

[163] *Consolidated Criminal Practice Direction*, available at http://www.hmcourts-service.gov.uk/cms/files/consolidated_criminal_practice_direction0405.pdf, [I.6.4].   [164] Ibid, [I.6.6].

[165] See *A-G v Hitchcock* (1847) 1 Ex 91, 154 ER 38.

In *R v Mendy*, while a detective was giving evidence at the appellant's trial for assault, a constable observed that a man in the public gallery was taking notes. This man then left the court, and was seen by the constable and a court officer discussing the case with the appellant's husband. This was apparently in order that the husband could describe more convincingly how he himself, rather than the appellant, had been responsible for the assault. When the husband testified, he denied in cross-examination that the incident with the man had occurred. The issue arose of whether the prosecution could call the constable and court officer to give evidence in rebuttal. The Court of Appeal held that this was possible, since the 'bias' exception to the collateral-finality rule applied: 'The witness was prepared to cheat in order to deceive the jury and help the defendant. The jury were entitled to be apprised of that fact.'[166]

The issue of cross-examination of police witnesses for the purpose of eliciting evidence of police malpractice[167] was considered by the Court of Appeal in *R v Edwards*.[168] This case is significant for what it says about two matters. First, it provides guidance on the extent to which a cross-examiner may seek to discredit a police witness by putting allegations of malpractice to him or her. Secondly, if allegations which the cross-examiner is permitted to put are denied by the witness, does an exception to the collateral-finality rule apply to allow the denials to be contradicted? On the first matter, the Court of Appeal stated:

> The police officers could certainly be cross-examined as to any relevant criminal offences or disciplinary charges found proved against them.
>
> . . .
>
> We do not consider that it would have been proper to suggest to the officer in the present case that he had committed perjury or any other criminal offence by putting to him that he had been charged but not yet tried. Nor do we think that complaints to the Police Complaints Authority which have not been adjudicated upon would properly be the subject of cross-examination. It would not be proper to direct questions to an officer about allegedly discreditable conduct of other officers, whether or not they happened to be serving in the same squad.
>
> There remains the problem of other cases in which the witness has, so to speak, unsuccessfully given evidence. . . .
>
> . . .
>
> . . . The acquittal of a defendant in case A, where the prosecution case depended largely or entirely upon the evidence of a police officer, does not normally render that officer liable to cross-examination as to credit in case B. But where a police officer who has allegedly fabricated an admission in case B, has also given evidence of an admission in case A, where there was an acquittal by virtue of which his evidence is demonstrated to have been disbelieved, it is proper that the jury in case B should be made aware of that fact. However, where the acquittal in case A does not necessarily indicate that the jury disbelieved the officer, such cross-examination should not be allowed. In such a case the verdict of not guilty may mean no more than that the

---

[166] (1977) 64 Cr App R 4, 6 (decision of 1976).

[167] See generally J Dein, 'Police Misconduct Revisited' [2000] *Criminal Law Review* 801.

[168] [1991] 1 WLR 207. See generally R Pattenden, 'Evidence of Previous Malpractice by Police Witnesses and *R v Edwards*' [1992] *Criminal Law Review* 549.

jury entertained some doubt about the prosecution case, not necessarily that they believed any witness was lying.[169]

On the second matter, the Court considered, distinguishing *Busby*, that no exception to the collateral-finality rule would be applicable.[170] Thus, should the police officers deny the allegations of malpractice in cross-examination, it would not be possible for rebuttal evidence to be called. The Court noted that *Busby* had been cited in *Funderburk* as falling under an exception to the collateral-finality rule which permits evidence to be called showing that the police are prepared to go to improper lengths to secure a conviction. The Court in *Edwards* thought, however, that the 'true basis' of the decision in *Busby* 'may well have been the suggestion of bias against *those particular defendants in that particular case*'.[171] In other words, the decision in *Busby* should be viewed as an application of the 'bias' exception. It was apparently considered by the Court in *Edwards*, however, that this exception would be inapplicable where what was at issue was possible police malpractice *in other cases*. Such an interpretation of the 'bias' exception would seem to confine it within rather narrow bounds.

4.4.2.4 Incapacity

Evidence of a witness's incapacity is admissible as an exception to the collateral-finality rule:

> If a witness purported to give evidence of something which he believed that he had seen at a distance of 50 yards, it must surely be possible to call the evidence of an oculist to the effect that the witness could not possibly see anything at a greater distance than 20 yards, or the evidence of a surgeon who had removed a cataract from which the witness was suffering at the material time and which would have prevented him from seeing what he thought he saw.[172]

4.4.2.5 General Reputation for Lack of Veracity

Finally, there is a controversial and little-used exception enabling evidence of general reputation for lack of veracity to be admitted as an exception to the collateral-finality rule. Thus circumstances may arise where a party which feels that it has failed to discredit a witness sufficiently in cross-examination will seek to call such evidence. There

---

[169] [1991] 1 WLR 207, 216–17. See also *R v Meads* [1996] Crim LR 519; *R v Malik* [2000] 2 Cr App R 8, 11–12 ('There is . . . a balance to be struck between the need to make sure that points fairly to be made about a police officer's previous misconduct are before the jury when his credibility falls to be judged in a later case and the need to avoid a smoke screen of unsubstantiated suspicion, innuendo and attempts to smear unfairly. . . . If there is clear evidence that a police officer, whose credit and credibility are significant in the case before the jury, has been guilty of serious malpractice on an earlier occasion, that necessarily damages his credibility when it falls to be judged on the second occasion, even though the malpractice alleged on the second occasion is of a different kind. We do not therefore think that it is a ground for denying cross-examination that the type of malpractice in issue is different. We do however think it necessary to consider how significant in the case the police officer's evidence is and what past misconduct he is shown to have committed'); *R v Twitchell* [2000] 1 Cr App R 373.   [170] [1991] 1 WLR 207, 220.

[171] Ibid, 215 (italics added).

[172] *Toohey v Metropolitan Police Commissioner* [1965] AC 595, 608.

are strict rules concerning the questions which may be asked of a witness who is called to testify to a previous witness's general reputation for lack of veracity:

The legal position may be thus summarised:

1. A witness may be asked whether he has knowledge of the impugned witness's general reputation for veracity and whether (from such knowledge) he would believe the impugned witness's sworn testimony.

2. The witness called to impeach the credibility of a previous witness may also express his individual opinion (based upon his personal knowledge) as to whether the latter is to be believed on his oath and is *not* confined to giving evidence merely of general reputation.

3. But whether his opinion as to the impugned witness's credibility be based simply upon the latter's general reputation for veracity or upon his personal knowledge, the witness cannot be permitted to indicate during his examination-in-chief the particular facts, circumstances or incidents which formed the basis of his opinion, although he may be cross-examined as to them.

This method of attacking a witness's veracity, though ancient, is used with exceeding rarity.[173]

That a party seeking to discredit a witness should be permitted, after cross-examining that witness, to call evidence of general reputation for lack of veracity has not escaped criticism. It has been stated in the House of Lords:

From olden times it has been the practice to allow evidence of bad reputation to discredit a witness's testimony. It is perhaps not very logical and not very useful to allow such evidence founded on hearsay. None of your Lordships and none of the counsel before you could remember being concerned in a case where such evidence was called. But the rule has been sanctified through the centuries in legal examinations and textbooks and in some rare cases, and it does not create injustice.[174]

After the evidence of general reputation for lack of veracity has been adduced, the other party is entitled to rebut this by leading evidence to bolster the creditworthiness of the witness in question.[175]

4.4.3 Reform

The collateral-finality rule represents one of the more problematic areas of the law of evidence. For one thing, the distinction between relevance to a fact in issue and relevance to credit, upon which the entire rule is premised, is far from clear. The decision in *R v Nagrecha*, for example, is regarded by some as questionable. It has been seen, furthermore, that the precise basis of the decision in *Busby* (did the cross-examination go to a fact in issue, or did an exception to the collateral-finality rule apply, and if so, which

---

[173] *R v Richardson* [1969] 1 QB 299, 304–5 (italics in original).

[174] *Toohey v Metropolitan Police Commissioner* [1965] AC 595, 605–6. See also *R v Colwill* [2002] EWCA Crim 1320.

[175] It is impermissible for a party to anticipate the adduction by the other party of evidence of general reputation for lack of veracity by calling evidence to bolster creditworthiness *in advance of* that evidence: *R v Beard* [1998] Crim LR 585.

exception?) remains the subject of differing views. This is unsurprising if it is appreciated that 'credibility is not something separate (a separate issue) which is somehow suspended between the witness's statement and the fact asserted therein'.[176] Something a witness says about a fact in issue has relevance to that fact only because of the witness's creditworthiness. It has even been acknowledged judicially that 'the distinction between matters going directly to the primary issue and those going to the credit of those who give evidence on the issue is hard to operate in practice, and possibly unsound in theory'.[177]

A further difficulty with the current state of the law is suggested by the decision in *Edwards*: it may presently be impermissible to call rebuttal evidence in situations in which this should be permitted. It is strongly arguable, for example, that police officers' denials, under cross-examination, of allegations of malpractice should not be treated as final (as *Edwards* suggests they should be), but that the defence should be permitted to call rebuttal evidence.[178]

There are, essentially, three possible reform options.[179] First, given that the distinction between relevance to facts in issue and relevance to credit may in any event be illusory, it may be possible to take a broad and functional approach to what constitutes relevance to facts in issue. To treat cross-examination as going to a fact in issue would mean that the collateral-finality rule would not be applicable in the first place. In *Funderburk*, the Court of Appeal acknowledged that the answer to the question whether evidence is relevant to a fact in issue or merely to credit may well be 'an instinctive one based on the prosecutor's and the court's sense of fair play rather than any philosophic or analytic process'.[180] Indeed, in *O'Brien v Chief Constable of South Wales Police*, Lord Phillips of Worth Matravers expressed reservations about the decision in *R v Edwards*:

> Evidence which indicates that a police officer has fabricated admissions in a previous case is not evidence 'as to credit alone', if it is alleged that the same officer has fabricated evidence in a subsequent case. The position is now governed by section 100 of the [Criminal Justice Act 2003] which renders admissible, with the leave of the court, evidence of the bad character of a person other than the defendant if, and only if, it has substantial probative value in relation to a matter which is in issue in the proceedings and is of substantial importance in the context of the case as a whole.[181]

---

[176] A A S Zuckerman, *The Principles of Criminal Evidence* (1989) 95–6. See also J McEwan, 'The Law Commission Consultation Paper on Previous Misconduct: (2) Law Commission Dodges the Nettles in Consultation Paper No 141' [1997] *Criminal Law Review* 93, 99: 'Once the notion of credibility is extended to the credibility of a particular defence, we are dealing with the issue of guilt.'

[177] *R v Wright* (1990) 90 Cr App R 325, 333 (decision of 1989). See also *Thomas v Comr of Police* [1997] 1 All ER 747, 764: 'when the question is whether the party is telling the truth on a central issue in the case, then his creditworthiness is bound up with the decision on that issue itself'. Cf S Seabrooke, 'Current Topic: The Vanishing Trick—Blurring the Line Between Credit and Issue' [1999] *Criminal Law Review* 387.

[178] See R Pattenden, 'Evidence of Previous Malpractice by Police Witnesses and *R v Edwards*' [1992] *Criminal Law Review* 549, 557.

[179] See generally M Newark, 'Opening Up the Collateral Issue Rule' (1992) 43 *Northern Ireland Legal Quarterly* 166, 176–7.   [180] [1990] 1 WLR 587, 598. See also *R v Tobin* [2003] EWCA Crim 190, [32].

[181] [2005] UKHL 26, [2005] 2 WLR 1038, [41].

Secondly, it may be possible to treat the list of exceptions to the collateral-finality rule as not closed. This was an option mentioned in *Funderburk*: 'It may be that the categories of exception ... are not closed. It is impossible to tell the circumstances in which some problems may arise in the future.'[182] The third option is to acknowledge openly that, ultimately, the aim is to achieve a fair balance between the considerations of convenience and justice in the circumstances of the particular case. Thus a flexible approach, rather than the current approach of recognizing a firm rule subject to exceptions, should be taken. Such an approach, which has much to commend it, has been advocated by Newark:

> The advantage of a discretionary approach would be that it calls for a more open balancing of the inconvenience and danger of opening up the collateral issue against the dangers of not doing so. Thus contradiction on trivial details which are likely to be hotly contested, wasting much time, requiring adjournments in fairness to the other side, confusing or misleading the jury, could be prevented, while contradictions on matters vitally affecting the reliability of the witness's testimony which can be quickly and fairly resolved, can be allowed. Of course, there will be difficult cases in between; but the argument in favour of discretion is based on the assumption that all sensible, fair-minded judges, without being able to formulate any general rule on the matter, can intuitively recognize those side issues that ought to be explored and those that ought not. Greater latitude could be granted to an accused seeking to contradict a prosecution witness than to a prosecutor seeking to contradict a defence witness.[183]

---

[182] [1990] 1 WLR 587, 599.

[183] M Newark, 'Opening Up the Collateral Issue Rule' (1992) 43 *Northern Ireland Legal Quarterly* 166, 176.

15

Evidence: The Future

The law of evidence in England and Wales is undeniably at a major crossroads. On the one hand the Civil Procedure Rules and the Human Rights Act 1998 have begun to make a substantial mark. On the other hand we have yet to witness the full impact of the radical changes introduced to the law of evidence by the Criminal Justice Act 2003. The coverage in this book of the major topics of character evidence and hearsay evidence is based on the 'new' law on these topics which is contained in the 2003 Act and which, as at mid-2005, has taken effect only fairly recently. Thus it has not been possible to discuss the 'new' law with reference to a full body of appellate case law interpreting the relevant provisions. A steady stream of such case law is inevitable and is awaited with interest.

We have seen that the law of civil evidence has in recent years become increasingly influenced by the Civil Procedure Rules. This is especially the case with expert evidence. In criminal cases the spate of legislation introduced since the 1990s has meant that the law of criminal evidence is arguably now governed more heavily by statute than by the common law.[1] A number of major statutory modifications of the common law have followed considerations of the law by bodies such as the Law Commission, the Runciman Royal Commission, and Lord Justice Auld's Criminal Courts Review. A cynic might note, however, that recommendations made by such bodies have been accepted and implemented by the legislature only where they had the potential to assist the prosecution by shoring up its armoury. Thus we have seen, for example, that the recommendation by the Runciman Commission that the right to silence at the pre-trial stage should not be watered down[2] and the Law Commission's recommendation that the similar fact rule be effectively retained[3] were not accepted. On the other hand, Runciman's recommendation that a corroboration or supporting evidence requirement for confessions need not be introduced,[4] the Law Commission's recommendation that the hearsay rule in criminal cases be substantially liberalized,[5] and the provisional thoughts expressed by Auld on the desirability of allowing the freer admissibility of evidence of a defendant's bad character[6] have all been accepted.

The evidence-handling ability of the jury, the trier of fact in serious criminal cases, is an especially pertinent consideration in the context of character evidence and hearsay evidence. Yet the law must proceed on the basis of assumptions which are inherently

---

[1] See, eg, the relevant provisions of the Criminal Justice and Public Order Act 1994, the Criminal Procedure and Investigations Act 1996, the Youth Justice and Criminal Evidence Act 1999, and the Criminal Justice Act 2003.

[2] See Ch 3.   [3] See Ch 8.   [4] See Ch 2.   [5] See Ch 9.   [6] See Ch 8.

difficult to test empirically. This is highlighted sharply by the issue of evidence of a defendant's bad character. It was traditionally assumed that such evidence was so prejudicial that there should be a general rule prohibiting its admissibility on the issue of guilt. Indeed, the view that such evidence is by its very nature prejudicial would appear to be supported by empirical evidence. Yet the law has been changed in the Criminal Justice Act 2003 to embrace what appears to be a fundamentally different assumption—that juries are in fact quite capable of evaluating bad character evidence appropriately (and that in fact the exclusion of such evidence might prove prejudicial). A shift in assumptions also underlies the hearsay provisions of the 2003 Act: the traditional assumption that juries were incapable of evaluating hearsay evidence properly has given way to the assumption (for which there is in fact some empirical support) that they may in fact be quite competent at doing so.

Attempts by the law to strike an appropriate balance, in the context of a particular type of prosecution evidence, between trusting juries on the one hand, and protecting the defendant on the other, can lead to complex results. The *Turnbull* guidelines on identification evidence,[7] which generally require warnings to the jury but also require the withdrawal of the entire case from the jury in certain circumstances, provide an example.

The Human Rights Act 1998, 'incorporating' as it does the European Convention on Human Rights into domestic law, has altered in a fundamental way the level of discourse associated with judicial discussions of evidence doctrine. There are now major decisions of the House of Lords or the Privy Council dealing with the role of Article 6 of the European Convention in the context of the privilege against self-incrimination,[8] entrapment,[9] special measures for vulnerable and intimidated witnesses,[10] sexual history evidence,[11] reverse-onus provisions,[12] and disclosure and public interest immunity.[13] These decisions typically contain much more thorough discussions of issues of principle, the law in other jurisdictions, and the academic literature than were traditionally encountered in appellate decisions.

This book will be supported by an Online Resource Centre providing six-monthly updates.[14] It is hoped that this will prove useful in assisting readers to keep abreast of developments in this fast-moving area of the law.

---

[7] See Ch 4.   [8] See Ch 3.   [9] See Ch 5.   [10] See Ch 11.   [11] See Ch 11.
[12] See Ch 12.   [13] See Ch 6.   [14] http://www.oxfordtextbooks.co.uk/orc/choo/.

Index